To H... ...
many thanks for your
generous help and
support

July 10, 1975

Rudolf Bilek

DISSENT IN THE USSR

This study was prepared under the auspices of the Research Institute on Communist Affairs, Columbia University.

DISSENT IN THE USSR

POLITICS, IDEOLOGY, AND PEOPLE

EDITED BY **RUDOLF L. TŐKÉS**

THE JOHNS HOPKINS UNIVERSITY PRESS

BALTIMORE AND LONDON

The Johns Hopkins University Press, Baltimore, Maryland 21218
The Johns Hopkins University Press Ltd., London

Library of Congress Catalog Card Number 74-24391
ISBN 0-8018-1661-0
Library of Congress Cataloging in Publication data will be found on the last printed page of
this book.

For Anne and Adam

CONTENTS

PREFACE

The idea to undertake a study of Soviet dissent came to me ten years ago when I first read the transcript of the trial of the Russian poet Josif Brodsky in the August 30, 1964, issue of *New Leader*. At that time I was preparing lecture notes for my first course on Soviet politics at Wesleyan University. The Brodsky story was exciting to me because it evoked memories of similar confrontations between the authorities and the rebellious intellectuals on the eve of the Hungarian Revolution of 1956. And it was frustrating, too, especially when I tried to incorporate the case of the imprisoned yet strangely defiant poet into my carefully prepared lecture plan. I found that the behavior and ideas of Brodsky and, some months later, those of Sinyavsky and Daniel did not fit any of the elegant models of communist politics that I proposed to teach my students.

After all, in a totalitarian system political prisoners do not argue with, let alone denounce, the prosecutor and the judge in an open courtroom. If they do, as Brodsky did, the political system must be something less than totalitarian or, at any rate, is different from what I have been led to believe from the scholarly literature and, indeed, from my personal experiences as a law student in pre-1956 Hungary.

These apprehensions were reinforced by the phenomenal growth of the Soviet dissident movement in the late 1960s. My doubts about the validity and intellectual honesty of much that the Western academic experts had to say about contemporary Soviet politics became compelling concerns. Perhaps unduly sensitive to the dissonance between these new realities of Soviet life and the conventional scholarly wisdom seeking to explain them, I decided to undertake a systematic study of the social roots, ideational content, and political significance of unorthodox behavior in the USSR.

Aided by a senior fellowship from the Research Institute on Communist Affairs, Columbia University, in 1969–70, I devoted several months to the study of dissent in communist systems and sketched out some tentative hypotheses about this matter. These I discussed with several colleagues then in residence at the institute, including Severyn Bialer, Phillip Gillette, Peter Ludz, Michel Lesage, and David Williams. With the benefit of their friendly criticism and useful advice I subsequently developed a set of propositions about the salient features of heterodox political ideas and behavior in the posttotalitarian Soviet Union. When I attempted to synthesize these ideas into a more general scheme, however, I realized that the limited skills of one individual were inadequate to utilize properly the flood of Soviet samizdat data. A different kind of research strategy was needed. At the end I decided to pursue a more modest and more realistic goal: that of helping to initiate a collective scholarly inquiry into the various manifestations, the sociopolitical significance, and the prospects for dissent in the Soviet political system.

In the planning stage of such a joint undertaking it is customary to seek support from a foundation or some other institution for a conference. I felt that in a period of "official détente" in Soviet-American relations, however, the unorthodox and "policy-sensitive" nature of the subject matter indicated a different approach. Accordingly I sought out colleagues in different disciplines with established interests in this area of research with the request that they, without the benefit of foundation or government research support, prepare an original study on some aspect of Soviet dissent. I was most fortunate to enlist the cooperation of a group of distinguished students of Soviet politics, literature, philosophy, history, and law, and I secured their commitment to participate in this venture.

Although the authors and the editor endeavored to utilize the most recent data on Soviet dissident activities and generally to bring their narrative up to date, the volume as a whole does not discuss events beyond the winter of 1973–74. February 1974, the month of Alexander Solzhenitsyn's involuntary departure from the USSR, seemed to me an important milestone in the history of contemporary Soviet dissent as well as an appropriate termination point for the chronological coverage of most essays. The arrival in the West of growing numbers of prominent Soviet dissidents and the likelihood that most will, perhaps in the near future, publish their personal accounts was another factor in favor of this particular date. Moreover, the continued activity in the USSR of prominent spokesmen like Andrei Sakharov and the appearance of new participants on the Soviet scene suggest that the subject of this book is likely to remain open-ended and to require continued attention. These limitations notwithstanding, it is my belief that the timeliness of the subject matter and its intrinsic importance to members of the concerned public as well as to serious students of Soviet affairs will not diminish appreciably because of the unavoidable delays associated with the publication of these studies in book form.

In acknowledging my indebtedness to various individuals who have helped to bring this volume into being, I first wish to thank the contributors for their splendid cooperation and willingness to accommodate my sometimes less than reasonable editorial suggestions through the various drafts of their chapters. The authors and the editor of this volume are indebted to Zbigniew Brzezinski and Peter Reddaway for their thorough and searching critique of an earlier draft of the manuscript. Mr. Reddaway's profound familiarity with the actors, events, and the documentary record of the democratic movement in the USSR and his willingness to share his knowledge with the authors of this volume have been of great help that I am anxious to acknowledge.

Gene Sosin and the editor wish to thank Dmitri Pospielovsky and Keith Bosely for their kind permission to quote the text of their translation of Bulat Okudzhava's "Paper Soldiers" that originally appeared in Dmitri Pospielovsky, Keith Bosely, and Janis Sapiets, *Russia's Underground Poets* (New York and Washington: Praeger, 1969), pp. 55–56.

On a personal note I wish to thank Professor Brzezinski, the director, and the members of the board of the Research Institute on Communist Affairs (RICA), Columbia University, for the stipend that enabled me to devote full time to the study of Soviet dissent. Since some of the authors are former RICA fellows and are active or former members of the Columbia University Seminar on International Communism, it seemed fitting that this volume be offered to RICA for publication under its imprimatur. My thanks go to members of the institute's Publications Committee for their positive response.

I am also grateful to Dean Hugh Clark and the council of the University of Connecticut Graduate Research Foundation for their generous and sustained support given to my research activities connected with this project. For several stimulating discussions, thought-provoking comments and an exhaustive and most helpful critique of my introductory chapter I would like to express my gratitude to Frederick C. Barghoorn. All authors of this volume are greatly indebted to Mr. Charles Pepper for his painstaking and thoughtful editing of what *we* thought was our final text. Finally, thanks are due to Mrs. Kathleen Lambert Burns for her cheerful and unstinting help in seeing the several drafts of my chapter and several others through to a completed typescript and to Miss Florence Selleck for her valuable assistance with the administrative details of the entire project.

Responsibility for views expressed in each study belongs to the individual authors. The editor assumes responsibility for the volume's conceptual framework and, along with each author, for the accuracy of facts (especially samizdat material) cited in their studies.

R. L. T.

A NOTE ON SELF-PUBLISHED (SAMIZDAT) SOURCES

Several studies in this volume draw on information contained in self-published, clandestinely circulated and reproduced documents that were originally written and read by participants and sympathizers of the contemporary Soviet dissident movement. Since the late 1950s more than 1,500 such documents have reached the West. Some of these were published in the original language by one of the several Russian, Ukrainian, and Lithuanian émigré publishing houses, daily newspapers, and socio-political and literary journals. Others were translated into Western languages and distributed by commercial publishing houses (book-length studies, memoirs, volumes of poetry) and by scholarly and current affairs journals (mostly article-length memorandums, essays, and open letters). Since the late 1960s, much of this scattered material as well as hundreds of other "less newsworthy" items have been collected and catalogued by the research staff of Radio Liberty in Munich. The systematic efforts of this U.S. government–sponsored broadcasting organization to collect and catalogue widely scattered samizdat material have resulted in the establishment of *Arkhiv samizdata* (Samizdat archive) for the purpose of authenticating, registering, and making available samizdat material to the scholarly community. Since 1972, by special arrangement with four American and four European repository libraries (see below), the processed contents of the Radio Liberty samizdat archives have been available to those interested in consulting these sources in the original languages.

Readers of this volume might wish to note that all references appended to the studies of this volume marked *AS* no. 000 refer to the Radio Liberty *Arkhiv samizdata* registry number and also that copies of the thus-identified documents can be purchased from one of the repository libraries.

Repository Libraries. In the United States: Slavic and East European Division, The Library of Congress, Washington, D.C. 20540; Center for Slavic and East European Studies, The Ohio State University, Columbus, Ohio 43210; Center for International Studies, Massachusetts Institute of Technology, Cambridge, Mass. 02139; and Hoover Institution, Stanford,

Source: Albert Boiter, ed., *Arkhiv samizdata, Register of Documents*, 2d rev. ed. (Munich, 1974), p. ii.

Calif. 94305. In Europe: Department of Printed Books, Slavonic & East European Division, The British Museum, London WC1, England; Osteuropa-sammlung, Die Bayerische Staatsbibliothek, Munich 34, Germany; Department of Printed Books, Slavonic Section, Bodleian Library, Oxford OX1 3BG, England; Oost-Europa Instituut, in cooperation with The Alexander Herzen Foundation, Universiteit van Amsterdam, Amsterdam, Holland.

DISSENT IN THE USSR

INTRODUCTION / **VARIETIES OF SOVIET DISSENT:**

AN OVERVIEW / RUDOLF L. TŐKÉS

This volume consists of twelve studies of various aspects of contemporary political, ideological, religious, and cultural dissent in the Soviet Union. The purpose of this collection is to analyze from the vantage point of five social science disciplines—politics, history, sociology, philosophy, and law—the Soviet dissidents' record since the early 1960s. The studies seek to subject the data emanating from dissident activities to objective scrutiny by placing the interaction between the dissidents and the regime in a perspective of continuity and change in Soviet society and politics. In doing so, the volume supplements the material previously available and in certain cases seeks to correct some misperceptions about the nature and significance of the Soviet dissident movement. The collection provides new evidence derived mainly from unofficial *samizdat*, or self-published, sources. Some of this might lead to a partial reconceptualization of some generally accepted theories about the dynamics of Soviet political development, patterns of political socialization, political communication, and techniques of crisis management in the posttotalitarian USSR.

To bring these objectives into proper focus, this introduction offers a summary of the contents of this volume, an explanation concerning its scope, and the rationale for the omission of certain themes of inquiry. Problems of evidence, explanation, and conceptualization that seem applicable to the study of dissent are discussed, following which an effort is made to relate the findings of this volume and other evidence relevant to the study of this phenomenon to certain Western social science theories on the general subject of opposition and political protest. The concluding part is addressed to the political and moral dilemmas posed by Soviet dissent for East-West détente and for the future of the free flow of people and ideas in an ideologically divided world.

DISSENT: SCOPE OF INQUIRY

This volume has been designed to provide answers to four questions: What is the political significance of Soviet dissent? What are the ideas and beliefs that motivate dissident activities? How are dissident beliefs communicated to the Soviet public and the world? And finally, who are some of the groups and individuals who constitute the dissident movement? Thus the studies in this collection are addressed to four general themes—politics, ideas, communication, and personalities and groups.

Although all these themes have been discussed in the rapidly growing body of Western literature concerned with dissent, most writings of this kind have left much to be desired in terms of balance, emphasis, methodological sophistication, intellectual rigor, and ideological bias. Many authors, some with only marginal interest in the matter, have written about this phenomenon in recent years. As a result, the study of dissent in the USSR still seems to be the domain of political journalists rather than that of the community of scholars with proper qualifications for the objective study of Soviet society and politics.

Each of the volume's four parts consists of three essays that focus on a set of related themes. The first part is addressed to the political context in which the interaction between the regime and the dissidents takes place.

Barghoorn's study analyzes the origins and development of official Russian/Soviet attitudes toward "different-mindedness" and describes the ways in which the Soviet regime has sought to prevent and punish unorthodox political behavior. The attitudes of both officials and average citizens toward politically deviant thinking and behavior have, of course, been conditioned by Russia's "subject" political culture. But Barghoorn discerns an emerging pattern of strategies and policies employed by the regime—a pattern appreciably different from those employed by Stalin when faced with comparable challenges in the 1920s and 1930s. Indiscriminate terror and massive coercion have been replaced in the post-Khrushchev era by a mixture of selective intimidation, manipulation, and cajolery. "Positive incentives" such as economic and psychic bribery of active and would-be dissidents are widely used. Instead of routinely meting out sentences of twenty-five years of forced labor (often amounting to a death sentence), the regime has developed a wide range of legal and extralegal measures with which to thwart the efforts of both leaders and followers of the Soviet protest movement. Barghoorn finds that the punishability of what the Communist Party elite considers anti-Soviet activity is often determined by a variety of factors such as the political resources that are available to each side to influence the other. The relative weight of such factors is determined by the regime's current policy dilemmas at home and abroad and by the politically and ideologically destabilizing potential of the dissidents' self-published appeals to the party leadership, the Soviet people, and world public opinion. While the outcome of the hundreds of documented confrontations between the regime and its opponents has never been in doubt, one can argue, as Barghoorn does, that the intimidation, incarceration, and forced emigration of the regime's critics have neither eliminated dissent nor resolved the issues that give rise to it.

Biddulph's essay focuses on the "problem of the powerless" and the techniques they develop in formulating strategies of protest. Because the

Soviet dissidents have no way of directly influencing the policy-making process, their protest strategies may be studied as unique methods of interest articulation. Biddulph employs a model of protest aims and audiences to interpret and analyze the protest activities of the "democratic movement of the USSR." After reviewing the dissident groups' salient characteristics (shared values, degree of interaction, techniques of interest articulation, etc.), Biddulph outlines the characteristics of the strategies they employed, beginning with the Sinyavsky-Daniel trial in 1965. Protests articulated in this and subsequent campaigns were both of the "public" and the "nonpublic" kind. Biddulph suggests that the protest movement was occasionally quite successful in achieving its short-run goal of controlling or mitigating official repression and reserves judgment as to the success of the dissenters' long-term objective, which, as he puts it, is "alliance building" among all the regime's opponents.

Friedgut's study is based on interviews with forty Jewish émigrés from the USSR who succeeded in obtaining exit permits and settled in Israel. Virtually all interviewees came from similar backgrounds in the intelligentsia and had worked as university lecturers, scientific researchers attached to one of the institutes of the USSR Academy of Sciences, creative artists, journalists, or minor administrators. Some of the respondents had been active dissenters while others had not participated at all in the Democratic Movement. Friedgut sought responses to some of the following questions: "What is the Democratic Movement?" "What is the democrats' program?" "What is your reaction to samizdat writings?" "How important is nationalism among the dissidents?" and invited speculation about the number and location of the regime's active critics throughout the USSR. Friedgut's conclusion offers a tentative assessment of the democrats' appeal, tactical and strategic strengths and weaknesses, and their place in Soviet society.

The second part of the volume seeks to place the phenomenon of dissent in the broad context of social structure, political philosophies, and religious beliefs. The essays attempt to develop linkages between the traditional and the modern in Russian/Soviet social, political, and religious thought.

Connor views the rise of dissent as symptomatic of strains generated by the "command" mode of integration—that is, the domination of the polity over other functionally differentiated spheres of the Soviet system. "Command" integration, which served the regime well in earlier "mobilizational" phases, has failed to function effectively in the postmobilization period. A highly structured society has been created in which representatives of various "spheres" now demand degrees of autonomy that the Soviet system cannot provide without threatening its own survival as a going concern. Notwithstanding these difficulties, which the more analytically inclined dissenters accurately depicted in their writings, Connor maintains that the congruence or fit of the traditional Russian and the contemporary

Soviet political culture has created enormous stability and, with it, virtually insurmountable odds for those wishing to reform or overthrow the present system. While nothing is permanently fixed in the USSR, the chances for significant change will remain quite small for the foreseeable future.

Kline's study offers a comparative analysis of the philosophical writings of three prominent dissident intellectuals: Alexander Yesenin-Volpin, Valery Chalidze, and Grigory Pomerants. The discussion focuses on Yesenin-Volpin's "On the Logic of Moral Sciences," Chalidze's "Reflections on Man," and Pomerants' "The Man from Nowhere," written respectively in 1970, in 1971, and between 1967 and 1969. Although many differences— generational, professional, disciplinary, and indeed philosophical— distinguish the authors, all three are unmistakably independent thinkers. They dissociated themselves from the values of the official orthodoxy and, each in his own chosen field of philosophical inquiry, committed themselves to higher standards of morality, ethical validity, and spiritual self-realization. In doing so they inevitably transgressed the permissible limits of intellectual nonconformity and were compelled to pay the price for their ideological misconduct.

Opposition by religious believers as a mode of dissident behavior is the subject of Jancar's study. The analysis focuses on four related aspects of the matter: (a) religion as a counterideology, including a discussion of the writings of Levitin-Krasnov and Boris Talantov; (b) programmatic statements by spokesmen of the Baptist and Russian Orthodox movements with emphasis on the relationship of religion and civil rights; (c) the linkage of religion and nationality as it can be inferred from the record of the Moslem and Jewish protest activists; and (d) an analysis of the Lithuanian Catholic case as a special variant of the civil rights and nationality dissent. Jancar's concluding remarks suggest that tensions arising out of religion, nationality, and civil rights have an enormous potential for political mobilization, with far-reaching consequences for the stability of the USSR.

The third part of the volume offers three studies that focus on dissent as a form of communication with political, cultural, and legal content. Although the discussion is primarily concerned with self-published political tracts, popular ballads, belles-lettres, and the legal constraints on the dissemination of such material in the USSR and abroad, each author approaches the matter from a different disciplinary viewpoint.

Drawing on the Western literature of communications theory, Hollander first outlines the ideological underpinnings and operational characteristics of the post-Stalin partial reorganization of the official political communications system in the USSR. Next she describes the innovations and alternative communications methods that the dissidents introduced in order to outwit official censorship and police surveillance of their writings. According to Hollander, dissident communications take many forms and may be classified as descriptive, suggestive, and interpretive. The authorities have employed many sophisticated measures to repair this breach of their communications monopoly, but they have yet to succeed in eliminating unorthodox thinking, especially among university graduates and the scientific intelligentsia.

Sosin's account is addressed to the traditional, yet very contemporary, phenomenon of word-of-mouth communication through underground music, poetry, and ballads. The authors of such works have used these art forms as effective vehicles for the articulation of universally shared political and moral concerns of the Soviet people, young and old, worker, peasant, and intellectual alike. Through a detailed analysis of the text of ballads and songs of three famous Soviet bards (Bulat Okudzhava, Alexander Galich, and Vladimir Vysotsky) and two who are less well known (Mikhail Nozhkin and Yuli Kim), Sosin presents an overview of the political philosophies of the contemporary popular counterculture in the USSR.

Soviet legal controls on the spread of samizdat works, especially into foreign countries, is the subject of Maggs's essay. The USSR's accession to the Universal Copyright Convention in 1973 has created a number of still unresolved legal, political, and moral problems for the authors, publishers, and to some extent the readers of samizdat writings. In his concluding remarks Maggs outlines the legal options and remedies available to Soviet authors who wish to publish their uncensored works in the West, particularly in the United States.

The concluding, fourth part of the book is entitled "People of the Democratic Movement." Although individuals and groups of people associated with the dissident cause have been discussed in virtually all the foregoing chapters, essays in this part attempt to define the human dimension of the various forms of political opposition in the USSR. The subjects of the authors' inquiry are three identifiable groups of dissidents— professional historians, natural scientists, and a group of young Moscow intellectuals—and the first two essays focus specifically on the evolution of the philosophical and political posture of Roy Medvedev and Andrei Sakharov, who have been the most prominent spokesmen of the first two groups.

Slusser's study discusses the political and intellectual dilemmas of contemporary Soviet historians and offers a guided tour to samizdat literature on history, politics, science, and belles-lettres. He also provides a critical evaluation of Medvedev's approach to the recent Soviet past in his book *Let History Judge*.

Dornan traces the evolution of Sakharov's political posture (and, through it, that of the liberal Soviet scientific community) by comparing and contrasting some of the leading propositions advanced in four of his memoranda written between 1968 and 1972. In conclusion, Dornan analyzes several of Sakharov's public statements and interviews from 1973 and 1974 that prompted an officially sponsored publicity campaign against him.

The concluding chapter by Feifer takes the reader to the intellectuals of Moscow, with whom contemporary Soviet dissent originated. Here the author describes the life style and intellectual proclivities of his Moscow acquaintances—warts and all—and offers some unorthodox explanations as to why most educated Soviet citizens *do not* wish to join the dissident movement.

As is apparent from the foregoing, neither the individual studies nor the volume as a whole are intended to provide exhaustive coverage of the many facets of contemporary Soviet dissent. A comprehensive treatment is an unrealistic goal that would inevitably lead to unacceptable compromises in standards of analysis. The editor instead encouraged the choice and development of certain themes of inquiry that held the promise of making an *original* contribution to the study of dissent. Therefore many significant subjects are not discussed in this symposium. For example, it may be argued that nationality dissent is an enormously complex issue that no single individual, unless he or she is an exceptional linguist and is extremely fortunate in locating the necessary data, can profitably investigate within the confines of one chapter.

Because of a variety of legitimate doubts about the reliability of the presently available evidence—both samizdat and official—the time does not seem ripe for a comprehensive account of the dissident activities of certain elites. These include the military, university students, lawyers, professional economists, creative and performing artists, "liberal" party bureaucrats, and the entire community of research scientists. Similarly, the ideologically unorthodox or otherwise officially disapproved activities of members of broad social strata and occupational groups such as factory workers, collective and state farm peasants, the population of eastern Siberia (especially those living in the new industrial towns), inmates of distant penal colonies, and so on are extraordinarily difficult to document in an academically acceptable fashion.

Moreover, no attempt has been made to relate the stories of many prominent individuals of the dissident movement. Apart from limitations of space, the cases of the writers Alexander Solzhenitsyn, Andrei Sinyavsky, Yuli Daniel, Alexei Kosterin, Josif Brodsky, Andrei Amalrik, Alexander Tvardovsky, Vladimir Maksimov, and Natalya Gorbanevskaya; of civil rights activists Peter Grigorenko, Peter Yakir, Valery Chalidze, Vladimir Bukovsky, and Anatoly Marchenko; of nationality spokesmen Svyatoslav Karavansky, Ivan Dzyuba, and Vyacheslav Chornovil; and of scientists Zhores Medvedev, Igor Shafarevich, Pavel Litvinov, and others are generally well known from their published writings and from the coverage accorded to them in the Western news media.

Finally, the volume does *not* include samizdat documents, a biographical directory, or a compendium of Soviet laws relevant to regulating unorthodox political behavior. Material of this kind can be found elsewhere.

Rather, it provides a set of original studies that, on the basis of new evidence, seek to identify the form, substance, and human dimension of the contemporary Soviet dissident movement.

UNCENSORED WRITINGS: EVIDENCE AND ITS LIMITATIONS

Secretiveness and an almost obsessive fear of the dissemination of unauthorized information of a political, social, military, or economic nature have been characteristic features of Russian and Soviet policies with respect to public communication, even on literary or scientific subjects.[1] Official attitudes toward free speech and uncensored expression of personal beliefs have not changed at all since the tsarist days. The mixture of zeal, suspicion, and fear displayed by police officials whom the Marquis de Custine encountered during his Russian journey in the 1830s is still typical of the reaction of high Soviet internal security officials when confronted with unorthodox political ideas and their proponents.[2]

Until the large-scale appearance of samizdat in the late 1950s, Soviet efforts to suppress uncensored information were on the whole quite successful. In fact, information about life in the USSR available to Western students was censored material that had successfully passed the scrutiny of several guardians of official orthodoxy. This is not to suggest that information so screened is, by definition, unreliable and useless for research purposes.[3] Rather, it is to emphasize the importance of *lakirovka*, or the official meddling with the facts as they are, and the Russian propensity to exaggerate success and to minimize or remain silent about failures, which created significant handicaps for those interested in applying Western social science methodology to the study of the USSR. Therefore all attempts at scientific reconstruction and analysis of the salient features of Soviet

1. It is worth noting that the much-maligned tsarist censorship had been considerably more tolerant than Glavlit, its Soviet successor. While much of the writings of Marx, Engels, Lenin, Plekhanov, and the Russian radical and revolutionary left did pass censorship, Glavlit has been known to censor not only the writings of the regime's suspected critics or opponents but those of Lenin, Stalin, and their successors when the political exigencies of the day required it. For a detailed exposition on the workings of contemporary Soviet censorship see Zhores A. Medvedev, *Ten Years after Ivan Denisovich* (New York, 1973). For a useful collection of studies on historic, philosophical, and administrative aspects of censorship in the USSR, see Martin Dewhirst and Robert Farrel, *Soviet Censorship* (Metuchen, N.J., 1973).

2. A recorded conversation between Andrei Sakharov and Mikhail P. Malyarov, first deputy prosecutor general of the USSR, provides several clues to visceral official responses to unorthodox arguments. "The Sakharov Dialogue," *New York Times*, August 29, 1973. For a perceptive analysis of the regime's legal biases toward unauthorized dissemination of dissident ideas, see Dietrich A. Loeber, "Samizdat under Soviet Law," *Index* 2, no. 3 (Autumn 1973): 3–24.

3. Robert Conquest's introduction to his *Power and Policy in the USSR* (London, 1962), pp. 3–78, offers probably the most perceptive discussion on the nature of censored "kremlinological" evidence for the study of Soviet politics.

realities—whether kremlinology, behavioral or revisionist models, or research strategies—have, at best, succeeded in producing limited, most often speculative, and generally unverifiable explanations lacking predictive potential and comparative usefulness for the study of other political systems.

The sudden availability of more than 1,500 uncensored self-published documents that have been smuggled out of the USSR by sympathetic Western travelers (many others have yet to reach the West) touching on virtually all aspects of Soviet life should, therefore, compel us to take a fresh look at the state of the arts and reconsider some of our possibly outdated views about the nature of Soviet society and politics.

This was not the first time that uncensored Soviet material became available for scrutiny by Western scholars. For example, the Harvard Project on the Soviet Social System drew upon the recollections of substantial numbers of former Soviet citizens, and its findings as reported in several studies did result in a modification of scholarly opinion on the USSR.[4]

Complementary, and by the nature of the enterprise transcending the significance of this project, was the undertaking by the late Merle Fainsod, whose results were published in 1958 under the title *Smolensk under Soviet Rule*. Fainsod's study was based on a "random selection of more than 5,000 files containing approximately 200,000 pages of documents" that had been taken by German army units from the archives of the Smolensk regional party committee in July 1941. The documents were shipped to Germany and subsequently captured by U.S. forces at the end of the war. After thorough perusal of this body of uncensored "official use only" material, Fainsod characterized it as "a mirror of Soviet reality" that enabled him, in some instances for the first time, to determine "how Russia was ruled." He found that Soviet politics as seen through internal party documents had been infinitely richer and far more complex than the official image hitherto available to the analyst had suggested. He also suggested a definite linkage between opposition and dissent in the 1930s and the 1960s:

> The Smolensk Archive provides a record in miniature of these profound social and political changes. It registers the gradual consolidation of Communist power in a region where the underlying disposition of economic forces offered formidable barriers to Communist control. It reveals the capacity of the regime to manipulate and discipline the new social forces which its grandiose experiment in social engineering released. But it also lays bare the vast human costs and bitter resentments which Communist rule entailed. The Archive may serve to remind us, if reminder is needed, that the totalitarian façade concealed a host of inner contradictions, that the yoke which Communism imposed left its legacy of smoldering grievances, and that the suppressed aspirations of yesterday may yet become the seedbed of tomorrow's fierce debates.[5]

4. Raymond A. Bauer, Alex Inkeles, and Clyde Kluckhohn, *How the Soviet System Works* (Cambridge, Mass., 1956).
5. Merle Fainsod, *Smolensk under Soviet Rule* (Cambridge, Mass., 1958), p. 454.

The very existence of the post-Stalin reform movement and the samizdat it generated provides evidence that the Soviet system's "inner contradictions" and the "fierce debates" they evoked represent enduring patterns of ruler-subject relationships in the USSR. It also suggests that, just as Fainsod's study helped to undermine (quite unintentionally, we might add) the then-dominant totalitarian model, new samizdat data should raise questions concerning the validity of many currently fashionable theories about the nature of the Soviet system.

Although both shed light on previously little-known matters, there are four important differences between the Smolensk and the contemporary samizdat material. One obvious difference is that the purpose of the former was to defend, maintain, and strengthen the status quo in accordance with instructions received from above—ultimately from Stalin himself. Apart from their natural proregime bias, governing responsibilities of this kind tended to impose political, ideological, and psychological limitations on the decision-makers who wrote many of the Smolensk documents. In contrast, nearly all the individuals we are able to identify as samizdat authors have no direct access to political power and wield, at best, a scarcely measurable influence on Soviet policy-making processes. This remoteness from power and the responsibility it entails tends to render their arguments not only critical but often impractical as well.[6]

The second difference follows from the first and lies in the factual reliability of the two kinds of uncensored material. While we may assume that both contain the best available evidence *as it is known* to the respective authors, it is obvious that, for example, statistical reports released by Smolensk officials, even with allowances for the vagaries of bureaucratic politics, tend to be more reliable than the often second-hand or third-hand statistical data that dissidents use in support of their arguments. As Western analysts have pointed out, dissident figures on Soviet defense expenditures, statistics on the inner workings of the Communist Party and the government, and samizdat studies of Soviet national income, living standards, and the like are frequently inaccurate or distorted to suit the author's purposes.[7]

Unlike official communications, both confidential and nonrestricted, self-published writings are produced, duplicated, and distributed under

6. Sakharov's proposal to levy a voluntary surtax on all industrial nations to aid the developing world may be cited as one example of this kind of dissident policy proposal.

7. A careful analysis of two samizdat essays—A. Babushkin, "The Results of the Implementation of the Eighth Five-Year Plan of the National Economy of the USSR," and A. Kazakov, "On the Problem of Comparing the Standards of Living of Workers in [prerevolutionary] Russia, the USSR and the Capitalist Countries," in *Svobodnaia mysl'*, no. 1 (Dec. 20, 1971), Radio Liberty (Munich) *Arkhiv samizdata* (hereafter cited as *AS*) no. 1180, reveals many crude errors in computation and conceptualization and careless use of published statistical evidence. Similar observations are made by Keith Bush, "Unofficial Soviet Estimates of the Defense Burden," *Radio Liberty Dispatch*, August 3, 1973. See also Paige Bryan, "Concerning Economic Grievances from Samizdat," *Radio Liberty Dispatch*, July 7, 1972.

conditions that are extremely vulnerable to manipulation by secret police and party "disinformation" experts. There is no completely reliable way of verifying the authorship of many samizdat documents, even when they are signed. In the absence of convincing proof of the genuineness and, more importantly, the representative character of several underground memoranda—especially of the politically more polemical variety and those involving the nationality question—one must refrain from drawing far-reaching conclusions from them.[8]

Both types of evidence, however, reflect the values, mores, and intellectual preferences of two distinct, yet in many ways compatible, Russian/Soviet political cultures. The Smolensk data mirror the contemporary Soviet officials' political prejudices, authoritarian intolerance, and reckless disregard of humane values—in short, the substance of what we have come to know as Stalinism, Bolshevik political style, and Leninist norms of party life. Dissident writings, though varying widely in style, content, and level of intellectual sophistication, also reveal the values of what might be called a contemporary Soviet political counterculture. These include a profound concern for people as human beings, pronounced sensitivity toward moral and spiritual values, a sense of righteous indignation over injustice of any kind, civil courage in the face of official lawlessness, and a deep though not widely shared sense of confidence in the inevitability of change for a better life in the USSR.

These two orientations, irreconcilable though they may seem, are united by a set of shared concerns about the common destiny of the Soviet people, their country, and the ruling Communist Party in the nuclear age. The historic legacy of authoritarianism in politics, of backwardness in economics, and of a propensity for extremism in the realm of political, cultural, and religious beliefs appears to be the most important unifying bond between the regime and its dissident critics.[9] Russia's epic voyage from backwardness, insecurity, and feelings of inferiority to modernity and global influence has taken a grave toll; it has deformed and made mutually

8. An example of suspected "disinformation" manipulation with unauthorized writings is provided by the first volume of the Khrushchev memoirs. For controversial analysis of that case see Victor Zorza, "The Khrushchev Memoirs," *Manchester Guardian Weekly*, February 6, 1971, pp. 11–13. The authorship of the important *Program of the Democratic Movement of the Soviet Union* (Amsterdam, 1972; signed by "Democrats of Russia, the Ukraine, and the Baltic Region") is at best ambiguous and at worst suspicious in view of the contents of that document. See also "KGB—Samizdat," RFE *Research*, Communist Area, 1015 (May 18, 1971), and Dimitry Pospielovsky, "The Zubatov Experiment and Its Relevance to Today's Soviet Union" (Paper delivered at the annual meeting of the Northeast Chapter of the American Association for the Advancement of Slavic Studies, Montreal, May 5, 1971).

9. Barghoorn points to a "number of other factors [that are] also relevant to the nature of opposition and dissent in the USSR" such as the "despotic Jacobin elements introduced into the Russianized Marxism of Lenin, the hostility toward the capitalist social system . . . and the premium on toughness, guile, suspiciousness and vigilance." Frederick C. Barghoorn, "Factional, Sectoral and Subversive Opposition in Soviet Politics," in *Regimes and Oppositions*, ed. Robert A. Dahl (New Haven, Conn., 1973), p. 33.

dependent the politics, methods and aspirations, and human relationships of the regime and its subjects. As a result Western standards in politics, values, and the qualities of human relationships often seem inadequate to measure and analyze the interaction between the regime and the dissidents in today's USSR.

These caveats about the limitations and the often *sui generis* properties of uncensored official and unofficial evidence will, it is hoped, place the data on which the individual essays of this volume are based in realistic perspective and allow the reader to form his own judgments from the record and the record alone.

DISSENT: CHRONOLOGY, TAXONOMY, AND TERMINOLOGY

Although the entire volume is devoted to the subject of dissent, a brief historical sketch of its origins and stages of development seems helpful at this point. A classification of schools of dissident ideologies will then be offered and an attempt made to define the term "dissent" as a specific form of opposition.

Political dissent in the Soviet Union had its origins in the reactions of both the people and the party elite to the Communist Party's philosophy and methods of dictatorship and terror in the years of the Russian civil war. After a brief struggle, the regime's intraparty critics, or to use the title of R. V. Daniels' seminal study "the conscience of the revolution," were silenced, exiled, or shot, and virtually all known noncommunist dissenters were eliminated during the Stalinist purges in the 1930s.[10]

The kind of dissent that this book analyzes began at the end of the Second World War, gained momentum after Stalin's death, and surfaced as a popular movement in the mid-1960s. Its development may be divided into four phases. These may be called (1) "subversive-militant" (1946–54), (2) "political counterculture" (1956–64), (3) "nationwide movement" (1965–71), and (4) "retrenchment and ideological polarization" (beginning in 1971).[11]

The classification of each phase denotes the organizational characteristics and political style of the dissident movement in specific periods of time. For example, typical of the first two phases was an organizational scheme resembling that of the underground conspiratorial societies of exiled political prisoners and university students in tsarist times. Imprisoned Red Army officers, communist intellectuals, members of religious sects,

---

10. R. V. Daniels, *The Conscience of the Revolution* (Cambridge, Mass., 1960); Robert Conquest, *The Great Terror* (New York, 1968). See also Stephen F. Cohen, *Bukharin* (New York, 1973).

11. This periodization is developed in greater detail in my "Dissent: Politics for Change in the USSR," in *Soviet Politics and Society in the 1970s*, ed. Henry W. Morton and Rudolf L. Tőkés (New York, 1974), pp. 11 ff.

suspected nationalist separatists, and their underground study circles constituted the first wave of postwar dissent. Partly as a reaction to the events of 1956 in Poland and Hungary, these were followed by the formation of secret discussion groups of Leningrad and Moscow students who also published samizdat journals containing poetry, short stories, and political satire.[12]

These earlier efforts, aided considerably by widespread domestic and foreign protest against the trial of Andrei Sinyavsky and Yuli Daniel in 1965, developed into a nationwide movement. The appearance of scores of signed statements and new self-published journals and newsletters and the large-scale influx of many hitherto politically passive elements into the movement, especially between 1966 and 1968, represented the high-water mark in the history of postwar protest. With the systematic campaign of repression that began in 1970–71 all but a few dissidents were driven underground and the rest were either exiled or forced to emigrate from the USSR. Thus it appears that the era of open protest and public contestation with the Soviet party, the government, and the state security organs had ebbed by the end of 1973 except for unprecedented episodes like those involving Solzhenitsyn and Sakharov.

Rather than attempt to forecast the future of Soviet dissent—a task that has been undertaken by all authors of this volume in their respective areas of inquiry—it seems useful to discuss next a related matter, that of the types of philosophies and programs that constitute the ideological dimensions of the protest movement.

The scholarly literature on the taxonomy of the ideational components of dissident thought can be briefly summarized. Feuer distinguished between two main schools of thought, "Scientific Opposition" and "Literary Opposition." Amalrik found three: "Genuine Marxism-Leninism," "Christian Ideology," and "Liberal Ideology." So did Biddulph in an earlier study, calling them "Fundamental," "Integral," and "Specific Policy"-related dissident ideologies. Yuri Glazov listed eight separate ideological trends in the Democratic Movement: "Neo-Communist," "Constitutionalist," "Neo-Slavist," "Christian Socialist," "Liberal," "Christian Democratic," "Civil Rights Activist," and the "Jewish Activist."[13]

Rather than adding to the considerable semantic confusion surrounding the subject, we propose a less ambiguous and perhaps more comprehensive

12. The pre-1965 phases of dissent are well documented in Hugh McLean and Walter N. Vickery, eds., *The Year of Protest 1956* (New York, 1961); George Lichtheim and Walter Laqueur, eds., *The Soviet Cultural Scene 1956–1957* (New York, 1958); *Samizdat 1, la voix de l'opposition communiste en U.R.S.S.* (Paris, 1969); and Patricia Blake and Max Hayward, eds., *Half-Way to the Moon: New Writings from Russia* (New York, 1964).

13. Lewis Feuer, "The Intelligentsia in Opposition," *Problems of Communism* 19, no. 6 (November–December 1970): 4–10; Andrei Amalrik, *Will the Soviet Union Survive until 1984?* (New York, 1970); Howard L. Biddulph, "Soviet Intellectual Dissent as a Political Counter-Culture," *Western Political Science Quarterly* 25, no. 3 (September 1972): 522–33; "Embryo of a Social Democratic Party?" RFE *Research*, Communist Area, 1516 (August 21, 1972), pp. 1–2.

approach. To begin with the simplest possible classification, we could categorize dissident ideologies along a left-center-right continuum. One such scheme was devised by Brzezinski in the larger context of a "policy spectrum USSR."[14] In it he expanded his threefold division by adding the categories of "Systemic Left" and "Systemic Right" to the opposite ends of his spectrum and, for purposes of *his* analysis, defined those belonging to this expanded center as "marginalists." In this scheme we find at the extreme right Molotov, Kaganovich, and the secret police and, at the other end, such improbable individuals and groups as Malenkov, the spokesmen for the consumers' goods industry, and the Moscow-Leningrad intellectuals. But this particular model does not appear to be helpful for the classification of dissident ideologies.

One plausible way of ordering the amorphous mass of dissident thinking is to define tentatively the dissidents' characteristics, stated goals, and manifest behavior as displayed in the way they pursue their objectives vis-à-vis the political authorities. By placing the matter in a cultural and historical perspective of intellectual continuity between traditional Russian methods of opposition and their latter-day manifestations we can, at the outset, identify three basic ideological positions. These can be called moral-absolutist, instrumental-pragmatic, and anomic-militant.[15]

By *moral-absolutist* dissident ideologies we mean programs and programmatic statements that represent alternative conceptions of morality and ethical validity and an unconditional reaffirmation of spiritual values over expedient, pseudoscientific philosophies justifying man's inhumanity to man in the name of modernization and technological progress or the attainment of a utopian end-state of political development. Such ideologies seek to reshape the beliefs of those segments of the population (mainly the intellectuals and the youth) that are thought to be susceptible to the devolution of the political regime's authority on ethical, religious, intellectual, and cultural grounds. Representatives of this kind of ideology include religious thinkers, moral philosophers, and most writers, poets, and humanistic social critics.

By *instrumental-pragmatic* ideologies we mean programs, statements, and other forms of public or semipublic communication that represent competing interpretations of the Marxist classics (particularly Lenin); alternative methods of modernization and scientific progress; and a commitment, expressed in language ranging from the aesopian to the most explicit, to experimentation free of political control, pursuit of scientific (that is, empirically verifiable rather than ideologically orthodox) truths, and, most importantly, demands for the unconditional official endorsement of the principle of intellectual autonomy in scientific matters. Proponents of

14. Zbigniew Brzezinski, "The Soviet Political System: Transformation or Degeneration," *Problems of Communism* 15, no. 1 (January–February 1966): 10.
15. These categories are developed in greater detail in Tőkés, "Dissent: Politics for Change," pp. 10, 15 ff.

such ideologies most often address their messages to members of the political elite whom they hope both to criticize and to persuade, in order to promote the creation of conditions conducive to the optimum development of science and a society that benefits from the fruits of scientific endeavors. Ideas of this kind are found in the writings of many distinguished Soviet scientists, such as Peter Kapitsa, Lev Landau, Igor Tamm, Zhores Medvedev, and Andrei Sakharov, and in those of scores of less well known people.

By *anomic-militant* ideologies we mean programs and statements that represent affirmations of national identity or spiritual autonomy or expressions of extreme alienation from the political philosophies, institutions, laws, and governing practices of the Soviet system. Ideologies of this kind do not seek accommodation with the status quo. Rather, without any real hope of obtaining satisfaction, they seek to confront and combat existing realities, such as officially sponsored or tolerated practices of religious, ethnic, and racial discrimination, policies of cultural russification, and the still unresolved legacy of the stalinist past. Their goal is to obtain the benefits of first-class citizenship and, with it, the totality of rights and privileges that the *letter* of the USSR Constitution confers on all Soviet citizens. Anomic-militant ideological spokesmen are the spiritual leaders of persecuted religious believers, articulate Ukrainian, White Russian, Baltic, and Central Asian intellectuals, and Jewish dissidents seeking to leave the USSR for Israel. This cluster also includes those politically estranged groups and individuals—often located at the extreme right of the ideological spectrum—who wish to overthrow the regime and restore an earlier, more authoritarian, and more traditionally Russian form of government. Neo-Slavophiles, unreformed stalinists, and visceral anti-Semites seem to belong to the category.

Each of these three dominant ideological orientations accommodates a remarkably complex set of explicit beliefs and political action programs that defy classification and, indeed, any attempt at a systematic analysis. One way to overcome these difficulties is drastically to oversimplify these matters and to present a tentative spectrum of documentable dissident ideologies depicting the *approximate position* of various groups and individuals toward what might be termed the Soviet collective leadership's policies and ideological posture during an arbitrarily chosen period in the late 1960s (table i-1).

Because of its focus on a limited period rather than on the entire postwar era, this scheme tends to conflict to some extent with the ideological postures that the several authors of this volume assign to the protagonists of their essays. It still may be argued, however, that even this kind of rudimentary classification is preferable to viewing dissident ideologies as totally amorphous and not amenable to classification along lines of traditional Russian/Soviet political beliefs. It will be noted that the list

TABLE I:1 Ideologies of Dissent in the USSR (1966-70)

Moral-Absolutist		Instrumental-Pragmatic		Militant-Anomic	
The Essential Left	Left	Center	Right		Fundamental Right
	PHOENIX 66	SOCIAL PROBLEMS	NOVY MIR	OKTIABR' Kochetov	Stalinists "Russian Patriots"
Galanskov	Yakir	POLITICAL DIARY	Yevtushenko		
Delone	Krasin	Chalidze	Ehrenburg		
Bukovsky	Nozhkin	Solzhenitsyn			INFORMATION (Tatar)
Amalrik	Kim	Sakharov	LITERATURNAYA GAZETA	Osipov	DIET
Ginzburg	Galich	Tvardovsky	TEATR Rendel		THE NATION'S WORD
Gorbanevskaya	Yesenin-Volpin	Rostropovich	Levitin-Krasnov		
Yakhimovich	Grigorenko	Roy Medvedev	Talantov		
Kosterin	Gabay	Zhores Medvedev			
Khaustov	Razumny	Voznesensky	EXODUS (Jewish)	HERALD OF SALVATION (Baptist)	
Fainberg		"Constitutionalists"		FRATERNAL LEAFLET (Baptist)	
Marchenko	"The Democrats"	CHRONICLE OF CURRENT EVENTS	All-Russian Christian		
Petrov-Agatov		Sociologists	Socialist Union		
Pisarev	Action Group for the	Revisionist Historians		Lithuanian Catholics	
	Defense of Civil Rights	Liberal Scientists			
		Educational Reformers			
		Liberal Economists			
		Moscow Human Rights Committee			
			Moroz		
	Agursky		Chornovil	Crimean Tatars	
	Malyshko	Dzyuba	Karavansky		
			Strokataya		
	Mandelshtam	UKRAINIAN HERALD			
CRIME AND PUNISHMENT					
	Okudzhava	Union of Fighters for			
	Vysotsky	Political Freedom			

THE SOWER — Litvinov, Chukovskaya, Plyushch, Pimenov

includes names of individuals and groups, titles of samizdat and legitimate publications, and arbitrarily defined collective entities such as "sociologists" as well as references to individuals and groups that are not discussed thoroughly or even at all in this book. In any event, the addition of categories of the "essential left" and "fundamental right" to the ideological spectrum—as well as the overlap of the scope of the above-discussed three main schools of ideological persuasion with more than one position along the "essential left–fundamental right" continuum—seems to provide some much-needed flexibility to the unavoidably static scheme.

OPPOSITION AND DISSENT

It is axiomatic that the soundness and explanatory potential of social science analysis depends on the correct and consistent use of semantic tools with which problems are identified, hypotheses posed, evidence marshaled, cases argued, and conclusions offered.[16] The study of Soviet society and politics, perhaps even more than other contemporary political subjects, is vulnerable to semantic confusion and ideologically biased interpretation. The intrinsically controversial nature of its political and ideological context and the doubtful factual reliability of Soviet data have created unusual latitude for the introduction of dubious evidence and contradictory interpretation that Western observers have all too often accepted at face value.[17]

Apart from ongoing discussions about "models," "isms," "paradigms," and other theoretical explanatory devices in Soviet studies, the state of the arts is such that many frequently used terms and concepts are still not defined so as to convey an unambiguous meaning. To be sure, communist studies are not alone in this dilemma. As Inkeles has suggested: "Our great problem in the social sciences is that so much of the time we are so imprecise in our language and so casual in our use of it, not because we are incapable of doing better, but because we have not developed the technique or habit of exact and precise expression."[18]

In a most general sense the term "dissent" conveys disagreement about something. It implies, beyond mere nay-saying, the existence of a contrary belief or opinion expressed in the form of an alternative or, at any rate, a different position on the matter. Opposition, in the sense of formal logic, denotes "the relation of exclusion or inclusion which exists between propositions having the same subject and predicate but differing in quality,

16. Robert Brown, *Explanation in Social Science* (Chicago, 1963); Abraham Kaplan, *The Conduct of Inquiry* (San Francisco, 1964), especially pp. 34–83.

17. For a useful discussion on this matter see Ellen Mickiewicz, "Uses and Strategies in Data Analysis of the Soviet Union: Cleavages in Industrialized Society," in *Handbook of Soviet Social Science Data*, ed. Ellen Mickiewicz (New York, 1973), pp. 1–47.

18. Alex Inkeles, "Models and Issues in the Analysis of Soviet Society," in his *Social Change in Soviet Russia* (New York, 1971), p. 431.

quantity, or both."[19] If we reduce the differences between the two to degree and kind, or quantity and quality, we may arrive at a set of characteristics with which to compare and contrast the respective meanings of dissent and opposition in the Soviet political context.

Let us begin with a general proposition about opposition, the more general phenomenon of the two. According to Skilling, "The process of opposition may be regarded . . . as a universal one, characteristic of all political systems, but its importance and the forms which it takes vary widely from country to country and from period to period." When he applied this proposition to the communist regimes of Eastern Europe, Skilling discerned four types of opposition: (1) "integral," meaning the total rejection of the political system and appropriate overt or covert oppositional behavior associated therewith; (2) "factional," that is, the kind carried on by groups or individuals belonging to the ruling elite for the purpose of affecting personnel and policy changes in the ruling hierarchy; (3) "fundamental," that is, opposition aimed at changing or negating certain policies that are basic to the political posture of the incumbent leadership; and (4) "specific," meaning "loyal opposition, seeking to change or influence public policy by criticizing established policies, offering different measures from those proposed, or suggesting future courses of action."[20]

Writing in the same volume on the Soviet case, Barghoorn identified three basic forms of opposition: (1) "factional," referring to "efforts by members of the highest party and governmental decision-making bodies to change the personnel or policies of the party-state"; (2) "sectoral"—a kind of loyal "interest group politicking"; and (3) "subversive"—implying demands for the "drastic alteration or even total abolition of the established order."[21]

Since both sets of definitions appear to be based on a thorough survey of the theoretical literature of opposition in communist polities, there is no need to search for additional definitions for the purposes of the following arguments.

In comparing Skilling's and Barghoorn's typologies, one is struck by their common image of the various kinds of opposition: they call them signs of a seamless continuum. It begins with relatively harmless and loyal disagreements about the regime's policies ("specific" and "sectoral" opposition, respectively) and progresses through the stages of "factional" or "fundamental" to the end of the spectrum labeled "integral" and "subversive" opposition. What neither author appears to consider is the basic epistemological difference between "within-system" and "system-rejective" kinds of opposition. The first is aimed at effecting changes *in* the system and

19. *Webster's New World Dictionary of the American Language* (Cleveland and New York, 1959), p. 1029.
20. H. Gordon Skilling, "Opposition in Communist East Europe," in Dahl, *Regimes*, pp. 90, 92–94.
21. Barghoorn, "Opposition," p. 39.

the second at change *of* the system.[22] The difference between the two is in fact a difference between reform and revolution as methods of effecting political change. Reformist change implies attempts at influencing or manipulating political power, and revolutionary change means its forcible acquisition and exclusive possession. Political activity leading to change of the system does, therefore, entail an unconditional commitment to overthrowing a political regime and establishing a new one in its stead.

The relevant social science literature on which Skilling's and Barghoorn's excellent studies depend to a considerable extent for conceptual support seems to fail to distinguish between "within-system" and "system-rejective" opposition as two related but analytically distinct phenomena. By subsuming both under the broader term "political change," arguments stemming from this approach have tended to obliterate the parameters and obfuscate the normative content of both kinds of behavior in established political systems.[23]

In view of the foregoing, it should be apparent that the present writer is inclined to view all instrumental-pragmatic, most moral-absolutist, and some anomic-militant dissent as "within-system" variants of opposition. In this context, however, even those ideologies that may be called "system-rejective" can be regarded as revolutionary only in the rhetorical sense of the word. Even with the will to power—and very few dissidents display this kind of determination—lack of resources prevents them from qualifying as revolutionary in any practical sense.[24] Revolutions require not only will and resources but *leadership* that, in alliance with the dissident masses, can challenge the incumbents with the hope of success. Barring a cataclysmic event such as a nuclear war, the formation of this kind of revolutionary anti-regime alliance in the USSR must be treated as extremely unlikely in the foreseeable future.

If dissent is viewed as a type of within-system opposition loyal to some aspects of the status quo (such as the regime's impressive record in industrialization, education, welfare, etc.) and critical of others (for instance, the *way*, especially the human cost, in which these results were achieved), then we can consider it as a form of interest articulation with a normative

22. Stanley A. Kochanek, "Perspectives on the Study of Revolution and Social Change," *Comparative Politics* 5, no. 3 (April 1973): 313.

23. Much of the "modernization and political development" literature shares the blame for this undifferentiated approach to revolutionary and reformist ideologies. For interesting examples, see Leonard Binder *et al.*, *Crises and Sequences in Political Development* (Princeton, N.J., 1971); Samuel P. Huntington, *Political Order in Changing Societies* (New Haven, Conn., 1968); and Samuel P. Huntington, "The Change to Change: Modernization, Development and Politics," *Comparative Politics* 3, no. 3 (April 1971): 283–322.

24. This reasoning does not, of course, deny the *potentially* revolutionary character of much that we normally associate with contemporary Soviet dissident ideologies and behavior. Rather, it emphasizes that the option to reenact the Bolsheviks' own prerevolutionary strategy and tactics as a way to overthrow the Soviet government is simply not available to any dissident group in the USSR.

content of which three types were identified in an earlier part of the analysis. Interests expressed in the samizdat literature are as complex and thematically heterogeneous as their authors' socioeconomic backgrounds and the grievances for which they seek remedy. In any event, the documentary evidence suggests that adherents of all three dissident ideological persuasions have a set of *shared interests* in advocating reforms in the areas of political democracy, nationality rights, socialist equality, and human rights. These are supplemented by and, in certain instances, subordinated to demands by specific groups focusing on "constituency-specific" grievances such as religious persecution, violations of artistic freedoms, and critical arguments about economic problems and the quality of life in the USSR.[25]

Thus, as the following essays will make clear, Soviet dissent is not merely a protest movement seeking to criticize the leadership, denigrate its authority, or weaken its power. Nor is it an opposition carried on for the psychic benefit of defying the authorities.[26] Rather, it is an ideologically heterogeneous political reform movement that is motivated by both shared and constituency-specific grievances with which the dissidents have sought to promote change by making demands on the political leadership to alleviate or eliminate unacceptable conditions.

DISSENT AND THE SOCIAL SCIENCES

In a recent essay on "The Politics of the Study of Revolution," Sheldon Wolin suggested that American social scientists have been partial to problem-solving methods that failed to capture the essence of rapid political changes, such as revolutions, and tended to attach a negative interpretation to the motivation of groups and individuals actively promoting unconventional methods to bring about desired social changes. "The tradition of social science," Wolin proposed, "is that of a science of *order*" (my emphasis). Given this preoccupation with stability and "orderly change," Wolin says, Western social science from Comte through Weber to Talcott Parsons has consistently upheld the existing scheme of things by refusing to accord legitimacy and separate existence to ideologies and movements that

25. For a useful listing of dissident demands based on a sample of over 500 samizdat documents, see Gerd R. von Doemming, "A Guide to Proposals for Systemic Change in the USSR Offered by Soviet Citizens," *Reference Handbook*, no. 82, Research Department, Radio Liberty (Munich, August 1971). See also Frederick C. Barghoorn, "The General Pattern of Soviet Dissent," in *Papers and Proceedings of the McMaster Conference on Dissent in the Soviet Union*, ed. Peter J. Potichnyj (Hamilton, Ont., 1972), especially pp. 14–25.

26. David Bonavia, the former Moscow correspondent for the *Times* (London), provides ample information, especially on Peter Yakir (whom he calls "Pavel"), to substantiate Solzhenitsyn's and Roy Medvedev's charges of "irresponsible," "provocative," and "amoral" behavior on the part of certain dissidents. See David Bonavia, *Fat Sasha and the Urban Guerilla: Protest and Conformism in the Soviet Union* (London, 1973), especially pp. 25–37, 119–28, and 140–52.

tended radically to alter or overthrow the social-political status quo. Although Parsons did attempt to accommodate revolution in his social system model as a species of "social change," he refused "to probe the sources of revolutionary discontents, by classifying the revolutionists as deviants bordering on the psychopathic, or by discounting the radical nature of revolutionary ideology."[27]

Few would dispute that works written under the influence of the dominant intellectual trends in the 1950s as well as those inspired by the so-called behavioral revolution in the social sciences were, to some degree, hostages to Parsonian problem-solving methods in their approach to the study of Soviet society and politics.[28] Methods of inquiry have a way of affecting the substance of findings. Scholarly efforts to impose an intelligible and philosophically unbiased order through the application of heuristic analytical constructs upon the confusing and, for most observers, morally repugnant Soviet sociopolitical reality thus have resulted in a "tendency to overvalue any given status quo"[29] and ignore or downgrade the importance of antiestablishment forces in communist systems.

This is not to say that works inspired by the Cold War image of seething, enslaved masses waiting for their eventual liberation failed to take the role of Soviet nonelites into account. Rather, it is to suggest that this was an undifferentiated view of the common people living under communism that attributed apocalyptic anticommunist proclivities to all Soviet nonelites.[30] In any event, the fact remains that the *ideas* of the politically powerless never appealed to Western Soviet specialists, most of whom have tended to dismiss them as subjects fit only for journalists and unscientific "area experts."

Research preferences of this kind were also shared by the behavioralists. To them, the political behavior of elites—factory managers, regional party secretaries, government bureaucrats, Young Communist League officials, and members of other highly educated occupational groups—offered more documentable and certainly more quantifiable kinds of evidence than that of the masses far removed from the policy-making process. In an age of "dying" or, at any rate, eroding ideologies, public contestation in communist systems that was confined solely to the realm of ideas seemed to most social scientists to be a futile exercise by politically irrelevant intellectuals and uneducated (and probably antimodernizing) masses. Moreover, one suspects, the impact of radical student activism on United States campuses in the late 1960s,

27. Sheldon S. Wolin, "The Politics of the Study of Revolution," *Comparative Politics* 5, no. 3 (April 1973): 349–50.

28. For a stimulating discussion on these matters, see Alvin W. Gouldner, *The Coming Crisis of Western Sociology* (London, 1971), especially pp. 246–85 and 412–46.

29. Kochanek, "Perspectives," pp. 318–19.

30. For a perceptive critique of Cold War images of communist politics, see Robert Burrowes, "Totalitarianism: The Revised Standard Version," *World Politics* 21, no. 2 (January 1969): 272–94.

which was carried on right on the doorsteps of many academic Sovietologists, may have been responsible for the audible silence or skepticism with which information about comparable Soviet events was received by the scholarly community. Subconscious empathies of establishment thinkers at either end of the East-West ideological spectrum seem to work in mysterious ways.

For example, the sociologist Zygmunt Bauman, a leading Western student of communist societies, identified seven types of conflict in communist Eastern Europe that in his opinion had been responsible for the known dimensions of dissent in that part of the world. These were conflicts between: (1) the "preindustrial crowd" and the stalinist political establishment (here Bauman refers to the peoples of Poland and Hungary in 1956); (2) educated experts and marginally qualified political time-servers; (3) incumbent officeholders and frustrated young office seekers deprived of opportunities for social mobility; (4) "trade interests," or specialists, and (political) personnel managers; (5) those with established social status and others without one; (6) ideas of nationalism and those legitimating Soviet domination; and (7) the intellectuals and their political censors.[31]

Thus, apart from nationalism, which is a significant factor in Soviet nationality dissent though perhaps not so important as in Eastern Europe, we are given a choice between viewing dissent as a family dispute among members of the establishment and considering it either as the politically ineffectual protest of rootless intellectuals or the mindless rage of preindustrial masses against the temporarily "stupefied power system." Ideals of freedom, democracy, and justice as motivating forces of political dissent in both communist and noncommunist systems are conspicuously absent from this taxonomy of the sources of political conflicts.

Another way of looking at dissent is to regard it as an expression of conflict between the ruling communist party and certain interest groups over the allocation of power and influence in the policy-making process. In the burgeoning literature on interest groups in Soviet politics we find many such conflicts described.[32] According to Skilling's and Griffith's important collection of studies on the subject, "A political interest group [is] an aggregate of persons who possess certain common characteristics and share

31. Zygmunt Bauman, "Social Dissent in the East European Political System," *Archives européennes de sociologie* 12, no. 1 (1971): 41–50.

32. The following works are indicative of the thematic scope of the recent literature on interest groups in Soviet politics: Carl A. Linden, *Khrushchev and the Soviet Leadership, 1957–1964* (Baltimore, 1966); Sidney Ploss, *Conflict and Decision-Making in Soviet Russia* (Princeton, N.J., 1965); Jeremy A. Azrael, *Managerial Power and Soviet Politics* (Cambridge, Mass., 1966); Roman Kolkowicz, *The Soviet Military and the Communist Party* (Princeton, N.J., 1967); Milton Lodge, *Soviet Elite Attitudes since Stalin* (Columbus, Ohio, 1969); Werner G. Hahn, *The Politics of Soviet Agriculture, 1960–1970* (Baltimore, 1972); and William E. Odom, *The Soviet Volunteers: Modernization and Bureaucracy in a Public Mass Organization* (Princeton, N.J., 1973).

certain attitudes on public issues, and who adopt distinct positions on these issues and make definite claims on those in authority."[33] The participants, in addition to the party, are most often the military, the economists, the managerial elites, the Komsomol, the intellectual community, and so on.

What is striking about the groups whose activities are described in the relevant literature is that, in the best Parsonian tradition, the kinds of interests they advocate are inherently system-supportive. Thus even if these interests are labeled "dissident," they most often fall in the "within-system" category of dissent. From this it follows that the normative legitimation of interests advanced by such groups represents merely "occupation-group-specific," hence permissible, variations on the regime orthodoxy. To be sure, allowances are made for the existence of "left" and "right" opinion groups within each unit of Soviet interest-group politics. However, apart from the traditionally rebellious writers and artists, there is no room for genuine nonconformists such as Maj. Gen. Peter Grigorenko in the military and Sakharov in the scientific community or for many less well known dissident spokesmen in other occupation groups. Moreover, nonelites such as ethnic and religious groups, though certainly meeting the requirements for consideration as interest groups (after all, interest articulation and aggregation through samizdat and mass petitions do represent definite claims on those in authority), are also excluded from the purview of the interest group approach to Soviet politics.

In conclusion, it may be noted that the motivations attributed to participants in Soviet interest-group politics are said to consist of status and power rather than (or in addition to) some kind of positive ideological commitment to concepts of freedom, justice, or a good society under socialism. Although motivations of the latter kind belong to the nonquantifiable realm of beliefs and ideas, they do represent relevant political data without which the study of Soviet politics remains at best incomplete or at worst becomes an intellectually barren exercise in semantics.

DISSENT, DEMOCRATIZATION, AND DÉTENTE

Until the invasion of Czechoslovakia in August 1968, Soviet dissent was essentially an internal dispute between the increasingly bold intellectuals, young people, and religious believers on the one hand and the uncharacteristically hesitant Soviet internal security apparatus on the other. However, when a handful of demonstrators on Moscow's Red Square protested the Soviet invasion of Czechoslovakia, they united, perhaps unwittingly, the cause of domestic reform aspirations in the USSR with that in other socialist

---

33. H. Gordon Skilling and Franklyn Griffiths, eds., *Interest Groups in Soviet Politics* (Princeton, N.J., 1971), p. 24.

countries and, through them, with all opponents of political dictatorship throughout the world. The crushing of freedom in Prague also prompted sharp criticisms from groups and individuals who had never before expressed an interest in internal Soviet developments. Protest came from several unexpected sources. For example, Maoist Chinese newspaper critics, revisionist Italian and French communists, and conservative Western politicians simultaneously expressed concern about injustices in the USSR and suddenly escalated the matter to the level of an "international problem."[34]

These unanticipated reactions to what the Soviet leadership considered purely domestic matters were further complicated by a variety of international developments that tended, for a time at least, to shield and protect the Soviet regime's domestic opponents. Of the several factors that seem relevant at this juncture, we may list five that probably influenced the Politburo's responses to manifestations of internal democratic opposition in the USSR. These were: (1) the position of the USSR as the leader of the international communist movement, which made the regime and the handling of its domestic affairs vulnerable to conflicting, yet in some ways mutually reinforcing, attacks, expectations, and criticism from China, Eastern Europe, and the nonruling communist parties, respectively; (2) European and U.S. public opinion that could have adversely influenced— but did not—official Western government attitudes toward foreign policy questions that the USSR deemed vital to its long-term security, including the eventual outcome of West Germany's new *Ostpolitik*, the continued development of trade relations with capitalist countries, and, most importantly, prospects of U.S.-Soviet rapprochement in several outstanding matters; (3) the unfavorable outcome to the USSR of the 1967 Arab-Israeli war, which not only enhanced the sense of religious identity and prompted the development of "emigration consciousness" among Soviet Jews but greatly sensitized foreign public opinion to the plight of religious communities in the Soviet Union; (4) the persecution of many articulate intellectuals whose only crime was their nonconformity to the official orthodoxy, which generated unexpectedly strong negative response from the Western media whose influence was thought to be decisive in shaping public opinion toward the USSR (unlike the purge trials of the 1930s, which might, after all, have been considered family feuds among Russian communist

---

34. Leopold Labedz, "Czechoslovakia and After," *Survey*, no. 69 (October 1968), pp. 7–21; Kevin Devlin, "The New Crisis of European Communism," *Problems of Communism* 17, no. 6 (November–December 1968): 57–68; Edward Czerwinsky and Jaroslav Piekalkiewicz, eds., *The Soviet Invasion of Czechoslovakia: Its Effects on Eastern Europe* (New York, 1972), especially pp. 64–80 and 140–58; and Joseph C. Kun, "Chinese Communist Reaction to Czechoslovak Crisis," RFE *Research*, Communist Area (August 27, 1968). An abbreviated and revised version of the following arguments was first published as "The Dissidents' Détente Debate," *New Leader* 57, no. 5 (March 4, 1974): 11–13.

leaders); and finally, (5) the body of written evidence—memoirs, novels, poems, and philosophical treatises on the particulars of the Soviet movement—that reached the outside world and tended to generate a momentum of its own by keeping the "Soviet question" alive and serving to devalue Russia's carefully nurtured image in the eyes of the world.

It became increasingly obvious to Moscow that all these were undesirable developments that, if left unchecked, could affect adversely both the internal stability of the country and the eventual success of its foreign policy priorities.

Over the years Soviet dissidents developed several channels of communication through which they sought to publicize their case to the outside world. These included holding press conferences; giving at least one television interview; making samizdat material available to foreign correspondents; and addressing direct appeals to such forums of foreign public opinion as the United Nations, heads of Western governments, participants in international conferences (both scientific, such as a meeting of psychiatrists, and political, such as the European Security Conference), influential private organizations such as Amnesty International, the World Council of Churches, the International PEN, and the Nobel Prize Committee, prominent intellectuals, and even legislative bodies such as the United States Senate.[35]

Facilitated by the retransmission of many of these messages through the British Broadcasting Corporation, the Voice of America, Deutsche Welle, and most prominently by the U.S. government–sponsored Radio Liberty, beginning in the late 1960s, there developed among Soviet dissidents a substantial body of opinion about foreign policy issues as they affected the cause of reform in the USSR.

---

35. For a representative sampling of dissident communications efforts to the outside world, see Hedrick Smith, "Solzhenitsyn Tells of Struggle to Write Despite Soviet Pressures," *New York Times*, April 3, 1972; the text of a CBS television interview with Amalrik, Yakir, and Bukovsky in *Survey*, no. 77 (Autumn 1970), pp. 128–45; a movie, *Human Rights in the Soviet Union*, featuring Mme Grigorenko, Levitin-Krasnov, Yakir, and four others, which was first shown in London in September 1971 (*New York Times*, Sept. 19, 1971); Susan Jacoby, "Andrei Amalrik, Rebel," *New York Times Magazine*, July 29, 1973, pp. 12–13, 36–40; Mstislav Rostropovich, "An Open Letter to *Pravda*," *New York Times*, October 16, 1970; "Appeal at Helsinki Parley Asked for Soviet Historian [Amalrik]," *New York Times*, June 26, 1973; Sylvia Zalmanson, "Otkrytoe pis'mo v Komitet po pravam Cheloveka pri OON" [Open letter to The Human Rights Commission of the United Nations] (March 1973), in *AS* 1442; Komitet prav cheloveka, "Zaiavleniie s sviazi s otkazom mezhdunarodnogo s"ezda psikhoterapevtov v Oslo obsudit' praktiku psiskhiatricheskoi gospitalizatsii po politich. motivam, prinimiaemoi v SSSR i v stranakh Vost. Evropy" (July 9, 1973) [The (Moscow) Human Rights Committee, statement in connection with the refusal of the Oslo meeting of the International Congress of Psychiatrists to consider the practice of psychiatric confinement for political motives in the USSR and in countries of Eastern Europe], *AS* 1446 (July 23, 1973); "Aninomnoe pis'mo Kongressu SShA o polozhenii evreev, zhelaiushchikh repatriirovat'sia iz SSSR v Izrail'" [Anonymous letter to the Congress of the United States concerning the situation of Jews wishing to repatriate from the USSR to Israel], *AS* 1433 (July 10, 1973).

The first person who consciously linked the question of political democratization in the Soviet Union to the larger issue of peaceful coexistence and global economic progress was Andrei Sakharov. His major statement, "Reflections on Progress, Peaceful Coexistence, and Intellectual Freedom," is analyzed in detail in Dornan's study, below, so its propositions need not be repeated here. Instead, it might be more useful to juxtapose Sakharov's interview with Western newsmen (August 21, 1973) with two other thematically related writings by Alexander Solzhenitsyn and Roy Medvedev.

Solzhenitsyn's position on international affairs may be reconstructed from his Nobel Prize acceptance speech (which he could not deliver personally), his August 1973 interview with Associated Press and *Le Monde* correspondents, and his letter of nomination of Andrei Sakharov for the 1973 Nobel Peace Prize.[36] Solzhenitsyn is a writer in the classical tradition of the Russian intelligentsia; therefore, by definition, he is a moral philosopher with a set of priorities about society, politics, and government. Being a Russian intellectual, he assumes the posture of keeper of his people's moral conscience and guardian against the corrupt and inherently immoral politicians who rule them.

Solzhenitsyn's contempt for professional politicians is not reserved for the Soviet leadership but is extended to powerful hypocrites of all nations. These include avaricious leaders of nonaligned nations, apologists for bloody "national liberation wars," those seeking to profit from the Watergate scandal, officials of the International Olympic Committee, those who in the name of ending the Cold War wish to muzzle free international broadcasting, and even the Nobel Peace Committee for possibly awarding its prize to appeasers like Neville Chamberlain. Solzhenitsyn deplores "the mistake of defining peace as the absence of war, rather than as the absence of violence," and urges the leaders of world public opinion to expose those who are content with fraudulent peace as the only alternative to violence and destruction. There is more to peace than the silence of the guns. "Coexistence on this tightly knit earth," he writes, "should be viewed as an existence not only without wars—that is not enough!—but also without

36. Alexander Solzhenitsyn, "Nobel Lecture in Literature 1970," in *Les Prix nobel en 1971* (Stockholm, 1972), pp. 153–65; "Not One Step Further: An Interview with Solzhenitsyn," *New York Review of Books* 20, no. 15 (October 4, 1973): 11–15; and Alexander I. Solzhenitsyn, "Peace and Violence," *New York Times*, September 15, 1973. Solzhenitsyn's *Letter to Soviet Leaders*, originally written in early September 1973 and made public (with minor revisions designed to soft-pedal some of Solzhenitsyn's critical statements about the quality of domestic politics in the U.S.) on March 5, 1974 in the *Sunday Times* (London) (also in book form by Harper & Row, 1974), does touch on Soviet foreign policy issues such as the danger of war with China and the problem of the Soviet Union's East European satellites. Apart from the difficulty of incorporating the contents of the letter into the narrative, its foreign policy–related arguments are fully consonant with Solzhenitsyn's other publicized statements on this matter. Therefore no attempt is made to include this document in the purview of the following analysis.

violence, or telling us how to live, what to say, what to think, what to know, and what not to know."[37]

The linkage in Solzhenitsyn's arguments for peace and democracy, his criticism of the moral duplicity of "evenhandedness" in condemning both the Greek colonels and the masters of the Gulag empire as if their crimes were of the same or even of comparable magnitude, amounts to a moral-absolutist definition of international public order as well as to an unqualified repudiation of an East-West détente as it has been practiced in the post-Vietnam era.

Détente without adequate guarantees, Solzhenitsyn argues, resolves nothing and only prolongs the danger of war and violence on a global scale.

There seems to be little doubt, as many now realize, that what is going on in the USSR is not simply something happening in one country, but a foreboding of the future of man, and therefore deserving the fullest attention of Western observers.

No, it is not any difficulties of perception that the West is suffering, but a desire not to know, an emotional preference for the pleasant over the unpleasant. Such an attitude is governed by the spirit of Munich, the spirit of complaisance and concession, and by the cowardly self-deception of comfortable societies and people who have lost the will to live a life of deprivation, sacrifice, and firmness.[38]

Sakharov's views on détente, in addition to several passages from his writings that are cited in Dornan's essay, may best be summarized by quoting from what might be considered his most detailed formulation of the matter, given to a group of Western reporters on August 21, 1973—on the fifth anniversary of the occupation of Prague.

Détente without democratization, détente in which the West in effect accepts the Soviet rules of the game, would be dangerous. It would not really solve any of the world's problems and would simply mean capitulating in the face of real or exaggerated Soviet power. It would mean trading with the Soviet Union, buying its gas and oil, while ignoring all other aspects.

I think such a development would be dangerous because it would contaminate the whole world with the antidemocratic peculiarities of Soviet society, it would enable the Soviet Union to bypass problems it cannot resolve on its own, and to concentrate on accumulating still further strength.

As a result, the world would become helpless before this uncontrollable bureaucratic machine. I think that if détente were to proceed totally without qualifications, on Soviet terms, it would pose a serious threat to the world as a whole. It would mean cultivating a closed country where anything that happens may be shielded from outside eyes, a country wearing a mask that hides its true face.

37. "Peace and Violence."
38. *Ibid.* In his *Le Monde* interview Solzhenitsyn placed a more generous interpretation on this matter: "The West by its publicity has already done much to help and save many of our oppressed, but it has not drawn the full lesson; it has not had the strength of feeling to realize that our persecuted are not only grateful to be defended, but also provide a high example of self-sacrifice at the very moment of death and under the syringes of psychiatric murderers." "Not One Step," p. 13.

I would not wish it on anyone to live next to such a neighbor, especially if he is at the same time armed to the teeth.[39]

Indeed, Sakharov "is no enemy of détente," as I. F. Stone said in his insightful analysis "The Sakharov Campaign." "On the contrary, complete and genuine détente, ideological as well as political coexistence, has been one of the two objectives of the extraordinary campaign that he has been waging since 1968. The other is the democratization of the Soviet Union."[40]

Paradoxical as it may sound, Sakharov is a supporter of a balance-of-power approach to international peace and stability. What he has been objecting to throughout has been a suspected devil's pact between the two superpowers at the expense of their democratic opponents at home and of their militarily less powerful client states abroad. Although an antimachiavellian in the general area of international politics, he is an astute tactician who is prepared to use every legitimate lever (such as the Jackson Amendment, which places political conditions on the granting by the United States of a "most favored nation" status to the USSR) to promote what he considers his prime objective, the democratization of the USSR.

Whether Sakharov's views on international relations represent a typical "instrumental-pragmatic" posture seems to be a moot point here. What matters is that his exalted social status because of his responsibility for the development of the Soviet hydrogen bomb (as of October 1973, he still had access to a chauffeur-driven limousine to attend a weekly seminar on theoretical physics) has added considerable weight to his arguments and has made him a spokesman—though an admittedly reluctant one—for the Soviet scientific community.[41]

Roy Medvedev's samizdat essay, "The Problem of Democratization and the Problem of Détente," is the third and, in some ways, most interesting contribution to current Soviet dissident debates on protest strategies and appropriate ways of influencing the Soviet leadership.[42] Unlike Solzhenitsyn and, as we may surmise, Sakharov, Medvedev is a Marxist who expects the

39. This passage is quoted in Hedrick Smith, "The Intolerable Andrei Sakharov," *New York Times Magazine*, November 25, 1973, pp. 47–48. See also "Sakharov Warns on Dealing with Soviet," *New York Times*, August 22, 1973.

40. I. F. Stone, "The Sakharov Campaign," *New York Review of Books* 20, no. 16 (October 8, 1973): 3. See also "The Sakharov Dialogue," *New York Times*, August 29, 1973; "Sakharov Reveals Agonies of Conscience," *New York Times*, September 10, 1973; "Sakharov: This, Not That," *New York Times*, September 12, 1973; and "Text of the Sakharov Reply to Lawyer," *New York Times*, October 8, 1973.

41. News of his request for permission to leave the USSR to accept a visiting appointment at Princeton was received with a sense of disappointment by some dissidents. According to an artist, "If he really goes it means they have won." Another Moscow intellectual felt that he was "the one person who has spoken out in defense of everyone." "Sakharov Decision Deplored in Soviet," *New York Times*, December 2, 1973.

42. R. A. Medvedev, "The Problem of Democratization and the Problem of Détente," full text in Radio Liberty *Special Report*, RL 359/73 (November 19, 1973). Excerpts were published in the *New York Times*, November 17, 1973, under the title "Arriving at Democratization and Détente."

impetus for democratic reform to come from gradual personnel and policy changes in the top party leadership rather than from outside pressures. Also, unlike Sakharov, Medvedev tends to downgrade the positive results achieved by open dissent, and he is sharply critical of the "immorality" and "provocative" behavior of certain dissidents such as Yakir and Krasin.[43]

In addition to these concerns, his essay "The Problem of Democratization and the Problem of Détente" was prompted by what Medvedev considers the politically counterproductive radicalization of several leading spokesmen of the dissident intelligentsia. These people, Medvedev argues, "have begun to express more extreme views and to make still less constructive proposals, guided more by emotions than by considerations of political appropriateness."[44] The examples of this kind of allegedly imprudent behavior seem to point to at least three identifiable individuals. One is the writer Vladimir Maksimov, who, in an open letter to the German novelist Heinrich Böll, denounced Chancellor Willy Brandt's *Ostpolitik* as a fraud and described its architect as a "mediocre apologist for a new Munich who takes himself for a great politician."[45] Another is Sakharov, who is taken to task for his endorsement of U.S. trade restrictions on the USSR. A third is Solzhenitsyn, for comparing favorably the South African government's treatment of imprisoned blacks with that accorded to Grigorenko by the Soviet authorities when they confined him to a hospital for the criminally insane as punishment for his political protest.[46]

Medvedev admits that there might exist a causal relationship between the relaxation of East-West tensions and the growing repression of dissidents. He feels, however, that the advantages of détente may outweigh, in the long run, the present difficulties experienced by the regime's critics. The responsibility for such retrograde policies belongs, in Medvedev's words, to "our hawks" and "right wing circles" within the ruling Communist Party Central Committee. With the removal of conservative Politburo members Shelest and Voronov, these forces, Medvedev intimates, have lost their leaders and are helpless to prevent the further easing of East-West relations.

43. The relevant passage is worth quoting in full: "The statements and testimony of such degraded persons as Yakir and Krasin, who were viewed by many organs of information for a long time as 'heroic fighters on behalf of civil rights,' were used for the dissipation and demoralization of oppositional tendencies which had developed in past years, although the immoral and objectively provocative character of their activities was already clear to many people in our country several years ago." R. A. Medvedev, "Problem of Democratization," p. 3.

44. *Ibid.*, p. 4.

45. See "Soviet Dissident Says Brandt Appeases East," *New York Times*, August 10, 1973.

46. R. A. Medvedev, "Problem of Democratization," p. 14. Writing in late January 1974, however, Medvedev chose to endorse and identify himself with the leading propositions of Solzhenitsyn's *Gulag Archipelago*, and three weeks later he went on record as calling the writer's expulsion from the USSR a "moral defeat" for the regime. See "O knige Solzhenitsyna 'Arkhipelag—Gulag' " [On Solzhenitsyn's book *The Gulag Archipelago*]; For an English text, see "Gulag Archipelago," *Ramparts* 12, no. 11 (June 1974): 49–55; and Robert G. Kaiser, Medvedev Deplores Writer's Exile," *Washington Post*, March 5, 1974.

The cessation of jamming of foreign Russian-language broadcasts in September 1973, the ratification by the Supreme Soviet of two United Nations covenants on social and political rights, the continued outflow of Jewish emigrants, the de facto suspension of the notorious "education tax," and generally pragmatic foreign policies especially toward the United States represent, in Medvedev's mind, positive steps in the right direction. He credits them, moreover, to mutual détente-inspired compromises rather than to efforts of the regime's domestic critics.

While not discounting the importance of Western public opinion as a factor in influencing Soviet policies at home, Medvedev offers advice concerning practical limitations on the efficacy of dissident protest aimed at foreign countries.

In general, the opportunities for pressure on the Soviet Union from the point of view of interstate or economic relations should not be overestimated. Not only because the Soviet partners in the talks will reasonably protest against interference in Soviet domestic affairs, but we generally doubt very much that the majority of Western leaders are really seriously concerned with problems of political and human rights in the USSR or China. In the long run, Nixon, Pompidou, and Heath defend the interests of the ruling classes of their countries, and it is not axiomatic that capitalist circles in the United States, England, France, and the FRG are so interested in the most rapid development of socialist democratization in the USSR or in speeding up economic, social, and cultural progress in the Soviet Union.

Therefore, Soviet "dissidents" who turn to Western countries for support must consider carefully the "address" to which they direct these appeals.[47]

The trouble, as Medvedev sees it, is that dissident appeals provided Western "rightist" circles with too much comfort and did not give enough encouragement to "leftist social organizations which are most interested in the evolution of genuine socialist democracy in our country." In any case, he suggests that "it would be an illusion to think that Western public opinion will sometime become more concerned with internal Soviet problems than with internal problems of its own." In conclusion, he reminds his fellow intellectuals "not to fall victim to a peculiar Moscow-centrism and fail to see that in many other countries there are just as severe, and in many instances still more severe, internal problems than those that exist in the USSR."[48]

Disagreements among dissident Soviet intellectuals about ways of putting pressure on the party leadership tend to overshadow their remarkable consensus about the nature of contemporary international relations and the place of the USSR in the community of nations. All seem to agree that some kind of change is inevitable in the way the USSR coexists with the rest of the world. None of them has false illusions about Western political institutions and the capitalist market economy that shape the daily lives of political

47. *Ibid.*, p. 11.
48. *Ibid.*, p. 14.

leaders, intellectuals, and the common people on the "other side." They all oppose political extremism and ideological demagoguery, and they are greatly concerned about the prospects of a lasting peace that is "more than the absence of violence." They are fearful of the Soviet "military-industrial complex" and tend to be skeptical about the wisdom of its political masters (or representatives?) sitting in the all-powerful Politburo.

According to their individual philosophical temperament, they all seek solutions from different constituencies at home and abroad. Solzhenitsyn probably speaks to the largest audience: to everyone who dreads war, cruelty, and the rule of faceless bureaucrats over the destinies of mankind. Sakharov's recent remarks seem to be addressed to political decision-makers, educated elites, and those who believe in the superiority of scientific reasoning over the blind passions of anachronistic ideologies. Medvedev might be called the honest broker between the other two in trying to reconcile his comrades' pleas for sympathy and help from the outside with the forbidding political realities of the Soviet Union where, he argues persuasively, all reforms must begin.[49]

These men and, we may surmise, many others like them in the USSR are becoming increasingly aware of the global context in which Soviet internal political developments are taking place. They are a new breed of Soviet internationalist democrats. They are deeply loyal to the country of their birth but have transcended the intellectual limitations of their environment and have chosen to identify themselves with the international community of men and women who have liberated themselves from the burdens of cultural insularity and political xenophobia.

CONCLUSIONS

It should be apparent from the foregoing as well as from the following studies that contemporary Soviet dissent is an extremely complex, multifaceted, and often contradictory phenomenon—just like the country where it has been taking place in the last twenty years. Thus no single volume, however broadly conceived, can possibly do justice to more than a

49. In the spring of 1974 the dissidents' debate on the future of the USSR took a new turn. As a reaction to the unprecedented expulsion of Solzhenitsyn from his native land, some former dissidents such as Yevgeny Yevtushenko felt compelled (perhaps temporarily) to rejoin the ranks of the regime's critics, while others such as Viktor P. Nekrasov refused to sign critical official statements about the Solzhenitsyn affair. More importantly, however, the Gulag book and Solzhenitsyn's *Letter to Soviet Leaders* prompted a potentially far-reaching debate among the dissenters over issues that—especially Marxist-Leninist ideology and Solzhenitsyn's Slavophile notions about Russia's future destiny—in the long run could irreparably polarize the leaders as well as the followers of the contemporary democratic movement in the USSR. See "Soviet Writers' Union Publicly Criticizes Yevtushenko," *New York Times*, March 7, 1974; "Soviet Expels Dissident Backer from Moscow to His Kiev Home," *New York Times*, March 23, 1974; and "Book on Solzhenitsyn Affair [*Live Not by the Lie*] Circulating in Moscow," *New York Times*, March 21, 1974.

few aspects of it. The themes of politics, ideas, communications, and people that are the foci of inquiry in this collection of studies could and, as more documentary evidence becomes available, undoubtedly will be expanded into other still-uncharted areas of Soviet society and politics. This book, then, is no more than a beginning of what one hopes will be a new look by Western scholars at the human condition and the political, social, and cultural forces that shape it in the USSR.

In symposia of this kind it is customary for the editor to offer a set of concluding remarks purporting to represent the consensus of the individual contributors to his volume. For at least three reasons a stock-taking of this sort seems inappropriate in this case. First, it is argued that political dissent is not merely an act of protest but an existential experience for both the participant and the beholder. This is particularly true in cases of confrontations that pit fellow human beings against their dehumanizing political environment. Once the issue is perceived in this manner, views, however objective and scholarly, tend to become matters of personal ethic and philosophical preference. Second, Soviet dissent, notwithstanding the latest waves of repression or, perhaps, because of them, is a still-unfolding process. Only the most tentative kinds of broad hypotheses and propositions about the nature of changes in the Soviet system may be attributed to dissent. And finally, a summary list of findings is not possible because, by editorial design, the individual authors, in the best tradition of Soviet studies, represent a wide range of opinion (in some instances irreconcilable) about the significance, dimensions, and future implications of their subject.

It is therefore the hope of the editor of this volume that both the short-comings and the merits the readers may find in it will stimulate additional work and even more painstaking analysis of Soviet dissent.

1 DISSENT: STRATEGY AND TACTICS

CHAPTER ONE / THE POST-KHRUSHCHEV CAMPAIGN TO SUPPRESS DISSENT: PERSPECTIVES, STRATEGIES, AND TECHNIQUES OF REPRESSION / FREDERICK C. BARGHOORN

INTRODUCTION

In the heyday of what Nikita S. Khrushchev called "the cult of personality of J. V. Stalin" it was probably as dangerous for a Soviet citizen to dissent from his government's policies or even to be suspected of dissent as it ever has been anywhere. During Stalin's rule open disagreement with or criticism of the autocrat, his policies, his interpretation of the official ideology of Marxism-Leninism, and the like entailed enormous risk of exile, imprisonment, torture, or death. So did membership in suspect ethnic or social groups or even suspicion that a citizen might be less than whole-hearted in his devotion to the leader. Punishment, moreover, not only was draconian; it was frequently capricious. All too often persons innocent of any crime suffered a worse fate than the "guilty." A frightening arbitrariness also characterized the relationship between the gravity of offenses and punishments meted out to their alleged perpetrators. The harshest penalties were frequently applied to those who had committed the mildest offenses or none at all, while others convicted of far graver crimes were treated more leniently.

The oligarchs who have ruled the USSR since Stalin died in 1953 have also sternly repressed dissent whenever it seemed to them to be dangerous to political stability, elite privilege, and their personal power. Their policy toward dissent differs significantly, however, from that which prevailed under Stalin, particularly during the twenty-odd years of his personal dictatorship (roughly 1934–53). Arbitrary coercion by no means vanished with Stalin, but its scope was considerably reduced. Yet the degree of "unfreedom," to borrow Felix Oppenheim's term, of Soviet citizens *vis-à-vis* the political authorities remained great. There were still many glaring discrepancies between official ideology and reality as perceived by some citizens. Alienation and moral outrage impelled some independent-minded men and women to petition for, or even to indignantly demand, changes in policies and institutions. Such dissent, especially if it seems to challenge the legitimacy of the political order or involve aggressive advocacy of structural

For financial assistance indispensable both to the preparation of this chapter and to his ongoing study of Soviet dissent, the author wishes to express his appreciation to the Stimson Fund of Yale University, the John Simon Guggenheim Memorial Foundation, the American Philosophical Society, the ACLS–SSRC, and the Research Institute on Communist Affairs at Columbia University.

change, may still lead to socioeconomic sanctions if the authorities regard it as relatively harmless or to exile, prison, labor camps, or special psychiatric hospitals if they consider it flagrant.

Still, today's disaffected, potentially rebellious citizens are fortunate in one important respect in comparison with their predecessors under Stalin. They apparently know reasonably well what the consequences will be of challenging official policies and norms openly, vigorously, or (most dangerous of all) in an organized fashion. Moreover, the limits of permissible dissent, while still narrow, have widened somewhat. They seem, however, to have again contracted after Khrushchev's ouster in 1964. Certainly, dissent became increasingly sharp and voluminous after Khrushchev's fall, presumably indicating that dissenters felt a more urgent need to criticize. Then too, severe sanctions against relatively high-status intellectuals, which Khrushchev had usually avoided (his allowing Boris Pasternak to be publicly hounded after publication abroad of *Doctor Zhivago* is a major exception, but in that case Khrushchev seems to have been misled by advisers he later repudiated) became increasingly frequent, especially after the Soviet-organized military operation against Czechoslovakian "socialism with a human face" in 1968. Perhaps most important, denunciations of Stalin's abuses of power and violations of "socialist legality" petered out a year or two after Khrushchev's departure. Perhaps the gradual tightening of control was the sort of behavior that one should expect from an authoritarian political system after a succession crisis has been weathered and political normalcy achieved.

The surprising degree of freedom that had been available under Khrushchev was the product of both personality and situational factors. To a degree that irked and alarmed most other CPSU (Communist Party of the Soviet Union) leaders, Khrushchev's political style was experimental, improvisational, and unbureaucratic. His habit of personally deciding issues of cultural policy, such as his authorizing publication of Alexander Solzhenitsyn's novella about life in a Stalin-era labor camp, *One Day in the Life of Ivan Denisovich*, contrasted sharply with the bureaucratic orthodoxy of his successors. Decision-making powers in such matters are now exercised by conservative cultural officials, in, for example, the Union of Soviet Writers. The leadership has not interfered with the normal and severe routines of the censorship and other control agencies. The relative "liberalism" of the Khrushchev era can also be attributed in part to the effects of succession crisis and factional strife. Khrushchev was impelled to seek support among social groups, including the literary-artistic intelligentsia, whose views had previously not been accorded much respect by the Soviet supreme political leadership.[1]

1. Reliable evidence supporting the above hypothesis is available in Zhores Medvedev's book *Ten Years after Ivan Denisovich* (New York, 1973), especially pp. 57–63, 76, 120.

This study focuses on the policy of the CPSU toward dissent, with special attention to the post-Khrushchev period, when for the first time an abundance of dissenters' *samizdat* (self-published) material became available. Based on both samizdat and official Soviet data, it analyzes the attitudes and beliefs that underlie the regime's effort to prevent, contain, or suppress dissent as well as the administrative and legal processes of repression.

Variance over time in regime-dissenter relations in the USSR has been considerable. For the student of comparative politics, however, this "intra-system" variance is less significant than "intersystem" differences between regime-dissenter relations in "hegemonies," such as the USSR, and other communist regimes, and in "polyarchies," such as Britain, Canada, the United States, etc. Robert Dahl defines hegemonies as "regimes that impose the most severe limits on the expression, organization, and representation of political preferences and on the opportunities available to opponents of the government." Polyarchies, in his lexicon, are states that "impose the fewest restraints" on opponents. They protect "most individuals, in their right to express, privately or publicly, their opposition to the government."[2] In a word, the political process is biased in the former toward unity and strict conformity, in the latter toward autonomy and diversity, provided that no faction or group press demands so extreme as to threaten anarchy or subversion.

In "communist" or "Leninist" systems, much of the activity of the political socialization and communication structures involves systematic indoctrination of the citizenry in a version of Marxism-Leninism tailored to the ongoing political needs of the leadership. They may be regarded as a subset of the class of "hegemonic" systems, which in turn is a subset of the larger set of authoritarian polities. In Leninist systems demands for political and ideological conformity are exceptionally frequent and insistent.

Typical of such demands made by the authorities upon citizens—in this case addressed primarily to CPSU members—is a statement published in 1973 in an organizational journal: "Of special relevance today are Lenin's words that if the party's guiding, educational, and organizational roles are weakened, this can only lead to the triumph of bourgeois counterrevolution.'"[3] Warnings of this kind are traditional in the USSR and other

2. Robert A. Dahl, ed., *Regimes and Oppositions* (New Haven, Conn., 1973), pp. 4-5. Also useful to scholars interested in the comparative study of dissent and, more generally, in fitting systems of the Soviet type into a "taxonomy" of political systems are Dahl's *Polyarchy: Participation and Opposition* (New Haven, Conn., 1971); Barrington Moore, Jr., *Terror and Progress, USSR* (Cambridge, Mass., 1954); and Samuel P. Huntington and Clement H. Moore, eds., *Authoritarian Politics in Modern Society: The Dynamics of Established One-Party Systems* (New York and London, 1970).

3. Unsigned report on a conference of Soviet and East European social scientists, under the auspices of the Academy of Social Sciences attached to the Central Committee of the Soviet Communist Party, entitled "Internatsionalny kharakter leninskikh printsipov partiinogo stroitelstva" [International character of Leninist principles of party-building], in *Partiinaya zhizn'*, no. 16 (August 1973), p. 58.

Leninist regimes. But they apparently were sounded with special urgency after "détente" had spurred Moscow to fashion strategies for maximizing the benefits while minimizing the costs of expanding contacts with the "bourgeois" world. Their persistence indicates how difficult it is for hegemonic systems, in their treatment of dissent and opposition, to escape the "self-fulfilling prophecy" described by Dahl:

> Since all opposition is potentially dangerous, no distinction can be made between acceptable and unacceptable opposition, between loyal and disloyal opposition. . . . Yet if all oppositions are treated as . . . subject to repression, opposition that would be loyal if it were tolerated becomes disloyal because it is not tolerated. Since all opposition is likely to be disloyal, all opposition must be repressed.[4]

However, the fact that there have been significant differences in treatment of dissent within and among the Lenin, Stalin, Khrushchev, and Brezhnev periods of Soviet history reminds us that a range of policy options is available to the leadership of even a hegemonic polity, a category to which, we assume in this essay, the USSR has belonged since the consolidation of Soviet power following the Bolshevik victory in the Civil War of 1918–21.

It is arguable, to be sure, that before the consolidation of Stalin's dictatorship the Soviet regime resembled what Dahl calls a "near-hegemony." Certainly in the post-Stalin period the top leadership has been more oligarchic than autocratic. This change in structure has been accompanied by some relaxation of control over articulation of dissent—but only when it did not challenge the consensus prevalent among the rulers regarding the limits of permissible public political discourse. Vigorous action has been taken against all who seriously violated the rule that nothing must be allowed to undermine the Politburo's control over the interest articulation function[5] and thus, in Soviet jargon, to diminish the "leading role" of the CPSU.

The factors fostering hegemony and inhibiting dissent in the USSR seem to include at least the following apparently synergistically related elements:

1. *The heritage of tsarist Russia's "subject" political culture.*[6] Compliance with the tsar's commands was fostered by the established Russian Orthodox Church, a vast bureaucracy, and a brutal political police. The harsh conditions of political struggle imposed by autocracy led Lenin to design a

---

4. Dahl, *Regimes*, p. 13.

5. The foregoing, in our opinion, is not incompatible with the stress placed by Stephen F. Cohen in his brilliant biography *Bukharin* (New York, 1973) on the wide range of alternative policies advocated during particular historical periods—especially the 1920s and the post-Stalin era—the rival leaders of the CPSU, and the striking differences in regime structure and policy at different times.

6. Gabriel A. Almond and Sidney Verba, in *The Civic Culture* (Princeton, 1963), indicate that typical individuals in a polity with this type of culture have a passive orientation to the system. Or—in terms somewhat different from theirs—"subjects" accept as normal a situation of dependency upon a government the policies of which they cannot influence. See pp. 17–18, 20–24.

party "which by its discipline, could survive against the forces of Tsarism."[7] Thus, "Bolshevism as a movement was an indigenous, authoritarian response to the environment of Tsarist absolutism which nurtured it."[8] Yet the extent to which Lenin's belief that the conquest of power by revolutionaries in autocratic Russia must be a quasi-military operation facilitated Stalin's creation of a hegemonic system remains controversial. Lowenthal has observed: "Without the pre-existing 'party of a new type,' the first state of the new type could not have been built up; with that party once victorious, the tendency for its leaders to establish dictatorial, monopolistic rule was given—to be brought out—'by events.'"[9] Insightful also is Trotsky's assertion that "the army of the Soviet Thermidor was recruited essentially from the remnants of the former ruling parties. . . . Members of the old classes were taken into the State machine and quite a few even into the Party."[10] The heritage of the tsarist traditional political culture, in whose rhetoric such concepts as orthodoxy, autocracy, and nationality loomed large, was certainly one factor in the emergence of Stalin's "subject-participatory" culture. This is evident in the latter's *vozhd* (equivalent to the German *Führer*), its hierarchical political structure, its official creed of Marxism-Leninism, and, especially for the "masses," a new Soviet nationalism.[11]

2. *Russian underdevelopment.* Before the outbreak of World War I, Russia had experienced rapid industrial growth for several decades. Yet when the empire fell in 1917 she was the least developed of the world powers. Contrary to the Marxist belief that capitalism everywhere would, as E. H. Carr put it, "run its full course," in fact "it was a nascent and immature capitalism which succumbed easily to the first revolutionary onslaught."[12] The struggle to build socialism in an underdeveloped country, exhausted by years of war, civil war, and foreign military intervention, created desperately difficult problems. Stalin's attempt to resolve the USSR's problems by a crash program of forced modernization entailed deprivations which set in motion a vicious circle of coercion-resistance-repression, culminating in the great purges of 1936–38 and the enduring pall of fear they cast upon the population.

The developmental gap between the USSR and the West and the lingering national inferiority complex that accompanied it perhaps spurred the regime to compensate by claiming for Soviet socialism moral superiority

---

7. Saul N. Silverman, ed., *Lenin* (Englewood Cliffs, N.J., 1972), p. 45.
8. Merle Fainsod, *How Russia Is Ruled*, rev. ed. (Cambridge, Mass., 1965), p. 3.
9. Richard Lowenthal, "Lenin and Totalitarianism," in Silverman, *Lenin*, pp. 190–91.
10. Leon Trotsky, *Stalin* (New York, 1946), pp. 404–5. Trotsky's interpretation is not incompatible with the careful analysis of early postrevolutionary party recruitment policy in T. H. Rigby, *Communist Party Membership in the U.S.S.R.* (Princeton, 1968), chap. 1, especially p. 87.
11. For a fuller presentation of the above, see Frederick C. Barghoorn, *Politics in the USSR*, 2d ed. (Boston, 1972), especially chap. 2.
12. Edward Hallett Carr, *The Bolshevik Revolution* (London, 1966), 1: 55.

to foreign capitalism. It was easy to move beyond these attitudes to xenophobic condemnation of "bourgeois" influences and to suspicion regarding the political loyalty of those who had unauthorized contacts with foreigners. But for some Soviet intellectuals the rigid pattern of prescriptions and prohibitions embodied in the official political culture seemed intolerably incompatible with Marxist doctrine or with the liberal values to which, despite regime pressures, a minority clung. Only by postulating the survival during the Stalin era of latent cultural and ideological diversity can we understand post-Stalin dissent. And this latent protest was in part, at least, a reaction to the strategies chosen by—or forced upon—the regime in its effort to cope with inherited underdevelopment.

3. *The foreign threat.* It is a truism that governments preoccupied with achieving military security tend to be intolerant of dissent. Certainly the Soviet authorities have always been so preoccupied. This preoccupation, sometimes amounting to obsession, was shaped by ideological and economic factors and, as much as anything, by historical experiences, in particular the bitter and destructive civil war that followed the Bolshevik seizure of power and the second struggle for survival against the onslaught of Hitler's hordes during World War II.

Trotsky identified a crucial aspect of the civil war legacy when he asserted that "Stalin, like many others, was moulded" by its "environment and circumstances."[13] According to Rigby: "As it was, in encouraging the *de facto* proscription of other parties and the concentration of initiative and decision making . . . the Civil War fostered that dictatorship of the central party leadership which has been the keystone of the Soviet political order ever since."[14]

The trauma of World War II probably confirmed for most Soviet citizens the truthfulness of earlier propaganda regarding the aggressive nature of "imperialism." In recent years growing concern over the intentions and military capabilities of Communist China has helped to sustain old fears of foreign "encirclement."

The link between economic underdevelopment and military security was dramatized by Stalin's well-known warning, in a speech to industrial executives in 1931, that unless the Soviet Union overtook the advanced capitalist countries in ten years it would be destroyed. This concern also inspired frequent admonitions to Soviet citizens to be vigilant in helping the authorities to ferret out "imperialist spies." It helps to explain, though not to justify, the readiness of the Soviet political police to accuse citizens who had been in contact with foreigners, including foreign communists, of conspiracy against the state. Such accusations, which can easily result in criminal prosecution, were sometimes pretexts for measures against individuals who

13. Trotsky, *Stalin*, pp. 404–5.
14. Rigby, *Party Membership*, p. 58.

had in no way sought to assist hostile foreign governments or émigré Russian organizations but who had incurred official displeasure because of dissent regarded as objectionable. To suspicious Soviet party and police bureaucrats, however, it has sometimes seemed that dissent, since it was not legitimate (we shall have more to say on this later), must have been instigated by foreign intelligence services for sinister purposes.

It should be added, however, that the CPSU's modernization effort generated massive support for the Soviet system. Patriotic pride was engendered and vested interests created by mass political mobilization, rapid industrialization and concomitant rapid social mobility, and impressive achievements in science, education, public health, and other welfare services. These achievements and the systematic Soviet socialization programs they made possible and to which they contributed help us understand why, in spite of hardships and frustrations, the level of articulated dissent has usually been low in the USSR.

Now Marxist-Leninist ideology, of course, is neither coterminous with Soviet political culture nor the only source of the regime's legitimacy. Patriotism, tradition, and the achievements of the CPSU in a wide range of domestic and foreign policy activity contribute. Most Soviet people, including most members of the intelligentsia, also seem to be chiefly concerned with status, job security, and more material goods and services for the nation and themselves. Alienation arising from conflicts between communist ideals and the regime's failure to fulfill them thus may well be confined to a very small minority of the population.

Yet for the authorities the existence of an official doctrine regarded as necessary for their legitimacy virtually forces them to punish bold and open critics on pain of seeming to appear weak and irresolute in its defense. Thus the ideological aspects of the Soviet type of political culture may play some part in generating both dissent and repression.

4. *Ideals and realities.* Account must also be taken of a problem peculiar to systems in which the authorities base their claim to legitimacy partly on the assertion that in the conduct of public policy they apply Marxist theory. This problem arises from the contradictions some intellectuals perceive between the observable realities of political life and the values embodied in Marxist thought. At least some idealistic persons have always regarded these values not as mere rationalizations for the power of the ruling elite but as personal moral commitments.

5. *The directed economy.* We accept the proposition that a socialist economy is not necessarily incompatible with toleration of dissent provided it is not highly centralized and is associated with a pluralistic political and social order.[15] The history of regimes of the Soviet type, however, indicates

---

15. For perceptive discussions of relations between socialism and political freedom, see Moore, *Terror and Progress*, pp. 170–73, and Dahl, *Polyarchy*, pp. 57–61.

that a centralized, state-directed economy tends to severely limit dissent. Although much research might be necessary to develop this argument, it seems plausible without extensive elaboration. Interest groups, for instance, which play a major role in articulating dissent in societies with market economies—where dissent flourishes—are weak in Soviet-type societies; and so is dissent. It also makes sense to think that dissent is weaker without the relative economic independence provided to a substantial segment of the population by ownership of property and the availability of alternative sources of employment in societies with market economies.

Finally, as will become apparent in our discussion of "extrajudicial repression," the price of dissent may be economic disaster. Conversely, intellectuals whom the regime regards as basically loyal and useful but who occasionally display a disquieting independence of spirit may be cajoled into a degree of conformity by a combination of threats and rewards.[16] Or so the Kremlin seems to calculate. The poets Yevgeny Yevtushenko and, to a lesser degree, Andrei Voznesenski apparently are examples. Be it noted, however, that Yevtushenko publicly protested after his telegram to Brezhnev opposing Solzhenitsyn's predeportation arrest was answered only by cancellation of a scheduled television appearance. While perhaps not indicative of a future protest wave, this and other reactions to the blow against Solzhenitsyn at least cast doubt on the validity of simplistic judgments about Yevtushenko and perhaps other "establishment" intellectuals and demonstrated once again the complexity and unpredictability of responses to repression.

By May 1972, when Nixon and Brezhnev held their first summit meeting in Moscow, regime pressures had silenced most of those who had persisted in openly articulating dissenting opinions over the preceding five or six years. Once unleashed, the quietly deadly effort to intimidate dissent, begun in 1965 with the arrests of Andrei Sinyavsky and Yuli Daniel, never ceased. However, it attained special intensity in 1968–69 in connection with Moscow's action against Czechoslovakia and again in 1972, as the détente between Washington and Moscow bore fruit. By the fall of 1973 a few leading dissenters such as Yuri Galanskov were dead—Galanskov probably because of harsh punishment and neglect of his need for proper medical care. Many, such as Vladimir Bukovsky, had begun serving long terms in prisons and labor camps. Others, among them the war hero Maj. Gen. Peter Grigorenko, had been confined for years in "special psychiatric hospitals" administered by psychiatrists serving the secret police. Peter Yakir, long thought to be immune from arrest out of respect for his martyred father

16. See, for example, I. Ignatev, "The Fortieth Birthdays of Ye. Yevtushenko and A. Voznesenski as Seen by Soviet Critics," *Radio Liberty Dispatch*, July 23, 1973, and Anatoly Kuznetsov's discussion in *New York Times*, October 1, 1969, on the economic and other consequences to Soviet writers of agreeing or refusing to collaborate with the KGB. See also Robert Conquest, "The Politics of Poetry," *New York Times Magazine*, September 30, 1973, and Yevtushenko's above-mentioned protest, *New York Times*, February 18, 1974.

(Iona Yakir, one of the top Soviet military commanders murdered at Stalin's behest), fell victim in August 1973 to a Stalin-like "show trial" after having been held in jail since June 21, 1972. A number of important leaders of the "Democratic Movement" (most, but not all, of Jewish or partly Jewish ancestry) such as Alexander Yesenin-Volpin and Zhores Medvedev had been permitted or forced to leave their homeland. Others—the physicist Andrei Sakharov and Solzhenitsyn were the most notable examples—persisted in lonely and perilous defiance of the immense power arrayed against them. They were sustained by the force of their moral convictions and protected somewhat by the moral support of thousands of prominent admirers and well-wishers abroad. It seems likely that the Soviet regime's decision to deport Solzhenitsyn on February 13, 1974 was heavily influenced by concern over the impact that even harsher measures against him would have produced in wide circles of world public opinion. Despite Western protests, the action was probably a shrewd move, since it deprived an already decimated dissident community of its most heroic, skillful, and inspiring leader. Solzhenitsyn left behind him thousands of political prisoners, some of whom, like the scientists Leonid Plyushch or Yuri Shikhanovich, the historian Andrei Amalrik, and General Grigorenko, were also men of remarkable courage, talent, and devotion to intellectual and moral freedom.

The Kremlin's resort to selective terror against dissenters, especially from early 1972 on, indicated that Brezhnev and his fellow oligarchs viewed the silencing of dissonant voices as less costly than a more tolerant policy. It is worth noting that both when official relations with the West were strained during the Czechoslovakian crisis and when they had significantly improved following the Nixon-Brezhnev meetings of 1972 and 1973, the Soviet authorities were willing to risk the damage to the Soviet image abroad—not to mention that inflicted on the morale of the Soviet intelligentsia—that they must have known would be among the costs of persecuting dissenting intellectuals.

This cost was kept to tolerably low levels by such methods as censorship and propaganda attacks—often, to be sure, crude and inept—on dissenters and their supporters abroad. It was also held down by the expectation of powerful interests in the West that vast economic and political benefits would flow from relaxation of tensions between the socialist and the capitalist worlds. It is not demonstrable that an even more forceful expression of moral support to the Soviet civil rights movement than was manifested in the West—especially in Britain and, in the case of the related cause of the right of Soviet Jews to emigrate, in the United States—would have produced a fundamental change in Soviet treatment of dissenters. But it does seem certain that, at least in the case of Jewish emigration, the moral force of an aroused world opinion—or of the elements thereof that took the trouble to act—helped to push Soviet policy toward at least partial, selective amelioration of punishments already decreed and abandonment of some projected acts of repression. The permission to allow some Jews to emigrate, which resulted by mid-1973 in departure of some 60,000, mostly to Israel, was, of course, a striking concession.[17]

Another striking indication that Soviet concessions may be forthcoming if resistance to repression is vigorous, at least if the Kremlin is not convinced that its prestige is heavily at stake, was furnished by the release from a psychiatric hospital of the biochemist Zhores Medvedev in 1970 after extensive protests by Soviet and foreign intellectuals.[18] While the struggle between dissenters and the Soviet authorities has shaped mainly by internal political factors, both sides, particularly the former, have persistently sought to present their case in as favorable a light as possible to the outside world. In view of the elaborate controls over information emanating from the USSR it is not surprising that dissidents were especially concerned to present their case to the non-Soviet world—or that the authorities regarded their efforts to do so as one of the most objectionable, indeed criminal, aspects of their behavior.

In very broad terms, the confrontation between Soviet dissenters and a leadership dedicated to "monolithism" constitutes a chapter in the age-old struggle, perhaps inherent in all political life, between the principles of political elitism and democracy. Of course, an axiom of official Soviet doctrine is that "socialist democracy" is superior to the lower, "bourgeois" form of democracy. But if one accepts Robert Dahl's conception of democracy as "a political system one of the characteristics of which is the quality of being completely or almost completely responsive to all its citizens," then one is forced to conclude that some Soviet dissenters rather than the leadership and bureaucracy aspire to democratic values and practices.[19] Some of the critics of official democracy petitioned the authorities with programs for the "democratization" of Soviet society; also, of course, the dissidents who disseminated the *Chronicle of Current Events* beginning in 1968 and organized the Action Group for the Defense of Human Rights in 1969 were often referred to by the term "Democratic Movement." Analysis of the professed values and goals, the self-images, the activities, and the strategies of the participants in this unequal duel may shed some light on the differences between "hegemonic" and "polyarchic" styles of rule and, more immediately, on the tensions and vulnerabilities of the "powerful yet insecure" post-Khrushchev USSR.[20]

---

17. For a perceptive comment on this development, see Anthony Lewis, "Soviet Words and Deeds," *New York Times*, June 21, 1973.

18. On the events that led to Medvedev's release, see Roy and Zhores Medvedev, *A Question of Madness* (New York, 1971), pp. 70, 117, 132, 169.

19. Quotation in Dahl, *Polyarchy*, p. 2.

20. See Hedrick Smith, "Soviet Union under Brezhnev Powerful yet Insecure," *New York Times*, June 17, 1973 for perceptive comment on some of the strengths and weaknesses of the contemporary USSR.

THE IDEOLOGICAL-HISTORICAL CONTEXT

As we have already indicated, public dissemination of opinions sharply at variance with official policy is, as a rule, dangerous or impossible in the USSR. Open defiance of official norms or, worse yet, of explicit warnings to remain silent—a fairly frequent phenomenon in post-Stalin and especially post-Khrushchev practice—is illegitimate political behavior in the eyes of the regime and in some cases is tantamount to treason. Since the domain of the "political" in the USSR is still enormous, punishment can follow the expression of aspirations, views, demands, and sometimes even esthetic preferences.

But of course the situation of dissenters, and indeed of citizens who are too prudent to express unorthodox or forbidden opinions, is not as difficult as it once was. Under Stalin, mere suspicion of nonconformity or even membership in a suspect social or ethnic group could be fatal.[21] As a rule Soviet citizens since then have been in a position at least to know what kinds of behavior would risk official reprisal and what would not. Following Khrushchev's dismissal, however, statutes prohibiting "anti-Soviet agitation and propaganda," which once were rarely applied, were invoked more frequently, often against persons of greater standing than before.

Tőkés has listed the dimensions involved in decisions as to whether dissent is to be treated as "legitimate, semi-legitimate, or illegitimate." These are, he suggests, (*a*) issue-area, (*b*) target (intended recipient), (*c*) affective content (mobilizing potential), (*d*) style of articulation, (*e*) mode of aggregation, and (*f*) agent's (articulator's) ascribed political and social status.[22] Thus the regime may evaluate an alleged offense as innocuous or extremely objectionable, as weakly or strongly expressed, as tolerable or intolerable in manner, as organized (hence more dangerous) or not, and finally as committed by persons of good repute or of suspicious character.[23]

Since even in a highly centralized system such as the Soviet Union the dispositions of enforcement officials vary, as do local conditions, and since laws and policy directives are often vague, even contradictory, it is not surprising that policy toward dissent sometimes seems inconsistent. Parameters, however, seem discernible.

21. Alexander Dallin and George W. Breslauer explore a wide range of practices in communist systems regarding the uses of terror and related practices to control dissent and other behavior objectionable to the authorities in their study *Political Terror in Communist Systems* (New York, 1971).

22. Rudolf L. Tőkés, "Dissent: Politics for Change in the USSR," in *Soviet Politics and Society in the 1970s*, ed. Henry W. Morton and Rudolf L. Tőkés (New York, 1974), p. 32.

23. See Dahl, *Polyarchy*, p. 15 for the axioms underlying this analysis: "The likelihood that a government will tolerate an opposition increases as the expected costs of toleration decrease," and "The likelihood that a government will tolerate an opposition increases as the expected costs of suppression increase."

Judging by the evidence of judicial proceedings against dissenters—to be examined later—especially severe sanctions are likely against those who challenge the legitimacy of Soviet rule (for example, by attacking official policies or, worse, institutions as unjust) or who threaten to undermine the credibility of the regime's authority. Severe penalties fall upon citizens whose views, disseminated abroad, tend to tarnish the official image of the Soviet way of life, especially if the foreign dissemination apparently resulted, as in the Sinyavsky-Daniel case, from a deliberate choice. Any overt criticism that the authorities regard as directed against the "Leninist nationality policy," by which the present leadership professes to be guided, draws harsh treatment. Here again, one motive appears to be concern for the Soviet image abroad. Even unconventional interpretations of historical events, such as Roy Medvedev's indictment of Stalin's abuses of power in his monumental study *Let History Judge* or devastating critiques of the official esthetic of "socialist realism" like Sinyavsky's are likely to be ruled out of bounds.

Finally, some dissenters who possess such assets as domestic and foreign prestige, although subjected to deprivation and harassment, have suffered much less grievous penalties for roughly similar offenses than more vulnerable persons of lower status.

Regardless of the Soviet Constitution's qualified acceptance of the principles of freedom of expression, civil rights, and legality, the leaders of the CPSU have always reserved the right—like the tsars before them—to determine which kinds of speech acts may or may not be tolerated or punished. Seldom have the Lenins, Stalins, Malenkovs, Khrushchevs, or Brezhnevs—or, for that matter, even the Trotskys or Bukharins—been willing to concede that anyone outside the CPSU supreme command has a right to dissent from the infallible party's policies.

Prior to the Tenth Party Congress in 1921, two streams of dissent were, as Schapiro points out, at least partially tolerated. These were the doctrines of the non-Bolshevik socialist parties (the Mensheviks and the Left Socialist Revolutionaries), who were, "if only barely, tolerated while the [civil] war was raging, and destroyed . . . after [it] had been won," and those of various dissident Bolsheviks. Lenin at that point labeled dissent not as the mere expression of alternative interpretations or opinions but as opposition or, to use the party jargon of those days, as "fractional" political activity.[24] Stalin and his successors, of course, invoked this precedent when they desired to warn or intimidate critics within or outside the party.

Within the party controversial issues were discussed rather openly until 1928. Although this discussion was subject to party control, the atmosphere in which it was conducted differed enormously from that which took shape

---

24. Leonard Schapiro, "Putting the Lid on Leninism," *Government and Opposition* 2, no. 2 (January–April 1967): 183–89.

after Stalin's victory over the "right opposition," headed by Nikolai Bukharin. This victory paved the way for what Moore called the "transformation of rulers." As Moore observed:

> Despite his dogmatism . . . Lenin had permitted direct criticism of his major assumptions by his Party colleagues. . . . But now Party doctrine, formulated by a very small elite, was to be regarded as above and beyond criticism. . . . In time the conception of Stalin as an infallible leader emerged.[25]

The foregoing helps us to understand why Khrushchev sometime contrasted "Leninist methods of persuasion and explanation" with Stalinist repression of intraparty differences.[26]

Khrushchev's advocacy of "Leninist persuasion" probably was inspired in part by the continued vitality of what might be called a "reformist Leninist" perspective on dissent. That this tradition survived Khrushchev's ouster is indicated by statements contained in Roy Medvedev's *Book on Socialist Democracy*. Medvedev's interpretation differs substantially from that of Schapiro, referred to above. Thus Medvedev argues that Lenin intended the famous Tenth Congress unity resolution as an emergency measure, as "a temporary violation of certain important principles of internal party democracy." He accuses Lenin's successors of having ignored the antibureaucratic aspects even of this resolution, which he admits was one of Lenin's most restrictive measures. He concludes: "In the activity of the party leadership since the death of V. I. Lenin such a vast burden of mistakes has accumulated that analysis and correction are impossible without open political discussion."[27]

Soviet dictionaries define a "dissenter" (rendered in Russian as *inakomysliashchi*) as a "differently minded" person or as one holding or having "a different way of thinking."[28] Other Russian equivalents for the English words "dissenter," "dissident," and "dissentient" include *dissident, raskolnik* and *sektant*, which—like *inakomysliashchi*—have, or originally had, religious connotations. Unfortunately the Soviet dictionaries do not provide examples or illustrations that might shed light on the way in which these terms are used in contemporary ideological and political contexts.

To the surprise of nobody familiar with Soviet political life, official Soviet publicists, on the rare occasions when they use *inakomysliashchii*, do

25. Barrington Moore, Jr., *Soviet Politics: the Dilemma of Power* (Cambridge, Mass., 1951), p. 158.

26. For example, in his last major speech to the Twenty-second CPSU Congress, in 1961. On this point, see Frederick C. Barghoorn, "Soviet Political Doctrine and the Problem of Opposition," *Bucknell Review* 12, no. 2 (May 1964): 1–29, at p. 18.

27. Roy Medvedev, *Kniga o sotsialisticheskoi demokratii* [Book on socialist democracy] (Amsterdam and Paris, 1972), pp. 71–74.

28. See, for example, A. I. Smirnitsky, *Russian-English Dictionary*, 3d ed. (New York, 1959), p. 272; S. I. Ozhegov, *Slovar russkogo iazyka* (Moscow, 1960), p. 242; O. S. Akhmanova *et al.*, *Russko-angliiskii slovar* (Moscow, 1962), p. 272; V. K. Muller, *Anglo-russkii slovar* (Moscow, 1963), p. 297.

so pejoratively. For example, according to an article "The Subversive Strategy of the War of Nerves," published January 13, 1972 in *Pravda* under the name of V. Bolshakov, those to whom the term apply fall into two groups: "ideologically unstable" individuals, and those who want "to restore capitalism" and are, in effect, "counterrevolutionaries." To be sure, we found in a source of the Khrushchev era—a legal treatise rather than a newspaper—an example of its use with a less pejorative connotation. The preface to a symposium on "especially dangerous state crimes," in an attack on Stalin's legal theoretician and prosecutor Andrei Vyshinsky, pointed out that, during the heyday of that "monopolist," all legal thinking contrary to his point of view was suppressed, and "the dissenters themselves paid dearly for their boldness."[29] But, a more recent publication distributed by an elite training center for party cadres asserts the party cannot "permit a part of its membership to withdraw into a dissenting [inakomysliashchuiu] group, or fraction, with its political line or group discipline separate from the party."[30]

As is to be expected, the term is used in a more positive sense by Soviet dissenters. Roy Medvedev, for example, asserts that it is absolutely essential to establish, "in our country and in the party", mechanisms facilitating dialogue "with dissenters and among dissenters" as well as "between the majority and the minority" in view of the fact that "various political tendencies" have developed both inside and outside the CPSU.[31]

The foregoing survey suggests at least two hypotheses. First, the efforts of the Soviet authorities to eliminate dissent have thus far proved unsuccessful. Second, its rulers have in the past and may be expected in the future—barring fundamental changes in the political system—to deploy their vast powers to prevent and abort dissent; to conceal or contain it; and whenever prevention and deterrence fail to harass, discredit, and punish its exponents.

"SYMBOLIC" CONTROLS: SOCIALIZATION AND PERSUASIVE COMMUNICATION

In his study *Dimensions of Freedom*, Felix Oppenheim did much to clarify the interrelated concepts of "control" and "unfreedom." Control he defined as "any process by which one actor causes another to act in a certain way." Influence, deterrence, conditioning, restraint, and prevention are subcategories of control. Prevention and punishability are the main subcategories of unfreedom, a concept overlapping somewhat with control. Unfreedom is

---

29. V. I. Kurliandesky and M. P. Mikhailov, eds., *Osobo opasnye gosudarstvennye prestupleniia* [On especially dangerous state crimes] (Moscow, 1963), p. 6. Perhaps it is significant that in the passage cited *inakomyslyashchie* is placed within quotation marks.

30. I. I. Pronin and S. A. Smirnov, comps., *Zhiznennaia sila leninskikh printsipov partiinogo stroitelstva* [The living force of Leninist principles of party-building] (Moscow, 1970), p. 15, in a chapter by Smirnov. Published by the CPSU Higher Party School.

31. R. Medvedev, *Kniga*, p. 51.

defined as "social unfreedom, signifying a relationship . . . expressed: 'with respect to y, x is unfree to do x'.' "[32]

One of the merits of Oppenheim's conceptual scheme is that it helps the student of authority-dissent relationships to perceive fundamental issues. The exposition that follows is partly inspired by this scheme but employs a somewhat different terminology and breakdown of the relevant topics.

First we shall examine the "positive" control functions—the inculcating of socially approved values, beliefs, and behaviors, which in systems of the Soviet type are prescribed by the supreme leadership of the hegemonic political party. Where Oppenheim applies such terms as influence and conditioning to these processes, political scientists—borrowing from sociologists—have come in recent years to call them "socialization" and "political communication." We reserve "negative" and "preventive" methods of control, involving administrative and legal procedures and the application of sanctions, for subsequent sections.

Let us grant that, as Berger and Luckmann point out, socialization performs in all social systems the function of maintaining "symbolic universes," or "institutional definitions" of reality. In a "monopolistic" pattern of socialization, such as prevails in the USSR, "a single symbolic tradition maintains the universe in question." A different pattern prevails in the "pluralistic" order prevalent in most other modern societies, where there is "a shared core universe, taken for granted as such, and different partial universes coexisting in a state of mutual accommodation."[33]

The "symbolic tradition" of Marxism-Leninism is the official legitimating and integrating doctrine of the hegemonic Soviet system. The Soviet rulers maintain, in effect, that they have achieved in Soviet Marxism a codification and synthesis of the highest values that can be pursued by political authority. Soviet citizens are frequently instructed by the highest political authority to rededicate themselves to ideological fundamentals. Typical was the inclusion in a CPSU Central Committee resolution in 1968—more than fifty years after the "Great October Socialist Revolution"—of Lenin's statement that "any neglect of socialist ideology . . . signifies . . . the strengthening of bourgeois ideology."[34]

As is well known, Soviet agencies of mass communication, and other institutions transmit, in addition to carefully sifted information, officially prescribed socialist values and beliefs.[35] As Bronfenbrenner notes, home and school are expected to imbue even the very young with the "superordinate

---

32. Felix E. Oppenheim, *Dimensions of Freedom* (New York, 1961), pp. 28, 67.

33. Peter L. Berger and Thomas Luckmann, *The Social Construction of Reality* (New York, 1967), pp. 92–172, especially pp. 121, 125.

34. *Pravda*, October 6, 1968.

35. See, for example, Barghoorn, *Politics in the USSR*, chaps. 4–6; Urie Bronfenbrenner, *Two Worlds of Childhood* (New York, 1970); Gayle Durham Hollander, *Soviet Political Indoctrination* (New York, Washington, and London, 1972); Ellen P. Mickiewicz, "The Modernization of Party Propaganda," *Slavic Review* 30, no. 2 (June 1971): 257–76.

goals" codified in "communist morality."[36] Building on these foundations, the network of "schools of communism" deployed throughout Soviet society—high schools, universities and technical schools, the Communist Youth League (Komsomol), the trade unions, military training programs, the mass media, and many other institutions—socialize and resocialize the citizenry. This program for the "construction of reality" is vast and is still growing.[37]

But how effective is it? This is a basic question for the student of dissent. On its answer depends, in large part, our evaluation of the cohesiveness of the Soviet political system. But this answer is difficult to provide. Even in the most "open" societies such as Britain or the United States, it is not easy to gauge—especially over time—the subtler aspects of public opinion. In the case of "closed" systems such as the Soviet Union, topics of investigation and research methods available to foreign social scientists remain subject to severe restrictions. Native researchers, if they are prudent, are ever mindful of Kremlin ideological directives. The margin of possible error is thus far greater.

It is therefore not surprising that in this area the findings of informed observers differ substantially. Even when they are in part the outcome, as is true of those cited below, of considerable experience in the USSR, these findings reflect extremely limited, scattered, and almost certainly biased samples of a complex and highly differentiated society. And of course they are inevitably influenced by the preconceptions of their authors.

Jerome Gilison asserts that "contemporary Soviet society is built upon a solid foundation of regime support" generated by "the regime's tight control and regulation of school curricula, supervision of the entire output of the mass media, isolation of the entire Soviet society from most outside (foreign) influences, and effective penetration of group activities to force individual conformity to regime-sponsored group norms." Gilison refers to "the small minority of dissidents, who have escaped the web of indoctrination," but sees them as "rendered ineffective" in the face of "the orthodox indignation or mere indifference of the vast majority of their fellow citizens."[38]

Useful for analyzing Soviet dissent is a typology offered by L. G. Churchward who has had unusually wide contacts with Soviet scholars and other professionals. In respect to the "political approaches" of dissenters he identifies four broad types: "careerist professionals" (broken down into the three subtypes of "party-minded loyalists," "pure careerists," and "loyal oppositionists"); the "humanist intelligentsia," "who are at present reacting against the narrow specialist training" in higher education; "open oppositionists"—he believes that "while some individuals undoubtedly draw on non-Communist belief systems for moral reinforcement, in the main their

36. Bronfenbrenner, *Two Worlds*, pp. 37–49.
37. On its expansion and adaptation since Stalin's death to changing internal and foreign conditions, see the works of Hollander and Mickiewicz cited above.
38. Jerome M. Gilison, *British and Soviet Politics* (Baltimore, 1972), p. xi.

witness is to the humanism of the underlying ideals of Communism"; and the "lost intelligentsia," whose members are "fully alienated from the Soviet system"; they "seek individual solutions by 'opting out' of the system." According to Churchward, probably only one in three or four hundred Soviet intellectuals would accept the risks faced by open oppositionists and only a small minority of the careerist professionals belonged to the loyal oppositionist subcategory as of 1970.[39]

Thus, like Gilison, Churchward concludes that the regime has thus far enjoyed considerable success in its effort to prevent or contain dissent. He attributes this success to such factors as CPSU commitment to the "rapid extension of Soviet science and culture," "the public recognition given to intellectuals through awards and honors," and other incentives. He also cites effective socialization into what he characterizes as the "specialized leadership role" of the intelligentsia, supplemented, where necessary, by control by the KGB's Fifth Section—which, he indicates, "steadily expanded" in the 1960s. The result, he says, is a pattern in which "most Soviet intellectuals seem to accept the socialist system and are prepared to work within the Communist political system, to observe its rules and to respect its restraints."[40]

But Churchward perceives a process of growing disidentification of Soviet intellectuals with at least some aspects of the polity. He reports that intellectuals are increasingly running the risks associated with urging reexamination of basic institutions and policies and in so doing are going beyond their assigned role of "serving as organizers of technological progress." He reports that specialists "under thirty-five in 1970" are likely to be more critical than their parents and, while they are careerist, "their careerism is often less individually-centered and is more likely to be influenced by the ethics of their professions." He even reports that "during the 1960s the number of 'alienated intellectuals' was certainly increasing."[41]

Bronfenbrenner, whose field research on Soviet childhood socialization is more systematic than that of any other foreign social scientist, points out that "deviance is interpreted as emotional betrayal and is responded to by withdrawal of acceptance." This pattern, he finds, produces highly dependent children, less prone than their Western counterparts to antisocial

---

39. L. G. Churchward, *The Soviet Intelligentsia* (London, 1973), pp. 136–39.

40. *Ibid.*, chaps. 4, 6–8, especially pp. 54, 90–92, 104–7, 128–34. Quotations are found on pp. 128 (first two quotations), 90, 144, 128. On the role and ethos of the intelligentsia, Churchward's views resemble those of George Fischer, "The Intelligentsia and Russia," in *The Transformation of Soviet Society*, ed., Cyril E. Black (Cambridge, Mass., 1960). Fischer asserts, p. 207, that Soviet economic development "greatly accentuated the general modern preponderance of the elaborately organized and differentiated technical professions over the 'free' and 'humanistic' professions." There is also considerable similarity between Churchward's appraisal of the "loyal opposition" and "open oppositionists" and portions of F. C. Barghoorn's "Factional, Sectoral and Subversive Opposition in Soviet Politics", in Dahl, *Regimes*, pp. 53–82, dealing with "sectoral" and "subversive" opposition.

41. Churchward, *Soviet Intelligentsia*, pp. 84, 103–4, 504.

behavior but also less disposed "to telling the truth and seeking intellectual understanding."[42]

Gilison's, Churchward's, and Bronfenbrenner's conclusions are salutary counterweights to the proneness of some Western analysts to exaggerate the failures of Soviet political socialization. It should be noted, however, that other well-informed scholars, partly on the basis of research done in the USSR, have arrived at different conclusions. Katz, for example, observes that Soviet sociologists' studies of youth attitudes "have shown present-day Soviet youth to be lacking in some, if not all of the qualities that they should supposedly have acquired."[43]

Although Churchward's observations are very useful, his failure to provide an analytic framework to explain the growing discontent he reports is distressing. The "alienation" noted by Churchward undoubtedly existed during the Stalin era, especially after Stalin's unleashing of mass terror. Khrushchev's destalinization measures and the preoccupation of the regime with the politics of the succession crisis allowed a critique of past injustices to develop. In the case of some young intellectuals it assumed forms that Khrushchev regarded as so extreme as to require suppression. Nevertheless, Khrushchev's policies nourished expectations that an irreversible process of reform had begun with prospects for expanding freedom of expression and other rights guaranteed by the Soviet Constitution but hitherto honored mainly in the breach. When Khrushchev's successors dashed these hopes, some intellectuals were alarmed and outraged. A few threw prudence to the winds and openly challenged official policies. We lack the data necessary to explore these developments in terms of the sophisticated formulations of "alienation" and "relative deprivation" applied by some social scientists to political protest in the United States. Employed judiciously, however, these formulations may shed light on the process to which Churchward calls attention.

Finifter, building on an interpretation of "alienation" most fully elaborated by Melvin Seeman, defines it as "one end of a continuum whose opposite extreme is . . . support or integration." She distinguishes "four different ways in which alienation toward the polity may be expressed": (1) "political powerlessness," or "an individual's feeling that he cannot affect the actions of the government"; (2) "political meaninglessness," a state of mind in which "political decisions are perceived as being unpredictable"; (3)

---

42. Bronfenbrenner, *Two Worlds*, p. 69. Hollander, *Indoctrination*, p. 9, similarly notes that "Soviet citizens are not encouraged to be open-minded, fair, independent, self-reliant, or to exhibit a spirit of compromise."

43. Zev Katz, "Sociology in the Soviet Union," *Problems of Communism* 20 (May–June 1971): 22–40. Hollander, *Indoctrination*, pp. 20, 168, refers to "discontinuity" and "inconsistency" in Soviet socialization and cites David Powell's article "The Effectiveness of Soviet Anti-Religious Propaganda" in the Fall 1967 *Public Opinion Quarterly* on the lack of success of such propaganda.

"perceived political normlessness," or "the perception that the norms or rules intended to govern political relations have broken down, and that departures from prescribed behavior are common"; and (4) "political isolation," or "a rejection of political norms and goals that are widely held and shared by other members of a society."[44]

The third and fourth of these "modes" may shed light on alienation in the USSR. The concept of perceived normlessness helps to explain the moral indignation that pervades the "democratic" Soviet dissent literature, especially that concerned with violations of legal rights. The feeling of political powerlessness presumably is far more widespread among all but high-level members of the political elite in Soviet-type systems than in polyarchies. It may also be potentially true for the USSR, as Finifter hypothesizes for the United States, that a high rank on both the powerlessness and normlessness scales is conducive to "extreme disengagement," likely to be manifested in some cases by participation in "separatist and revolutionary movements" and in other cases by "complete withdrawal."[45]

The concept of relative deprivation, most fully developed by Gurr, is helpful in explaining the heightened anger and despair experienced by dissenting Soviet intellectuals when Khrushchev's dismissal was followed by intensified repression. Gurr defines relative deprivation as "a perceived discrepancy between men's value expectations and their value capabilities." He posits that "conditions that increase the . . . level or intensity of expectations without increasing capabilities," or that "decrease . . . value position" without decreasing expectation, "increase deprivation, hence the intensity of discontent." He also suggests that "short-term deterioration in a group's conditions of life" can have such effects.[46]

Ever since Stalin set in motion his "revolution from above" in 1929, the Kremlin has pursued what might be termed a policy of ideological-cultural protectionism. Its rationale, if there is one, presumably is to permit a "socialist" culture to develop behind a wall of measures that exclude subversive "bourgeois" influences. The party's culture-building effort benefited from its monopoly control of socialization and communication facilities. The ultimate weapon, however, was the political security police, vested

44. Ada W. Finifter, "Dimensions of Political Alienation," *American Political Science Review* 64, no. 2 (June 1970): 390–91.

45. *Ibid.*, p. 407.

46. Ted Robert Gurr, *Why Men Rebel* (Princeton, 1970), p. 13. On p. 47 Gurr discusses "decremental deprivation," "in which a group's value expectations remain relatively constant but value capabilities are perceived to decline, condition sometimes accompanied by "loss of faith in the society's integrating structure of beliefs." On p. 113 he notes that a "period of improvement generates expectations about continued improvement. If those expectations are frustrated by declining value output or repressive governmental action, violent protest is a likely consequence." In post-Khrushchev Russia violence was absent, but perhaps some dissident strategies such as appeals to foreign public opinion over the head of the Soviet authorities and organized circulation of samizdat might be regarded as a relatively prudent functional equivalent in some sense.

with the authority to excise from the body politic persons or groups deemed capable of obstructing or reversing the building of the new culture, which the rulers insisted upon calling "socialist."

In fact, as we know from the statements of many Soviet dissenters over the years, much in the regime's record was difficult to square with fundamental tenets of Marx's original doctrine, such as the belief that a reduction in coercion would accompany progress toward the construction of socialism. The regime's insistence that all citizens enthusiastically propagate its doctrine and equate the elitist-bureaucratic structure created by Stalin with socialism tended to alienate thoughtful and morally sensitive citizens.

Grievances were created among some members of ethnic and religious subcultures by the centralizing, assimilationist, and Russifying thrust of Soviet cultural policies. The very success of industrialization and modernization, which brought increased differentiation and specialization, also generated aspirations and perspectives incompatible in some respects with the norms of the dominant bureaucratic political culture.

The considerable diminution in the use of coercion as an instrument of social control since Stalin's death and increased reliance on techniques of persuasion may indicate an increase in voluntary acceptance of the official culture and political system by the citizenry. But, the persistence of a closed intellectual system—to be sure in a somewhat less crude and restrictive form than that which prevailed under Stalin—and the scope, range, and intensity of dissent in the post-Khrushchev era cast doubt on the success of the socialization effort and on the homogeneity and stability of the political culture.

PREVENTION

Censorship No socialization program is ever completely successful. This fact poses problems in all societies, but it creates special difficulties for the rulers of single-party, ideologically legitimated dictatorships. Any refusal to support their policies and accept their doctrines tends to undermine the authority of rulers who have linked their legitimacy to established symbol structures. Hence it is not surprising that they institute elaborate censorship and other controls over communication.

In the USSR, the formal censorship (which, despite the various bureaucratic redesignations it has undergone, is still apparently known in the USSR by its traditional name *glavlit*) is a massive structure, subordinated to the CPSU Central Committee, with an estimated 70,000 employees strategically placed in administrative centers, newspapers, publishing houses, and the like throughout the country.[47] Organized censorship is almost as old as the

47. Leonid Vladimirov, "Glavlit: How the Soviet Censor Works," *Index*, autumn-winter 1972, pp. 31–43. Vladimirov is the pen name of Leonid Finkelstein; he also contributed under the latter name to the special issue entitled *The Soviet Censorship* in *Studies on the Soviet*

Soviet regime, although it began as an "emergency," "temporary" practice.[48] Doubtless because its practice is embarrassing to a regime that claims to be guided by democratic principles, the very existence of censorship is subject to censorship.[49]

Some courageous Soviet writers sometimes succeed in "beating the censorship and communicating something of value to the reader," as the Soviet refugee writer A. Anatoly puts it. But as the late Arkady Belinkov pointed out, writers sometimes spend years rewriting censored works, only to die with their labors unfinished.[50]

Resisting the censorship requires a kind of courage and endurance possessed by only a few writers such as Solzhenitsyn. Apparently most Soviet writers succumb, though not always completely, to "self-censorship," accommodating to the demands and responding to the handsome material rewards offered conformists, especially talented but unscrupulous ones.[51]

In at least some cases, however, the regime pays a price for the frustrations inflicted on creative people by censorship. Indeed, as Dewhirst points out, the rise of samizdat can in large part be attributed to "the immense difficulty experienced by Soviet citizens in publishing . . . about really controversial subjects."[52] In turn, the regime's effort to eliminate samizdat by coercion, with which we shall deal in the next section, tarnished its image abroad.

In 1973 the USSR announced its intention to adhere to the Universal Copyright Convention. This move after decades of resistance apparently boded ill for Soviet dissenters. A Supreme Soviet decree issued shortly afterward indicated that all Soviet works—as the *Wall Street Journal* put it, "even those not published" but "found on the territory of the USSR in any objective form"—would be covered. Hence the decree was "clearly directed at *samizdat*." Further, "Under this law a writer could be prosecuted if he admitted authorizing foreign publication of his work. If he denied authorizing foreign publication . . . Russia could bring legal action against the foreign publisher for violating the copyright convention."[53]

Union n.s. 11, no. 2 (1971). This issue, the best single source of information on the subject, originated as a round-table symposium in London in 1970. The participants included the late Arkady Belinkov, Natalia Belinkova, Anatoly Kuznetsov (A. Anatoly), Max Hayward, Martin Dewhirst, and other specialists.

48. See David E. Powell, "Controlling Dissent in the Soviet Union," *Government and Opposition* 7, no. 1 (Winter 1972): 87; Vladimirov, "Glavlit," p. 31; *Soviet Censorship*, pp. 6–7.

49. Powell, "Controlling Dissent," p. 87, and *Soviet Censorship*, among others, note that in two articles in *Izvestiia* for May 30 and August 20, 1970 attacking the London censorship symposium "the subject to which it was devoted was not mentioned or even hinted at."

50. Anatoly Kuznetsov [A. Anatoly], in *Soviet Censorship*, p. 30; see also Belinkov's remarks *passim*.

51. *Ibid.*, pp. 26–49.

52. Martin Dewhirst, in *ibid.*, pp. iv–v.

53. "From Russia with Vengeance," editorial in *Wall Street Journal*, March 29, 1973.

Other Communications Controls The shaping and channeling of information in the Soviet Union involves many agencies and techniques other than formal censorship. An attempt to describe the total process even summarily would be inappropriate here. We shall mention only a few particularly significant aspects about which information is available.

Although restrictions on foreign travel have relaxed considerably since Stalin's death, it is still extremely difficult. Citizens of noncommunist countries find it much easier to visit either communist or noncommunist states than do Soviet scholars, scientists, and other professionals, especially if they wish to go as tourists rather than on official government business.[54] Even the acceptance of an official invitation to attend a scientific conference abroad can involve running a gauntlet of incredibly complicated and humiliating bureaucratic procedures.[55]

Because of the strict Soviet internal passport regime, internal travel and freedom of choice of residence and employment are severely restricted. The overall economic and cultural development of the country is adversely affected.[56]

Even when Soviet citizens are permitted to have contacts with foreigners at home or abroad, the effects may be restricted because of caution engendered by indoctrination, briefings, and the frequent published warnings regarding the alleged use by the "imperialists" of cultural exchanges as an instrument for ideological subversion.[57] Of course the situation is somewhat more "normal" now, especially in "nonideological" fields, than during Stalin's reign.[58]

PUNISHABILITY

Legal Prescriptions and Proscriptions. Defining the process "making it punishable for someone to do something," Oppenheim says: "Y makes it

---

54. Abundant statistical documentation is in Mary Jane Moody, "Tourists in Russia and Russians Abroad," *Problems of Communism* (November–December 1964): 3–13. Unfortunately no similar study for a later period is available. But in view of the tightening of Soviet political controls since Khrushchev's fall, the current situation is probably similar or even less favorable.

55. See Zhores A. Medvedev, *The Medvedev Papers* (London, 1971), pp. 7–292. R. Medvedev, *Kniga*, pp. 257–58, refers to the "humiliating" procedures to which Soviet citizens desiring to visit not merely "capitalist" but also other "socialist" countries are subjected. He asserts that for Soviet citizens travel abroad is not a right but a privilege, granted at the pleasure of the authorities.

56. R. Medvedev, *Kniga*, pp. 259–62.

57. Frederick C. Barghoorn and Ellen P. Mickiewicz, "American Views of Soviet-American Exchanges of Persons," in *Communication in International Politics*, ed. Richard L. Merritt, (Urbana, Ill., 1973), p. 163; Hollander, *Indoctrination*, p. 195; Paul Wohl, "Soviet Worry: Flowing In of West's Ideas," *Christian Science Monitor*, June 7, 1973.

58. See Barghoorn, "Factional, Sectoral and Subversive Opposition," pp. 53–70; Alex Nove's remarks in *Soviet Censorship*, pp. 122–23; H. Gordon Skilling and Franklyn Griffiths, eds., *Interest Groups in Soviet Politics* (Princeton, N.J., 1971), and review thereof by Erik Hoffman, *American Political Science Review* 67 (March 1973): 283–85.

punishable for X to do x to the extent that, were X to do x, X would be penalized for having done x as a result of some action y of Y."[59]

In analyzing authority-dissent relations in the Soviet type of system it is useful to supplement the general notion of punishability with the concept "terror." Terror is defined in a recent study as "the arbitrary use, by organs of political authority, of severe coercion against individuals or groups, the credible threat of such use, or the arbitrary extermination of such individuals or groups."[60]

Oppenheim points to the "unfreedom" relation between government and citizen, which is common to all known polities. Dallin and Breslauer call attention to a phenomenon characteristic of dictatorships and particularly of the "Stalinist" stage of development of communist systems: the extreme inconsistency with which rules are often applied and the psychological trauma that often results. They also point out, "As Communist systems pass beyond the mobilization stage, the incidence of political terror as an instrument of public policy tends to decline sharply." But the Soviet regime has continued to apply it to "dissidents among the cultural intelligentsia and particular ethnic minorities."[61] Of course, many members of the scientific, technical, and other sectors of the Soviet intelligentsia have also been victims of coercion in the post-Stalin era. As I have indicated, however, sanctions have usually been applied as part of a relatively "rational," predictable pattern of reprisals for actual rather than suspected or potential violations. The post-Stalin, particularly the post-Khrushchev, leadership nevertheless shared Stalin's aversion toward dissenters. As Yesenin-Volpin recently wrote, "In the Soviet Union, in order to go to prison for a long time, it was always sufficient to boldly criticize—without necessarily calling for any action—the principles of the established order, whatever they were, and the authorities."[62]

Perhaps the most significant negative changes since Khrushchev's ouster have occurred in the sphere of legal prescriptions and their application. Khrushchev's liberalization encouraged a degree of freedom of expression perhaps not intended by Khrushchev himself and certainly abhorrent to his successors. The period since his ouster saw a partial, carefully controlled return to the norms and practices of the Stalin era. But it also witnessed challenges to authority of a kind that did not occur under Khrushchev, such as the establishment of the Moscow-based Human Rights Committee. It should also be borne in mind that while in literature there was greater freedom under Khrushchev than afterward, Brezhnev and his fellow oligarchs perhaps did not subject religious believers to as severe persecution as he did.

59. Oppenheim, Dimensions, p. 77.
60. Dallin and Breslauer, *Political Terror*, p. 1.
61. *Ibid.*, p. 88.
62. Alexander Yesenin-Volpin, "Posle Stalina" [Since Stalin], *Novoe russkoe slovo*, March 13, 1973.

While the lot of advocates of "democratization" worsened after Khrushchev's ouster, the differences should not be exaggerated. An oppressive degree of unfreedom prevailed during both periods. Moreover, many of the critics who were punished with draconian severity by the Brezhnev regime had earlier suffered not insignificant penalties. Vladimir Bukovsky, Alexander Ginzburg, and Yuri Galanskov, for example, were sentenced in 1967 and 1968 to, respectively, three, five, and seven years in labor camps. But while Khrushchev was still in power they served time in camps or (in Bukovsky's case) in mental hospitals for dissident statements. It is interesting that Bukovsky declared during his 1967 trial that he began to oppose the rampant "oppression and concealment" in 1961 after three of his friends had been tried as criminals for producing a handwritten appeal.[63] Nor should it be forgotten that it was in 1961 that the persecution, by psychiatric commitment, of General Grigorenko began—apparently for demanding with too much zeal, the "restoration of Leninist principles."[64]

Basic to the relation between law, justice, and dissent in the USSR is the enduring tradition that subordinates legal policy, like other aspects of social and cultural policy, to the Kremlin's political goals. The party command determines legal policy partly through manipulating the doctrine of "socialist legal consciousness," which as Stephen Weiner has pointed out requires in effect that Soviet judges be guided by party policy in deciding "whether a given statute governs a certain pattern of established facts."[65] Party chieftains, including Khrushchev and Brezhnev, have regularly included in their reports to CPSU congresses statements tantamount to directives regarding the function of law as an instrument of party policy.

Political control of justice is of course especially tight in respect to behavior regarded as "socially dangerous." Crimes such as treason, espionage, "terroristic acts," and "anti-Soviet propaganda and agitation" are ranked at the top of the "social danger" scale and have been characterized since the legal reforms of the late 1950s and early 1960s as "especially dangerous state crimes." Previously they were termed "counterrevolutionary" crimes. This redesignation reflects the doctrine that, with the suppres-

---

63. On the 1968 sentencing of Ginzburg and Galanskov as well as their and Bukovsky's earlier punishment, see Pavel Litvinov, comp., *The Trial of the Four* (London, 1972), English text ed. Peter Reddaway, pp. 5–11, 210–20. On Bukovsky's reaction to what he regarded as an injustice to his friends, see Pavel Litvinov, comp., *The Demonstration in Pushkin Square*, trans. Manya Harari (Boston, 1969), p. 73. For the best account of the early stages of development of post-Stalin nonconformist attitudes and the Khrushchev leadership's countermeasures, including expulsion of thousands of students from universities after the Hungarian uprising of 1956, see Cornelia Gerstenmaier, *Die Stimme der stummen* (Stuttgart, 1972), pp. 61–74, English trans., *The Voices of the Silent* (New York, 1972); also Gunther Hillmann, *Selbstkritik des Kommunismus* (Munich, 1967), pp. 208–15.

64. Peter Reddaway, *Uncensored Russia* (New York, 1972), p. 128.

65. Stephen M. Weiner, "Socialist Legality on *Trial,*" in *In Quest of Justice*, ed. Abraham Brumberg (New York, 1970), p. 48.

sion of exploiting classes and the consolidation of socialism in the USSR, all possibility of counterrevolution has vanished.[66]

It is still considered necessary, however, to strictly enforce legal safeguards against actions detrimental to the social order and the state. According to Soviet legal doctrine only actions detrimental to society are punishable, not thoughts or opinions. But, some of the relevant statutes, as we shall see, are loosely drafted and on occasion are still more loosely interpreted and applied. The result is that, in practice, thoughts, opinions, and even attitudes are indeed punished.[67] Dissident activists such as Bukovsky took the position that some of the statutes designed to combat "anti-Soviet agitation and propaganda" and related offenses, in particular articles 70 and 190-1 of the Criminal Code of the Russian Soviet Federated Socialist Republic (and their counterparts in the criminal codes of other republics), were in fact directed against freedom of thought and expression and were therefore unconstitutional. This position was supported by a number of distinguished Soviet scientists and other leading intellectuals, some of whom addressed a petition to the highest party and state authorities in 1966 demanding that the then newly adopted articles 190-1 and 190-3 be repealed. The ground for the demand was that the articles opened "the way to the subjective and arbitrary interpretation of any statement as deliberately false and derogatory to the Soviet state and social system" and were "contrary to the Leninist principles of social democracy" and to the "exercise of liberties granted by the Constitution of the USSR."[68] The authorities ignored such protests. In the years that followed, Bukovsky and others who persisted in "criticizing the Soviet laws and the activities of the KGB" were subjected to increasingly severe repression. In 1967 he was sentenced to three years in a labor camp and in 1972 to a deprivation of freedom totaling twelve years.[69]

Both the nature and application of Soviet legal rules governing "political crimes" probably shock most Americans and others who live under legal systems that include safeguards of civil rights. But it must be remembered that even in "political" cases official Soviet legal behavior after Stalin was an improvement over earlier practices. The 1926 Criminal Code of the RSFSR (Russian Republic) and subsequent laws reflected Stalin's intensified

66. The concepts are discussed in V. I. Kurlyandsky and M. P. Mikhailov, eds., *Osobye opasnye gosudarstvennye prestupleniia* [On especially dangerous state crimes] (Moscow, 1963), pp. 9–32, especially pp. 13–15.
67. For the official doctrine that only acts, not thoughts, are punishable, see *ibid.*, p. 18.
68. Litvinov, *The Demonstration in Pushkin Square*, pp. 14–15.
69. Quotation in *ibid.*, p. 126. R. Medvedev, *Kniga*, pp. 184–88, gives a cogent critique of articles 70, 190-1, and 190-3. Medvedev points out that in prosecutions under these articles prosecutors and judges have sometime paid no attention to the question of the truthfulness of allegedly anti-Soviet statements with the dissemination of which defendants were charged and have otherwise misapplied the law. He presents the texts of several protests against violation by the authorities of legal and constitutional provisions, including one addressed in April 1968 to Brezhnev, Kosygin, and Podgorny by 150 "representatives of the Ukrainian intelligentsia."

struggle against crimes "directed against the foundations of the Soviet system." Many were punishable by death. Following vigorous debates over law reform in the 1950s, the adoption of new Fundamental Principles of Criminal Legislation of the USSR in 1958 and of a new criminal code of the RSFSR in 1960 substantially moderated the draconian penal pattern.[70] The notorious doctrine of "analogy," according to which an act not covered in existing law could be punished under laws against "similar" offenses, was repealed.[71] Article 3 of the 1960 code provided that no person could be punished unless he had committed a crime provided for by law. Under the previous rule "social danger itself" was the "key to judicial sanctioning."[72] The death penalty, formerly applicable to several "counterrevolutionary crimes," was replaced for some offenses by lesser penalties. The Special Board (Osoboe soveshchanie) of the MVD, which had sentenced millions of "kulaks" and members of other "socially dangerous" categories to long terms in labor camps without regular legal procedure, was abolished in 1954. These and other measures reducing the impact of arbitrary police power support Dallin's and Breslauer's judgment regarding the drastic diminution of terror in the postmobilization stage of communist systems.[73]

Nevertheless some wide loopholes were carried over from the old legal codes to the new. Chief of these is article 70 of the RSFSR Criminal Code, which penalizes "agitation or propaganda carried on for the purpose of subverting or weakening the Soviet regime or of committing particular, especially dangerous crimes against the state, or the circulation, for the same purpose, of slanderous fabrications which defame the Soviet state and social system, or the circulation or preparation or keeping, for the same purposes, of literature of such content."[74]

Seven months after the conviction in February 1966 of the authors Sinyavsky and Daniel under article 70, articles 190-1 and 190-3 were added to the RSFSR Criminal Code. Article 190-1 covers behavior similar to that penalized by article 70 but does not require proof of subversive intent. Presumably it was intended to blunt in future cases the widespread adverse comment occasioned by the clash between the writers' assertion that they had not intended to weaken Soviet authority and the court's insistence that they had. Article 190-3, "a response to group demonstrations that took place

---

70. Harold J. Berman, Introduction, in *Soviet Criminal Law and Procedure* (Cambridge, Mass., 1966), trans. Berman and J. W. Spindler, p. 26.

71. However, G. A. Kriger, in his contribution to *Razvitie sovetskoi demokratii i ukreplenie pravoporiadka na sovremennom etape* [The growth of Soviet democracy and the strengthening of contempary legality], ed. A. N. Vasilev (Moscow, 1967), asserted that "analogy" had played a positive role in its time in the struggle against anti-Soviet elements.

72. Harold J. Berman, Introduction, in *Soviet Criminal Law and Procedures*, 2d ed., trans. Berman and J. W. Spindler (Cambridge, Mass., 1972), p. 21.

73. Dallin and Breslauer, *Political Terror*, p. 81.

74. Berman, *Soviet Criminal Law*, 2d ed., pp. 153–54. More severe penalties are provided if these acts are committed in wartime.

after the Sinyavsky-Daniel trial," makes punishable "organization of, and likewise, active participation in, group actions which violate public order in a coarse manner," or "clear disobedience of the legal demands of representatives of authority." Both articles carry penalties of not more than three years of deprivation of liberty. Other aspects of this case aroused comment, of course, especially the fact that it was the first trial in Soviet history in which the production of works of fiction displeasing to the authorities was formally treated as a crime. Under Stalin, surely, the punishment would have been exile or execution without a court trial.[75] Article 72, on "organizational activity directed to commission of especially dangerous crimes against the state," is another law that has frequently been invoked against dissidents. So has Article 142—"violation of laws on separation of church and state and of church and school"—especially against nonconformist Baptists for providing religious instruction to children. According to such quantitative data as are available, articles 142, 70, 190-1, and 190-3 have been invoked more frequently against dissenters than any other statutes.[76]

PUNISHMENT AND THE RATIONALE OF ITS APPLICATION

Extrajudicial Repression. In samizdat sources such as the *Chronicle of Current Events*, the expression "extrajudicial repression" (*vnesudebnye repressii*) refers to measures short of arrest and trial visited by the authorities on those whose political attitudes have incurred official displeasure. Of course the ultimate sanctions are "judicial repression" in the form of prosecution followed by years of confinement in labor camps or prisons or by commitment to prisonlike mental hospitals. The extrajudicial measures, however, also constitute a formidable array of deprivations. Reflecting the situation before 1972, Reddaway noted that the authorities after Stalin had "normally arrested only those civil rights activists who have most persistently refused to conform." He characterized this policy as "hesitant repression."[77] In hindsight, especially in the light of the 1972–73 crackdown on dissent, this assessment may seem an understatement. When formulated, however, it was not unfounded. Moreover, it may help to explain an antidissent policy that was certainly more complex and differentiated than Stalin's though considerably harsher than Khrushchev's. Relative leniency and differentiation are indicated by the fact that many high-ranking

---

75. See *ibid.*, pp. 82, 181, and Max Hayward, ed. and trans., *On Trial: The State versus "Abram Tertz" and "Nikolai Arzhak"* (New York, 1966).

76. Texts of above in Berman *Soviet Criminal Law*, 2d ed., pp. 72, 169; Reddaway, *Uncensored Russia*, p. 11. The judgment regarding relative frequency of application of laws is based on examination of the extensive data compiled by Radio Liberty Research in its massive *Reestr osuzhdennykh v borbe za prava cheloveka v sssr* [Register of detainees in the struggle for human rights in the USSR] (New York, 1971).

77. Reddaway, *Uncensored Russia*, p. 27.

intellectuals who associated themselves with public criticism of such actions as the Sinyavsky-Daniel trial but then, under pressure, ceased to express dissent went unscathed or suffered only minor penalties. But because of defectiveness of data we cannot be very sure about the specific measures resorted to in particular instances.

In the absence of compelling evidence to the contrary, it is logical to assume that the authorities' decision to resort to coercion—abroad in Czechoslovakia, at home in the arrests of Grigorenko, some of the Action Group leaders, and others—was the principal factor in the diminution or withdrawal from participation in open expressions of dissent by almost all "establishment intellectuals" after 1969. To be sure, Sakharov, Valery Chalidze, the Medvedev brothers, Solzhenitsyn, Yakir, Amalrik, and others continued to expose and publicize, for example through interviews with foreign correspondents, what they regarded as major abuses and defects of Soviet life. How dangerous this strategy of radical disclosure could be to its practitioners is suggested by the severe treatment that Amalrik, Bukovsky, and Yakir received after they were interviewed by William Cole, a CBS television reporter, in May 1970.

Besides coercion or its threat, other factors may have persuaded most of the Soviet intelligentsia to drop out of what must have seemed an increasingly hopeless struggle. These factors included the stepped-up "mobilization of party members and supporters," new measures to tighten inner-party discipline (which culminated in a grant of power to party primary organizations power to supervise scientific research institutes), tightened controls by professional unions, and the rationalization and systematization of political indoctrination inaugurated and vigorously pushed by Brezhnev and his associates.[78]

Perhaps the major inhibiting factors, however, were the continued isolation of the Soviet intelligentsia from the "masses" of ordinary office and factory workers and farmers, combined with a conformism and timidity in part inherited from the tsarist and Stalinist past but also reflecting, as Amalrik pointed out "the psychology of government workers" who "regard the regime as a lesser evil than the painful process of changing it."[79] Amalrik's analysis may help us to understand the relative weakness of Soviet intellectual dissent. It also suggests that if Brezhnev was far less savage in suppressing dissent than Stalin, his relative leniency reflected his and Soviet officialdom's confidence that the threat of dissent was more potential than

78. Churchward, *Soviet Intelligentsia*, pp. 139–43, discusses political and administrative controls employed in what he characterizes as the party's drive during the 1960s to "maintain its hegemony over Soviet intellectual life." On the strengthening of political indoctrination, see Barghoorn, *Politics in the USSR*, pp. 117–18, 127–28; Ellen P. Mickiewicz, "The Modernization of Party Propaganda in the USSR," *Slavic Review* 30 (June 1971): 257–76; Hollander, *Soviet Political Indoctrination*, pp. 165–66, 193–96.

79. Andrei Amalrik, *Will the Soviet Union Survive until 1984?* (New York, 1970), pp. 19, 21, 33–37.

actual. The leadership appears to have reckoned, correctly, that most intellectuals could be kept under control if an example were made of a few. Those selected were the most vulnerable by virtue of the extreme nature of their actions or utterances or in some instances because of known defects of character.

One gets the impression that, in sharp contrast to Stalin's crude use of terror, the Brezhnev regime pursued a policy of graduated, incremental reprisals. It sought to fit the severity of punishment to the "social danger" represented by specific kinds and acts of dissent. But other considerations, such as the effect of a measure on the regime's image at home and abroad also carried weight.

We can take as an example the twenty distinguished scientists, writers, and other intellectuals who in 1967 protested against what they regarded as the unconstitutionality of articles 190-1 and 190-3 of the RSFSR Criminal Code. As of around early 1971, six had been subjected to reprimands or other relatively mild forms of extrajudicial repression. Even in these cases the action appears to have been taken not for the protest in question but for later acts of protest. Yakir and Sakharov were among the signers of the petition in question, and of course they were later subjected to reprisals. On the other hand, the composer Dmitri Shostakovich, also a signer, visited the United States as a member of an elite Soviet good will group in 1973. Most of the signers apparently engaged in little or no further activity objectionable to the authorities and, as a result, suffered no penalties.[80] What pressures they may have received aside from those already described here are unknown to this writer.

We should note the somewhat anomalous cases of two high-status intellectuals—Lidia Chukovskaya, daughter of the famous children's writer Kornei Chukovski and herself a respected writer and critic, and the Ukrainian poet Andrei Malyshko—as examples of persons who within limits were allowed to protest publicly against official policies without incurring severe penalties. Chukovskaya is well known for her stinging rebuke to Sholokhov for his speech at the Twenty-third CPSU Congress expressing satisfaction over the punishment of Sinyavsky and Daniel, for powerful statements in defense of Solzhenitsyn in 1968, and for other outspoken expressions of dissent. The Moscow section of the Union of Soviet Writers reprimanded her and thirty-four colleagues in May 1968 after they had signed a declaration condemning the treatment of Ginzburg and Galanskov.[81] More seriously, however, the authorities forbade publication

80. The text of the petition and the names of its signers are in Litvinov, *Demonstration in Pushkin Square*, pp. 14–15. The conclusion here is based on research by Reddaway for *Uncensored Russia.*

81. Reddaway, *Uncensored Russia*, p. 90. The union charged, among other things, that such statements as the one Chukovskaya "might be exploited by bourgeois propaganda for purposes damaging to the Soviet Union."

of her book *The Deserted House* (written in 1940 and evoking the atmosphere of Stalin's purges, it was published only in the West long after the dictator's death). Then in January 1974, reportedly in frail health and almost blind, she was expelled from the Writers Union because she had defended Sakharov against the attacks made on him in autumn 1973. This measure, of course, subjected the sixty-six-year-old writer to severe psychological and financial deprivations.[82]

As for Malyshko, a Radio Liberty Research study distributed in 1969 pointed out that he had usually pursued a "middle course." But he was among the first to sign a petition addressed to the leadership of the Ukrainian Communist Party regarding the mass arrests of Ukrainian dissidents in 1965 and 1966. Thereafter he was severely criticized at times. Nevertheless in 1969 he was awarded the Lenin Prize for literature.[83] Since no further information is available on Malyshko, we can assume that he has not engaged in dissent in recent years and hence has not been molested.

In contrast to the relatively mild treatment of Malyshko are the actions taken against the founding members of the Action Group (in Russian *Initsiativnaia*, or initiative group) for the Defense of Human Rights, founded in early 1969. By mid-1973 fourteen of the fifteen had been subjected to extra-judicial repression—in the form, for example, of minatory "prophylactic chats" in KGB offices—or to sentences to camps or commitment to special psychiatric hospitals. The remaining member was the biologist S. Kovalev, who, as Reddaway noted, "drops from the Chronicle's purview altogether."[84] Presumably he like Malyshko did not continue his dissenting activity long enough to incur severe sanctions.

The Action Group was formed almost immediately after the arrest of the militant civil rights leader Peter Grigorenko. Reddaway suggests that the group was organized because of a desire to coordinate the members' civil rights activities following the loss of Grigorenko's leadership. The combination, however, of a rudiment of organization and the Grigorenko style of militancy apparently was particularly objectionable to the authorities. Moreover, the Action Group appealed again and again to Western public opinion through, for example, the United Nations. General Grigorenko himself had gone so far as to accuse the political leadership of "criminal" behavior for concealing from the Soviet public the truth about what he regarded as Stalin's inept military leadership during World War II and for failing to right the wrongs done to the Crimean Tatars by the dictator.[85]

82. *New York Times*, January 13, 1974.
83. Stephen D. Olynyk, "1969 Lenin Prize for Literature Goes to Andrei S. Malyshko," *Radio Liberty Dispatch*, Dec. 8, 1969.
84. *Uncensored Russia*, p. 153.
85. For details, see P. Grigorenko, *Mysli sumasshedshego* [Thoughts of a madman] (Amsterdam, 1973).

Solzhenitsyn, of course, became as objectionable as Grigorenko, especially after publication in December 1973 of part of his study of Soviet political prisons and camps. This is indicated, among other evidence, by the fact that just before his expulsion the authorities formally accused him of treason. But in contrast to Grigorenko, Solzhenitsyn was extremely careful to conduct himself in a fashion calculated to make it as embarrassing as possible for the regime to move against him, and he was a world figure. Grigorenko was probably treated with exceptional harshness because militant dissent by an army officer must appear to the Kremlin as an exceptionally dangerous type of behavior.

In contrast to these cases, the Soviet authorities displayed relative leniency toward the members of the Human Rights Committee organized by Sakharov, Chalidze, and a few others, mostly scientists, in November 1970. By the fall of 1973 the Human Rights Committee, like the Action Group, was virtually moribund. Sakharov, who had become increasingly outspoken, was in deep trouble with the authorities; his colleagues Igor Shafarevich and Grigory Podyapolsky were under severe pressure; and Chalidze, who had been the most active member of the group, was in the United States, where he remained after having been officially deprived of Soviet citizenship. Even so, as long as the members scrupulously observed Soviet law and assumed the role of respectful petitioners rather than militant complainers they were treated considerably better than the Action Group.

These observations, though not rigorously systematic, point to correlations between dissenter behavior and regime responses. Not surprisingly, it appears that militant, fundamental, persistent dissent is likely, other things being equal, to be treated more harshly than the limited, respectful, "within-system" variety, especially if the latter is expressed infrequently.

Nothing said here indicates that post-Khrushchev treatment of dissent is necessarily more humane or benevolent than was Stalin's. Depending on one's point of view, recent policies might seem more humane, more sophisticated, or more insidious than earlier ones. They are clearly more rational and perhaps more effective. The widely differentiated tactics described in this chapter bespeak shrewdness. It is certainly difficult to establish clear patterns and correlations in such a complex and fluid situation, but it is possible that by pursuing a policy of selective and differentiated repression the Soviet authorities drove a wedge between the more militant, dissenters and the more cautious liberals. It is striking that many "establishment intellectuals" supported their more militant colleagues in the 1966–68 period but then fell silent. Another significant aspect of "wedge-driving," perhaps, was selective alteration of the traditional rigid ban on emigration. Departure for the West of some of the most militant dissenters not only deprived the Democratic Movement and the Jewish resistance of some of their ablest, most energetic leaders; it also must have aroused morale-destroying feelings of abandonment among those left behind to carry on an increasingly unequal struggle.

But regardless of whatever rationality and sophistication one may see in Brezhnev's policy, it is the same policy as Stalin's pursued by other means more appropriate to a new situation. Means change, but Brezhnev, Stalin, even Khrushchev all agreed that the rights and freedoms citizens might enjoy were a matter that the leaders of the CPSU alone should decide. Challenges to this basic principle were still matters for the Kremlin and its KGB enforcers to deal with. Herein as always lay the basic difference between the Soviet dictatorship and all varieties of democracy.

Now as Reddaway's study and other sources show, the arrest and trial of a nonconformist are likely to culminate an exhausting campaign of harassment and intimidation. In many cases the authorities can silence a protester before reaching the final stage. Lesser reprisals can be psychologically rending, and the regime can inflict dire poverty on offending intellectuals by denying them access to the market. As Churchward notes, "There are many cases over recent years of outstanding intellectuals, including writers, artists, teachers, and scientists, who have been forced to accept poorly paid manual work because professional employment was denied them."[86]

Some of the deprivations visited on protesters are expulsion from the CPSU or the Young Communist League, dismissal from jobs or educational institutions, denunciation by colleagues at rigged "self-criticism" sessions, illegal search of homes, seizure of personal papers and books, interrogations in KGB offices, surveillance or disconnection of telephones, verbal abuse and threats by mobs, and physical beatings. Churchward suggests that the number of intellectuals subjected to such penalties runs into thousands.[87]

86. *Soviet Intelligentsia*, p. 143. Yuri Glazov, in "Samizdat: Background to Dissent," *Survey*, Winter 1973, points out that as a result of dismissals, demotions, and transfers from jobs, the signers of protest petitions in 1968 "found themselves if not utterly isolated then at least in the peculiar position of hunted men" despite the fact that their "letters had expressed only a hundredth part of the indignation that was choking the ordinary citizen in his own home."

87. Churchward, *Soviet Intelligentsia*, p. 144. Reddaway, *Uncensored Russia*, pp. 72–90, 122, 143–45, 390, 411–18, 420, contains scores of examples, most of them reported in *Khronika tekushchikh sobytii* [Chronicle of current events]. The issues of this samizdat journal that appeared after Reddaway completed his compilation report on hundreds of additional cases.

For the reader unfamiliar with these sources, a word on their nature and availability may be helpful. In 1969 the émigré journal *Posev* (Frankfurt) began publishing the *Chronicle* in Russian in special supplements. *Posev* and its sister publication *Grani* have distributed much other important samizdat material. Reddaway, *Uncensored Russia*, presents in English, with useful notes and commentary, the contents of *Chronicle*'s first 11 issues. Amnesty International in London has published in English translation all issues beginning with no. 16. In 1973 there appeared in New York the first issue of *Chronicle of Human Rights in the USSR*, edited by Peter Reddaway and Edward Kline and published by Khronika Press in Russian and English.

Examples of extrajudicial repression include the expulsion from the CPSU in 1969 of the historian Roy Medvedev; expulsion from the Writers Union of Solzhenitsyn in 1969 and in 1973 of Vladimir Maksimov, a writer who had briefly employed Bukovsky as a research assistant and had addressed a petition to the authorities protesting Bukovsky's brief 1971 commitment to a psychiatric institution; the withdrawal in 1967 of permission to the poet Voznesensky to travel to America; the cancellation for a time of foreign concert tours of the cellist Mstislav Rostropovich, a friend of Solzhenitsyn, and renewed harassment of Rostropovich in connection with heightened pressures against Solzhenitsyn in 1973; the lifting of Sakharov's security clearance after his 1968 essay *Progress, Coexistence, and Intellectual Freedom*, the first episode in a campaign including—in 1973—denial to his stepchildren of enrollment in schools, jobs in the USSR, and permission to travel abroad. A startling example of the almost unimaginable pettiness often displayed by the authorities in punishing dissent not considered serious enough for judicial action occurred in the science center Obninsk in 1968. Mere attendance at the funeral of a young physicist who had been expelled from the CPSU for applauding the Czechoslovakian leader Dubcek was made the pretext for the expulsion of a number of his colleagues.[88] Only slightly less shocking was an occurrence in Saratov in 1970. There, because they had helped Yuri Vavilov, the son of the famed geneticist N. I. Vavilov, to erect a monument to his martyred father in a local cemetery, several scientists were given "intraparty reprimands."[89]

Official hostility toward dissidents can extend to their attorneys if they defy the taboos imposed by ideology and protocol. A defense lawyer's role in a dissent trial can amount to virtual collusion with the prosecution in "reeducating" the defendant and the praising of socialist justice. It appears to be dangerous in such cases to attempt to disprove prosecution arguments that literary or other works and materials written by, disseminated by, or found in the possession of defendants are slanderous. In this situation a lawyer may resort to the strategy of arguing that, while the works in question were indeed "anti-Soviet," the client was unaware of this and hence his motive was not malicious. D. I. Kaminskaya, Galanskov's attorney at his trial under article 70 in 1968, went as far as to argue that the trial proceedings had validated the correctness of the statements made in one of Galanskov's works, called by the prosecution a "slander on Soviet reality." This was a bold action under Soviet conditions. But she did not seek to

---

Numerous items relevant to this and other aspects of this study have also been published in *Survey* (London), the New York émigré newspaper *Novoe russkoe slovo*, and other journals.

88. Reddaway, *Uncensored Russia*, p. 412.
89. Reported in *Chronicle*, no. 17 (English-language version), pp. 77–78.

defend Galanskov's action in including in one of his samizdat collections
Sinyavsky's article "What Is Socialist Realism?" since the sentence passed on
Sinyavsky and Daniel had deprived her of the right to "argue about the
definition of it as 'criminal.'"[90] Boris Zolotukhin, Ginzburg's counsel in the
same case, as the first issue of the *Chronicle of Current Events* pointed out,
"convincingly refuted all the prosecution's evidence and—for the first time in
many years' experience of political trials—called for the complete acquittal
of his client." As a reward he was expelled from the party and from his post
as head of a legal consultation office.[91]

In 1972, Kaminskaya was refused a special pass that the authorities—apparently illegally, as Bukovsky charged in his final statement at this
trial—sometimes require for entering the courtroom in politically sensitive
trials. As a result she was unable to act as Bukovsky's advocate.[92] V. Ya.
Shveisky, another attorney experienced in dissent trials, also found it
impossible in 1973 to undertake the defense of Amalrik, against whom new
political charges had been brought by fellow prisoners in his labor camp in
Siberia.[93]

Another obstacle facing dissident defendants and their lawyers is the
frequent refusal of judges to permit them to call witnesses whose testimony,
in their opinion, would tend to prove them innocent. This action is documented in a number of samizdat trial records.[94]

If often happens that a dissident whose conduct has been unorthodox
enough in the opinion of the authorities to justify admonishment but not
arrest is called into the offices of the political police for an ostensibly friendly
"chat" (*beseda*). For example, the KGB called in Pavel Litvinov after
learning of his intention—which he did nothing to conceal—to make public
the documents he had assembled on the January 22, 1967 demonstration to
protest the arrest of Ginzburg and Galanskov. Litvinov was warned that if
such a report was produced, even by someone else, he would be held
responsible. One peculiar aspect of this episode, as Litvinov pointed out to
his KGB interlocutor, was that not the KGB but the procuracy was

90. Litvinov, *Trial of the Four*, p. 185.
91. Reddaway, *Uncensored Russia*, p. 85; *Posev*, August 1969, p. 16.
92. "The Case of Vladimir Bukovski," *Survey* 18, no. 2 (Spring 1972): 127.
93. See Valery Chalidze, "New Sufferings Await Amalrik," *New York Times*, July 11, 1973.
But M. P. Malyarov, the first deputy USSR procurator general, told Sakharov on August 15,
1973 that Shveisky had "attended" Amalrik's new trial. As a result of Sakharov's having made a
record of his conversation with Malyarov, incidentally, the world learned that Amalrik had
been sentenced to an additional three-year term.
94. Rachel Welber assembled a mass of data demonstrating and elaborating on the taboos
and pressures that severely circumscribe the role of defense counsel in dissent cases in an
unpublished study submitted in May 1973 to be undergraduate Russian and East European
Studies Program at Yale University. She analyzed 29 samizdat accounts of dissent trials and
other sources.

responsible for conducting investigations under Article 190-1, which the interlocutor said applied to the case.[95]

Yakir and Chalidze were among the prominent civil rights activists subjected to harassment and attempted intimidation by the security police and then to more serious penalties. Yakir, after years of persistent but relatively petty harassment and three KGB warnings, was finally arrested in June 1972. Chalidze, while in the United States, was deprived of his Soviet citizenship the same year.[96] According to Andrei Dubrov, a political émigré and former activist in the civil rights movement, Yakir, his wife, and several friends fell victim to a KGB tactic shortly before Yakir's arrest in 1972. This was the poisoning of alcoholic beverages ostensibly given them by friends. This tactic seems to be fairly frequently employed against persons the police wish to injure, warn, or perhaps get rid of.[97]

The spring and summer of 1973 witnessed a veritable cascade of harassments directed against Andrei Sakharov. They included calling him to a KGB office in March and the crude threats made to him by the first deputy procurator general, M. P. Malyarov, in the latter's office on August 15.[98]

Judicial Repression. The legal prescriptions for dealing with "especially dangerous crimes" outlined above are so vague and general that they seem to have been designed to make the prosecution of critics easy and their defense difficult. Such a hypothesis is powerfully supported by the records of the trials of Sinyavsky and Daniel, Ginzburg and Galanskov, Bukovsky and Victor Khaustov, Litvinov, Amalrik, Revol't Pimenov, Kronid Lyubarsky, Yakir, Victor Krasin, and dozens of other civil libertarians. It is also buttressed by what is known about the numerous obscure trials of Ukrainian, Crimean Tatar, and other protesters accused of "nationalist" agitation as well as by those of Jews tried on a variety of pretexts but in essence because they sought to emigrate.

One of the most valuable contributions of the samizdat materials is the glimpse they provide behind the veil of secrecy that has traditionally

95. Text of the "chat," in Russian and English, is in Karel van het Reve, ed., *Dear Comrade: Pavel Litvinov and the Voices of Soviet Citizens in Dissent* (New York, 1969), p. 1–17.

96. On KGB cajolery and admonishment of Yakir, see, e.g., Robert Conquest's introduction to Yakir's *A Childhood in Prison* (New York, 1973).

97. See Andrei Dubrov, "Poslednie dni P. Yakira na svobode" [Peter Yakir's last days in liberty], *Novoe russkoe slovo*, April 21, 1973. Dubrov asserts in this dispatch that in a period of two years the KGB called Yakir in three times. He believes the drugging was intended to convey a sense of the KGB's omnipotence and the folly of continued resistance. On the harassment of Chalidze, see *Volnoe slovo* (issued by the publishing house Possev in Frankfurt November 22, 1972), pp. 55–101. Among other things, it describes what appears to have been a KGB attempt to exploit statements allegedly made to its agents by an arrested Belgian citizen, Hugo Sebrechts, in contriving a criminal case against Chalidze.

98. On these episodes, see Hedrick Smith, "K.G.B. Is Reported to See Sakharov," *New York Times*, March 24, 1973; "The Sakharov Dialogue," *ibid.*, August 29, 1973.

concealed the systematic repression of dissent in the Soviet Union. The objectivity and fullness of the accounts of judicial repression that appeared in the *Chronicle of Current Events* and other publications differ enormously from the sparse, slanted accounts in the official press.[99]

From the point of view of the Soviet political leadership, not only dissent but disclosure of information about official action against dissenters to Soviet citizens—and still more so to foreigners—is a form of subversive activity. Probably for this reason the prime targets of the 1972–73 crackdown were the civil libertarians active in compiling and distributing the *Chronicle of Current Events*.[100]

Such unofficial accounts make clear that a salient feature of "socialist legality" is the "educational" function assigned by the CPSU to prosecutors and judges and also, be it noted, to defense attorneys. Education of some sort is probably common to legal systems everywhere, along with punishment and deterrence. In the USSR and similar systems this function is construed as a propaganda task of demonstrating the superiority of socialist to capitalist justice. This is not surprising in a system where all political structures have some ideological-propaganda role. But it is peculiarly

99. In addition to the sources cited in n. 87 above, the fuller, more detailed accounts of trials of dissenters include Hayward, *On Trial*; Litvinov, *Demonstration in Pushkin Square; idem, Trial of the Four*; Reddaway, *Uncensored Russia*; and Natalia Gorbanevskaya, *Red Square at Noon*, trans. Alexander Leven (London, 1970). Much information is also contained in Abraham Rothberg, *The Heirs of Stalin* (Ithaca, N.Y., 1972).

100. *Chronicle of Human Rights in the USSR*, no. 1 (1973), pp. 7–8, 11–14; *Chronicle of Current Events* (1972), p. 226; *ibid.*, no. 27 (1973), pp. 290–92. The first item reports that one of the charges against Lyubarsky was "possession and distribution" of *Chronicle*. The letter addressed to the *Times* of London by five leading dissenters, including Yuri Shtein, a former member of the Action Group, and Alexander Yesenin-Volpin, referred to a "command from on high" to close down *Chronicle*. The letter was released in Moscow in early March and was published in *Posev* in the same month (it is cited here from the Russian text in *Arkhiv samizdata* 1105). On the Kremlin's determination to silence *Chronicle*, see also Murray Seeger, "Case 24: KGB vs. Underground Soviet Bulletin," *Los Angeles Times*, November 1, 1972, and Anatole Shub, "The Escalation of Soviet Dissent—and of Soviet Repression," *New York Times Magazine*, September 10, 1972, p. 92. Both refer to a reported Central Committee directive to the KGB in December 1971 to give top priority in the new campaign to silence dissent to stopping *Chronicle*. As the editors of the English translation of issue 27 of *Chronicle* pointed out, the fact that the time that elapsed between its appearance in Russian (in Moscow, about November 9, 1972) and that of no. 26 was—by more than a month—longer than the interval of two months, give or take a few days, since the *Chronicle* began circulating in April, 1968, "suggests a more irregular appearance pattern for the future, or even that the *Chronicle* might cease to appear, at least for a time." In his dispatch "Soviets harass dissident holdout" in *Christian Science Monitor*, May 4, 1973, Leo Gruliow asserted that "The KGB evidently now has stamped out the Chronicle." Yakir and Krasin, he wrote, had "broken" under interrogation and provided the KGB with "detailed information," while Yakir's daughter Irina "reportedly admitted having helped to produce the *Chronicle*." Other victims of the KGB's operation against *Chronicle*, often referred to as "case 24," were the mathematical logician Yuri Shikhanovich, who was officially declared insane in early 1973 after more than a year of solitary confinement, and the literary scholar Gabriel Superfin. Apparently one of the pretexts for the stepped-up pressure against Sakharov in 1973 was an offer he and his wife had made to act as surety for Shikhanovich.

difficult for Soviet prosecutors and other personnel to demonstrate the advantages of the Soviet way of life in the field of criminal justice, for the mere occurrence of crime, particularly "political" crime, is embarrassing in what is officially described as a "developed socialist society."[101] Not surprisingly, prosecutors and judges resort to the tactic of portraying dissenters as persons imbued with "anti-Soviet" views or even as moral degenerates who inexplicably prefer to live off the black market or even on handouts from anti-Soviet émigré organizations and "imperialist" intelligence services rather than by honest toil. Fanciful though such charges seem to all who take the trouble to study the relevant facts, they probably seem plausible to the audience of woefully uninformed Soviet citizens whom they are intended to impress.

Political nonconformists in the USSR are likely to be tried twice, once in the courtroom and again in the news media. Civil libertarians usually appear in the media as horrible examples of moral viciousness and political immaturity.[102]

The Sinyavsky-Daniel trial was perceived by many Soviet and foreign intellectuals, including such hitherto faithful communists as the French poet Louis Aragon, as an outrage and a menace. In comparison with official arbitrariness at subsequent dissent trials, that of Sinyavsky and Daniel was conducted with a certain restraint and decorum. Nevertheless legality clearly played second fiddle to politics. The prosecution's method of applying article 70 was to assume rather than to prove that Sinyavsky and Daniel had deliberately "maligned" and "slandered" the Soviet system in works sent abroad for publication—this through words they put in the mouths of fictional characters. The prosecutor and the judge conspicuously ignored the argument of both writers that it was absurd to judge their political views by the statements of fictional characters.[103]

The fact that Sinyavsky's and Daniel's works were published abroad was emphasized, though this in itself was not a crime under Soviet law. Their works, it was brought out, were excerpted by foreign radio stations, praised by "reactionary" foreign critics, handsomely printed, issued in attractive

---

101. The proclamation of the achievement of a "developed socialist society" in the USSR and other Warsaw Pact countries dates from a conference in Prague in 1970, the results of which were reported in the journal *Problemy mira i sotsializma*, 1970, no. 12. The authorities' exasperation with continued "especially dangerous state crimes" is reflected in such statements as the following in an authoritative law school textbook: "The social danger that they pose has perhaps diminished slightly from an objective point of view . . . but their ideological harmfulness has even increased and Soviet citizens' attitude toward them has become one of complete intolerance." Vasilev, *Razvitie sovetskoi demokratii*, p. 95. Certainly such an attitude is displayed throughout the criminal justice process from arrest through incarceration.

102. See, for example, press items that accuse Ginzburg and Galanskov of being paid agents of anti-Soviet foreign organizations in Litvinov, *Trial of the Four*, pp. 283–306. Also see Powell, "Controlling Dissent," p. 96, and Berman, *Soviet Criminal Law*, 2d ed., pp. 87–89.

103. Hayward, *On Trial*, pp. 49–50, 158.

jackets, and sold in vast numbers.[104] The insinuation was that both authors hoped to make a great deal of money out of the foreign publication of their works. But this line was not pressed hard, probably because the defendants easily demonstrated its groundlessness.

Access to the courtroom where the Sinyavsky-Daniel trial took place was restricted to a selected "public," many of whom were ordered to attend. Yet, according to Roy Medvedev, "many members of the scientific and literary communities who had urgently expressed a desire to personally follow the proceedings were refused access."[105]

Doubtless the compilation and worldwide dissemination of remarkably full and accurate records of the proceedings of this and other trials despite such restrictive measures angered officials and heightened their determination to suppress protest and disclosure. The issues of legality and freedom of information thus became intertwined for both dissenters and authorities.

Two minor writers, Arkady Vasilev and Zoya Kedrina, played an active role as "public accusers" in the Sinyavsky-Daniel trial. They seem to have displayed even more hostility toward the defendants than the prosecutor. But no "public defenders" were present.

As for the press coverage of the case, the keynote was sounded before the trial began when the critic Dmitri Eremin wrote in *Izvestiia*: "The first thing you feel in reading their works is disgust."[106] Comment during and after the trial was in the same vein. Foreign journalists, even communists, were barred from the proceedings.

The vindictive atmosphere and calculated disregard of the rights of the accused that marred the trial of Sinyavsky and Daniel recurred, in some respects in aggravated form, in later political trials. Some defendants committed the heresy of attacking official political doctrines in the courtroom. Indignant prosecutors and judges responded with threats rather than with legal arguments.

Thus Vladimir Bukovsky said during his trial in 1967: "We demonstrate, for instance, in defense of Greek political prisoners—are we to remain indifferent to the fate of our own?" His prosecutor replied: "It seems . . . that you don't repent of anything that you have done, yet seven months in solitary confinement might have made you change your attitude toward Soviet laws."[107] Later Bukovsky drew a comparison between Spanish and Soviet attitudes toward political demonstrations. The judge termed the parallel "an outrage." He then attempted to discredit and obstruct presentation of Bukovsky's argument that the case against him was based on unconstitutional law, arbitrarily applied. Warned against "criticizing the

104. *Ibid.*, pp. 66, 114, 125, 128–29, 131.
105. *Ibid.*, pp. 1, 12; R. Medvedev, *Kniga*, pp. 180–81.
106. Hayward, *On Trial*, p. 23.
107. Litvinov, *Demonstration in Pushkin Square*, p. 74.

laws and activities of the KGB," Bukovsky replied: "The KGB has discredited itself so effectively that there is nothing we can add."[108]

Though convicted, Bukovsky received the relatively light sentence of three years in a corrective labor camp. But his more submissive codefendants, Vadim Delaunay (also often transliterated as Delone) and Yevgeny Kushev, both received only suspended sentences of one year. And Bukovsky was given a much more severe sentence under article 70 in 1972—twelve years of deprivation of freedom (two in prison, five in labor camps, five in exile). The court revealed part of the motive for this severity when it pointed out that during the investigation and trial he "refused to cooperate with the enquiry and refused to admit his guilt."[109]

In keeping with the propaganda purposes of Soviet justice, accused persons are expected to admit their guilt and express repentance. Doing so will contribute to the political education of their fellow citizens, especially those who might be contemplating "criminal" behavior similar to that of the accused in question. It follows that the authorities view with extreme disfavor a vigorous rebuttal of charges.

The treatment of Ginzburg and Galanskov in connection with their January 1968 trial was even more extreme than that of Bukovsky and the others already described. The accused were held incommunicado for pretrial investigation almost three months beyond the normal legal maximum of nine months.[110] Although it is obvious from the proceedings and press reports that Ginzburg was tried for having compiled a "White Book" on the Sinyavsky-Daniel trial and Galanskov for his activities in connection with the samizdat journal *Phoenix 66*, the state charged them and their codefendants, the typist Vera Lashkova and Alexei Dobrovolsky, under article 70, with "establishing links" with the Russian émigré organization NTS, with (in Ginzburg's case) "harboring two songs of an anti-Soviet nature," with receiving "anti-Soviet pamphlets from abroad," and the like. Galanskov was also charged with violating currency regulations. The prosecution built its case largely on the testimony of Dobrovolsky, who had turned state's evidence and received a sentence of two years, while Ginzburg received five years and Galanskov seven. Yet Dobrovolsky was an admitted liar, and his testimony was uncorroborated and was contradicted by other defendants and witnesses.[111] The authorities also relied on the testimony of Nicholas

---

108. *Ibid.*, pp. 116–27.
109. "The Case of Vladimir Bukovsky," *Survey* 18, no. 2 (Spring 1972): 123–60; quotation at p. 160. On Bukovsky's earlier sentence in 1967, see Litvinov, *Demonstration in Pushkin Square*, pp. 155–56.
Alexander Ginzburg said at his trial under article 70 in 1968 that he was certain to be convicted "because so far no one accused under article 70 has been declared innocent." Litvinov, *Trial of the Four*, p. 210. So far as the author knows this still applies to all the articles invoked against dissenters.
110. Litvinov, *Trial of the Four*, pp. 35–39.
111. *Ibid.*, pp. 53, 194–204, 316–23.

Brocks-Sokolov, a young Venezuelan of Russian parentage. Brocks, an NTS adherent, came to the USSR in December 1967, long after Ginzburg and Galanskov had been put behind bars. Arrested as a spy, he asserted that he had been sent by the NTS to help the defendants. Yet both the prosecution and the press treated his irrelevant testimony as proof of the defendants' guilt.[112]

Among the features of the case of these participants in the August 25, 1968 demonstration in Red Square against the Warsaw Pact invasion of Czechoslovakia, were the commitment of Victor Fainberg to a psychiatric hospital, where as far as this writer is aware he is still; the beatings administered to participants, including Fainberg, whose teeth were knocked out; the dispensing of free liquor to a crowd that gathered near the entrance to the courtroom; the abuse heaped by the mob on well-wishers of the defendants—and also, while the participants were being roughed up on Red Square, the anti-Semitic sentiments expressed by some of their assailants.[113]

One of the most puzzling and foreboding of all post-Stalin dissent trials was that of Yakir and Krasin in August 1973. By itself, the decision to apply judicial repression to the hitherto immune Yakir, who in his youth and early manhood had spent fourteen years in camps, indicated the regime's increasing readiness to undertake stern measures against its critics. In 1961, Khrushchev, in his concluding remarks at the Twenty-second CPSU Congress, had in the course of a eulogy of one of Stalin's victims, Army Commander Iona Yakir, gone out of his way to refer in a friendly way to his son Peter.[114]

In 1973, Peter Yakir and Victor Krasin stood trial on charges that they had violated article 70 of the RSFSR Criminal Code. They were accused of links with the NTS, of having helped to organize the Action Group, of involvement in composing and distributing the *Chronicle of Current Events*, and of having received funds from abroad. As Andrei Dubrov pointed out (in an article based on information received by telephone from Vienna to Moscow dissenter sources), accusing dissidents of connections with the NTS is a favorite KGB ploy designed to play on the antipathies toward that organization of Soviet patriots and foreign leftists.

The charges and the careful stage management of this trial resembled those used in that of Ginzburg and Galanskov five years earlier. Like those

112. *Protsess chetyrekh*, pp. 25–26, 187–93, 356–60, 450–55, 548–50.
113. Natalia Gorbanevskaya, *Red Square at Noon* (London, 1970), pp. 55–104, 161, 238–54. Gorbanevskaya, a young poet, participated in the demonstration, but was soon released, perhaps because she was the mother of two small children. Later, however, she was committed for a time to a mental institution. Her careful account also reveals that close relatives as well as friends of the accused were not allowed to attend the trial of the demonstrators. A Moscow newspaper, however, reported that workers of Moscow enterprises attended the trial. They felt that the accused were attempting to "attract the West's attention." This report indirectly confirms, as dissident sources charged, that access to the trial was determined by political considerations. See *ibid.*, pp. 127, 235.
114. *XXII s"ezd kommunisticheskoi partii sovetskogo soiuza* [(Proceedings of) The Twenty-second Congress of the Communist Party of the Soviet Union] (Moscow, 1962), 2:586.

of religious writer Anatoly Levitin-Krasnov and Vladimir Bukovsky a year or two earlier, the trial was held in Lyublino, a suburb remote from the center of Moscow, where earlier dissent trials had taken place. Lyublino was tightly cordoned off by police, and foreign correspondents could not pick up bits of information even by stationing themselves near the courthouse. Control over access to the courtroom was so tight and the premises so packed with KGB men that it may have been impossible for sources favorable to the defendants to put together a record such as we have for earlier dissent trials.[115] But by far the most startling feature of the trial was the defendants' collaboration with the prosecution in an obvious attempt by the KGB to exploit the affair for propaganda purposes.

The defendants pleaded guilty and in return received comparatively mild sentences—three years' deprivation of freedom, including the time in prison while under investigation, plus three years of exile. In appraising the sentence one should keep in mind the fact that Yakir and Krasin had done nothing that would have been considered at all illegal in any country where civil liberties are protected. Furthermore, as the *New York Times* pointed out editorially, it was "only through TASS dispatches and the reports of a Soviet Foreign Office briefing official that the world is being apprised of these prisoners' alleged 'confessions.'" Yakir and Krasin went on public display a few days later "to recant once more in public," as Theodore Shabad noted in his report on the exercise filmed by Soviet TV. The "illegal activities" listed in the defendants' reported statements included "clandestine meetings with foreigners." Shabad's dispatch noted: "Newsmen's questions about which provisions in the Soviet criminal code viewed meetings with foreigners as criminal went unanswered.[116]

One can only guess what methods were employed to bring to such a pass a steadfast dissenter like Yakir. To be sure, as the American press reminded readers, Yakir had once said that he might be made to admit anything under interrogation, but "you will know that it will not be the real me speaking." It was widely reported that Yakir, who was known to drink heavily, might have caved in once alcohol was denied him. But this hypothesis does not account for Krasin's behavior. A better explanation may be that Yakir and Krasin made a deal not only to save themselves from a worse fate but to alleviate the lot of associates, including Yakir's daughter, Irina, who were involved with the *Chronicle*.[117]

115. See Androi Dubrov, "Pervy den protsessa", [First day of the trial], *Novoe russkoe slovo*, Sept. 1–2, 1973. Dubrov's account was superior in insight and detail to those published in the *New York Times* and other English-language newspapers.

116. Editorial: "Charade in Moscow," *New York Times*, August 31, 1973. Dispatch: Theodore Shabad, "Soviet Dissidents Recant in Public," *ibid.*, September 6, 1973.

117. In his article "Two Men: One Exhausted, One Threatened" in the *New York Times*, September 7, 1973, Chalidze asserted that the KGB promised Yakir that in return for furnishing information desired by them "there would be no more new arrests." If so, the authorities broke the promise by arresting Irina Belogorodskaya, Victor Khaustov, and Gabriel Superfin in 1973. Also relevant is Sakharov's statement to Western correspondents regarding "widely printed warnings

A disturbing feature of the Yakir-Krasin trial was the attempt made during it to link Sakharov and Solzhenitsyn with some of the defendants' activities. The aim presumably was to justify repression of the latter. The KGB had paved the way as far as Sakharov was concerned by having a letter allegedly written by Yakir sent to Sakharov. The letter said that the author would be "extremely glad if what I have written permits you to avoid those mistakes and delusions which I unfortunately have not avoided and which I recognized too late."[118]

Of course the controlled Soviet information media afforded Sakharov or Solzhenitsyn no opportunity to explain their views or to defend themselves against the torrent of accusations and insinuations directed against them. Instead they sharply criticized Western radio stations that sought to supply their Soviet audience with information on these matters. These machinations made the hopes expressed a few years earlier by Soviet civil libertarians for further progress in "cleansing away the foulness of Stalinism" seem sadly unrealistic.[119]

An optimist might derive some consolation from the thought that even the grim spectacle presented by Soviet justice in the summer of 1973 was still far from full-fledged Stalinism. Indeed the regime was, to a degree, on the defensive, as indicated by the failure at that time to take decisive action against Sakharov and Solzhenitsyn. Some of Sakharov's friends also came to his defense in statements widely reported in the West, and others, such as the famed seventy-nine-year-old physicist Peter Kapitsa, refused to sign denunciations of Sakharov (Kapitsa, it was reported, was nevertheless permitted to proceed to Finland to attend a conference).

There is a substantial body of evidence indicating that the treatment of dissenters outside Moscow tends to be even harsher than in the capital.[120] One important factor has probably been the limited but not insignificant opportunities available in Moscow for exchanging information with foreigners and for transmitting it to the outside world, which must put a degree of

---

that for the appearance of every new issue of the *Chronicle* appropriate persons would be arrested," quoted by Theodore Shabad, "Soviet Dissidents and Confession," *ibid.*

118. Text in *A Chronicle of Human Rights in the USSR*, no. 2 (April–May 1973), pp. 11–12. The editors pointed out that Yakir's letter was delivered by a KGB officer, which "has created the impression that the investigators are anxious to make known Yakir's position." But they also noted that there was no indication of whether or not the letter was composed with the help of Yakir's investigators.

119. Andrei Sakharov, *Progress, Coexistence, and Intellectual Freedom* (New York, 1968), pp. 54–55. In the years that followed the release of this essay Sakharov became steadily less optimistic about the prospects for a renovative, regenerative process, which he had once apparently hoped it would encourage.

120. See especially Michael Browne, ed., *Ferment in the Ukraine* (London, 1971), and Vyacheslav Chornovil, comp., *The Chornovil Papers* (Toronto and London, 1968). Also see John Kolasky, *Education in Soviet Ukraine* (Toronto, 1968) and *Two Years in Soviet Ukraine* (Toronto, 1970), and, for light on the ideological foundations of protest by Ukrainian intellectuals against Moscow's cultural policy, Ivan Dzyuba, *Internationalism or Russification?* (London, 1968).

restraint on the authorities. The offensive of 1972–73 against Soviet citizens who maintained relations with foreigners may have erased the difference, but at least in the period before then the treatment of dissenters in Moscow seems as a rule to have been somewhat more lenient than in, for example, Kiev or Lvov. Other reasons for the greater coercion in the non-Russian national units of the USSR are probably the ethnic tensions between Russians and non-Russians and Moscow's traditional concern over any political activities that might threaten its tight control over the strategically sensitive borderlands. Hence it is not surprising that draconian sentences have been imposed on Ukrainian intellectuals accused of "nationalism."[121]

There have been two—or perhaps three—major waves of arrests of Ukrainian intellectuals since Khrushchev's ouster. In 1965 some twenty-five writers, artists, teachers, and other professionals were arrested and tried (for the most part secretly). Several received very long sentences. One was Svyatoslav Karavansky, a linguist-translator who had already served almost seventeen years of a twenty-five-year term in labor camps until he was released under a 1960 amnesty. At the request of the KGB he was sent back in 1966 to serve out the remainder of his term. Born in 1920, Karavansky had been arrested in Odessa in 1944 as a member of the OUN, a Ukrainian nationalist organization, but apparently he was not accused of collaboration with the Rumanian occupation forces. His return to the Mordovian labor camps followed his criticism of what he regarded as discrimination against Ukrainians in access to higher education in the Ukrainian Republic. Undoubtedly the authorities' anger was heightened by the fact that in petitions addressed to high officials he demanded criminal prosecution for Dadenkov, Ukrainian minister of higher and secondary education, and Rudenko, chief procurator of the USSR.[122] In 1969 Karavansky received an additional sentence for allegedly conducting "anti-Soviet propaganda" in the dreaded Vladimir prison.[123]

Most of the other Ukrainian dissenters arrested in 1966 were men about thirty years of age with good ideological credentials and prospects for successful careers. These young writers, historians, scientists, and other professionals could not convincingly be charged—as the "jurists" and the protesters of the Stalin era had been—with plotting the Ukraine's secession

---

121. Thus in 1961 seven Ukrainians, known as the "jurists" because some of them had legal training, received sentences ranging from death—later commuted to 15 years—to 7 years in camps for various alleged political acts that amounted in essence to demanding that what the defendants called Moscow's "colonial" policy toward the Ukraine be replaced by a policy of "socialist democracy." See Browne, *Ferment*, pp. 16–17, 31–93. Amazingly enough, not a word about this case appeared in the Soviet press, and it was almost unknown to Soviet citizens until the literary critic Ivan Svitlychny circulated a report on it in 1966. This report became known in the West in 1967 through a reference in an article published by Chornovil in a Paris-based Ukrainian-language publication. *Ibid.*, p. 31.

122. *Chornovil Papers*, pp. 5, 65–67, 81, 87–88, 93, 166–180, 214–19.

123. Browne, *Ferment*, p. 236.

from the Soviet Union. Their dissent, according to the available evidence, was the "within-system" sort. Leninist in terminology, it demanded an end to what the dissenters perceived as Muscovite cultural imperialism and violations of "Leninist nationality policy." The charges against Vyacheslav Chornovil, Valentin Moroz, and others ranged from reading, or even merely possessing, Ukrainian-language works published in Russia before 1917 or in the United States and Canada since then to criticism of the abolition of compulsory instruction in the Ukrainian language of the children of Ukrainian parents in the Ukrainian Republic. The dissenters also objected strongly to Moscow's practice of transporting Ukrainians convicted of "state" crimes to labor camps located not in the Ukraine but in Mordovia and other units of the Russian Republic. And they expressed bitter indignation over the systematic lawlessness practiced against even the mildest of critics by the agents of law enforcement. As Moroz has put it, "If we follow to the end the paths along which the KGB men entered our reality, we will find ourselves in the nightmarish thicket of the Stalinist jungle." The data he adduces about interrogation methods, treatment of prisoners in camps, and the "self-characterizations" of KGB men that he recalls from his own contact with them validate his assertion.[124]

It is not surprising that Moroz and Chornovil have paid a high price for their efforts to make known the systematic repression of critical thought and freedom of information in Soviet Ukraine. Moroz, a promising historian born in 1936, was sentenced in 1966 to five years. Released in 1968, he was again sentenced in November 1970 to six years in prison, three years of labor camps, and five years of exile.[125] Chornovil, a television journalist and a former activist of the Young Communist League, born in 1938, was sentenced in 1967 after he had angered the authorities by protesting against violations of the legal rights of protesters whose cases he had been assigned to cover. After his release in 1969 under an amnesty he continued his protest activities. Rearrested in January 1972, he was sentenced under article 62 of the Ukrainian Criminal Code (equivalent to article 70 of the RSFSR Code) to seven years' deprivation of liberty in a strict-regime camp plus five years' exile.[126]

Moroz and Chornovil are representative of hundreds of Ukrainian intellectuals repressed by the authorities since Khrushchev's ouster alone. Soviet dissident sources and the Western press have reported that in 1972 more than a hundred Ukrainian civil rights activists were arrested. Many

124. Valentyn Moroz, "A Report from the Beria Reservation," in Browne, *Ferment*, p. 127. Abundant corroboration of Moroz's picture may be found elsewhere in Browne. At pp. 191–95, for example, is the English text of the protest of 139 Ukrainian "intellectuals and workers" against violation of the "principles of legality and publicity." The letter asserted that "symptoms of Stalinism" were manifested "even more overtly and grossly" in the Ukraine than in Moscow. See also *Chornovil Papers* and the other works on the situation in the Ukraine cited earlier as well as Reddaway, *Uncensored Russia*, pp. 280–97.
125. Browne, *Ferment*, p. 236.
126. *Chronicle of Human Rights in the USSR*, no. 1, p. 8.

were sentenced to long terms in camps. One, the critic Ivan Dzyuba, suffered from tuberculosis. He had been spared imprisonment earlier despite his protests against Russification in the Ukraine and against persecution of fellow intellectuals. Nevertheless, he was sentenced in early 1973; but later, after reportedly recanting, he was apparently released from prison. The brilliant Ukrainian mathematician Leonid Plyushch, born in 1939, was committed by a Kiev court in January 1973 to a prison psychiatric hospital. The trial was secret, and even his wife was not permitted to attend. It followed more than a year of enforced psychiatric observation during which the notorious KGB psychiatrist Lunts found him to be suffering from "reformist delusions."[127] In view of these events the charge of excessive toleration of local Ukrainian national pride leveled against P. Yu. Shelest by V. V. Shcherbitsky in April 1973—though, as is common in Soviet practice, it did not name the target of criticism—seems ironic.[128]

The examples, which we regard as typical, of repressive actions against civil rights advocates in Moscow and the Ukraine that we have examined above tend to confirm that repression is even harsher in the provinces than in the capital. Presently we shall present other data in support of this contention. Before doing so, however, it might be well to emphasize that local and temporal variations in the application of repression are far less significant than the essence and totality of this coercive system. In general, it appears, the Soviet authorities tend to behave as ruthlessly as they feel they need to and as opportunities and circumstances permit. It would be a mistake to conclude from the record to date that Moscow dissenters will always be treated better than Ukrainians. In this connection it is pertinent to recall some events of 1973—in particular, the reindictment of Andrei Amalrik for "slandering" the Soviet system instead of his release after completion of his three-year term in a labor camp, during which he contracted meningitis and was declared an invalid. A well-informed veteran of the civil rights struggle in the USSR pointed out that Amalrik faced a device that had been applied in "many similar cases" that is, a new case was brought against him on the basis of the testimony of "camp guards and common criminals who are dependent on the camp administration."[129]

127. The best account of this case seems to be that of Andrei Sadykh in *Novoe russkoe slovo*, July 10, 1973.

128. Shcherbitsky's charges were contained in a report to the Central Committee of the Ukrainian Communist Party that was published in *Pravda ukrainy*, April 20, 1973. Shortly thereafter Shelest, who had been replaced as first secretary of the Ukrainian party organization in May 1972, was retired from the Politburo. While interpretation of such matters must inevitably be speculative, the treatment of Ukrainian dissenters does seem to have become harsher after Shcherbitsky replaced Shelest. There are indications that the Ukrainian KGB was restrained from going all out to crush dissent during Shelest's administration. On this point see, for example, Browne, *Ferment*, pp. 61, 14. Also see *Chornovil Papers*, p. 72, where Chornovil notes that Shelest had praised the poet Ivan Brach while KGB officers had reviled him.

129. Chalidze, "New Sufferings." Among other aspects of his prognosis for Amalrik's fate, Chalidze noted that Amalrik's right to legal defense had been violated—his attorney had "not

Nevertheless, it seems to this writer that nonconformists fare worse in the provinces than in Moscow. (Amalrik's 1970 trial, incidentally, was held not in Moscow, despite the fact that the crimes of which he was accused had presumably occurred there, but in Sverdlovsk a thousand miles to the east.) If so, this difference is highly significant, for the Ukraine, for example, with several times the population of Moscow and the special factor of nationality discontent, probably contains far more dissidents than the capital.

Mykhaylo Masyutko, a teacher who was one of the victims of repression in the Ukraine in 1965–66, wrote a petition to the Supreme Soviet of the Ukrainian Republic that somehow was smuggled out of his Mordovian camp. In it he asked why in the camps of Mordovia, thousands of kilometers from the Ukraine, the percentage of Ukrainians among the political prisoners was "60 or even 70 percent."[130] Another protester, the Russian Anatoly Marchenko, has said on the basis of experience in labor camps and prisons that "there are particularly many Ukrainians and people from the Baltic republics." Amalrik also told the American correspondent Anatole Shub in 1969 that "more than half the prisoners in our camps these days are . . . Latvians, Lithuanians, Georgians, Ukrainians and the rest."[131]

Of the ethnic groups numerous members of which have been punished for "anti-Soviet agitation" and other "state crimes," perhaps the best known are the Jews and the Crimean Tatars. Because their experience is relatively well known we shall treat it only briefly. Of course in the case of these two ethnic groups, the character of Soviet justice reflected the same contradiction between, on the one hand, the effort to project an image of formal legality and on the other, the far weightier factor of *raison d'état* that, obviously, determined the outcome in Moscow "mainstream" dissent trials and in the Ukraine. These cases, however, confronted the Soviet leadership with special problems and, in the case of the Jews, with perhaps its most successful challenge.

The Jews in the Soviet Union were deprived by Stalin and his successors of even the limited cultural autonomy enjoyed by Soviet nationalities. All too often they are derogated in the mass media and in ostensibly scholarly studies by attacks on Judaism, even though most Jews have no affiliation with the organized forms of the religion.[132] Jewish attempts to assert what in

consented to defend him this time due to unlawful limitations on his rights as a lawyer." Amalrik, perhaps because of foreign protests, was subsequently provided with a research job but remained in exile in a remote part of Siberia.

130. Browne, *Ferment*, p. 19. Ostensibly on the charge of "preparing . . . anti-Soviet documents" but doubtlessly because he had written the petition and other essays on nationality questions, Masyutko in December 1966 was placed in the camp prison for six months and then, although he was seriously ill, was transferred to the rigorous Vladimir prison. See *ibid.*, p. 10, and *Chornovil Papers*, p. 140.

131. Browne, *Ferment*, p. 19, referring to Anatoly Marchenko, *My Testimony*, and to Anatole Shub's article in the *International Herald Tribune*, March 31, 1969.

132. Zvi Gitelman, "The Jewish Religion in the USSR," *Synagogue Council of America* (New York, 1971), demonstrates, especially on pp. 17–19, the spillover from attacks on the Jewish religion to inculcation of anti-Semitic sentiments directed against Jews as an ethnic community.

most modern societies would be regarded as normal sentiments of group identity and pride have frequently been characterized officially as manifestations of "Zionist" and "anti-Soviet" activity. Operationally, as two American prosecutors traveling in the USSR in 1971 to inquire into arrests and impending trials of Jewish prisoners were told by a Soviet official, "anti-Soviet activity" is defined as "Any publication of news about Israel by an unofficial or unauthorized source."[133]

The six-day Arab-Israeli war of 1967 triggered official pressure on Soviet Jews to publicly denounce Israeli "aggression." But increasing numbers of Jews began to demand the right to emigrate. These included many young people who, as the young engineer Kochubievsky said in a statement that helped cause his arrest, knew "nothing about Jewish culture and language, who are mostly atheists" but who felt proud of their national heritage. Amazingly enough in view of previous Soviet policy, which had in effect viewed leaving the USSR as a crime, by mid-1973 some 60,000 Jews had been allowed to leave. Most went to Israel under regulations that permitted the emigration of Jews who had relatives abroad.[134]

Many times that number probably want to emigrate, including many highly qualified Jews of Moscow and other big cities whose departure is resisted on both economic and prestige grounds. Nevertheless the departure clearly constitutes the greatest success to date of the "resistance movement" in the USSR. The most significant factors seem to be the existence of the state of Israel as a homeland outside the USSR, something other non-Russians do not have; the exceptionally strong sense of identity and militancy displayed by Jews after 1967; and the very great interest in and support for their cause abroad. The limited but significant concessions made to the Jews tend to support the view that even the Kremlin can be moved by internal resistance supported by world opinion. But this tentative conclusion must be cautiously interpreted. In many ways the situation of the Jews is special. Other ethnic groups and the civil rights movement generally, however, can learn and draw comfort from the example.

The Jewish emigration struggle may have been partly inspired by the Democratic Movement. The struggle of Jews against discrimination and affronts to group dignity was hailed by civil rights leaders.[135] Many Jews, like others whose conception of their legal rights differed from the official interpretation, have been dismissed from jobs and arrested, and a number have been sentenced to long terms in camps.

The harshest act of judicial repression of Jewish activists was the Leningrad "hijacking" trial of December 1970. This trial, like that of

133. Richard Cohen, ed., *Let My People Go* (New York, 1971), p. 247.
134. The text of Kochubievsky's statement, including the quotation, is in Moshe Decter, ed., *A Hero for Our Time* (New York, 1970). Kochubievsky left for Israel in 1972 after imprisonment in a camp.
135. On these points, see, for example, Reddaway, *Uncensored Russia*, pp. 298–300, and Sakharov, *Progress*, pp. 65–66.

Kochubievsky, was apparently designed to discourage demands by Soviet Jews for emigration. It caused such an outcry internationally that the death sentences imposed on two of the eleven defendants were commuted to fifteen-year terms in labor camps of the strictest regime. Some of the other sentences were reduced. The wife and daughters of Mark Dymshits, the alleged ringleader of the plot, apparently struck a bargain with the state prosecutor and were released. But one witness who testified vigorously for the defense was sentenced to three years in a camp, and at least one Leningrad Jew who protested was immediately arrested.

The defendants were charged only with planning, not with attempting, a hijacking. There were serious grounds for doubting that they had even planned one. Indeed, in many ways the whole affair smacked of KGB provocation. In support of this hypothesis one can cite, for example, the suspicious and virtually unprecedented speed of Soviet press publication of the announcement of the crime.[136]

The entire Crimean Tatar nation of some 200,000 people was deported to Central Asia in 1944 on charges of collaboration with the Nazi occupying forces. It was one of eight deported ethnic groups about which information became widely known only after Stalin's death. Indeed, the facts regarding the deportation of one of these peoples, the Meskhetians, did not become known until 1969. The Tatars apparently lost 46 per cent of their number as a result of the deportation and the other peoples also suffered severely.[137]

In 1967 a decree apparently published only in Uzbekistan, where most of the Crimean Tatars resided, absolved this small nation of the blanket charges made during the war. The decree referred, however, not to "Crimean Tatars" but to "Tatars who had previously lived in the Crimea."[138] The wording is significant, for it cut athwart the wish of many Crimean Tatars to return to their ancestral homeland, which, together with recovery of the political status of autonomous republic, abolished in 1944, was a major goal of an extremely active national pressure group campaign. Indeed, probably nothing like the Tatars' mass street demonstrations and other organized protest activities had been seen in the USSR since the 1920s. The Tatars were not permitted, however, to return to their home in the Crimea, which had been reassigned to Russians and Ukrainians. When the Tatar leaders persisted in organizing demonstrations and in collecting signatures on

136. See the account of the trial in Cohen, *Let My People Go*, pp. 81–118, and of the second trial of nine alleged accomplices of the Leningrad eleven as well as of other related trials in other parts of the USSR, pp. 245–71. The second trial involved such familiar irregularities and violations of Soviet law as holding of defendants *in camera* beyond the legal limit, barring of friends and relatives from attendance, and moving a trial from Riga to a distant suburb.

137. For indispensable background information see Robert Conquest, *The Nation Killers* (New York, 1970). See *Uncensored Russia*, chaps. 12–13, for the *Chronicle*'s coverage of the struggle for their national rights waged after their official "rehabilitation" by the Crimean Tatar and Meskheti peoples. See also the careful study prepared by Ann Sheehy for the Minority Rights Group, *The Crimean Tatars and Volga Germans: Soviet Treatment of Two National Minorities* (London, 1971).

138. The text is in *Current Digest of the Soviet Press* 19, no. 36 (1967): 3.

petitions despite official warnings, the authorities cracked down hard. Hundreds of Crimean Tatars were arrested on minor charges such as "petty hooliganism." Many families were expelled from the Crimea, and many petitioners who had gone to Moscow were deported and in some cases beaten. The top leaders, including the renowned physicist Rollan Kadiev, were sentenced in 1969 to labor camps on charges of slandering the Soviet state. Although numbers of Crimean Tatars continued to protest in the 1970s, their movement seems to have been weakened by the crackdown and its grievances were not satisfied.[139]

The cause of the Crimean Tatars was supported in various ways by leading Moscow dissenters, including the late Alexei Kosterin, Sakharov, Litvinov, Larisa Daniel, and most actively General Grigorenko. Grigorenko's arrest and subsequent incarceration in a special psychiatric hospital at Chernyakhovsk came after he had been tricked into going to Tashkent in 1969 with the intention of testifying at the trial of Kadiev and his associates.[140] He was released from confinement on the eve of former President Nixon's visit to Moscow in June 1974.

Clearly this protest movement has been less successful than that of the Soviet Jews. The Crimean Tatars lacked the Jews' advantages of support abroad and a foreign homeland, and the Kremlin might be reluctant to grant the demands of a group that might remain actively discontented within the USSR. Then too, in view of the example their success might have set to other non-Russian ethnic groups, it is not surprising that Moscow reacted violently to Crimean Tatar pressures.[141]

Labor Camps. Anatoly Marchenko wrote as a veteran of six years in prisons and camps, including the Mordovian camps for political prisoners: "Today's camps for political prisoners are just as horrific as in Stalin's time. A few things are better, a few things worse."[142] As Marchenko's account and Reddaway's extensive study show, "The most powerful means of influencing the prisoners is hunger"—imposed "in the hopes that prisoners will either become submissive and publicly denounce their own views, actions and friends, or die through illness or some desperate act brought on by permanent weakness."[143]

139. On a major protest in 1971 addressed to the CPSU'S Twenty-third Congress, see Sheehy, *Crimean Tatars*, p. 16.

140. *Ibid.*

141. As Leonard Schapiro has pointed out, in the case of Soviet Jews also "the real problem is presented not by the Jews who will be allowed out but by those who will remain behind." "The Soviet Jews," *New York Review of Books*, July 19, 1973, p. 4.

142. *My Testimony*, trans. Michael Scammell (New York, 1969), p. 3. The translation in Reddaway, *Uncensored Russia*, p. 186, differs slightly.

143. The first quotation is from a letter by Marchenko to Soviet officials, reproduced in Reddaway, *Uncensored Russia*, pp. 185–90; the second is from Peter Reddaway, "The Soviet Treatment of Dissenters and the Growth of a Civil Rights Movement," in *Rights and Wrongs: Some Essays on Human Rights*, ed. C. R. Hill (London, 1969), p. 85.

To be sure, the camps operate on a much smaller scale today than during the Stalin era. There is abundant evidence, however, that for those unfortunate enough to be sentenced to a term in a "corrective labor colony," as the camps are officially designated, life is hungry, humiliating, often degrading, and not infrequently short—especially for political prisoners.[144]

Control over camp inmates is effected by an elaborate system of controls, including, as one would expect, the setting of prisoners to spy and report on one another. One of the most potent controls is manipulation of prisoners' fear of reclassification up the scale of deprivations minutely prescribed for each of the four labor colony "regimes": ordinary (*obshchii*), hard (*usilenny*), strict (*strogii*), and special (*osoby*).[145] There are also gradations of regime in prisons; prisons are generally regarded as more severe than camps and are reserved, as are the two severer grades of camp regime, for persons convicted of serious political offenses.[146] Marchenko observes in a comparison of "normal" and "strict" regime in Vladimir prison: "The differences between these regimes might seem infinitesimal to someone who hasn't experienced them on his own back, but for a prisoner it is enormous. On normal regime there's a radio, on strict regime not; on normal regime you get an hour's exercise a day, on strict regime half an hour, with nothing at all on Sundays; on normal regime you're allowed one visit a year lasting thirty minutes. . . . ." Also according to Marchenko, "In practice any con that the authorities take a dislike to is liable to end up on special regime or in prison—if he's too difficult, say, or independently minded."[147]

144. On the discrimination practiced against "politicals," see Marchenko, *My Testimony*, especially pp. 90–100, 261–75, 300–19. Reddaway's judgment that regulations governing life in the camps are "clearly designed to cause physical suffering and loss of dignity" is confirmed by abundant evidence. See *Uncensored Russia*, p. 203. For a detailed description of the labor camp system based on samizdat sources, see *ibid.*, pp. 185–226, and Reddaway, "Soviet Treatment of Dissenters," pp. 79–120. The nightmarish quality of life in the camps and the Kafkaesque mentality of the KGB overlords in charge of them are most vividly conveyed by Marchenko, who suffered further punishment after his revelations were published, and by Chornovil, Moroz, and other Ukrainians cited above.

145. Reddaway, "Soviet Treatment of Dissenters," p. 85; also *idem, Uncensored Russia*, p. 206, and E. L. Johnson, *An Introduction to the Soviet Legal System* (London, 1972), p. 151. Johnson translates *usilenny* not as "hard" but as "strict."

146. According to Reddaway, the authorities almost invariably send those convicted under article 70 or others governing punishment for "especially dangerous state crimes" to "the toughest camps in Mordovia" or to the notorious Vladimir prison. See *Uncensored Russia*, p. 206.

147. Marchenko, *My Testimony*, pp. 115, 85. The second statement is confirmed, insofar as it refers to official regulations, in N. A. Struchkov and V. A. Kirin, eds., *Kommentarii Kosnovam ispravitelno-trudovogo zakonadatelstva soiuze ssr i soiuznykh respublikh* [Commentary on the principles of corrective labor legislation in the USSR and in the Union republics] (Moscow, 1972), p. 86—where, incidentally it is revealed that prisoners confined to the punishment cell (*kartser*) get no exercise at all. Generally this official description of the regimes confirms the reports of Marchenko and other dissident sources. But it attributes rather different characteristics to the camp system than do Marchenko and others who have experienced it.

It is significant that labor colony authorities are legally empowered by article 77-1 of the RSFSR Criminal Code to impose penalties, including the death penalty, for "disorganizing" the work of a camp or other offenses if these are committed by "dangerous recidivists or persons

Contrary to officlal claims regarding the "progressive" nature of the Soviet penal system, Reddaway asserts—and an abundance of evidence supports him—that "The sufferings of Soviet political prisoners do not end on their release from prison or camp." They are severely limited in employment opportunities, for example, and they may be denied the right to reside in major cities or ports or border areas.[148] New charges based on behavior while a prisoner are also possible, as in the cases of Karavansky and Amalrik.

The Scope of Repression: A Quantitative Note. Statistical data on the numbers and categories of dissenters subjected to repression are incomplete, are of dubious reliability, and are difficult to verify and analyze. If one casts a wide net one may arrive at a very large figure. Sir John Lawrence, for example, states: "There are certainly some tens of thousands and perhaps a hundred thousand political prisoners, taking the phrase to include all prisoners of conscience." Even this number is almost minuscule in comparison with Conquest's estimate of "5½ million deaths from hunger and from the diseases of hunger" as a result of the "purely man-made famine" in the Ukraine in 1932, the "wiping out" of some 10 million "kulaks" (mostly falsely labeled), the detention of 8 million persons in labor camps in 1938, and a figure of more than 20 million dead "as the debit balance of the Stalin regime for twenty-three years" for operation of the labor camps.[149]

One careful recent estimate by Boris Lewytzkyji, based on samizdat sources, of the number of persons "sentenced between 1960 and 1971 on political grounds" is 670. The figure would be larger by perhaps several hundred as of 1973 had Lewytzkyji taken account of "hundreds of arrests" reportedly made by the KGB in the winter and spring of 1972, especially in the Ukraine.[150] Another compilation by the research staff of Radio Liberty, also based on samizdat sources, yielded a figure of some 3,000 arrests or sentencings of persons engaged "in the struggle for the rights of man in the USSR" in the period from Stalin's death through February 1971.[151]

As far as this writer knows, no study of the scope of judicial repression that exploits all the relevant samizdat sources has been made. But even though a careful study of this character would be most useful, it would not resolve the problem described by Reddaway as "the difficulty of knowing how many politicals have been sentenced on trumped-up charges under non-political articles, and indeed of defining, in Soviet conditions, the very

---

convicted of grave crimes." See Berman, *Soviet Criminal Law*, 2d ed., p. 155, and Vasilev, *Razvitie sovetskoi demokratii*, p. 47, for text and commentary respectively.

148. *Uncensored Russia*, pp. 222–26.

149. Sir John Lawrence, *Russians Observed* (Lincoln, Neb., n.d.; reprint ed., London, 1969), p. 179; Robert Conquest, *The Great Terror* (New York, 1968), pp. 22–25, 333–36, and app. A.

150. *Opposition in der Sowjet-Union* (Munich, 1972), p. 39; Editorial "Rising Soviet Tensions," *New York Times*, June 25, 1972.

151. Radio Liberty Research, *Reestr*, p. 1.

concept of a political offense." He appears to believe, however, that if exiles are included the order of magnitude of tens of thousands of "prisoners of conscience" is valid.[152]

Political Psychiatry. Perhaps an even harsher form of punishment than confinement in prisons or labor camps is "indefinite compulsory treatment" in prison psychiatric hospitals. This can be the lot of a political nonconformist accused of a crime, as Reddaway says, "if the K.G.B. thinks he may have committed the crime in a state of legal non-accountability (nevmeniaemost'), or if it wants to frame him and thus avoid an open trial which might involve his spirited self-defense and also provoke demonstrations."[153] A mass of highly convincing samizdat evidence supports this statement.

General Grigorenko, Ivan Yakhimovich, Vladimir Bukovsky, Natalya Gorbanevskaya, Victor Fainberg, Vladimir Borisov, and Vladimir Gershuni are among the best-known dissenters who have been committed under criminal procedure.[154] A civil commitment procedure was used against Zhores Medvedev, Yesenin-Volpin, and others; an appeal is easier under it.[155]

Roy Medvedev wrote in 1971 that the practice of psychiatric hospitalization had been illegally applied in several dozen cases in recent years and was being applied with increasing frequency. Like other dissenters, he regarded this procedure as a means by which the authorities could bypass normal

---

152. *Uncensored Russia*, p. 205.

153. *Ibid.*, p. 234. This passage asserts that under the criminal procedure psychiatrists produce diagnoses and prescriptions for treatment desired by the KGB. That Reddaway does not exaggerate is indicated by the official doctrine governing forensic psychiatry as described in a translation of a Soviet text. This source says its task is "to give an expert evaluation, on assignment from investigatory agencies and courts . . . and to recommend measures for the prevention of socially dangerous acts by the mentally ill." G. V. Morozov and Ya. M. Kalashnik, *Forensic Psychiatry*, trans. Michael Vale (White Plains, N.Y., 1970), p. 24. Judge David Bazelon's Introduction, p. xiii, expresses the opinion that the quoted passage and the fact that "no mention is made for any role of the forensic psychiatrist in protecting the rights of the mentally ill" indicate an explicit bias in favor of the government. See also V. N. Kudryavtsev ed., *Vyiavlenie prichin prestupleniia i priniatie predupreditelnykh mer po ugolovnomu delu* [Concerning the cases of criminality and the use of preventive measures in criminal cases] (Moscow, 1967), p. 51, which recommends that criminal investigators be alert to possible mental problems of the accused. The Soviet authorities maintain secrecy regarding this matter. The results of an extensive investigation conducted by a commission of the CPSU Central Committee in 1955–56, for instance were suppressed. The group was headed by Sergei Pisarev, who had spent two years in a mental institution because he sent a report to Stalin criticizing KGB fabrication of the notorious "doctors' plot" case. The commission found that "hundreds of absolutely healthy persons" had been kept in institutions for years. See Reddaway, *Uncensored Russia*, p. 232, and Medvedev and Medvedev, *Question of Madness*, p. 198, fn.

154. On their cases and several others, the most recent information available is in "Abuse of Psychiatry for Political Repression in the Soviet Union." Testimony of Dr. Alexander Sergeevich Yesenin-Volpin and Constantin W. Boldyreff, U.S., Congress, Senate, Committee on the Judiciary, 92d Cong., 2d sess., Sept. 26, 1972.

155. See on these cases, respectively, Medvedev and Medvedev, *Question of Madness, passim*, and Reddaway, *Uncensored Russia*, pp. 81–83, 234–35.

court procedure in dealing with inconvenient persons. He characterized it as "an enormous danger" to the prospects of Soviet socialist democracy.[156]

There appears to be a tendency to resort to this form of repression in cases where there is reason to believe the accused would defend himself in a court so vigorously and effectively as to seriously embarrass the authorities (e.g., Grigorenko). It also tends to be used against persons whose background and conduct are appropriate targets from the point of view of the Soviet bureaucratic elite. To the average bureaucrat, any person who chooses to run the risk of losing the privileges enjoyed by upper-income professionals must belong in a mental institution.

Perhaps the best sense of the impact of psychiatric confinement on an individual is conveyed in the personal accounts of Grigorenko and Bukovsky. Grigorenko observes: "A psychiatric hospital is terrifying for the sane because they are thrown among people who are psychologically disturbed. Yet the total absence of civil rights and the hopelessness of their position are no less terrifying." He points out that in these institutions, which are infested with KGB informers, even a sympathetic and honest doctor may be of no help to a prisoner. Bukovsky, in testimony at his 1972 trial, described the sadistic punishments he had observed being administered at the Leningrad Special Psychiatric Hospital where he was confined in 1963–65. The strongest condemnation of psychiatric confinement is probably Solzhenitsyn's statement that "the incarceration of free-thinking healthy people in madhouses is spiritual murder" more cruel than the Nazi gas chambers.[157]

CONCLUSIONS

In terms of norms appropriate to polyarchies, Soviet attitudes and practices toward dissent are harsh and vindictive. In the United States, laws roughly equivalent to articles 70, 190-1, and 190-3 of the RSFSR Criminal Code have been in force, as a rule, only during national emergencies.[158] Unfortunately nothing approaching a full-scale comparison of the treatment of political nonconformity in polyarchical and hegemonic systems can be

156. R. Medvedev, *Kniga*, p. 189.
157. Crigorenko's account is in Gorbanevskaya, *Red Square at Noon*, p. 277. Bukovsky's is in "The Case of Vladimir Bukovski," *Survey*, Spring 1972, pp. 128–30. Bukovsky landed in the institution after a copy of Djilas' *The New Class* was found in his possession. He was tried in 1972 under article 70 for, among other charges, "maintaining that in the USSR sane people are placed in mental hospitals where they are subjected to inhuman treatment" and for providing foreign correspondents with information in the same tenor. The quotation by Solzhenitsyn is from a statement in defense of Zhores Medvedev contained in the *Chronicle of Current Events*, no. 14 (June 1970), translated and published in Leopold Labedz, ed., *Solzhenitsyn* (London, 1970), pp. 171–72.
158. Mark W. Hopkins, in *Mass Media in the Soviet Union* (New York, 1970), p. 130, asserts that "Article 70 is similar to the 1798 Sedition Act in the United States" and to the American Sedition Act of 1918.

attempted here. Not only would such an effort distract us from our central task; it is scarcely feasible at present since much of the data that would be necessary is unavailable.[159] It may be useful, however, to specify some of the dimensions that might be explored in a systematic comparative study. These include legal rules and procedures defining the nature and limits of permissible dissent and penalizing their violation; the political structures and processes involved in making, applying, and adjudicating such rules; and the fundamental factors of political culture and climate of opinion that shape the context in which laws are formulated and applied. Obviously such a study would also have to be concerned with the numbers of individuals penalized under the laws against dissent.

Those who share this writer's individualist and pluralist biases will doubtlessly regard continued repression of dissent after Stalin's death and its intensification after Khrushchev as evidence that only substantial, perhaps fundamental, changes in the political culture and structure of the USSR can establish and guarantee "public contestation."[160]

Now we know that serious violations of civil rights, especially but not only those of ethnic minorities, have occurred at times throughout American history, particularly in periods of acute international or domestic tensions. These failures indicate how difficult it is, even under relatively favorable conditions, to preserve the vitality of polyarchy, including those aspects that Thomas I. Emerson has described as "the system of freedom of expression" (as distinct from "action," which can be controlled). Nevertheless the words of Justice Robert Jackson stand as the norm: "If there is any fixed star in our constitutional constellation, it is that no official, high or petty, can prescribe what shall be orthodox in politics, nationalism, religion or other matters of opinion or force citizens to confess by word or act to their faith therein.[161] The contrast with "Leninist" systems, where the political authorities unabashedly seek not only to shape citizens' beliefs but to create a "new man," is too obvious to require comment. As for the Watergate affair, the public disclosure and condemnation of the violations of traditional American rights offer good grounds for confidence in the American political system.[162]

159. Some of the necessary data has been assembled in Paul Hollander's useful study, *Soviet and American Society* (New York, 1973). But it is more on the level of the social system than in the spheres of politics and law.

160. In *Regimes*, p. 2, Dahl associates public contestation, or liberalization, with "the extent to which institutions are openly available, publicly employed, and guaranteed to at least some members of the politicsl system who wish to contest the conduct of the government." See also Dahl's *Polyarchy*, chap. 1, on the relations among democracy, an as yet unrealized ideal; contestation; "participation," the proportion of the population entitled to participate in public contestation; and "democratization," movement toward increases in both contestation and participation—and, finally, the specification of opportunities and institutional guarantees necessary, according to Dahl, for democratization to take place.

161. Emerson, *System of Freedom of Expression*, pp. 17, 29.

162. In an address to the freshman class at Yale, President Kingman Brewster perceived "a new respect for skeptics; a new welcome for critics; a new tolerance of heretics." *New York Times*,

But for the Soviet Union, it now seems clear that no hope for improvement can realistically be entertained for the next few years. Not only freedom of expression but even freedom from incarceration are threatened as never since the death of Stalin.

Why? How can one explain the paradox of the increasing military power and external security of the USSR at the same time as a growing concern to prevent criticism that the political leadership regards as subversive? The answer may lie in enduring features of the dominant Soviet political culture that are unlikely to respond to short-term changes in the international arena, though they may do so in the long run.

Judging by political communication in the USSR, the elite believes that the clichés and quotations that dominate the official creed remain indispensable for the preservation of the dominant political culture and the system of rule associated with it. But this ritualized doctrine is potentially extremely vulnerable to criticism, as the censorship and legal sanctions against dissent indicate. Its weaknesses include dullness and irrelevancy. It is also so inconsistent that, one suspects, it would disintegrate if subjected to public criticism and would soon be supplanted by a variety of schools of thought.

One of the obvious contradictions in the official political culture lies between bureaucratic-elitist and democratic-egalitarian symbols. Those who, like Grigorenko, reject the elitist values run the risk of being declared insane if they persist in pursuing consistency or "Leninist" truth as they see it. Another glaring assault on reason is the requirement that official Marxism-Leninism be uncritically accepted as a "science." In addition, as every user of Soviet mass media with access to independent sources of information is aware, their fairy tale version of events at home and abroad make Madison Avenue seem, by comparison, a model of veracity and objectivity. No wonder that, as the well-known Soviet political joke has it, "There is no truth in *Pravda* and no news in *Izvestiia*" (the names mean, respectively, "truth" and "news").

One wonders why the Soviet leaders themselves do not gradually "phase out" official ideology, or at least modernize it and render it more intelligible and appealing. Perhaps there are as many answers to that question as there are students of Soviet politics. Among those that may make sense are the following. The legitimacy of the regime is largely based on what the Yugoslav philosopher Svetozar Stojanovic calls "the statist myth of socialism." In the Soviet type of "monolithic" communist system, he points out, "The truth of authority replaces the authority of truth."[163] Unfortunately for those who hope for democratization of Soviet politics, the pattern is deeply

---

September 6, 1973. One hopes that he is right rather than Noam Chomsky, who wrote at about the same time: "There is little prospect for a meaningful reaction to the Watergate disclosures." *New York Review of Books*, September 20, 1973.

163. *Between Ideals and Reality*, trans. Gerson S. Sher (New York, 1973), pp. 37, 87.

rooted not only in Stalinism but also in prerevolutionary Russian tradition. These influences have conditioned most Soviet citizens—especially, it seems, the Great Russians and some other peoples of the USSR—to conform much more pliantly to authority than most of the peoples of the communist countries in Eastern Europe and such Soviet minorities as Jews and Crimean Tatars. If it is difficult in the pragmatic political culture of the United States for a president, for example, to admit error, how much more difficult must it be for rulers reared in the Russian tradition, which imputes sacredness and infallibility to political authority. But in such a system not only the rulers but the ruled tend to accept the legitimacy of authority, however despotic. Stalin's rule did not arouse as much popular discontent as a westerner might have expected. Neither does the milder rule of today, as Amalrik, Roy Medvedev, and other dissenters have ruefully admitted.

Then too, in a way, the status quo serves the interests and the egos of the Soviet elite as a whole, including the intelligentsia. It provides them with comfort and security, and it confers on the most eminent scientists and artists a share of prestige and respect enjoyed by no other social stratum. If such were not the case, Sakharov, when he was attacked in the press in 1973, might have received the support of more than a handful of the hundreds of thousands of "scientific workers" of whose existence the regime is so proud.[164] Under the circumstances it is noteworthy that the blast emanating from the USSR Academy of Sciences had only forty signatures, about 10 per cent of the total membership, and that these apparently were party members required by party discipline to sign. It is also pertinent that the recommendation for reforms addressed in 1970 to Brezhnev and his colleagues by the physicists Sakharov and Turchin and the historian Roy Medvedev asserted that a majority of the intelligentsia and youth understood the necessity of "democratization."[165]

Khrushchev, of course, learned to his sorrow that attempts by top leaders to revise the official ideology and established organizational structures are likely to generate dangerous factional opposition in elite circles.

In sum, an array of mutually reinforcing factors facilitates repression in the USSR and inhibits resistance, dissent, and reforms. All this indicates how enormously difficult it would be for a system of the Soviet type to relax its controls even slightly, let alone for it suddenly to permit public contestation and legitimate opposition. This does not mean that socialist systems must forever repress opposition and dissent. But it helps to underline the significance of the fact that Brezhnev's Russia, despite retrogression since

164. As of 1966, according to Ellen P. Mickiewicz, *Handbook of Soviet Social Science Data* (New York, 1973), p. 154, there were 712,400. According to Mervyn Matthews, *Class and Society in Soviet Russia* (London, 1972), p. 144, the "scientific and cultural" intelligentsia as of 1959 numbered more than 5 million.

165. See "Po voprosu imeiushchemu bolshoe znachenie" [About a question of great significance] (Turin, n.d.), p. 13.

Khrushchev's ouster, is more rational and hence less given to excessive use of coercion against dissenters than was Stalin's. A very important change is that after Stalin's death "the government began to prosecute people—as a rule—only for things they had actually done," while under Stalin "the Soviet authorities were, year after year, jailing and killing completely innocent people by the hundreds of thousands."[166] If the prosecution still all too often distorts and misrepresents the "crimes" with which dissenters are charged, the reduction in arrests has nevertheless lessened the suffering experienced by the mass of Soviet citizens.

A steady rise in the gross national product, however, has increased the regime's capacity to reward conformity. Intellectuals may therefore learn to calculate the potential results of their statements and actions more carefully and to practice a conformity that pays material dividends. We should recall that some of the angry young men of the late 1950s and early 1960s, such as Yevtushenko, have reconciled themselves to becoming, in effect, Kremlin public relations agents. Moreover, as Dev Murarka has pointed out, the campaign against Sakharov and Solzhenitsyn was joined by "people who had thus far steadfastly refused to sign this type of letter against anyone."[167]

It gives pause to recall that as recently as 1970 Yakir expressed guarded confidence in a letter to Amalrik, with whose deeply pessimistic position he disagreed, about the future of the "democratic movement." Among other things, wrote Yakir, "the ideas proclaimed by it have begun to spread widely throughout the country, and that is the beginning of an irreversible process of self-liberation."[168]

It is evident that the cautious optimism that still survived among some Soviet dissidents and foreign observers in 1970 gave way to the deep pessimism of 1974 mainly because of the authorities' ruthlessness and skill in discrediting, isolating, and repressing, and sometimes expelling dissenters.

---

166. Karel van hat Reve, Introduction, in Litvinov, *Demonstration in Pushkin Square*, p. 8.

167. Dev Murarka, "The Soviet Dissidents' Mistake," *New Statesman*, September 7, 1973, p. 303. Murarka's analysis is perceptive in pointing to the support for the regime generated by Soviet nationalism and xenophobia and by the gulf between the "affluent" dissidents and the "average," uninformed, antiintellectual Soviet common man. But it is unfair in underestimating the overwhelming advantages of the authorities and neglecting the despair this unequal condition naturally induces in the dissenters' mind. Murarka mentions academicians Frumkin and Engel'gardt, writers Aitmatov and Ganzatov, and composers Shostakovich and Khachaturian as former supporters of Sakharov or Solzhenitsyn who signed letters attacking them. Others whom he does not mention are Konstantin Simonov and Venyamin Kaverin.

An even more negative line of speculation than Murarka's is in Anatoly Kuznetsov's article "Dozhivet li Amalrik do 1984? [Will Amalrik live to see 1984?], in *Novoe russkoe slovo*, July 29, 1973. He argues that an increasingly sophisticated and confident KGB relies wherever possible on persuasion rather than coercion—one might say on positive rather than negative reinforcement. He asserts that many dissidents known to him ceased their activities after being called in by the KGB and notes that some protesters well known to the outside world such as Ivan Yakhimovich have become silent. On this basis he concludes, "Today one may speak of the end of the movement."

168. Text in Amalrik, *Will the Soviet Union Survive?* p. 120.

Some prominent dissidents attributed this powerful repressive thrust to the Soviet-Western "détente." The fact that as early as January 1969 a knowledgeable journalist reported that "a new kind of purge" involving "economic degradation and isolation" and including removal of hundreds of protesters from large cities to small towns had begun casts doubt on the validity of such charges.[169] They are not, however completely incorrect. Stalin, we recall, proclaimed his "most democratic" constitution in 1936 just as he prepared to unleash mass terror. So today, it appears, repression feeds on the failure of both governments and public opinion in the West to exert maximum pressure on behalf of the exponents of freedom in the USSR. Such a proposition is not necessarily inconsistent with the view, expressed earlier in this chapter, that one basic motive for repressing dissent is to prevent disclosure of information incompatible with official images of Soviet reality.

The relationship between repression of dissent and denial of access to information deserves further comment. The most sinister explanation of this strategy would be that it arises from the expansionist nature of Soviet foreign policy, which seeks to lull foreign suspicion about domestic coercion and thus facilitate coercion abroad—of the kind applied in 1968 in Czechoslovakia—when the time is ripe.[170] Ideological messianism, however, is not necessarily the main motive of the Kremlin. Rebroadcasting by foreign radio stations of critical statements by Soviet citizens—often the only way the Soviet public hears them—has long been a significant feature of the contemporary pattern of international political communication. Thus *samizdat* ("self-published") material becomes *tamizdat* ("published there") and partially undermines the Kremlin's monopoly over internal political communication. This process threatens to some degree the secrecy vital to the survival of the official political belief system.

This last observation brings us to what appears to be the dominant factor in Soviet repression of dissent; that the leaders believe it is incompatible with the optimum functioning and, ultimately, the very existence of their type of political system. Only this hypothesis explains, for example, the striking fact that even in time of peace stricter controls are exerted over dissent in the Soviet type of system than is the case during wartime in constitutional democracies like Britain, Canada, and the United States.[171]

169. Paul Wohl, "Soviet Dissenters Hit by 'Purge,'" *Christian Science Monitor*, January 20, 1969.

170. In this connection it is interesting that Soviet foreign policy was criticized as "expansionist" and "messianic" in the letter addressed in May 1970 to Brezhnev, Kosygin, and Podgorny by Sakharov, Turchin, and Roy Medvedev. "Po voprosu," p. 20.

171. During the war in Vietnam, according to Emerson, *System of Freedom of Expression*, p. 68, "it had become clear that general opposition to the war or defense effort, no matter how vigorously asserted, was constitutionally protected." He notes on p. 90, however, that "various forms of harassment appeared at certain points throughout the system."

By the spring of 1972 the KGB choked most of the life out of the Soviet civil rights movement. During the next two years the Kremlin's inquisitors continued to tighten the screws. It is scarcely surprising that the guardians of absolutism can today celebrate a victory of sorts over the advocates of democratization.

Yet, this victory was purchased at the price of disgrace, disarray, and dismay—the first so far as Soviet standing among all who value human rights is concerned; the second in the ranks of many European communists, especially in Italy; the third, perhaps, in Soviet leadership circles, startled by the unanticipatedly vigorous Western response to the 1973 campaign of threats and defamation against Sakharov, Solzhenitsyn, Maksimov and other dissidents.

By mid-1974 it appeared that the selective terror directed by the KGB against dissenters since 1971 had produced substantial but inconclusive and, perhaps, only temporary results. Although the *Chronicle of Current Events* ceased publication with issue no. 27 in October 1972, an issue no. 28 that appeared in May 1974 announced that distribution had been resumed despite the risks because "continued silence would amount to at least passive support for the hostage tactics" pursued by the police. In a foreword to the issue distributed in the United States, Pavel Litvinov, recently arrived in this country, wrote movingly of the "sad picture" of official lawlessness and persecution to be found in its pages but affirmed the moral obligation to expose injustice and comfort its victims. In this and other sources were recorded new arrests, for example of Armenian dissidents; new sentences, such as those of the literary scholar Gabriel Superfin and the psychiatrist Gluzman (the latter obviously the victim of his insisting that Grigorenko was sane); and new torments inflicted on men like Moroz, Bukovsky, Shikhanovich, Plyushch, and many others already locked away in prisons, camps, and police-run 'psychiatric" institutions. In the meantime a few dissidents who were well known in the West, such as Solzhenitsyn and Litvinov, left the USSR, and it was rumored that a number of other prominent independent thinkers and artists had applied for permission to leave.[172] Such events, of course, weakened the Soviet "democratizers," but they also exposed the Soviet ideological bankruptcy.

In the confrontation that has been the subject of this essay, the political actors committed to preserving essentially unchanged the system shaped by Stalin's "revolution from above" controlled overwhelming resources. Between these "conservatives" and the "democrats" were the "masses," politically apathetic but, to all appearances, passively loyal to and, in any case, dominated by a regime skilled, as Hollander argues, in manipulating a

---

172. "*Khronika tekushchikh sobytii,*" no. 28 (December 31, 1972) (published by Khronika Press, New York, 1974); Robert Kaiser, "Emigration Becoming a New Soviet Option," *Washington Post*, June 14, 1974.

people conditioned by harsh experience to prefer bread and a modest increase in consumer goods to freedom.[173] The Democratic Movement for its part lacked organizational and communications resources and popular support. It was also extremely heterogeneous and hence lacked cohesion. Some of its activists and supporters displayed astonishing heroism. But others apparently were scared off by the police, succumbed to blandishments, or responded to propaganda portraying dissent as a tool of Western imperialism.

Under what conditions might a future "democratic movement" have a better chance of achieving its goals than did that of the 1960s? To answer this question we must consider aspects of recent and current dissent that we have not yet touched on. The Democratic Movement was in essence the product of the succession crisis that followed Stalin's death. Its impetus was derived from wide and deep revulsion against Stalin's use of terror as an instrument of rule. The destalinization measures pushed by Khrushchev, impelled partly by his own convictions and partly by his desire to exploit the "Stalin issue" against political rivals, imparted respectability to moderate dissent. Finally, many talented and articulate former inmates of Stalin's camps such as Yakir and Solzhenitsyn were released, and they were determined to do everything possible to expose the terrible evils of the past and to prevent their recurrence in the future. For a time, their efforts were shielded from reprisals by Khrushchev.

Khrushchev is now officially at best a semiperson. The protests he encouraged or condoned began to be suppressed shortly after he fell from power. The new roar of protest engendered by the leadership's decision to end destalinization has, at least for the time being, been mostly silenced.

In the light of this record it appears that to succeed a reform movement would have to enjoy at least the degree of sponsorship provided for a time by Khrushchev, but over a longer time span and exercised with a clearer vision, greater skill and more determination than he provided. In addition it would need more, and more powerful, allies and supporters within the party apparatus and other sectors of the political elite than the mainly nonparty Democratic Movement ever had. Probably it would also require a higher level of consensus regarding goals and strategies than the protesters of the 1960s were able to achieve. The probability of success would vary, one suspects, with the disorientation and disorganization in the political leadership accompanying succession crisis. Finally, the movement would need to build a much broader base of public support than that of the late 1960s and early 1970s ever succeeded in fashioning.

The historical status of the Democratic Movement will depend, however, only in part on whether its activists are mourned as martyrs or honored as prophets. All who seek understanding of the nature of Soviet communism

173. Hollander, *Soviet and American Society*, pp. 388–92.

already have reason to be grateful to the dissenters for works of scholarly analysis that shed brilliant light on previously obscure aspects of the Soviet system. Dissenting intellectuals have also performed a valuable service to truth by demonstrating that concepts such as openness, democracy, and freedom can have meaning even in a largely closed society. The dissenters inaugurated a process of myth deflation and a regeneration of critical judgment. Unable to cope intellectually with dissent, the authorities resorted to repression. But the vigor and tenacity displayed for several years by the dissident movement may be more significant for the future than the Kremlin's victory. Some Soviet intellectuals have shown that they believe a society with advanced technology must also be politically modernized. In essence this is what the demand for "democratization" means. If repression flourishes and reform languishes, alienation and frustration will eventually affect more and more of them.

No one can predict just when a new wave of protest and resistance may arise. The shape of the future will be determined by the will, resolution, and skill of the rulers and the emerging forces of opposition. There will probably be succession crises in the future, and one of them may be accompanied by conditions more favorable to dissent and even opposition than those in the past. If, on the contrary, control and orthodoxy prevail indefinitely, the cost to Soviet society in terms of waste of talent and impairment of performance will be enormous.

One thing seems certain. Unless the frustrations that generate protest are attended to by correcting the conditions underlying them, the Soviet regime will continue to confront an unpleasant choice between toleration of dysfunctional dissent and suppression, with all the costs it entails at home and abroad.

CHAPTER TWO / PROTEST STRATEGIES OF THE SOVIET

INTELLECTUAL OPPOSITION / HOWARD L. BIDDULPH

This essay is an attempt to interpret and analyze the protest activities and strategies for effecting political changes that were employed within the so-called Democratic (or Human Rights) Movement[1] in the USSR during the period 1967–71.

The concept of protest has been variously employed in political and social analysis. Jackson and Stein, Lipsky, and Masotti and Bowen all agree on two basic factors that distinguish the concept of political protest from revolution or insurrection, and I shall use them here. The first involves objectives: unlike insurrection, protest, whether violent or nonviolent in form, is directed toward achieving change through the prevailing political order instead of toward destroying or suspending it. Second, protest is primarily directed not toward displacing the incumbent political leaders but toward winning concessions from them.[2]

Protest thus is conceptualized here as a set of strategies of interest articulation for those who perceive themselves as relatively "powerless" in resources of influence and access to the decision-makers. To exert effective impact on the decision-makers the protesters perceive that they must build political resources through some unusual, dramatic, and often nonconventional means of communication.[3] I shall distinguish protest from the direct confrontation tactics of powerful groups such as the mobilization of the military by oppositionist generals or well-organized boycotts by labor.

---

1. These terms have been used interchangeably not only by Western interpreters but also by the participants, as evidenced within the pages of *Khronika tekushchikh sobytii* [Chronicle of current events], hereafter cited as *Chronicle*. See also *Programma demokraticheskogo dvizheniia Sovetskogo Soiuza* [Program of the Democratic Movement in the Soviet Union](Amsterdam, 1970) and Andrei Amalrik, *Will the Soviet Union Survive until 1984?* (New York, 1970), pp. 9–21.

2. Robert J. Jackson and Michael B. Stein, eds., *Issues in Comparative Politics* (New York, Toronto, and London, 1971), pp. 266–67; Michael Lipsky, "Protest as a Political Resource," *American Political Science Review* 62, no. 4 (1968): 1144–46; Louis H. Masotti and Don R. Bowen, *Riots and Rebellion: Civil Violence in the Urban Community* (Beverly Hills, Calif., 1968), p. 14.

3. See especially Lipsky, "Protest as a Political Resource," p. 1146. Lipsky's concept of protest provides part of the basis for the conceptual framework of this essay.

Protest, as used here, is limited to articulating and dramatizing the "message" in ways that will appeal to the normative orientations of the intended receivers.

It will also be useful to distinguish two general types of protest. In *nonpublic protest* the communication is addressed directly to the decision-making group. The protesters seek to increase their access and the credibility of their political goals through special "appeals" to the authorities. The increase in their political resources of influence is made by successfully "selling" the legitimacy or credibility of their value priorities to the decision-makers. The term "nonpublic" signifies that the protest group avoids the attempt to activate additional publics in influence building; but it is not meant to suggest that the message will forever escape public knowledge. In *public protest*, on the other hand, the protesters have lost confidence in their ability to increase their influence by direct appeals to the authorities. The activists here seek to overcome powerlessness by activating third parties to intercede for them or by "movement building."

The effort to activate third parties differs from movement building in that the former does not aim to recruit new members or allies for the movement. The strategy is to motivate third parties, who are seen to have greater credibility, legitimacy, or prestige with the authorities than the protesters, to intercede. The first problem is to identify appropriate third parties who may be sympathetic to the grievances of the protesters and who also have potential influence on the decision-makers. The second is to locate a communications channel. The third is to frame a "message" in such a way as to appeal to the value orientations of the third party.

The "movement building" strategy involves an attempt by the protesters to increase their political resources by increasing their numbers or by establishing a coalition with another group. Resource building in this case is a matter of multiplying numbers of direct supporters and building overt political consciousness. It is hoped that in building a large, vocal, visible constituency for the protest movement the authorities will be induced to respond to the grievances being dramatized.

Naturally the distinction between activating third party intercessors and movement building is largely analytical, and any protest group might use some combination of these strategies rather than one exclusively. Both strategies are examples of *public* protest inasmuch as they involve attempts to activate additional publics in influence building in relation to the decision-making arena. These additional publics might be internal (i.e., within the political system) or external (i.e., in the system's international environment).

This conceptualization of protest activity provides a framework for interpreting the oppositional behavior in a polity. Now we are prepared to examine the Democratic (or Human Rights) Movement of the USSR.

THE DEMOCRATIC MOVEMENT AS A
POLITICAL GROUP

The Democratic Movement lacked the cohesion that formal organization would have provided. While smaller circles such as "The Action Group for the Defense of Human Rights in the USSR" gained a certain amount of organizational cohesion within the larger movement, there was no evidence of large-scale organization.[4] In the present Soviet political habitat it would be impossible to sustain a large-scale organization for protest purposes. Participants in the "movement" also lacked uniform occupational identity, although between 80 and 90 percent of the more than 1,000 signatories of protest letters and petitions between 1967 and 1970 belonged to professions under the general rubric of the "technical and cultural intelligentsia of the USSR."[5]

The term protest group is appropriate, however, in a more informal sense. First, activists within the movement appeared to share a sense of group identity. They employed the terms Democratic Movement, Human Rights Movement, and Civil Rights Movement as means of self-identification.[6] The pronouncements issued in samizdat, or self-published materials, also reflected a sense of collective responsibility and mission. In its formal platform, for example, The Action Group for the Defense of Human Rights describes itself as composed of persons "united by a feeling of personal responsibility for that which occurs in our country," who "affirm the absolute worth of the individual," and who have a determination to "act openly in the spirit of legality" to secure the "progress of freedom."[7] This same sense of collective responsibility is reflected in the open letter of Ilya Gabai, Yuli Kim, and Peter Yakir to the "critical intelligentsia."

. . . we appeal to you people of creative labor, people in whom our nation places its unlimited trust: raise your voices against the imminent danger of new Stalins and Ezhovs. The fate of future Vavilovs and Mandelshtams is on your conscience. You are the heirs of the great humanistic traditions of the Russian intelligentsia.[8]

One encounters this sense of collective mission for the movement in the last appeal of Ivan Yakhimovich, a former collective farm chairman, before his arrest in 1969: "The mighty of the world are strong because we are on our knees. It is time to stand up!" The same attitude is expressed in the slogan at

---

4. *Chronicle*, no. 8 (June 30, 1969). Cf. Peter Reddaway, ed., *Uncensored Russia: The Human Rights Movement in the Soviet Union* (London, 1972), pp. 150 ff.

5. See Howard L. Biddulph, *Opposition in The Communist Polity* (forthcoming), pt. 2.

6. See n. 1 above.

7. *Chronicle*, no. 8; cf. English text of this petition in Cornelia Gerstenmaier, *The Voices of the Silent* (New York, 1972); pp. 421 ff.

8. From the English translation in Abraham Brumberg, ed., *In Quest of Justice: Protest and Dissent in the Soviet Union Today* (New York, Washington, London, 1970), p. 161.

the end of the "open letter to the citizens of the Soviet Union" signed by Gennadi Alexeev (the Baltic naval officer Gavrilov): "Russia is waiting for new people!"[9]

Another ground for regarding the Democratic Movement as a political group is the increasing body of evidence that the participants shared a distinct community of values even though they displayed a remarkable diversity of political orientations. These values I have designated elsewhere a deviant subculture or political counterculture. Members of the movement tend to reject the inevitability of utopia and the infallibility of political authority. They appear to affirm a pluralist conception of the right of political expression and criticism and an "autonomous participant" conception of ideal citizenship. They affirm the desirability of a responsive government, whose authority is limited in scope and procedural operation and that operates according to an established tradition of the "rule of law."[10]

This shared value system produced a marked consensus of political goals among activists within the movement. (1) They shared the goal of establishing a tradition of the rule of law based on a literalist, democratic interpretation of the existing Constitution of the USSR. They saw themselves as defending the constitution against arbitrary official acts and statutes that suppress individual freedom. (2) They shared the desire to establish the freedom to obtain and distribute political information independent of the officially controlled media of the USSR as a basis for making intelligent political evaluations. (3) They sought the broadening of the freedom of political expression and social criticism and the abolition of censorship. (4) They advocated a greater safeguarding of the rights of the accused in criminal cases and the suspension of the powers of the security organs (KGB) to intervene in the life of the private citizen. (5) They championed the rights of minority nationalities such as the Crimean Tatars and Meshketians to return to their homelands and of Jews who so desire to emigrate to Israel. In general they advocated a more pluralist right of the minority nationalities to self-determination. (6) They supported the aspirations of religious groups to greater autonomy and freedom from state interference and persecution. (7) They were strongly critical of the interference of the great powers in the internal affairs of smaller nations and were particularly concerned about foreign policy of the USSR in this regard. The invasion of Czechoslovakia by Soviet and Warsaw Pact troops in 1968 mobilized one of the most vehement and widespread outpouring of protest within the short history of the movement.[11]

9. Gerstenmaier, *Voices of the Silent*, pp. 417, 447.

10. Howard L. Biddulph, "Soviet Intellectual Dissent as a Political Counter-Culture," *Western Political Quarterly* 25, no. 3 (September 1972): 522-33.

11. The following contain primary source materials in English that document the generalizations: Brumberg, *In Quest of Justice*; Reddaway, *Uncensored Russia*, especially chaps. 1-4, 11-16; Vyacheslav Chornovil, comp., *The Chornovil Papers* (New York, 1968); Andrei

In addition, some objectives were stated but did not receive a consensus of support within the movement. For example, the samizdat journal *Kolokol* advocated in 1965 a plural party system, and *The Program of the Democratic Movement* made the same proposal.[12] But the overwhelming majority of oppositionists have not expressed themselves favorably on this matter. Peter Grigorenko has called for competitive elections and others for economic decentralization and market socialism,[13] but no consensus has been evidenced on these proposals either.

The third and most important ground for considering the movement a political group is the degree of interaction its participants displayed in the pursuit of the above goals. While no visible organization coordinated the various protest activities, samizdat communications exercised a remarkable unifying and catalyzing effect on the participants. Mutually supportive protest activities sprang up from the Baltic republics to Siberia and Central Asia during and following such events as the political trials in Moscow and the Ukraine from 1966 to 1969, the Soviet invasion of Czechoslovakia, the internment of dissidents in psychiatric hospitals, the arrest of prominent personalities within the movement, and the repression of political activism among the minority nationalities. The unifying effect of the bi-monthly samizdat journal *Khronika tekyshchikh sobytii* (Chronicle of current events) during 1968–71 was probably considerable. Julius Telesin recalls that the events recorded in the *Chronicle* were "for me landmarks on the road of the transformation of many people from apes into men," progressive stages in the "learning of inner freedom."[14] The results of this quasi-spontaneous but mutually supportive interaction of protesters was summed up by Anatoly Yakobson in late 1968. Since the trial of Sinyavsky and Daniel in 1966, "not one single arbitrary act of despotism and force on the part of the administration has gone unchallenged." Yakobson describes this "honorable tradition" as the "beginning of the self-liberation" of Soviet man.[15]

Public protest demonstrations, "white books" detailing grievances, the exposure of official acts of repression in the *Chronicle* and other samizdat publications, personal and group letters of protest to Soviet officials and to the internal and external media, and legal briefs and formal protests to international agencies all are considered facets of the group protest activity

---

Sakharov, *Progress, Coexistence, and Intellectual Freedom* (New York, 1968); Gerstenmaier, *Voices of the Silent*, pp. 309–545, particularly pp. 493–504. For detailed documentation of each of these goals consult Howard L. Biddulph, "Soviet Intellectual Dissent as Interest Articulation" (paper delivered at the meeting of the Pacific Northwest Political Science Association, Tacoma, Wash., April 30, 1971), especially pp. 12–22.

12. *Kolokol* (Leningrad), no. 4 (1965), as reported in *Posev*, 1968, no. 4 (cf. Gerstenmaier, *Voices of the Silent*, pp. 480–85); *Programma*, pp. 20–31.

13. Cf. Gerstenmaier, *Voices of the Silent*, pp. 397–99; *Chornovil Papers*, pt. 2; Sakharov, *Progress, Coexistence*, p. 77.

14. Reddaway, *Uncensored Russia*, p. 51.

15. Gerstenmaier, *Voices of the Silent*, p. 383.

of the Democratic Movement insofar as they supported one or more of the seven basic goals outlined above. All these activities are not of equal significance. Signing a collective letter of protest is not as serious a gesture as participation in a public protest demonstration, which in the present Soviet context would probably result in imprisonment. Nevertheless, it takes courage to sign a document that may circulate widely through samizdat and even reach the external media of the "enemies" of the USSR. Judging from current Soviet practice, anyone signing a protest letter will probably incur some social sanctions ranging from loss of a job or expulsion from the Communist Party, to an official "reprimand," which is recorded on one's work record, and other informal sanctions. Such an action is sufficient to activate a personal file in the offices of the KGB. Furthermore, one must assume that the signer subscribes to the message in the protest letter. For this reason, and because the costs of participation are well known to Soviet dissidents, the signing of a protest letter is included as a supportive action within the group protest activity of the Democratic Movement.

THE POVERTY OF POLITICAL RESOURCES

As previously outlined, protest may be conceived as a strategy by a relatively powerless group to build political resources for influencing the decision-making process. It is appropriate, therefore, to examine the movement in relation to the political influence resources that are available in the USSR.

Formal interest group politics (*gruppovshchina*), like factionalism within the Communist Party, has long been explicitly rejected by the dominant political culture of the USSR as illicit behavior.[16] In recent years, however, Western analysts have recognized what has long been a reality of Soviet politics, that a certain type of interest articulation exists de facto and is even encouraged in the USSR. Official scholarship has acknowledged approvingly the consultation of leading policy-makers with specialist-elites on issues relating to the expertise of the latter.[17] Philip Stewart's study of political influence in the Stalingrad party provincial committee (Obkom) has documented the participation of trade union, economic, Komsomol, military, and local party officials in the public sessions of the deliberative process through their membership on party committees concerned with policy formation. Schwartz and Keech provide one case study where the judgments of a particular specialist-elite (the educators) succeeded in

16. Consult *Fundamentals of Marxism-Leninism* (Moscow, 1963), pp. 599 ff; and *Sovetskaia sotsialisticheskaia demokratiia* [Soviet socialist democracy], ed. M. B. Mitin (Moscow, 1964), p. 211 ff. See also the Preamble of the *Rules of the CPSU* (Moscow, 1971).

17. See, for example, Ia. Umansky, B. Baianov, and M. Shafir, *Sovetskaia sotsialisticheskaia demokratiia* [Soviet socialist democracy] (a different book from the one of the same title cited in n. 16) (Moscow, 1968), pp. 216–22.

significantly modifying the policy proposal of a Soviet leader (Nikita S. Khrushchev's theses on school reform in 1958).[18]

Interest articulation in the USSR is, nevertheless, much more informal than in Western pluralist societies because of the illegitimacy of formal associational interest groups and the lack of subsystem autonomy. The party controls the appointment of personnel and material resources of all legitimate social entities and undertakes either to manage or to control the activities of all formal social organizations. For this reason interest articulation is not only more informal but also more fragile and dependent. It is more frequent and effective at the fact-finding stage of the policy process, when expert opinion is solicited, than it is in initiating policy deliberation.

The foregoing studies seem to indicate, however, that some individuals and groups outside the policy-makers do have resources that at least sometimes permit successful influence on the decision-making process. The principal resources of influence available to these "intermediate actors" in the Soviet political setting are: (1) access—the right and opportunity to consult with policy-makers; (2) expertise—acknowledgement that they possess expert knowledge that is needed to make rational decisions; and (3) legitimacy—the perception that their claims are compatible with the values of the political authorities. Lindblom correctly observed that the impact of interest groups on policy-makers is dependent on the "weight" assigned to them by the fundamental values of the decision-makers to whom they appeal.[19]

Donald Kelley's comparative analysis of the education reform of 1958 and the industrial reorganization of 1957 concludes that the *political sensitivity* of the issue is a key variable. It accounts, he finds, for the difference in impact of the articulations of the educators in 1958 and the industrial managers in 1957. On this basis he hypothesizes that if the top elite perceives the issue to be politically sensitive, the effectiveness of the resource of expertise is drastically reduced or eliminated.[20]

Furthermore, specialist-elites are held to be credible only when testifying on matters within their acknowledged professional competence. An example of this attitude was Khrushchev's retort when he heard that the famed scientists Peter Kapitsa and Lev Landau opposed certain party policies on the arts: "That is not why we admire Kapitsa and Landau."[21] In other words,

---

18. Philip Stewart, *Political Power in the Soviet Union; A Study of Decision-Making in Stalingrad* (Indianapolis, 1968); Joel J. Schwartz and William R. Keech, "Group Influence and the Policy Process in the Soviet Union," *American Political Science Review* 62, no. 3 (September 1968): 840–51.

19. Charles Lindblom, *The Policy-Making Process* (Englewood Cliffs, N.J., 1968), p. 68.

20. Donald R. Kelley, "Interest Groups in the USSR: The Impact of Political Sensitivity on Group Influence," *Journal of Politics* 34, no. 3 (August 1972): 863.

21. Priscilla Johnson, *Khrushchev and the Arts* (Cambridge, Mass., 1964), p. 11.

scientists must be consulted on issues concerning science and technology but not in other areas. On sensitive political questions the party alone is competent.

As we have seen, the participants in the Democratic Movement have been, for the most part, dissident members of the socially privileged technical and cultural intelligentsia. The movement has counted within its ranks some notable scientists and literary figures. Their potential influence was nullified, however, by the political sensitivity of their chief concerns. Soviet leaders do not acknowledge any credible expertise of scientists, teachers, or cultural workers on such questions as the correctness of the decision to topple the Dubček government by military force, the permissible limits for expressing dissent, the proper treatment of those officially classed as deviant, or the wisdom of party policy toward national and religious minorities. On these sensitive political issues the party alone is competent. The legitimacy of consultation and the credibility of expert judgment of intermediate articulators apply only to more technical issues. The political sensitivity was, in fact, greatly increased by the fact that the Democratic Movement did not simply articulate positions but sharply criticized official party policy in all these areas. The morality of party policy in domestic and foreign affairs was perceived by the political leaders to have been seriously questioned.

Those individuals and groups that enjoy relative access to Soviet decision-makers have quite modest resources of influence in comparison with Western pluralist standards. The Democratic Movement, however, lacked the legitimacy of being consulted on the issues with which it was most concerned and was denied the resource of expert credibility. Even in the more restrictive Soviet context, therefore, the movement must be considered relatively powerless in terms of access to normal resources of influence. The alternatives for the movement were protest for the purpose of creating resources of influence—or silence. In choosing protest, the human rights activists inaugurated a new behavioral dimension in Soviet politics: open, public opposition.

THE STRATEGY OF NONPUBLIC PROTEST

The predominant (though by no means exclusive) strategy of influence building in the early stages of the Human Rights Movement following the Sinyavsky-Daniel trial of 1966 was nonpublic protest. There are plausible reasons for this. Nonpublic protest would be closer to the established mores of the dominant political culture. Mao Tse-tung's mobilization of mass publics for the purpose of waging policy conflict and leadership struggle with his opponents during the Great Proletarian Cultural Revolution is quite foreign to the Soviet political tradition. One of the first principles of

Soviet politics is rather that conflict and grievances are not aired publicly except where criticisms of individuals can be used to serve the goals of political socialization. The results of political conflict between the leaders are publicized selectively only following their resolution. It is understandable that the Soviet civil rights activists would be strongly influenced by this tradition.

Furthermore, as discussed above, it would be obvious to the activists that public protest runs a greater risk of incurring severe personal costs than nonpublic protest. It would be rational to try the least costly form of protest first provided that there is some chance that it will produce a positive effect. The trial of Sinyavsky and Daniel obviously represented a fundamental shift away from the liberalization and destalinization policies of the Khrushchev era, in which reformist intellectuals were considered allies of the political leadership. Because of their previous access to the political leadership many of these individuals were not yet ready to conclude that all efforts at nonpublic protest would be in vain.

The campaign conducted against Sinyavsky and Daniel in the media before the trial was protested by several intellectuals. Others wrote testimonial letters for the defense of the accused during the trial. The conviction and sentencing of the accused produced an outpouring of nonpublic protest letters, some collectively signed and others individually authored.[22]

Typical of these was a letter signed by sixty-three Moscow writers, many of them prominent, addressed to "The Presidium of the Twenty-third Congress of the CPSU, the Presidium of the Supreme Soviet of the USSR, and the Presidium of the Supreme Soviet of the RSFSR." While the text became widely known afterward (in large part because of the open attack upon the sixty-three signers delivered by the writer Mikhail Sholokhov at the Twenty-third Party Congress), it is clear that the writers intended the protest for the Soviet leadership directly rather than for other reference publics. The message is phrased in urgent but moderate language, and the arguments are calculated to appeal to the values of the political leaders. The letter concedes that the defendants were lacking in "prudence and tact" in their writings and expresses disapproval of the "means by which these writers published their works abroad." But it disagrees that the trial proved their works to be "anti-Soviet." The trial of writers for their writings, it maintains, "creates an extremely dangerous precedent and could impede the progress of Soviet culture." The trial "causes us [i.e., the USSR] more harm than did any of their [the defendants'] mistakes." The signatories beg the release of Sinyavsky and Daniel "on our surety." Such an act of magnanimity "is dictated by the interests of our country, the interests of the world and those of the world Communist movement."[23]

22. Max Hayward, *On Trial: the Soviet State Versus "Abram Tertz" and "Nikolai Arzhak"*, rev. ed. (New York, 1967), pp. 233–73.
23. *Ibid.*, pp. 284–86.

Another notable example of nonpublic protest following the trial was a letter from five scholars addressed directly to General Secretary Leonid I. Brezhnev. Although the tone of this letter is more stridently critical, again the arguments used and the proposals offered are clearly calculated to try to appeal to the perceived values of the Soviet leader. The protesters attempt to show that the trial will do more harm to the image of the USSR than the defendants could possibly have accomplished. In the prosecution of writers for what they write, the letter affirms, the trial is unprecedented in Russian and world history. The pretrial vilification of the defendants in the official media is also strongly condemned. The protesters propose that: (1) "philosophers and sociologists" be given the task of investigating the "social causes" of the actions of the two writers; (2) their trial be reexamined and a pardon granted; and (3) a serious reconsideration of official policies toward the treatment of intellectuals be undertaken to avoid benefiting "bourgeois propaganda," as the trial had done.[24]

No direct responses were communicated to the protesters by the political leadership. But sanctions, meaning primarily loss of jobs, were imposed on many of the less well-known writers in the group. The harsh line taken at the Twenty-third Party Congress indicated that there would be no reversal of the new course.[25]

The trial of Alexander Ginzburg and Yuri Galanskov in January 1968 was the other major event that generated widespread nonpublic protest. This form of protest was overshadowed, however, by a dramatic public outcry. The publicity given the arrest and trial by the new journal *The Chronicle of Current Events* helped stimulate both public and nonpublic protest.

Protest petitions and letters concerning the Ginzburg-Galanskov trial were sent to a wide range of authorities by artists, writers, teachers, engineers, doctors, mathematicians, physicists, librarians, high school students, university students, a collective farm chairman, a retired general, and factory workers. The total number of signers of protest letters concerning the Ginzburg-Galanskov trial and the invasion of Czechoslovakia in 1968, but excluding the protest movements among the national and religious minorities of that year, was between 800 and 900. The *Chronicle*, which painstakingly researched this nonpublic protest activity after the fact, reported that not one of these petitions was answered by any of the officials to whom they were addressed.[26]

There was a response, however, of a special kind. It took the form of systematic reprisals against those who had participated in the protest movement during 1968. Those involved in public demonstrations suffered the most severe reprisals. The participants in nonpublic protests were

24. *Ibid.*, pp. 291–99.
25. Reddaway, *Uncensored Russia*, chap. 3; cf. *Chronicle*, nos. 1–2.
26. *Chronicle*, nos. 1–3; Reddaway, *Uncensored Russia*, chap. 3. Also see documents in Brumberg, *In Quest of Justice.*

normally not arrested, but they were expelled from the party (if they held membership), fired from their jobs, dismissed from their union, or expelled from the university (in the case of students). The first and second issues of the *Chronicle* listed the names of 91 who had experienced this kind of "extrajudicial reprisal," and the fifth issue in December reported 63 new names. Some prominent writers developed a strategy of "countervailing power" by pledging their mutual solidarity and notifying the Writers Union that if it expelled even one of their number all would resign en masse. One report put the number of this solidarity group at 100, another as high as 150. The tactic prevented the expulsion of any of the group, but lesser sanctions were meted out to them on a graduated scale: the "severe reprimand," the "reprimand with an endorsement," the "severe rebuke," the "strong warning," and finally the "warning."[27]

In addition to the protest letter, the *programmatic essay* or *brief* was apparently used by both nonpublic and public protesters. This form of communication combines the protest language of the letter with a more sophisticated and detailed argument and presentation of data. Admittedly many essays and briefs are hard to classify as public or nonpublic. *The Chornovil Papers* on the prosecution of Ukrainian dissident intellectuals is clearly an example of public protest. Chornovil formally addresses this extensive document to the "Public Procurator of the Ukrainian SSR, the Head of the Supreme Court of the Ukrainian SSR, the Chairman of the State Security Committee, and the Council of Ministers of the Ukrainian SSR." But the opening statement reveals that he is really appealing directly to mass publics: "I am not asking you [the authorities] for anything. Numerous enquiries, demands, and intercessions have crashed against the cold wall of your indifference."[28]

It is more difficult to classify Ivan Dzyuba's *Internationalism or Russification?* This programmatic essay is a detailed examination of the Soviet nationalities problem with emphasis on the Ukraine. Addressed formally to the first secretary of the party in the Ukraine, P. Yu. Shelest, it might also have been intended to influence Ukrainian public opinion toward more nationalist views. If so, Dzyuba's essay is an example of public protest. He phrases his argument in Leninist rhetoric, attempting to show that Soviet federalism and nationalities policy have departed from Lenin's original conception of pluralistic national self-determination.[29]

The remarkable brief of March 19, 1970 by the Soviet physicists Andrei Sakharov and Valery Turchin and the historian Roy Medvedev is quite clearly an example of nonpublic protest. It is addressed to Brezhnev, Alexei

27. *Chronicle*, nos. 1, 2, 5; Reddaway, *Uncensored Russia*, pp. 84–85.
28. *Chornovil Papers*, p. 2.
29. Ivan Dzyuba, *Internationalism or Russification? A Study of the Soviet Nationalities Problem* (London, 1968).

Kosygin, and N. V. Podgorny in their respective positions of general secretary of the CPSU, chairman of the Council of Ministers, and chairman of the Presidium of the Supreme Soviet. The authors protest the reversal of liberalization by the post-Khrushchev leadership but do so in a skillful manner calculated to appeal directly to the leaders' values. The tone is relatively moderate, with the appeal to reason that is characteristic of Sakharov's writing. The essay defends each of the seven basic goals to which the movement is committed, arguing in the manner of the Czechoslovakian intellectuals during the spring of 1968 that democratization is necessary to avoid bureaucratic and technological stagnation. Its plea for the end of the persecution of intellectuals rests more on pragmatic than on moralistic grounds: "Under conditions of a modern industrial society, in which the role of the intelligentsia becomes increasingly important, such dissension can only be described as suicidal." Democratization will not only stimulate technological development but unite the "best intellectual forces of the country" behind the party for the solution of economic and social problems. Without that support the party will find it difficult to solve the challenging technological problems of the future.[30]

While some members of the movement have continued to emphasize the value of nonpublic protest, the failure of this strategy to elicit any favorable response from the regime during the 1968 campaign resulted in disillusionment and an increasing resort to public opposition techniques. Direct appeals had failed to establish any legitimacy or credibility for the Democratic Movement in the eyes of the political rulers of the USSR.

THE STRATEGY OF PUBLIC PROTEST

The Sinyavsky-Daniel trial also motivated several cases of more public protest. Alexander Ginzburg, a young Soviet poet, had had previous public protest experience. He was sentenced in 1960 for editing the samizdat journal *Syntax* and was rearrested in 1964 for organizing with Alexander Yesenin-Volpin the demonstration on "Constitution Day," December 5, 1965.[31] Ginzburg's preparation of a white book on the Sinyavsky-Daniel trial for public dissemination was one of the first steps toward kindling the public protest activities afterward. Two public demonstrations in Moscow in January 1967 demanded the release of Sinyavsky and Daniel and the repeal of article 70 of the Russian Republic's Criminal Code (because of its alleged violation of the freedom of political expression clause in article 125 of the Soviet Constitution). These protests resulted in the arrest of Victor Khaustov, Vladimir Bukovsky, Vadim Delone (or Delauney), and later in the year Yevgeny Kushev. Pavel Litvinov, grandson of the commissar of foreign

30. Gerstenmaier, *Voices of the Silent*, pp. 493–504.
31. Hayward, *On Trial*, p. 274.

affairs during the prewar Stalin era, publicly distributed the text of Bukovsky's remarkable "final plea" at the trial. These more public actions by a handful of individuals, along with the inauguration of the *Chronicle*, helped galvanize the dissident intellectuals for the public protest activity that erupted in 1968–69.

As Lipsky's paradigm shows, a group undertaking public protest faces three problems: (1) choosing a viable and receptive reference public (or publics), (2) developing a credible and effective communications medium (or media) for conducting the protest, and (3) presentation of the message in a manner sufficiently appealing to the perceived values of the receivers to impel them to intervene on behalf of the protest group.

These problems are particularly formidable in the Soviet political environment. Public protest defies the tradition previously described that conflict is conducted and resolved nonpublicly. Rather than building political resources, therefore, this strategy presents the real risk of being counterproductive. The political loyalty of a protest group using public methods would be seriously questioned not only by the authoritative decision-making group but by other internal publics socialized to the prevailing mores. One of the Democratic Movement's big problems all along has been how to establish its credibility as a loyal, noninsurrectionary group.

Second, there is the problem in a nonpolyarchical system of locating third parties with sufficient resources to be influential on decision-makers. Unless the third parties possess autonomous resources, an appeal to them is not qualitatively different in effect from protesting directly to the political rulers. Yet the party undertakes to monopolize political resources, to interpenetrate and coopt into its own elite those entities enjoying the resource of expertise.[32] External publics may also be sought (i.e., outside the USSR), but this effort risks damaging again the credibility of the movement's assertions of loyalty. The movement is open to the charge of aiding foreign "bourgeois propaganda" in behalf of "enemies" of the USSR.

Third, access to a communications medium is a particular problem in the USSR. The regime controls the regular public media so that they will deny access to protest messages. Public protest is difficult in a modern mass society where newspapers, television, and radio are prevented from giving coverage to the message, where strict censorship prevails over all forms of written publication, and where unofficial protest demonstrations and unauthorized dissemination of political views are severely punished as a matter of course. Subformal communications exists in all bureaucratic environments and in all societies;[33] but mutually supportive political action, and especially

32. On cooptation, see Frederic J. Fleron, "Co-optation as a Mechanism of Adaptation to Change: The Soviet Political Leadership System," in *The Behavioral Revolution and Communist Studies*, ed. Roger Kanet (New York, 1970), pp. 125–45. Also see Fleron's essay in Carl Beck et al., *Comparative Communist Political Leadership* (New York, 1973), pp. 43–79.

33. Anthony Downs discusses this point in *Inside Bureaucracy* (Boston, 1967), pp. 113–15.

public protest, depends on the establishment of credible regular channels of communication.

The birth of the *Chronicle* on April 30, 1968 as a regular bimonthly samizdat journal was one of the principal devices used to solve this communications problem. Samizdat publications have provided a channel for political and cultural communication intermittently throughout the Soviet period as well as in nineteenth century Russia. The samizdat journals *Syntax* (edited by Ginzburg, 1958–60), *Phoenix* (edited by Yuri Galanskov, 1961, 1966), and *Sphinxes* (edited by Tarsis, 1965) were all precursors of the *Chronicle* in the post-Stalin era, but they were chiefly concerned with political-cultural essays and poetry while the *Chronicle* concentrated on journalistic reporting on the protest movement. The latter provided a regular channel through which the communication of political information and protest messages could be conducted to a developing journal audience within the USSR and abroad. It thus provided the dual function of alliance building among the dissident intellectuals and public protest aimed at additional audiences.

The editors of the *Chronicle* sought to establish the credibility of this communications channel through two policies: (1) an insistence on scrupulous accuracy of its published factual information and (2) a moderate, unemotional, "facts without embellishment" style. Issue no. 8 contains the following statement of editorial policy:

The *Chronicle* makes every effort to achieve a calm restrained tone. Unfortunately the materials with which the *Chronicle* is dealing evoke emotional reactions, and these automatically effect the tone of the text. The *Chronicle* does and will do its utmost to ensure that its strictly factual style is maintained to the greatest degree possible, but it cannot guarantee complete success. . . . In certain cases one is obliged to give an appraisal of the facts, otherwise their true significance might escape the unsophisticated reader. . . . The *Chronicle* is expressly devoted to the question of human rights . . . but like other samizdat is an example of freedom of speech and the press, of creative freedom and freedom of conscience, put into practice.[34]

By presenting accurate information and through the device of striking an objective pose, the *Chronicle* was quickly successful in acquiring a reputation for credibility. The moderate, factual tone also served to create the

---

34. *Chronicle*, no. 8; cf. Reddaway, *Uncensored Russia*, p. 55. On the editorial policy toward accuracy, issue no. 7 affirms: "The *Chronicle* aims at the utmost reliability in the information it publishes. In those instances when it is not absolutely certain that some event has taken place, the *Chronicle* indicates that the piece of information is based on rumor. But at the same time the *Chronicle* requests its readers to be careful and accurate in the information they provide for publication. A number of inaccuracies occur during the process of duplicating copies of the *Chronicle*. There are mistakes in names and surnames, in dates and numbers. The quantity of these grows as the *Chronicle* is typed and retyped again and again, and they cannot be corrected according to the text as can other misprints," Reddaway, *Uncensored Russia*, pp. 58–59. Given the manner in which the *Chronicle* is produced, its level of accuracy is remarkable.

impression of legality and legitimacy in its audience. The *Chronicle* proclaimed itself to be a "legal" journal on the grounds that it is simply recording events and facts. In what respect could it be considered libelous merely to report the truth?

The *Chronicle* is in no sense an illegal publication, and the difficult conditions in which it is produced are created by the peculiar notions about law and freedom of information which in the course of long years have become established in certain Soviet organizations.[35]

In this fashion the *Chronicle* sought to establish its legality and credibility in the mind of the reader while at the same time communicating a highly emotional and moralistic public protest. In this manner it was able not only to communicate public protest through reporting demonstrations, written pleas to Soviet and world opinion, platforms, and programmatic essays, but also to convert what were originally nonpublic protest letters, unanswered by the authorities, into public protest documentation.

The informal channel through which protest information was conveyed to and from the *Chronicle* is described as follows:

. . . the *Chronicle* cannot, like any other journal, give its postal address on the last page. Nevertheless, anybody who is interested in seeing that the Soviet public is informed about what goes on in the country, may easily pass on information to the editors of the *Chronicle*. Simply tell it to the person from whom you received the *Chronicle,* and he will tell the person from whom he received the *Chronicle*, and so on. But do not try to trace back the whole chain of communication yourself or else you will be taken for a police informer.[36]

The public protest activities of the dissidents were aimed at both internal and external publics. An examination of a few selected protest petitions will reveal their strategies for reaching these publics.

EXTERNAL PUBLICS

In communicating with the outside world, the movement followed the tactic of appealing for third-party intercession. There were four different external publics the dissidents attempted to activate.

First, an attempt was made to gain the intercession of foreign communist and workers parties: On February 24, 1968, a letter of protest was sent to the Budapest "Consultative Conference of Communist and Workers Parties of the World," which was preparing for a world conference later that year. The letter was signed by twelve dissenters, among them some of the leading personalities in the movement—Alexei Kosterin, Larisa Bogoraz, Pavel Litvinov, Yakir, Victor Krasin, Ilya Gabai, Peter Grigorenko, Anatoly

35. *Chronicle*, no. 5; cf. Reddaway, *Uncensored Russia*, p. 54.
36. *Chronicle* no. 5.

Levitin-Krasnov, Yuri Glazov, Zampira Asanova, Boris Shragin, and Yuli Kim.[37] Because of the invasion of Czechoslovakia the world conference was postponed, but the consultative conference did not respond to the petition. When the world conference did convene in Moscow in 1969, a demonstration of Crimean Tatars occurred on Mayakovsky Square to dramatize the grievances of this group to the international assemblage.[38] Other letters were sent to Western communist media. One was Natalya Gorbanevskaya's appeal after the arrest of the Red Square demonstrators who had protested the invasion of Czechoslovakia. It went to *Rude pravo, L'Unita, L'Humanité, The Morning Star,* and other organs but was published first by the noncommunist media.[39] While Western communist media expressed some disappointment and criticism of circumstances in the USSR, there is no evidence that any of them specifically interceded with Soviet leaders on behalf of the Democratic Movement.

The second external public was the Western intellectuals. They would have less access to Soviet leaders than the Western communist parties but would be more sympathetic with the movement's values. Western intellectuals did intercede publicly for their Soviet brethren, but the leaders of the USSR were able to ignore or dismiss these efforts. One such petition from W. H. Auden, A. J. Ayer, Cecil Day-Lewis, Jacquetta Hawkes, Julian Huxley, Mary McCarthy, Yehudi Menuhin, Henry Moore, Bertrand Russell, Paul Scofield, Stephen Spender, and Igor Stravinsky expressed support for the Soviet dissident intellectuals but was able to offer no concrete assistance because of lack of access to the political leadership of the USSR.[40] The intellectual protest demonstrations conducted in the West informed public opinion but, except in some special instances cited below, failed to have visible impact.

The third external public the Soviet dissidents sought to activate was international agencies. Anatoly Marchenko's appeal to the International Red Cross concerning the treatment of political prisoners and conditions in Soviet prisons is one example of this technique.[41] The appeal of the Action Group for the Defense of Human Rights in the USSR to the United Nations Commission on Human Rights represented a more dramatic example of this approach. The commission was requested to look into the alleged violation by the Soviet government of the UN Declaration of Human Rights in suppressing political expression in the USSR. Five appeals were

37. *Ibid.*, no. 1.

38. Reddaway, *Uncensored Russia*, chap. 13.

39. *Chronicle*, no. 3. Cf. Natalya Gorbanevskaya, *Midday: The Case of the Demonstration of August 25th, 1968 on Red Square* (London, 1972).

40. *Chronicle*, no. 2, offers appreciation for the attempts of Western intellectuals to intervene on behalf of Soviet dissenters.

41. Marchenko is the author of an exposé on Soviet penal institutions, *My Testimony* (London, 1969).

made to the UN on this question without avail. Finally Secretary General Thant ruled that charges could not be considered that were presented only by private individuals.[42]

The fourth external public to which the protesters appealed was simply "world public opinion." Numerous protests are addressed to Western media, encouraging their publication and wide dissemination. No doubt the dissidents took comfort in reports of the dissemination of their views in the West and in some of the demonstrations that occurred, one of which was made by three students from England and Scandinavia in Moscow's GUM department store; but these had little effect. One important issue in the USSR, the right of Soviet Jews to immigrate to Israel, was no doubt favorably affected by Western opinion—although it is impossible to measure political influence on Soviet decision-making empirically, given its lack of visibility.[43] Strong Zionist influences in some Western government circles and publics may have favorably affected the result, but it is also possible the Soviet leaders simply concluded that more liberal emigration policies on Jews would effectively export some of their problems.

INTERNAL COMMUNICATION OF PROTEST

In its communications within the USSR, the Democratic Movement does not appear to have activated any significant third-party intercessors. Instead it followed the tactic of alliance building to strengthen its political resources. This is not surprising considering the fact that to play the role of third-party intercessor a group must possess some significant autonomous resources. In the USSR, when the political leadership is strongly committed to a particular position, third-party broker-politics is extremely unlikely to be feasible among the institutional groups enjoying access because of the lack of autonomy of their political resources. The political resource this strategy seeks to develop is numbers—more citizens who are committed to the goal of further democratization in the USSR and who refuse to submit quietly to the suppression of individual political expression and autonomous participation. When the number of such activists reaches a certain level, according to this expectation, the regime will finally be compelled to respond to the demands for a fundamental enlargement of political freedoms.

A wide variety of public protest activities have been utilized for alliance-building and for the display of dissident opposition: (1) public protest

42. *Chronicle*, no. 8. See also Reddaway, *Uncensored Russia*, chap. 7.
43. For a discussion of the problems of measuring political influence on the Soviet decision-making process, consult Stewart, *Political Power*; Franklyn Griffiths, "A Tendency Analysis of Soviet Policy-Making," in *Interest Groups in Soviet Politics*, ed. H. Gordon Skilling and Franklyn Griffiths (Princeton, N.J., 1971), pp. 335–77; and Howard L. Biddulph, "The Interest Group Approach and Soviet Policy-making: A Critical Reappraisal," MS prepared for publication.

demonstrations, (2) public appeals circulated through samizdat, (3) political "platforms" circulated and discussed by samizdat journals, and (4) programmatic essays.

The demonstration of Pushkin Square in support of Ginzburg and Galanskov in January 1967 was the beginning of the use of the street demonstration. The demonstration on Red Square in August 1968 to protest the invasion of Czechoslovakia helped to stimulate many less-publicized demonstrations and public opposition activities throughout the USSR. According to the *Chronicle*, the district party committees in Leningrad alone reported at least fourteen public activities of this type following the Moscow demonstration. The Crimean Tatars conducted a number of activities of this type, including the one in Mayakovsky Square, in support of their demand to be reinstated in their Crimean homeland. Another highly unusual form of public demonstration, at least for the USSR, was a "tent city" the Crimean Tatars erected near the village of Marino outside Simferopol to dramatize their demands.[44]

In addition to a number of petitions to "public opinion" and to fellow members of the intelligentsia, the dissidents published in samizdat several "white books" of official "illegalities." These included Ginzburg's white book on the trial of Sinyavsky and Daniel, Chornovil's documentary record of the trial of Ukrainian dissenters, and Gorbanevskaya's account of the aftermath of the Red Square demonstration. Political platforms began to appear in 1969, the most celebrated being *The Program of the Democratic Movement*. Among the many programmatic essays that were publicly circulated for discussion, Sakharov's treatise and Roy Medvedev's study of Soviet development and Stalinism are notable.[45]

All four of these forms of public protest served the function of alliance building as well as "opposition through publicity." Whether or not the efforts of the dissidents to publicize every act of repression committed by the political leadership had any restraining effect on what the authorities would otherwise have done is impossible to establish or even analyze, but this was at least one short-run purpose of the protest.

The "long-run" objective was alliance building. It is also impossible to measure the success of the movement in recruiting the resource of numbers during the period, 1967–70, but the breadth of news covered in the *Chronicle* gives evidence that its scope was nationwide, although likely still microscopic in comparison with truly mass organizations. Some of the moral supporters of the movement expressed quite pessimistic opinions about its ever attaining its objectives. Amalrik was representative of this view.[46]

---

44. *Chronicle*, nos. 9, 7.
45. See Hayward, *On Trial*; *Chornovil Papers*; Gorbanevskaya, *Midday*; *Programma*; Sakharov, *Progress*; Roy Medvedev, *Let History Judge* (New York, 1971).
46. Amalrik, *Will the Soviet Union Survive until 1984?*

Others remained optimistic, their self-confidence growing as the "movement" spread, until the official crackdown of 1972–73. Yakir expressed the optimistic view in these words: "Although at the present its social base is indeed very narrow and the movement itself has been forced to operate in extremely difficult conditions, the ideas proclaimed by it have begun to spread widely throughout the country, and that is the beginning of an irreversible process of self-liberation."[47]

In the early 1970s, however, the official policy of repression was accelerated. The movement was disrupted through the imprisonment or incarceration in psychiatric wards of almost all its leading personalities. The arrest of Yakir and Krasin silenced the *Chronicle*, and their public trial (with full "confessions") symbolized the effective termination of the Human Rights Movement.

Robert Dahl has stated what he calls the "self-fulfilling prophecy of hegemonic regimes":

Since all opposition is potentially dangerous, no distinction can be made between acceptable and unacceptable opposition, between loyal and disloyal opposition, between opposition that is protected and opposition that must be repressed. Yet if all oppositions are treated as dangerous and subject to repression, opposition that would be loyal if it were tolerated becomes disloyal because it is not tolerated. Since all opposition is likely to be disloyal, all opposition must be repressed.[48]

Dahl's generalization is useful in accounting for the rise of the democratic opposition movement in the USSR. By treating the cultural dissent of the early 1960s as political opposition to be suppressed, official Soviet policy helped to generate the Human Rights Movement—a genuine political opposition—after the Sinyavsky-Daniel trial. Once a political opposition movement was in existence, it was the official policy of repression that deepened the cleavage. In the beginning the movement was primarily committed to specific policy opposition. But the behavior of the regime produced a commitment to more fundamental changes among the intellectual dissidents during 1968–70, as reflected in the platforms and programmatic essays of this period. The suppression of what was largely a nonpublic protest movement in 1966 and 1967 led by 1968 and 1969 to the first public opposition movement of significant proportions since the early 1920s. While the movement remained noninsurrectionary in its methods and objectives, by the 1970s it had become committed to fundamental systemic changes in the Soviet polity.

The strategy of public opposition employed by the Democratic Movement cannot be fully evaluated for several reasons. First, the movement was suppressed before its full potentialities were evident. Second, as previously

47. P. Yakir, "An Open Letter to Amalrik," *Survey* no. 74–75 (Winter–Spring, 1970), p. 111.
48. Robert Dahl, *Regimes and Oppositions* (New Haven, Conn., 1973), p. 13.

emphasized, the lack of visibility of decision-making in the USSR makes it extremely difficult to measure the operation of political influence. Third, the dimensions of the movement are not adequately visible to an outside observer. Any concluding evaluation must therefore be highly impressionistic.

It appears that the Democratic Movement succeeded in becoming a highly visible opposition in Soviet society but did not achieve mass support for its political objectives. It appears to have failed in its attempt to project an image of a loyal, noninsurrectionary group working to improve the existing body politic. Part of the reason for this failure, no doubt, lay in the fact that public opposition violates one of the most important mores of the political culture, as previously discussed. Furthermore, it appears in hindsight that the emphasis given to communicating with external publics had the effect of damaging the internal strategy of alliance building while it also failed to activate third parties effectively.[49] The dissidents seemed to overestimate both the willingness of the external publics to intervene and the susceptibility of Soviet leaders to foreign influence on such issues. This tactic provided ammunition for charges of disloyalty, which undoubtedly exercised a persusasive appeal against them in public opinion. The overreliance on external communication with third parties was therefore not only unproductive but counterproductive to the objectives of the movement.

In spite of the failure of the Democratic Movement to achieve its specific objectives, it would be a mistake to evaluate its political impact as nil. During the five years of its existence the movement's use of public protest inaugurated a new dimension of political behavior in Soviet society that, like the influence of the Decembrists on nineteenth-century Russia, may yet provide an inspiring example for future generations of dissenters.

49. For a thoughtful analysis and assessment of this problem, consult the essay by the dissident Soviet historian Roy Medvedev, "Problems of Democratization and Détente," *New Left Review*, no. 83 (January–February, 1974), pp. 27–40.

CHAPTER THREE / **THE DEMOCRATIC MOVEMENT:**

DIMENSIONS AND PERSPECTIVES / THEODORE FRIEDGUT

Fascinating questions all too often prove to be fruitless either for lack of sufficient research material or because they add little to the main body of knowledge in their field. What a satisfaction, then, to find an abundance of rich source material coming available that allows us to deal with matters relevant to the essence of the Soviet polity.

While Karel van het Reve may exaggerate somewhat in saying that it is more important to read *Khronika* than *Pravda*,[1] there is no doubt that the materials distributed through the self-publishing channels known as *samizdat* yield new and often startlingly refreshing perspectives on Soviet politics. A dissenting intelligentsia has been identified with the struggle for political reform in Russia for the past two hundred years, and it was almost with the joy of seeing a prophecy fulfilled that Sovietologists detected an increasingly overt ferment of literary and political ideas rising out of the dull and viscous morass of verbiage that characterized so much of Soviet thought of the Stalin period.

The burgeoning literature of protest, particularly of political protest, led by what is commonly called the Democratic Movement,[2] has provided shelves full of studies. The wonders of modern technology (described by horrendous neologisms) have also introduced *kinizdat* and *magnitizdat* into the lexicon of protest along with the now well-known *samizdat*. We are thus familiar with the programmatic works of the Democratic Movement, and this article is not intended as an examination of their content.[3] Personal

1. Karel van het Reve, "Ideologies and Programs of Soviet Dissenters," in *Papers and Proceedings of the McMaster Conference on Dissent in Soviet Politics*, ed. Peter J. Potichnyj (Hamilton, Ont., 1972), p. 246.

2. For the purposes of this article, the term Democratic Movement is used to describe those who advocate general political change in the Soviet Union and express their opinions outside the framework of the Communist Party. This distinguishes the democrats from reform communists acting only within the party, on the one hand, and those interested primarily in specific changes—freedom of emigration for Jews, specific national or religious rights, etc.—on the other. There are, of course, some overlaps in which persons campaigning for particular rights also press for general political reform.

3. A concise Soviet analysis will be found in Andrei Amalrik, *Will the Soviet Union Survive until 1984?* (New York, 1970). For a non-Soviet summary, see Gerd R. von Doemming, *A Guide to Proposals for Systemic Change in the Soviet Union Offered by Soviet Citizens*, Radio Liberty Reference Handbook no. 82 (Munich, 1971). Van het Reve, "Ideologies and Programs," is a succinct and deeply penetrating insight into the values and motivations of the democrats. Zev Katz, *Soviet Dissenters and Social Structure in the USSR* (Cambridge, Mass.,

memoirs that are unusual in that they deal with contemporary events rather than the more or less distant past give us the taste and texture of the tightly knit circles of democrats, mirroring the personal qualities of individuals and their interpersonal relations.[4] Many documents of the movement have been gathered and published in whole or in part, first of all within the USSR, in the twenty-seven issues of the *Khronika tekushchikh sobytii* published from April 1968 to November 1972, and outside the USSR in the Radio Liberty *Arkhiv samizdata*.[5]

The element missing from the democratic literature is that of self-analysis. Quite understandably (and quite in keeping with tradition), the democrats are preoccupied with questions of *chto delat'* (What is to be done?) and of survival to the virtual exclusion of concern for their place in the realities of the existing Russian society. The notable exception to this is Andrei Amalrik, whose attempted analysis of the size, social structure, and prospects of the democrats indicates something of the valuable knowledge to be gained by pursuing this line of inquiry.[6]

The Democratic Movement should be seen not only through the outsiders' reading of its writings. These are, after all, often polemical and hortatory, written in the heat of battle with the regime and with conscious intent to create the "mystification" commonly practiced by the nineteenth century intelligentsia. In every case they are produced under the stultifying limitations of the Soviet political milieu. There is much that can be learned from the perceptions of democrats about themselves and from the images that members of the Soviet intelligentsia outside the Democratic Movement have of the democrats.

From material hitherto available, rough estimates have been made of the size, geographical distribution, and social composition of the Democratic Movement, usually following the lead given by Amalrik.[7] A central difficulty

---

1971) analyzes the social outlooks reflected in democratic programmatic writings. Abraham Rothberg, *The Heirs of Stalin* (Ithaca and London, 1972) is a full-length study of the emergence of the democrats out of post-Stalin dissidence.

4. Once again the list is lengthy and generally well known. A comprehensive bibliography of works dealing with dissent and the democrats can be found appended to the Amnesty edition (see n. 5 below) of the *Chronicle of Current Events* nos. 22–23, pp. 101–7, and in Potichnyj, *Papers*, pp. 266–74. This author found three works particularly valuable for the insights they gave into the personality and social structure of the democrats: Anatoly Marchenko, *My Testimony* (London, 1969); Andrei Amalrik, *Involuntary Journey to Siberia* (New York, 1970); and Natalia Gorbanevskaya, *Red Square at Noon* (New York, 1970).

5. The *Khronika tekushchikh sobytii* has been translated into English and published as *Chronicle of Current Events* by Amnesty International. Possev Verlag, Frankfurt, has published the original Russian texts. When cited as *Chronicle*, the reference is to the Amnesty edition. In addition, Peter Reddaway has edited and annotated eleven issues of the *Chronicle* under the title *Uncensored Russia* (London, 1972). At the time of writing this study, I had not had an opportunity to consult subsequent issues of *Chronicle* that reached the West in 1974.

6. Amalrik, *Will the Soviet Union Survive?*, pp. 13–17.

7. *Ibid.*, pp. 15–16. Cf. Frederick C. Barghoorn, "The General Pattern of Soviet Dissent," in Potichnyj, *Papers*, pp. 7–10; Reddaway, *Uncensored Russia*, p. 23; Katz, *Soviet Dissenters*, pp. 10–12. These estimates are discussed below and compared with results of my own research.

in forming such estimates has always been the question of evaluating the latent support available to the democrats from passive sympathizers. Factors influencing the creation and expression of such support will be examined here. Beyond this, it has proved possible to gain some understanding of the motivations and perceptions of those who undertake active participation in the Democratic Movement and, no less important, of those who abstain from participation. These perceptions have to do with the democrats' various programs and with their relations to the rest of Soviet society. Finally, some insights into the mechanisms of the spread of the movement and the spectrum of regime reaction to dissidence can help us estimate its prospects for growth.

The information presented here was derived from discussion with forty people, former Soviet citizens, all of whom were students or members of the intelligentsia. Of these, eight had been actively identified with the Democratic Movement at some time. The interviews ranged in length from a half-hour to four hours and were unstructured, but in each case a common core of questions was presented that was intended to derive the interviewee's perceptions of the above subjects.

The reader should immediately be aware that all those interviewed, whether active democrats or not, ultimately opted for emigration rather than for continued residence and hope for change in the USSR. While this should not affect the factual information gleaned from the interviews, the evaluative and attitudinal information supplied may be biased by the nature of the sample. To check this point, I asked the interviewees to estimate the representativeness of their opinions by comparing themselves with former colleagues still in the USSR. In virtually every case the response indicated that the views expressed in the interviews were in no way unique and that within the interviewees' circle of friends in the USSR numerous people could be found with similar perceptions of the democrats. It can therefore be suggested that the elements that recur frequently in the responses of the interviewees can be used with a high degree of confidence in constructing a picture of the Democratic Movement's place in Soviet society.

"WHAT IS THE DEMOCRATIC MOVEMENT"?

The first point emphasized in virtually every response is that there is no Democratic *Movement* but rather small groupings of democrats that, except for the Chalidze-Sakharov-Tverdokhlebov Human Rights Committee,[8] have no formal structure, membership, or regulations. The interviewees thought it perfectly understandable that a totalitarian authority would

---

8. The greater part of the interviewing was done before Chalidze's journey to the United States (November 1972) and the subsequent revoking of his citizenship by the Soviet authorities.

prevent autonomous groupings that might prove to be the nucleus of an organized opposition. Particular emphasis was given to the idea that when any such grouping succeeded in disseminating information independently, it became particularly dangerous to the authorities and was sure to be suppressed. In this regard, the clandestine *Chronicle of Current Events* was considered more of a challenge to the authorities than the Chalidze committee's open journal *Social Problems*.

The attempt to use a detailed knowledge of Soviet law as a shield for democratic activity was appreciated by those interviewed mainly for the perplexities it sowed among Soviet officials. One of the most prominent opinions held about Soviet officials (which will be discussed in detail) is that they lack intelligent understanding of their duties. The challenge of using the law to frustrate their arbitrary repression of civil rights is thus viewed at once as a moral imperative for Soviet society and as an amusing experiment to see how the officials will respond. The game is played not so much with the hope of winning as to see whether it is possible to score a few points and keep alive the concepts of civil rights. Both democrats and others freely admitted that despite their sympathies few had the courage and the principles needed to play this dangerous form of bear-baiting. For the overwhelming majority, the lack of weight and organization of the democrats discourages the growth of their ranks. Natalia Gorbanevskaya makes this point quite clearly in her account of the Red Square demonstration against the invasion of Czechoslovakia: "The 'pointlessness' and the 'inappropriateness' of the demonstration were the talk of . . . that 'left wing, radical and liberal' Moscow . . . which completely agreed with our attitude to the fact of the invasion."[9]

The absence of organized democratic expression is not only a matter of relations with the regime. It is an expression of a broad range of programmatic diversity as well. Perhaps the only point on which all democrats and dissenters agree is the recognition that political change in the Soviet Union over the past twenty years is not yet sufficient to guarantee that Stalinism cannot return. After 1956, hope arose that there could be an alternative polity in the USSR.[10] Yet the shadow of Stalin still broods over the consciousness of virtually the whole intelligentsia. Yuli Daniel used the fear of a return of Stalinism as a defense in his trial,[11] and Roy Medvedev bases his whole research effort on the need to root out its remnants.[12] Frederick C. Barghoorn notes seven themes common to various programmatic docu-

9. *Red Square at Noon*, p. 281.

10. Amalrik, *Will the Soviet Union Survive?*, p. 11, writes that only after 1956 did Soviet dissenters begin to think of programs to replace Stalinism.

11. See Max Hayward, ed., *On Trial: The Soviet State versus "Abram Tertz" and "Nikolai Arzhak,"* rev. and enl. ed. (New York and Evanston, 1967), p. 54. Daniel states: "not only I, but any person who thought seriously about the situation in our country—was convinced that a new cult of personality was about to be established."

12. Roy A. Medvedev, *Let History Judge* (New York, 1971), p. xxvii, writes: "Stalinism remains a real threat, in open as well as disguised forms."

ments of Soviet dissenters. First among these is fear of the resurgence of Stalinism, and criticism of Maoism is next.[13] On this subject the opinions expressed in samizdat appear to coincide closely with those of the interviewees.

Beyond this limited basis of agreement we find that there are numerous ideological, factional, and personal divisions like those familiar to all from the history of the liberal and revolutionary movements of tsarist Russia. Some of this is expressed in the relatively genteel intellectual tone of the samizdat writings, but it much goes deeper and is said to weaken the democratic effort. Interviewees cited the case of Solzhenitsyn, who in some circles is regarded as a neo-Slavophile and thus not truly democratic.[14] Among national minorities the question of participation in the democratic effort is often a source of factionalism.[15] The same is true, sometimes even more sharply, between groups of various tendencies—different nationalities, differing religious groups—and all of these *vis-à-vis* the democrats.

Disunity, with the consequent danger of infiltration and informers, was offered in several cases as a reason for nonparticipation of individuals in democratic politics. Creation of a united front, or even of any extensive degree of coordination, was seen as dependent on a single person who could bridge the gap between groups. The only candidate for this, the only man who was thought to know everyone and to have channels of communication with all groups, was Peter Yakir. More than any other person he was seen as the personification of the Democratic Movement, though this, as will be shown later, had negative as well as positive aspects.

PROGRAMMATIC PROBLEMS

Interviewees, even those who themselves had been active dissenters, were highly reluctant to categorize the ideas of the various individuals or groups of democrats. Three reasons were given for this. First of all, the ferment of dissent and the constantly changing political climate within which the democrats live produce a constant flux of their own individual ideas. As one person pointed out, many of those who are seeking a democratic philosophy must make their way through two millenia of political thought without the

13. Barghoorn, "General Pattern," p. 17. Criticism of Maoism is closely linked with the fear of resurgent Stalinism. Several interviewees in discussing their views on China stated that in the event of a clash they would support "Russian totalitarianism against Chinese totalitarianism, not out of patriotism but as the lesser of two evils."

14. For an expression of this see Mikhail Grobman, "Solzhenitsyn Does Not Deserve His Reputation as Lover of Liberty," *Jerusalem Post*, November 10, 1972, p. 12. A number of Jews still living in the USSR later wrote a letter to the editor defending Solzhenitsyn and emphatically denying the charges of anti-Semitism that Grobman raised.

15. See, for instance, George S. N. Luckyj, "Polarity in Ukrainian Intellectual Dissent," *Canadian Slavonic Papers* 14, no. 2 (1972): 269.

benefit of intimate acquaintance with the practical history of various outlooks.[16] A second reason is that many samizdat documents, particularly those prepared with the intention of seeking legal publication in the USSR, are written in carefully restrained if not Aesopean language and may not reflect accurately the extent of political reform actually championed by the author. A final reason given was that some basic documents circulated in samizdat were either forgeries not originating within democratic circles or were "mystifications," deliberately aiming at creating the impression of existence or size for nonexistent or minuscule groups.

Two such documents are the memorandum "To Hope or to Act," known as the Memorandum of the Estonian Technical Intelligentsia Group,[17] and the "Program of the Democrats of Russia, the Ukraine, and the Baltic Lands."[18] Among Democrats interviewed were some who had systematically inquired as to the origins of both these documents, without success. It is perhaps typical of the response of almost all interviewees that without knowledge of the individuals associated with these documents no serious analysis of their content or significance is undertaken. That there are persons who advance the ideas of political, moral, and social reform advocated in these two documents is undisputed, but several interviewees when asked about these documents said they simply doubted that any substantial group of Estonians would take an interest in general political reform.[19] The fact that this appears to be a commonly held opinion is of some significance whether or not the view is correct.

If there is hesitation regarding evaluation of many ideas current among democratic dissenters, this hesitation disappears when the question of neo-Slavophile thought is raised. The trend of Russian patriotism that easily leads to Great Russian chauvinism appears to be a nightmare for many democrats. They see in the appearance of the journal *Veche* and the essay

---

16. For evidence of this changing of ideas see an interview in which Sakharov is quoted as considering himself no longer a Marxist but a liberal, *Newsweek*, November 13, 1972, p. 13. Roy Medvedev, still a Marxist communist at the time of the completion of his study on stalinism, was recently reported to be engaged in research on social and political trends within and without the Communist Party under the title "Democracy and Socialism"; *New York Times*, August 19, 1972.

17. *Arkhiv samizdata* no. 70. Subsequent references to this archive use the abbreviation *AS*.

18. Published as *Programma Demokraticheskogo Dvizheniia Sovetskogo Soiuza* (Amsterdam, 1970).

19. Reddaway, *Uncensored Russia*, p. 172, expresses some doubts as to who and how many people might have composed the Estonian Memorandum, while Barghoorn, "General Pattern," p. 34, n. 16, states that some believe it to have been composed by Russian intellectuals. Van het Reve, "Ideologies and Programs," p. 247, is skeptical as to the exact origins of the "Program," and Ukrainian democrats later stated that they had not participated in its formulation. Rudolf L. Tőkés, "Soviet Dissent: Problems and Research Scenarios," in Potichnyj, *Papers*, p. 40, and Katz, *Soviet Dissenters*, p. 48, discuss the "Program" as a document reflecting accurately relations and programs of Soviet democrats.

"Slovo natsii" a rising wave of chauvinist feeling that is attracting a large following in intelligentsia circles.[20] A number of fears were expressed regarding these ideas. They are considered a counterpart among the intelligentsia of the Russian nationalism that has replaced a moribund Marxism as the actual ideology of the Soviet Communist Party, leading to chauvinist reaction's domination of any possible liberal reforms. The idea that nationalist pride might corrupt the intelligentsia by providing it with a politically safe avenue of self-expression and identification with the regime was expressed with considerable agitation. The fear was also expressed that the Christian Democratic trend of dissent might easily be drawn toward the nationalist trend, forming the democrats' only link with any mass group but costing them all liberal characteristics. In general, the trend of the Soviet Union towards Great Russian chauvinism was viewed as the coming catastrophe for Soviet society as a whole.[21]

While there is certainly a real basis for these anxieties, they also reflect a different democratic limitation, the abyss between the universalist democratic striving for reform and the particularist aims of national and religious minorities. In examining this relation we quickly see that it is asymmetrical. The democrats will act openly and forcefully in support of any particularist movement for freedom, but this support is not always publicly accepted and reciprocated. Andrei Sakharov, among others, has both written and acted in support of emigration rights for Jews, and Peter Grigorenko has devoted great energy to furthering the claims of the Crimean Tatars for repatriation. Interviewees, however, reported that the Tatar movement's leaders had some misgivings as to the wisdom of being identified with the democrats. Within the Jewish emigration movement there is an ongoing discussion over support for the democrats. Some oppose it on tactical grounds, asserting that the demand for repatriation to Israel should be their sole activity so that the grounds on which the authorities might oppose and repress their movement will be narrowed. Others advance more general separatist grounds, stating that the mistake of many Jews fifty years ago was to tie their future to the reform of Russian society. In practice, the fact that democrats such as Boris Tsukermann, Julius Telesin, Raisa Palatnik, and numerous others have crossed over to the emigration movement has created

---

20. For *Veche*, nos. 1 and 3, see *AS* 1013 and 1108 respectively. *Veche*, no. 2 (*AS* 1020) is summarized in *Chronicle*, no. 20, p. 257. "Slovo natsii" is *AS* 590. For a review of the content of these publications see Dmitry Pospielovsky, "The *Samizdat* Journal 'Veche': Russian Patriotic Thought Today," Radio Liberty Research Paper no. 45 (Munich, 1971).

21. Harrison Salisbury, in the introduction to Gorbanevskaya, *Red Square at Noon*, p. 7, writes of a "revival in lightly concealed form of the kind of anti-intellectual chauvinistic spirit which was epitomised in the last fifty years of the Romanov regime by the *chernaia sotniia*." A. Yakovlev, writing in *Literaturnaia Gazeta*, no. 46 (November 15, 1972), p. 5, criticizes the recent republication of a nineteenth century Slavophile poem attacking the revolutionary intelligentsia of that time as "people not of us, people not Russian." The existence of the informal "*Rodina* Club" among writers is cited as part of this trend.

close personal ties between the two groups and has resulted in de facto cooperation and a lively exchange of information and moral and material aid.

Nationalist influences are reported far to outweigh that of the democrats in the Baltic states and the Ukraine. The skepticism that greeted the purported democratic expressions from Estonia is typical of this perception. In Tartu University, the democrats among the students were all from Moscow. The local students paid no attention to the democrats and responded only to appeals for their own national independence. Interestingly, Baltic students studying in Moscow were much more responsive to the ideas of the democrats. In the Ukraine, a speaker at a democratic gathering provoked a storm by including the demand "*bez zhidov i Moskalei*" (without Jews and Muscovites) in his speech, and he was not allowed to finish. But even within the less extremely nationalist Ukrainian democratic circles national consciousness and suspicion find strong expression. Thus the *Ukrainskii visnik* (Herald of the Ukraine, roughly the Ukrainian equivalent of the *Chronicle*) is quoted as criticizing the *Chronicle* for insufficient attention to the national aspirations of minorities and characterizes it as "a publication of Russian (and possibly to some extent, Jewish) circles."[22] It is generally felt that the nationalist movements have a wider appeal to the local population than does democratic activity and that the national movements are larger in scope.[23]

DEMOCRATS: HOW MANY AND WHERE?

The number of active democrats is more a matter of conjecture than of measurement, for not only are the numbers always changing but the nature of the groups involved is such that knowledge of the movement as a whole is limited. Two facts stand out. The active democrats are at best a tiny percentage of the intelligentsia, and the number of people active shrinks rapidly with every act of repression by the regime. To elicit estimates of the number of active democrats I used a definition that might fit Peter Reddaway's "mainstream members."[24] An active democrat was taken as one who was active in the production and distribution of the *Chronicle*, the writing and dissemination of political samizdat, or the signing and circulating of petitions for human rights. Interviewees' responses to this definition ranged from "a few hundred" to a maximum figure of 3,000, with the majority of responses clustered below 1,000. Barghoorn estimates that well

22. Quoted in *Chronicle*, no. 22, p. 45.
23. Perhaps indicative of this is the *New York Times* report of December 11, 1972, that in the latter part of the year 1972 eight people were arrested for democratic activity and a hundred for Ukrainian nationalist activity.
24. Reddaway, *Uncensored Russia*, p. 23.

over 1,000 can be listed from signatures to appeals, while Reddaway estimates nearly 2,000.[25]

The low numbers of activists generally reported may appear surprising when we consider Amalrik's notation that 738 people signed petitions in connection with the Galanskov-Ginzburg case alone.[26] This may be explained, however, by the fact that during the period of the Galanskov-Ginzburg trial (January 1968), the regime's response in most of Moscow (though not, for instance, in Novosibirsk) was comparatively mild; relatively few people were expelled from their work. The signing of petitions was considered fashionable and a sign of moral quality involving only marginal danger. Later the repression grew, and we have already noted the reluctance of many people to join in overt expression of their revulsion at the invasion of Czechoslovakia, although this was clearly a crisis point that stirred great interest and feeling. Thus though a cumulative count of signatures may yield 2,000 over a span of five or six years, the majority of these people may not have been active in any continuing way.

The rapidity with which a KGB campaign can drive the democrats underground (though not destroy them permanently) is evident from the events of the second half of 1972 in Moscow and elsewhere. In 1969, Yevgenia Ginzburg was said to have found a group of 40 active democrats in the city of Kazan. A year later only 5 remained, the others having been arrested, moved elsewhere, or fallen silent.

The situation of the great Novosibirsk science center, Akademgorodok, is perhaps typical in several ways. First, it exemplifies the growth of democratic ferment wherever there is any group of intelligentsia. Until a KGB "hunting campaign" in late 1972 cut it off, there was general and almost open reading of both literary and political samizdat, with the overwhelming majority of the more than 4,000 scientists taking interest in it. The *Chronicle* passed from hand to hand, and documents from Moscow were reproduced and circulated. Discussions of social and political problems were ubiquitous and continuous, though carried on within discreet circles of close friends with little intermingling among members belonging to different circles. Some persons were said to "live for the readings and discussions." Yet following the mass expulsions of the 46 who signed petitions on behalf of Galanskov and Ginzburg or protested in support of Sinyavsky and Daniel, democratic activity hardly went beyond talk and reading.[27] Little if any samizdat was created at Akademgorodok, and petitions and protests did not

---

25. *Ibid.*; Barghoorn, "General Pattern," p. 7. Barghoorn, p. 33, n. 4, says that an early draft of Reddaway's work "noted only slightly over a thousand." An unfinished work under way at the Russian and East European Research Centre at the Hebrew University of Jerusalem has less than 1,000 persons in an examination of samizdat published in Russian. The criterion for listing a name here is at least two separate appearances in connection with democratic activity, exclusive of solely religious or national groups.

26. Amalrik, *Will the Soviet Union Survive?*, p. 15.

27. For the "Letter of the 46" from Novosibirsk in support of Galanskov and Ginzburg see *AS* 21. For the reprisals taken by the regime see Reddaway, *Uncensored Russia*, p. 396, and

circulate. The fear of losing positions or worse and the faint prospect of any effective action sufficed to keep most dissent on a theoretical level.

The dismissal and transfer of active democrats from Akademgorodok presumably should have generated dissent in other institutions, and interviewees indeed reported knowledge of new democratic contacts in smaller centers to the east as a result of migration of Akademgorodok scientists.[28] Nevertheless the weight of the democrats in regular academic institutions outside Moscow appears to be even less than the tiny percentage in the capital city. At the Electro-Technical Institute in Novosibirsk no democratic activity of any sort was in evidence. In the Minsk Polytechnical Institute a former head of a department noted that there was much alienation from the regime and that discontent was frequently aired among friends. No petitions were circulated, however, and he had no knowledge of the existence of the *Chronicle*. Foreign broadcasts were the source of knowledge of samizdat, and few manuscripts were available in the institute.

In Riga, one source estimated that there were thirty or forty persons interested, though not necessarily active, among the democrats. Almost all were Russians or Jews, with very few Latvians. These were concentrated within the university, although two were in the music conservatory, generally considered a conservative stronghold. The *Chronicle* arrived from Moscow regularly and circulated in this group. It did not, however, appear to reach the students, nor was there creation of samizdat or organization in the student body beyond a few short-lived attempts to create small discussion groups on social and philosophical problems. Even Ilya Rips's dramatic self-immolation in protest against the invasion of Czechoslovakia, though it was the talk of the town, aroused no response and only limited sympathy.

The apathy of Soviet students as reflected in the *Chronicle* is commented upon by Reddaway[29] and is generally confirmed by students interviewed. Although small local groups of many sorts—Cheist, Maoist, neo-Marxist, and so on—are to be found in the universities, and although samizdat is eagerly consumed, such activity is sporadic and generally short-lived, often ending with graduation and the assumption of employment and family responsibility. Students do, however, play an unseen but important role in supporting the democrats and particularly the *Chronicle*. Students travel to the provinces frequently and were often the source of information regarding arrests, trials, and unrest. In addition, they assisted in such mundane but essential matters as buying quantities of onionskin paper for the copying of the *Chronicle* without attracting undue attention.

---

n. 50 on p. 481. Although only 17 of the 46 signatories are noted here as having been punished, an interviewee from Novosibirsk claimed that all those associated with the letter had suffered expulsion from the party, their studies, or their employment.

28. Such a spreading of dissent is reminiscent of the spreading of the news of "Bloody Sunday" in 1905 when the tsar exiled leaders of the demonstration to various parts of Russia.

29. Reddaway, *Uncensored Russia*, pp. 32–33.

In the numerous large research institutes and cultural and administrative centers in Moscow little encouragement is to be found for the democrats. The Central Institute for Mathematical Economics was said to have perhaps 4 active democrats. The rest of the scientific staff was either afraid or apathetic. A similar situation was reported from the Scientific Research Institute of the State Committee for New Inventions. Of the 900 employees, most of whom had higher education, 3 had engaged in democratic activity while perhaps 20 or 30 others had some sympathy for the democrats. The Documentary Film Studio of the Ministry of Higher Education had a professional staff of 100, but no democratic activists were among them and no samizdat was circulated there. The Plekhanov Institute of Economic Research, with close to 1,000 scientific employees, has only passive and fearful sympathizers with the democrats. In the Institute of the History of Art in Moscow, 4 or 5 of the 100 workers signed petitions at various times, but when 2 of them were dismissed all activity stopped.

An interesting comparison can be made between the two following cases. The Institute of the Peoples of Africa and Asia in the Academy of Science is known as a "dissident institute." Of 200 employees, some 26 signed a petition against censorship and 9 signed a protest in connection with the Galanskov-Ginzburg trial. In the Leningrad branch of that institute, only 2 or 3 of the 300 employees had signed petitions while 6 or 7 more either distributed samizdat or had sent individual letters on controversial subjects to newspapers or the authorities. The employees of the institute in Moscow all knew some foreign language and had regular access to the foreign press as well as to restricted-distribution Tass summaries of social and political problems. These were used in the preparation of factual and evaluative position papers for the use of the Central Committee of the CPSU. Both the fact of access to the foreign press and the analysis of world affairs were said to have had their effect in forming democratic consciousness within the institute.

The above may be compared with a purely administrative office with close to 1,000 employees. None of these expressed any democratic sympathies, and many of the older employees were open neo-Stalinists whose chief public complaint against the regime was that it was not sufficiently forceful in maintaining law and order.

The numbers of people engaged in democratic activity are thus small not only within the population as a whole but within the scientific, creative, and administrative intelligentsia. Moreover, the regime has thus far been able to check the growth of democratic groups by depriving a relatively few people of employment or freedom. Peter Reddaway's optimism regarding the democrats' growth is not shared by the interviewees, and his denial that they are "a small and dwindling band of dissidents," written before the democrats' debacle of 1972 (interviewees used the world *razgrom*, "destruction") does not stand up in the light of recent history.[30]

30. *Ibid.*, pp. 31–32.

Nevertheless, two points are made repeatedly in this connection. The first is that the importance and even the influence of the democrats goes far beyond their numbers.[31] The second is that cycles of repression recur periodically, but that the expression of democratic ideas returns as soon as the regime's attention is diverted elsewhere.

The principal centers of democratic activity are Moscow and Kiev, followed at some distance by Leningrad. Leningraders spoke of the peculiarities of the city's tightly knit circles of intelligentsia as well as of a tradition of harsh police and Communist Party surveillance as responsible for their city's surprisingly low level of dissident activity.

Moscow is the undoubted center of the democrats. As the Soviet capital it attracts foreign diplomats, newsmen, tourists, and students whose presence is essential to the transmission of democratic information abroad. Foreigners are also a source of non-Soviet literature and information, stimulating the democrats' thinking and encouraging them to develop their ideas.

Outlying centers must depend on chance, personal acquaintances, and a *kommandirovka* (official travel order) to Moscow to gather encouragement, information, and the latest samizdat. By all accounts the authorities are less inhibited by legal strictures outside Moscow. Nevertheless, modern conditions of communication have created a situation far different from that in which the tsarist Premier Kokovtsev could say in 1913, "A hundred kilometers from the large centers and thirty kilometers from the provincial capitals they know nothing of these [revolutionary] politics."[32]

The relations between Moscow and the provinces are, however, largely one-way. Information comes, via foreign broadcasts or as a result of an individual's visiting the capital, but much less information flows to the center. So much depends on personal contact that where this is lacking, groups, journals, and samizdat creations may exist without their existence becoming known elsewhere until the persons involved are arrested and sentenced. Thus we find a number of instances in which the *Chronicle* reports that a single issue of a journal or a leaflet has turned up bearing the signature of an unknown group.[33]

Part of the paradox of existence of the democrats is that if they express their ideas publicly they invite suppression, but if they keep them clandestine they lose all hope of being politically effective. Different groups have differing solutions. The small circle that prepared the *Politicheskii dnevnik* over a period of six years remained totally unknown to the democratic

31. The idea that the Bolsheviks were a small faction in February 1917 must surely occur to the authorities in their consideration of the democrats. Avraham Yarmolinsky, *Road to Revolution* (New York, 1962), p. 227, notes that the total membership of the *Narodnaia volia* was estimated at 500 and that a list of all those associated however tenuously with the movement reaches 2,200 names.

32. Quoted by S. S. Oldenburg, "Impressive Progesss since 1905," in *Russia in Transition, 1905–1914*, ed. Robert H. McNeal (New York, 1970), p. 95.

33. E.g., *Chronicle*, no. 23, p. 97. There is evidently an immense quantity of as yet unknown samizdat material.

"public at large" and kept the journal's circulation strictly limited.[34] Chalidze's bimonthly *Obshchestvennye problemy* goes to the other extreme, publishing openly, distributing by mail, but avoiding topics of current Soviet happenings. The *Chronicle* chooses a different path—attempting to spread its net of readers and informants as widely as possible, deploring the need for secrecy, but with its chief editors kept deep in the underground and reportedly abstaining from any public expressions of dissent.

REGIME RESPONSES

The regime's response to democratic activity has varied greatly from time to time and in various places.[35] Only in the latter half of 1972 could democrats' arrest and trial be predicted confidently. Explanations of why the regime did not sweep all suspected democrats into the prison camps vary widely. Some opinions support Amalrik's contention that "the regime is simply growing old and can no longer suppress everyone and everything with the same strength and vigor as before."[36] Others suggested conflict within the regime and a growing sophistication of the KGB as reasons for the erratic nature of repression. Nevertheless the fear of judicial or extrajudicial retribution is clearly central to the response of almost all the nonparticipants in democratic activities. Whatever other reasons were linked to inaction—personality, ideology, a sense of futility, and the like—fear was present, both in the personal calculations of the respondents and in their evaluation of other nonactive colleagues. Clearly there is a difference between the fear of loss of employment and possible arrest as retribution for democratic activity, which is expressed here, and the terror of arbitrary imprisonment or execution that was a cornerstone of the Stalinist polity. Atomization of society by fear and suspicion nevertheless remains one of the totalitarian characteristics that persist in the Soviet Union today.

The potential of fear is maintained at a high level through active networks of informers, both paid and volunteer. These, whether KGB agents, party members, or simply busybodies, suffice to keep track of all personal contacts within any institution. Students assumed that if any discussion groups were formed, informers joined them. An employee of a scientific institute estimated that 15 to 20 percent of his colleagues were active as informers. Another stated that once he was known as a democrat he could rely on a dozen persons' reporting his every contact to the director.

34. Twelve of the 72 known issues of the *Politicheskii dnevnik* have been read outside of the USSR (*AS* 1001–12). A list of the contents of these issues and an analysis of the journal may be found in Albert Boiter, "Notes on the 'Political Diary,'" Radio Liberty Research Paper no. 43 (Munich, 1971).

35. See n. 27 above for the severity of reaction to protest in Novosibirsk. In comparison, Amalrik, *Will the Soviet Union Survive?*, p. 26, writes that only 15 percent of all those who protested in connection with the Galanskov-Ginzburg trial suffered immediate dismissal.

36. Amalrik, *Will the Soviet Union Survive?*, p. 30.

One of the aims of such a system is to protect against democratic expansion. If a known democrat consorts with new contacts, the new person is summoned to the director's office or to the party secretary. In exceptional cases he is called before a "troika" of the director, the party secretary, and the head of the "first section" (security) of the institution. There the "waverer" gets a friendly admonition that association with undesirables is not to his benefit. This talk generally has the required effect. If not, black marks are chalked up against the miscreant's name until such a time as he commits some overt act or until a vigilance campaign leads to the dismissal of unreliables.

The delivery of such warnings often appears to frustrate and infuriate potential democrats, for it embodies many of the elements of Soviet power that alienate the intelligentsia. Moreover, party secretaries and KGB representatives appear to be almost universally crude and boorish and to arouse all the contempt that Russian intellectuals express for a leadership that systematically eliminated culture and talent from its ranks, replacing them with brute force and corrupted values.[37] But respondents were fascinated by reports of what has come to be known as the "Andropov Gambit." Yuri Andropov, chairman of the KGB, is said to have recruited a cadre of intelligent and well-read agents whose task it was to persuade dissidents that nonpublication of many literary and social works stemmed from the authors' stylistic and intellectual shortcomings rather than political calculation. This attempted use of reason in place of thinly veiled terror earned Andropov a certain measure of admiration as a "liberal" innovator in police work.

RATIONALES OF PASSIVITY

The fear that breeds dissociation from dissident activity is not always expressed as a fear of direct retribution. A response that occurred a number of times was a fear of association with the democrats because they are "possessed" (*beshenye*) people. Their obsession with justice wipes out all prudence, and they are capable of destroying both themselves and everyone about them in a rash outburst of idealism. George S. N. Luckyj uses the same term when he writes that only those who are truly "possessed" will be brave enough to raise their voices in dissent.[38] When this feeling was probed it turned out in each case to be related to Yakir and those most closely associated with him.

Further questioning regarding views on Yakir revealed that he was the center of much controversy. Admittedly the most prominent figure among

---

37. Expression of this idea will also be found in *Ibid.*, p. ix: "I cannot listen to the Soviet radio. I cannot read *Pravda*. It is crude, stupid and full of lies." See also Medvedev, *Let History Judge*, pp. 314–15.
38. Luckyj, "Ukrainian Dissent," p. 277.

the democrats, he was viewed with disfavor by many nonactive respondents not only because he was regarded as "possessed" but because of his heavy drinking and the reputed wildness and coarseness of behavior of his immediate circle. In contrast, Bukovsky was described as "saintly" and other figures such as Chalidze as "cultured people." Those interviewees who had been in any way close to Yakir and all those who had been active democrats had only admiration for his integrity and actions.

A third variation on the theme of fear links it with Soviet patriotism. A few interviewees stated that they thought the democrats, whether or not they were aware of it, were being used by foreign agencies hostile to the Soviet Union.[39] Association with the democrats thus seemed to them to entangle one in possible espionage charges as well as to offend their sense of patriotism. While those raising this point were fully aware that the charge of being a tool of foreign agencies might well be entirely a KGB ploy, the combination of fear, prudence, and patriotism and a total lack of sympathy for émigré agencies such as the NTS evidently made such an approach palatable to the interviewees.

Democratic contacts are thus almost always based on close personal bonds of friendship and long association. Only with persons of intimate understanding and trust can fully frank political conversations be held. This is true also of the circulation of samizdat. Where personal contact exists, transfer of material is rapid. The *Chronicle* reached Tartu University three days after its appearance in Moscow. We have already mentioned, however, the lack of contact between university teachers and students in Riga, which resulted in an interested student traveling to Leningrad to read the *Chronicle* for lack of entrée into Riga democratic circles. Reports of lengthy travels for the purpose of reading samizdat came from several sources.

This isolation results in a very spotty and uneven distribution of both literary and political samizdat. One Moscow democrat was pleasantly surprised to find that within the course of a year a statement of his assailing anti-Semitism and censorship had become known among students and writers in Murmansk, Kiev, and Tashkent.[40] The formation of links with the lesser centers are unpredictable and unstable, however, and foreign broadcasts appear to be a more frequent source of information for remote cities than direct distribution.[41]

39. This theme is reported as being used by the KGB to weaken Yakir in his interrogations late in 1972. See *New York Times*, December 11, 1972, p. 26.

40. For a comment on the geographical spread of sources for the *Chronicle* see Reddaway, *Uncensored Russia*, p. 30.

41. Not only does the Soviet public show considerable interest in broadcasts of the BBC, VOA, and Radio Liberty, but the Soviet authorities have reacted to this interest. This reaction is not limited to the great jamming campaign the Soviets have mounted. Interviewees from three different areas (Moscow, Czernowitz, Vilna) reported the implementation of separate research projects in which people were asked the principal source of their information. In the Moscow

The interest shown in samizdat varied widely. Those who tended toward democratic activism read both political and literary samizdat. The nonactive, while enthusiastic about reading literary material, described political samizdat such as the *Chronicle*, protest letters, and trial reports as "uninteresting." In general they would not carry such material or keep it at home, although some stated that they would occasionally read it at a friend's house. Among the nonactive people were those who had active democratic friends to whom they would pass on information if they had it. Thus the potential sources of information for a journal such as the *Chronicle* are more widespread than its active supporters.

THE DEMOCRATS AND SOVIET SOCIETY

All of what has gone before deals with the status of the Democratic Movement among the intelligentsia, whether active supporters or passive, skeptical sympathizers. What about other groups in Soviet society? How is the relation of the Democratic Movement to them perceived?

With the exception of the Christian-oriented groups among the democrats (as exemplified by Levitin-Krasnov), there appears to be no attempt to proselytize among the Soviet masses. In part this is due to prudence, for cases were cited in which an attempt to reach out to workers resulted in denunciation to the police. The most prominent reason cited, however, was the total lack of community of values between the democrats, who are virtually all in the intelligentsia, and the working people. Most interviewees spoke much in the vein of Amalrik, who wrote: "To the majority of the people, the very word 'freedom' is synonymous with disorder. . . . As for respecting the rights of an individual as such, the idea simply arouses bewilderment."[42] One interviewee who took part in the protests outside the courthouse during the trial of Galanskov and Ginzburg noted that though the majority of those harassing the demonstrators were mobilized *druzhinniki* (volunteer police auxiliaries) from a Moscow auto plant, passersby spontaneously joined in denouncing the protesters. An eyewitness to the Red Square demonstration against the invasion of Czechoslovakia reported a similar spontaneous hostility.[43]

Some interviewees raised the separation from the mass to the level of principle, as reflected in the statement: "It is high time we were freed from the foolishness of populism. The most important thing is the individual and his rights." Only one interviewee, not a former activist, spoke against this

project 6 percent of the 16,000 citizens polled reported foreign radio as a principal source. It was believed, however, that the actual percentage was higher, for some respondents were not asked to put their names on the questionnaires, and of these 17 percent named foreign broadcasts.

42. Amalrik, *Will the Soviet Union Survive?*, p. 34.

43. See Gorbanevskaya, *Red Square at Noon*, p. 29. Note her own comment, however, that to her the crowd appeared more neutral; p. 31.

view. He maintained that contact could and should be made with the elite of technically trained workers whose superior education and standard of living made it possible for them to compare the situation of Soviet citizens with others and to compare the regime's performance with its promises.

As regards the nondemocratic intelligentsia—a much larger group than the democrats and their passive and hidden sympathizers—they are viewed as totally apathetic, oriented only to material benefits and career advancement, thereby giving stability and strength to the regime. A saying attributed to Bruno Jasiensky that was popular among the disillusioned democrats in Novosibirsk was quoted by an interviewee: "Fear not your enemy—at the worst he can kill you. Fear not your friend—at the worst he can betray you. But fear apathy, which permits the spread of killing and betrayal in our world."

What was particularly disturbing to the interviewees was the feeling that a significant section of this apathetic intelligentsia desired some point of identification with the regime to overcome its traditional alienation. These were seen as people who could be moved by nationalist blandishments and in a euphoria of patriotism brought to overlook the regime's violations of human rights as the cracked eggshells that are inevitable in making an omelet.

In the search for influence the democrats have not overlooked the possibility of reform within the party. The entire neo-Marxist tendency of the democrats (Kosterin, Yakhimovich, Medvedev) stood on the premise that there can exist a healthy ideological foundation on which a democratic communism can be built. In particular, after 1956 people like Roy Medvedev saw reform through the party as a real hope for the USSR. It is important, however, to see that the one punishment that quite consistently followed any public and collective democratic activity was expulsion from the party. Hopes of reform from within were totally crushed at the time of the invasion of Czechoslovakia. At present the prevailing view is that the few reform-minded individuals who remain active in the party in hope of better times are totally isolated and cannot let their opinion be known. As for the growth of a new generation that might bring in democratic ideas, the process of selection is such that by the time any young person advances to a position of party influence he has so adapted to the system that there is little likelihood of his taking initiative to reform it.[44]

From all the above the democrats' position in Soviet society is clear. Though the essence of their values is firm, the ways in which they express them and define themselves is very much in flux. So too are the groupings and numbers of those who are active and sympathetic to democratic ideas. At the time of writing the democrats were very much in retreat, and the

---

44. An examination of the Soviet leaders who have come up through the Komsomol—Shelepin, Semichastny, and others—is food for thought in this respect.

evaluation offered by Rothberg appears to fit the realities of Moscow. He emphasizes the isolation of the democrats from any popular base and points out that neither the party, the workers, the peasants, government bureaucrats, nor even a majority of the intelligentsia feel any need to press for systemic change.[45]

CONCLUSIONS: THE DEMOCRATS' ROLE AND FUTURE

It is in the light of this isolation and the differences of opinion among themselves that the function of the democrats in Soviet society must be understood. It may be natural that interviewees viewed the lack of unity among dissenters as unfortunate, but it is perhaps instructive that none of them thought of it as a natural phenomenon in any large group of freely thinking individuals.

Quite clearly the democrats are not a political force in terms of offering an alternative regime, for they do not and cannot rally mass support for a defined program. They do, however, offer an alternative idea and a critical consciousness with which to examine the realities of Soviet life.

In this function, the *Chronicle* may be compared not so much to *Iskra*, as Barghoorn suggests,[46] but to a generation of radical publications of a much earlier time, which first brought new values and ideas to the attention of the Russian people. The dissemination of accurate information and the formulation of thought free of censorship, the revival and sustenance of respect for moral integrity and truthful reporting of events, the reminder that the intellectual stultification of Orwellian "doublethink" and "newspeak" is not the only genre open to the intellectual—these are the invaluable contribution of the few who dare to commit themselves to democratic action.

In the cycle of repression and relaxation that runs through Soviet life, much as it has been noted in previous Russian history, the democrats are the "yeast" that transfers the ferment of consciousness to a new generation. Thus should a crisis shake the existing regime, alternative ideas and values could be presented to the society and could develop into a political movement for reform. Even the current wave of exile and imprisonment and the interruption of the *Chronicle* do not signal the end of the dissidence or a final silencing of the democrats.

What emerges strongly in the present period is that the regime is fully prepared to use repression and fear to prevent the spread of democratic ideas and the coalescence of independent groups. Moreover, it is clear that these weapons are effective in containing the democrats and maintaining their near-total social isolation. The great majority of the intelligentsia, confronted by the overpowering hostility of the state, lapses into political

45. Rothberg, *Heirs of Stalin*, pp. 380–81.
46. Barghoorn, "General Pattern," p. 13.

apathy. The regime, through control of employment and economic benefits, networks of informers, and a variety of sanctions ranging through physical force, applies itself energetically to maintaining its power monopoly. In this sense a strong element of totalitarianism continues to dominate the Soviet system. It is perhaps this element more than any other that highlights the difficulties underlying any potential transformation of the Soviet system. It also gives a perspective to the limited nature of political change in the Soviet Union since Stalin's death and suggests that if we wish to project a timetable of liberal reform we should look ahead several generations rather than expect any swift change when the present generation of leaders leaves the scene. At present any nonregime demand for reform evokes some form of repression, for it is virtually the only response to which all levels of the party and government apparatus are attuned. As long as reform demands have no social basis to give them political weight, those articulating them are vulnerable to the regime's repression, and the demands remain outside the sphere of legitimate society. The wonder of democratic existence, then, and the human significance that far exceeds the democrats' limited numbers, is that in such circumstances there continue to exist people who surrender to neither terror nor apathy.

APPENDIX

Characteristics of Sample of Soviet Intelligentsia Interviewed

(N 40)

Age		*Party Membership*[1]	
20–29 years	9	Party	8
30–39 years	10	Nonparty	32
40–49 years	11		
50 and over	10		

Sex		*Place of Residence*	
Male	26	Moscow	23
Female	14	Vilna	4
		Kiev	3
Education		Minsk	2
Complete higher	31	Riga	2
Incomplete higher	6	Odessa	2
Secondary and technical	3	Leningrad	1
		Novosibirsk	1
Occupation		Perm	1
Teaching in higher education	8	Kishinev	1
Scientific research	10		
(Science and engineering)	3		
(Humanities and social science)	7	*Dissent Activity*	
Creative arts	6	Democratic activists[2]	8
Administration	8	Active sympathizers	6
Student	6	Passive sympathizers	21
Journalism	1	Nonsympathizers[3]	5
Worker	1	Activists in Jewish exodus movement[4]	14

[1]Six of the members had joined the Communist Party before or during World War II. The other two were young people who joined in the early sixties.

[2]Degree of activity was determined by examining participation in the following activities: preparation and distribution of *Khronika*; signing of petitions; writing samizdat of a democratic nature; regular reading of *Khronika*.

Persons who participated in *two* of the above were considered activists.

Persons participating in *one* type of activity were classed as active sympathizers.

Persons who did none of the above but expressed sympathy for the general aims and activities of the Democrats were classed as passive sympathizers.

Those who criticized the democrats as "wild," "possessed," "not serious," "ineffective" without expressing sympathy or admiration were classed nonsympathizers.

[3]The Nonsympathizers were:

Two former long-time party members;

One activist in the Jewish exodus movement;

Two nonparty and not active in other groups.

[4]Four of the activists in the exodus movement were also classed as democratic activists.

Attitudes on Great Russian Chauvinism

In discussing prospects for Soviet society, 13 individuals raised the question of Great Russian chauvinism as a major problem. The 13 were the following:

Dissent Activity		Place of Residence		Age	
Democratic activists	3	Moscow	10	30–39 years	4
Passive sym- pathizers	7	Vilna	2	40–49 years	4
Nonsympathizers	3	Kiev	1	50 and over	5
Activists in Jewish exodus movement	8				

A Note

1. On the subject of the extent of and prospects for the democrats' having close links with other sectors of Soviet society (nondemocratic intelligentsia, workers, peasants), the answers were as follows:

Democrats isolated with no prospect of influence	31
No clear answer	8
Educated sector of workers can understand and sympathize	1

2. On the subject of contact between the democrats and other dissenting groups (national and religious minorities), answers were as follows:

—Fuller cooperation can and should be sought.	6
—Cooperation should be limited for tactical reasons and should be kept hidden.	3
—Against intergroup cooperation on the grounds that energy devoted to broader and more diffuse goals of the broader movement are irrelevant to the more particular movement.	8
—Cooperation is ineffective because national and religious minorities have no general interest in democratic aims.	9
—No clear answer.	14

3. All the forty respondents claimed an interest in literary samizdat. Sixteen respondents read *Khronika* with some regularity. Three respondents had produced manuscripts of a democratic nature.

2 SOCIETY, IDEOLOGY, RELIGION

CHAPTER FOUR / DIFFERENTIATION, INTEGRATION, AND

POLITICAL DISSENT IN THE USSR / WALTER D. CONNOR

The aims of this essay are fairly straightforward, but at the outset something needs to be said about what it does not purport to do. It is not a review of the growth of dissent and opposition since the mid-1960s, and the watershed of the Sinyavsky-Daniel trial. Nor does it attempt to describe, in their full detail and diversity, the varieties of dissent and the various spectra of opinion they represent. Least of all is it an effort to analyze the complex interactions of the dissenters on the one hand and their opponents—the KGB, the officials of special psychiatric hospitals, the middle- and high-level bureaucrats of the legal system, and those who delegate to all these their responsibilities—on the other. These are all treated elsewhere in this volume.

What is offered here is a loose and tentative framework, but hopefully a useful one. Within it political dissent is viewed as a symptom of the socioeconomic changes that have taken place over a lengthy period. These changes allow us to speak of the USSR in comparison with the world's other nations as a relatively mature society. A major issue is the nature of the polity's response, in its role as manager of the whole social system, to this societal maturity. It is on this issue, to be elaborated at greater length below, that the present inquiry into the origins, nature, and potential impact of dissent in shaping the Soviet future is focused.

COMPLEXITY AND THE
PROBLEM OF INTEGRATION

The USSR is a complex society manifesting, like other modern societies, a high degree of structural differentiation. While the modernity of the USSR relative to other modern societies is a matter of some debate[1] (and is, in a sense, one of the issues of this paper), it is of a degree sufficient to place the

---

1. The meaning of this question and the answers depend, of course, on the definition of modernity. This essay does not attempt to resolve the question in any general way. But the material that follows does touch on one criterion for judging modernity—the degree of structural differentiation in a society. Soviet society *is* highly differentiated. Is this modernity? Some would say yes. Others would be less ready to agree, noting that the differentiated parts lack the autonomy they see as characterizing modern Western societies. This criterion is certainly not the only nor necessarily the most important of modernity, but it is one to which several of the authors cited herein attach considerable importance.

Soviet Union squarely among those nations whose complexity creates serious problems of coordination or integration.

Integration in traditional or primitive societies is less problematic, since such labels *signify* less differentiated, less complex systems. The distinct structural entities in such societies are relatively few and tend to be multifunctional. The family as the basic unit of production, consumption, education, and socialization is a textbook example here. Modernization of such societies—the processes of industrialization, urbanization, and the like—involves a continuing structural differentiation, a diminution of the importance of multifunctional units, and the rise of more specialized units better fitted to the performance of needed activities. Roles as well as the structures in which they are nested become more specialized. As the dissimilarity of human activities increases, so also do integrative problems. Modes of integration rooted in custom and tradition that are adequate to the integrative needs of simpler systems no longer suffice. New modes are needed if the adaptive capacity of the society is to increase. As a nation struggles, or is pushed, toward modernity, the problems of integration may become major foci of struggle in the political arena,[2] and the choice, conscious or not, of an integrative strategy may be a critical juncture in nation-building.

The choice and the potential for success of integrative strategies seem to depend in large part on three factors: the degree of differentiation (or "modernity") of the society in question in the period prior to the choice of a strategy; the content and relative vitality of the antecedent political culture (i.e., its chances of persistence); and the objectives of modernization itself. The Soviet case presents interesting divergences from the usual modernizing nation in each of these regards.

The Russian society of 1917, though severely disrupted by war and governmental collapse, was substantially more modern than it had been thirty years before and was more modern than the societies of Africa and Asia that embarked on modernization after World War II. Substantial industrialization, development of communications and transport systems, and a rate of GNP growth sufficient to move the nation near the takeoff point had been achieved since 1885.[3] The Bolshevik "modernizing elite" faced a society already fairly complex; the integrative task would be of commensurate complexity.

While war and revolution brought the end of tsarism, the political culture that was both its product and support survived. This culture was characterized by parochialism and passivity on the part of the masses, a quasi-

2. See S. N. Eisenstadt, *Modernization: Protest and Change* (Englewood Cliffs, N.J., 1966), p. 37.

3. See, on prerevolutionary development, Theodore H. von Laue, *Sergei Witte and the Industrialization of Russia* (New York, 1963). See also the essays by von Laue and Alexander Gerschchenkron in *The Transformation of Russian Society*, ed. Cyril E. Black (Cambridge, Mass., 1960).

mystical mode of relating to the tsar-autocrat, and an acceptance of the state as the promoter, coordinator and doer of a broad range of social and economic matters in the absence of a strongly developed entrepreneurial tradition.[4] Under such conditions, as Brzezinski has noted, "a democratic Russia—either liberal or socialist—does not seem to have been a real alternative."[5] A political formula, if it is to "fit" a society must be consistent with the cultural peculiarities, the level of civilization, and the prevailing notions about the bases of political obligation that characterize that society.[6] The Bolshevik formula fit fairly well, even allowing for the obvious differences between its dynamic "totalitarian" direction and that of tsarist authoritarianism.

The objectives of the Bolshevik modernization program were both transformational and defensive. The Marxist-Leninist value system clearly implied the necessity of a transformation from tradition to modernity, but national security was of no less importance. Stalin's enumeration of the defeats Russia had suffered in the past as the price of backwardness, and the objective of "socialism in one country," echoed the concerns of defensive modernizers stretching back to Peter the Great. Added to the centralism so dominant in the political culture, this concern virtually guaranteed that the system, as it grew more differentiated, would be integrated in a centralistic, "command" fashion and that *control* would become an obsessive concern of the bureaucracy that emerged to rule the society. Whether control eventually acquired the character of an end or remained a means is a matter of some debate that we need not enter here.[7] It suffices to note that control was so critical an element in the structuring of the Soviet system during its modernization that general agreement prevailed among Western analysts into the late 1950s on the totalitarian nature of the system.[8] Totalitarian

---

4. For a treatment of political culture, Russian and Soviet, see Frederick C. Barghoorn, "Soviet Russia: Orthodoxy and Adaptiveness," in *Political Culture and Political Development*, ed. Lucien W. Pye and Sidney Verba (Princeton, N.J., 1965), pp. 450–511. For another comment on cultural influences on development in tsarist and Soviet Russia, see Reinhard Bendix, *Nation-Building and Citizenship* (Garden City, N.Y.: Doubleday, Anchor Books, 1969), pp. 183 ff.

5. Zbigniew Brzezinski, "The Soviet Past and Future," *Encounter*, March 1970, p. 6.

6. See Leonard Binder, "National Integration and Political Development," *American Political Science Review* 58, no. 3 (September 1964): 625.

7. To what degree, e.g., is Hollander correct in arguing that Soviet bureaucracy "has developed primarily as a device of control and only secondly as an instrument for the management of modernization?" Can the rapid increase of state penetration into every area of life in the period after 1928 be explained as an outgrowth of a conscious commitment to maximize totalitarian control almost as an end in itself, as a result of Stalin's pathological suspicion and distrust, or as an incremental outcome of ad hoc responses to resistance against developmental objectives (e.g., the resistance to forced collectivization)? See Paul Hollander, "Politicized Bureaucracy: The Soviet Case," *Newsletter on Comparative Studies of Communism* 4, no. 3 (May 1971): 14.

8. See Carl J. Friedrich and Zbigniew K. Brzezinski, *Totalitarian Dictatorship and Autocracy*, 2d ed. (Cambridge, Mass., 1965). See also Carl J. Friedrich, ed., *Totalitarianism* (Cambridge, Mass., 1954).

integration shaped the Soviet system. Yet in a sense the nature of its tasks also shaped the totalitarian structure, the "command-centralist" style. With the successful completion of those tasks (narrowly construed, "capital accumulation;" more broadly, "system building") basically behind it, the polity underwent no marked change in substance or style until the death of Stalin. The reliance on terror declined sharply after that event, raising questions about the continued applicability of the totalitarian label. Whatever the role of terror, however, the political system's claim to command the specialized sectors of a complex Soviet society underwent no moderation. This persistence raised the question of the efficiency of such a mode of integration when extended into a period of relative societal maturity.

THE SOVIET PATTERN OF INTEGRATION

As the vogue of the totalitarian model declined among Western analysts of Soviet affairs, new models and approaches were advanced in an attempt to construct the conceptual apparatus necessary for a clearer understanding of the post-Stalin system. Among the many contributions, a few are striking in the degree to which their authors, though in different terms, concern themselves directly with the same problem of differentiation and integration.

T. H. Rigby's approach classified societies into three types—traditional, market, and organizational—according to whether the prevailing mode of integration, or coordination of social effort, was custom, contract, or command. In the customary coordination typical of traditional societies, the roles of individuals, the statutes, and the place of elites and of masses are seen as fixed and given. Neither elites nor masses negotiate for changes in the traditional definitions. Modern, complex societies typically operate by contract. Here the political elites, other elites, the labor force (through its unions), and other groups, *negotiate* the terms of their cooperation under "market" conditions. In the command mode an asymmetry of power produces a group, typically the political elite, that determines with minimum negotiation the terms of coordination, producing an organizational society. In Rigby's view, the industrial societies of the West are largely market in nature. The USSR, however, is organizational; the state-party bureaucracy *commands* other specialized sectors and does not negotiate with them.[9]

Mark Field, focusing on the processes of structural differentiation that accompany modernization, sees this differentiation as implying "a fair amount of autonomy for the differentiated spheres and the development of criteria of action specific to these spheres; it also raises the important question of the *integration of these different areas through a system of exchange of*

---

9. T. H. Rigby, "Traditional, Market, and Organizational Societies and the USSR," in *Communist Studies and the Social Sciences*, ed. Fredrick J. Fleron, Jr. (Chicago, 1969), pp. 170–187 (originally published in *World Politics* 14, no. 4 (July 1964): 539–57).

outputs [emphasis mine]." Autonomy, however, is only a tendency, and among the outcomes of differentiation is that of " 'constricted' development, a situation in which one of the differentiated spheres will attempt to dominate the others coercively by restricting and regimenting their tendencies toward autonomy." The USSR, in Field's view, is in a state of "constricted development." The various specialized spheres—science, education, the arts, communications, industry, and so on—are dominated by one sphere, the polity, which does not operate on a quid pro quo basis, does not "exchange outputs."[10]

Frederick Fleron characterizes political systems as monocratic, adaptive-monocratic, cooptative, and pluralist, depending on the way political elites acquire or gain access to essential skills that generally are in the hands of other "specialized" elites. The spectrum runs from monocracy, wherein the political elite can coerce all the skills it needs, to pluralism, where unitary, self-perpetuating political elites are absent. Fleron locates the USSR toward the middle, as a cooptative system. Such a view is open to dispute, but more critical here is his characterization of the problem faced by systems with a strain toward monocracy, the risk that "these specialized elites might attempt to trade their skills for some degree of participation in the political policy-making process."[11]

"Contract," "exchange of outputs," the "trade" of skills: fundamentally these three analysts are posing the same questions, in rather similar language, and they agree on the importance of the mode of integration in complex societies. The USSR, with a history of command integration during its construction, shows a persistence of command into its mature phases and, all in all, little movement toward contract.

Nor is this persistence difficult to explain. The state-party bureaucracy continues to be very distinct from other, "functional" elites—distinct in a number of ways that minimize the possibility of its ever being able to enter contractual or exchange relations with them. One aspect of this distinction is caught nicely in Boris Meissner's observation that there are two types of power, even in Soviet society: "the power of the top bureaucrats rests in the *positions* they hold, while that of the intelligentsia is rooted in the authority and prestige inherent in the *functions* it performs."[12]

The political elite is distinct from the other elites by virtue of the basis it claims for its own legitimacy and the recruitment practices that flow from it.

10. Mark G. Field, "Soviet Society and Communist Party Control: A Case of 'Constricted Development,' " in *Soviet and Chinese Communism: Similarities and Differences*, ed. Donald W. Treadgold (Seattle, 1967), pp. 189–90.

11. Frederick J. Fleron, Jr., "Toward a Reconceptualization of Political Change in the Soviet Union: The Political Leadership System," in Fleron, *Communist Studies*, pp. 222–43 (originally published in *Comparative Politics* 1, no. 2 [January 1969]: 228–44). The quotation is on p. 232.

12. Boris Meissner, "Totalitarian Rule and Social Change," in *Dilemmas of Change in Soviet Politics*, ed. Zbigniew Brzezinski (New York, 1969), p. 77.

The former involves assertions whose nature and language are essentially "untestable"—that the party is the sole correct interpreter of Marxism-Leninism, that Marxism-Leninism itself is the sole correct vehicle for interpreting history and the social process, that guided by it the party will make the right decisions and achieve, for the society as a whole, the best possible net balance of consequences in any situation.

It follows that those who join the political elite will be willing to accept these notions and to use them to rationalize their positions of command. The bureaucracy has little need of overly inquiring, critical minds—an essential quality in the scientific and creative intelligentsia. It does need, and does find and use, persons willing to live within the terms of this "mystification" of their dominance in return for the privileges and benefits their share of power will confer. Other performances—those of the specialists, those of the workers—can be and largely are judged by merit principles. But the performances of the bureaucratic ruling class are not. As Parkin has observed, the *"raison d'être* of the hegemonic party is to preserve political control in the hands of a social group which could not legitimate its power and privileges by reference to the same criteria which govern the distribution of rewards among the population at large."[13] These, however, are descriptions of the system at rest. With such a quality and style of leadership, what is the Soviet system's direction when this mechanism is in motion? This, essentially, is the question raised at the end of the last section of this essay, and one that Soviet political dissent of its very nature raises as well. We can now turn to examine some thoughts of analysts and dissenters alike on this question.

COMMAND AND PARASITISM

Something of a diagnostic consensus on the ills of the Soviet system was reached by a number of scholars in their contributions to a discussion in *Problems of Communism* in 1966–68 that was initiated by an essay by Brzezinski.[14] The "greater institutional maturity of Soviet society," he argued, had been important in prompting the abandonment of violence in political competition. But pattern-breaking moves by the polity had also grown more difficult, since the society was "far more developed and stable, far less *malleable* and atomized" than in the past. The party's function was less clear, the question of its relevance to the USSR of the 1960s sharply posed.

---

13. Frank Parkin, "System Contradiction and Political Transformation," *Archives euro-péenes de sociologie* 13, no. 1 (1972): 60.

14. Zbigniew K. Brzezinski, "The Soviet Political System: Transformation or Degeneration?", *Problems of Communism* 15, no. 1 (January–February 1966): 1–15. This and the other contributions to the discussion appear in book form as Brzezinski, *Dilemmas* (see n. 12 above). Pagination in citations to Brzezinski's and others' articles corresponds to that in the book version.

Soviet history in the last few years has been dominated by the spectacle of a party in search of a role. What is to be the function of an ideocratic party in a relatively complex and industrialized society, in which the structure of social relationships generally reflects the party's ideological preference? To be sure, like any large sociopolitical system, the Soviet system needs an integrative organ. But the question is, What is the most socially desirable way of achieving such integration? Is a "strong" party one that dominates and interferes in everything, and is this interference conducive to continued Soviet economic, political, and intellectual growth?[15]

Conquest saw the USSR as a nation "where the political system is radically and dangerously inappropriate to its social and economic dynamics." Barghoorn, though disagreeing with Brzezinski on the urgency of the "transformation-degeneration" dilemma, agreed that the "existing Soviet political structures and the ideology which serves as a major source of their legitimacy are increasingly irrelevant to a more and more diversified society."[16]

The substantial measure of Soviet success in the system-building phase had, in fact, created a situation in which the problems of system management were complex beyond the coordinating capacities of a political structure clinging to a "penetration" strategy when it was no longer creative.[17] Such coordination required a favorable balance of innovative over conservative tendencies in political institutions—a balance that seemed to be lacking.[18] Conquest saw in the confrontation of polity and society the "conditions of a classical Marxist prerevolutionary situation."[19]

The problems that evoked such alarming diagnoses from Western observers (and that are reflected in the less systematic but, perhaps, richer content of samizdat) seem to be reducible to two, which are interrelated: first, the quality of bureaucratic management of the economy and the larger society, and second, the style of political recruitment in a differentiated system ruled by a politicized bureaucracy.

The party elite, in the view of Western observers and some dissenters as well, lacks the expertise, flexibility, and perceptiveness necessary for the creative coordination of social and economic forces. It contributes little to the society, and, to return to a theme touched upon earlier, has few relevant "outputs" to exchange with other specialized sectors. In Meissner's words, the

15. Brzezinski, "Soviet Political System," pp. 13, 20, 26.

16. Robert Conquest, "Immobilism and Decay," in Brzezinski, *Dilemmas*, p. 72; Frederick C. Barghoorn, "Changes in Russia: The Need for Perspectives," *ibid.*, p. 41.

17. Alfred G. Meyer makes this point eloquently in his essay, "Political Change through Civil Disobedience in the USSR and Eastern Europe," in *Political and Legal Obligation: Nomos XII*, ed. J. Roland Pennock and John W. Chapman (New York, 1970), p. 423.

18. For a discussion of conservative and innovative tendencies and their importance, see Eisenstadt, *Modernization*, pp. 40, 149–50.

19. Conquest, "Immobilism," pp. 70–71.

ruling power elite is increasingly regarded as parasitic, for two reasons. In the first place, it represents a foreign body in the fabric of the elite structure of an industrialized society, since it does not submit to the economic rationality that is characteristic of an industrial merit society. The goal of promoting the conditions for existence and growth is only of secondary relevance to it. Its primary objective is the consolidation and expansion of its power base.

Second, the ruling elite is immensely exploitative of the other social groups. Through its absolute monopoly of power and unrestricted control over the means of production and property of the state, it is in a position to divert a disproportionately large share of the social product to the achievement of its political objectives, and at the same time to secure a higher personal income for its members.[20]

The Soviet dissidents S. Zorin and N. Alekseev, in their samizdat pamphlet "Time Will Not Wait," further develop the themes of exploitation and parasitism.[21] They focus on the *nomenklatura* system, which gives the Communist party control of a vast array of personnel matters and elevates the "managers" to a position virtually unassailable and remote from the masses. *Nomenklatura* is seen as a form of *property*, a kind of vested right to a well-paying job, "as inalienable as capital in a bourgeois society. It serves as a legal basis for our system much in the manner of the law of private property under capitalism." The new nomenclatured class is vertically differentiated—each level takes orders from the one above and gives them to the one below. There is no right of appeal. Career-making is the watchword in the system; success is reported upward, failure is concealed. Misinformation at the top is the result, and the exercise of elite power consequently is not necessarily integrative in effect. Zorin and Alekseev see the system as one in which "there is no proprietor, but there is an all-powerful and voracious consumer—the party-state bureaucracy."[22] The political elite emerges as the main extractor of "surplus value" in the Soviet system. Scholarly and samizdat diagnoses, then, have a common implication: the bureaucracy must rule by command rather than contract because, having no outputs to exchange, it can scarcely enter into contractual relationships.

The elite is certainly aware of the problems it faces: modest economic growth rates and recurrent agricultural crises, reconciliation of the halting degree of autonomy granted economic managers with the eternal strain toward control, and comprehending the sources, the "style," the acts of the ever-more-publicized dissidents. Its response to the latter has indicated relatively little change of perspective: an on-again, off-again campaign against dissent via the labor camp or the mental hospital, the linking of dissenters with Western imperialism and "international Zionism," and other variations on familiar themes. Amidst innovations such as the issuance of visas and

20. Meissner, "Totalitarian Rule," p. 83.
21. This pamphlet is discussed and cited in Dimitri Pospielovsky, "Programs of the Democratic Opposition," Radio Liberty Research Paper no. 38 (Munich, 1970).
22. *Ibid.*, pp. 6–9, quoting "Time Will Not Wait."

"advice" to emigrate to some dissenters, calls continue for increasing the ideological vitality of the party, for even more tough-tempered, uncompromising stands against alien ideas. Yet at the present stage, as the demands of continued economic development and adaptation press harder, it is unclear that ideology itself is relevant as a base for continued party dominance.

What of the patterns of recruitment to this troubled elite? We know little about them, less than we should like to know. Generally, we can judge the efficiency and quality of recruitment not in process but only in outcome. Who is in power, how knowledgeable are they, how successful are they, in responding to the problems they confront? Observers may well differ in their answers, but few would deny that qualities not necessarily related to objective performance—loyalty, subservience, adaptability to an often arcane set of game rules, connections and efficient use of them—are more important for advancement in the Communist Party of the Soviet Union than in bureaucracies less "politicized."[23] Such qualities are unlikely to be accompanied by readiness to pay attention to interests and pressures that may be highly significant in the long run but are not yet represented institutionally at the high-level bargaining table. Brzezinski doubts that the CPSU can remain vital when its personnel policy renders it, "almost unknowingly, inimical to talent and hostile to political innovation."[24]

The foregoing picture of parasitic mismanagement and recruiting practices emphasizing subservience and mediocrity is indeed bleak. But it is easy to go too far in reading portents of the future in it. Surely, many talented and potentially innovative persons are driven away from politics to seek careers in other sectors. But many of them remain, with their skills, ready to be tapped by the elite when they are needed.[25] If the talented do not seek political-bureaucratic careers, given the conditions of Soviet life they nonetheless cannot easily retreat into inaccessibility. Another important point involves our lack of information concerning the postwar generation of *apparatchiki* (party and government bureaucrats). Are they like their elders, or do generational factors account for more than the training and socialization (still in the hands of the elders) that marks initiation into a party-state bureaucratic career? Such questions are surely worth asking. Whatever the answer, one thing remains clear: political dissent seems to be linked in a number of ways now to be specified to the whole complex of issues, from command-centralist integration to its outcomes in a particular style of rule and recruitment. In the absence of answers to such future-oriented questions as the one raised above we can at least examine the shape of the present.

23. See Meissner, "Totalitarian Rule," pp. 77–78.
24. Brzezinski, "Soviet Political System," p. 10.
25. The evidence for the existence of coalitions of politicians *and* experts on opposing sides of policy conflicts, rather than a simple confrontation of politicians *versus* experts, provides some support for such an assertion.

DIFFERENTIATION, INTEGRATION, AND DISSENT

Soviet political dissent, it seems to me, can be regarded as both product and symptom of those aspects of the Soviet system discussed earlier: increased structural and role differentiation as a result of modernization and a response to the integrative problems thus produced that has been radically different from that developed in most Western societies. Command rather than contract has been the predominant Soviet mode of integration, and one may view the emergent complex society as a case of constricted development.

This constriction can be seen as a major cause of two distinct but related varieties of dissent. The first is the demands for more autonomy presented by members of the scientific-technical intelligentsia. Some of these demands are couched in "efficiency" terms. The costs to the social system (about whose broad outlines and direction agreement is presumed to exist) of the bureaucracy's interference in "expert" areas are cited. But increasingly the demands seem to involve claims to a larger role in goal *definition*. Critics of contemporary American society have presented their calls for restructuring of priorities in the form of "counterbudgets" and the like, and Andrei Sakharov, as one example, has done much the same. Nor is it accidental that such proposals should emerge from the intelligentsia rather than from the economic managers, a group upon whom, not too long ago, many rested their hopes of a gradual rationalization and, perhaps, liberalization of the system. By the very nature of the system in which they operate, the managers are not entrepreneurs but administrators, closer in outlook to *apparatchiki* than to other groups. The skills and abilities that provide them with the security and perquisites of their jobs are specific to the Soviet system. Their "viability" in a Western industrial society is a matter of great doubt, as it would be in a debureaucratized Soviet society. Such is not, decidedly, the case with the intelligentsia, the nature of whose work renders them marketable across ideological borders. The managers, all in all, have a stake in stability, the scientific-technical intelligentsia in change.[26]

Secondly, on a broader base, the continuing commitment to maintenance of a monolithic unity in Soviet society—in basic values, in belief systems, and in citizenship—evokes protests from the creative intelligentsia, from religious groups such as the Baptists, and from national minorities such as the Crimean Tatars. Each of these foci of protest reflects elements of complexity, or differentiation—the diverse, idiosyncratic visions of reality that lie at the base of artistic creativity, the presence of religious belief along with official atheism, the ethnic diversity of the USSR itself. While the latter two are forms of differentiation not directly related to the functional differentiation upon

26. See Parkin, "System Contradiction," pp. 54–55 for further amplification of this point.

which the argument here is largely based, they are no less important targets of a command system. A potentially critical quality of religious and national dissent is the fact that, in contrast to the dissent of the scientific-technical and creative intelligentsias, these contain the seeds of mass movements. In varying degrees they link members of the intelligentsia to the rank and file. We shall return to this point later.

In any case, it is this generalized domination by the polity that the authors of "Time Will Not Wait" attack, and it provides Sakharov as well with one of his main targets. While the party was indeed a major force, perhaps the principal force, in driving Soviet society to modernity, the result is a peculiar form of modernity, one that Shils has characterized as a "tyranically deformed manifestation of potentialities inherent in the process of modernization."[27] One of the manifestations of this deformity is a peculiarity in the way divergent interests (which are divergent by virtue of differentiation) are articulated. While in the past many would have thought interest articulation itself incompatible with a Soviet type of system, most today would probably agree with Francis Castles's observation that "totalitarian regimes are not so much antipathetic to the articulation of interests, as to the formation of groups."[28] In liberal-democratic systems (and it is in their perspective that Shils seems to find Soviet modernity deformed) the outside dissenters would move toward the formation of *associational* interest groups. But in the USSR, insofar as dissenters are organized, they are outside the law. *Institutional* interest groups—the armed forces, the police, (some) industrial managers—have a monopoly on group representation. Here is where the deformed modernity affects the articulation of political demands. The Soviet Union is highly differentiated. The existence of differentiated spheres of activity produces "criteria of action specific to these spheres" for those who perform functions within them. Yet the Soviet system provides an incommensurately small number of mechanisms for expressing demands dictated by these criteria.[29]

The recognition that institutional interest groups articulate their needs at high levels of the bureaucracy raises an interesting question: Is it possible that, at the Central Committee level or above, the party itself is penetrated by dissenting reformists—potential articulators of the interests of noninstitu-

27. Edward Shils, "Further Observation on Mrs. Huxley," *Encounter*, October, 1961, p. 45.
28. Francis G. Castles, "Interest Articulation: A Totalitarian Paradox," *Survey*, Autumn 1969, p. 127.
29. The quoted phrase is from Field, "Soviet Society," p. 190. Kornhauser's remarks are suggestive with regard to problems the Soviet system might face in a time of major crisis due to this small number of "mechanisms" (generally, recognized groups) through which interests can be articulated. "Multiple independent social groups support authority by sharing in it, that is, by themselves acting as intermediate authorities capable of ordering limited spheres of social life. In the absence of effectively self-governing groups, the state not only lacks restraint; it also lacks support." William Kornhauser, *The Politics of Mass Society* (New York, 1959), p. 136.

tional groups? Does dissidence affect some within the power structure as well as outside? On the possibility of an underground "democratic" opposition within the leadership, one student of Soviet affairs says the following:

> If, despite the persecutions and arrests, a process of democratization is in progress among the post-Khrushchev leadership, it has its own peculiar dialectical logic. The reactionary elements of the leadership (and it is they who are in power, or else there would be no persecutions) are made very uneasy by the hierarchical proximity of their more democratically inclined colleagues. In the absence of absolute autocracy, which would permit the supreme dictator to eliminate all such top-level "heretics" individually, Brezhnev, Suslov and company can only permit themselves to persecute low-level democratic and opposition circles at the present moment. Thereby they probably reckon on depriving their more democratically inclined colleagues of support among wide sections of the intelligentsia, after which it should not prove too difficult to remove these colleagues. This was exactly the method once used by Stalin against the Trotskyites and other intra-Party oppositionals: first there was a purge of the low level Party opposition, then action was taken against Trotsky, Zinoviev, Bukharin, etc.[30]

Supporting evidence for this idea may be found in the mode of approach of top-level scientists such as Sakharov. Given their experience of (relatively) close acquaintance with the corridors of power, they may have reason to believe that they contain "reasonable and moderate circles."[31] The survival of the *Chronicle of Current Events* has also caused some to wonder if the KGB itself may not be penetrated by persons sympathetic to the dissidents. Yet it seems dangerous to rely on such evidence too heavily. Such views may simply be wrong, and the KGB's failure to prevent the resurfacing of the once-suppressed *Chronicle* might be subject to other, less optimistic interpretations. In a matter so speculative, where new data, to say nothing of rumors, outdate one's observations so readily, it seems to me that thus far the burden of proof must remain with those who claim that the top leadership includes reformist elements with links to, or support in, the population of dissidents outside.

Social complexity is mirrored as well in the variety of dissent itself. Not all dissidents criticize the same aspects of the system, nor for the same reasons. The spheres of the system in which a nondissident works and lives determine to a significant degree the way he sees the world. Surely there are marked differences of this sort between a senior scientist at Akademgorodok and a general in the Soviet Army. The dissidents, of course, show similar differences. Similarly, the protests of religious and ethnic groups, reflecting non-occupational-professional fissures in Soviet society, differ from those of the scientific or artistic intelligentsia. Dissidents like Sakharov with high positions in a specialized elite—insiders—hold a certain authority rooted in

30. Pospielovsky, "Programs," p. 13.
31. *Ibid.*

the functions they perform. Their style and their prescriptions for change differ markedly in many cases from those of the outsiders like Amalrik and Marchenko. Such people have no handle by which to grasp the system, the Politburo might observe that society in no way really needs them.

For one like Sakharov, protest, logically enough, took the form of persuasion aimed at the political elite. Hence his manifesto, radical as it may be in content, is an attempt to convince the leadership, to make them see that a continuation of current policies will be counterproductive.[32] Amalrik's *Will the USSR Survive until 1984?* is a very different sort of document, part exposé, part gloomy "futurology." It and other documents such as "Time Will Not Wait" reflect the style, viewpoint, and position of outsiders, whose usual contact with the elite is through the KGB.

But dissent ranges even further than the boundaries thus far indicated. There is dissent and grumbling as well from the neo-Slavophiles (Great Russian "nationalists" and other groups *some* of which might be lumped together as a "right wing"). *Veche*, the neo-Slavophile journal, is in no sense, given the current state of Soviet internal policy, "reactionary." But manifestos such as "A Nation Speaks"[33] contain strong elements of aggressive nationalism, anti-Semitism, and racism. They thus apparently occupy a position on the spectrum of Soviet dissent similar to that of Moczar and the Partisan faction in Poland. This direction of dissent reflects, it seems, disgust and disgruntlement at even the sham internationalism of the CPSU, the foreign aid extended to "brotherly socialist countries" (which made adherents of this line strong supporters of the invasion of Czechoslovakia in 1968), and at any increase in the role played by minority nationalities even in the symbolic structures of government. These "Russites," of course, are a more easily tolerated opposition; much of their program makes them supporters of Politburo and Central Committee hard-liners. One feels that they must be well represented in the military and the KGB. Certainly the predominant ideology of the former, its rhetoric, and its criteria of action seem more nationalist than anything else.[34] Indeed, it is possible that circles within the elite encourage such an opposition as a counterweight to the democratic movement and because they realize the weakness of the phrase-mongering of contemporary official ideology as a basis for any kind of emotional linkage with the regime.[35] But to whatever degree the Russites may be manipulated by the leadership (or elements therein), it seems beyond question that their response to the Soviet system is as authentic as that of the democratic

32. Andrei D. Sakharov, *Progress, Coexistence, and Intellectual Freedom* (New York, 1968).

33. For commentary on *Veche* and on "A Nation Speaks," see D. Pospielovsky, "The Samizdat Journal *Veche*: Russian Patriotic Thought Today," Radio Liberty Research Paper no. 45 (Munich, 1971).

34. See Michael Scammell, "Soviet Intellectuals Soldier On," *Survey*, Winter 1971, p. 100.

35. See Jonathan Harris, "The Dilemma of Dissidence," *ibid.*, p. 121.

opposition. The currents of aggressive nationalism, anti-Semitism, and xenophobia are strong, and the brand of Marxism-Leninism communicated to the masses over the years has, if anything, tended to encourage them.

PRESENT AND FUTURE

The political dissent that has arisen in recent years, so impressive in its volume and in the persistence and courage it manifests, has been viewed here as emerging from an interplay of growing societal complexity and the polity's resistance to demands for autonomy based on various facets of that complexity such as technical competence, ethnic identification, and religious differentiation. This, it seems to me, is a useful way (but not the only useful way) to view dissent. It seems less clear, however, that the USSR's alternatives, at least with respect to the relatively near future, can be summarized by any such term as transformation, degeneration, adaptation, or decay.

One is forced to recall that the USSR is, after all, a very stable system.[36] The institutional framework that crystallized under Stalin by the mid-1930s remains essentially unaltered. Despite all that has been said about insecurity in office as a characteristic hampering rational administration in the USSR, the average apparatchik seems, rather, to have a tight grip on his job and thus a real stake in the system. And, in a century when most revolutions have been buried by history, few systems can boast such staying power. One that can would seem an unlikely candidate for "degeneration" at a time of relative tranquillity.[37] Though such a characterization of the present indicates reservations about the quality of change that may come in the next ten years, it is worthwhile to explore, in some measure, the future. Let us examine three of the possibilities—not an exhaustive enumeration, to be sure, but nonetheless one that will raise a number of relevant issues.

Trauma. The specter of a massive challenge to the Soviet system from exogenous pressures—most realistically, protracted and violent conflict with China—surely is present in the rhetoric of the Kremlin leadership. The probability of such an occurrence depends on so many imponderables that it must remain beyond our consideration here. Assuming such a trauma, however, what might the outcome be? Amalrik himself is unclear on this question.[38] But it seems safe to say that there is no reason to expect the rise of any democratic polity from the ashes. What might well be expected is a

36. For an eloquent argument supporting the prospective stability and staying power of the Soviet polity and institutional structure, see Tibor Szamuely's contribution to the symposium "The USSR Since Khrushchev," *Survey*, Summer 1969, pp. 51–69.

37. One might, however, raise the question (without resolving it here) of whether the Soviet system, which through so much of its history has viewed itself, often accurately, as encircled and embattled, is not more fit to remain stable under such perceived external pressures than in a situation of tranquillity promoted by a relative détente with the West.

38. Andrei Amalrik, "Will the USSR Survive until 1984?", *Survey*, Autumn 1969, pp. 76–78.

partial decomposition of the system along ethnic lines, with the larger Central Asian republics going their own way, or attempting to do so. It is well-nigh impossible to estimate the level of separatist sentiment in, let us say, Uzbekistan. But the mass nationalist feelings among Crimean Tatars and some other groups caution us not to underestimate its strength under conditions that might make secession attractive. It may well be that Soviet modernization, in its impact on educational levels, economic life, and general living standards of non-Slavic, historically "underdeveloped" nationalities, has helped create dangerous national consciousness where little existed at the time when the boundary lines of the present-day Union republics in Central Asia were drawn.

For the more developed Western nationalities, the Ukrainians and the peoples of the Baltic, the possibilities during a conflict with China are diverse. Part of the Soviet rear in such a conflict, they are likely to be well secured. Furthermore, their leanings would scarcely be pro-Chinese. Despite the evidence of nationalist sentiment in these areas, secession or disengagement from the USSR hardly seems likely; the realities of politics dictate otherwise. The situation would provide opportunities for a great deal of maneuvering on the part of the East European states but not for the Western territories of the USSR itself.

All these, however, are speculations based on a speculation of a violent Chinese-Soviet conflict. Such towers of speculation are arguably of little use at present. Nationalist dissent is a fact of Soviet life today and is ever more evident, for the growth of ethnic-national currents within samizdat is striking. But it is probably most reasonable to say that the issues it raises will be dealt with in a Soviet system at peace in the more or less foreseeable future.

Transformation of the Elite. The possibility that recruitment to the elites of the late 1970s and the 1980s will produce a new sort of leadership deserves attention. Two bases of such a transformation have claimed the attention of many analysts: the simple fact of generational change and, for want of better words, the "technologization" or "professionalization" of party leadership.

Would a generation raised in the post-Stalin era be more responsive than the present leaders to a diverse set of interest groups, many of which are now denied legitimacy? Jonathan Harris notes the feelings of some of the younger intelligentsia that a new generation, while "now obliged to repeat the slogans of their superiors," does this as dissimulation and "will be more willing to dismantle the controls over intellectual life when it takes over the reins of leadership in the 1970's and 1980's. As one student insisted, the coming generation of CPSU leaders will be as receptive to new ideas as to jazz and mini skirts."[39] Hopeful optimism, indeed—and, given our limited access to Soviet society, such hopes, held by those who are part of it, should be taken

39. Harris, "Dilemma of Dissidence," pp. 118-19.

seriously. Yet some pessimism is in order as well. The CPSU is, after all, very much a minority of Soviet society, and the segment of it that occupies the seats of real power is even smaller. It has been careful in the matters of intake and promotion. Even if a gap exists in the USSR between older and younger political generations, with most of the youth on the relatively liberal side (and this is still quite questionable), there will certainly be a sufficient supply of younger cadres similar in outlook to the current *apparat* to allow continuity of the current pattern well into the 1980s. Such persons, it seems to me, are the current recruits. Can we assume that their "repetition of slogans" is merely an instrument of self-protection, or is it evidence of the same poverty of ideas that marks their elders? Aging men in the Politburo and the Central Committee oppose today a movement of dissenters generally younger than they. Is it not possible that tomorrow groups more closely matched by age will still oppose each other? We have little evidence, but what we do have surely does not demonstrate the contrary.

What of the other possibility, a "technologized" elite? First, it should be noted that this implies a very different, more profound change than a gradual rise in the educational levels of the bureaucracy. The latter is a fact, pointed to with pride in the USSR. The scenario is, rather, one of a realization that control can only be maintained on the basis of the elite's having a command of knowledge and skills equalling that of the intelligentsia, to be ensured by recruiting only persons with equivalent education and training. Yet, as Parkin observes, such a change would involve "the risk of secularizing the party"—changing the base of its legitimacy and making problematic the rationale for its continued separate existence as integrator.[40] We see little readiness for this in today's USSR, despite the growth of the rhetoric of "scientific management" (*nauchnaia organizatsiia truda, nauchnoe upravlenie obshchestvom*). The qualifications of cadres may rise constantly, but, in Parkin's words,

> As long as the attainment of the party's historic mission is felt to depend on men with distinctive attributes of loyalty and obedience, then the party apparatus is likely to continue to choose its own successors with care. And men whose primary commitment is to the political bureaucracy, whose rewards and privileges, authority and influence are dependent on this commitment are, by this very fact, a clearly demarcated social group, whatever purely technical qualities they may have in common with other men.[41]

As general levels of education continue to grow in the USSR, there is no compelling reason to feel that the supply of such men will be insufficient.

Persistence and Stability. The most obvious and direct indications we possess as to the shape of the future are rooted in the past and the present. As noted above, the past has shown that the Soviet system is impressively

40. Parkin, "System Contradiction," p. 59.
41. *Ibid.*, p. 61.

stable. The "birth traumas" of industrialization at a forced pace and collectivization were successfully negotiated; during the purges, the war, and the aftermath the system retained its essential shape. In the present, within this system, the apparatchiki, however unappealing and mediocre their style and appearance, are firmly in control. If there is dissent in the top levels of party and state, the conservatives seem to have the advantage over any reformist elements. The status quo–oriented elite is scarcely in a state of paralysis, whatever the novelty of the challenges it has faced since 1965. Nor does it appear likely to lose that advantage when one considers three aspects of the system today: interest articulation, political culture, and the balance of resources.

Interests do get articulated in the Soviet polity—not all interests, but certainly those that seem critical for the survival of the system. The large institutional interest groups are, one way or another, taken care of. They are not ignored, for they are important stays of this very stable system as presently constituted. This is scarcely the case with the dissenters. The system has, in general, ignored them and their demands without thus far incurring costs it cannot bear. Once again the burden of proof seems to fall on those who argue that failure to respond to the dissidents' demands must have important consequences.

Political culture links the bureaucratic elite and the masses more closely than it links the dissidents to either. The antecedent political culture of tsarist Russia fit relatively well with the emergent Stalinist institutional framework at the most critical points. To all appearances, the contemporary political culture still fits this largely unchanged institutional pattern quite nicely. Soviet political culture, as expressed in the attitudes and the general mental set of the masses toward the polity, might be said to be in a state of arrested development when compared with some other successfully modernizing countries. The masses do not demand legality, representative institutions, freedom; these are unfamiliar and exotic concepts. Their economic demands are modest—housing, consumer goods, food—and they are being satisfied, albeit with interruptions. Many, certainly, have never been better off. Most have never heard of the dissidents so well known in the West. Those who have react with hostility or incomprehension, in either case hardly justifying the relative optimism some (but by no means all) dissidents have about the "popular masses."[42] Dissent and dissenters may be a natural product of over fifty years of Soviet history, but just as natural is their failure to strike a responsive chord among the masses. The interest in freedom and the rule of law is not broad enough, is not sufficiently a "mass" interest, to make its accommodation critical.

Finally comes the problem of resources—resources of the sort that, mobilized, equal power. No extended discussion of the nature of such resources in the Soviet case can be attempted here; yet a quick look may

42. See Pospielovsky, "Programs," pp. 15–17.

serve to make the point. Who controls finance, jobs, the preponderance of information available to the masses? Who has legitimacy in the masses' eyes, insofar as this can be measured? Who presently commands enough specialized expertise to keep the system running? In each of these cases the answer seems clear—the party-government elite, which, despite the absence of any institutionalized arrangements for the transfer of power at the top, has proved durable and able to replenish itself. By comparison, the resources of those who would change the system are meager. One can accept Robert Dahl's assertion that advanced economies "automatically distribute political resources and political skills to a vast variety of individuals, groups, and organizations" but still, along with Dahl, acknowledge the looseness of fit between economic levels and political systems.[43] The technical intelligentsia has essential skills, but most of its members cannot be numbered among the dissidents. The dissidents often show courage, idealism, an ability to invent ways to challenge the bureaucracy; yet the bureaucracy still commands the forces of coercion.

FINAL CONSIDERATIONS

The image of the ruling bureaucracy as immobile is a striking one. As we have seen, the tendency of analysts has been to ascribe various critical consequences in the Soviet system to this immobility. Yet to say that the bureaucracy "is at once a barrier to significant change and a major pillar of the frozen stability of Soviet society"[44] is not to indicate that the situation must or will change drastically. Stability may be conserved in ways that involve neither immobilism nor transformation.

Indeed, the notion of an immobile polity has been subjected to challenge on a number of grounds, most notably by Jerry Hough. While space does not permit a detailed discussion of his arguments supporting a view of the Soviet system as more adaptive, his observation that the notion of an immobilized system is vague is one worthy of attention. In the end, the question of whether the system is immobile or not "is not susceptible of a definitive answer, except perhaps by a future historian who will have the advantage of knowing what has occurred during the rest of this century."[45]

It is, of course, always easier to predict "stability"—the persistence of contemporary patterns—than to pick the most plausible among radical departures from these patterns. This course in essence has been the one adopted in the present essay's treatment of the Soviet future. Yet such predictions seem doomed to error at some point, since all things change,

43. Robert A. Dahl, *Polyarchy: Participation and Opposition* (New Haven, Conn. and London, 1971), pp. 71–80.
44. Hollander, "Political Bureaucracy," p. 18.
45. Jerry Hough, "The Soviet System: Petrification or Pluralism?", *Problems of Communism* 21, no. 2 (March–April, 1972): 41.

even though the USSR changes more slowly than other large societies. Moves toward more rational administration in the Soviet system are evident. "Scientific organization of labor" and "scientific administration of society" are not simply rhetoric, though their impact thus far is difficult to gauge. Similarly, the broad profiles of Soviet society are changing rapidly: as one sociologist observed in 1969, the average annual increase of "scientific workers" amounted to 12.3 per cent, that of industrial workers only 3.5 per cent. The number of scientific workers doubled between 1950 and 1960 and doubled again between 1960 and 1966.[46] Should one then look for a time when broad claims will be advanced on the part of a large intelligentsia against the political bureaucracy, as they were in Czechoslovakia during the "Prague spring"? One such claim was Pavel Machonin's critique of a society where the "complexity and quality" of a person's work do not at all correspond to his share of social management and where differentials in rewards and a share in determining the direction of society ran in the wrong direction and were insufficient for a "mature socialist society" and its immediate needs.[47] The Sakharov manifesto seems to hint at a similar point, noting the desirability of establishing "unified wage rates based on the social value of labor and an economic market approach to the wage problem."[48] To do so, it seems, would subject the bureaucracy itself to the same criteria of performance it imposes on the rest of society, and this has not yet happened in either society.

Thus while one can, even within a general framework of stability, see changes occurring that presumably will not be without effect, it is well-nigh impossible to predict what that effect will be. The Czech reform movement brought together, if somewhat uneasily, the intelligentsia and the workers; but, as Zygmunt Bauman has observed, this circumstance reflected the special character of Czechoslovakia, where the "socialist revolution" had not been, as it was in the USSR and most other East European states, a modernizing force.[49] If the Soviet intelligentsia, or its dissident sections, can ever find a common cause with the workers, one may expect surprising and perhaps revolutionary events. But for now that base is missing, and if it ever develops this will happen only in the distant future.

46. See S. A. Kugel', "Izmenenie sotsial'noi struktury sotsialisticheskogo obshchestva pod vozdeistviem nauchno-tekhnicheskoi revoliutsii" [Changes in the social structure of the socialist society under the impact of scientific-technical revolution], *Voprosy filosofii*, 1969, no. 3, pp. 18–19.

47. Pavel Machonin, "Sociální rozvrstvení naší společnosti" [Social classification of our society], *Nová mysl*, 1968, no. 4, pp. 466–74; English trans., *JPRS Political Translations on Eastern Europe*, no. 351 (May 31, 1968), pp. 42–53.

48. Sakharov, *Progress*, p. 77.

49. Zygmunt Bauman, "Social Dissent in the East European Political System," *Archives européenes de sociologie* 12, no. 1 (1971): 49.

CHAPTER FIVE / RECENT UNCENSORED SOVIET

PHILOSOPHICAL WRITINGS / GEORGE L. KLINE

1

This chapter is devoted to only three authors: Alexander Sergeyevich Yesenin-Volpin, Valery Nikolayevich Chalidze, and Grigory Solomonovich Pomerants. I do not include Andrei Sinyavsky for two unrelated reasons: I have already discussed some of the central themes of his *Mysli vrasplokh* (Thoughts taken unawares) of 1966,[1] and his new book, *Golos iz khora* (A voice from the chorus), published in England in September 1973, was not available to me when I was writing this essay.

In contrast to Soviet philosophical writings subject to the censorship (both self-censorship and *glavlit*-type censorship), which exhibit a depressing uniformity,[2] these three authors show considerable diversity of both views and style. Volpin and Chalidze are fairly similar and are about equally distant from Pomerants. This is not simply a result of age differences. Both Pomerants (b. 1917) and Volpin (b. 1925) came to intellectual maturity at the height of Stalinism; Chalidze (b. 1938) reached intellectual maturity in the post-Stalin era (the late 1950s). The works I shall focus on were all written within a period of three or four years: Volpin's "O logike nravstvennykh nauk" (On the logic of the moral sciences) in late 1970, Chalidze's "Razmyshleniia o cheloveke" (Reflections on man) in mid-1971, and Pomerants's "Chelovek niotkuda" (The man from nowhere) between 1967 and 1969.[3] All three men share a concern with the disciplines of ethics and social philosophy; all three are deeply committed to the defense of human freedom. All three display considerable irony and wit—features conspicuously

1. See my "Religious Ferment Among Soviet Intellectuals," in *Religion and the Soviet State: A Dilemma of Power*, ed. Max Hayward and William C. Fletcher (New York, 1970), pp. 59–60; and, for a more detailed discussion, which includes Sinyavsky's fiction and his introduction to the 1965 Moscow edition of Pasternak's poetry, see my "Religious Themes in Soviet Literature," in *Aspects of Religion in the Soviet Union: 1917–1967* ed. Richard H. Marshall, Jr., *et al.* (Chicago, 1972), pp. 162–63, 167–68, 170–74.

2. Two noteworthy exceptions: (1) the late Oleg Drobnitsky, though militantly Marxist-Leninist in his views, possessed a crisp, forceful, and sometimes sparkling style. (He died young in the crash of a Soviet jetliner in October 1972.) (2) Alexander Ianov, a literary critic and historian of ideas, has written knowledgeably, concisely, and often wittily about certain nineteenth-century Russian thinkers. See, for example, his "Slavianofily i Konstantin Leont'ev," *Voprosy filosofii*, no. 8 (1969): 97–106, and my discussion in "Religion, National Character, and the 'Rediscovery of Russian Roots,' " *Slavic Review* 32 (1973): 29, 30, n. 6, 34–36. (Ianov left the Soviet Union late in 1974 and now lives in the United States.)

3. I shall refer to certain other essays and sketches by Pomerants that date from the middle and early 1960s. All are collected in G. Pomerants, *Neopublikovannoe* (Frankfurt, 1972).

absent from "official" Soviet philosophy. Pomerants is characteristically eloquent but sometimes vague; Volpin and Chalidze are characteristically precise but sometimes austere.

Volpin and Chalidze are more interested in questions of logic and methodology than Pomerants.[4] They aspire to rigor and system, at least in the sense of connected and sequential exposition.[5] They are secularists[6] and rationalists. Because of their active involvement in the dissident movement in defense of human rights, they pay a good deal of attention to problems of law and jurisprudence. But Pomerants isn't much interested in those subjects. He aspires to insight and wisdom. His exposition tends to be essayistic and aphoristic. He is a deeply religious man, although his religious convictions include Buddhist, and even Vedanta, as well as Christian elements. His position thus contrasts with that of Solzhenitsyn and Sinyavsky, both of whom are wholly committed to Russian Orthodox Christianity. Pomerants accepts one kind of rationality (*razumnost'*) but is critical of "dry, abstract, manipulative rationality [*rassudochnost'*]." He frequently, and pejoratively, employs the Slavophile terms *rassudok* and *rassudochnost'*, terms not used by Volpin and Chalidze, for whom there is only one reason, *razum*, and one rationality, *razumnost'*.

It would be tempting to call Volpin and Chalidze neo-Westernizers (*novozapadniki*) and Pomerants a neo-Slavophile (*novoslavianofil'*). But Pomerants, more forcefully than anyone else I know, has repudiated the general xenophobia and the particular anti-Semitism of both the nineteenth-century Slavophiles and—especially—the contemporary Soviet neo-Slavophiles or neo-*pochvenniki*.[7] Thus he must be grouped among the critics of Slavophilism. But he is no ordinary Westernizer, and his writings give evidence of a deeper immersion in Russian culture than either Volpin's or Chalidze's. He cites, usually with clear approval, such Russian thinkers and writers as Dostoevsky, Solovyov, Rozanov, Berdyaev, Tsvetaeva, and Mandelshtam. In their works considered here Volpin and Chalidze cite *no* Russian thinkers or writers.

Some of these differences are no doubt due to differences in education and professional specialization. Pomerants is an orientalist, with training in history, philosophy, and the study of religion; Volpin is a logician and

---

4. However, Pomerants touches on methodological questions in two essays, "Dve modeli poznaniia" [Two cognitive models] and "Tri urovnia bytiia" [Three levels of existence], in *ibid.*, pp. 53–71 and 73–87. Pomerants's approach to methodology is perceptibly more "speculative" and less "analytic" than that of either Volpin or Chalidze.

5. In an earlier essay Volpin is quite unsympathetic to systematic philosophers. He claims that philosophers do not have to be, and perhaps cannot be, systematic. See A. S. Yesenin-Volpin, "Svobodnyi filosofskii traktat" [A free philosophical treatise], in his *A Leaf of Spring* (New York, 1961), p. 110.

6. Volpin is militantly secularistic and anticlerical, but Chalidze shows both tolerance and sympathy for religious beliefs and practices.

7. See my "Religion, National Character," especially pp. 30–32, 37, 39.

mathematician who has specialized in mathematical logic and the foundations of mathematics; Chalidze is a theoretical physicist. A further difference is that, since 1972, Volpin and Chalidze have been involuntary exiles, living in the United States; Pomerants remains in Moscow.

In what follows I discuss the writings of Volpin (sec. 2), Chalidze (sec. 3), and Pomerants (sec. 4), and then make some comparative and generalizing remarks by way of conclusion (sec. 5).

2

In the Afterword of his "Free Philosophical Treatise" (1959), Volpin reported the remark of a friend who, having heard a summary of the work's arguments, said to him: "Then you believe only in thought and reason?" Volpin responded: "Yes, for of course there is nothing else to believe in. And in fact one doesn't have to *believe* in these things. You shouldn't believe in reason. For a thinking human being it is enough to *be* rational."[8]

This is a fair statement of the extreme rationalism which permeates Volpin's 1970 work. He begins by asserting that:

[In this system] the primary role should be allotted to the struggle against the necessity of [religious or ideological] faith and the development, as far as possible, of universal and irreproachable methods of proof.[9]

In building a foundation for any science faith must be wholly eliminated. But Volpin admits—somewhat grudgingly, I think—that faith "may be necessary in various spheres of human activity" and adds that the "right to have faith constitutes an inalienable part of freedom of thought" (p. 7).

Sounding as self-confident and as unhistorical as an eighteenth century *philosophe*, Volpin declares that "in the history of human thought the need for faith was called forth by a weakness in the ability to reason and to argue, a weakness that can be overcome only by widening and deepening logic" (p. 8). As for 'faith' in the sense of 'shared belief'—whether that of a religion or a secular ideology—Volpin notes that "faith is demanded as a necessary condition for the continuation of joint activity among people" and admits that "such demands have a practical use." But, he hastens to add, "they limit freedom of doubt as well as freedom of thought in general" (p. 8). Further, "any moral system, any legal system demanding even the smallest degree of faith limits freedom of thought," and there is "no rational basis for having confidence in the judgments" of one who accepts such demands (p. 9).

---

8. "Svobodnyi," p. 170.
9. "O logike nravstvennykh nauk," p. 3. Later Volpin adds that faith or belief (*vera*) involves accepting a proposition as true without proof; hence faith always involves the risk of error (p. 7). Page references to "O logike," given in parentheses in the text, will be to the Russian typescript in *Obshchestvennye problemy* (Moscow, 1971), pp. 3–68. I shall use the unpublished English translation by Elaine Ulman and Karen Andreason, with certain terminological revisions, for direct quotations.

Volpin insists that everyone must have the unlimited right to ask "Why?"—"the question that destroys faith"—and to demand proof. By *proof* of a proposition Volpin means any honest method (here 'honest' means 'not characterized by either force or fraud'; these two concepts remain undefined, though Volpin promises to define them in a future work) that renders the proposition incontestable.

By 'moral sciences' (*nravstvennye nauki*), Volpin tells us, he means ethics and jurisprudence, the theoretical disciplines that have as their subject matter morality and law, respectively. He is confident that the development of the "logic of the moral sciences" will produce "important preconditions for moral progress," even though theorizing will have to be supplemented by active struggle—in particular the struggle against falsehood and deception, the first and worst of human vices because they serve to screen all the others.

Volpin distinguishes between *rules* (which include permissions, demands, and prohibitions), *goals* or *ends* (*tseli*), and *requests, commands*, and the like (p. 6). He goes on to develop what he calls the "logic of confidence [or trust]" (*logika doveriia*), including the "critique of confidence" (*kritika doveriia*) (pp. 12–14). I omit details and turn to what Volpin says about the role of modal logic in the moral sciences.[10] He distributes the modalities of possibility, actuality, and necessity among five kinds of logic: (1) "deontic" logic ('deontic' meaning 'having to do with obligations'), where 'possible' means 'permitted' or 'allowed' and 'necessary' means 'required'; (2) "optative" logic (which deals with ends or goals and the means for realizing them); and, finally, three kinds of "alethic" ('truth-related') logic: (3) "instrumental" logic (translating Volpin's *organicheskii*, which clearly refers to *organon* in the Greek sense of 'tool' or 'instrument' rather than to organism in the biological sense), (4) epistemic logic, and (5) ontological logic (p. 15). I forego further discussion of the last three; it is the deontic and optative kinds of modal logic with which Volpin is most concerned.

Modalities, he insists, are always related to circumstances. What is possible in certain circumstances may be impossible in others. The circumstances that face an agent, when described with sufficient precision, are termed his "situation." Volpin writes:

> In situation S, to follow the rule permitting or requiring one to perform act A *in S* means to perform A in S. Only a requirement can be violated, and breaking the requirement A in S consists of performing the *opposite* act in S (i.e., not-A, or B, if A is not-B) (p. 19).

Rules are not judgments, hence they are neither true nor false.

According to Volpin, a given act A may be simultaneously prohibited and permitted in a given situation S. But if permission for A turns out to be

---

10. He had noted the need to develop such logics more than a decade earlier. See "Svobodnyi," p. 166.

inapplicable in *S*, then one must obey the prohibition, which now "represents a demand" (pp. 21–22).

He notes that:

in jurisprudence one runs across such *clashes* between permissions and prohibitions fairly often, in fact it would be difficult to avoid them. . . . But there is a need to distinguish such cases of permissions [*razresheniia*] from the rest. For this reason I will call the *allowance* [*pozvolenie*] or *authorization* [*dozvolenie*] of *A* in *S* (from the method side) the presence (in that method) of permission for *A* in *S* in the absence of the prohibition of *A* in *S* (p. 22).

In the sphere of deontic modalities we must, Volpin insists, distinguish between the impossibility of act *A* and the obligatoriness of not-*A*.

A method may be "incomplete" in two different ways:

(1) It may permit several different acts, such as *A*, *B*, . . ., in situation *S* without indicating any grounds for choosing between them. Such a situation Volpin calls "Buridanian" (after Buridan's ass, which is supposed to have starved when placed between two equidistant piles of hay). It is not always possible to perform all of the permitted acts; they may be mutually incompatible. If taste (a "tactic of preference") decides, as Volpin suggests, then it would seem that the choice is arbitrary.

(2) There may simply be no rule that is applicable to act *A* in situation *S*. In such cases the incomplete method is completed either by the "principle of liberalism," according to which everything not prohibited by the method is permitted by the regime, or else by the "principle of despotism," according to which everything not permitted by the method is prohibited by the regime (pp. 23–24).

In the first case the distinction between permissions and authorizations does not play any role (that is, permission automatically leads to authorization), but in the second case what is not permitted must be specified (since what is permitted but not authorized has already been prohibited by the method) (p. 24).

According to Volpin, there is a general confusion of the concepts 'not permitted' and 'forbidden'; this confused identification rests on the assumption that every act is either permitted or forbidden. In fact, such an assumption is justified only in the case of a "complete" method.

For any activity and any of its situations *S*, authorization of *A* in *S*, "contained" in the rules of the activity, is the *basis* [or ground; *osnovanie*] for performing act *A* in *S* (pp. 25–26).

The demand that every phase of an activity be completed only after the basis for that phase has been demonstrated Volpin calls—using a rather odd term—the "fundamentary [*fundamentarnyi*] regime of the activity" (p. 26).[11]

---

11. Volpin goes so far as to distinguish between what he calls the "despotic" and the "fundamentary" senses of the adverb *tol'ko* (only) (p. 27).

Aiming for maximal freedom and the elimination of all unnecessarily limiting rules, one must subordinate activity in the establishment of morality (i.e., systems of rules of conduct) to the fundamentary regime so that only grounded limitations enter into morality. The same is true in relation to legislative activity (p. 26).

In jurisprudence, the principle *nullum crimen sine lege* ("there is no crime without a law") corresponds to the principle of liberalism. But it would be premature to conclude, Volpin says, that everyone has the right to perform any act not expressly forbidden. For example:

The law does not prohibit anyone from becoming the victim of a crime, but at the same time the law cannot require a court to grant the suit of anyone who insists on his right to become [such] a victim (p. 28).

Volpin's discussion of freedom is original, complicated, and in some respects puzzling. He stipulates the meaning of the term *svobodnyi* (which I shall translate as 'free$_1$') as 'unobstructed' and the meaning of *vol'nyi* ('free$_2$') as 'uncoerced' or 'uncompelled' (*nevynuzhdënnyi*). Thus *svoboda* ('freedom$_1$') means 'unobstructedness'; *vol'nost'* ('freedom$_2$') means 'uncoercedness'. It follows, for Volpin, that an agent or an act can be free$_2$ because uncoerced but at the same time unfree$_1$ because obstructed; or free$_1$ because unobstructed but still unfree$_2$ because compelled (pp. 39–40).[12]

Ordinary language uses these terms inconsistently, creating a powerful obstacle to their correct usage. Therefore a term is needed designating the combination of freedom$_1$ and freedom$_2$; I will designate this combination by the Greek word *eleutheria* ('freedom'), and I will call free$_1$ and free$_2$ acts or activities, as well as free$_1$ and free$_2$ agents, *eleutheric* (p. 40).

Thus an eleutheric act or agent is both uncoerced and unobstructed and eleutheria is a complex (relational) quality combining uncoercedness with unobstructedness.

Volpin recognizes that the terms 'eleutheria' and 'eleutheric' are not entirely felicitous—and not just because they are Greek. He suggests a narrower sense of the terms, which would make 'eleutheric' synonymous with 'both free$_1$ and independent' (p. 40). This is a narrower (more restrictive?) sense because, according to Volpin, independence is a narrower (more limited?) quality than freedom$_2$. Thus the quality which results from combining independence with freedom$_1$ would be narrower in this sense than that which results from combining freedom$_2$ with freedom$_1$.

---

12. Volpin does not use subscript numerals. But since standard English has only two possible candidates for the roles of *svoboda* and *vol'nost'*, namely 'freedom' and 'liberty,' and since (1) these terms are synonyms and (2) 'liberty' lacks an adjectival form parallel to 'free,' some such distinguishing device is needed. (*Svoboda* and *vol'nost'* are also synonyms in standard Russian.)

Volpin considers it an analytic truth, one based on the "principle of deontic-instrumental necessity,"[13] that the better is always preferred to the worse. But tastes (or "tactics of preference") differ; cases of apparent choice of the worse involve evaluations of better and worse based on a tactic of preference distinct from that employed by the observer to whom the choice appears the worse. Put more simply: A chooses X, which seems to him better than Y; B judges that A has chosen the worse, since to B, Y seems better than X. This explanation strikes me not only as positivistic and relativistic in the extreme, but also as thin and unconvincing.

According to Volpin, human action (*deiatel'nost'*) may take the form of either a field of action (*poprishche*) or a particular activity (*aktivnost'*), which in turn is made up of a series of connected acts (*postupki*). The field of action he characterizes, somewhat austerely, as an "abstract process formed by all possible acts of a given sort performed within the limits of conceivable activities" (p. 42). For example, a given chess game is a particular activity, consisting of moves performed in succession according to definite rules, while the game of chess as such is the chessplayer's field of action.

Since acts obstruct each other, thus restricting the freedom$_1$ of their agents, limitations must be introduced. These limitations "primarily concern the freedom$_1$ of acts necessary for the field of action or for its goals, but also for the goals of the activities being carried out in this field" (p. 44). In general, according to Volpin, the freedom$_1$ of given acts is more important than independence or freedom$_2$ for the goals of the field of action.

In formulating a moral system, Volpin asserts, one must follow a fundamentary regime. But if the acceptance of one demand creates a dead end, exceptions may be allowed.

A system of morality or a legal code is just, for Volpin, if every one of its demands as well as any permitted exceptions to these demands is well grounded. In such a case, he says, the "principle of sufficient reason" has been applied to morality or law in the general form of a demand that every rule be grounded.

Volpin sees the principle of equality before the law, or equality of rights, not as essential to justice but only as an important way in which justice is manifested in the contemporary world. A commanding general and a common soldier have equal rights only in the (weak) sense that anyone who is a commanding general has the same rights and responsibilities as anyone else occupying that role, and anyone who is a common soldier has the same rights and responsibilities as anyone else occupying *that* role. But this is an "emasculation" of the principle of equal rights. Nevertheless, those who seek justice today (rightly) accept this "emasculated" principle.

---

13. The full statement of this principle is: "If process E is described by method M, the rules of which include a demand that act A be performed in situation S, then it is instrumentally [*organicheski*] necessary for the continuation of E in S that A be performed in S" (p. 29).

Rather than setting up a demand to tell the truth, or the "whole truth," Volpin would simply prohibit intentional lying. There are various (perhaps trivial) cases, he explains, where failure to tell the truth, or the whole truth, does not involve lying—for example, when a mathematician adopts a false premise in order to refute it or when an actor refers to himself on stage as "Hamlet."

The struggle against falsehood is basic to morality, but it must be carried on fairly. Thus, Volpin writes:

Each individual must be protected by legislation from false accusations of lying, and lying itself must be prosecuted by means more just than criminal penalties. The natural punishment for a liar is to be exposed [as such] and (for a reasonable period) denied confidence (p. 62).

Eleutheric morality, according to Volpin, must either evade or resist ideological power—where 'ideology' means 'a system of prejudices significant for morality' (p. 52). Volpin admits that what he calls "ideological moralities"—presumably including various religiously based moralities— seek to further mutual aid among human beings. Eleutheric morality should not oppose this tendency but should emphasize noninterference in other people's affairs.

The "principle of rational choice," as applied to means, gives preference to those means that do not preclude the eventual adoption of other, temporarily excluded, means. This principle is often violated in the name of the "principle of urgency" (*nasushchnost'*), which gives preference to those means that are obviously effective in the immediate situation. This, according to Volpin, is a special case of the "preference of the interests of the present over those of the future," a principle which can be rationally grounded only when neglect of present interests threatens the very continuation of a field of action.

The principle of rational choice gives preference to those rights that help to protect other rights. When normal life is threatened, as by war or natural disasters, generally recognized rights may (justly) be limited, but only to the extent necessary to meet such threats.

Volpin lists a number of rights that, he maintains, must be upheld by eleutheric ethics, according to the principle of rational choice:

(1) *The right to the defense of every* (other?) *right* must be recognized as the supreme right.

In relation to recognized rights, this supreme right must include recognition of the right to fight against any threat to violate recognized rights and to fight for their restoration wherever they have been violated (p. 54).

This recognition must include the recognition of the right to struggle to assert unrecognized rights.

(2) Next in importance is the *right to freedom$_1$ and freedom$_2$ of thought* (i.e., the unobstructed and uncoerced right to form and express opinions).

This right, Volpin asserts somewhat puzzlingly, entails recognition of the *right to life and health*. But since life, according to Volpin, should be free$_2$ as well as free$_1$ (i.e., uncoerced as well as unobstructed), the recognition of the right to life must be accompanied by a recognition of the *right to suicide*.

(3) The *right to leave a given society* must be universally recognized, since participation in the life of any society must be uncoerced. This right is "limited only by the demand that the fulfillment of obligations stemming from just demands of the morality and laws of that society be guaranteed" (p. 55).

(4) The *right of association with others* to attain one's goals or to exercise one's rights must be universally recognized and is limited only by just demands intended to prevent the formation of associations that threaten the eleutheria of others.

Volpin goes on to list a number of more specific rights—of freedom of travel, expression, assembly, choice of a field of action and one's role within that field, the right to fair trial, to public-health care, and so on.

Apparently assuming the deterrent force of punishment, Volpin says that legislators in setting penalties should go no further than is necessary to produce a "loss of the desire to commit a crime . . . on the part of a potential criminal" (p. 56). He sees contemporary criminal law as greatly exceeding such limits. Attempts to justify a five-year prison term for a given crime rather than a four-year or a six-year term are futile, he remarks, since "in the overwhelming majority of cases" *any* prison term at all is unjust.

What Volpin somewhat controversially calls "logical" connections should, he insists, be established between the seriousness of each crime and the severity of its punishment. He says, for example, that "logic" can help remove such present injustices as harsher penalties for rape than for first-degree murder. He gives no example of a criminal code with this characteristic.

Volpin admits that criminal law must forbid not only criminal acts but also whatever tends toward them, since "the chief end of criminal legislation is precisely the prevention of crime" (p. 58). The attempt to commit a crime may itself be considered a crime; but this principle must not be carried too far. Acquiring poison in order to commit murder, for example, is a dangerous attempted crime. But to punish the would-be murderer for acquiring the poison would unjustly penalize an attempt at an attempt. Volpin insists that one must call a halt long before the point is reached where it would be considered a criminal act to walk toward a pharmacy with the intention of inquiring about how to obtain poison.

Repressive criminal laws are often accepted by an indifferent public because they do not seem to affect its interests directly. Most people do not wish to leave the country of their birth, so they passively accept intolerable limitations on this right. Volpin offers a more fanciful example that combines his present point with the earlier one: No one can jump over his house, so a law prohibiting such an act would be taken very casually. But if such a law also forbade the attempt to commit this "crime," then a policeman who saw someone running toward his house might suspect him of such an attempt.

According to Volpin, statutes of limitation rest on two sound principles: (1) moral agents change with the passage of time, and (2) it is wrong to punish an agent who is not guilty of a given crime. The clear implication is that, say, A, who committed a crime at time t_1, is no longer the same moral agent and hence is not culpable at time t_2 if the interval between t_1 and t_2 is sufficiently long. Volpin does not specify a minimum time lapse but mentions that it would be "awkward" to punish a person for a crime which he had committed twenty years earlier. Of course, the difficult and controversial cases concern not twenty but three, five, or seven-year periods. Volpin says nothing about these nor about differences among moral agents in maintaining "personal identity" in the required sense through given time periods.

Volpin insists that the rules of judicial procedure must be scrupulously observed and must be made public. Violations of the principle of "the public's right to know" (*glasnost'*) make possible further violations in judicial procedure such as improperly assigning the burden of proof or failing to respect the presumption of innocence. *Glasnost'* is the most important necessary condition though not the only one for just judicial procedures.

The *glasnost'* of legislation must be expressed not only in generally available publications, but also in codifications which give everyone the opportunity to verify that some law exists and, in case it is missing, to refer to this fact as a manifestation of the will [i.e., intention?] of the lawmaker. Codes are sufficient for this purpose; collections put together by jurists are not always sufficient (p. 61).

Each code of laws, according to Volpin, should include a glossary of unfamiliar terms and rules for interpretation. Brevity is a virtue, but clarity and completeness of formulation are even more important.[14] "Every inexactness in the formulation of a criminal law must be interpreted by the courts in favor of the accused (this is one manifestation of the presumption of innocence)" (p. 57).

Volpin sees no need to try to ground or justify existing social and political institutions "logically," since "they will certainly change" and in many cases should be substantially improved. Sounding very much like Locke, he claims

---

14. Volpin sees a dangerous inexactness in the ordinary Russian use of *ne dolzhen* for *dolzhen ne* and *ne khochu* for *khochu ne* (p. 63). The distinction between the first two expressions is difficult to capture in English; both expressions would normally be translated 'should not'. One might distinguish—accurately but awkwardly—between 'does not have to' and 'has to not'. The second distinction is between 'I do not want [to]' and 'I want not [to]'. In any case, Volpin's point would appear to be of dubious generality.

that the state has value "only as a juridical institution which protects the rights, interests, and lives of its citizens and other residents of its territories" (p. 64). By extending their demands beyond these limits, states turn honest citizens into enemies.

Volpin envisages a worldwide sociopolitical system: "A free distribution of societies following various just systems of morality and legislation in their inner lives and intermingling in cities." Isolated conflicts or crimes, he says, would be treated by local authorities. But Volpin admits that such a world order "assumes a level of ethical development higher than that reached by any human society" up to the present (p. 65).

Summing up, Volpin notes that his basic intention has been to show that the rules of ethics and jurisprudence admit of a far stricter grounding than has usually been thought possible. He confesses that much that he finds of value in his discussion may seem "trivial and generally known," but adds: "Just rules and systems *should* become trivial and generally known" (p. 66; italics added). To make them such is the task of the ethical and legal theorist.

In the past, explanations of the development of morality and law have stressed historical, sociological, psychological, and other factors to the neglect of the "logical" factor. Volpin concludes:

Now let logic in its development show everyone what freedom₁ [unobstructedness], freedom₂ [uncoercedness], and justice are, and may the very spread of the ideas of eleutheric ethics constitute an important historical and social factor preparing for the victory of those ideas (p. 66).

3

Volpin focuses almost exclusively on the relations *among* people. Chalidze, however, extends his view to *include* the human individual. He looks within this atom of society to see what makes it function as it does.

Chalidze's essay "Reflections on Man" is divided into four chapters of unequal length. Chapter 1, "Manifestation of the Will," is nine pages long; chapter 2, "Human Conduct," is forty pages; chapter 3, "Society," is twenty-nine pages; and chapter 4, "The Overcoming of Unfreedoms," is eleven pages. Chapter 1 is divided into five sections, the fourth of which has five subsections; 2 is in seven sections, the sixth of which has seven subsections; 3 has thirteen sections; and 4 is not further divided. In what follows I shall discuss only briefly the rather complicated content of chapter 1 and the beginning of chapter 2 and shall concentrate my attention on the second half of chapter 2 and especially on chapters 3 and 4.

Chalidze discusses questions of (1) philosophical anthropology, (2) social and political philosophy, and (3) legal philosophy. The central concept in each of these areas is (1) the "automatism of the will," (2) hierarchy, and (3) individual freedom and the "collective will."

Chalidze leaves the notion of will undefined but says (*a*) that he means by it something like what Schopenhauer meant by *Wille* (though it is clear that, in contrast to Schopenhauer, he has no doctrine of cosmic will), and (*b*) that it is something like life force or psychic energy. He insists that any "manifestation" of a human being is a manifestation of his will.[15]

Chalidze claims that each limb and organ in a living organism has a "local" or "localized" will.[16] The will of the individual enters into relations with its localized wills that are analogous to its relations to external wills—attention-getting, for example, or evaluation, rivalry, and subjugation.

Chalidze uses the rather unwieldy expression 'automatism of the will' to designate any "manifestation" of an organism other than its conscious will, such as instinct, tropism, or reaction. Automatisms help to maintain the stable state (homeostasis) of individual organisms and of the species as a whole. There are automatisms of many different kinds ranging from pain avoidance, warmth-seeking, isolation, and sex to rivalry, submissiveness, kindness, "corporateness" (i.e., sociability and cooperativeness), and the "evaluative" and "cognitive" automatisms.

Automatisms interact; the stimulation of one may either obstruct or facilitate the stimulation of others. When a manifestation of the will satisfies an automatism, the result is a feeling of joy or pleasure (*radost'*); when such satisfaction is blocked or precluded, the result is pain or sorrow.

Chalidze envisages a three-stage process: (1) an automatism is stimulated by an external factor, (2) will-energy is expended to "satisfy" the stimulated automatism, and (3) a state of satisfaction is reached in which the organism is no longer sensitive to external factors of the given kind.

The strength of an encountered will is gauged by the "evaluative automatism." 'Evaluation' (*otsenka*) in Chalidze's usage is a broad term that includes alertness, the discovery and analysis of the characteristics of the encountered will, and interpretation of its "language." The evaluative process is relatively easy in the case of wills that are familiar but is difficult in the case of unfamiliar wills.

The "language of the will" may be deceptive. A strong will, for instance, may use symbols (including words and gestures) that make it appear weak. Survival is facilitated by the principle of "maximal evaluation" of unknown wills—assuming them to be very strong until they prove otherwise.

When wills clash, what Chalidze calls the automatism of "rivalry" or "competition" (*sopernichestvo*) is stimulated. Rivalry appears only where

15. Chalidze also speaks of the 'will-manifestation of the self" or "manifestation of the self through the will." "Razmyshleniia o cheloveke" (unpublished typescript, Moscow, 1971), p. 3. Further page references will be to this typescript.

16. Chalidze even speaks of the "will" of a single cell, at least with respect to the "stimulation of receptors" (p. 5).

the wills are of comparable strength. A strong will reacts to a weaker one by either subjugating or ignoring it.

The automatism of "submissiveness" (*pokornost'*) stimulates the automatism of kindness and "corporateness" on the part of stronger wills. If a very weak will—say, that of a child—inadvertently stimulates the automatism of rivalry in a stronger will, it will be saved from injury by activating the "automatism of laughter." Laughter provides a form of will discharge that prevents the stronger will from concentrating on rivalry.

Chalidze discusses will "surrogates"—that is, substitutes that economize both physical energy and will-energy, such as lighting a fire by striking a match instead of rubbing two sticks together. He distinguishes four kinds of surrogates: (1) "informational," (2) "material," (3) "will surrogates," and (4) "energy surrogates" (p. 10). The first includes accumulated information about one's own and others' wills, about "will language," and the like. The second includes accumulated food supplies, tools, and techniques. The third includes the use of other wills—those of animals, slaves, or free men. The fourth includes such energy sources as wind, water, steam, and electricity.

Chalidze speaks of an automatism of "increased scope of will" manifested in the accumulation of subjugated wills[17] as well as of "informational," "material," and "energy" surrogates. An individual's "effective scope of will," or simply "scope of will," includes the scope of his accumulated surrogates.

Individual wills interact not only with each other but also with what Chalidze calls the "collective will" (*kollektivnaia volia*) of the society.[18] Only in the simplest cases, he insists, does this represent a mere summation of individual wills,[19] although its character reflects the "averaged" characters of the wills of individuals. The collective will requires submission by individuals—to traditions, customs, rules of behavior, and public opinion. It thus restricts the possible modes of manifestation of individual wills despite the fact that one of its functions is to ensure the satisfaction of individual automatisms.

"Will exchange" (*volevoi obmen*) involves mutual aid among individuals as well as the exchange of will surrogates. The collective will regulates this exchange on the basis of the principle of "equal value" or "equality of value" (*ravnotsennost'*). If *A* and *B* provide goods or services for each other, *A*'s expenditure of will-energy (and physical energy) for *B* must not be greater than *A*'s expenditure would have been if he had provided the goods or services himself. For example, Chalidze says, to avoid spending time and trouble shopping, I buy from a door-to-door salesman, but only so long as

17. Subjugated wills presumably include one's own "localized wills" as well as the wills of others.

18. It bears an obvious analogy to Rousseau's *volonté générale*, although Chalidze does not refer to Rousseau in this context.

19. Cf. Rousseau's *volonté de tous*.

his markup is not greater than my expenditure of energy in shopping would be. Chalidze admits that each person involved in such a will exchange can evaluate only his *own* expenditure of energy, not that of the other person. This would seem to raise the difficult question of the comparability and quantifiability of units of will-energy.

At this point Chalidze introduces the concept of *hierarchies*, asserting that the automatism of "increase of [scope of] the will manifests itself . . . as a striving to rise in a hierarchy" (p. 11). Various hierarchies have their own dominant characteristics, and there is a hierarchy of hierarchies. Each of the many strata of a given hierarchy has its own characteristic modes of manifesting the will and its own "will language."

In a will exchange where the parties differ in their evaluations of their respective hierarchical positions, disagreement as to what constitutes "equal value" is likely. A doctor, for example, may consider his five-minute consultation equal in value to a full day's work by a stevedore; but the stevedore may not agree!

In his discussion of the role of deception in the exchange of information about will states (including information conveyed by the "glance"[20]), Chalidze refers to lying, humor, and irony.[21] He reports but does not endorse the common view that lying is permissible if the harm that will result from it will be less than that from telling the truth in the given situation—for instance, if lying is the only way to save an endangered human life. According to the "principle of reciprocity," it is permissible to lie to a liar. There is a presumption that the strong do not lie (to the weak), since they can impose their wills without lying; but they do lie to each other.

Chalidze stresses the difficulty of moving from lower to higher levels of a given hierarchy, partly because of the incomprehensibility of the "will language" of the higher strata. "It is not enough," he writes, "to be able to lift weights to move into the hierarchy of weightlifters; one must also accept a certain system of norms [i.e., rules]" (p. 29, n. 1). To violate these rules is to disqualify oneself as a weightlifter, whatever one's physical capacities. Such rules are enforced by one's sense of honor, by conscience, and by shame.

According to Chalidze, the formation of new hierarchies is now more frequent than it used to be. If someone cannot compete successfully for leadership in an existing hierarchy, he can form a new one and be first in it. There is specialization in science, sports, new trends in art, new civic organizations. One could, Chalidze suggests, become a collector of objects found in the stomachs of elephants killed by hunters and, at least in the beginning, be first in such a hierarchy!

Hierarchical structure appears in any random group of interacting persons. What Chalidze calls the "dominant parameters" of the hierarchy

---

20. Cf. Sartre's discussion of *le regard* in *L'Être et le néant*.
21. He includes protective coloration and mimetic behavior in animals and insects among the deceptive modes of conveying will-information.

are usually taken from tradition. But they may be created on the spot—among young people, for instance, based on the ability to imitate animal noises or blow smoke rings.

Children, according to Chalidze, "constitute the lowest [hierarchical] stratum for the adults around them." Being keenly aware of their status, they manifest their wills in ways characteristic of lower hierarchical strata such as lying (p. 31 n).

The separation and mutual isolation of hierarchies is today much less marked than formerly. Hierarchies are so numerous and varied that it is reasonable to assume that each individual will find at least one hierarchy in which he can gain a higher position than in others "wholly on the strength of his natural capacities" and character (pp. 31, 32).

Reaching the top in one hierarchy does not end the struggle. Competition with past or potential rivals continues. One attempts to move to a higher hierarchy, to increase the importance of one's own hierarchy in the hierarchy of hierarchies, or to be first in several hierarchies at once. For example:

Stalin, having taken first place in the party-state hierarchy, consolidated the dominant position of this hierarchy in the society, strengthening his own primacy, and destroying rivals—both those who had once been rivals and those who might turn out to be such in the future. He claimed first place in the hierarchy on the basis of other qualities (military skill, kindness, science and scholarship), he raised the position of the nationalities of his country in the hierarchy of nations by their achievements and, in an illusory way, by rewriting history: Russian arms, it turned out, were always the most successful, Russian scholars and scientists the first inventors and discoverers, etc. (p. 32 n).

Shame has been viewed—by Vladimir Solovyov, whom Chalidze does not mention, and others—as a moral feeling that distinguishes man from the animals. In fact, it may be only a defense mechanism against possible will-losses or hierarchical downgrading. (According to Chalidze, we have no basis for denying that animals experience shame.) (1) Shame impels us to avoid letting others watch acts that require special concentration of the will, such as defecation and coitus, since the concentration makes it difficult to respond adequately to an unexpected challenge.[22] (2) Shame prevents us from becoming involved in activities that would lower our hierarchical status such as lying or being stingy or dirty.

Chalidze sees the "cognitive automatism" as an evolutionary development of the "automatism of evaluation of an encountered will," made more complex by the capacity to "model" will situations (p. 47). In simple cases the correctness of one's evaluation of an encountered will is confirmed by the practical outcome. One should overvalue just enough to avoid the risk of

---

22. Chalidze notes that satisfaction of the "automatism of isolation" has, with time, taken on an ethical coloring, although its requirements may be met in "illusory" ways. For example, Moslem ethics requires that one cover one's face when sleeping if actual privacy is unavailable.

will-losses from competing with a will which is stronger than one had assumed it to be. One should not overvalue excessively—presumably because that would cause one to forgo competition for no good reason. According to Chalidze, individuals who undervalue encountered wills perish and those who do not make optimal evaluations fail.

Differing opinions often lead to disputes conducted in different languages—"the words have different meanings for the various disputants, to say nothing of the fact that they may be quarreling about the evaluation of will situations which are not the same"—since the will states of the disputants differ and the evaluator of a will situation is himself a part of that situation (pp. 49–50).

Disputants tend to assume, however, that in any given situation there is a "uniquely correct opinion." This assumption has led to the search for what philosophers call "truth." The belief in "truth" is supported by the fact that opinions sometimes coincide and that there are cases in which the will state of the observer plays a minimal role. Instances are the interpretation of a repeated scientific experiment and cases in which the situation is deliberately "modeled" so as to eliminate both the "influence of the observer's will state and the ambiguity of terms," as in formal systems (p. 50).

Noting that the "authority of logic is extremely high," Chalidze goes on to make a critical remark directed implicitly at Volpin (see pp. 160–61 above):

The pride of [members of] the cognitive hierarchy is such that the hope is even expressed that following logical rules will guarantee the correctness of thought, and there is an extreme opinion that in such cases one can do without acts of faith (p. 51).

According to Chalidze, individuals have a "natural subjective right" to manifest their wills. But this right, as Hobbes saw, is always limited by the "right of the powerful." The "collective will" has emerged as a defense of individuals against the powerful, thus limiting the rights of the latter. But since the collective will is itself much stronger than any individual will (another Hobbesian point), its right is also a "right of the powerful" (p. 53).

Chalidze defines law (*pravo*)[23] as a "system of principles of uniform [*edinobraznyi*] limitation of individual wills by the collective will" (pp. 53–54). He provisionally characterizes the demands expressed within a given hierarchy as *ethical* and those that issue from the collective will of the society as a whole as *legal*. In this sense ethics may be regarded as "intrahierarchical" law. But the distinction between law and ethics is not sharp, since each hierarchy has its own "collective will."

The basic purpose and function of the collective will (Chalidze adds, sounding very much like Locke) is to protect individuals from other wills

---

23. The Russian term *pravo* (like the German *Recht* and French *droit*) means both 'law' and 'right'. In this passage Chalidze uses *pravo* in the sense of 'law', but in the immediately preceding and following passages he uses it to mean 'right'.

and (in Chalidze's technical language) to help them "satisfy" their various "automatisms." Chalidze distinguishes sharply between the collective will and the will of the de facto rulers of a given society. The latter "express" the collective will but "do not always express it adequately" (p. 55), that is, they may fail to defend and help individuals and may even exploit or oppress them. In the latter case Chalidze refers to those who exercise "political authority" (*vlast'*) as "usurpers of the collective will."[24] He uses this expression frequently with reference to Stalin as well as to the current rulers of the Soviet Union.

The principle of equal value in will exchange has generated the negative rule, "Do not do to others what you do not want them to do to you." The concept of justice is linked to the "nontrivial sense of equality which takes individual differences into account" (p. 56). Formal equality involves injustice, since it fails to take such differences into account. Thus it would be unjust, Chalidze maintains, to tax the rich and poor equally; it would be more nearly just to take some fraction of each individual's "will surrogate" as a tax. Or again, formal equality in the treatment of prisoners, which imposes the same regime on all, is unjust. An imprisoned vagrant may be quite happy with a narrow bunk while for an imprisoned intellectual it would be a real hardship.

Chalidze asserts that in recent times the attention of the "collective will" of societies has turned to the "defense of the rights of members of lower hierarchical strata" (p. 57). Opposition to racial and national discrimination is growing; such opposition no longer involves "substantial [will-]loss" to the hierarchies that previously followed discriminatory practices. (This last claim seems highly questionable; Chalidze does not offer specific examples of what he has in mind.) He expresses skepticism about the success of measures intended to combat discrimination in (third-world?) societies that are "close to the primary will hierarchy" and where there is intense competition between sharply differentiated hierarchies (pp. 57, 58).

He speculates that in ancient times the ethics of the one protohierarchy may have constituted the law of the (specific) society. In the process of breakup of that hierarchy, law became "suprahierarchical," although even today (he says) certain social hierarchies may be favored by the law.

Chalidze discusses legal interference in such personal matters as homosexual relations between consenting adults (punishable in the Soviet Union, as he has noted in more recent writings, by a five-year prison term), suicide, and self-mutilation (e.g., to avoid military service). He notes that under Stalin a Soviet prisoner who attempted but failed to commit suicide received

24. Chalidze defines the "usurpation of hierarchical position" as "advancement [in a hierarchy] which involves violation of the principle of equal value [in will-exchange]" (p. 70). He adds that everyone, not just the hierarchical usurper, has an interest in preventing the advancement of hierarchical inferiors to his own level in the hierarchy.

an additional term, since he had "sabotaged" the official decision establishing the period of his "deprivation of freedom."

Chalidze says that, although he himself is not sympathetic to the idea of breaking laws, he recognizes that anyone has the right to commit an illegal act and to take responsibility for it—so long, presumably, as he also accepts the prescribed punishment.

He admits that the evaluation of criminal acts committed for "lofty" motives, such as euthanasia and the exposure of deformed infants, is and probably always will be controversial. It is doubtful, he says, that even in the distant future the "collective will" will come to an unequivocal resolution of such thorny questions.

In one of his rare favorable comments on "socialist law," Chalidze writes, apparently without irony: "The socialist system of law has succeeded in preventing some people from having abnormally much in order that more should remain for the others" (pp. 62–63). He adds that "society's rational concern for the lowest hierarchical strata" is a socialist idea (p. 86).

Restitution to victims of crimes involves, where possible, the restoring of the situation that existed prior to the crime. This entails taking from the criminal any advantage he may have gained from the crime and returning it to the victim. But this is not possible where the victim's "will-loss" involves his reputation or his disappointed hopes—or, one might add, his life. Originally, cash payments were made to victims of irreparable injury (Chalidze does not make clear *who* made the payments—whether it was the convicted criminal or his family or society as a whole.) Now, however, a person who inflicts "irreparable will-loss" is considered punishable but is not expected to make restitution. His victim is thus left without remedy except in the rare cases of payment of medical bills or the award of a pension (presumably by the authorities, not the criminal).

Where the criminal and his victim occupy dissimilar hierarchical positions, a lesser injury to the superior requires a greater injury to the inferior to restore the original will relation. Thus, traditionally, if a slave "offended the ears" of his master, his own ears were cut off. This, according to Chalidze, is a form of retribution or retaliation, not punishment. The corresponding punishment, intended to destroy the offender's "localized will," would be the cutting out of the slave's tongue. (Cf. *Code of Hammurabi*, paragraphs 282, 192.)

According to Chalidze, punishment typically involves both the absolute hierarchical downgrading of the wrongdoer and elimination of his presumed evil will by "isolating it from the society." Earlier this was done by ostracizing or executing the offender. Sometimes a limb or organ such as the hand or tongue was excised as "locus of the evil [localized] will." (Cf. *Code of Hammurabi*, paragraphs 196, 218, 253.) Castration and exorcism, Chalidze adds, involve similar assumptions about localized evil wills.

The "hierarchical downgrading" involved in punishment includes the removal of medals and insignia, confiscation of property, public display of prisoners, and confinement in dirty cells. It also includes public undress and subjection to humiliating searches and to the authority of people of lower hierarchical status such as prison guards.

Punishment has always influenced the criminal's further hierarchical advance. Former convicts are treated with suspicion and in some hierarchies face legal obstacles to advancement.

Prisoners naturally attempt to shorten or end their period of confinement by good behavior, bribery, and escape. According to Chalidze, while they should be held responsible for any new crime (e.g., bribery, assault) committed in the course of attempts to escape, they should *not* be punished for the attempt itself. Only the guards or warden should be held responsible for a successful escape, since this indicates a failure on *their* part.

Chalidze claims that the role of enforcers of the principle of equal value in will exchange has traditionally been played by those (usually old men) who are not themselves involved in hierarchical competition, who stand (hierarchically) far above those whom they judge, and who possess an abundant "informational surrogate." Disinterestedness and honesty are still considered qualities essential to those who "judge others in the name of the collective will" (p. 68).

Groups of judges drawn from various hierarchies are more apt to be impartial than single judges. The "presumption of the honesty of the powerful will" is extended to judges, but not blindly or uncritically, as is clear from such principles of trial procedure as the public's right to know (*glasnost'*) and the oral presentation of evidence at a hearing (*ustnost'*). Other requirements—that the judge carefully study the matter in dispute, for example, and that both parties may call witnesses—were formalized later.

Chalidze anticipates that certain methods of hierarchical stabilization will continue to receive legal sanction but that others, such as racial and religious discrimination, will not.

Even in totalitarian societies, what Chalidze calls the "preaching of freedom" may be effective if it helps people avoid will dissatisfaction and choose "non-norm-bound (*nenormirovannyi*) modes of will discharge. "It sounds blasphemous," Chalidze writes, "but the distribution of pornographic postcards is a more powerful method of propagandizing for freedom than preaching exalted ideas about human rights" (p. 73, n. 2).[25]

Totalitarian political systems impose unity, suppressing hierarchies that "are not inscribed in the planned unified structure" (p. 73). In contrast,

25. In another passage Chalidze partly clarifies this rather cryptic statement. The will-dissatisfaction produced by restraints on direct competition, he asserts, is offset in the advanced industrial countries by the greater frequency and intensity of will discharge resulting from "increased sexual freedom" (p. 81).

democratic political systems flourish in societies with a "powerfully developed polyhierarchical structure" (p. 71). Democratic governments permit the development of a "hierarchy of hierarchies," allowing more or less free interhierarchical competition for "will surrogates" and for participation in the expression of the collective will. There is a constant breakup and reforming of hierarchies, accompanied by growth in the "freedom of hierarchical competition (including the individual's freedom to choose or reject hierarchies), and freedom from interference by that hierarchy which at a given moment participates in the expression of the collective will" (p. 74).

For Chalidze, the family is one of the key hierarchies making up a "polyhierarchical society." Historically, the establishing of a family was an important step in the process of the "individualization of the human person" (*individualizatsiia lichnosti*), a process grounded in the "automatism of increased scope of will." Having acquired priority in a hierarchy of his own creation, the founder of a family discovers that his "freedom and degree of individuality increase with his hierarchical position." According to Chalidze, standard questions of "hierarchy evaluation" include: "Are you married?" and "How many children do you have?"—which attests to the importance of family status for the "automatism of hierarchical growth" (p. 76).

Chalidze admits, however, that the *contemporary* stage of the process of "individualization" involves, if not the breakup of the family, at least a tendency to attribute less importance to hierarchical demands within it.

He sees a close connection between the struggle for individual freedom and the breakup of social hierarchies generally, although he admits that it is not clear which process is cause and which effect.

Chalidze insists that the "individualization of the human person" is an essential component in historical progress even though it is not recognized as such by communists, who in contrast advocate the increased "correlativity"[26] of individual behavior. Communists see "communism" as the "inevitable future of mankind." But, according to Chalidze, they inconsistently claim (1) that the inevitability of communism follows from the objective laws of social development, and (2) that men should make sacrifices to realize the goal of communism even though it will be realized ("by history") independently of human efforts.

More generally the "usurpers of the collective will" preach that everyone has a moral duty to serve progress. They set up their own conception of progress as an (absolute) end that justifies their "usurpation, their violation of the principle of equal value in will exchange, and their curtailment of human rights" (p. 79). But, Chalidze warns (sounding rather like Alexander Herzen, to whom he does not refer), after "love of God" and "love of

---

26. *Korreliativnost'*—a term which means something like 'dependence on [or conditioning by] the social environment'. In any case, it contrasts sharply with *individualizatsiia*.

Caesar," devotion to progress may serve as a kind of "fetish" in the preaching of human goals. What Chalidze calls the "dictation of goals" influences the individual's hierarchical evaluations and limits his freedom, especially in the choice of hierarchies.

After suggesting "competition" between men and machines as a possible way of counteracting the boredom and exhaustion of contemporary factory workers, Chalidze adds, echoing Mikhailovsky (though not mentioning him): "I am not interested in the increase of labor productivity. I am concerned about the permanent suffering of human beings, the accumulation of [will] dissatisfaction, and the danger of social tragedies . . ." (p. 80 n).

Chalidze sets the tone of his final chapter, "The Overcoming of Unfreedoms," with his opening statement: "*Liudiam ochen' trudno zhit'*" (Human life is very difficult) (p. 82). He sees a twofold reason for this: (1) much will-energy is expended on the satisfying of primary automatisms (such, as that of pain-avoidance, presumably), but because of biological adaptation such "satisfaction" does not give pleasure; (2) although the striving for happiness leads to a striving for freedom, the gaining of freedom paradoxically does not bring happiness. In "freely" suppressing an automatism, subjecting it to his conscious will, a man leaves himself dissatisfied, deprived of "localized pleasures." The connection between freedom and suffering is clear even in the simplest cases: freeing oneself from automatic, "unambiguous" causal reactions, one suppresses the stimulated automatism by a conscious volition. Such "freedom in the choice of reaction" causes suffering because it leaves the automatism unsatisfied.

Chalidze speaks sympathetically of the "image of Christ carrying the cross"—an image in which freedom and atonement through suffering are fused. "In contrast to the forced torments on the cross," he writes, "the path to Golgotha symbolizes the willingness to suffer—i.e., the highest indetermination [*nedeterminirovannost'*] of conduct, the highest freedom, as distinguished from the [lower] freedom of seeking ways to avoid suffering" (p. 83).

Human society is not "norm-bound" (*normirovannyi*), as are the totalitarian societies of the social insects, in which what Chalidze calls the "natural rights" of individual insects are sacrificed to social homeostasis. Even in the most flourishing human societies some people will commit crimes, be punished, commit new crimes, and thus spend most of their adult lives in confinement.[27] This, says Chalidze, is a tragic fact. We can hope that future societies will think as constructively about such people as past societies have done about the poor.

---

27. Although Chalidze does not say so explicitly, his assumption that crime will continue indefinitely contradicts the Marxist-Leninist view, according to which crime is a consequence of economic deprivation and will disappear in an affluent and nonexploitative society.

In Chalidze's view, one who tries to free himself without violating the principle of equal value will be unwilling to gain his own freedom by limiting the freedom of others. If he accepts such self-restraints, he will be able to seek "ways of optimizing emancipation" so that it will not result in a new enslavement (p. 87).

Anyone who seeks to be free, according to Chalidze, must be convinced that his intended freedom will be a hierarchically higher condition than dependence on current prohibitions and that it will compensate him for his suffering and will dissatisfaction. Generally this is not the case, and many people know that real freedom is more effectively achieved through hierarchical advancement. But much trouble and effort, which involve a certain unfreedom, are needed to maintain the higher position.

Chalidze disclaims having made any attempt to discover or advocate *new* ways of gaining freedom. He has merely surveyed the *old* ways. But he is concerned that freedom be preserved in the very process of emancipation, since many proposals for gaining individual freedom have involved new forms of unfreedom. Instead of "extrahierarchicality," they have preached "success in new hierarchies" (p. 93).

Chalidze is left with a difficult theoretical problem, since he insists that "freedom in any case remains illusory, [and] we cannot expect other than illusory freedom" (p. 88). In an earlier passage he had maintained that neither classical determinism nor the doctrine of free will can be established on either rational or empirical grounds, adding that "for a sense of . . . freedom of the will it is enough for the individual to assume that he could have acted otherwise. . . ." (p. 4 n). Yet Chalidze says repeatedly that such a "sense of freedom" is "illusory," even though the "illusion of freedom is . . . justified, since any degree of ability to control one's automatisms increases . . . both internal and external freedom. . . ." (p. 19).

These are puzzling claims, especially in view of Chalidze's assertion that the manifestation of conscious will provides a "sense of the illusion of freedom of the will" (perhaps he meant to say "an illusory sense of freedom of the will," though that would not have helped with the main difficulty) (p. 17).

Chalidze seems to me to move uneasily between the common-sense assumption that freedom is real and related to the conscious will and the incompatible positivist assumption that freedom is an illusion.[28] His closing words express appreciation for those theories of freedom that "do not prevent our becoming aware of the *illusory* character of any specific degree of attained freedom" (p. 93; italics added).

---

28. I suspect that Chalidze would agree with Mikhailovsky's deliberately paradoxical formulation: "Perhaps [freedom] is a delusion, but history is moved by it," *Soch*, III, 437.

In his rich and compact essay Chalidze touches, often with marked originality and perceptiveness, on many topics I do not have space to discuss: art, religion, sex, politeness, profanity, vandalism, corporal punishment, torture. Perhaps such topics can be discussed in some future, more extended study.

4

Unlike Volpin and Chalidze, Pomerants at one time published several articles of philosophic relevance in such Soviet publications as the journal of oriental studies *Narody Azii i Afriki* and the philosophy journal *Voprosy filosofii.*[29] Only two pieces have appeared in the latter, the first in 1960, the second in 1966. The first, entitled "An Ancient but Terrible Weapon,"[30] is a review of Russian translations of four "classical" texts in atheistic and antireligious literature: Lucretius' *On the Nature of Things*, selected satires of Lucian, selected writings of Ulrich von Hutten (1488–1523), and Holbach's *Letters to Eugène*. Pomerants takes a fairly standard Marxist-Leninist line on religion, theology, and the church, although he writes with more erudition and subtlety than most Marxist-Leninist antireligionists.

The second publication[31] is less significant for two reasons: (1) it is signed by three authors besides Pomerants, and there is no way to identify Pomerants's specific contribution to the collective effort; (2) the article is simply a survey without interpretive or critical comment of eight works by African authors, all of whom profess sympathy for Marxist-Leninist "scientific socialism." The authors range from luminaries of the hour such as Kwame Nkrumah and Sékou Touré to obscure ideologists of "African socialism." It seems likely that Pomerants served mainly as a translator and summarizer of French and English texts.

The "man from nowhere" in the title of Pomerants's most important philosophical essay is the contemporary Soviet intellectual or, more accu-

29. Volpin has published technical papers on mathematical logic in *Voprosy filosofii*; Chalidze has published in *no* Soviet philosophy journal.
30. "Staroe no groznoe oruzhie," *Voprosy filosofii*, no. 7 (1960): 177–79. Pomerants's title is borrowed from a line in Mayakovsky's poem, "Vo ves' golos" (At the top of my voice).
31. "Problemy sotsializma v Afrike" [Problems of socialism in Africa], *Voprosy filosofii*, no. 1 (1966): 172–79, signed by "workers of the section on the countries of Asia and Africa of the Fundamental Library of Social Sciences of the Soviet Academy of Sciences: S. Ia. Berzina, Iu. I. Komar, S. I. Kuznetsova, G. S. Pomerants."
One reason why Pomerants has published no philosophical essays in the Soviet Union since 1968 (the other being that his philosophical position has moved impermissibly far from Marxism-Leninism) is that in that year he signed a letter protesting the Ginzburg-Galanskov trial. Among the letter's 169 other signers were Natalya Gorbanevskaya and Vitaly Rubin, both currently experiencing serious difficulties in the Soviet Union; Julius Telesin, Yuri Gendler, and Anatoly Yakobson, all now in exile in the West; and Gabriel Superfin, sentenced in May 1974 to five years of forced labor and two years of (domestic) exile. For the text of the letter and list of the signatories, see Abraham Brumberg, ed., *In Quest of Justice: Protest and Dissent in the Soviet Union Today* (New York, 1970), pp. 164–69.

rately, member of the Soviet *intelligentsia*.[32] Pomerants is obviously aware of the long tradition of controversy concerning the Russian *intelligentsia*; but, curiously, he refers to the principal theorist and historian of that phenomenon, R. Ivanov-Razumnik, only once and in passing, crediting him only with the identification of the *intelligent* as a "critically thinking individual." In fact, Ivanov-Razumnik borrowed that expression, as he freely acknowleged, from Peter Lavrov, who had first given it currency in his *Historical Letters* of 1868–69. I shall return to Ivanov-Razumnik's detailed characterization of the *intelligentsia* and its relation to the people (*narod*) a bit later. But I want first to consider Pomerants's "downgrading" of the *narod*,[33] which occupies the opening pages of his essay.

Pomerants declares that the peasantry, having left a profound mark on the moral and esthetic consciousness of mankind, is now disappearing. In Russia only remnants of the *narod* are left, like patches of melting snow in the corners of dense forests in springtime. Here and there we find a Matryona or an Ivan Denisovich;[34] but the *narod* as a great historical force, a phenomenon that inspired Pushkin and Gogol (and Tolstoy, one might add), is no more. The few remaining "peasant" countries are hungry countries. Where the peasantry has disappeared, hunger has been wiped out.

Not everyone who works the land is a peasant, Pomerants is quick to add. Farmers in the United States (and he notes that they represent only 7 percent of the population,[35] fewer than the university students and professors) do not have a "peasant mentality." Nor do farmers in Israel, where the members of certain *kibbutzim* have organized a "league for struggle against religious pressures," a typical expression of the "scientific" and "urban" mentality.

According to Pomerants, the *narod* has been replaced in the economy, though not in the cultural or spiritual life of the country, by the urban and rural proletariat. More picturesquely expressed, the grandchildren and great-grandchildren of Russian peasants have been "trampled down" by historical "progress" into a faceless "mass of plumbers, steamfitters, and bookkeepers."[36] But the peasant exodus from the land is for Pomerants a "progressive" phenomenon. The Australian bushmen, he says, were wrong

32. I shall treat *intelligentsia* as a Russian word and regularly italicize it in order to be able to use the Russian noun *intelligent* ('member of the *intelligentsia*'). As we shall see, *intelligent* is not synonymous with 'intellectual'.

33. I shall use the Russian word *narod* rather than the English 'people', 'common people', or 'folk', all of which it can mean. Traditionally *narod* has been taken as equivalent to *krest'ianstvo* (peasantry).

34. These are characters in, respectively, Solzhenitsyn's short story "Matryona's House" and his novel *One Day in the Life of Ivan Denisovich*.

35. The fact that half of the Soviet population is engaged in agriculture results, according to Pomerants, not only from the notorious inefficiency of Soviet farm labor but also from the fact that peasants are forced to remain on the land through the system of internal passports.

36. The Russian expression is *slesarno-bukhgalterskaia massa*. See G. Pomerants, "Chelovek niotkuda," *Neopublikovannoe*, p. 128. Subsequent page references in the text will be to this collection.

in regarding the transition to peasant labor as sacrilegious, and peasants are wrong to regard the giving up of the dominance of "land, blood, kinship and 'the faith of their fathers'" as sacrilegious (p. 127).

As for the famous sense of debt and duty[37]—the moral guilt felt by so many nineteenth century "repentant noblemen" toward *muzhiks* and poultry maids—Pomerants will have none of it. It still makes some sense in underdeveloped countries but no longer makes any sense at all in developed ones. Pomerants offers a comparative wage table (see table 5.1) to back up his point. (He does not cite his sources, but I have no reason to doubt the figures he gives. Those for the United States seem about right for the period 1967–69.)

Pomerants concludes that in developed countries skilled blue-collar workers are better paid than average white-collar workers.[38] Thus a sense of guilt toward the *narod*, though it makes sense in India and Lebanon, doesn't make much sense in Japan and is quite absurd in Sweden or the United States. Pomerants does not say where the Soviet Union would fall on such a table, but Moscow, at least, must be fairly close to Belgrade in the comparative earnings of skilled blue-collar and average white-collar workers.[39] In the Soviet Union, according to Pomerants, it makes more sense to feel guilty when you flush a toilet than when you eat an egg. Sewer technicians are much worse off—at least in terms of the unpleasant conditions of their work, if not their wages—than poultry maids.

Pomerants does not deny that many scientists and scholars are time servers and "prostitutes," and he admits that those who have sold out or prostituted themselves should feel guilty. But *not*, he insists, exclusively toward *poultry maids*! When an *intelligent* expresses guilt toward the *narod* he simply reinforces the popular prejudice that intellectual work is a form of *barstvo*—the unproductive, parasitic life of the landed gentry.

On the contrary, Pomerants insists, intellectual and white-collar work is difficult and demanding. Tolstoy, he reminds us, chose to plow and reap with his peasants; but no one ever freely chose either to make galoshes out of stinking rubber or to compile an index for a book. His own creative intellectual work, Pomerants says, has not brought him any monetary reward; he has earned his living as a "stevedore" or "post horse" of intellectual labor (p. 134).

In his apologia for the *intelligentsia*, Pomerants recurs to the slightly ambiguous historical examples of Poland in 1956 and Czechoslovakia in 1968. Is it the peasantry or the *intelligentsia*, he asks, which, when it gets

---

37. The Russian word *dolg* includes both meanings.

38. In at least one place, presumably under American influence, Pomerants speaks of "white-collar" and "blue-collar" workers (p. 135). But he normally uses the jargony Soviet pleonasm *rabotniki umstvennogo truda* (literally, 'workers of intellectual labor').

39. Pomerants notes that the wage structure in Madrid is very similar to that in Belgrade despite sharp differences between the Spanish and Yugoslav sociopolitical systems.

TABLE 5:1 Weekly Earnings in Dollars

City	Occupation		
	Construction worker	Bookkeeper	Secretary
New Delhi	3.33	40.00	18.50
Beirut	20.00	180.00	115.00
Madrid	28.00	42.00	53.00
Belgrade	25.00	40.00	30.00
Tokyo	44.00	40.20	50.00
Stockholm	122.64	94.64	88.02
New York	248.00	127.50	125.00

Source: From G. Pomerants, "Chelovek Niotkuda," *Neopublikovannoe* (Frankfurt, 1972), p. 132.

what it wants for *itself*, helps society *as a whole* to change for the better? After the Polish October of 1956, Pomerants maintains, the peasants got what they wanted: an end to the forced collectivization of ariculture. Today (1968–69) the Polish regime, based on the "conservative village," is "one of the most reactionary in Eastern Europe" (p. 129). It might be objected that such an account ascribes a disproportionate influence to the peasantry in the shaping of Polish policy, and—with hindsight—that when Gomulka was deposed as a result of uprisings by Polish *workers*, a moderate "liberalization" of the regime was accomplished without significant alteration in the position of the peasantry.

Pomerants more plausibly analyzes the events of the Prague Spring as a gaining of free speech by the Czech *intelligentsia*, which opened a path to political freedom for the whole Czechoslovakian people. He does not here comment on the Soviet invasion and occupation of Czechoslovakia. I am not sure how Pomerants would react to the plausible claim that in the early 1970s the Czechoslovakian, not the Polish, government is the principal contender for the title of "most reactionary government in Eastern Europe" (always excluding Albania, as Pomerants presumably did when he made the parallel claim for Poland). Pomerants might protest that the Czech *intelligentsia* is not to blame for the Soviet invasion. But again it could be argued that their unrealistic demands and overhasty actions made the invasion almost unavoidable, given the nature of the Soviet government and of the "fraternity of socialist nations."

Yet, Pomerants seems to me right in his claim that, despite the many faults of the *intelligentsia*, "only in it does the demand for freedom of speech arise." The demand is neither expressed nor felt by peasants, workers, or bureaucrats. Furthermore: "Where the *intelligentsia* is enslaved, all are slaves . . . [and] if the problem of the *intelligentsia* is not solved, the country as a whole will remain in darkness" (pp. 129–30).

Moving to a sociological analysis, Pomerants notes that the eighteenth century physiocrats were wrong in assuming that *peasant* labor would always be the dominant form of human labor. But the nineteenth century political economists—presumably including Marx, though Pomerants does not mention him in this connection—were also wrong in assuming that *industrial* labor would always be the dominant form. What is dominant today, Pomerants declares, is the "production of scientific-technological information." But other forms of "work" will replace this in the future, perhaps the production of "creative states" of consciousness through art, ritual, yoga, zen, mystical exercise, or "psychotechnics" (p. 137).

In his reaction to the *muzhik*-worship of nineteenth century *narodniki* and their contemporary followers, Pomerants sometimes waxes polemical, even abusive—as when he writes:

In wartime, when the government permits him to be brave, the Russian peasant pulls himself together and becomes a human being. In peacetime, when the government does not permit this, he loses his self-respect, does vile things, drinks, and behaves insolently while drunk (p. 172).

The quest for truth and justice, which is what was valuable in the traditional *narod*, now lies in tatters. And what we most need today—art, love, and the contemplation of natural beauty—is aristocratic in its roots and has always been foreign to the *narod*. Pomerants here offers a suggestive digression on "work, holidays, and leisure," the upshot of which is that there must be a balance between serious work (*delo*) and holiday (*prazdnik*), not a predominance of work as in Roman and modern times nor a predominance of the holiday as in the Middle Ages.[40] Then, Pomerants writes, it was considered a much greater sin to fail to go to church on a holiday than to do slovenly work. He insists that a holiday, as opposed to mere leisure or nonwork, entails giving oneself up with reverence to something higher than work.

In the case of the New Year holiday—the only one left in the Soviet Union, as Pomerants comments with some bitterness—if you take from it the moment of reverence, the mystical tremor as the clock hands approach midnight, all that remains is socially "getting drunk" (*p'ianka*), sometimes preceded by officially "being bored" (*skuka*) (p. 141). But under contemporary conditions the most important holiday he says, is the "inner holiday," and the *narod* never had that.

In characterizing the *intelligentsia* more closely, Pomerants agrees implicitly with Ivanov-Razumnik (without mentioning him in this connection) that cultivation, erudition, sensitivity, even creativity are not enough to make one

---

40. Pomerants refers to Max Weber and the "Protestant work ethic," and he cites Marx's well-known Eleventh Thesis on Feuerbach: "The philosophers have only *interpreted* the world in various ways; the thing, however, is to *change* it." But he finds Marx's views about the importance of leisure for human freedom (in *Capital*, vol. 3) "more profound" (p. 141).

an *intelligent*.[41] Ivanov-Razumnik had defined the *intelligentsia* ethically by its opposition to *meshchanstvo*[42] and sociologically as a group, marked by a sense of continuity, that is not confined to any single class or "estate" and that is characterized by "the creation of new forms and ideals and their active introduction into life, in the direction of the physical and intellectual, social and personal liberation of the individual person."[43] *Meshchanstvo* is narrow, shallow, and impersonal; the *intelligentsia* is broad, deep, and vividly "personal."[44]

So far as I can see, Pomerants would accept all of this. What he quite clearly repudiates is Ivanov-Razumnik's corollary claim that the *intelligentsia* in its "creativity" and its "ideals" is the "living nerve of the *narod*," the "real organ of popular consciousness," and the "totality of the living energies of the *narod*."[45] Pomerants sees no such relationship. Rather, as he puts it, the *intelligentsia* is itself what some of its members had at various times mistakenly assumed the *narod* or the proletariat to be—the fermenting force that moves history. Less metaphorically put, the *intelligentsia* is that part of the educated stratum of society in which "spiritual or cultural growth [*dukhovnoe razvitie*]" occurs, the locus of the disintegration of old values and the emergence of new ones.

The hope for social and cultural renewal, Pomerants is convinced, lies uniquely with the *intelligentsia*. It is the "twig" which, when inserted into a supersaturated solution, will initiate the process of crystallization of new value structures.[46] Shifting the metaphor, Pomerants likens the *intelligentsia* to a field of radiant energy with a center of maximum intensity but no outer limits. The intense center is what Pomerants calls the "animate or ensouled [*odushevlënnyi*]" *intelligentsia*. The "inanimate or soulless" *intelligentsia* is morally indistinguishable from the *meshchanstvo*, although in favorable

41. But, somewhat inconsistently, Pomerants says that the "chosen people" of the twentieth century are those engaged in "creative intellectual work" (p. 130). And in his contribution to a volume dedicated to Academician V. P. Vasilyev, the noted nineteenth-century sinologist, Pomerants goes further, asserting that the modern intellectual and *intelligent* differ from the medieval scribe in distinct ways: "The intellectual by his logical-scientific or technological-scientific turn of mind and the *intelligent* by his vivid sense of alienation from the cosmic and social order." (G. Pomerants, "Shen'shi kak tip srednevekovogo knizhnika," in *Istoriia i kul'tura Kitaia* [Moscow, 1974], p. 381.) This characterization of the intellectual seems unduly narrow; it would appear to displace poets, artists, critics, and speculative thinkers to the ranks of the *intelligentsia*.

42. Sociologically speaking, *meshchanstvo* means "middle class"; ethically or culturally speaking, it is "philistinism." Pomerants distinguishes three groups within the "educated stratum of society": (1) *intelligentsia*, (2) *meshchanstvo*, and (3) "cadres." The second and third groups are quite close, he says, and both are remote from the first.

43. R. Ivanov-Razumnik, *Istoriia russkoi obshchestvennoi mysli* [A history of Russian social thought] (St. Petersburg, 1906), 1:12.

44. *Ibid.*, pp. 17, 22.

45. *Ibid.*, p. 12.

46. Pomerants admits that the current Soviet *intelligentsia* does no such thing. Rather it is a "stuffing for the meat-pies" of the "contemporary Russian kitchen" (i.e., regime), which can be steamed, fried, or eaten raw, "with blood, in its own juice" (p. 147).

circumstances it is capable of appreciating and even sharing in the values and goals of the animate or ensouled *intelligentsia*.

Pomerants admits that his "model" does not explain why *intelligenty* who begin by struggling for freedom often end up in *shigalëvshchina*[47]—that is, a totalitarian utopia of absolute equality in which geniuses are to be destroyed in infancy. To explain this fact and to explain why so many dictators are artists *manqués*—Hitler a painter, Nasser a novelist, Stalin and Mao poets—another "model," that of the Fall, must be added. Intellectual freedom, according to Pomerants, is like atomic energy; it can either save or destroy the world. "The victory of the *intelligentsia* over tradition is an opportunity for a new and higher degree of freedom and [also] the possibility of a more terrible slavery" (p. 150).

Pomerants is troubled by the fact that a part of the *intelligentsia* has become a "political counterelite" and that fighters against despotism have begun to use despotic methods. In Africa, he notes drily, this process is greatly speeded up: At the age of eighteen "Numa Pompilius" is a student whose head is filled with ideas of freedom; at twenty he is a minister; at twenty-two he builds a gold bathroom in his palace; at twenty-four the tyrant is overthrown! At least, Pomerants adds, there are fewer corpses in such cases. In contrast, the number of those who have been shot to death in Russia and China would equal the entire population of several new African states.

Pomerants insists that the core of the *intelligentsia* does not, and presumably *should* not, aspire to political power. Its proper role in political life is in *dialogue* with the political authority. "The realm of the spirit and the realm of Caesar," he writes, "should have something in common but should not be united under a single crown" (p. 156). The *intelligentsia* should be represented politically by an association (Pomerants does not call it a party) having a press but taking no part in government, at least in the executive branch.

"The peoples (*narody*) must be transfigured, the Old Adam must die so that a new [Adam] may be born" (p. 175). In other words, the old *narod* should give way to the new *intelligentsia* and be enlightened by it. But the *intelligenty* should remember that "before enlightening others one must become a light, must cease to be a human mass, a particle of darkness" (p. 167).

At times Pomerants seems rather pessimistic about the prospects for such a self-renewal of the *intelligentsia*. In particular, he seems not to share Ivanov-Razumnik's faith in the *intelligentsia* as a historically continuous social *group*. Sounding very much like the Pasternak of *Doctor Zhivago*, he

---

47. An abstract noun formed from the name 'Shigalev'. Shigalev is a fanatical revolutionary in Dostoevsky's *The Possessed*.

writes: "Everything great has been initiated . . . by single individuals who have refused to howl [with the pack]. I count upon such single individuals" (p. 168).[48]

In a 1965 paper read at a meeting of the Institute of Philosophy in Moscow but never published in the Soviet Union, Pomerants raised the hoary question of the "Moral Character of the Historical Individual"[49] and its corollary, the question of the ends and means of historical action. Pomerants's essay is remarkable for the frankness of its repudiation of Stalinism and the bluntness and urgency of its warning against re-Stalinization, which by 1965 was already well advanced. But he makes *no* critical remarks about Lenin or Leninism, pursuing instead the essentially Trotskyite line that Stalinism was a "perversion" and "distortion" of the Leninist legacy (see pp. 215, 217). Defining the true revolutionary as a "passionate struggler for justice," Pomerants clearly means to include Lenin in this lofty category. In contrast, Stalin—as Lenin warned the party—loved "expropriation, terror, etc. for their own sakes" (p. 221). This distinction simply will not wash, as every reader of Solzhenitsyn's monumental *Gulag Archipelago* must by now be vividly aware. But in 1965 Pomerants was still writing as a Marxist-Leninist, even though he ventured to brand as false two key Stalinist (and, one must insist, Leninist) assumptions: (1) the moral character of an historical agent is of no importance, only his deeds matter; and (2) "progress justifies everything" (p. 210).

Pomerants's initial example is from Oriental history. He compares the "gentle" emperor Asoka of India with the "cruel" emperor Ch'in Shih Huang Ti of China, referring ironically to the "humanism" of the former as "petit-bourgeois" and to that of the latter as "authentic" and based on a "progressive scientific theory" (p. 209). It might be more helpful to distinguish between a "humanism of principles" that refuses to treat living human beings as means to future historical ends and a "humanism of ideals" that is quite prepared to instrumentalize living human beings for such ends. In other words, Asoka's "humanism of principles" is present-oriented and ethical; Ch'in Shih Huang Ti's "humanism of ideals" is future-oriented and instrumental.[50]

---

48. Pomerants uses the same term, *odinochka*, that Pasternak used in his celebrated rebuke to those who cluster into political parties or philosophical schools: "*Istinu ishchut odinochki* [Truth is sought by single individuals]."

49. "Nravstvennyi oblik istoricheskoi lichnosti," *Neopublikovannoe*, pp. 207–25. A free and somewhat abridged translation of this essay is included in Brumberg, *In Quest of Justice*, pp. 323–30. To the best of my knowledge, this is the only English translation of any of Pomerants's philosophical writings. A French translation had appeared earlier under the title "Le rôle de l'individu dans l'histoire" in *Samizdat 1: La Voix de l'opposition communiste* [sic] *en U.R.S.S.* (Paris, 1969), pp. 253–63.

50. I have developed this distinction with reference both to Marx's own position and to Marxism-Leninism in an article, "Was Marx an Ethical Humanist?" in *Studies in Soviet Thought* 9 (1969): 91–103.

Finally, a word about Pomerants's views on religion. In 1965 as well as in 1960 he was ready to claim that the "scientific world-view"—that is, Marxism-Leninism—had "undermined the world religions" (p. 225). But he added that such a world-view cannot create images of moral integrity and beauty comparable to those of Buddha or Christ. That is a task for poetry and may take a very long time. The "Red Guard" (i.e., primitive and violent) attack on religion has given way to a dialogue with the great world religions—religions that have produced the art of Bach, Rublev, and Dante.

In the 1967–69 period Pomerants was willing to go a bit further, declaring that in order to restore ritual to its proper place in modern civilization there is no need to revert to paganism. "It will be enough to stop hounding the church and to restore its natural role in contemporary culture, following the example of other civilized countries" (p. 142).

5

My concluding remarks will be grouped under four general heads: (1) the respective topics of the three authors; (2) their respective styles; (3) some of their more problematic concepts; (4) some tentative suggestions about the direction in which an unfettered and uncensored Soviet philosophy might develop.

(1) The topics upon which Volpin and Chalidze focus stand largely *outside* the tradition of Russian social thought: the structure and relationships of law, rights, and obligations, and—in the case of Chalidze—the nature of the "automatisms" of the will, social hierarchies, and the "collective will."

In contrast, the topics upon which Pomerants focuses stand largely *within* the tradition of Russian social thought, which centers on the philosophy of history and culture. Thus his topics are the nature and relationships of the *intelligentsia* and the common people (*narod*), the character and direction of progress, and the "role of the individual in history."

As we have seen, Pomerants reverses one traditional view (that of the nineteenth century "populists" and of Ivanov-Razumnik) concerning the relationship of *intelligentsia* to *narod*. But he continues the traditional obsession of the Russian *intelligent* with the role of the Russian *intelligentsia*.

(2) The manner in which these topics are treated is more original, even idiosyncratic, in Pomerants's case and more straightforward in the cases of Volpin and Chalidze. Pomerants writes allusively, metaphorically, with abundant irony, and many literary and historical references, some of them rather exotic. Volpin and Chalidze write in a "scientific" and analytic mode and make few historical or literary references although, as we have seen, they can be both witty and ironic.

(3) Most of the key concepts used by all three authors strike me as problematic in the sense of requiring more precise definition, clarification, and theoretical grounding than is provided in the works under review.

(*a*) In Volpin's case, I think the concepts of rationality, logic (including modal logic[51]), right, permission, and prohibition, though fairly carefully defined, need to be more clearly related to one another and more adequately grounded.

(*b*) Chalidze's most problematic concepts are automatism, will (including "evil will" and "collective will"), hierarchy (including "hierarchy of hierarchies"), responsibility, punishment, restitution, and finally (as indicated above, pp. 178–79) freedom, including "freedom of the will." The relation of "genuine" to "illusory" freedom stands in special need of clarification.

(*c*) Pomerants does a good deal to make clear what he means by *intelligentsia* and 'people' (*narod*), but more needs to be done, in particular a clarification of the relation of the preurbanized to the posturbanized peasantry and the relation of the *intelligent* to the "intellectual." As suggested above, Pomerants's discussion of humanism (which dates from a period when he was in effect still defending the "authentic humanism" of Lenin while sharply repudiating the "false humanism" of Stalin) would be helped by some such distinction as that between a "humanism of principles" and a "humanism of ideals." There also seems to be too much of the Marxist, and general nineteenth century, commitment to "progress" in Pomerants's thought. On this point Chalidze's position stands in welcome contrast.

Having made these critical comments I wish to emphasize that all three authors have *many* things to say that are of great interest and value.

(4) It has sometimes been claimed that if Soviet philosophers were freed of ideological constraints, including censorship of the spoken and written word, they would, in revulsion against the required system of speculative thought—Marxism-Leninism—lapse into an antispeculative and antisystematic, "positivistic" or skeptical philosophy.

There is some evidence of this in Volpin's position, which is, indeed, both skeptical and positivistic. The evidence is less clear in the case of Chalidze who, though he shows traces of positivist influence, uses a mainly "analytic" *method* (in the sense of "conceptual" rather than "linguistic" analysis) although his *doctrine* is fairly systematic. However, it is important to note that both Volpin and Chalidze focus their philosophical "analysis" on important human problems: the nature and relations of law and morality,

---

51. I am aware that Volpin has discussed the technicalities of modal logic in various papers, but I am not convinced that what he says there clarifies the relationship of logic in general, and modal logic in particular, to the structure and functioning of the "moral sciences."

the structure of rights both moral and legal, the principles of trial procedure, punishment, and the like.

In none of these essays do I find evidence of a turn toward a "Marxist existentialism"[52] of the kind developed in the early post-Stalin period by Eastern European Marxists such as Kołakowski in Poland, Kosík in Czechoslovakia, and Petrović in Yugoslavia. This position, though understandably attractive to young thinkers emerging from the ideological straitjacket of Stalinist Marxism, is beset by theoretical tensions and would probably strike the more sophisticated Soviet philosophers as not presenting a viable theoretical option for the 1970s.

"The Man from Nowhere" contains few traces of Pomerants's earlier Marxist position. He seems to have been measurably influenced by certain non-Marxist Russian thinkers (e.g., Berdyaev) and by certain Russian poets (Mandelshtam, Tsvetaeva). There is also more than an undercurrent of Eastern thought: Vedanta and Buddhism, including Zen. This occasionally brilliant essay in social philosophy, *Kulturkritik*, and philosophy of history is written in an informal, "literary," and aphoristic style. Its polemical edge is often keen.

The direction in which Pomerants's thought has moved between the middle and late 1960s is promising. But whether he has in his unpublished writings of the last five years made good on the considerable theoretical promise of "The Man from Nowhere" cannot be decided until those writings become available. One can hope that this event will not be long delayed.

---

52. One would not expect either Volpin or Chalidze to flirt with Marxist revisionism since neither was a Marxist in the first place. Pomerants seems not to have been much attracted either to the "young Marx" or to revisionist attempts to graft Kantian, Heideggerian, or Sartrean conceptions of individual freedom and responsibility onto a Marxist theory of history and society. For further discussion see my "Leszek Kołakowki and the Revision of Marxism" in *European Philosophy Today*, ed. G. L. Kline (Chicago, 1965), pp. 113–56.

CHAPTER SIX / RELIGIOUS DISSENT IN THE SOVIET

UNION / BARBARA WOLFE JANCAR

In the latter half of the 1950s* Nikita Khrushchev's government launched the third religious persecution in the history of the Soviet Union. The virulence and brutality of this campaign rivaled its notorious predecessor of the 1930s. No faith escaped: Christian, Jew, Moslem, Buddhist, all fell victim to Khrushchev's determined effort to eradicate religion from Soviet life. Opinions differ as to why the Soviet leaders chose that particular time in history for this attack.[1] Its most significant effect, however, was the extraordinary opposition it generated among believers. The early 1960s saw the development of religious dissent for the first time in Soviet history.

Yet the role of the religious element in Soviet dissent has received virtually no attention. While studies of religion in the Soviet Union have been steadily increasing both in this country and abroad, none attempts to analyze the possible impact of this type of dissent on Soviet society as a whole.[2] Now the importance of religious dissent can no longer be ignored. It is responsible for more than a third of the available registered *samizdat* (self-published) material. In addition, 17,000 signatures to a 1972 memorandum protesting religious persecution, a 400-person sitin before the Central Committee building in Moscow, and the publication of some thirty-nine dissenting religious periodicals indicate considerable flexibility and breadth to the movement.

The main problem in an inquiry of this kind is that we do not know the extent to which the Soviet public is involved. We have no figures on religious dissenters. Even the data on religious membership are unreliable, since many

---

In memoriam Bernard Yarrow. The author would like to thank Gretchen Brainard, information officer, and the library personnel of Radio Liberty and the Russian Research Center of the Massachusetts Institute of Technology for their assistance to me in locating documents. My special thanks go to Dr. Paul Anderson and Dr. William C. Fletcher for answering my many queries on the status of religion in the Soviet Union today.

1. By general consensus Khrushchev launched the campaign (1) to show the USSR's ideological purity in the confrontation with China and (2) to strengthen his position in the Soviet Communist Party. See Michael Bourdeaux, *Faith on Trial in Russia* (New York, 1971), p. 61, and Joan Delaney Grossman, "Khrushchev's Anti-Religious Policy and the Campaign of 1954," *Soviet Studies* 24, no. 3 (January 1973): 374–86.

2. The exception might be William C. Fletcher and Anthony H. Stover, eds., *Religion and the Search for New Ideals in the USSR* (New York, 1967). This book attempts to analyze the impact of religious values on the search for new ideals launched by destalinization. The editors' general finding is that organized religion appeared to exert a minor role while the religious values embodied in Western culture played a much greater one.

believers are not members of registered congregations. Furthermore, many of those of Jewish or Moslem heritage do not practice those faiths. But some idea of the numbers of participants in the major religions can be gained from table 6:1.

Owing to the Soviet persecution of Judaism, organized Jewish religious societies constitute only the visible fraction of the whole. For this reason the figures given for Jews represent nationality rather than adherence to an active faith.[3] Otherwise the numbers are probably conservative. There are doubtless many more unregistered or nonpracticing people who believe in one faith or another to various degrees.[4]

But no approximation of membership, of course, provides a clue as to the numbers of dissenters in each religious grouping. When one tries to count the signatures on the various petitions that have come to light and assign them to cities and towns, the dissenters seem to be swallowed up in the Soviet countryside. Hence any quantitative study based on membership participation is impossible.

What is more feasible is a substantive analysis of religious dissent. The focus here becomes not numbers of believers but numbers, kinds, and frequency of issues raised. Here I believe one can identify at least three major areas of concern that have been broached by dissident elements within the major religions over the past ten years: (1) religion as a counterideology, (2) religion as a question of civil rights, and (3) religion as tradition and culture. Every recent manifestation of religious dissent appears capable of classification under one of these categories. All dissenters have raised the question of ethics and values. The Baptists and Orthodox have been much concerned with civil rights; the Jews and Moslems have been particularly involved in the attempt to preserve religious tradition and culture; and the Lithuanian Catholics constitute a special variant uniting both civil rights and the nationality issue.

In this chapter I shall investigate the substance of religious dissent during the 1960s by means of these categories. First I shall present a statistical analysis of the issues raised relative to the dissenters of the various faiths, then examine each of the various issues, and finally attempt to evaluate their significance in the larger context of dissent in the Soviet Union.

---

3. For a discussion of Soviet persecution of the Jews, see Joshua Rothenburg, "Jewish Religion in the Soviet Union," in *The Jews in Soviet Russia since 1917*, ed. Lionel Kochan (London, 1970), pp. 159–87.

4. In 1954 the official organ of the Evangelical Christians Baptists (ECB) identified 5,400 congregations and 512,000 baptized believers. The journal added that if one included members of believers' families and "other people close to our brotherhood" the number would come close to 3 million. *Bratsky vestnik* [Fraternal Herald], 1954, nos. 3–4, p. 91. The smaller Protestant sects, such as the Mennonites and the Lutherans, and the Georgian and Armenian national churches are not included in the table. The Protestant sects have been permitted no legal recognition and the latter are primarily national religious institutions whose membership has not participated in the recent dissent movement.

At the outset it is proper to recall briefly the present status of organized religion in the Soviet Union. Without a picture of the permissible parameters of religious activity it is difficult to understand what the religious ferment is all about.

Soviet legislation on religion can be seen as a progressive attempt to undermine the temporal and spiritual power of the various faiths. While the first decree on the subject in 1918 established the theoretical separation of church and state and permitted citizens to give or receive religious instruction in "a private way" (article 9), it dealt a grave blow to the faiths' economic power by pronouncing the property of all religious associations the property of the people (article 13).[5] The confiscation of religious property affected the Orthodox Church most severely and served as a pretext for the subsequent campaign to liquidate the church during the 1920's. The Baptists and other Protestant sects fared better mainly because they were relatively recent comers to the Russian religious scene and because their persecution under tsarism gave them no identification with autocracy. For the Jews, the 1918 decree meant the abolition of the Kehilah (Jewish communal council) and the beginning of the attack on Judaism by the Evsektsiia, or Jewish Section of the Communist Party. The future of the Moslems of Central Asia was still at issue. By a decree of November 24, 1917, the Soviet government promised all Moslems who supported the Revolution that their "beliefs and customs, national and cultural institutions" would "be henceforth free and inviolable." Subsequent proclamations in 1920 to 1922, established Friday as the day of rest and permitted continuance of the Shariat (or Moslem canon law) courts. These steps further encouraged Moslems to believe that their religion would be protected by Soviet law. But these illusions were shattered in 1925 and 1926 when the Shariat courts were gradually liquidated and the religious schools closed throughout Moslem Central Asia. Until the end of the twenties, the chief religion to suffer a coherently organized persecution was the Orthodox Church. The pattern of destroying Orthodoxy from within by "divide and conquer" through the Soviet creation of a rival Orthodox church, the Living Church, found its counterparts in the Soviet tolerance of controversy within the Protestant sects and the regime's efforts to promote disunity within Islam, Judaism, and Buddhism.[6]

---

5. For the text of the decree see Boleslaw Szczesniak, ed. and trans., *The Russian Revolution and Religion, 1917–1925: A Collection of Documents Concerning the Suppression of Religion by the Communists* (Notre Dame, Ind., 1959), pp. 34–35.

6. Steve Durasoff, *The Russian Protestants, Evangelicals in the Soviet Union, 1944–1965* (Rutherford, Madison, and Teaneck, N.J., 1969), pp. 61–74, and Zvi Gitelman, "Soviet Jewry: The Early Years," in *Aspects of Religion in the Soviet Union, 1917–1967*, ed. Richard H. Marshall, Jr. (Chicago, 1971), pp. 323–40. In 1923, the Moslem schismatics of Dagestan held a congress urging revision of the Shariat (Robert Conquest, ed., *Religion in the USSR* (London, 1968), p. 70), while an attempt was made to create a Soviet Buddhist center among the Buriats (J. J. Gaponovich, "The Siberian Tribes," in Marshall, *Aspects of Religion*, pp. 429 ff.).

The major campaign to eradicate religion got under way with the First Five-Year Plan. In 1929 a law was enacted to regulate religious associations that remains the basis of religious organization today.[7] Among its most important provisions are an injunction against religious education of minors and highly restrictive regulations regarding the registration of religious associations.[8] This law initiated a system of direct control by the Soviet authorities over local religious communities. The law thus may be considered the second step in the regime's program to uproot religion from the USSR.

The third step came in the form of agreements and regulations made with the various faiths during the 1941–44 period. These agreements imposed hierarchal religious organizations paralleling that of the Orthodox Church on the Baptist and Moslem faiths.[9] No such agreement was ever reached with Judaism or Buddhism.

This third step of the Soviet regime injected two new elements into religious life in the Soviet Union. It put the religious leadership as well as local religious communities under close Soviet control and thus opened up unprecedented opportunities for communist penetration of the religious hierarchies. It also sanctioned the uneasy *modus vivendi* of the atheistic state with the faiths it had pledged to destroy, thus creating the conditions under which believers could legally appeal discriminatory government actions. For while the 1936 constitution theoretically gave back their civil rights to believers, the terrible purges of the thirties almost succeeded in wiping out organized religion of any kind.[10] Through their sanction of legal religious organizations, the agreements reached in the forties legitimized the practice of religion in the Soviet Union.

In 1960–61, then, the issuance of a new set of regulations in conjunction with renewed persecution profoundly affected the life of all religious

7. The text of the Law on Religious Associations is in William B. Stroyen, *Communist Russia and the Russian Orthodox Church, 1943–1962* (Washington, D.C., 1967), pp. 121–27. Also see Dietrich A. Loeber, "The Legal Position of the Church in the Soviet Union," *Studies on the Soviet Union* 9, no. 2 (1969): 16–39.

8. If a group wants to worship, at least 20 believers of the same faith must petition the local authorities for permission to register as "a religious society." If the petition is approved locally, it then goes upward through the Soviet administrative hierarchy to the Council for Religious Affairs in Moscow. If the council approves the petition, the association may be considered registered and legal. The religious leader of the community must also be registered. State control does not end with registration. Article 14 empowers the registration agencies, i.e., the local authorities, to remove individual members of the association's executive body at any time. Opportunities for penetration of religious organizations by communist sympathizers under this provision are only too obvious. Finally, there can be no evangelism beyond the church doors (articles 17, 18, and 19). A pastor, priest, or rabbi may preach only in his own religious building, while the state retains control over all religious publications.

9. An account of the agreements made by the Soviet government with the Orthodox, Baptist, and Moslem faiths during this period is in Alexandre Bennigsen and Chantal Lemercier-Quelquejay, *Islam in the Soviet Union* (New York, 1967), pp. 171–83; Durasoff, *Russian Protestants*, pp. 117–73; and Stroyen, *Communist Russia and the Orthodox Church*, pp. 32–47.

10. William C. Fletcher, *A Study in Survival* (London, 1965).

communities. This was the immediate cause of the emergence of Baptist and Orthodox dissent. Long-standing deprivation had combined with a new onslaught of political strictures to convince some believers that if their religion was to survive, it had to be fought for.

THE ISSUES

Data for the kinds of issues raised by the dissenters in the major religious faiths have been culled from the Arkhiv samizdata of Radio Liberty. This source was chosen because of the general acceptance of both its authenticity and its serialization system. Material emanating from religious dissenters in the collection comes from the Orthodox, the Baptists, the Jews, and the Lithuanian Catholics. Unfortunately no documents primarily concerning Moslem dissent have come through samizdat, and thus this analysis of issues does not embrace it. Something will, however, be said about Islam later. Here it should be noted that while the case of the Crimean Tatars has Moslem overtones, it is, in my opinion, essentially a problem of nationality, not religion.

The same argument could be advanced in the case of the Jews; but here, I believe, the distinction between nationality and religion is more difficult to make. The very word Israel has highly religious connotations. Moreover, Jewish identity has been to a considerable degree a product of the historical persecution of an ethnic group primarily for its religious faith. Hence, at the risk of some distortion, I decided to include all Jewish contributions from the samizdat archive in my analysis. Since Buddhist dissent has been relatively marginal, I have reluctantly omitted it from the study. Finally, it should be stressed that the data presented here do not represent all samizdat religious literature nor all material having to do with religious dissent that may have appeared in the USSR but only registered documents from the Arkhiv samizdata.[11] No attempt is made to present a sample universe in order to "best guess" actual proportions of religious dissident activity in the Soviet Union because such statistical methods are inappropriate in this situation. The concern is to provide some picture of the types of issues raised, by whom, and in what form.

As can be seen from figure 6:1, by far the largest input into samizdat has come from the dissident Baptists, or the *initsiativniki* as they became known to the Soviet authorities.[12] The reader must be cautioned on interpreting

11. A broader selection of documents is contained in the Documentation Service on Religion in the Soviet Union compiled by Michael Bourdeaux in England.

12. The name derives from the original action group, or *Initsiativnaia gruppa*, which formed after 1961 for the purpose of convening a Baptist congress. While the dissenters changed their name to "Organizing Committee" after 1962, the Soviet press continued to call them *initsiativniki*. In 1965, with the development of a real schism between the dissidents and the parent organization, the dissenters called themselves the Council of Churches of the Evangelical-Christians Baptists. Michael Bourdeaux, *Religious Ferment in Russia: Protestant Opposition to Soviet Religious Policy* (New York, 1968), p. 21.

these figures. The calculations are based on numbers of documents emanating from the various faiths, not on numbers of signatures. In the latter respect the Lithuanian Catholics would probably achieve a very high percentage in view of their 17,000 signatures to one document alone. Still, the findings suggest that the input of Baptists, and to a lesser extent of Jews, has been well above their numerical size within the country as a whole (compare table 6:1). The dissent activity of the Orthodox, on the other hand, is much less than might be anticipated from the estimate of believers. The proportionately lower level of dissent initiative among the Orthodox gives some support to the argument that the Orthodox Church, despite persecution by the regime, has held a more privileged status than the other faiths—witness the 1945 agreements.

Table 6:2 provides a four-way breakdown of the raw data by kind of issue; by whether it was primarily designated for consumption at home or abroad; by religious faith; and by whether the document was written by a group or an individual. Summaries of the raw data are provided in tables 6:3 and 6:4, and by figures 6:2 and 6:3. In the categories of issues, "monographs" include any kind of commentary not listed under another category, such as

FIGURE 6:1

Percentage Participation of Major Religious Faiths

in Samizdat Archives to May 1973

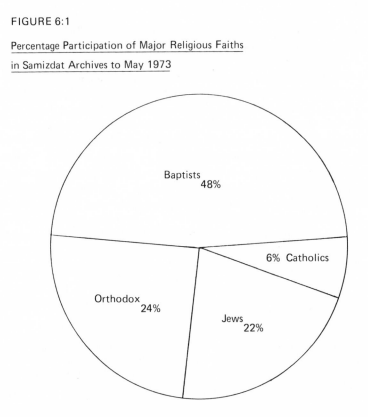

TABLE 6:1   Estimated Membership in Major Religions in the Soviet Union, 1970

Faith	Number of members	Faith	Number of members
Orthodox	50,000,000	Jewish	2,268,000
Baptist	500,000	Moslem	30,000,000
Roman Catholic	5,000,000	Buddhist	253,000

Sources: Orthodox, interview with Dr. Paul Anderson, who was given it by prominent Orthodox churchmen during his most recent visit to the USSR. Baptists (including full baptized and nonbaptized members), Alexander Karev, general secretary of the church, in *Bratsky vestnik*, 1966, no. 6, p. 17. Catholic, *East-West Digest*, 1970, no. 6. Jews, the figure for Jewish nationality from the 1959 census (rather than the 1969 census, which appears less reliable). Moslems, James Critchlow, "The USSR's Moslem Republics: Nationalist in Form and Nationalist in Content" mimeographed (1970). Buddhists (Buriats), 1959 census.

poems, long personal letters, and Easter greetings; "trial records" include court transcripts and official sentences; "affidavits, arrests, trials, sentences" include petitions filed under these headings as well as certifications by officials of the conduct of the accused at work; "persecutions and church closings" cover individual as well as group persecutions, such as the closing of the monasteries; "prison conditions" and "prisoner lists" are self-explanatory; "civil rights and religious freedoms" involve documents that specifically mention these issues. (While the violation of legality is very much at issue under the persecution and arrest categories, the civil rights heading means that the writer has drawn immediate attention to this issue. For example, much of the Jewish dissent in this area involved Jews writing to the Soviet authorities to renounce their Soviet citizenship or refusing to vote in elections because of their second-class status. Rather predictably, the Jews showed themselves most sensitive to this problem.) "Publications" include periodicals published by the religious dissenters under samizdat. "Internal appeals and church affairs" refers to the Catholic bishops' appeals to the faithful for caution in signing petitions and, most importantly, writings involving constitutional or canonical matters in the organization of a religious institution.

Certain features of the data are immediately striking. Petitions and accounts of persecution occur with the greatest frequency, and in the case of the Baptists and the Catholics they represent the highest percentage of dissent documents. Not quite so expected is the high frequency of monographs. As table 6:3 indicates, monographs on religious subjects rank highest among the Orthodox, primarily because of the large inputs from Anatoly Levitin-Krasnov.[13] Less prominent among the issues overall but

13. Peter Reddaway has informed the author that the Baptists have also written at length on theology. Not so many of their items have reached the West, however, nor have all of those that have been registered.

TABLE 6:2 Typology of Religious Dissent in USSR

Type of subject of Document	Baptists G^a	I^a	Orthodox G	I	Jews G	I	Catholics G	I	N
Monographs (incl. poems, etc.)	2	11	2	57		7			79
Trial records	6	11		2[b]	5			4	28
Arrests, trials, sentences	24[c]	16	3	3	6	11	2	4	69
Persecution, church closings	35	11	6	12	8	2	7	2	83
Prison conditions	11	5		1	2				19
Prisoner lists	9				2				11
Civil rights, relig. freedom	1	1		3[d]	3				8
Publications	39				6		4		49
Internal religious affairs	12	1	4	15[e]			2		34
Treatment of children	8	8			1				17
Emigration					27	20			47
	147	64	15	93	60	40	15	10	
Totals	211		108		100		25		444

Source: Albert Beiter, comp., "A Serial Register of the Arkhiv Samizdata," mimeographed (Munich: Radio Liberty, 1972) and the author's own review of AS 1127–1242.

Note: Mentions of religious activity in *Chronicle of Current Events* are not included, since they did not come from the religious groups themselves.

[a]G = groups (3 or more persons), I = individuals.
[b]Includes transcript of trial of Patriarch Tikhon in 1924.
[c]Includes only petitions addressed to persons abroad; does not include open letters.
[d]Includes Levitin-Krasnov's letter to the Human Rights Groups.
[e]Includes three letters involving persons abroad.

especially important for the Orthodox and the Jews respectively have been canonical matters and the question of emigration.

A second important fact is the degree to which the various faiths carried on their dissent in groups (three or more) or as individuals. Despite the difference in hierarchical structure between Jews and Catholics, the tendency to group or individual action is relatively the same. The organizing capacities of the Baptists indicated in figure 6:3 have historic precedent and have been commented upon by Bourdeaux and by Fletcher.[14] The capacity to organize would seem to have contributed in no small degree to the dissident Baptists' success in gaining concessions from the Soviet authorities, as did the Jews' organized campaign. In the latter case the data indicate a more concentrated attack focused on one particular issue as contrasted with the Baptists' more diversified effort.

14. Bourdeaux, *Faith on Trial*, chap. 4. William C. Fletcher, "Protestant Influence on the Outlook of the Soviet Citizen Today," in Fletcher and Stover, *Religion and the Search for New Ideals*, pp. 62–82.

TABLE 6:3 Frequency Distribution of Dissent Issues by Religious Faith

	Baptists		Orthodox		Jews		Catholics	
Kind of Issue	N	%	N	%	N	%	N	%
Monographs	13	6.2	59	54.7	7	7	0	0
Trial records	17	8.0	2	1.8	5	5	4	16
Petitions	40	18.9	6	5.5	17	17	6	24
Persecution	46	21.8	18	16.7	10	10	9	36
Prison complaints	16	7.6	1	.9	2	2	0	0
Prisoner lists	9	4.3	0	0	2	2	0	0
Civil rights	2	.9	3	2.8	3	3	0	0
Publications	39	18.5	0	0	6	6	4	16
Internal church	13	6.2	19	17.6	0	0	2	8
Children	16	7.6	0	0	1	1	0	0
Emigration	0	0	0	0	47	47	0	0
Total	211	100.0	108	100.0	100	100	25	100.0

Source: Table 6:2.

What is most significant is the individual initiative shown among the Orthodox. The high incidence of individual action does not mean a large number of persons involved; rather it refers specifically to the prolific writing of Levitin-Krasnov and Boris Talantov as well as letters and pleas by the priests Nicholas Eshliman, Gleb Yakunin, and Sergei Zheludkov and by Alexander Solzhenitsyn and a few others. There seem to be at most ten individuals, both intellectuals and priests, who constitute the vocal dissent in Russian Orthodoxy today. The church hierarchy as a whole has remained silent, as has the great mass of Orthodox believers. This finding suggests two complementary explanations. (1) The strict control over the choice of priests, which has been objected to by Eshliman and others, has succeeded in producing a compliant priesthood, and the line between compliance and

TABLE 6:4 Frequency Distribution of Religious Samizdat Documents Designated for the USSR or Abroad by Religious Faith

Faith	Abroad	USSR	% Abroad
Baptists	21	190	10
Orthodox	7	101	6
Jews	33	67	33
Catholics	1	24	4
Total	62	382	14

outright collaboration may be a small one, as the Osipov affair revealed.[15] (2) Except for the monastery and church closings, the mass of Orthodox believers appear to perceive no grievance against the present state of affairs of sufficient importance to unite for action.

A cautionary note is urged here. Lacking the disciplined approach by the Baptists and being accustomed to a strong hierarchical church structure, the

15. A. A. Osipov was an Orthodox priest who left the priesthood amid much publicity in 1959. He suddenly saw the "light," he said, and realized the childishness, emptiness, and pettiness of the religious life. He was subsequently defrocked and excommunicated by Patriarch Alexii, an action that cost the patriarch his position.

A reading of the documents gives strong substance to the contention that Osipov was in fact a plant by the Soviet government to discredit the church. A translation of the relevant documents can be found in Michael Bourdeaux, *Patriarch and Prophets: Persecution of the Russian Orthodox Church Today* (New York, 1970), pp. 46–57.

FIGURE 6:2

Frequency Distribution of Types of Religious Dissent

Found in Samizdat Documents

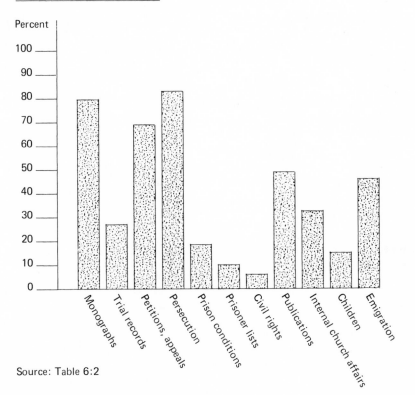

Source: Table 6:2

Orthodox would be less likely candidates for organizational initiative than their Protestant counterparts. Significantly, those who have chosen to dissent are among the better educated. By contrast, large numbers of Baptists of less education, such as the Sloboda family, have united to dissent. A second factor in the individual rather than group action of the Orthodox dissenters may be the historic fact that Orthodoxy has traditionally been the established church in Russia. Thus the ordinary Orthodox believer has had little prior experience in the management of dissent. By contrast, Jews, Catholics, and Baptists are continuing to experience a persecution similar to what they knew under the tsars.

A third finding of importance relates to the range of alternative types of dissent and the direction of this dissent to the audience at home and abroad. In both categories the Baptists and the Jews utilized ten of the eleven types

FIGURE 6:3

Percentage Distribution of Religious Dissent by Faith and by Group or Individual

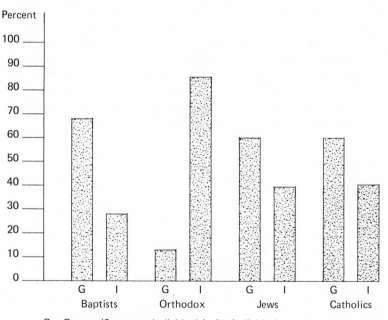

G = Groups (3 or more individuals), I = Individuals.

Source: Table 6:2

of dissent indicators, the Orthodox used seven, and the Catholics adopted only five. In their foreign appeals the Jews, as might be expected, concentrated especially on trying to reach officials at the UN and in Israel. It must also be remembered that most of their dissent periodicals have been published abroad. The comparative success of the Jews and the Baptists in being heard by the Soviet government leads one to hypothesize that a wide choice of dissent channels plus deliberate direction of this dissent abroad may be more productive than a more conservative approach.

Again a word of caution. Because of their history of persecution, the Jews and Baptists most probably expect little to be gained from negotiations with the Soviet authorities. Orthodox leaders, on the other hand, may feel that the best approach for the dominant religious group is not opposition but cooperation, with the possibility of quiet maneuvering.

Since the data presented here are a total population rather than a sample it is impossible to generalize from it. Nevertheless a certain pattern emerges as to the characteristics of dissent among the various faiths. (1) Organization, flexibility in the use of dissent techniques, and appeal beyond the Soviet attentive public are indicative of the Baptist and Jewish modes of operation, which suggests more integrated, goal-oriented movements. (2) Individual initiative, a more rigid application of dissent techniques, and a primary concern with the relevant Soviet audience indicate a weaker thrust to Orthodox dissent. (3) Because the Lithuanian Catholics are latecomers to the dissent scene, it may be too early to attempt to characterize their behavior pattern. On the basis of the data, however, it may be seen as midway between (1) and (2). On one hand it shows relatively strong organization; on the other it has been the most conservative in its dissent techniques and has made, at least in terms of percentages, the smallest effort to communicate with the non-Soviet world.

RELIGION AS A COUNTERIDEOLOGY

There is much force to Nicholas Berdyaev's argument that the dedication of the Soviet regime to the elimination of religions cannot be understood if one interprets communism purely as a social and economic philosophy.[16] The USSR is not a secular society. Atheism has replaced theism as the ruling faith. Traditional religion is thus placed in an untenable position of confrontation with the new ideology, with its insistence on the absolute of the earthly city, its liturgy of production figures and economic triumphs, and its pagan festivals. There are many dimensions to the challenge of religion to the communist life style. At the risk of oversimplification, it appears that they can be summarized under two headings: the need to reintegrate tradition into modern Soviet life, and the knowledge that some truths are not relative but eternal.

16. Nicolas Berdyaev, *The Russian Revolution* (Ann Arbor, Mich., 1961), pp. 1–47.

Religion and Tradition. The appeal of religion as part of the cultural heritage has been noted in several studies dealing with religion in the Soviet Union.[17] No one can read Brodsky, Boris Pasternak, Solzhenitsyn, or Anna Akhmatova without being sensitive to the pervasive religious imagery of their work. From the Arkhiv samizdata we have seventy-nine monographs analyzing the role of religion in contemporary Soviet society. Most of these are by two Orthodox believers, Levitin-Krasnov and Talantov. If the analysis that follows appears to overrely on the work of Levitin-Krasnov, it is because he has been the most prolific contributor to the intellectual life of religious dissent. Therefore it is to him we must turn for the main ideas while realizing that he must in no way be considered as representative of the various religious currents but as writing from his own beliefs.

A major appeal to tradition is to be found in Levitin-Krasnov's *Svataia Rus'* (Holy Rus.). For Krasnov, "Holy Rus'" is not a geographic or political term. It is primarily cultural, serving as an identity link between the past and present. "Holy Rus'" is "spirit and life, the collective expression of those blessed qualities that live in the soul of the Russian people and that are preserved in modern times only among believers, who alone demonstrate love, goodness, and suffering."[18]

Such a view contains strong overtones of traditional Russian messianic mysticism. A similar belief in the saving mission of the Russian Church is to be found in I. Denisov's "The Word of an Apostate," where the author reviews the history of the Russian Church, locating its tragedy in the fact that since Peter the Great it has never taken an initiatory position in the life of the country but has always stood to one side. The author sees the church in an analogous position today, unable to be the center of what he terms "the consolidation of the healthy forces of the country."[19] The failure of the church to live up to its mission in 1927, is the subject of Boris Talantov's monograph *Sergievshchina.* For Talantov, the then Patriarch Sergei's compromise was indefensible, for it created a "false division of all the spiritual needs of man into the purely religious and the purely sociopolitical." The agreement between an atheistic power bent on its destruction and the Orthodox Church was an attempt at communion between light and darkness, between Christ and Antichrist, which found its proper punishment in the outbreak of the Second World War.[20]

17. Zinaida Shakovskaya, "The Significance of Religious Themes in Soviet Literature," in Fletcher and Stover, *Religion and the Search for New Ideals*, pp. 119–29; George L. Kline, "Religious Themes in Soviet Literature," in Marshall, *Aspects of Religion*, pp. 157–86; Maurice Friedberg, "Jewish Themes in Soviet Russian Literature," in *The Jews in Soviet Russia since 1917*, ed. Lionel Kochan (London, 1970), pp. 208–15.

18. A. E. Levitin-Krasnov, "Holy Rus' in These Times," October 21, 1964, AS 719.

19. I. Denisov, "The Word of an Apostate: An Article on the Situation of the Russian Orthodox Church under the Soviet Regime," n.d. [probably around 1970], AS 1061.

20. Boris Talantov, "Sergievshchina or Compromise with Atheism (The Leaven of Herod)," August 1967–March 1968, AS 745. A good writeup in English may be found in John B. Dunlop, "The Recent Activities of the Moscow Patriarchate Abroad and in the USSR," mimeographed, (Jamaica Plains, Mass., 1970), pp. 109–116.

Solzhenitsyn draws on the same messianic vein of Orthodoxy in his Lenten letter to Patriarch Pimen, in which he criticizes the church's contemporary leadership for its failure to lead. "The lesson of Russian history over the last centuries confirms that it would have passed incomparably more humanely if the church had not renounced her independence. . . . Alas, . . . we have lost forever the bright esthetic Christian atmosphere upon which for a thousand years have rested our morals, our outlook on life, our world-view, folklore, even the very name of our people." Solzhenitsyn sees the possibility of church renewal only in return to the sacrifice and sufferings of early Christianity.[21]

The Orthodox appeal to an older tradition finds its echoes in Soviet Islam. The recent proliferation of literature dealing with Islam's past has been one of the central features of Central Asian writing in the past decade. While the relationship of Islam to Central Asian nationalism is left to another section, one example of the kind of appeal being made to the Moslem past is worth citing here. The work of an Uzbek poet, it attempts to link contemporary Central Asia with the Islam of Samarkand and Bukhara.

My cradle was the territory of Great Asia,
The cradle that rocked Ulughbek and Avicenna,
The light in whose eyes has spanned a thousand years
This is the world that led the caravan of history
This Samarkand, this Bukhara—these two universes.
This is the cradle of communism in the bosom of the East.[22]

The poem is clearly not a celebration of progress over a backward religion but an assertion of Islam as a superior historical force.

Similar appeals to their cultural past have been given by Jews seeking to leave the Soviet Union for Israel. *Exodus*, the Jewish samizdat periodical, displays an appropriate quotation from a psalm: "If I forget you, O Jerusalem, let my right hand wither away." Indeed, the main contention of Jews desiring to emigrate is that they have been cut off from their heritage.[23]

---

21. Alexander Solzhenitsyn to Pimen Patriarch of All Russia ("Lenten Letter . . . on the Situation of the Church in the USSR"), 1972, AS 1087, published in *Russkaya mysl'*, March 30, 1972.
22. Jämol Kämol, "Aamarquandu Bukhara bu . . . " [Samarkand and Bukhara, these . . .], *Shärqu Yulduzi* (Tashkent), no. 9 (1969), p. 117, as cited in James Critchlow, "Signs of Emerging Nationalism in the Moslem Soviet Republics," *The Soviets in Asia* (Mechanicsville, Md., 1972), p. 21.
23. The psalm quoted here is 136 in the Russian psalter, 137 in English versions. Here it is translated by the author from the Russian.
Mention should be made here of a member of the Communist Youth League. Alla Milikina, *Iskhod*, no. 2 (1970) published her letter to the 16th Komsomol Congress in which she relates that she is an orphan and wants to join her relatives in Israel. For this she is called a betrayer and is ostracized by her former loyal Komsomol friends. "I am Hebrew," she writes. "My fate is indissolubly linked with the fate of my people." She further regrets that she has no knowledge of Hebrew history, language, or culture, and calls on Soviet youth to help her. The letter is dated May 25, 1970.

Moral and Spiritual Values. While tradition seems to be a strong factor in the appeal of religion in Soviet Russia, the evidence suggests that the spiritual "truths" of religion carry even more weight.

In a letter to Pope Paul VI, Levitin-Krasnov gives us a clue concerning the current attraction of religion. The third generation under communism, he contends, no longer hates the church because of its association with tsarism, as did the first generation, and it is no longer indifferent to religion as was the second generation. Rather it is an unhappy generation for whom religion is part of its passionate search for truth.[24] This new type of believer is young and concerned. The Baptist dissent movement is primarily a movement of people under forty.[25] Young Soviet Orthodox intellectuals write: "Today again, there rises before the Russian conscience, weary from idolatry, the eternal problems of God, good and evil, death, the building of a just society."[26] A memorandum written by a young Soviet and recently received in the West indicates that the most sought-after books by young people in the Soviet Union after the Bible or the four Gospels are the writings of the Russian Christian philosophers.[27]

A major factor in the moral appeal of religious dissent is the poverty of the official atheistic creed. The official teaching is that the life of the individual and of all humanity has no meaning that is given beforehand and that does not depend on men. It is man who created the meaning of life. The Soviet citizen is told that the only way to realize this meaning is through the struggle to build Communism.[28] The rooting of the communist ethic in "devotion to the cause of communism and the love of the socialistic fatherland" makes the highest good the victory of communism.[29]

To accept such a proposition one has to believe that Soviet communism really is the highest good. What the religious dissenters offer is a kingdom not of this world, but nevertheless a kingdom brought a little nearer by the realization of a more humane, just, and honest community on this earth. Levitin-Krasnov, for example, argues for "neohumanism," which in his view is a "stateless, truly free, classless society, liberating man from need, fear, and force." This new type of body politic will be a true "theocracy," or rule of God.[30]

24. A. E. Levitin-Krasnov to Pope Paul VI "On the Situation of the Russian Orthodox Church," n.d. [probably ca. September 26, 1967], AS 389.
25. Gennadi Kryuchkov was just 40 at the time of his arrest in 1966, while Georgi Vins was only 38. Of the 212 prisoners given on the 1968 Baptist prisoner list, 33 percent are under 40, and 10 percent in their 20s. Bourdeaux, *Religious Ferment*, pp. 211–29.
26. AS 83. The letter was published in *Novoe russkoe slovo*, January 19, 1969.
27. The memorandum was written by a Soviet citizen 27 years of age who came to the West in early January 1973.
28. "A Conversation on the Meaning of Life," *Nauka i religiia*, 1965, no. 7, pp. 7 ff.
29. *Moralny kodeks stroitelia kommunizma*, [Moral code for the building of communism] (Moscow, 1964), pp. 29–30.
30. In a quasi-Christian socialist appeal, he affirms that "the living God will triumph when the earthly gods perish," when the advent of the international of neohumanism brings about the downfall of every kind of exploitation of man by man. A. Levitin-Krasnov, *Stromati* (Frankfurt, 1972), pp. 152–53.)

In a Western context such a message may seem trivial, justifying the accusation that the Soviet religious dissidents are not giving new breadth to their faith. But the samizdat literature leaves little room to doubt that what the Soviet believer wants is not a new religion but the old one purged of its complicity with power.

If such an argument has any validity, the second and perhaps most important aspect of religious dissent's moral appeal stems from the character of the dissenters themselves. The strength and integrity of such men as Archbishop Yermogen, Georgi Vins, Talantov, Levitin-Krasnov, and Solzhenitsyn stand out in sharp contrast to the behavior and practices of the various church hierarchies. There is an inherent moral righteousness about the dissident, and continued persecution by the authorities only reinforces it and makes it more appealing. Good confronts evil in Baptist leader Georgi Vins's final speech to his judges in the fall of 1966:

Not for robbery, nor for gold—
Do we stand before you.
Today here, as in Pilate's day,
Christ our Savior is being judged.[31]

Prison is an important factor in the strengthening of the moral position of the religious dissenters, as it has been in the case of other dissidents as well. One has only to read the poems of nineteen-year-old Aida Skripnikova[32] and Georgi Vins[33] to appreciate the profound impact of prison experiences on their faith. There is a strong temptation on the part of the Western observer to distance himself from the tales of torture and horror emanating from the camps. As Talantov pointed out in his complaint to the procurator general about religious persecution, there may be no law against holding a religious belief, but woe to the man who actively professes a faith![34] Prison would seem to be an experience that transforms the believer either into a determined militant or an apostate. The outsider can only look with humility on the individuals who have borne their imprisonment in the unshakable belief that this was their way to bear witness.[35] In this context, it should be noted that the man arrested for his faith appears to get more support from

31. As cited in Bourdeaux, *Faith on Trial,* pp. 128–29.
32. For one of Aida Skripnikova's poems, see "Privet vam, druzia!" [Greetings to you, friends], AS 841.
33. One of Georgi Vins's prison poems, which Aida Skripnikova managed to send out of the country before she herself was arrested for the second time, is translated in Bourdeaux, *Faith on Trial,* pp. 149–50.
34. Boris V. Talantov, "Complaint to the Procurator General of the USSR, R. A. Rudenko, Concerning the Persecution of the Church in Kirov Province and Also Concerning the Lying Campaign Undertaken Against It in the Press," April 26, 1968, AS 58.
35. Boris Talantov prophetically writes in his "Complaint": "Over the course of my whole life, I have expected that I would be arrested without any guilt on my part 'to rot in prison' or to be fired from work." *Ibid.,* pp. 5–6.

ordinary people than the intellectual. Bourdeaux even speaks of a "fraternity of support" coming from all sides, not just from Christians, for the Christian prisoner.[36]

The sense of witnessing for the truth appears to have provided strong motivation for the attacks on the canonicity of the Orthodox hierarchy and for the initsiativniki's dissent against the official Baptist endorsement of the notorious letters of instruction in 1961. It is one thing when the Soviet government blandly states that no Soviet citizen has ever been persecuted for his faith. It is another when the church hierarchy swears upon the Gospels that no such persecution exists and that no churches are being closed against the wish of believers.[37] Such obvious falsehoods make credibility in church leadership problematical if not highly suspect.

The defense of the Orthodox hierarchy that is willing to speak is eminently reasonable but not entirely convincing. It is the age-old argument that the church in its fight for continued existence must come to terms with every circumstance no matter how difficult. Can one really assume that the patriarch and his associates had no knowledge of the closing of churches and the persecution of believers? Or are they in fact practicing What Levitin-Krasnov has termed "*tsezaropapism*," or complete submission to civil power?[38] The line between an untenable situation and positive cooperation can be drawn too finely.

The question of being on the side of truth or Satan can pose serious problems for any believer. While on balance another Orthodox schism would seem unlikely and might indeed be disastrous for the church, it cannot entirely be ruled out.[39] The Baptist dissidents broke with the legal church institution over this very issue and, from available statistics, appear to have

36. As quoted in *U.S. News and World Report*, June 5, 1972, p. 30.

37. Patriarch Alexii went on public record as swearing that persecution did not exist at the Conference of Disarmament in London, February 16, 1960. In his complaint to Rudenko, Talantov made much of this statement and provided ample evidence to the contrary.

38. Sergei Zheludkov to Solzhenitsyn, Easter (April) 1972, AS 1167, in reply to Solzhenitsyn's Lenten letter cited above. Levitin-Krasnov discussed *tsezaropapism* (which might also be rendered "caesaropapism") in "Bolnaia tserkov" [The ailing church], August 27, 1965, AS 886.

39. Dr. Paul Anderson has talked with many of the Orthodox Church leaders and on that basis tends to minimize the support of the Orthodox dissenters within the church as a whole. In his opinion the central factor in Orthodoxy is the correct celebration of the liturgy as it has always been done. The first great schism under Peter the Great occurred over the issue of changes in the liturgy. Soviet support of the Living Church was only contributory proof of the diabolic nature of the movement, it was not central to disaffection with it. Thus, Anderson believes that so long as the church rites are celebrated with the traditional pomp and ritual the Orthodox dissidents will never gain a wide number of believers to their side. Personal interview with Anderson, April 18, 1973. Michael Bourdeaux, on the other hand, argues to the contrary. In his opinion, a rigged election of a new patriarch acceptable to Moscow but unacceptable to the faithful might widen the credibility gap between the rank and file and the hierarchy to the extent of a schism. Bourdeaux, "Dissent in the Russian Orthodox Church," *Russian Review* 28, no. 4 (October 1969). William C. Fletcher tends to agree with Bourdeaux. Fletcher to Jancar, April 30, 1973.

drawn about half the registered membership with them.[40] When we talk about religious dissidents we have to distinguish between at least four different types: (1) those who may not be practicing believers but nevertheless have a faith; (2) those who worship underground; (3) those who may be members of a legally recognized religious institution but conceal their lack of sympathy with its leaders; and (4) the active dissidents. Only the last group is visible; the other types represent a large reserve of latent popular disaffection with Soviet religious policies that may be susceptible of mobilization. It is this as yet passive, faceless populace that is attracted by the cultural and moral appeal of the different faiths, incarnated, so to speak, in the lives of a few heroic individuals.

RELIGION AND CIVIL RIGHTS

The issue of civil rights has been perhaps the most salient factor of religious dissent. Table 6:2 indicates that eight of eleven dissent indicators involve a civil rights issue, not to mention the many references to violations by the Soviet government of legal norms in the religious dissent publications. The main thesis of the Baptist and Orthodox letters and appeals to the Soviet authorities as well as their dealings with their own religious hierarchies was that illegality had been perpetrated and had to end. The Lithuanian Catholics protested their right to religious education, even though this right was specifically proscribed by the 1929 law, while the Jews protested the arbitrary manner in which visas were granted to would-be emigrants and their status of second-class citizens. Since the Jews were not so much concerned with changing injustice in the Soviet Union as escaping from that injustice to Israel, civil rights for them was not the major issue. Arkhiv Samizdata records no protests by the Moslems regarding infringement of their religious rights. Hence the Baptist and the Orthodox dissidents provide us with the richest data for the civil rights issue.

The Baptists. The springboard for the Baptist civil rights movement may be found in two documents issued by the All Union Council of Evangelical Christians Baptists (AUCECB) in 1960. These are the new statutes and the letter of instructions.[41] As the original statutes of 1944 and the 1948 revision of them were never made public, we cannot compare them with the 1960 version. A cursory look at the new statutes, however, indicates many areas where state interference is not only likely but invited.

40. Anderson estimates that about half the organized congregations, or 250,000 members, have gone over to the initsiativniki. His calculations are based on the number of delegates to the 1969 Tula conference relative to their proportionate representation among the membership.

41. The full text of the new statutes can be found in Bourdeaux, *Religious Ferment*, pp. 190–210. The full text of the letter of instructions is not available in the West, but references to it may be found in *Bratsky listok*. nos. 2–3 (February–March 1965). An excerpt from it is in Bourdeaux, *Religious Ferment*, pp. 20–21.

Article 4 says that the AUCECB shall consist of ten members, the "most experienced, active" members of the Evangelical Christians Baptist Church. Who determines the experience and activity of these individuals is not specified. None has to be an ordained minister. Article 11 leaves control of church officers with the council through the power of appointment, while article 12 gives these officers the right to impose discipline upon their local church. The AUCECB further maintains contact only with registered churches (article 13) and helps with the training of ministers through practical advice and instructions (article 15). Members of the AUCECB are elected at special conferences of responsible representatives (article 18). Again, criteria for "responsibility" are not given. Changes in the statutes are made by a two-thirds vote of the council (article 20). Among the duties of the presbyter is to watch over the religious activities of each registered community, especially with regard to the admission of new members and the character of religious services (article 22). One wonders whether the presbyter is the servant of the church or the state in this capacity. At all events, the presbyter's activities are reported to and examined by the AUCECB (article 24).

The new statutes were clearly designed to assert the supremacy of the AUCECB over the entire Baptist community. Given the traditionally loose organization of the Baptist Church prior to 1944, there is little doubt that such regulations ran counter to its fundamentalist, democratic spirit. More importantly from the civil rights standpoint, the dominance of the council in the life of the church, the imprecise methods by which it was to be chosen, and the lack of criteria for membership were positive openings for the Soviet authorities to intervene.

The letter of instructions complements the "hard line" policy of the new statutes. Primary among its stipulations (and these were issued by the AUCECB, it must be remembered) were an end of "zealous proselytization"; a reduction of baptisms between the ages of eighteen and thirty to a minimum; a prohibition against children attending services; and an injunction to the senior presbyter not to enlist new members nor to get too involved in his preaching but "to check unhealthy missionary tendencies." The two documents taken together made the governing council of the Soviet Baptist Church party to its own demise. They further provided substantial justification for the question posed by the three leading Baptist dissenters, Alexei F. Prokofiev, Georgi Vins, and Gennadi K. Kryuchkov, as to whose side the council was really on.

The revisions to the statutes presented by the Baptist dissenters is a truly extraordinary document to come out of the Soviet Union. Carefully it proceeds to change those articles that permit excessive state intervention into the life of the Baptist Church and give total control to the ECB Council. In essence it provides for a real separation of church and state, which theoretically is guaranteed by the Soviet Constitution. As such it contradicts Bourdeaux's contention that the initsiativniki initially presented no chal-

lenge to the Soviet state. Fundamental to Prokofiev's, Vins's, and Kryuchkov's dissent was the contention that the state had interfered where it had no
constitutional right. To rectify the situation, the revisions called for the
election of the council by a Baptist congress. Control of amendments would
also be taken from the council and vested in the congress.

Direct evidence that the Baptist dissent leaders definitely saw the problem
as a church-state issue comes from the letter Kryuchkov wrote to Khrushchev reviewing Soviet Baptist history and recent persecution by the Soviet
authorities. While assuring the Soviet leader that Baptists "remain unshaken
in their relationship to the state," Kryuchkov goes on to say:

This does not mean that . . . we should admit "the powers of this world" into the
leadership of our church. *Whatever state law might be* [italics mine], the church
must remain free from the interference of the world and the secular authorities in
her internal life. . . .

The state is now exerting a definite and *unlawful* opposition to this precise task of
purifying the ECB Church, which compels us to make a more thorough analysis of
the deprivation of rights to which the ECB Church has been subjected in our
country.[42]

The formal demand for guaranteed civil rights came in 1965, this time in a
letter addressed to Leonid Brezhnev in his capacity as President of the
Commission on the Constitution. The appeal asks for a revision of article
124 of the Soviet Constitution and cites Lenin, the decree of January 23,
1918, and the Declaration of Human Rights in support.[43]

The second Baptist thrust for civil rights derives from the petitions and
appeals against individual arrest and persecution drafted by those of the
Baptist rank and file who had chosen the path of dissent. On the basis of the
data presented in table 6:2, 65 percent of the Baptist dissent literature from
the Arkhiv samizdata, excluding material in the periodicals, involves
accounts of illegalities on the part of the Soviet government. While the bulk
of these comes from groups, a surprisingly large number, particularly in the
case of appeals from arrest or sentence, comes from individuals. The types of

---

42. Italics added. The full text of the letter to Khrushchev is given in Bourdeaux, *Religious
Ferment*, pp. 53–63.

43. The full text is to be found in *ibid.*, pp. 105–13. The letter made three specific demands:
(1) to guarantee de facto the separation of church and state; (2) to repeal the April 8, 1929 law
on religious associations; and (3) to clarify the formulation of the article on freedom of
conscience to include freedom of religious propaganda. A case could be made that the
American heritage of Soviet Baptism played a major role in helping the two men work out their
constitutional theory. The American influence was particularly evident during the 1920s when
Ivan Stepanovich Prokanov, a representative for Westinghouse, was a leading Baptist figure.
Significantly, one of the foremost Soviet researchers in religion, A. I. Klibanov, suggests that
the Baptist declaration of loyalty to the Soviet government coming at the same time as the
recognition of the Soviet Union by the British and the American governments was no
coincidence. Klibanov, *Religioznoe sektanstvo i sovremennost'* [Religious sectarianism and
contemporary society] (Moscow, 1969), p. 8.

injustices reported range from the inability of a congregation to gain legal registration to tales of children being taken from their parents and sent to orphanages because they were being given religious education in the home. The most serious accusations involve the deliberate torture of prisoners in the labor camps.[44]

The most significant development to emerge from the tragic litany of torture, beatings, harassment, monetary frauds, trials, and imprisonments has been the Council of Relatives of Imprisoned Baptists. Organized early in the reform movement, it was the direct result of the prison murder of Khmara. As was the case with Vins's and Kryuchkov's constitutional ventures, the council marked a new departure in Soviet history, and antedated its Czechoslovak counterpart, *K*-231, by four years.[45] Among the council's many activities, all of which have been carried on under incredibly difficult circumstances, should be noted the organization of relief and support for the prisoners' families; the publication of lists of those Baptists actually in prison; and the publication of a Bulletin that gives information to relatives about the prisoners' condition as well as hope and strength to carry on the fight.

The council has been very active in promoting the interests of its constituents by petitioning world organizations as well as Soviet authorities for help for prisoners in the camps. Among its most politically significant actions was its role in organizing the May 16, 1966 demonstration before the Communist Party Central Committee building in Moscow, when some 500 Baptists congregated to petition Brezhnev to allow them to hold a free all-Union ECB Congress composed of both registered and unregistered associations.[46] The evidence suggests that from its very inception the council has

44. One evidence of registration difficulty is AS 764, a 1970 petition by 1,454 believers in Naro-Fominsk (Moscow oblast) for official registration. Appeals like this are made for years with no positive response from the authorities. The best-known case of child removal is that of the Sloboda family; AS 615, 616, 845. Their story was widely reported in the Western religious press. A more recent case was that of 21 Baptists of Barnaul who wrote Kosygin and the local authorities explaining that their children were no longer in school because of cruel persecution by their classmates; AS 1225. Other religious parents were forced to take their children out of school because of inhumane treatment by teachers and classmates; AS 909, 1068, 1225. A celebrated incident in a labor camp was the brutal murder of Nicolai Kuzmich Khmara, an account of which was published in *Congressional Record* 110, no. 184 (September 24, 1964): 1. A more recent and equally bloody example was the alleged torturing to death of Ivan Vasileevich Moiseev in July 1972; *Bulletin of the ECB Council of Prisoners' Relatives*, no. 9 (1972), p. 59, AS 1205.

45. A brief description of Klub 231 is given in Barbara Jancar, *Czechoslovakia and the Absolute Monopoly of Power* (New York, 1972), pp. 203–4.

46. According to article 12 of the decree of 1929 and the 1961 amendment of the statutes of 1945, authorization must be obtained for all general meetings of members of religious associations. An account of the events preceding the demonstration and the brutal treatment of the demonstrators by the police is given by Bourdeaux, *Religious Ferment*, pp. 113–24. A fascinating aspect of the story is that apparently the KGB had been looking for Vins and Kryuchkov for some time and had been unable to find them. The arrest of the two took place on May 25, 1966, when they walked into the Presidium of the Supreme Soviet with a petition to hold the congress.

performed the functions of an interest group. It thus constitutes the first such group actively promoting civil rights in the communist world. Despite, or perhaps even because of, intense persecution, the group continues to operate. When a member is arrested new members appear from his family and the organization carries on. It is the council that forms the core of Bourdeaux's "fraternity of support."

To the Baptists, then, belongs the credit for two crucial components of the civil rights movement: the constitutional and legal analysis of the religious question made by its leaders, and the spontaneous organization of an interest group from below to work actively toward a civil rights end. It should not be thought that the two elements are separate entities; they are part of a complementary process to achieve the mutually desired goal of the end of state interference in religious practices.

The Orthodox Dissenters. Dissent in the Orthodox Church, as figure 3 shows, has displayed much less organization than the Baptist movement. But, since a split in the Orthodox Church involves some 50 million people, as opposed to a possible 3 million Baptists, Orthodox dissent represents a potentially more serious threat to the Soviet leadership. The slow evolution of the Orthodox movement bears out Bourdeaux's contention that it most probably was inspired by the Baptist initiative.[47] It had its origins in two post–World War II trends within the church: the Soviet government's exploitation of the patriarchy for its foreign policy objectives, and the silence of the patriarchate on the closing of churches and monasteries, which started in the late 1950s.[48] These two trends, coupled with the Osipov affair, might be thought to have been of sufficient concern to alarm members of the Orthodox clergy. But the immediate impetus to dissent came, as with the Baptists, in new political strictures contained in the acts passed by an extraordinary synod of bishops on July 18, 1961.[49]

Like the Baptist documents, the acts of the synod of bishops were aimed at reducing the independence of the church and promoting more control of religious activities by the state. The primary objection was to the elimination of the parish priest from the vestry or local church council. The acts provide an executive council consisting of three people: the elder, his assistant, and a treasurer, all elected by the congregation (article 3). The duties of the priest were limited to the performance in the church of public services (article 9) and the "spiritual guidance" of his flock. The executive council, on the other

---

47. Bourdeaux, *Religious Ferment*, pp. 183–89.

48. For a discussion of the role of the Orthodox Church in Soviet foreign policy, see Yury Marin, "The Moscow Patriarchate in Soviet Foreign and Domestic Policy," *Bulletin for the Study of the USSR* 8, no. 2 (February 1961): 32–38; and John Dunlop, "The Political Role of the Moscow Patriarchate," *ibid.* 7, no. 9 (September 1960).

49. The acts of the synod of bishops of the Russian Orthodox Church (July 18, 1961) are published in full in Bourdeaux, *Patriarchs and Prophets*, pp. 44–46.

hand, was given full control of the temporal affairs of the church, including finances, for which it was answerable to the civil authorities (article 5). In addition, article 4 stipulated that parish meetings of the entire congregation could be held only at the discretion of the local soviet, while article 12 required strict adherence by the clergy and the parish to civil legislation on the church.

The formulation of a protest to these measures, which were passed apparently in a great hurry and with no serious consideration, was four years in coming. On November 21, 1965, the Reverend Nicholas Eshliman and the Reverend Gleb Yakunin, both of the Moscow Diocese, sent a twenty-four-page letter to Patriarch Aleksii about the interference of the state in church affairs. On December 12 they addressed an eight-page letter to Podgorny describing the violation by officials of the Council for Russian Orthodox Church Affairs (CROCA) of the separation of church and state.[50] On November 25, 1967, Archbishop Yermogen wrote a six-page declaration to the patriarch in which he supported the position of the two priests.[51]

The documents indicate that the initial position of the Orthodox clergymen was considerably more radical than Kryuchkov's and Vins' original amendments to the Baptist new statutes. The letter to the Soviet authorities specifically defines eight areas where Soviet officials have acted illegally: (1) the registration of the clergy, whereby no priest can be ordained, assigned, or transferred without prior approval having been given *orally* by CROCA; (2) the campaign of the closing of churches and monasteries and the liquidation of religious societies;[52] (3) the registration of baptism and other church rites as a de facto introduction of the registration of religious affiliation of Soviet citizens prohibited by the Soviet Constitution; (4) the restriction of freedom to practice religious cults; (5) the violation of the principle of freedom of conscience in respect of children; (6) the violation of the principle of separation of church and state by means of administrative interference in the financial life of church communities; (7) the de facto limitation of a religious society to between twenty and thirty members, thereby denying to masses of believing citizens their legal rights to participate in managing the administrative and economic life of the Russian Orthodox Church; (8) the limiting of the staff of clergy, inhibiting the celebration of religious rites.

---

50. AS 7, 22, 723 and 724. English translations of the documents were published as *A Cry of Despair from Moscow Churchmen* (New York, 1966). A shortened version is to be found in Bourdeaux, *Patriarchs and Prophets*, pp. 189–223.

51. AS 75.

52. Metropolitan Nikodim made a statement on BBC on October 9, 1966 to the effect that between 1961 and 1964 10,000 churches had closed in the USSR due to a "lack of funds." Boris Talantov, "The Calamitous Situation of the Orthodox Church in the Kirov Region and the Role of the Moscow Patriarchate," AS 58; English trans., Bourdeaux, *Patriarchs and Prophets*, p. 144.

The letter to Patriarch Alexii is even more specific on all the points made to the Soviet authorities. As regards the registration of baptisms, Eshliman and Yakunin accuse the patriarchy of a "grievous sin" in supporting a practice for which there is no written law. They further implicate the patriarchate in complicity in the forced closing of churches and monasteries and censure the church leadership for its silence regarding the cessation of services in homes and the restriction of religious education for children.

The most powerful of the priests' accusations comes in their interpretation of canon law. The interference of secular officials, they assert, makes every ordination or election of church officials null. More important, the exclusion of the parish priest from the executive council and his election by the people utterly violate traditional canonical regulations on the duties and nature of the parish priest. This subordination of the priest to secular control is destroying parish life and dividing Orthodox Christians. Throughout their presentation, Eshliman and Yakunin make it clear that the submission of the patriarchate to the wishes of the Soviet authorities in these crucial areas has not been the result of legal legislation but merely a matter of *oral* agreement and habit. Like the Soviet authorities, the Moscow patriarchate is violating civil legislation as well as permitting the entrance of the "rules of the world" into the life of the church.

The Arkhiv samizdata gives us no evidence of any spontaneous movement of rank-and-file Orthodox to support the priests' position. Their greatest defenders have been Talantov and Levitin-Krasnov. Some historical reasons for the lack of Orthodox initiative have been cited earlier. Here it is well to recall two sociological realities of modern Orthodoxy. William Fletcher estimates that the present base of the institutional church is about a quarter of its pre-1927 base.[53] A great many would-be dissenters have most probably either joined the underground church or became indifferent to the controversy within the established institution. Their support or nonsupport of the patriarch may be just a matter of terminology. Secondly, there is the practice stressed in Eshliman's and Yakunin's letter of Soviet screening and approval of all clerical appointments. Under such conditions the likelihood that the majority of the priests will break with the state cannot be considered very great.

To the Orthodox dissenters belongs the credit of having linked up with the Moscow civil rights movement. The Arkhiv samizdata provides at least ten examples of cross-fertilization, among which should be mentioned Levitin-Krasnov's appeals to the chairman of the Russian Republic's Supreme Court during the Galanskov-Ginzburg trial and his article in defense of Vladimir Bukovsky;[54] his essay "A Light in the Window" on the occasion of the arrest of Maj. Gen. Peter Grigorenko, who had been active

53. Fletcher to Jancar, April 30, 1973.
54. February 9, 1968, AS 52, and "Not with Sword and Spear," April 7, 1971, AS 693.

in pushing the return of the Crimean Tatars to their homeland;[55] his letter to the Moscow Human Rights Group congratulating them on their formation;[56] Sakharov's letter to Podgorny on behalf of Krasnov;[57] the letter of Valery Chalidze to Patriarch Pimen on behalf of a group of believers in Naro-Fominsk;[58] and a letter by Chalidze, Sakharov, and Andrei Tverdokhlebov to the Presidium of the USSR Supreme Soviet asking pardon for nine Jews sentenced in the Leningrad trial.[59] The exchange of letters between Solzhenitsyn and Father Zheludkov may be seen as a further link in the chain.[60] Perhaps because of Krasnov's activism, the Moscow based *Chronicle of Current Events* started its coverage of the religious scene with Orthodoxy beginning in December 1968. The first reporting on the Jewish question came in 1969 and the Lithuanian Catholics and the minor Protestant sects were brought in in August 1970. Despite the extent and volume of the Baptist protest, the *Chronicle* did not give full coverage to the initsiativniki until October 1970.

In summary, the Baptists may be said to have provided the constitutional initiative and the grass roots organization for the civil rights issue. On their part the Orthodox performed the highly critical function of making contact with other dissident groups linked to the civil rights movement.

RELIGION AND NATIONALITY

While the dissent movement in the other three of the Soviet Union's major religions has had to do with the suppression of civil rights, its main expression has been focused on the question of national identity. Both the Jews and the Lithuanian Catholics have published widely in samizdat. The Moslems, however, appear to be isolated from the central core of religious dissent. What I will say about them here will thus be mainly conjecture, since I have no acquaintance with the languages of Central Asia and must rely on the reports of others. In the case of the Jews and the Moslems, the dissenters appear to hold the position that to be a Jew, or an Uzbek, Kazakh, etc., carries identification with a specific religion. As with Western Europe, religion for the peoples of Central Asia has been for centuries the traditional framework of a whole way of life that has survived fifty-odd years of communism.

55. In the essay, Levitin-Krasnov compares General Grigorenko to the Good Samaritan of the parable, who did not pass by the man who had fallen among thieves. The implication is that Christians have fallen behind in their manifestation of the Christian spirit toward their neighbors. May 24, 1969, AS 269.

56. Published in "An Addendum to *Chronicle*," December 30, 1970, AS 524.

57. May 23, 1971, AS 685.

58. February 26, 1971, AS 599. This was the Baptist group that has tried unsuccessfully to get their churches registered. See n. 44 above.

59. AS 625.

60. Solzhenitsyn's "Along the Oka" (n.d., probably about 1964) lamenting the closing of the churches should also be mentioned; AS 721.

The Jews. Of the hundred documents published by Jews in samizdat, forty-seven are specific appeals having to do with the difficulties individuals and groups have experienced in trying to get permission from the authorities to emigrate to Israel.[61] The Jews here would seem to be touching on a civil rights issue. Closer scrutiny of the appeals suggests, however, that what is actually being contested is not the general right of all to emigrate but the specific right of the Jews to return to their homeland. The several lengthy monographs on the Jewish question and anti-Semitism in the USSR support this contention. Roy Medvedev has written that the creation of the state of Israel radically altered the "Jewish problem" throughout the entire world so that the question of Jewish assimilation and "repatriation" are today entirely different. "Jews," he says, "have their *national* state."[62]

The discussion of the Jews' right to emigrate *qua* Jews seems to place the Jewish question squarely in the framework of nationality dissent. Yet further study of the documents suggests there is a point where something more than nationality enters in. The Soviet authorities themselves are not quite sure where to place the "Jewish question." At times Soviet ideologues label it an intrinsic part of the class struggle. In this view, Zionism is an attempt by international capitalists "to divert the toiling Jews away from the inter-national revolutionary struggle" with the help of the Americans and the European powers. The support of the Jewish masses is enlisted by the use of Jewish religious slogans relating to the "chosenness" of the Jewish people and the "advent of the promised land."[63] At other times the Jewish question is seen as a nationality problem that can be easily overcome by assimilation.[64] At still others, the Soviet regime gives the issue a religious cast.[65]

The ambivalence of the Soviet authorities as to the nature of the Jewish problem finds its analogy among the Soviet Jews themselves. Anti-Semitism in the USSR has focused on the elimination of the Jews both as a nation and as a religion. While Judaism knew the bitter persecution of the 1920s common to the other faiths, there was no agreement made with it after

---

61. I have excluded the Galanskov-Ginzburg trial from this total, as my analysis of the trial document leads me to conclude that it had more to do with intellectual freedom than with the question of Jewishness or the persecution of Jews in general.

62. Roy Medvedev, "*Samizdat*: Jews in the USSR: Document: Soviet Union," as published in *Survey* 17, no. 2 (Spring 1971): 194.

63. I. Braginskii, "The Class Nature of Zionism," *Kommunist*, 1970, no. 9 (June), pp. 101–12.

64. The 1970 census reported an unexpected decline in the number of Jews to 2.15 million from 2.27 million in 1959. Official explanations centered on the fact than an increasing number of Jews declared themselves to be Russians or members of some other nationality. Jews have accused the Soviet authorities of manipulating statistics. *New York Times*, May 8, 1971.

65. G. Bakunuskii, "Zionizm i Sotsialnaia doktrina iudaizma" [Zionism and the social doctrine of Judaism], *Nauka i religiia*, January 1972, pp. 58–63; I. S. Ivanov, "Antikommunisti-cheskie ustremleniia sovremennogo Zionizma" [Anticommunist aspirations of contemporary Zionism], in *Religiia v planakh antikommunizma* [Religion in the plans of anticommunism], ed. M. V. Andreev (Moscow, 1970), pp. 197–221.

World War II for its continued existence. No Jewish seminaries were opened, and the authorities closed synagogues with perhaps more relish than Christian churches during 1961–64. Even graveyards were violated.[66] By the 1950s knowledge of Hebrew had virtually vanished, and the publication of Hebrew and Yiddish literature seems gradually to have come to an end after 1965.[67]

Under such conditions many Jews appear to have lost a sense of religious identity. One writer, Grigory Svirsky, describing his experiences in a samizdat work, wrote that he had always considered himself a Russian. However, in the aftermath of Khrushchev's antisemitism campaign against the Jews, in 1965, he found he could not get his books published. To his astonishment, the characteristic reaction to his protest against the anti-Semitic policies of the Writers' Union was, "How is it possible that a Russian writer is a Jew?" There followed a vicious campaign of harassment, investigation by the authorities, and other "administrative measures" against the author.[68]

This pattern was repeated throughout the 1960s in the USSR.[69] Individuals who had never thought of themselves as particularly Jewish started to identify themselves as Jewish because of persecution.[70] Although only vaguely defined, the religious element would seem to have played some part in this development. Witness the enormous crowds that have assembled around the synagogues, particularly in Moscow at Passover time, and the accounts of individuals who have been persecuted for teaching the faith and the Hebrew language.[71]

Apart from these scattered examples there is little evidence that religion did much to arouse the new national feeling of the Soviet Jews except for its direct association with Jewish culture and history. In the context of the total dissent movement, the distinguishing characteristic of Jewish dissent has

66. Twenty-six representatives of the Jewish intelligentsia to A. Snechkus, February 2, 1968, AS 64.

67. In 1959, after 11 years of procrastination, three books in Yiddish appeared in the USSR: the selected works of Mendele Moykher Sforim, Y. L. Perets, and the Sholem Aleichem. Publishing in Yiddish continued through 1964–65 but subsequently petered out. Ch. Shmeruk, "Yiddish Literature in the USSR," in Kochan, *Jews in Soviet Russia*, pp. 266 ff.

68. Grigory Svirsky, "Why?" as translated in *Survey* 18, no. 2 (Spring 1972): 161–67.

69. For other examples the reader is referred to Peter Reddaway, ed., *Uncensored Russia: Protest and Dissent in the Soviet Union* (New York, 1972), pp. 298–318.

70. Jews in Vilnius to Secretary General Thant of the United Nations, the U.N. Human Rights Commission, and Premier Golda Meir of Israel, May 18, 1970, published in *Iskhod*, 1970, no. 2, pp. 12–13.

71. *L'express* gives a good account of the Passover crowd of 400 young people near the synagogue on Arkhipova Street in Moscow, March 29, 1971. When the police tried to disperse them, they regrouped. In the melée that followed, one 15-year-old was stomped into a puddle. Thirty were later detained by the police for three hours. The magazine also carried the story of a doctor, Herbert Braunover, who, after being warned that he must stop teaching Hebrew and the Torah, was forced to leave his job as a physician. His wife, a pharmacologist, was fired, and the doctor was subsequently accused of vehicular homicide. *L'express*, June 28–July 5, 1971, pp. 4–5.

been its ability to appeal abroad (see table 6:4) and its success in mobilizing international resources to secure concessions from the Soviet authorities. In this effort its ethnic ties with international Jewry would seem to be paramount.[72]

The Moslems. To the best of my knowledge no specifically Moslem dissent movement has yet been organized. A great deal of documentation suggests, however, the emergence of a Moslem-based anti-Russian feeling in Central Asia. In this setting Islam has usually been considered an adjunct of a rising local nationalism rather than an independent force in its own right.[73] But a summary survey of the data suggests the possible evolution of a pan-Islamic consciousness simultaneously with the development of local national feelings.

Islam is similar to Judaism in its total identification with a way of life, but it is akin to Christianity in its acceptance by a diversity of peoples over the course of time. While the Moslems under Soviet rule have never been allowed a religious publication, as have the Baptists and the Orthodox, each union republic that once was part of the *umma*, the traditional nationless Moslem society, is permitted mass media. At present these are our most valuable sources of information about the religious renaissance that appears to be taking place in Soviet Central Asia.

The renaissance can be attributed mainly to two factors. The first is the rising sense of accomplishment and achievement experienced by the Central Asian nationalities as their republics have industrialized. Economic progress has increased anti-Russian feelings, especially among the Central Asian elites.[74] In their search for identity the logical starting point has been Islam.[75]

72. A popular documentation of this effort is Richard Cohen, ed., *Let My People Go* (New York, 1971).

73. Bennigsen and Lemercier-Quelquejay, *Islam in the Soviet Union*, and Alexandre Bennigsen, "Islamic or Local Consciousness among Soviet Nationalities?" in *Soviet Nationality Problems*, ed. Edward Allworth (New York, 1971). The first book is the only one available that deals exclusively with the religion of Islam as distinct from the nationality problem in Soviet Central Asia. Geoffrey Wheeler, on the other hand, points out that the present union republics are completely artificial entities and that there is thus an absence of characteristic indications of nationalism in Soviet Central Asia; *The Modern History of Soviet Central Asia* (New York, 1966), pp. 147–55. See also Critchlow, "Signs of Emerging Nationalism," and Grey Hodnett, "What's in a Nation?" *Problems of Communism* 15, no. 5 (September–October 1961): 2 ff.

74. One of the main irritants has been the dominance of Russians or Slavs in the key economic and political posts of Central Asia. In the 1920s the Soviet government preached a doctrine of *korenizatsiia*, or an assigning of Moslems to administrative posts proportionate to their number in the total population. In practice this has meant that the president of a republic's council of ministers or the first secretary of its communist party is a Moslem while the director of the planning commission, the minister of communication, or the second party secretary is a Russian. Thus while Moslems are admitted into the administration, their control is carefully restricted by the Russians. A discussion of this problem is in Bennigsen, *Islam in the Soviet Union*, pp. 210 ff.

75. The degree to which the Central Asian peoples have not mixed with the Slavic nationalities has been well documented. In every case, Turkic peoples have retained their mother tongue for use at home and among themselves while learning Russian as a second

Secondly, in a world of peaceful coexistence marked by Arab-Israeli tension and the Chinese-Soviet rift, Islam, like Orthodoxy, has been viewed by the Soviet authorities as an excellent propaganda vehicle. But if it was to serve this purpose a certain leniency toward the practice of the religion was necessary. Thus the Soviet leadership has been caught in a dilemma. On the one hand it must continue to assert that Islam is a vestige of the past that does "great harm to the Soviet people."[76] On the other it has to prove to potential and actual allies in the non-Soviet Moslem world, not to mention the Moslems in China, that there *is* religious freedom in the USSR.[77]

Islam thus finds itself in a position analogous to that of the Orthodox Church with one important distinction. Commentators on Islam tend to stress its nonhierarchial nature and essentially democratic structure. The believer is not dependent on the services of a church in order to practice his religion, as the mosque dispenses no saving sacraments which believers are obliged to attend. Since the strength of Islam lies in individual rather than group observance, unlike Orthodoxy or Catholicism, destruction of its institutions—the mosques, *madresahs* (higher educational establishments), and *mektebs* (schools attached to the mosques)—does not strike at the heart of the faith.[78]

The continuing vital hold of Islam on the Soviet Moslem peoples is borne out by the extent to which it is castigated in the local Central Asian press. Among the usual fulminations about inadequacies in antireligious propaganda and the persistence of barbarous customs and traditions, certain rudiments of protest can be discerned.

Two events in particular seem significant. The first is from the region of Narabad in the Tadzhik Republic. In September 1970 a group of men was tried for "destroying the social order." The inference was that they had attempted to organize a protest against religious persecution by sending letters to state and party organizations. While one can only speculate on influences, the outside protest method was similar to that of their Christian colleagues and the Crimean Tatars.[79]

---

language. In addition there is a tendency not to seek interracial marriages. A good study of this problem is Robert A. Lewis, "The Mixing of Russians and Soviet Nationalities," in Allworth, *Soviet Nationality Problems*, pp. 116–65.

76. *Kazakhstanskaia pravda*, March 16, 1961.

77. The Soviets are the first to admit that the role of Islam in the "national liberation" movement is a complicated and little-studied question. While sociologists are quick to point out the class character, the celebration of poverty, and the love of private property they interpret as central to Islam, they admit that "at times" Islam can play a positive role, as it did in Algeria. Under no conditions, however, can any kind of Islamic socialism be considered true socialism. G. M. Kermimov, "Islamskii antikommunizm na sovremennom etape" ("Islamic anticommunism at the present stage"), in Andreev, *Religiia v planakh*, pp. 170–96.

78. Louis Dardet and M. M. Anawati, *Introduction à la théologie musulmane: Essai de théologie comparée* (Paris, 1948), especially chap. 1; H. A. R. Gibb, *Mohammedanism* (New York, Oxford, London, 1969); Reuben Levy, *The Social Structure of Islam* (Cambridge, 1965), especially chap. 1, "The Grades of Society in Islam."

79. *Soviet Tojikiston*, September 23, 1970.

An even more incredible event took place in the village of Alar in the Azerbaidzhan Republic, also in September 1970. According to the official report, 5,000 or 6,000 persons assembled in this village to see a ritual play lasting three hours. It developed that the event had been organized with the consent of local party, state, and *kolkhoz* (collective farm) officials, who arranged for buses to collect the faithful and bring them in. When questioned every official from the top down insisted he knew "nothing about it," even though the play was an annual event. Although no mosque is legally registered in that area, according to the official account, there are in fact many underground mosques that are active centers of religious life. In addition, the custom of pilgrimages to the shrines of Moslem saints is very much alive.[80] The native authorities went through the motions of prosecuting the most visible offenders in the Alar case. The kolkhoz chairman who apparently had arranged the play was deprived of his job by the court. But two weeks later he was given the chairmanship of an even larger farm.[81]

The coverage given this case makes one wonder whether it might be one among many and to what extent they are organized in defiance of Soviet antireligious preachments. A further fascinating question is whether there is any relationship between the two events.

Aside from such specifically religious indications of dissent, another phenomenon closely connected with Islam has appeared: *mirasism*, from an Uzbek word meaning "traditional heritage." *Mirasism* focuses on the rehabilitation of Moslem culture and Moslem historical personalities, particularly those of the nineteenth century.[82] David Nisseman has identified three types of tradition operative in the Soviet Union: new Soviet-created traditions such as the wedding ceremony, "progressive" traditions that can be integrated into the Soviet world view, and "reactionary remnants" of the past.[83] In their quest to recover legitimacy for the past, Central Asians have tried to rehabilitate every important Moslem in their history under the label of "progressive." The difficulties they have encountered have been recorded by Robert Conquest and others.[84]

As an exponent of Islam's cultural heritage, *mirasism* rebuts the Soviet argument that Islam has consistently been a backward religion. It thus raises

80. A Soviet analysis of this custom may be found in V. N. Basilov, *Kul't sviatykh v islame* [The cult of saints in Islam] (Moscow, 1970).
81. Räfail Naghiyev, "The Event in the Village of Alar," *Kommunist* (Baku), September 4, 1970, as translated by David Nisseman for Radio Liberty Committee, mimeographed (Munich).
82. For an account of the renaissance of Islamic culture in nineteenth century Central Asia, see chaps. 13–15 in Edward Allworth, ed., *Central Asia: A Century of Russian Rule* (New York, 1967), pp. 349–485.
83. David Nisseman, "Turkic Nationality Tensions in the USSR," mimeographed (prepared for Radio Liberty Committee, 1968), pp. 2–5. See also Critchlow, "Signs of Emerging Nationalism," pp. 18–27.
84. E.g., the account of the rehabilitation of Shamil in Robert Conquest, "Some Further Rewriting," *The Nation Killers* (New York, 1970), pp. 164–78.

the whole problem of the interpretation of the Russian presence in Central Asia. By the end of the nineteenth century modernization in much of the old Central Asian *umma* was well under way, spurred on by the work of Moslem reformers, or *Jadids*, and inspired by the genius of Ismali Bey Gaspirali, the author of pan-Turkism. A valid argument could be made that at that moment the Central Asians were the leading Islamic proponents of the modernizing movement.[85] When the Revolution came, many progressive Central Asians saw in Bolshevism the only answer to colonialism and turned their thoughts to the derivation of new communist theory based on their experience. The best known of these, the Tatar Sultan Galiev, worked out a program that he believed would win the agrarian East to Marxism-Leninism. The crux of his plan was the organization of an all-Moslem federation of the Moslems under Russian rule. But the Soviet government totally rejected the idea in establishing the Union republics, and Galiev was subsequently liquidated.

The history of Moslem Central Asia's resistance to Russian imperialism and the present search for an identity to withstand Russification[86] give strong support to the argument that *mirasism* and the revival of Islam in the 1960s are not mere adjuncts of local ethnicity but are pivotal to the development of a collective anti-Russian consciousness among all the Moslem nationalities. Islam may not be serving a religious function as much as providing a focus for joint action by the Central Asian elites in their pressure on Moscow. The 1970 census showed the Islamic population growing three to four times faster than the Slavic.[87] Thirty million Moslems represent a formidable challenge to Moscow. "Moslem power," even though not specifically religious in tone, carries economic and political weight. Richard Pipes has suggested, and the 1969 Tashkent riots seem to substantiate, that to be Russianized and to be communist have been perceived as identical. If so, it is highly possible that Central Asia will never accept atheism.[88] In view of the fact that Islam did not acquire the connotations of despotism that accrued to the Orthodox Church under tsarism, the faith must be seen as the one unifying element of the Central Asian republics' cultural tradition about which there are probably few reservations. The

85. Hélène d'Encausse points out that Gaspirali's pamphlet "To the Moslems of All Russia," published in 1876, as well as two other works on Islam and modernization, argued that Muhammed's teaching, far from being reactionary and paralyzing, was dynamic, leading to progress. Hélène Carrere d'Encausse, "The Stirring of National Feeling," in Allworth, *Central Asia*, pp. 177–78.

86. The impact of Russification on Central Asia is well defined in Frederick C. Barghoorn, *Soviet Russian Nationalism* (New York, 1956), especially in chaps. 3–5.

87. The birth rate for the Russian Republic in 1970 was 5.9 per 1,000 persons. For the Kazakh Republic it was 17.3, for the Azerbaidzhan Republic 22.5, for the Uzbek Republic 28, and for the Tadzhik and Turkmen republics more than 29. Tsentral'noe statisticheskoe upravlenie pri Sovete ministrov SSR, *Narodnoe khozaistvo SSSR v 1970* (Moscow, 1971), pp. 50–51.

88. Richard Pipes, "Islam and Communism," *Baltimore Sun*, July 21, 1960.

centripetal implications of mirasism and an Islamic revival would seem to carry more explosive power than those of any other major religion in the USSR.

The Lithuanian Catholics. The actions of this last group of dissenters are representative of both the civil rights and nationality aspects of the dissent movement. Priority of importance goes to civil rights, as 60 percent of the documents in the Arkhiv samizdata relates to this area (see table 6:3). The letter to the secretary general of the United Nations signed by 17,054 Catholics paints the all-too-familiar picture of discrimination.[89] On the other hand, the documents make it quite clear that what is being discussed is the situation in Lithuania. This point is stressed by the Reverend Juozas Zdebskis's statements at his trial.[90] In view of the fact that the documents were written in Lithuanian and "Lithuanian" figures in the name of the dissent publication *Chronicle of the Lithuanian Catholic Church*, it has to be assumed that the movement is largely confined to those who are both Roman Catholic and Lithuanian.

Given the lateness of its beginnings, it is probable that the Lithuanian protest gained force as a consequence of the development of Baptist and Orthodox dissent. The use of petitions and appeals is similar to the methods of other Christian dissidents, while the Lithuanian complaints are virtually identical. As with the other religious groups, the Lithuanian Catholics' religious leaders—Fathers Seskevicius, Zdebskis, and Bubnis—have been tried and imprisoned. The activity of the Lithuanians, however, differs from that of the other religious dissenters in two important respects. The first is the sheer numbers of persons involved. According to Lithuanian sources, despite knowledge that there would be reprisals against Catholics who signed the memorandum to the United Nations, believers signed by the thousands. *Chronicle of the Lithuanian Catholic Church* informs us that the KGB rounded up many of those who were collecting signatures, confiscated texts of the memorandum, and threw away the signatures collected. So many more than 17,000 probably signed.[91] This is an incredibly high number of signatures for a single document anywhere in the world and particularly in the USSR. In sheer mass protest the only competition is the Crimean Tatars. The collection of the signatures alone attests to an amazing organizational ability and solid mass support.

A second aspect of the Lithuanian protest has no counterpart in other dissent movements. This is the use of violence: the self-immolation of Roman Kalanta in Vilnius prior to President Nixon's Soviet visit and the

---

89. December 1971–January 1972, AS 1091. In March 1973 I telephoned the secretary general's office to find out what had happened to the letter. The office was unable to locate it.
90. November 11, 1971, AS 1067.
91. *Chronicle of the Lithuanian Catholic Church*, no. 2 (1972), translated into Russian by Radio Liberty Committee, mimeographed (Munich), pp. 1–2.

two days of rioting it touched off. The incident was the more remarkable given Roman Catholicism's attitude toward suicide. When this factor is coupled with the severity of the riots we gain some appreciation of both the desperation and the hostility present in the Lithuanian situation, which do not seem to have been such critical factors in the other movements we are examining. The use of violence suggests the hypothesis of an embittered nationalism buttressed by an intense religious faith. Soviet sources accuse the Vatican's policy of *aggiornamento* of being "one of the basic causes preventing the final break of believers with religion. It is easier to battle with a decaying religion than with one that has been renovated."[92] Apparently the Lithuanian Catholic hierarchy has been highly successful in its efforts to modernize; hence the frustration of its priests and the continuing strength of Catholicism in Lithuania.

The injection of violence into the religious dissent issue raises the whole question of the degree of frustration experienced by believers of all kinds at a given moment and the threshold at which frustration may erupt. It is notable that in Soviet terms the participants in the Lithuanian riots were treated fairly leniently.[93] The absence of mass arrests suggests that the authorities were reluctant to inflame a highly volatile situation. If this is the case, one may hypothesize a threshold of frustration above which violence cannot be ruled out as a weapon in the arsenal of future religious protest.

EVALUATION

The foregoing discussion suggests at least three approaches to an evaluation of the religious aspect of dissent in the Soviet Union: (1) in terms of issues; (2) in terms of its ability to achieve stated goals; (3) in terms of its interaction pattern with other groups in Soviet society.

The Issues. The issues raised by the religious dissenters are among the main problem areas plaguing contemporary Soviet society. In this sense, religious dissent cannot easily be labeled either conservative or progressive. Religion has taken on a left-of-center posture with the Leningrad Christian socialists,[94] and the *Veche* group may be classed as conservative;[95] but the primary focus of the religious dissidents themselves has not been political

92. K. Rimaytis, article in *Sovetskaia Litva* (Vilnius), August 12, 1973, pp. 2–3.

93. The most active among them were arraigned as "hooligans" and sentenced accordingly. The apparent leader, a 17-year-old by the name of Richardas Truskhauskas, was also charged with group rape and received a ten-year sentence, while other possible ringleaders were sentenced under similar charges. "Deserved Punishment," *Sovetskaia Litva* (Vilnius), January 3, 1973, p. 4.

94. The program of the *Sotsial-Khristiane* (AS 525) was published in *Posev*, 1971, no. 1, pp. 38–43.

95. For an analysis of what might be called the Russian conservative, patriotic dissent movement, see Dmitri Pospielovsky, "The *Samizdat* Journal *Veche*: Russian Patriotic Thought Today," mimeographed, CRD 331/71 (Munich: Radio Liberty Research, November 5, 1971).

but ethical and procedural. Andrei Amalrik has expressed the viewpoint of many Soviet intellectuals in his belief that real liberation in the USSR is impossible in the absence of an alternative ideology generated from either above or below but rooted in some kind of moral principles.[96] As I have tried to show, religion has provided this alternative for Moslem and Christian alike. If one accepts Berdyaev's interpretation of Soviet Marxism-Leninism as essentially a religious belief, then the theistic religions would seem the more logical replacement to atheism than a secular philosophy. The acceptance by Solzhenitsyn and other Soviet intellectuals of Christianity supports this contention.

Talcott Parsons has argued that "a legitimation system is always related to and meaningful dependent on a grounding in ordered relations to the ultimate reality that is . . . always in some sense religious."[97] The question posed by Soviet society is whether the problem of meaning, in Max Weber's sense, can be solved by a materialistic faith whose absolute is the victory of earthly communism. The evidence suggests that official Marxism-Leninism has been incapable of providing satisfactory answers to the basic questions of man's mortality and of good and evil. Hence the revival of organized religious beliefs in the Soviet Union and the potential power of the religious dissenters. When this aspect of religion is combined with its thrust toward individual liberties and identification with national consciousness, it can be understood why the Soviet authorities are so determined to uproot theistic faiths from the minds and hearts of the Soviet people. The three issues raised by the religious dissenters also explain why religion cannot be considered an epiphenomenon that will wither away with the banishment of prejudice and superstition.

The Ability to Achieve Stated Goals. The dissident movement has demonstrated considerable ability in this domain. First place must go to the Baptist initsiativniki in getting the ECB statutes modified in 1963 and again in 1966. Considering the odds against them this was a notable feat. Among other things, the dissidents managed to include in the revised statutes a triennial church conference, the election by this conference of the executive council, the appointment of senior presbyters approved by the churches of which they are a member, the elimination of the paragraph on strict "church discipline," and the suppression of an article that permitted baptism only in the summer.[98] In the 1966 statutes the Central Executive Council was expanded to twenty-five with provision for the council's election of the ECB president and general secretary as well as the president and secretary of the

96. *Will the Soviet Union Survive until 1984?* (New York, 1970), pp. 36–41.
97. *Societies: A Comparative and Evolutionary Perspective* (Englewood Cliffs, N.J., 1966), p. 10.
98. The full text of the 1966 statutes can be found in Bourdeaux, *Religious Ferment*, pp. 190–210.

triennial congress. In addition, area superintendents were created to function between the council and their areas. Delegates to regional meetings were to be named by the churches, one representative for every fifty members. The expansion of the AUCECB and the creation of regional administrations indicates certain concessions to democracy on the part of the Soviet regime, although the regional organization seems to parallel CPSU structural lines. Perhaps the greatest concession was a provision that each church maintain its autonomy in deciding the most important internal church questions. Among these is excommunication, as Alexei Prokofiev had originally demanded in the revision of the 1960 statutes.

Further evidence of concessions came in the permission granted by the Soviet authorities to the ECB to hold congresses in 1966 and 1969. Most surprising of all was the state's allowing the initsiativniki to hold their own conference at Tula in December 1969. Twenty delegates reportedly attended, representing forty-seven different areas of the Soviet Union.[99] Why this congress was held is uncertain, for its leaders were promptly rearrested. But the fact that it was held at all suggests the authorities' awareness of the group's potential challenge, which consistent and ruthless oppression had failed to silence.

The Orthodox dissidents have also fared not badly. While Eshliman and Yakunin were originally deprived of the right to offer the liturgy, neither was sent to a prison camp. Eshliman now lives in retirement in a monastery, and Yakunin has apparently been allowed to officiate once again. A similar fate befell Paul Golyshev, archbishop of Novosibirsk. Educated in Paris, he returned to the Soviet Union only to tangle too soon with the authorities. Considered by some observers as the spiritual successor to Archbishop Yermogen, he alone of all the church hierarchs was denied permission to attend the synod of bishops that elected Pimen patriarch in 1971. He was not imprisoned, however, but merely retired to the diocese of Vologda for his dissent activities.[100] Perhaps the Soviet authorities feel they cannot risk another Orthodox schism like that of 1927 for fear of alienating the Slav population in the face of a rapidly increasing Turkic minority.

The success of the Jewish emigration movement is a matter of public record. By the fall of 1973, any improvement in United States–Soviet trade relations had become clearly linked to the Soviet government's permitting unrestricted emigration to all Soviet Jews desiring to leave the country.[101] The fate of Soviet Jewry had become an issue in international politics. To a

99. For an account of this meeting, see Michael Bourdeaux, "Baptists in the Soviet Union," mimeographed, Radio Liberty Research Paper no. 47 (Munich, 1972), pp. 6–8; and the letter of the conference delegates to Kosygin following the congress, AS 838.

100. *Le monde*, November 26–27, 1972, p. 7.

101. See my discussion of this point in "The U.S.-Soviet Trade Negotiations," prepared for the Foreign Policy Research Institute of the University of Pennsylvania, January 1973, pp. 24–28, as well as the intensive reporting in the *New York Times* on the issue, September–October 1973.

certain extent the same can be said of Islam. In its cultivation of the Moslems across the Chinese frontier and in the Near East the Soviet Union can ill afford a thorough purge of Islam within its borders.

Soviet religious policy over the past ten years has thus been a mix of persecution and concession, which has given the religious dissenters the possibility to maneuver and to gain strength from that maneuvering.[102]

Interaction Pattern with Other Groups of Soviet Society. The evidence suggests that the religious dissidents have been able to realize contact with three important segments of Soviet society: among themselves, with the dissenting intelligentsia's civil rights movement, and with the population at large. The data given in this paper, while not positive proof, does, in my opinion, provide an indication that none of the religious dissent groups were operating in ignorance of the activity of the others. In this sense it could be said that the Baptists provided the initiative, setting the framework of the debate, establishing representative organizations, and doing the groundwork to make contact among themselves and with the outside world. Because of the size of its membership and its privileged position in the Soviet Union, the dissenters of the Orthodox Church were able to receive more immediate publicity for their actions and to establish contacts in Moscow. The determination and courage of the Jewish dissidents as well as their international success served as an inspiration to the entire dissent movement.[103] The Lithuanian Catholics benefited from the combined experience of all the religious dissenters to move beyond dissent to add the new ingredient of violence. It is curious, however, that despite contact with one another each religious group remained separate, waging its own particular battle. In fact, except for Levitin-Krasnov,[104] no initiative has come from any of the faiths for unity of any kind. Apparently the encounter with common persecution and common suffering has a long way to go to break down traditional religious antagonisms.

There can be no doubt of a linkup between the religious dissenters and the intelligentsia. If the ten documents mentioned earlier are insufficient evidence, the treatment of religious dissent in *Chronicle* confirms that the two streams have reached out toward each other. In his essay on General Grigorenko Krasnov argues for the superiority of the democratic system with all its failings, while in "Holy Rus'" he outlines a specific program for

---

102. Witness the announcement by the initsiativniki of the formation of the underground Khristianin Publishing House in their open letter to Kosygin of June 1, 1971 (AS 878) and the appeal to prayer addressed to all ECB believers of June 10, 1971 (AS 879).

103. A point stressed by Julius Telesin in his introduction to Reddaway, *Uncensored Russia*, pp. 38–40.

104. In his letter to Pope Paul VI, Levitin-Krasnov addresses himself to the possibility of the unification of Orthodoxy with Catholicism. Elsewhere he speaks of the growth of Orthodoxy from a moribund Byzantium as compared with the dynamic evolution of Catholicism. AS 389, late 1967.

the guarantee of religious freedom in the Soviet Union. Solzhenitsyn's concern about the behavior of the Orthodox hierarchy betokens a positive flow from the intelligentsia to the believers. The making of common cause between the faiths and the intelligentsia is a possibility that neither side has yet seen fit to exploit, but the very fact that it is there would seem to strengthen both interests.[105] As Bourdeaux and others have pointed out, the Soviet intellectuals have traditionally had limited access to the dissident elements in the population. The thrust of religious dissent toward civil rights now makes such contact possible.

The strength of religious feeling among the general Soviet population has been well documented by Soviet researchers. Soviet statistics generally attempt to prove that the most educated segments of the population are by and large indifferent to religion. In an extremely interesting study made of the town of Lunino and the collective farm, "Forward to Communism," Soviet sociologists reported that 97 to 100 percent of those with a higher education identified themselves as nonreligious, while 74 percent and over of those specified as barely literate (*malogramotnie*) considered themselves believers.[106] The study further showed that the less-educated *kolkhozniki* clung more tenaciously to their religion than even the rural village dweller. Other studies attempt to demonstrate that only the countryside and the aging rural population still believe, while still others try to locate religious observance primarily among the working class, housewives, and pensioneers.[107] A 1967 survey of Kazan published in *Nauka i religiia* indicated that 21 percent of the population was religious; 34 percent of this group were members of the working class, 81 percent were women, and 42 percent were pensioners.[108] However, Talantov's letter to Podgorny on the situation of the churches in Kirov oblast as well as his letter to Pope Paul VI suggests that increasing numbers of educated young people of both sexes may be turning to religion but are afraid to be seen in church. Certainly Soviet statistics must be taken with caution, as they are required to demonstrate the official line that religion is only for the backward and uneducated. Religion may well be gaining ground in the more secularly oriented cities, although its main support still seems to come from the smaller cities and rural areas if one can judge from the origins of the samizdat protests and appeals.

105. William C. Fletcher comments on this point in "Solzhenitsyn and the Merger of Dissent," *Worldview*, August 1972, pp. 5–8.
106. Akademiia obshchestvennykh nauk TsK KPSS, Institut nauchnogo ateizma, *K obshchestvu, svobodnomu ot religii* [Toward a society free from religion] (Moscow, 1970), p. 90.
107. Akademiia nauk SSSR, Ministerstvo kul'tury RSFSR, Muzei istorii religii i ateizma, *Voprosy preodoleniia religioznykh perezhitkov v SSSR* [Questions concerning the overcoming the remnants of religiosity in the USSR] (Moscow, 1966), especially pp. 3–16, 31–52. In both these articles the authors argue that the solution to overcoming religious prejudices is more education.
108. As reported in *New York Times*, August 30, 1967.

TABLE 6:5 Proportion of Baptists and Orthodox Practicing Religious Observance in Penza Oblast, 1968, by Age

Age	Baptists	Orthodox
20–40	19.6%	16.2%
40–60	9.6	15.1
Over 60	70.8	85.8

Source: Institute on Scientific Atheism, as published in *The Christian Science Monitor*, December 27, 1970.

In the spread of religion, Soviet sources indicate that the Baptists again have been taking the initiative. A survey conducted in Penza oblast in 1968 by the Institute on Scientific Atheism indicated that 88 percent of those identifying themselves as Baptists attended church regularly and only 3 percent did not attend at all. Among the Orthodox the corresponding figures were 10.7 and 26.3 percent. Baptists also appeared to attract slightly more young people, as table 6:5 shows. A particularly interesting finding of the survey was that 20 percent of the respondents reported that they had once been atheists.

All these studies seem to support the contention that religion is very much a concern of all segments of the Soviet population. If this can be assumed to be the case, then religious dissent becomes the link that could unite the intellectual currents of opposition with latent popular dissatisfaction.

The findings of this chapter on the relation of religious dissent to other dissent movements within the framework of the total Soviet population can be summarized in the Venn diagram given in figure 6:4. Dahl has theorized that the likelihood that a government will tolerate an opposition increases as the expected costs of suppression increase.[109] It took more than 200 years for the religious wars generated by the Reformation to produce the recognition that toleration might be a civil necessity. It took another 100 years for the secular republic spawned by the French Revolution to come to terms with the Catholic Church. It is by no means axiomatic that the Soviet government's war on religion is irreversible. A proactive model of dissent assumes that participation in a social movement involves challenges by relatively powerless groups that represent the activist portion of some underlying solidarity group. The political struggle takes the form of a mass movement because the groups involved initially lack the scale of organization, access, and appropriate response to operate inside existing political channels. In

109. Robert A. Dahl, *Polyarchy, Participation and Opposition* (New Haven, Conn., 1971), p. 15.

other words, the groups lack institutional power.[110] In contesting the Soviet interpretation of the separation of church and state, the Christian dissenters are in fact fighting for the church as an independent political institution in a manner analogous to the anti-Russian confrontation of the Moslem republics. In both cases the underlying constituencies are numerically enormous.

110. Charles Tilly, "From Mobilization to Political Conflict," multilith (Ann Arbor, Mich., 1970); William A. Gamson and James McEvoy, "Police Violence and Its Public Support," *Annals of the American Academy of Political and Social Science* 391 (September 1970): 97–110.

FIGURE 6:4

Relation of Religious to Other Major Dissent Movements in USSR

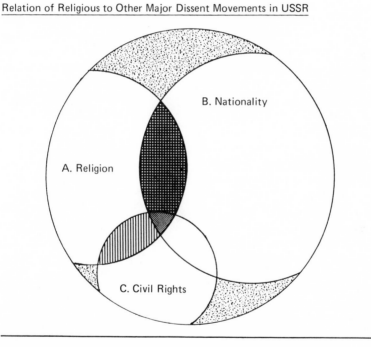

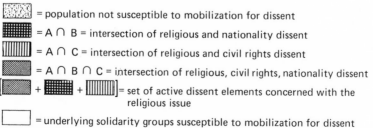

= population not susceptible to mobilization for dissent
= A ∩ B = intersection of religious and nationality dissent
= A ∩ C = intersection of religious and civil rights dissent
= A ∩ B ∩ C = intersection of religious, civil rights, nationality dissent
+ + = set of active dissent elements concerned with the religious issue
= underlying solidarity groups susceptible to mobilization for dissent

The Lithuanian Catholics and the Jews have demonstrated that continued frustration can result in negative domestic and international political consequences. Hence the religious dissent movement cannot be dismissed as peripheral to the overall dissent picture. As figure 6:4 attempts to portray graphically, its position may in fact be central. With its deep popular roots, its contacts with the dissenting elements among the Soviet elites, and its identification with the moral, civil rights, and nationality issues, religion at present may be the one dissent component capable of providing a base for a nation-wide opposition movement.

3 SAMIZDAT

AS POLITICAL COMMUNICATION

CHAPTER SEVEN / POLITICAL COMMUNICATION AND DISSENT IN THE SOVIET UNION / GAYLE DURHAM HOLLANDER

Public political communication is the nerve network of political life. The content that flows along it is the substance of politics. The political significance of either the process or the content of the transmission of information or policy is very broadly defined in the Soviet Union. In this context two crucial questions immediately arise: What are the extent and the nature of oppositional communications allowed within legitimate political life? And who are the opinion leaders? These are among the most essential questions in viewing the rise and spread of dissent in the Soviet Union because, in a sense, the existence of an extraofficial public communication network is what the struggle between the regime and the dissenters is all about.

The roots of Soviet concern with the leadership of political opinion go back to the early days of the Bolshevik faction of the Russian Social Democratic Labor Party. Among Lenin's foremost talents and concerns were the strategy and tactics of political persuasion; his theories of political organization are inextricably related to communications theories, many of them well ahead of his time. His formulalike articulation of an already well-known truth—"The newspaper is not only a collective propagandist and a collective agitator; it is also a collective organizer"[1]—set the tone for the

---

1. The original text, printed in *Iskra* (Spark) on May 6, 1901, gives a more exact idea of what Lenin had in mind when he spoke of a newspaper as a basis for political organization:
"The role of the newspaper is not limited, however, only to the dissemination of ideas, only to political education and the attraction of political allies. The newspaper is not only a collective propagandist and collective agitator, but also a collective organizer. In this last regard one can compare it with logs which one sets up around a building which is being raised, marking the contours of the construction, making easier the relationships between individual builders, helping them to divide the work and survey the overall results achieved by organized labor. With the help of the newspaper and in connection with it, a permanent organization will be built, occupied not only with local, but also with regular general work, training its members to follow events attentively, to evaluate their significance and influence on various strata of the population, and to work out purposeful means of influencing these events from the viewpoint of the revolutionary party. One technical problem: to guarantee a proper supply of materials to the newspaper and its proper distribution we are forced to create a network of local agents of one party, agents in active relationships with one another, knowing the general conditions of affairs, used to regularly fulfilling diverse functions of all-Russian work, trying their strengths at the organization of one set of revolutionary activities or another. This network of agents will be the skeleton of exactly the type of organization we need."—from "S chevo nachat," in V. I. Lenin, *KPSS O Pechati* [The CPSU on the press], ed. V. I. Vlasov et al. (Moscow, 1970), pp. 40–41.

entire structure and functioning of the Soviet mass media and agitation-propaganda apparatus. It is the nature of this communications system, with its extreme concern with control and the built-in illegitimacy of genuinely critical expression, that has provoked much of the activity of the current dissent movement. Leninist traditions have also affected communications among dissidents; for example, they are using periodicals more and more as a basis for their own organization.

Most of the dissidents find common cause in the form of their activities, many of which are explicit or implied protests against official repression of their efforts to become informed, exchange ideas, and influence others to join them. Their concern for creating a genuine public opinion rather than continuing to allow the Communist Party to monopolize all interest articulation has brought them into a head-on confrontation with party bureaucrats. Consequently much of the regime's response to dissidents has also taken the form of disrupting disallowed communications: breaking up demonstrations, intercepting and confiscating the self-published, uncensored publications known as *samizdat*, and isolating dissenters from their work milieu and ultimately from the population as a whole by confining them in prisons, camps, or mental hospitals.

The very definition of dissent is, of course, a matter of communication. Only when opposing views become a social phenomenon through transmission to other individuals or groups do they become very significant. This is especially true in a political system that has defined most criticism of the elite and of the basic nature of the system as treasonous.[2] When opinions contrary to the official version of reality are articulated, even among a restricted public, a limited sort of spontaneous public opinion begins to develop. It is the narrow range of legitimate criticism in the Soviet Union that defines an extremely broad range of expression as deviant or dissident.

Most discussions by dissenters point out the need for *glasnost'*, the open, free dissemination of information and ideas. Why is this such a persistent demand? The dissidents hope that by raising the informational level of thinking people they will also increase the general consciousness of political factors. Thus the renascent "critical intelligentsia" will be strengthened and enlarged. By emphasizing certain political trends and practices, they hope to promote the crystallization of public opinion on certain issues. The critical intelligentsia, then, seeks to act as an opinion leader to coalesce and intensify pressures growing among other segments of the population, particularly the specialist class from which the intelligentsia comes. All of this, of course, flies in the face of Leninist theory concerning public opinion and the leading role of the party.

2. For a good discussion of the development of Soviet policy toward opposition, see Leonard Schapiro, "Putting the Lid on Leninism," *Government and Opposition* 2, no. 2 (February 1967): 101–203.

In the Soviet Union it is particularly relevant to consider the opinion leadership role of the intelligentsia in the emergence of an alternative system of political communication. Although this group was small during the early and middle nineteenth century, its self-defined role as watchdog and critic of the political system made it important in bringing about political change. Mainly through literature and literary criticism it demonstrated that the oppressive characteristics of the government could be opposed, albeit not without cost, and that a movement for change could be sustained and even strengthened in the face of widespread repression. With increasing sophistication and ruthlessness, combined with important moral and material assistance from outside the country, it played an important role in generating enough discontent to undermine an already faltering political system. Hence the familiarity of the victorious survivors of that struggle with the power of underground communications networks and their recognition of the value of public demonstrations in awakening consciousness among a certain segment of the population is based on a long tradition. The profound mistrust and class antagonism of party bureaucrats toward the emerging critical intelligentsia in the post-Stalin period are part of an old Russian political pattern. Like the old intelligentsia in Russia, this new group is only a thin film on top of society; but also like that group, it is nurtured by support from outside.

Moreover, the more stratified class structure of present-day Soviet society works to the advantage of the new intelligentsia. Unlike the polarized class structure of tsarist autocracy, which left the critical intellectuals isolated from the masses, Soviet society is now composed of a number of layers through which waves of change may slowly pass with ever-broadening repercussions. Most important in this structure is a "specialist" class,[3] a large group of educated, skilled people, including academics, professionals, engineers, economic managers, and technical specialists. The talents of these people, especially of scientists and engineers, are needed by the nation, and they therefore possess some resources for bringing pressure on the government. It is from this crucial group that the critical intelligentsia, as well as the government bureaucracy, is recruited. Thus the critical intelligentsia is not only challenging the party's monopoly on the public expression of "truth" but is also competing for the attention and sympathy of people within the specialist class. Members of this group have become heavy consumers of communications as a result of the rapid development of mass media during the post-Stalin years. Therefore the role of the dissident channels is even more important in the competition.

Communication among people at variance with the system, no matter what their political orientation, is essential for the survival and growth of

3. Andrei Amalrik uses this term in his essay *Will the Soviet Union Survive until 1984?* (New York, 1970). See the discussion later in this chapter.

any genuine internal criticism. Opinions held in isolation often wither. The psychological and sometimes material support that comes from contact with others of like mind has much to do with how well one's convictions can be maintained and developed. Largely because of an official awareness of the power of a network for the expression and exchange of ideas, there is an immense gap between the rights of citizens to privacy, assembly, and freedom of speech and press as stated in article 125 of the Soviet Constitution (1936) and the very obvious facts of the repressive political culture (for example, the principle of "democratic centralism" as codified in the party statutes and the RSFSR (Russian Republic) Criminal Code, articles 58, 70, 190-1 and 190-2).[4]

Dissidents have been persistent in pointing out inconsistencies in official documents with regard to the freedom of expression or criticism. They have clearly attempted to evade the official definition of what is legitimate political activity, referring to both the constitution and the libertarian norms expressed in such documents as the Universal Declaration on Human Rights (which was signed by the Soviet government) to bolster their position.[5] Agents of the KGB have acknowledged the essential inconsistency of the official position several times in private interviews, pointing out that these documents were "written for people abroad."

OFFICIAL SOVIET POLITICAL COMMUNICATIONS

Some General Theoretical Considerations. The communications structure of any society performs four functions essential for the maintenance and development of its political system. One, in which mass media and face-to-face communications play an important part, is legitimizing the form of government, the regime in power, individual members of that regime, and the policies pursued by it.

Based on this is an integrative function: the fostering of unity, coherence, and continuity in the political culture.[6] Together the legitimizing and

---

4. The basic principles of "democratic centralism" are laid out in the 1961 Party Rules, Jan F. Triska, ed., *Soviet Communism: Programs and Rules* (San Francisco, 1962), pp. 168–69. According to Alfred Meyer, *Leninism* (New York, 1962), p. 304, the term was first used by Lenin in 1906 in "Tactical Platform for the Unification Congress of the RSDRS" (text in V. I. Lenin, *Sochineniia* [Moscow and Leningrad, 1926–32], 9:50).
   The full texts of these articles is given in Pavel Litvinov, *The Demonstration in Pushkin Square* (Boston, 1969), pp. 13–14.

5. The title page of *Khronika tekushchikh sobytii* [*Chronicle of current events*], the major dissident journal, usually carries the text of Article 19 of this declaration. The journal is cited hereafter as *Chronicle*.

6. Sidney Verba has defined "political culture" as "the system of empirical beliefs, expressive symbols, and values which define the situation in which political action takes place. It provides the subjective orientation to politics. . . . Looked at this way it can be seen that political culture

integrative functions form the process we call "political socialization." The content of political socialization has to do with ideas about how power is and should be distributed, progress and the nature and direction of historical change, the role of the nation in world affairs, the role of essential political organizations (in the Soviet case, the Communist Party) at home and abroad, and the citizen's ideal qualities and proper place in political life. In the Soviet Union there is a concerted effort to emphasize the didactic role (which is always seen as persuasive in nature) of the party in political communication and to downplay the initiative of the citizen.

A third major function is what Wilbur Schramm has called the "watchman" role: the scanning of the horizon and reporting back to the society.[7] This often means expanding the attention range of citizens as well as leaders; the context that is considered relevant for political opinions is broadened. Remote people and events are brought closer, and the attention of the audience is focused on certain objects selected as being of political importance. Often this makes possible comparisons unfavorable to the political system. Aspirations are thereby raised, creating a climate of susceptibility to change. There is good reason for a regime that seeks to control political change to try to limit this horizon-scanning function, at least as far as reporting back to the general citizenry is concerned. It is not surprising that providing access to forbidden subject matter has been a major preoccupation of dissident communicators, one that has intensified since the ouster of Nikita Khrushchev.

A final function that depends very much on how the others have been performed is the "policy" role. It consists of orchestrating, expressing, and translating into political demands the needs and wishes of various groups in the political community. In the Soviet Union these processes are totally monopolized by the party and are therefore another prime target for the efforts of dissidents in their communications activities.

The last two functions are closely related to what we mean by the role of "public opinion." It is part of the libertarian political tradition that public opinion is necessary for the government and the population to make sound judgments about how well the government is functioning. Hans Speier has defined public opinion as "opinion on matters of conern to the nation freely and publicly expressed by men outside the government who claim a right that their opinions should influence or determine the action, personnel, or structure of their government."[8] The existence of public opinion, he says,

---

represents a system of control vis-à-vis the system of political interactions. Political culture regulates who talks to whom and who influences whom. It also regulates what is said in political contacts and the effects of those contacts." Verba, "Comparative Political Culture," in *Political Culture and Political Development*, ed. Lucian W. Pye and Sidney Verba (Princeton, N.J., 1965), pp. 513, 517.

7. Wilbur Schramm, *Mass Media and National Development* (Stanford, Calif., 1964), p. 259.

8. "The Historical Development of Public Opinion," in Hans Speier, *Social Order and the Risks of War* (Cambridge, Mass., 1969), p. 323.

requires that the government be expected to disclose and explain its decisions so that citizens can think and talk about them; that the government not deny the assertion that the opinions of citizens on public matters are relevant for policy-making; and that there be access to information on the issues with which public opinion is concerned. There is a series of implied assumptions here about the population: that they possess the financial means and skills for access to the media and that they have sufficient leisure for discussion. This is what Speier means when he calls public opinion a "phenomenon of middle class civilization."

In contrast, Leninist theory on public opinion begins with the notion of "class consciousness." This can only be brought to the all-important class, the proletariat, from the outside, since workers are imbedded in capitalist society, prey to its pressures and insufficiently disciplined to develop more than a "trade-union consciousness." The tightly organized revolutionary party, composed for the most part of bourgeois intellectuals, earns its right to educate and lead the proletariat by its mastery of Marxism-Leninism: a knowledge of the laws of history and the correct path to communism. The party elite must "elevate the spontaneity" of the masses; rather than merely testing the state of mass thinking, it must propagandize to actively influence it. Lenin had a tendency to observe an increase in class consciousness among the masses when they responded favorably to his propaganda appeals.[9] The party can learn from the masses in a tactical sense only; it can sense from them the right timing and form for political action but not the goals of politics.

Opposition in the Soviet Context. Leonard Schapiro has distinguished between "opposition" as a political group that not only disagrees with the ruling group but wants to replace it, and "dissent" as the expression of views different from and critical of those of the ruling group, without necessarily setting oneself up as an alternative.[10]

The Soviet regime has a tradition of defining any dissent as opposition to be isolated and controlled or eliminated. Lenin's own intolerance toward differences of opinion within the Bolshevik faction of the Russian Social Democratic Labor Party can be traced back at least to *What is to be Done?* The "Decree on the Press" and "General Regulations on the Press" signed by Lenin on October 27 (November 9), 1917 prohibited the non-Bolshevik press and imposed censorship restrictions.[11] These measures were supposedly temporary, extraordinary measures, to be repealed "when public life returns to normal." This never took place. The most significant party decision portraying Lenin's attitude toward internal opposition is the resolution of the Tenth Party Congress in 1921 entitled "Concerning the Unity of the

9. See Alfred G. Meyer, *Leninism*, p. 47.

10. Schapiro, "Putting the Lid on Leninism," pp. 182–83.

11. See discussion of "Does Censorship Exist in the Soviet Union? . . ." a collection of documents from 1917–22 (Leningrad, 1970) in *Chronicle*, no. 14 (June 30, 1970), AS 407.

Party." Adopted during the crushing of the Kronstadt Revolt, it prohibited activity within the party by so-called fractions with special platforms and their own "group discipline." In its secret Point Seven, the resolution empowered the Central Committee to take the necessary measures (including expulsion from the party) against anyone who engaged in similar activity in the future.

In 1922, censorship was transferred from the political department of *Gosizdat* to *Glavlit* under the Commissariat of Enlightenment. The date of this decree, June 6, 1922, marks the introduction of official censorship, though de facto censorship had already been established since 1917.[12] Under Stalin, of course, dissent became coterminous with treason. Khrushchev used measures justified by the resolution of the Tenth Party Congress to deal with opposition within the party, and his successors have been more conservative than he. The principle of "democratic centralism," whereby the decisions of higher bodies are binding on lower bodies, facilitates the elimination of internal opposition, while party control over all organizations, especially communications institutions, facilitates the inhibition of expression of any opposition outside the party.

Characteristics of the Legitimate and Alternative Systems. Considering the functions a political communications system performs for its political system and the two very different views of "public opinion" we have just mentioned, it is interesting to compare the official system of mass media and the agitprop apparatus with the alternative or dissent network of communication. Clearly the latter is in some senses compensatory to the former. On five major dimensions the two systems differ considerably.

1. *The official system is monopolistic and highly controlled; the alternative one is pluralistic.*

The party reserves the right to transmit and interpret the truth according to Marxist-Leninist theory. It has a monopoly on institutionalized organization, with a visible, stable, self-perpetuating apparatus facilitating control over the economic and technical apparatus; personnel (through the *nomenklatura* system[13]); news sources (output of the domestic agencies TASS and NOVOSTI and the material coming in over foreign wire services); and a well-developed coercive apparatus (censorship; punishment; isolation by deprivation of employment, housing, or freedom; and so on) for backing up the persuasive system. Although communications policy under Khrushchev was rather liberal, the control apparatus remained intact and was never discredited. It has been used more actively since his ouster.

12. *Ibid. Gosizdat* is the acronym (in Russian) for State Publishing House for Political Literature. *Glavlit* used to stand for Principal Directorate for Matters of Literature and Art but now refers to the Principal Directorate for the Safeguarding of State and Military Secrets in the Press, attached to the Council of Ministers.

13. *Nomenklatura* is a list of appointments reserved for party jurisdiction. See Merle Fainsod, *How Russia is Ruled* (Cambridge, Mass., 1963), p. 224.

In contrast, the extraofficial system involves many different strains of dissent (national, ethnic, and various political interpretations) and is accessible to anyone who dares to obtain the necessary means, and become involved in it. There is no one ultimate interpreter of the truth. In fact, it has been noted that there is so little overlap among the subnetworks of the system that if one didn't observe key people who have access to different types of materials or didn't see them brought together in publications such as the *Chronicle of Current Events*, one could almost speak of many different alternative networks.

2. *The official system is extremely hierarchical, paralleling the party apparatus and monitored by it at all levels; the alternative network is non-hierarchical.*

Since there is no one political organization among dissenters, no one ideology or set of goals, and no one form of communication, there can be no way of setting up a hierarchy that encompasses the entire movement. Within certain groups there may be such tendencies, but they are not characteristic of Soviet dissent as a whole.

3. *Official communications are patterned with a massive top-to-bottom flow of content; the extraofficial network operates on a horizontal plane.*

In the legitimate network there is very limited bottom-to-top communication (letters to newspapers, readers' conferences, secret police informers, etc). Horizontal communication among groups and individuals below the elite level is severely and purposefully curtailed, inhibiting the development of any competing world-view or any serious modification of the elite version of reality except within the elite itself.

Among dissenters there can be none of this tight control of direction, for there is no organized hierarchy to create and maintain it. Some of the more open, symbolic acts are directed upward at the official elite, but by and large the flow of information is among various groups on a more or less equal basis or among individuals within these groups.

4. *Soviet mass media and the agitation-propaganda apparatus carry content that is primarily prescriptive; the unofficial system is concerned more with description and interpretation.*

The official system presents all material in a didactic manner with clearly defined implications for citizen reaction and behavior. As the nerve structure of the party, the system simultaneously transmits both esoteric messages to the apparatus and exoteric communications to the public at large. Controlled by the elite, it performs the "policy" role rather smoothly; the interests that are legitimately articulated are few, and even fewer are translated into policy and implemented.

Although in the alternative network there are programs and demands that contain prescriptive material, one of its notable features has been straight factual material presented with meticulous care (for example, in *Chronicle*) and interpretations of reality clearly at variance with the official versions. The dry, factual tone of *Chronicle* is a stylistic protest against the arrogant, repetitive exhortations of the official media.

5. *The official system is dualistic and highly coordinated; the alternative one is multiform and relatively uncoordinated.*

Mass media and the person-to-person official network of the agitation-propaganda apparatus are closely intertwined in function, form, and content. A two-stage communication process occurs naturally in many societies. In Western studies the process is called the "two-step flow"; under it opinions and information flow from the media to certain influential persons.[14] In the Soviet Union this two-stage communication has long been institutionalized to minimize uncontrolled interpersonal communications and to control the content and audience reaction to messages.[15]

Although the unofficial system employs both interpersonal contacts and printed materials as well as broadcasts (mainly foreign radio and some illegal domestic ham stations), these are not at all well coordinated. Often there is much duplication and waste of energy and talent.

The Soviet official political communications system, while thoroughly modern in its technical apparatus and organizational network, is clearly a part of the authoritarian rather than the libertarian tradition. The main identifying features of an authoritarian communications systems are that the state ranks higher than the individual in the scale of values,[16] the communications apparatus is hierarchical, and the source of truth restricted. This tradition waned considerably in the West during the second half of the eighteenth century. The model that replaced it was that communications should serve the individual before the state, that it should offer diversity rather than unity, that it should contribute to change as well as continuity, and that it has every right (even the duty) to criticize the government in power. The collection of groups and individuals that we call "dissenters" are challenging the authoritarian tradition with ideas long accepted, if never fully lived up to, in the West.

THE POST-STALIN
COMMUNICATIONS ENVIRONMENT

In considering the features of the post-Stalin period that most facilitate dissident communications, one is immediately struck by the tremendous growth in the mass media. It amounts to a "communications explosion." Table 7:1 shows the dramatic increase in accessibility of the media.

---

14. Elihu Katz and Paul F. Lazarsfeld, *Personal Influence* (Glencoe, Ill., 1955), p. 32.

15. For a fuller discussion, see Gayle Durham Hollander, *Soviet Political Indoctrination: Developments in Mass Media and Propaganda Since Stalin* (New York, 1972), pp. 165–68.

16. Wilbur Schramm, "Two Concepts of Mass Communications," in Schramm, *Responsibility in Mass Communications* (New York, 1957), pp. 62–77.

TABLE 7:1 Access to Mass Media in the Soviet Union

Type of access	1952	1959	1970
Copies of newspapers per issue (millions)	42	62	141
Per 100 people (ages 10–69)	–	40	97
Total radio sets (millions)	17.5	53.9	94.8
Per 100 people (ages 10–69)		34	60
Wired radio speakers (millions)	11.7	29.2	46.2
Per 100 people (ages 10–69)		19	29
Wave radio sets (millions)	5.8	24.7	48.6
Per 100 people (ages 10–69)		15	31
Television sets (millions)	0.1	3.6	34.8
Per 100 people (ages 10–69)		2	22

Sources: Broadcast media figures for 1952 and 1959: *Narodnoe Khoziaistvo v 1962 godu* (Moscow, 1963), p. 422. Newspaper figures for those years, *ibid.*, p. 604.
Broadcast media figures for 1970: *Narodnoe Khoziaistvo v 1970 godu* (Moscow, 1971), p. 466. Newspaper figures for that year, *ibid.*, p. 678. Per-100 figures based on calculations from above and census data by age group for 1959 from Tsentral'noe Statisticheskoe Upravlenie pri Sovetye Ministrov SSSR, *Itogi vsesoiuznoi perepisi naseleniia 1959 goda (svodny tom)*, (Moscow, 1962), table 12, 49; and for 1970 from *United Nations Demographic Yearbook*, Statistical Office of the United Nations (New York, 1971), 22d ed. pp. 398–99.
Note: Per-100 figures are missing for 1952 because of the lack of comparable census data.

The Soviet audience experienced a change from predominantly collective or public exposure to private access. This has had several implications. It has meant more flexibility in the timing and nature of exposure to the media. One can read or listen at will in the privacy of one's family or friendship circle, thus avoiding the often unsolicited interpretation of news by official party agitators who were usually present at collective readings or listening sessions. Individuals can now communicate their own private, sometimes unorthodox, reactions to others sharing similar opinions without official scrutiny. The mere possibility of doing this might strengthen the development of interpretations contrary to the party line. It also means that the function of propagandists and agitators, who had previously extended the scarce media channels (by reading newspapers to groups of workers during lunch breaks, for example), has been reduced to mere interpretation of the news to a more sophisticated and less interested audience. More private media exposure in a somewhat freer atmosphere has also meant better opportunities for exposure to foreign information sources, particularly radio. A rising standard of living means that more people can afford the shortwave sets (especially the less expensive transistorized models) that best receive foreign broadcasts.

Official policy also relaxed controls in certain areas. Jamming of foreign stations decreased and for some, like the Voice of America and the British Broadcasting Corporation, ceased altogether for a time between 1963 and 1968. This meant that the Soviet audience, especially during that period, has had much greater latitude in the choice of news sources. Long trapped in a relatively closed communications system and then exposed to alternative, sometimes anti-Soviet viewpoints, the audience experienced important changes in awareness and expectations (see below).

Radio is not the only Western source of information and values to which there has been greater access. Printed materials, foreign tourists, and Western journalists have all become more evident in European Russia and have sometimes even made their way to Siberian cities. Soviet citizens were also allowed for a time to go as tourists in greater numbers to Eastern Europe and some Western countries. This was almost always done in groups with KGB "companionship"; after the summer of 1968 travel became much more difficult. But this Western contact brought an increased awareness of other values, world-views, and political cultures. This expanded awareness is very much related to the growth of a readiness to accept change, a common characteristic of modern political cultures. The rapid changes of the outside world were quickly disseminated through the official and nonofficial communications systems and dovetailed with the direct experience of rapid and radical internal political changes during this time (destalinization, the ouster of Khrushchev, and so on).

As these changes occurred, the Communist Party system of education that produced speakers for the agitprop apparatus was being diluted organizationally. During the late 1950s and early 1960s the party turned away from strict indoctrination of members for propaganda work to mass political education. This meant greater numbers involved in party education work but much less control over the apparatus by the elite and therefore less orthodox presentations of the party line through official personal channels. The number of students enrolled increased tremendously, from 6.2 million in the academic year 1957–58 to 25 million in 1964–65. During the same period the proportion of students who were not members of the party rose (from 15 to 78 percent.)[17] There was a shift away from the study of fundamentals of Marxism-Leninism; in 1963–64, for example, less than a third of the students were studying party history, political economy, and philosophy. Younger people especially were avoiding these subjects.[18] Immediately after the ouster of Khrushchev, however, the new regime set about putting party education (the schooling of party leaders, particularly propagandists and agitations) on a "solid ideo-

17. For a complete discussion of the party education network to 1967, see Ellen Propper Mickiewicz, *Soviet Political Schools: The Communist Party Adult Instruction System* (New Haven, Conn., 1967), p. 10.

18. *Voprosy partiinoi ucheby* [Questions of party education] (Moscow, 1966), p. 17.

logical foundation." Following a reorganization of the ideological apparatus[19] the number of students registered dropped to 12 million, 75 percent of them members or candidate members of the party.[20] By 1971 the total enrollment in party education had increased to only 16 million.[21]

But the slackening of discipline in party education had already had its effect. People no longer felt such pressure to attend political meetings both because they could obtain their information directly from the media and because there was less emphasis on ideological purity in the propaganda apparatus. For outside events even the elite did not hesitate to seek and openly refer to foreign radio as a source of information. The new regime rapidly moved to correct what they saw as a dangerous laxity related to the liberalization in Czechoslovakia. They feared "contagion" from Eastern Europe, all the more since Soviet intellectuals were following events there with great interest and referring to them in domestic ideological disputes. Pressure to attend political meetings was stepped up along with the ideological campaign that began in March 1968, and by this time speakers were more orthodox in terms of party affiliation and training than they had been under Khrushchev.

One noteworthy attempt to increase the sophistication of speakers was the institution of a new category of ideological workers called "politinformatory" (political informers).[22] These speakers were supposed to cover more specialized matters than either agitators or propagandists. Even so the high costs of tight information control manifested themselves. One commentator remarked:

> The event has taken place, it is being discussed and sometimes interpreted the wrong way, but the politinformers are silent; they are waiting for "instructions." The leaders of the party and public organization are not always responsible for the weak activity of some of the politinformers, for their lack of timeliness. Sometimes the informer is silent and does not speak because he does not know what to say, he does not have enough material for a thorough speech. But the local as well as central newspapers and journals give such material sometimes with great delay.[23]

The development of sociology during the post-Stalin period also significantly changed the communications environment, contributing to the open expression of political dissent. Public opinion polls, primarily those conducted by *Komsomolskaya pravda*, also contributed to the climate of

19. See Hollander, *Soviet Political Indoctrination*, chap. 6.
20. A. Dmitryuk, "Nasushchnye voprosy Marksistko-Leninskoi ucheby kommunistov," *Politicheskoe samoobrazovaniie* 2 (1966): 85.
21. Leonid Brezhnev, speech at the Twenty-fourth Congress of the CPSU, *Pravda*, March 31, 1971, pp. 2–10; *Current Digest of the Soviet Press* 23, no. 14: 37 (hereafter referred to as *CDSP*).
22. See Hollander, *Soviet Political Indoctrination*, chap. 6.
23. K. Nikolayev, "Party Life: Operational Efficiency and Depth—How to Organize Political Information Better," *Pravda*, December 14, 1967, p. 2.

change, especially among the younger generation.[24] By asking people what they thought, they helped to legitimize public opinion as interpretation coming from the people, not only from the party elite, and thereby represented an erosion of Leninist theory. While the techniques used in these studies were unsophisticated at first, the net effect was to make people feel that their opinions, even the less orthodox ones, were in some sense legitimate and worthy of consideration. Many of the results of the polls were not published, largely because of a publishing bottleneck (especially in the social sciences) but partly because many of the results simply did not accord with official mythology about Soviet society and the state of mass consciousness. Even among the published polls there were some obvious gaps between myths and expressed opinions.[25] Some of these discrepancies had to do with the mass media themselves.[26]

A significant amount of sociological research was carried out by sociological research centers on behalf of central newspapers[27] and television stations in large cities. Audience studies showed that people had rather serious complaints about the type and quality of news they got from the media.[28] There was a notable lack of enthusiasm for articles about economic life, even though economics occupies a huge proportion of newspaper space. Readers indicated that they wanted more and better international news and items relating to their personal lives: moral themes, practical information, consumer services.[29] Television, although considered by the regime primarily as

24. These polls were carried out by the newspaper's Public Opinion Institute, then under the direction of B. Grushin.

25. To give but one example, a 1964–65 study of people in Gorky who had had their children baptized showed that 66 percent were skilled workers, the average monthly salary was higher than those who had not had their children baptized, and the majority enjoyed good living conditions (their own individual house or apartment), contrary to the party's assumption that unskilled and uneducated workers predominated in this group. Cited in Ellen Mickiewicz, "Policy Applications of Public Opinion Research in the Soviet Union," *Public Opinion Quarterly* 26, no. 4 (Winter 1972–73): 574.

26. For example, *Political Diary*, no. 63 (December 1969), *AS* 1010, reports that a *Literaturnaya Gazeta* poll of readers was not published because the results of the study were so displeasing to the editors.

27. Most of these studies were carried out by the Academy of Sciences' sociological research group under its Siberian Division. For a discussion in English of these studies see Mickiewicz, "Policy Applications," and *Problemy sotsiologii pechati* (Novosibirsk, 1969 on). These sources indicate that many of these studies, which were done after the 1964 party plenum, were a result of the removal of restrictions on subscriptions to periodicals. Since the newspapers now had to compete for readership, they sought to determine their strengths and weaknesses as well as to learn something about the makeup of their audiences.

28. For more information on the audience research studies, see Hollander, *Soviet Political Indoctrination*, and Nils H. Wessell, "The Credibility, Impact, and Effectiveness of the Soviet General Press," Ph.D. diss. in political science, Columbia University, 1972.

29. A study conducted over a ten-year period by an Estonian newspaper, *Edazi*, indicated that over half of its readers thought there was not enough attention in the paper to cases of embezzlement of state property and mismanagement. Seventy-two percent found too little information on accidents and other occurrences. More than 90 percent thought there was too much in the newspaper about the "Movement for Communist Labor." Reported in B. Firsov,

an instrument of political indoctrination, was looked upon by the audience first of all as a means of entertainment. This gap in expectations naturally resulted in considerable frustration at the heavy didactic nature of programming. A study of the television audience in Tallin (Estonian SSR) indicated that even when seeking political news and commentary, viewers turned first to Finnish television, then to Estonian television, and last to Moscow Central in Russian.[30] Intellectuals watched Finnish television more than any other group. Obviously the Soviet media frustrate their audience's needs in many ways, and it is not surprising that it turns to foreign sources.

One of the most noteworthy features of the post-Stalin period and one that has received little attention is the return to civilian life of millions of former prisoners, camp inmates, and political exiles. The significance of the dispersion of these people among the population is two-fold. First, those outside have experienced a direct confrontation with the personal experiences of friends, relatives, and acquaintances who were incarcerated or exiled. Perhaps the return of the "Lazaruses" to tell the tale has affected the legitimacy of the regime more than all the official changes in the party line during the post-Stalin period. Second, these returnees spread among the population some of the political culture of the camps, especially communications patterns helpful in carrying on underground resistance activity.[31] For many of these people, a separation of attachment to the Soviet system from attachment to its current leadership was a useful psychological defense, and this no doubt has spread since their return to civilian life. It would be reasonable to assume that the radical and unpredictable changes of post-Stalin political life further encouraged this capacity to compartmentalize political loyalties. In any case, the inmates' return has undoubtedly made it more difficult for many Soviet citizens to dismiss questions concerning the integrity and legitimacy of the leadership. It has also given some people the sense that they have the right, even the duty, to dispute the party's interpretation and to speak out on political matters.

Increased leisure time has also been an important factor. With less time spent on political meetings, more access to media, and the shortening of the work week in the early 1960s from six to five days, people have been able to engage in activities that are less political in content. A recent book on party propaganda lamented the fact that most of the free time gained by workers goes not for ideological self-improvement but for daily affairs and such

"Massovye kommunikatsiia," *Zhurnalist* 1967, no. 2, pp. 50–52. A *Literaturnaya Gazeta* study showed that its readers preferred only two of the topics that occupy the most space in the newspaper: sports and the work of trade unions. Mickiewicz, "Policy Applications," p. 570.

30. Rut Karemyaye, "Kak tiazholie pushki v boiu," *Sovetskoe Radio i Televideniie*, 1967, no. 7, pp. 30–35.

31. For references to these skills and techniques see especially Yevgenia Ginzburg, *Journey into the Whirlwind* (New York, 1967; Alexander Solzhenitsyn, *One Day in the Life of Ivan Denisovich* (New York, 1963); and Meyer Galler and Harlan Marquess, *Soviet Prison Camp Speech* (Madison, Wis., 1972).

unworthy diversions as playing chess and dominoes.[32] There is much more time for informal discussion among friends, greater access to information providing material for speculation, and no paucity of interesting political developments to interpret.

The Role of Word-of-Mouth Information. Word of mouth has always been used extensively for certain kinds of information, but it has assumed particular significance during the post-Stalin period. Both for people in important positions and for ordinary citizens it has acted as a channel of essential information that is not provided by the mass media or agitprop network. The media do not report on subjects that do not illustrate social and political processes that are supposed to be taking place. This amounts to a kind of "socialist realism" in journalism. Among significant topics omitted are advance news about the availability of goods in short supply (such shortages are rarely admitted publicly), news of economic failures (bad harvests, economic scandals, and so on), accidents and natural disasters, information about poor living conditions, critical political jokes, and all sorts of political news such as advance warnings of irregular political events, background on political events and personalities, information on spontaneous citizen demonstrations, news of dissident activities, and information about the coercive apparatus (informers, arrests, punishments, camp conditions, and the like). According to many Soviet citizens, word of mouth is necessary for them to interpret news from official channels intelligently.

Contrary to popular conceptions about "rumor," word-of-mouth information in the Soviet Union is known to be relatively efficient and reliable. The data reported by the Harvard Project on the Soviet Social System as well as interviews conducted by the ComCom Project at MIT indicate the extensive use and credibility of this channel for most people.[33] Moreover, the fact that it has been deliberately used on several occasions by the party to spread important and sensitive news would imply that the party considers it trustworthy. The ouster of Khrushchev, for example, was announced and explained only by word of mouth.[34] A group of Siberian sociologists studying the readership of *Trud* in the late 1960s pointed out that the role of rumor was

32. M. Dunchevska, "Svobodnoe vremia i organizatsiia propagandy" ["Leisure time and the organization of propaganda"] in G. L. Smirnova et al., *Voprosy teorii i praktiki partiinoi propagandy* [Problems of the theory and practice of party propaganda] (Moscow, 1971), pp. 1964–66.

33. See Raymond A. Bauer and David B. Gleicher, "Word-of-Mouth Communication in the Soviet Union," *Public Opinion Quarterly* 17, no. 3 (July 1953): 297–310 for the Harvard Project and Hollander, *Soviet Political Indoctrination*, p. 182 for the MIT data.

34. According to *Political Diary*, 50 (November 1968,) AS 1008, Anastas Mikoyan gave the following account: "When the Khrushchev issue was raised in the Presidium of the Central Committee, twenty-two people spoke in a business-like way, without abuse. Khrushchev defended himself. We did not make public the secret details about all this, not wanting to wash our dirty linen in public and not wanting to exaggerate it. We decided to inform the Party and the people by word-of-mouth." *New York Times*, August 22, 1971, p. 32.

very important in times of crisis but even in normal times was quite "active." They found that "acquaintances" played a more important part as an information source among the best- and worst-educated strata in Soviet society than among middle groups.[35]

People use word of mouth in different ways according to their social and political position. The Harvard Project reported that peasants, who have traditionally been hostile to the official system, use oral channels as a source for most news. Intellectuals, on the other hand, use word of mouth as an additional source rather than relying on it entirely. While they are closer to official sources, they need more supplementary information to perform their professional duties. This pattern seems to have continued throughout the post-Stalin period. Intellectuals are also more likely now to have access to non-Soviet sources of information, such as foreign radio and Western printed matter; both are available in the large European cities or "science cities" in which they reside. Dissidents are largely from the professional-intellectual (what we have called earlier the specialized) class; because of this and their particular information needs as well they use word of mouth much more than the ordinary citizen. This compensatory function of rumor illustrates Shibutani's definition: "Rumor is a substitute for news; in fact, it *is* news that does not develop in institutional channels. Unsatisfied demand for news—the discrepancy between information needed to come to terms with the changing environment and what is provided by a formal news channel—constitutes the crucial conditions of rumor construction."[36]

The official system of political communications, even with its post-Stalin modifications, has certain general characteristics that facilitate the development of an alternative or supplementary network. We have already implied that the information sources available to the population about both domestic and foreign political life are inadequate. The question of adequacy depends, of course, partly on subjective judgment. The Soviet population has become more informed, and more interested in specific political events. There has been a "revolution of rising expectations" with regard to the availability of information.

The fact that some of the information flow about domestic and foreign events (some foreign stations broadcast back to the Soviet Union information about internal events, since horizontal communications within the country is curtailed) has been stemmed during the last few years has caused a good deal of frustration among the Soviet audience. One Samizdat journal, *Political Diary* (no. 50, November 1968) mentions how difficult it would have been to find out what was going on in the Middle East without foreign radio.

35. V. E. Shliapentokh, ed., *Chitatel'i gazeta: Itogi izucheniia chitatel'skoi auditorii tsentral'nykh gazet* [The reader and the paper: Results of an audience survey for central newspapers] (Moscow, 1969).
36. Tamotsu Shibutani, *Improvised News* (New York, 1966), p. 62. It should be noted here that in Shibutani's framework distortion of messages is not a typical characteristic of rumor.

The interview of Pavel Litvinov with the KGB agent Gostev is revealing of the gap between the growing sense of a "right to know" and the government's position on the dissemination of sensitive information:

Litvinov: . . . Instead of starting a new case, you yourself should publish the record of this criminal trial [of Vladimir Bukovsky in September, 1967] and in this way kill the rumors circulating in Moscow.

Gostev: And why do we need to publish it? It is an ordinary criminal case of disturbance of the peace.

Litvinov: If so, it is all the more important to give information about it, to let all the people see that it is really an ordinary case.

Gostev: Vechernaya Moskva of September 4, 1967 gives all the information about the case. All that has to be known about that trial is in there.

Litvinov: In the first place, there is too little information: the reader who had heard nothing previously about this case simply would not understand what it is all about. In the second place, it is false and slanderous. Rather, the editor of *Vechernaya Moskva* or the person who gave such information should be charged with slander. . . .

Gostev: . . . Pavel Mikhailovich, keep in mind: *Vechernaya Moskva* has printed all that the Soviet people should know about this case and this information is completely true and we warn you that if not only you, but your friends or anybody makes this record, you specifically will be held responsible for it.[37]

A second inadequacy in the official system is insufficient access for the expression of citizen opinions that are not controlled by the party or that call its policies into question. The factors we have already mentioned account for the growing demand for such outlets, creating pressure for the conditions under which a "public opinion" can develop.

Another factor that might contribute to the rise of dissent in the USSR is the one-sided view of reality that has been presented to the Soviet population for so many years. Research on techniques of persuasion has shown that for educated people a one-sided presentation is less effective than a two-sided one, and that a two-sided view is the more effective when individuals are later exposed to propaganda for the other side. The two-sided presentation has a kind of inoculation effect against an opposing point of view.[38] It could be, then, that the Soviet population (especially its more educated strata), having been exposed only to the party's point of view for so long during the Stalinist period, was particularly susceptible to influence from the outside when it came. If so, this susceptibility was probably reinforced by the shock of the disclosures of the Secret Speech and the subsequent changes in the party line.

Finally, the post-Stalin period has been one of traumatic events for the population, particularly the well informed. Perhaps the most threatening

---

37. *New York Times*, December 27, 1967.
38. Carl I. Hovland, I. L. Janis, and H. H. Kelley, *Communication and Persuasion* (New Haven, Conn., 1953), p. 110.

events from the point of view of intellectuals have been the arrests and trials of various writers and the persecution of prominent dissenters among the scientific elite. The demonstrations, petitions, and other forms of illegitimate political activity associated with these events and the punishment by officials for protests have produced a backlash among the specialist class and others. The behavior of the defendents who refused to recant and even voiced their oppositional views in court and the fact that these speeches were disseminated by the underground publication network have undoubtedly had an inspiring effect on other potential dissenters. For example, the defense speech of Valentin Moroz, a Ukrainian intellectual arrested in 1965 and again in 1970, taunts officials with the effect of persecution:

Since 1965, you have put several dozen people behind bars. What have you achieved by doing this? . . . Have you, for example, stopped the stream of non-official literature which avoids censorship and is called SAMIZDAT? No, you are too weak to do that. SAMIZDAT is growing, is becoming richer and richer in form and direction, authors and new readers. . . . You wanted to put out the fire; instead you have thrown fuel on the flames. Nothing has contributed so much to intensifying political life in the Ukraine as your repression. Nothing has attracted so much attention to Ukrainian renaissance as our trials. In fact, precisely these trials have shown to the public at large that political life in the Ukraine has come to life again. . . .
Your dams are strong and because of them you think you are out of danger. The Spring tides have simply moved out of your way and found new channels. Your turnpikes are closed. But they hold up no one, for the routes bypassed you long ago. . . . In the Ukraine and in the whole Soviet Union the new processes of development are just beginning. . . . In an era when all men are able to write, when there are 800,000 students in the Ukraine alone, when all have radios, every important event becomes a mass event.[39]

THE ROLE OF THE NEW CRITICAL INTELLIGENTSIA IN PUBLIC OPINION LEADERSHIP

Among the most salient characteristics of the mainstream dissenters are their use of the nineteenth century Russian intelligentsia as a reference group and their desire to engender a genuine public opinion in the Soviet Union. There are many indications that Soviet critics of the regime consider themselves as the "conscience of the nation" in the tradition of Chernyshevsky, Dobrolyubov, Herzen, and others.

An author who writes under the name Semyon Telegin in "Who Is One to Be?" discusses the growth of a new, humanitarian culture, the basis of which is the importance of the individual as opposed to the state machine. In referring to the role of contemporary art and science in forming this culture, the author

---

39. "The case of Valentin Moroz: Valentin Moroz' Defense Speech," *Survey* 18, no. 1 (82) (Winter 1972): 219–21.

calls on the intelligentsia to carry to the people "culture for the emancipation of the soul."[40] Although exclusively concerned with a rational-scientific organization of society, the social-democratic samizdat journal *Seyatel'* (Sower) views the role of the intelligentsia in a similar way.

> If the basic part of the scientific intelligentsia stands behind the alternative program, if the wider circles of the intelligentsia relate to it with a degree of sympathy, and if the other social classes, especially the workers, have no reason to be antagonistic—then the goal will be reached already.[41]

Critical political expression in Russia has traditionally been the task of a certain group of intellectuals; "intelligentsia" in its original meaning referred to the politically aware, critically thinking segment of the educated class.[42] During the nineteenth century this group manifested an amazing resourcefulness at creating and maintaining clandestine information networks to serve as nuclei for organization and propaganda among the population. Its position lay between the autocracy and the peasant masses, but it stood outside the social structure and gained perspective from this relative isolation.

During the Soviet period the structure of the population has become much more differentiated. At the top is a relatively small elite, political rather than aristocratic in origin. Below it are ordinary party and government administrators, a specialist class (including academic, managerial, and professional people), a white-collar clerical class, and a stratum of skilled workers, followed by unskilled workers and the state and collective farm peasantry. Changes in the class structure, especially the growth of educated segments, can be seen in table 7:2. It is the specialist class that is of most interest to us in

TABLE 7:2   Class Composition of the Soviet Population, 1928–71 (percent)

Class	1928	1939	1969	1971
Workers	12.3	33.5	49.5	58
White-collar intelligentsia[a]	5.3	16.7	18.8	22
Intelligentsia[a]	(1926—3 million)			(30 million)
Collective farmers	2.9	47.2	31.4	20
Independent farmers & tradespeople	79.5	2.6	0.3	0.0

Source: Adapted from "Statisticheskie materialy: territoriia i naselenie," *Vestnik statistiki*, no. 6 (1972), table 10, p. 87.
[a]Workers occupied primarily with mental labor.

40. Discussed in *Chronicle*, no. 12 (February 28, 1970), *AS* 366.
41. "Declaration of the *Seyatel'* Group," *Seyatel'*, No. 1 (September 1971), in *Vol'noe slovo, Samizdat izbrannoe*, Documentary Series, edition no. 5 (Frankfurt, 1972), p. 70.
42. Martin Malia, in his article "What Is the Intelligentsia?" in *The Russian Intelligentsia*, ed. Richard Pipes (New York, 1961), pp. 1–18 points out the two overlapping uses of the word: the "critically thinking" segment of the educated class, or those who were actively oppositional.

this discussion, since it is from that group that the critical intelligentsia and part of the political elite are recruited. Because its skills are necessary for the functioning of a modern economic and political system, it has grown rapidly during the post-Stalin period. Any pressure (however loosely organized) toward an independent public opinion comes from this group.

The relationship of party officials with intellectuals and professionals has always been ambivalent at best. If an intellectual is one who is occupied with generating and analyzing ideas, and if a professional is one who exercises some autonomy of judgment in his or her field of expertise, then the basic Leninist idea of the indisputable leading role of the party is inherently antiintellectual and antiprofessional. We needn't review here the Stalinist destruction of the early Soviet intellectual-professional class, particularly its literary segment. Khrushchev, though indulgent compared to Stalin, never removed the basic restrictions on intellectual activity (censorship, after-the-fact censure, controls on access to jobs and housing, etc.). Yet given the task of building a modern industrial society and a politically powerful nation, the regime needed to engender some degree of commitment from these people. The tension between official antipathy toward this group and the need for its resources has become even greater in the post-Stalin period, when the Soviet Union has become more and more of a world economic and political power and its intellectuals have developed contacts with their peers in other modern industrial nations.

Soviet intellectuals have indicated that there has been a high degree of cohesion among intellectual friendship groups, particularly during the post-Stalin period.[43] Linked together, they form a kind of subculture marginal to the larger political culture, neither wholly of it nor entirely distinct from it. Both through their professional activities and their isolation in "science cities" like Akademgorodok and Obninsk, scientific intellectuals have greatly contributed to the development of a sense of class solidarity. This sense of common pursuit stems not only from their shared position vis-à-vis the party authorities but also from a recognition of important values like freedom of discussion and inquiry and cognitive rationality.

They are in touch with the world culture outside the Soviet Union more than any other group, aside from a small party elite involved in official contacts. Many of them have a working knowledge of a foreign language as

---

43. Yuri Glazov has described the growth of solidarity and group pressure during the post-Stalin period: "The more intellectual and spiritual a circle of friends, the tighter were the restrictions placed on membership. . . . For acceptance into a highly intellectual circle a complex system of recommendation and even a probationary period were required. When you became a member of this kind of circle you realized you had entered into an esoteric clan where everything was divided into "us and them." . . . The *sine qua non* of integrity demanded of each member of the circle imposes restrictions not only upon his behavior inside the circle, but upon his conduct outside it, that is, in society. . . . Members of an intellectual circle are solemnly required to conduct themselves honorably in a sphere of life." "*Samizdat*: Background to Dissent," *Survey* 19, no. 1 (86) (Winter 1973): 81–82.

well as limited access to foreign printed matter for professional use. Those who live in large European centers and the "science cities" also come into contact with foreign professionals in their respective fields.[44] Therefore they are uniquely qualified to perceive the relative isolation of Soviet society and the gap between reality as experienced in their own personal lives and depicted in foreign channels, on the one hand, and that pictured in the Soviet mass media on the other. This intensifies a realization of their own privileged position as well as a sense of being deprived of the information and collegiality that are crucial in maintaining their professional sophistication. Because of this compartmentalization, intellectual life is far more concentrated than in Western societies. More attention is focused on fewer cultural-intellectual events and objects; information about these travels very rapidly and reliably by word of mouth. There is also an unusually intense concern about intellectual freedom and professional working conditions. Politically imposed limitations exist because of the party's concern about the potential development of opposition among the intellectuals; but this concern becomes a self-fulfilling prophecy, since it heightens intellectual antipathy toward the party apparatus. The *Seyatel'* group has described the conflict:

Side by side with the administrative class, the scientific intelligentsia has an enormous significance in the state capitalist society. In all of history this is the first class . . . that consists by its very definition of thinking people for whom intellectual freedom and freedom of information are necessary conditions for the success of their socially useful productive activity. . . .

The administrative class fears broad application of the scientific principle. Its own absolute power and its privileges are founded on suppressing intellectual freedom, making the population stupid through propaganda, denying the right to information. Any serious reform threatens its own monopolistic position in society. As for the intelligentsia (above all the scientific intelligentsia), it feels the artificial nature of the existing situation; this engenders its dissatisfaction, which becomes a mood of opposition.[45]

The critically thinking intelligentsia, feel their ambivalent position most keenly. Because of this they lead a kind of double life in their communications behavior. They participate extensively in institutional and informal official networks. They have a high rate of exposure to the mass media, yet are most critical of it. The newspaper studies we mentioned earlier show that educated

44. In 1969 more than 3,000 foreign intellectuals reportedly visited Akademgorodok. See R. Yanovsky, "The Scientist's Ideological Convictions," *Sovetskaya Rossiia*, August 28, 1970 (CDSP 22, no. 46 [December 15, 1970]: 5) and Zhores Medvedev, "Secrecy of Correspondence is Guaranteed by Law," *The Medvedev Papers* (London, 1971) for a realistic discussion of scientific correspondence with non-Soviet colleagues.

45. "Declaration of the *Seyatel'* Group," pp. 59–61. The use of the term intelligentsia here is slightly broader than ours. This antagonism is also indicated in Sakharov's unfriendly references to the neostalinism of Sergei P. Trapeznikov, director of the Science Department of the Central Committee of the CPSU, in *Progress, Coexistence, and Intellectual Freedom* (New York, 1968), pp. 56–57.

readers in general are "harder to please, more critical, more interested in problems of science and the humanities. . . . . The more highly educated are also more critical of newspaper and television materials pertaining to news and national and international political issues." Among the readers of *Literaturnaya Gazeta*, those most dissatisfied with "discussion materials" are employees in the government bureaucracy, people in the arts, natural scientists, teachers of natural science, journalists, and professional people[46]—all people vitally involved in the social-political system and the group from whom the intelligentsia is recruited.

While the members of the intelligentsia seek official information for their professional and personal activities, they supplement it with additional channels for exchanging ideas and information in another idiom. They are among the most active participants in word-of-mouth communication. Nadezhda Mandelshtam, writing about the growing repression of intellectual life in the twenties and thirties, called this phenomenon "linguistic dualism."[47] A recent émigré intellectual has referred to it as "behavioral bilingualism."[48] Intellectuals are required to praise party authority and incorporate its political symbolism in their work and professional-social intercourse; but among trusted friends they revert to the everyday language of the intellectual-professional class, speaking without party jargon and often criticizing official authority. After the Hungarian revolution the rule of the game was made clear: you can speak as you like, but in private only. Pasternak broke this rule by allowing publication of *Doctor Zhivago* abroad. He was followed by Sinyavsky and Daniel, and their trial in 1966 stimulated a flood of public and private dissent communication.

The usual behavior of the more critical specialists is to move back and forth between the official and unofficial communications milieus as circumstances warrant and allow. Seen in this context, the "informer" (*stukach*) for the secret police is a middleman or "translator" who reports on private conversations to the official network. Some dissenters have taken the position that this back-and-forth dualism is intolerable. They have "come out" and now are "monolingual": they speak their own language in public, using it critically toward the official political culture. Once an individual has taken this step there is no need for the intermediary informer. The official political culture

46. G. I. Khmara, 'Pechat' v sistemye massovykh kommunikatsi," *Problemy sotsiologii Pechati* 1 (1969): 209–10 and "Literaturnaya Gazeta i ee chitatel'," *ibid.*, 2 (1970): 127–29, both mentioned in Mickiewicz, "Policy Applications," p. 574. It should also be noted that the second least satisfied group was workers, who, according to the hypothesis of Mickiewicz, react critically due to the obvious discrepancy between their daily lives and the official picture in the media (p. 572).

47. In *Hope against Hope: A Memoir* (New York, 1970), Mme Mandelshtam remarks: "It was clear that the youth was leading a double life and talked two different languages. At what point do people switch from bureaucratic and ideological jargon to ordinary everyday speech? Our leading playwright was always longing to write a play about this linguistic dualism and the critical moment at which people pass from one idiom to the other" (p. 89).

48. Glazov, *ibid.*

refuses to absorb these dissident monolinguals and ignores their petitions, remarks, and criticisms. A few, like Àmalrik, Medvedev, Solzhenitsyn, and Sakharov, have been allowed to exist temporarily in this state, but all have had to suffer severe sanctions. Quite correctly, the regime considers their compensatory political communications as a direct challenge and fundamental criticism of the Soviet system.

Rather than a common set of origins or purposes, a shared position vis-à-vis the political system and a common modus operandi bring together various types of dissidents. Certain forms of repression, most notably the dissenters' trials and the use of psychiatric repression, have elicited similar responses from people of very different views who might otherwise not have realized their common dilemma in communicating and mobilizing support. In a brief and bitter essay, Vladimir Osipov, editor of the Russian nationalist samizdat journal *Veche*, has remarked: "I personally find the freedom of certain opinions disgusting. But it must exist IN THE NAME OF LIFE. . . . One might agree that the freedom to govern is the preserve of the few. But the freedom to think and to dissent belongs to us all."[49]

Lenin's tight band of dedicated revolutionaries were bourgeois intellectuals who joined him to carry "class consciousness" to the proletariat. Gradually, however, under Lenin's intolerant style of leadership, they ceased to be "intelligents" and shed both their class origins and their critical faculties. Having achieved power, the party elite assumed control of the means of propaganda and expanded them to carry simplified, repetitive messages to the masses. As Stalin gradually purged the party of old Bolsheviks and intellectuals educated under the old regime, he consolidated his control of the agitprop apparatus and the means of coercion that backed it up. The intellectuals who were left became mere spokesmen for the party line as defined by Stalin and his sycophants, and those who refused to do so or erred in their judgment of that task were physically eliminated.

During the post-Stalin period the media have burgeoned and become more professionalized. Soviet journalists and other media and propaganda specialists have assumed the function of carrying out the party elite's directions with regard to the fostering of correct political ideas among the population.

At the same time, two major phenomena have worked to produce the renascence of a critical intelligentsia that conceives of itself as a leading group in the formation of public opinion. First, there have been many serious questions raised about the legitimacy of the party's guiding role amid radical changes beginning with the death of Stalin but having roots much farther back. It is understandable that in such a confusing period people seek opinion leadership for answers to questions about the very nature of the political system itself. But the population that formerly looked to the mass media and agitprop apparatus for a well-orchestrated vision of reality now found

49. "The Secret of Freedom," December 1971–January 1972, in *Chronicle*, no. 24, AS 1100.

inconsistency and disorganization there. No easy, credible answers came forth from the political elite. Those who needed guidance turned to the informal opinion leaders, and important among these were intellectuals in the process of forming their own views. Lipset and Dobson, in considering the role of intellectuals as critics of society, have hypothesized that certain intellectuals whose occupational task is the interpretation of experience showed themselves particularly sensitive to the normative ambiguity that accompanied the post-Stalin changes. "Others looked to them for a clarification of the meaning of the times; willingly or unwillingly, writers, artists, and others professionally concerned with the interpretation of experience found themselves in a position of social leadership."[50]

Secondly, the opening up of the communications system to greater variety and external influence helped intellectuals, who had the greatest access to foreign sources, become transmitters of unofficial interpretations of events. A growing specialist class, having the prerequisites suggested by Speier for the development of a public opinion (financial means and skills for access to communications and leisure for discussion), now existed. Among this group intellectuals enjoy a certain amount of prestige, and it is natural that other specialists should turn to the more knowledgeable and thoughtful members of their class for opinion leadership. When not only literary intellectuals but prominent scientists began to articulate their views publicly it was undoubtedly with a view toward influencing the leadership through the support of the specialist class. The intelligentsia thus attempted to take back from the media specialists and the party elite the function of politically educating the significant class in the population. That class is seen by them to be not so much the proletariat but the specialist class and possibly white collar and skilled workers.

Literary and scientific intellectuals are still the most likely candidates for dissent activity. Social scientists, while reported to be quite liberal and critical of the regime in private, are not very visible among active, publicly committed dissenters. Their work, however, has traditionally been under strict day-to-day party control. Until recently, social scientists have come from the disciplines of history, philosophy, and economics. Both their recruitment and work is extremely sensitive to changes in the party line. Sociology, a new and troubled discipline (partly because its very existence pushes against those former boundaries), has been more productive of criticism, both directly and indirectly, but most of its members' critical expression has been private. This group's main contribution has been the creating of conditions that may foster dissent: importing of Western social science literature and methodology, carrying out research on public opinion, audiences, and uses of leisure, and so on.

50. Seymour M. Lipset and Richard B. Dobson, "The Intellectual as Critic and Rebel: With Special Reference to the United States and the Soviet Union," *Daedalus*, no. 101 (Summer 1972), p. 156.

In a sense, the question of how broadly based among social classes is the Soviet dissident movement does not strike at the heart of its significance. Workers have never played an important decision-making role in Russian or Soviet politics. While their tacit acceptance of a given political position is probably necessary, their active support seems to have been less important in fact than in theory. The elitist orientation of the CPSU makes it sensitive to the power of public opinion among a rather specialized public.[51] At this stage in history the intelligentsia are not so isolated from "the masses," since the population as a whole, as we have seen, is much more stratified by education and standard of living. The immense gap between the privileges of the elite and the poor living conditions of most farm people is meliorated somewhat by the existence of several intermediate classes. It is very unlikely, however, that dissent could make any significant impact on the Soviet political culture, particularly its communications apparatus, without some support from the specialist class.

Andrei Amalrik has referred to the influence of the specialist class with regard to civil rights. He mentions the slow movement toward the rule of law during the post-Stalin years, impeded by a passive bureaucratic elite oriented toward self-preservation. The specialist class has been disturbed by the issuance of decrees (such as the antiparasite law and articles 190-1 and 190-3 of the Criminal Code) in direct contradiction to the Soviet Constitution and international conventions such as the Universal Declaration on Human Rights. While progress toward civil rights was bogged down at the top, however, the specialists began to demand that they be treated "not in accordance with the current requirements of the regime but on a legal basis." Amalrik refers to the "gray belt" of activities that the law does not specifically forbid but that are in fact prohibited by the authorities, such as contacts with foreigners, duplication of manuscripts, and spoken or written criticism of the system. Most of these are fundamental communications activities necessary for the development of any independent public opinion. The Soviet government has, in Amalrik's terms, tried to blacken the gray belt, while the specialist class has responded by trying to whiten it by doing things previously considered unlawful but guaranteed in the constitution and the Universal Declaration on Human Rights. By constantly referring to these documents they place the regime in an awkward position.[52]

The point has been made that some intellectuals are libertarian only in their criticism of the limits of political expression but are authoritarian in their

---

51. Although we often refer to "public opinion" as if the majority of the population had one collective predisposition toward all issues (which is also the Soviet view), V. O. Key, Jr. has made a useful distinction between special publics and the general public: "In actual politics one issue engages the attention of one sub-division of the population, while another arouses the interest of another group, and a third question involves still another special public." V. O. Key, Jr., *Public Opinion and American Democracy* (New York, 1961), p. 10.

52. Amalrik, *Will the Soviet Union Survive?*, pp. 17–25.

political views.[53] Since the range of political orientation is extremely broad among the intelligentsia (including some very right-wing views), this assessment is undoubtedly correct.[54] Nevertheless their verbal and behavioral affirmation of libertarian communications ideals is extremely significant. They pointedly ally themselves with the libertarian political tradition and confront the regime regarding its authoritarian position toward communication and opposition.

PATTERNS OF COMMUNICATIONS AMONG DISSENTERS

Because of the nature of legitimate Soviet political communications, dissenters have developed what amounts to an alternative or supplementary political communications network. It is shared to some degree by other Soviet citizens but is more intensively used by those who are critical of the regime and hope to build some sort of public opinion. All Soviet citizens learn to "read between the lines," making the most of the repetitive, formulary material in the official media. This is a particular communications skill developed in systems where censorship is widely practiced and where public media are used also as channels for esoteric communication (e.g., the dissemination of the party line and information on personnel changes to the party apparatus and rank-and-file members). By contrast, the audience's task in the West is to glean the most important information from a barrage of conflicting and often irrelevant facts.

Word of Mouth. As we noted earlier, most Soviet citizens use the word-of-mouth or unofficial person-to-person network for certain kinds of content. Ideas and information may be passed on serially from one individual to another or exchanged in small discussion groups among trusted friends. Used critically, this can have a "myth-busting" function, helping to cut through the official cant and extract facts from the politically orthodox context. It also produces interference for the official system by introducing more information and interpretation at variance with the party line. Informal word of mouth plays a particularly important part for critics of the regime because they trust the official media less than most people and need alternative channels for spreading information that could never be passed over the public media or official personal network. They use personal contacts heavily in the collection of information for, production of, and distribution of samizdat, especially the journals that report on dissident activities.

53. Jonathan Harris, "The Dilemma of Dissidence," *Survey* 16, no. 1 (78) (Winter 1971): 109.
54. For a partial survey see Dmitri Pospielovsky, "Programs of the Democratic Opposition: A Review and Analysis of the Political Ideas of Recent Samizdat Writing," Radio Liberty Research Paper no. 38, 1970.

Person-to-person networks are most useful for small communities or in large cities. Jerome Gilison, studying nonvoting and negative voting as a form of political dissent, concluded that "only in a small cohesive community could there be sufficient communication of the dissenting view prior to the election to assure each voter that he would actually be a member of the *majority* by voting 'no.' "[55] Much information does travel from urban areas to rural outbacks by direct personal contact, however. Soviet Jews who have emigrated report that they relied heavily on personal contacts, mainly through families, with information and documents transmitted by persons traveling long distances solely for that purpose. They could not, of course, trust the Soviet postal system, which practices censorship.[56]

Naturally much information is passed by telephone. A good deal of the support that was generated for Zhores Medvedev during his forcible confinement in a mental institution was initiated and transmitted in this manner.[57] It is also thought that much of the information that has appeared in the *Chronicle* and other samizdat journals is transmitted by phone, since it appears so soon after events in scattered, remote places. A new Soviet government restriction on internal phone conversations would seem to confirm this. It reads: "The use of telephone links (intercity, city, and rural) for purposes contrary to state interests and public order, is prohibited."[58] This prohibition will pose a major problem for samizdat journals reporting on illegitimate activities and official repression. Presumably it will also inhibit the transmission of information about activities in the provinces to Western reporters in Moscow. News of the Kaunas riot in May 1972, for example, reached Moscow immediately by telephone and was sent out by a foreign reporter to be given wide publicity outside the country.

Foreign Support. Dissenters have received a good deal of support for their activities from outside the Soviet Union. In a sense, Western reporters and foreign radio are for them a "transmission belt" to the larger world, particularly to people in their ethnic or professional groups whose support may be useful. Much of the openly political support is in the form of letters and petitions by foreign individuals and groups to important party or government bodies, and these are often broadcast to the Soviet population as well. Appeals and letters from Soviet citizens are often sent to foreign stations, which then broadcast them to the Soviet audience. Such documents of the internal opposition (which also include literary and other types of material) is

---

55. J. M. Gilison, "Elections, Dissent, and Political Legitimacy," *American Political Science Review* 62, no. 3 (September 1968): 357.

56. See Zhores Medvedev, "Secrecy of Correspondence."

57. Zhores and Roy Medvedev, *A Question of Madness* (New York, 1971).

58. Decree no. 655 of USSR Council of Ministers, August 31, 1972, addendum to article 74 of *Regulations of Communication of the USSR*, announced in *Sobranie Postanovlenia Pravitel'stva SSSR*, no. 19.

known as *radizdat*. Tape recordings of foreign broadcasts and other broadcasts and other materials circulate as *magnitizdat*. Foreign media thus have become an extension of the domestic alternative network, "amplifying" the activities and writings of the democratic movement.

Not surprisingly, the Soviet government views foreign stations broadcasting to the Soviet Union as hostile, aggressive organs of the intelligence services of the countries that harbor them. Several propaganda campaigns to discredit these stations have been launched during the post-Khrushchev period.[59] These efforts may deter some listeners among the general population, but they are unlikely to affect the behavior of members of the democratic movement, who have few alternative sources for these categories of information.

What proportion of radios in the Soviet Union are capable of receiving foreign radio broadcasts? Radio Liberty estimated in 1969 that about 27 million could of the 86.5 million total.[60] If the same proportion held true in 1970, out of 94.8 million, almost 30 million sets could be tuned to foreign broadcasts (the population at this time was about 245 million). In addition there were more than 20,000 licensed amateur or "ham" radios and several thousand more that operated illegally. Many of these are powerful and sensitive and can pick up almost any foreign broadcast (see below).

According to one commentator, the most listened-to station among intellectuals as of 1971 was the Voice of America in Russian. Others claim this honor for BBC, and still others would argue that dissenters listen most to Radio Liberty, which specializes in broadcasting critical material, including a good deal of dissent literature and information. The most-jammed stations are Radio Liberty (because it carries material openly critical of Soviet policies) and BBC (because it enjoys high credibility with the Soviet audience for general news).[61] Interviews conducted at Massachusetts Institute of Technology in the early and middle-sixties indicated that for three types of information—events in non-Communist countries, Soviet economic news, and political news in general—Soviet stations offered more news but foreign stations were considered more reliable sources.[62] Certainly today foreign radio must be considered one of the most reliable sources for news of political, ethnic, and religious dissidence, since Soviet media devote next to no attention to these subjects—the exceptions being brief, oblique references to foreign radio listening and short, misleading accounts of political trials.

A recent Soviet publication on propaganda indicates that Soviet officials are concerned enough about the influence of foreign radio to organize an active domestic radio counterpropaganda operation:

59. See Hollander, *Soviet Political Indoctrination*, p. 114.

60. *Guest in the Home*, Munich, 1969, mentioned by Lewis Feuer in "The Intelligentsia in Opposition," *Problems of Communism* 19, no. 6 (November–December 1970): 10.

61. Michael Scammell, "Soviet Intellectuals Soldier On," *Survey* 16, no. 1 (Winter 1971): 105–6.

62. For further information on types of news and reliability see Hollander, *Soviet Political Indoctrination*.

In order to deeply analyze and more correctly plan all work in the battle with bourgeois ideology and inimical propaganda, there has been created. . . a Public Council on Ideological Problems (in its ranks are fifteen prominent specialists in the field of social science and propagandists). Relying on the study of bourgeois propaganda materials, the council makes recommendations on the thematics of counter propaganda broadcasts. . . . This allowed us to mount a broad counterpropaganda [effort] earlier than the bourgeois radio stations and at the same time *prepare listeners for a critical reception of falsified materials broadcast by them.*[63]

Obviously, Soviet propaganda specialists have become aware of the advantages of preparing the population for information or interpretations contradictory to the party line. A clear impact has been made on Soviet programming by foreign radio stations. They also know that the version of an event that reaches the audience first is more likely to be believed (the "primacy" effect). This is one substantial adjustment of a formerly closed communications system that now has to cope with competition from outside.

How do Soviet dissenters feel about the support they receive from abroad? One source indicated that the highly placed people who produced and read *Political Diary* (see above) were not happy about the foreign broadcasts concerning their publication, though they released several issues to inform Westerners of their existence.[64] But the mainstream of the democratic movement does not seem to be at all embarrassed by the publicity given their efforts. To the contrary, at least three dissidents have publicly applauded the role of foreign radio, citing its supplementary role in the dissemination of political information within the Soviet Union. In his essay on Soviet penal policy Yuri Galanskov appealed for support from Western communists in particular and the outside world at large:

The Western press, and especially the Western radio stations broadcasting in Russian publicize the arbitrariness and acts of crude coercion by Soviet official personnel, and thus force the state bodies and officials to take action. In this way the Western press and radio are fulfilling the tasks of what is at present lacking in Russia, an organized opposition, and thereby stimulating our national development.[65]

Complaining to Chakovsky, the author of an article in *Literaturnaya Gazeta* of April 1968 about the Moscow campaign against the Galanskov-Ginzburg trial, Lev Kvachevsky wrote:

You yourself write that the letters were sent to Soviet organizations and "the West" is merely informing Soviet citizens that such an act has taken place. The content of any such letter is hardly likely to be a secret. But why is it that precisely the radio stations of England, America and Germany which have become the communications link

---

63. Ye. E. Vartanova, chief, Editorial Board for All-Union Radio, "Propaganda Marksizm-Leninizma po Radio i Televidenie," in Smirnova, *Voprosy teorii i praktiki*, p. 266 (emphasis added).

64. Anthony Astrachan, "Introduction: Documents: Soviet Union, *Political Diary*," in *Survey* 18, no. 3 (84) (Summer 1972): 210.

65. Cited by Peter Reddaway, *Uncensored Russia* (New York, 1972), p. 225.

between our people and a part of the intelligentsia? (You do not, I trust, doubt that the broadcasts of these stations are listened to by millions of Soviet people.) Has the Literary Gazette, which always writes in such detail about trials, . . . printed even one of the letters protesting against the judicial victimization of Ginzburg and Galanskov?[66]

And Solzhenitsyn praised Radio Liberty in his April 1972 interview for its role informing the world about developments among Soviet dissenters.

One of the most dramatic cases where foreign support (from radio and in the form of telegrams and letters from Western scientists and intellectuals) helped is that of Zhores Medvedev, who was confined in a mental institution for his "publicist" activities. His arrest was reported almost immediately on foreign radio stations and in Western newspapers. Sakharov's letter to Brezhnev of June 6, 1970 was also communicated abroad, and it increased the streams of telegrams from scientists all over the world. Medvedev felt that the Kaluga doctors were restrained from prescribing powerful depressants for him because they were "under pressure from outside opinion as it was without asking for more."[67] Of great importance in this case was the fact that his twin brother, Roy, had mobilized a number of personal contacts by word of mouth and phone and so could keep Western correspondents as closely informed as he himself was during his brother's ordeal. In the opposite direction, *The Chronicle of Current Events* prints a good deal of foreign material, such as materials from Eastern Europe or petitions in support of Soviet dissenters directed to official Soviet organizations.

An important source of unofficial communication in the Soviet Union that is often overlooked by outsiders is the amateur radio operator, or "ham." There is a strict system of control over radio parts and the training and licensing of Soviet hams, since this is considered a paramilitary activity. Nevertheless there is a good deal of extraofficial information passed along from foreign hams to their Soviet counterparts and among the Soviet hams in different parts of the Soviet Union. In 1965 there were about 15,000 or 20,000 licensed Soviet amateurs.[68] In addition, a number of illegal trans- mitters are in operation. The number of illegal stations apparently in- creased dramatically during the mid-1960s when a do-it-yourself handbook for radio amateurs was published; it sold out immediately. "*Samefir*" (again, patterned after the acronym *samizdat* [see below] using the word *efir* for ether or air waves) has become more and more political as time has passed, but apparently there has been a crackdown in this area. Stiff penalties were finally imposed, obliging the courts to deal with "radio row-

---

66. Cited by Reddaway, *ibid.*, p. 381. Kvachevsky lost his job two months after sending this letter.

67. Medvedev and Medvedev, *Question of Madness*, pp. 56, 150.

68. For a complete description of the organization and operation of legal amateur stations see F. Gayle Durham, *Amateur Radio Operation in the Soviet Union* (Cambridge, Mass., Center for International Studies, Massachusetts Institute of Technology, 1965).

dies" according to article 70 of the Criminal Code covering "anti-Soviet agitation and propaganda."

It is difficult to estimate the value of such stations for the development of Soviet dissent, but certainly they supplement the dull and tendentious official Soviet newscasts, and, operating on illegal wavelengths, are capable of transmitting important and sensitive information very rapidly. In August 1968, transmitters in the Ukraine told Soviet troops about the real situation in Czechoslovakia.[69] The stations seem to be spread out over the Soviet Union but are particularly dense in the European area, where it is easiest to obtain the necessary radio parts.

Samizdat. Perhaps the best-known method of dissent communication is the written word. Underground manuscripts circulating in typescript have been dubbed *samizdat*, meaning "self-publication." The word was apparently first used in the early 1960s, although it may have existed in very narrow circles earlier than this.[70] The phenomenon, however, goes much further back. In 1790 a customs official, Alexander Radishchev, wrote and had published on his own press by serfs an antiserfdom book, *A Journey from Petersburg to Moscow*. The book was eventually banned, and all but 17 of 650 copies were confiscated. The remaining ones circulated in private hands.[71] In the 1820s Pushkin and Griboyedov both circulated manuscripts privately to avoid the censor. Under Alexander II, Herzen published *Kolokol* (The bell) mostly in London and had copies smuggled back into the country. Unpublished political manifestoes and tracts began to circulate more and more as illegal political groups proliferated in the 1860s and 1870s. Notable in the effort to secure support for these activities from abroad was Sergei Kravchinsky (Stepniak), who settled in London in 1884 and in 1890 organized the Society of Friends of Russian Freedom. This organization published *Free Russia*, a journal supporting the Western publication of underground samizdat. Illegal Russian publications and Western support and "amplification" of them thus long antedates the Soviet regime or the development of the broadcast media.

Lenin's own involvement in underground publication led him to some of his organizational theories. He adapted the words of Wilhelm Liebknecht: "Teach, propagandize, organize; only a *party organ* can and must be the central point of this activity."[72] During the early years of the Soviet regime,

---

69. For a discussion of the illegal ham stations see Marianna Buten-Schoen, "Underground Airwaves Flourish Despite Officials' Strong Stand," *Springfield* (Mass.) *Union*, November 18, 1972.

70. Julius Telesin states that a Moscow poet used the term *samsebyeizdat* ("I publish myself") in the late fifties and later adopted *samizdat* ("I myself do the publishing," not necessarily of one's own work). "Inside *Samizdat*," *Encounter*, February 1973, p. 25. The word is modeled on *Gosizdat*, the Russian acronym for the State Publishing House for Political Literature.

71. Avrahm Yarmolinsky, *Road to Revolution* (New York, 1962), chap. 1.

72. V. I. Lenin, *Sochineniia* 4th ed. (Moscow, 1941–1952), 4:200.

censorship existed in fact but was not formally reimposed until 1921 (see above). With the reinstitution of censorship, poems, novels, and stories began to circulate underground. Nadezhda Mandelshtam vividly portrays the culture of this early Soviet samizdat (called Underwood after the make of the typewriter) and poignantly describes the arrest and eventual death of Osip Mandelshtam for an anti-Stalin poem that circulated only by word of mouth and in a few manuscript copies.[73]

After Pasternak broke the ice by allowing *Doctor Zhivago* to be published in the West, other well-known writers of various persuasions have engaged (sometimes unintentionally) in *tamizdat*, publication "there" (*tam* = in the West). This has become much more difficult with Soviet participation in the International Copyright Convention beginning in May 1973. Most of this material is reimported clandestinely and circulated among literary people and dissidents. Several unofficial journals were published in the late fifties and early sixties (*Sintaksis, Phoenix,* and *Sphinxes*). Many literary manuscripts circulated underground, either because the authors knew they would be rejected for publication or because this had already happened. Often the editors who rejected the manuscripts started the circulation process by making copies before they returned the manuscripts to the authors. In the summer of 1965 censorship tightened along with the general political atmosphere; the authors Sinyavsky and Daniel were arrested in September.

Rather than stemming the flood of samizdat, the policies of Brezhnev and Kosygin seem to have stimulated it considerably. In 1968 the *Chronicle of Current Events* began its regular bimonthly appearance. The arrests in late 1972 and early 1973 of many people involved in *Chronicle* seems to mean that there is an end to official tolerance or indecision regarding the journal and that its "demonstration effect" was too potent to offset any advantages its existence might have for the regime.

The content of samizdat at first was primarily literary. Literary intellectuals have a long tradition of using the written word for political purposes; before Lenin they understood that "ideas are weapons." They have also had to confront the issue of censorship in their daily professional activities even if they did not consider their orientation primarily political. More recently, scientific and technical people have produced dissent publications. Notable among these is Zhores Medvedev's *Rise and Fall of T. D. Lysenko*. Political tracts and manifestoes increasingly are included among the subjects of illegitimate publication, along with reports of political events such as trials and Writers Union meetings. The dry, factual tone of *Chronicle* has led to the conclusion that its authors and producers were primarily scientists rather than literary intellectuals.

The following list gives some indication of the scope and depth of material known to be circulating in samizdat (items may appear individually or in journals):

73. Mandelshtam, *Hope against Hope*, chaps. 1–9.

I. Literary works
   A. Novels, stories, plays, poetry
   B. Memoirs, autobiography
II. News and reports
   A. News notes on activities and persecution of dissidents at liberty in the USSR and manifestoes of support for the activity from abroad
   B. Stenographic reports and accounts of political events (searches, arrests, demonstrations, trials, meetings, "interviews" with KGB agents, psychiatric procedures, funerals of prominent literary people or dissidents)
   C. Reports from places of confinement: psychiatric hospitals, camps, and prisons
III. Appeals, declarations, and letters to officials by dissenters and their supporters in the USSR or abroad
IV. Analytic articles and philosophical treatises on various subjects (such as analyses of events in Czechoslovakia and Yugoslavia, the development of dissent, the position of Jews or Crimean Tatars, and so on)
V. Official documents (treaties, declarations, and pacts signed by the USSR, reprints from the RSFSR Criminal Code and Code of Criminal Procedure, texts of secret orders, and so on)
VI. Pornography
VII. Reviews of samizdat materials—e.g., collections of reviews of Solzhenitsyn's *August 1914* and a review, titled "Confrontation with Oneself," of a samizdat survey of the Soviet press of 1967–71 on the Middle East known as *Our Middle Eastern Friends*, both mentioned in *Chronicle*, no. 24.
VIII. Miscellaneous
   A. Reviews of Soviet press on particular topics (to give readers some historical perspective on the official treatment of a given subject)
   B. Reprints of certain old newspaper articles of interest (for example, Julius Telesin mentions the reprint from *Sovetskaya Sibir'* for 1938 of a report of a trial of local NKVD and procuracy officials who carried out repressive measures against 160 children; "Inside '*Samizdat*,'" *Encounter*, February 1973, p. 26)
   C. Lists of cuts made by censors in legitimately published works
   D. Reprints of interesting passages published in legitimate works
   E. Reprints of articles published abroad, especially in Czechoslovakia (such as V. Skutina's "Prisoner of the President" from April 1968 issue of the Czech journal *Reporter*; for this article the author was persecuted and accused of calling Novotny a "tyrant, a scoundrel, and an idiot" (mentioned in *Chronicle*, no. 23)

It would be interesting to do a comparative content analysis of all samizdat materials and of a sample of Soviet legitimate publication to determine what topics are omitted officially but are represented in the underground literature. We do have available a large number of samizdat publications in the West and can make some rough guesses at the most important areas of content in underground communications (or rather that portion of it that has reached the West). But Westerners were almost totally unaware of the *Political Diary* (1964–71) until after it ceased production; therefore it is risky to assume that the samizdat we do have access to is representative. We can tell something about the areas of interest, however, by what is available.[74]

A count of items in the serial register of the Arkhiv samizdata (Radio Liberty, Munich) indicates that most of the material is directed toward influencing either public opinion (domestic or international) or the official representatives of the regime (newspapers, government and party officials, and so on). It might be argued that, since the regime has a rather poor record of responding to such appeals, many of these items are in fact directed primarily toward public opinion and are only formally addressed to the regime.[75] Categorizing the same materials by type of content, we find that the overwhelming majority of them (479) is directly concerned with socialist legality or civil rights; the rest relate to these areas indirectly (against neo-Stalinism, on Czechoslovakia, nonofficial critiques of socialism or Marxism-Leninism). Judging by its printed production, then, Soviet dissent is concerned mainly with trying to establish some broader legitimate boundaries of the political culture. To use Amalrik's phrase, its participants want to "whiten the grey belt."

How does the samizdat network operate? Usually an author, an editor (to whom the manuscript may have been submitted for publication), or a friend comes into possession of a typescript. He or she types up a few copies (usually from three to twelve, depending on the thickness of paper available, the skill of the typist and the length of the manuscript) and passes them on to friends who might be able to make more copies or to someone for whom it would be useful. The original person generally keeps a copy and sometimes returns the original, perhaps with an extra, to the person from whom he or she obtained it. Each person who receives a copy makes a few more, and by a geometric progression hundreds of copies come into existence. The author of the original manuscript generally has no control over the number of copies made and no real knowledge of the impact of his or her work because contact with

---

74. They have been collected by Radio Liberty, Munich, and are available at several places in the United States and Europe. See pp. xii–xiii for information about public access to samizdat material.

75. The count of items yields the following breakdown by form (no item is counted in more than one category):

Petitions and letters to Soviet government officials or bodies: 181	Short stories or collections of stories: 7
Petitions, addressee not mentioned: 11	Poems: 21
Letters to newspapers: 35	Essays, treatises: 73
Letters to individuals or groups in various professions: 45	Miscellaneous articles, anthologies: 26
Letters to non-Soviet communists or Communist parties: 5	Issues of underground journals: 44
	Accounts of events (trials, searches, etc.): 51
Public statements of opinion: 92	Official records (of trials, meetings, etc.): 50
Appeals to "world public opinion": 9	Trial statements by dissidents: 8
Letters to dissenters: 2	Records of official meetings denouncing or levying sanctions against dissidents: 4
Belles lettres:	Records of press conferences or meetings by dissidents: 4
Novels, autobiographies: 17	Texts of speeches: 8

the manuscript is lost after one or two links in the chain. Often the author "publishes" pseudonymously. A real exchange of ideas is difficult under these circumstances.

The usual method of reproduction has been by typewriter. Typewriters in the Soviet Union are no longer so closely controlled and scarce as they once were, and literary and research workers often have access to them at work or at home. Most samizdat typing is done at home. Since it is a laborious task, typists usually try to make as many copies as they can at one sitting. Therefore they try to use very thin paper. Since onionskin paper is relatively scarce in the Soviet Union, it looks somewhat suspicious to go into a store and buy several reams of it. Typists and authors usually get several friends to buy smaller amounts.

Sometimes one copy of a manuscript is read in group fashion by a number of people gathered together. As the first person is finished, he or she passes individual pages on to the next; those who enter the room last are handed the first sheets of the manuscript.[76]

Photography is also sometimes used, and since many Soviet people have photography as a hobby, this is a promising method for duplication. Its advantages are that it is very rapid and many more copies can be printed from one original than by typewriter. But the original from which the photocopies are made must be of good quality, and many *samizdat* typescripts are poor, either from being the tenth or eleventh copy in a set or from being handled by too many people. The finished copy also takes up a lot of storage space since photographic paper is relatively thick. A fairly recent article in the journal *Free Thought* extolled the virtues of photography and included detailed instructions on the type of equipment that should be used, its prices, and where it can be purchased.[77]

An article by a writer calling himself S. Topolev in the same journal analyzed the disadvantages of the current organization and duplication method of samizdat for the dissident movement. He mentions the problem of getting committed, reliable typists; the fact that authors do not get much feedback and therefore have no sense of participation in an intellectual dialogue; and the duplication and scattering of intellectual energies. Storage of samizdat is a problem, both because the housing shortage leaves little space and the materials are highly incriminating. Yet people store up copies of items they don't need in order to trade them for materials that do interest them; hence, samizdat has developed its own underground barter system. Topolev's solution to many of these problems is *kolizdat* (collective publishing): uncensored materials printed in journals with regular periodicity and a known list of subscribers, editorial boards, and the use of duplicating equipment. The

---

76. See Telesin, "Inside *Samizdat*," p. 31.
77. K. Glukhov, "Photography as a Method of Reproducing Textual Documentation" *Svobodnaia Mysl'*, no. 1 (December 20, 1971), AS 1180.

last suggestion is one of the most radical, since such machines are tightly controlled in the Soviet Union precisely to prevent such a proliferation of underground material. Topolev calls on scientists and engineers in the movement to solve this problem. The journals would carry only materials not otherwise circulating in samizdat so that there would be a high incentive to subscribe and the storage of other materials would not be necessary.[78] *Free Thought* itself seems to embody some of Topolev's suggestions; it is devoted to publishing thematic articles and, by organizing itself in the most efficient way possible, to building a more solid political organization for the articulation of dissenters' interests.

Late 1971 seems to have marked a turning point for at least a segment of the dissident movement. At the same time *Free Thought* appeared, the social-democratic journal *The Sower* (*Seyatel'*, mentioned above) also began publication. It is interesting to compare the basic assumptions and priorities of the two journals. Both agree that there is a crisis in the movement. *Free Thought*'s editorial board, however, devotes a good deal of space to the problems and solutions involved in improving the immediate organizing capacity of the journals circulated underground. *The Sower*, on the other hand, rejects for its own group the more open symbolic behaviors (such as petitions and demonstrations) and sees the construction of a comprehensive program as the item of highest priority. It also emphasizes the importance of samizdat, seeing it as the fundamental instrument of agitation and propaganda for the movement, but warns against its becoming an end in itself rather than a means. *The Sower*'s program calls for directing the basic agitation-propaganda effort "towards the intelligentsia and semi-intelligentsia, simply because the most immediate response can be expected there as a result of greater education and psychological readiness." It warns, however, against a "caste spirit." Most important it puts forth a rather naive tentative program based on the "scientific-democratic management" of society by experts.[79]

Symbolic Behavior as Political Communication. Public political rituals are patterned symbolic representations of various aspects of a political culture. Parades, party congresses, and other such displays periodically reaffirm the legitimacy of the regime and its incumbents. The institutionalized roles of citizen and leader, linguistic formulas ("fascist beasts," "socialist legality"), and physical representations (pictures of current leaders, military equipment) emphasize mutual expectations so that leaders and population can predict one another's behavior. The habitualization of such symbolic aspects of life to some extent frees both (but especially leaders, since they are in a position to commit arbitrary and illegal acts against citizens) from a

78. S. Topolev, "Ot Samizdata k Kolizdatu," *ibid.*, pp. 6–17.
79. The first two issues of *Seyatel'* are available in Russian, published by Possev in Frankfurt. The first issue has been translated by Michael and Gretchen Brainerd in *Intellectual Digest*, January 1973.

continual reassessment of their position as a background to political interaction. In the Soviet Union, manifestations of rules and folkways of politics are subject to a high degree of control both because a high premium is placed on citizen conformity and because the regime is strongly aware of the socializing aspect of such rituals.[80]

In this context, one of the most important aspects of the dissenters' communications is that they signify the adoption of public behaviors either at variance with official expectations of the citizen role or, in their more extreme forms, in direct violation of written or unwritten prohibitions. The most active and committed Soviet dissenters have adopted the technique of public demonstrations to communicate their views and a rejection of their clandestine status to the population and the authorities. This type of act has been most important in challenging the Soviet officialdom's monopoly on the control of public political behavior, pointing out the gap between rights as "guaranteed" in the constitution and inhibited by the regime.

Several other kinds of acts have had great symbolic value, since they represent behavior that for so long has been beyond the pale in the Soviet Union. Andrei Sakharov at an international genetics conference in Moscow in 1970 picked up a piece of chalk and wrote on a blackboard: "Academician Sakharov is soliciting signatures for the support of Zhores Medvedev." Medvedev had been arrested and put in a mental hospital a few days earlier. Sakharov's appeal attracted only a few signatures, but it was an act of unprecedented boldness, since the behavior of Soviet scientists at international gatherings is closely watched and the public soliciting of signatures is obviously the sort of spontaneous act abhorred by the party.[81] Several self-immolations, most notably those in the Baltic republics and in Kiev, surely represent the ultimate in purely symbolic expression of political views (however desperate the actors may be considered in comparison with the rest of the population). Large gatherings of ethnic groups (Crimean Tatars for the birthday of Lenin, Jews dancing outside their synagogue during a holiday) represent officially disallowed public statements of solidarity and commitment to non-Russian ethnic traditions; most such demonstrations are dispersed with brutal force and many of the participants wounded or arrested. *Chronicle*, no. 22 (November 10, 1971) mentioned that on April 29 and 30, 1971, the yellow-and-blue flag of the Ukrainian People's Republic of 1917–20 appeared on a water tower in the town of Novy Rozdal.

In 1970 and 1971 Soviet dissidents expanded their communications activity again by appearing in two films intended for foreign consumption. One, made by the CBS correspondent William Cole, included interviews with

---

80. See Peter L. Berger and Thomas Luckmann, *The Social Construction of Reality* (Garden City, N.Y., 1966), pts. 1 and 2.

81. The incident is described in Medvedev and Medvedev, *A Question of Madness*, and in James F. Clarity, "Soviet Dissent Is Not Unified, but It Proves to Be Persistent," *New York Times*, June 14, 1970, p. 1.

Amalrik, Bukovsky, and Peter Yakir. The second was an example of *samokino* (or "self-produced" movies), if we may use yet another acronym: eight dissidents (including Anatoly Levitin-Krasnov, Yakir, Alexander Yesenin-Volpin, and Zinaida Grigorenko), some of them members or supporters of the Action Group for the Defense of Civil Rights, made appeals relating to the plight of the Crimean Tatars, the problems of Soviet Jews intending to emigrate, conditions of those sentenced to psychiatric hospitals, the necessity for freedom to enter and leave the USSR, freedom from censorship, and the need to observe the rule of law. Finally, in early June, 1972, some one thousand mimeographed pamphlets calling on workers to demonstrate and strike for better working and living conditions were left in Soviet mailboxes.[82]

Whether well-orchestrated manifestations of highly articulate political beliefs or spontaneous demonstrations of personal loyalties, all these forms of alternative political communications fulfill important functions for the Soviet population. At the very least they play a "consciousness-raising" role, focusing attention on certain issues and circumstances that most people might find more comfortable to overlook. People of like views can find one another and, though they must overcome a number of obstacles to do it, exchange ideas on political subjects, thereby stimulating analytic and critical thinking about Soviet society. The airing of opinions strengthens them in the minds of their holders, and common public participation further bolsters commitment to democratic or other ideals. Finally, the alternative communications network constitutes a skeletal political organization through which political action not controlled by the regime can be initiated.

Perhaps one of the most important functions of the alternative system of political communications in the USSR is the selection of content, particularly the legal topics and persons that are featured. Attention in the media confers status on certain issues, groups, and individuals. Conversely, the Soviet legitimate system is well-known for making certain people "unpersons" (such as Khrushchev after his ouster) by virtually ignoring them. Underground or alternative communications challenges the foci of the legitimate political culture by giving publicity to people who can serve as role models for a new type of political behavior and to issues that have been glossed over or ignored throughout the Soviet period, such as the right to dissent. In a sense, this returns us to our basic point: that the communications used by political dissenters directly challenges the party's monopoly on information and its interpretation of what is important and legitimate.

OFFICIAL REACTIONS TO THE ALTERNATIVE COMMUNICATIONS NETWORK

Although another chapter in this volume considers the question of the regime's reaction to dissent in general, a few remarks are in order here

82. Charlotte Saikowski, "Soviet Thumb Fails to Muffle Dissident Voice," *Christian Science Monitor*, June 21, 1972, pp. 1–2.

concerning the official response to some of the challenges we have pointed to in terms of communications theory. Soviet authorities have been faced with a difficult problem: how to inhibit the development of a dissident communications system without resorting to extensive overt physical force that might, among other things, have a boomerang effect. One can divide the regime's strategies into three main categories: passive or negative responses to extralegitimate communications, active tactics against foreign support, and active sanctions against the dissenters themselves.

Most of the numerous petitions, appeals, letters, and manifestoes addressed to individual officials or institutions have been met with a resounding silence. The official network has simply not accepted them as part of reality and has refused to dignify them by a response. The rare answers to individuals by specific offices such as the postal network have been extremely perfunctory and officious, including formal apologies for the "loss" of a letter that has obviously been intercepted by the security organs.[83] Another form of "nonreaction" is the failure to repress activities such as the production and distribution of *Chronicle*. In the last few months individuals involved with this journal have been arrested, yet for at least four years previous to this officials knew of its existence but took no effective action to suppress it.

We have already mentioned the active campaigns in the mass media against foreign radio stations and their listeners. Beyond these, there have been explicit and sometimes rather brutal warnings to foreign correspondents in Moscow to cease their contacts with dissenters. Several of them were followed and beaten up before or after prearranged meetings with their Soviet friends. In at least one instance, officials of the Foreign Ministry's press department warned Western correspondents that they could expect stern reprisals if they attended a news conference that had been called by the mother of Alexander Ginzburg and the wife of Yuri Galanskov in 1968.[84] Finally, Soviet dissenters themselves have been warned repeatedly not to meet with foreign correspondents and have been harrassed in their efforts to do so in spite of these warnings.

The few official reports of the trials of dissidents have consistently carried tendentious descriptions of the charges and abusive references to the defendants. In several cases the slanted coverage of such trials has backfired: Soviet citizens have reasoned that if the trials were aboveboard and the defendants really guilty, there would be no reason to exclude genuine public observers (the halls are usually packed with collaborators hired by the authorities to jeer at the defendants while relatives and friends of the accused are kept out "because there is no room") and more information would be given in the newspaper reports.[85]

---

83. See Zh. Medvedev, "Secrecy of Correspondence."

84. Raymond H. Anderson, "Soviet Warns Western Reporters on Dissidents," *New York Times*, January 19, 1968.

85. See Reddaway, *Uncensored Russia*, p. 119 for information about slanted newspaper accounts. An example of the result of this treatment is the reaction of Larisa Bogoraz-Daniel. In her final plea to a Moscow court she pointed to the sense of personal responsibility she felt: "I

Beyond the misleading accounts of trials, regular propaganda campaigns have been waged against specific individuals. These have taken the form not of references in the mass media but of special meetings (from which his friends were excluded) about people like Solzhenitsyn. In personal "interviews" with friends of dissidents the KGB has tried to discredit the relevant individuals. A second level of active response to dissidents is harrassment such as unsubtle, round-the-clock surveillance, attempts to provoke them into disorderly or illegal behavior, and cutting off normal channels of communications (telephone, interference with correspondence, and so on.)[86] Finally, for people who have assisted dissenters by some gesture of support (e.g., signing letters of protest) there are official reprimands.[87] More serious forms of repression include removal of residence permits to live in Moscow (or other large cities), dismissal from professional positions or other jobs, expulsion from professional unions, expulsion of children of dissidents (Sakharov is a good example) from educational institutions, and so on to actual arrest, interrogation, trial, and punishment by confinement in a prison, labor camp, or mental institution. The underlying strategy seems to be the isolation of dissenters from their normal social and professional contacts, thereby interrupting the flow of support and information.

CONCLUSION

Both the official Soviet system of political communication and its complementary alternative the dissident communication network are each in their

---

thought some public personages might speak publicly, but they did not. I was faced with the choice of acting on my own or keeping silent. For me, to have kept silent would have meant joining those who support actions with which I did not agree. . . . The prosecutor ended his summation by suggesting that the verdict will be supported by public opinion. I, too, have something to say about public opinion. I do not doubt that public opinion will support this verdict, as it would approve of any other verdict. The defendants will be depicted as social parasites and outcasts and people of different ideologies. . . ." "Excerpts from the Proceedings of Trial in Moscow," *New York Times*, October 15, 1968.

86. *Chronicle* reports, for example, that the dissident physicist Valery Chalidze's mail and telephone connections were obstructed in 1971 (no. 23, January 5, 1972). During the visit of President Nixon to the USSR May 22–30, 1972, the telephones of Yakir, a member of the Action Group; Sakharov and Chalidze, members of the Human Rights Committee; R. A. Medvedev and thirteen participants in the Jewish Exodus Movement were disconnected. By July these telephones had still not been reconnected. *Ibid.*, no. 26, July 5, 1972.

87. *Chronicle*, no. 1, *AS* 560, carries the item "Report from the Board Secretariat of the Moscow [Writers] Organization." At the session of May 20, 1968, the secretariat issued reprimands and warnings to a number of members for "political irresponsibility manifested in the signing of declarations and letters which, by their form and content, discredited Soviet laws and the authority of Soviet judicial organs, and for ignoring the fact that these documents might be exploited by bourgeois propaganda for purposes damaging to the Soviet Union and Soviet literature." Mikhail Romm was summoned to his district party headquarters and criticized for his telegram to the Kaluga Hospital concerning the enforced confinement of Zhores Medvedev there. Veniamin Kaverin was summoned to a similar meeting of the Writers Union for the same reasons, and saw on the table a list of other writers who had also sent letters or telegrams of protest about the Medvedev affair. (Z. and R. Medvedev, *A Question of Madness*, pp. 158–59). Many other examples of this category of intimidation could be given.

own ways legacies of Leninist theory on public opinion. The conception of the elitist party interpreting reality to the masses, raising the level of political literacy, and laying out the correct response to any given event precludes tolerance of serious internal criticism or active opposition in public communication. The extreme control of the mass media and agitation-propaganda apparatus as channels of esoteric and exoteric communications necessary for party activities and "ties with the masses" are as much a part of Leninist theory as they were when the Bolsheviks took power. The acceptance of official censorship is even greater today than it was then. On the dissent side, the use of illegitimate samizdat journals as a core for political organization is very much in the tradition of the Bolshevik prerevolutionary press. The idea of enlightened intellectuals imparting political consciousness to the nation is also in keeping with early Leninist theory. The difference is that Lenin's "bourgeois intellectuals" were to become dedicated, disciplined revolutionaries under the strict control of the party elite and to direct their efforts toward developing political consciousness among the proletariat. The new critical intelligentsia, in contrast, is more concerned with defining its own version of reality, without strict limitations on the variety of interpretations that may arise, and using political communications to convert members of the specialist class and a portion of the party elite. One of their goals is to strengthen the hand of liberals in the party elite; they aspire to the status of an interest group as they independently articulate their political views. Their concern with developing a genuinely critical public opinion as a check on government places them in the libertarian tradition, which is squarely opposed to the Leninist tradition of imposing on the population a monolithic view of reality subject to the vicissitudes of internal party intrigues.

Does the dissident network threaten the essential elements of the Soviet tradition of political communications? Indeed it does. Not only do dissident communications reject the notion that the party is the sole, infallible source for information and the interpretation of reality, but they actively propose alternatives to the party line. In so doing, dissenters challenge the legitimation and integration processes as conceived in the Soviet context and counteract official political socialization by presenting the population with alternative symbols and models for political behavior. The network seeks to undermine the willingness of citizens to play their parts as passive, cooperative units of a unified political community. One dissenter has put it rather graphically:

We are so used to Stalinism that we are afraid of a change. Afraid to straighten our backs, to draw ourselves up to our full height. Suppose we can't manage to stand up on our feet? We feel more secure on all fours. The Action Group, the Committee for Human Rights, open letters, [samizdat] journals—finally, thank God, we're beginning to overcome our fear. We are inspired by the courage of Grigorenko, Ogurtsov, Bukovsky. The courage of real men. Cowards do not speak out for the truth.[88]

---

88. "Cowards Don't Play Hockey," *Chronicle*, no. 24, January 7, 1972, AS 1100.

The notion of individual responsibility for political convictions and actions is slowly spreading among the specialist class not only by the content but also by the forms and methods of communication, which demonstrate the individual's capacity for questioning and resisting the authorities' presumption to articulate his or her interests. Just as important, the series of acts we have described has undermined the party elite's confidence that people will play by whatever set of rules the party puts forth even if the game tomorrow is different from what it was yesterday. In this sense, the alternative network interferes with the policy function of the official communication system: it boldly and consistently articulates individual and group interests at variance with the official line and pointedly brings the official line into question. Finally, by reporting on dissident and other political activities at home and abroad, the alternative network competes with the official system in the watchman role; it surveys the horizon, selects items different from those found in the official network, and confers status on events and personalities that are overlooked or disparaged by the official system.

For dissidents, the alternative network attempts to compensate for the deficiencies of the official political communications system, allowing them access to forbidden information and offering channels for expression of their views. It also impedes the effectiveness of the legitimate system by producing "noise," purposefully tries to break up myths of official presentation, lessens party control over the range of world-views presented in Soviet society, and ultimately undermines the party's legitimacy. For the party, it serves to let off steam and flush out dissidents; but in so doing it sometimes makes heroes of those who criticize the party and its policies.

The major problem of the party in stemming samizdat activity is to avoid the use of too much force. Although the party retains the monopoly on the use of coercion and has never denounced it as a method of political control, its large-scale application has several disadvantages. First is the knowledge that unless it is very carefully applied, force will generate still more daring dissent. Moreover, the regime hesitates to be seen as repressive in the eyes of Western countries with whom it hopes to improve relations as a buffer against China. Finally, the regime knows from experience that terror can get out of hand: as in the thirties, the first wave of oppressors is likely to be destroyed by the second wave of oppressors. On the other hand the dissidents may play the role of radicals in compelling the regime to use force, for if they are at all successful in undermining its legitimacy and credibility in the eyes of an important segment of the population like the specialist class they deprive it of some of its effectiveness in persuasion.

In the short run we can expect more intense repression of dissident communications activity. One can only hope that in the long run the new critical intelligentsia may win enough adherents to strengthen the hand of liberals in the party elite. The question is really whether the alternative communications network can survive in some form long enough seriously to alter the extreme control mentality of the present generation of leaders or to undermine their influence on a younger generation of leaders not so tainted by Stalinism. Any relaxation of controls on political communication will inevitably be associated with liberalization of the entire political culture.

CHAPTER EIGHT / MAGNITIZDAT: UNCENSORED SONGS

OF DISSENT / GENE SOSIN

Magnitizdat is the Russian contraction of the words *magnitofon* (magnetic tape recorder) and *izdatel'stvo* (publishing). Like *samizdat*, the word refers to the dissemination of works not approved by official Soviet censorship. Magnitizdat works consist primarily of uncensored songs of social commentary recorded by well-known Soviet bards to guitar accompaniment at informal gatherings.

Copied and recopied via tape recorder, they can gain wide circulation. The most famous and popular poet-balladeers are Bulat Okudzhava, Alexander Galich, and Vladimir Vysotsky. Their songs reveal the existence of a lively counterculture that has received great impetus thanks to the mass production of tape recorders during the 1960s. Since this period also saw the tightening of control over the arts following the relative liberalization during the early years of Khrushchev's era, magnitizdat songs have offered the poets and their admiring public a vehicle for candid statements about the quality of Soviet life that are difficult, and usually impossible, to express in officially controlled media. This chapter analyzes representative lyrics of songs by these three leading balladeers in order to determine some of the major themes of this unique genre of Soviet dissent. Mikhail Nozhkin and Yuli Kim will also be treated briefly in view of their increasing popularity with the Soviet public.

Before the 1960s the magnetic tape recorder was virtually unknown in the Soviet Union. Copies of forbidden jazz and sentimental gypsy romances were crudely scratched on medical X-ray plates and played on phonographs. Large-scale Soviet manufacture of tape recorders, beginning with the late 1950s, enabled mass reproduction of contemporary ballads otherwise unavailable through the open commercial channels of the state-owned

*I wish to thank Victor Kabachnik for his generous assistance to me in the preparation of this study. Mr. Kabachnik, who left Moscow in 1972 and now lives in New York, is a close friend of Alexander Galich and owns a comprehensive collection of tape recordings of songs that Galich performed during informal gatherings in Moscow. In addition, Mr. Kabachnik has shared with me his first-hand knowledge of the magnitizdat (also called *magizdat*) phenomenon in the Soviet Union as well as of the works of other poet-bards.

I also wish to express my appreciation to Misha Allen of Toronto for his valuable advice and his permission to reprint his excellent translations of Vysotsky's lyrics. Mr. Allen, a specialist in Russian culture and folklore, is perhaps the leading Western expert on magnitizdat.

Finally, my thanks to Professor Rudolf L. Tőkés of the University of Connecticut for encouraging me to undertake this study.

recording organization.[1] *Narodnoe khoziaistvo*, the official Soviet handbook, lists no figures for the production of tape recorders before 1960. In that year 128,000 were produced. The number rose to 453,000 in 1965 and to 1,064,000 in 1969. In 1970 the number of machines produced was 1,192,000.[2]

Bulat Okudzhava is acknowledged to be the first important bard of magnitizdat. In a samizdat document that appeared in the West in 1972, Semyon Telegin discussed the possibility of creating "under the conditions of a repressive regime a culture opposed to that regime." Telegin declared that the task was already being solved and offered as evidence the success achieved by Okudzhava in reaching the broad Soviet public:

We all remember the moment when a new art made its first breakthrough: Okudzhava's appearance before the people. A world suddenly was opened to us which we had never suspected existed. It was not somewhere far off, but here, in our souls, in our nighttime trolley-buses, in the Arbat . . . , in the drumroll of the capital [allusions to songs by Okudzhava]. We discovered the riches of our world. We realized the meagerness of the food they gave us [i.e., the guardians of official art]. The fashion for Okudzhava might end, but there was no returning to the past. It became clear that there was no use waiting for favors from the singers in the camp of Russian warriors, for we had to get to work ourselves. And I consider that the first sign of the new culture that came into being was the guitar-and-singing craze: no matter how condescendingly the professionals regarded it, it had authenticity, spontaneity, and human spirit.[3]

Telegin added that "contemporary music for the people is not to be found in the plenary sessions of the composers' union or on the radio, but in the long hours of tape recordings played at gatherings of intellectuals, and in the coaches of suburban trains."[4]

In his samizdat pamphlet *Will the Soviet Union Survive until 1984?* Andrei Amalrik described the appearance of a "cultural opposition" after Stalin's death in 1953. He called it "a new force, independent of the government" and added:

There appeared many young poets, artists, musicians and *chansonniers*; typewritten journals started to circulate, art exhibitions opened and songfests of youth were organized. This movement was directed not against the political regime as such but only against its culture, which the regime itself nevertheless regarded as its own component.[5]

1. Victor Kabachnik reports that the first Soviet tape recorder on the market was the "El'fa-6." It appeared in the mid-1950s and was a rather primitive machine. By 1958 other models such as the "Dnepr-3" and "Spalis" were available. Today tape recorders can be purchased in cities throughout the USSR. Later models include the "Yauza-10" (300 rubles) and the less expensive "Astra," "Yauza-5," "Yauza-6," "Chaika," and "Nota." Some foreign models are also available at higher prices.

2. *Narodnoe khoziaistvo* (Moscow, 1970), p. 251.

3. Semyon Telegin, "Kak byt'," pp. 1-2, Radio Liberty Arkhiv samizdata, AS 1151.

4. *Ibid.*, p. 3.

5. Andrei Amalrik, *Prosushchestvuet li Sovetski Soyuz do 1984 goda?* (Amsterdam, 1969), p. 4.

Amalrik explained that he had in mind such events as the public reading of poetry at Mayakovsky Square in Moscow, the circulation of Alexander Ginzburg's samizdat journal *Syntax*, and "the appearance of a great number of authors and performers of songs which were spread in millions of magnetic tapes, e.g., Okudzhava, Galich, Vysotsky, *el al*."[6]

Anatoly Kuznetsov, a Soviet novelist who defected to England in 1969, reported that he was among the first listeners to Okudzhava's songs in Moscow during the 1950s:

At that time only a scattered few were interested in tape recorders, which were a novelty, unwieldy and absurd. It was even impossible to suppose that a "tape recorder explosion" was soon to occur. . . . Soviet ideological organs, busy in the field of radio production, . . . completely failed to pay attention to such a seemingly innocent technical branch as the production of tape recorders. A demand existed and it was satisfied, and when at last the ideological firemen discovered the catastrophic breakthrough, it was too late. Now it is a rare home without a tape recorder, and an evening party or get-together without one is unthinkable.

Quite likely, billions of hours of complicated work in off hours have been spent by people in the Soviet Union in copying, acquiring, exchanging, and recopying Okudzhava and the galaxy of equally good singers around him.[7]

BULAT OKUDZHAVA

Okudzhava was born in 1924 in Moscow, the son of a Georgian father and an Armenian mother.[8] In 1942 he volunteered for the army and was wounded in battle.[9] In 1950 he finished his studies at Tiflis State University and taught in a village school in the Kaluga region, where he began to write poetry. His first volume, *Lyric*, was published in Kaluga in 1956. Okudzhava then moved to Moscow, where he joined the staff of *Literaturnaia gazeta*.[10] His second volume of poetry, *Islands*, appeared in Moscow in 1959.

By 1960 Okudzhava had already gained a reputation as a singer of ballads. One observer who was present at an unofficial concert he gave in

---

6. *Ibid.*

7. "Talks by Anatoly Kuznetsov," no. 17 in a series of Radio Liberty Russian broadcasts, March 10/11, 1973.

8. His father was shot as a "Japanese spy" during the great purges; his mother was imprisoned for 19 years in Siberia. Both were members of the Communist Party. She was rehabilitated in 1956 and returned to Moscow. See Mihajlo Mihajlov, *Moscow Summer* (New York, 1965), p. 106.

9. His story "Bud' zdorov, shkoliar!" in the liberal anthology *Tarusskie stranitsy* (which was published in 1961 but soon banned) is based on his wartime experiences. A translation appears under the title "Lots of Luck, Kid!" in *Pages From Tarusa*, ed. Andrew Field (Boston, Toronto, 1963).

10. He is believed to have played a role in the publication of Yevtushenko's famous poem "Babi yar" in 1961. See Priscilla Johnson, *Khrushchev and the Arts* (Cambridge, Mass., 1965), p. ix.

1961 reported that he established close rapport with his audience, a group of workers in the arts:

Okudzhava sang about what disturbed him, and every line of his verse breathed the truth of life. Whether he sang about love or war his words penetrated into the souls of people who were thirsty for real songs. For a long time nobody had been satisfied with the clichés of official songs filled with banal lyrics or primitive prefabricated patriotism. Bulat Okudzhava's fame grew as tapes spread his songs all over the country.[11]

The poet himself offered a clue to the reason for his popularity:

The love of folklore which I felt inside me stimulated my desire to sing some verse to the accompaniment of a guitar. I thought up the melody, and being almost unable to play the guitar or sing or read music I began to sing my verse without realizing what a scandal would burst out in a short time.

I liked to sing about what troubled me—about war not being a vacation or a parade, but a terrible, stupid inevitability; about women as something wonderful; about Moscow as amazing, sad, and not always happy; how I—a Moscow ant—am not always successful; how the Paper Soldier cannot, unfortunately, always make the world happy.

I sang about this, and it turned out that others were moved, not because it was brilliant, but just because most songs in vogue before that were official and semiofficial and cold, without a sense of man's fate; songs were steeped in cheap cheerfulness (this was called optimism), primitive, routine rhetorical thoughts about Moscow, about man, about the homeland (this was called patriotism).

The guitarists accused me of lacking talent, composers said I lacked professionalism, singers said I had no voice, and they all accused me of impudence, insolence and vulgarity. . . . The officials accused me of pessimism, antipatriotism and pacifism, and the press backed them up.[12]

The "paper soldier" mentioned by the poet refers to one of his best-loved songs:

Now once there was a soldier boy
Handsome and bold as bold can be
But he was just a children's toy:
He was a paper soldier, see.

---

11. Victor Kabachnik in "Magnitizdat," no. 8 in a series of Radio Liberty Russian broadcasts, August 1, 1972. Inquiries concerning Radio Liberty broadcasts or magnitizdat tapes should be addressed to Director, Information Division, Radio Liberty Committee, 30 E. 42d St., New York, N.Y. 10017.

12. Introduction to *Pauvre Avrossimov* (Paris, 1972), the French edition of Okudzhava's novel *Bedny Avrosimov*. Cited in I. Ignatiev, "Ternisty put' Bulata Okudzhavy" (Research Department, Radio Liberty, Munich, June 19, 1972), p. 11. See also Joseph Langland, Tamas Aczel, and Laszlo Tikos, eds. and trans., *Poetry From the Russian Underground* (New York, Evanston, San Francisco, London, 1973), pp. 241–44.

He wanted to remake the world
For all men to live happily
But round the bedpost he was twirled:
He was a paper soldier, see.

Ready amid the fire and smoke
Twice over he'd lie down and dee.
You looked upon him as a joke:
He was a paper soldier, see.

You didn't think he could be trusted
With things demanding secrecy.
And why? In case you're interested
He was a paper soldier, see.

But he would fret and curse his lot
Long for a life that's wild and free.
Fire! Fire! He begged. He quite forgot
He was a paper soldier, see.

Fire? Very well.
Here: come along!
And off into the fire went he
And burnt to cinders for a song.
He was a paper soldier, see.[13]

Here, as in many of his songs, Okudzhava expresses a viewpoint at variance with the false optimism found in the approved literature of socialist realism. He seems to identify himself with the altruistic paper soldier who wants to fight injustice and to remake the world but who is vulnerable and doomed to perish. In contrast to the outpouring of pompous, chauvinistic songs over Soviet radio and on public loudspeakers, Okudzhava deals with such themes as the senselessness of war. "How simple to become a soldier," he states ironically in a twelve-line poem that concludes: "And if something isn't right, it isn't our affair, / As they say, 'the Motherland issued the order!' / How nice not to be guilty of anything, / And just to be a simple soldier, soldier!"[14] Although Okudzhava did not identify the soldier with any particular country, he made a concession to sensitive authorities who might

13. In Keith Bosely, ed. and trans., with Dmitri Pospielovsky and Janis Sapiets, *Russia's Underground Poets* (New York, Washington, 1969), pp. 55–56. Unless otherwise noted, the translations of the magnitizdat lyrics quoted in this study are mine.
14. "Voz'mu shinel' i veshchmeshok i kasku" [I take my coat and rucksack and my helmet], in B. Okudzhava, *Proza i stikhi* (Frankfurt, 1964), p. 191.

not have permitted him to sing it at gatherings. He would announce the title as "Song of the American Soldier."[15]

"Don't believe in war, little boy," another short song begins. "It is sad, little boy, / And as tight as boots. / Your dashing steeds / Can accomplish nothing, / And you will wind up / Getting all the bullets."[16]

In another pessimistic song about war, Okudzhava tells the soldier that the boots are crashing and the drums are rolling, so it is time to bid his woman farewell. The platoon marches off into the fog, but the past is much clearer than the future. The soldier returns home expecting to be embraced, but the house smells of betrayal. Now, while one looks with hope to the future, the carrion crows fatten in the fields and war rumbles once again, calling the soldier to march off.[17]

In his "Ditty About the Infantry," Okudzhava complains that it is foolish to go off to war when spring is bursting over the land. "Don't believe the infantry / When it sings gallant songs. / Don't believe, don't believe, / When nightingales cry out in the gardens. / Life has not yet settled her accounts with death."[18]

The poet is capable of handling the theme of war not only in a melancholy, tragic mood but also satirically. An amusing ballad describes a king who prepares to set forth to battle against the enemy. His queen mends his mantle and gives him a bag of dry bread and three packs of Belomor cigarettes:

And placing her hands on the chest of her husband, the king,
She said, while encouraging him with a radiant look,
"I can't abide pacifists, so you must beat them up good,
And do not forget to get sweet cakes for me from the foe."[19]

The king departs with his army, consisting of "five sorrowful soldiers, five happy soldiers, and a corporal." The sorrowful ones are captured, but the victors manage to bring back a whole bagful of sweet cakes. Okudzhava concludes:

Now orchestra, play, and let singing and laughter ring out.
It's no use, my friends, giving way to a moment of grief.
There's really no sense keeping sorrowful soldiers alive,
Besides, then there wouldn't be cookies enough for us all.[20]

15. Victor Kabachnik says he attended a concert in Moscow at which Okudzhava announced this song with stress on "American." The statement was received with knowing laughter.
16. "Ne ver' voine, mal'chishka," Okudzhava, *Proza i stikhi*, p. 188.
17. "O voine" [About war], *ibid.*, p. 187.
18. "Pesenka o pekhote," *ibid.*, p. 189.
19. "V pokhod na chuzhuiu stranu sobiral'sia korol'" [A king once prepared to campaign on the enemy's soil], *ibid.*, p. 193.
20. *Ibid.*

Unlike Galich (see below), who often employs satire as a sharp political weapon, Okudzhava prefers to create a lyrical atmosphere in which to communicate his feelings and philosophy. The cumulative impression derived from listening to his songs and reading the texts is that he is not an "anti-Soviet" poet but that he nevertheless fails to fill the official Soviet prescription for "healthy" themes which serve the educational goals of Communist ideology.

For this reason Okudzhava quickly came under fire from Khrushchev's principal spokesman in ideology and the arts, Leonid Ilyichev. As chairman of the Ideological Commission of the Soviet Communist Party's Central Committee, Ilyichev held a meeting in December 1962 with 140 writers, artists, and cinema workers. Among those whom he criticized was Okudzhava:

> Let us understand, comrades composers, what is happening with songs. The Soviet people love songs. But side by side with songs with a broad civic motif, songs which sing the spiritual beauty of the Soviet people and reveal the purity of their souls, there are also vulgar songs which are designed to appeal to low and cheap tastes. In particular, the verses and songs of the gifted poet B. Okudzhava are out of keeping with the entire structure of our life. Their whole intonation—everything about them—does not come from purity of the soul but from spiritual breakdown. They say that these songs are loved by our youth. But what youth? Whose tastes are they intended for?[21]

The songs Ilyichev labeled as "vulgar" were actually evocations by the poet of the genuine attitudes of a new generation searching for sincerity and honesty after years of disillusionment with the phony cant of officialdom. In Okudzhava's "Ditty about Roosters" he points out that the rooster naturally cannot help crowing because he was created for that purpose. "But nobody goes to the yard, / It seems there are no longer fools / Who run to the crow of the cocks."[22] In other words, people are more discriminating today in their rejection of the empty crowing of sloganeers. In his "Ditty about Fools" Okudzhava deplores the state of affairs in which wise men are labeled fools so the real fools will not be conspicuous.[23]

Mihajlo Mihajlov, the young Yugoslav scholar whose book *Moscow Summer* became a *cause célèbre* in his country and led to his imprisonment, devoted a chapter to his friend Okudzhava. He recalled:

---

21. *Literaturnaia gazeta*, January 10, 1963. See also Patricia Blake and Max Hayward, eds., *Half-way to the Moon* (New York, Chicago, San Francisco, 1963), pp. 23–24.

22. "Pesenka pro petukhov," in *Bulat Okudzhava Sings His Own Songs*, ARFA Records, ALP 1015 (Chicago, n.d.). This Western disc reproduces songs with texts in Russian. Okudzhava made a record during a trip to Paris in 1967, produced by Le chant du monde, LDX 7 4358 (Paris, n.d.). A Polish recording company also produced a disc based on Okudzhava's performances in Warsaw: MUZA Polskie nagrania, XL 0482 (Warsaw, n.d.).

23. "Pesenka o durakakh," in Okudzhava, *Proza i stikhi*, p. 197.

Okudzhava was called before the Central Committee and was told, more or less: "You sing your songs so nicely; why did you have to go and compose this song *Fools*?" Okudzhava promised that he would not sing that song at concerts any more. A year later he composed another song, *The Black Tomcat*: a black tomcat lives in the dark gateway of a house; it's a long time since he caught any mice. Now, assisted by darkness, he preys on us instead. He does not ask for anything and he does not beg; we bring him everything ourselves and we say: "Thank you." It's probably because of this that our house is sad. We should have put up an electric bulb in the gateway, but we cannot get up enough money. Again Okudzhava was called in: You sing your songs so nicely; for example, a nice song like *Fools*. Why did you have to go and compose a song like *The Black Tomcat*?

"Well, that's the way it goes," Okudzhava says, and his optimism is completely justified.[24]

Alas, Okudzhava was too optimistic. His intensely personal approach lacked the "broad civic motif" as Ilyichev would define it. Okudzhava affirmed the right of the average Soviet citizen to his own private joys and sorrows apart from any connection with the party, state, collective, and similar approved objects of adulation. Instead he celebrated the eternal qualities of faith, hope, and love. In a song that begins "Please pull down the blue shades, nurse," Okudzhava urges Faith not to be sad because her "debtors still remain on earth"; he tells Hope not to despair, for "your sons are still on earth"; and he hears Love's voice reassuring him that she has not forsaken him.[25] In a poignant song entitled "François Villon," Okudzhava offers up a prayer to God to grant everyone that which he lacks, adding: "And do not forget about me."[26] In "Protect Us Poets, Protect Us," he appeals to unnamed leaders not to treat poets today as Pushkin and Lermontov were treated in tsarist times, when they were provoked into fighting duels and were killed.[27]

But the time inevitably came when the authorities would no longer tolerate this basically apolitical poet whose ditties honored nameless, ordinary Muscovites. After Mihajlov's book appeared in 1965 in the West, Okudzhava was summoned before the Central Committee. They demanded that he publicly repudiate a statement made by Mihajlov that the Soviet authorities were preventing the production of Okudzhava's records and censoring his radio broadcasts. The poet refused, arguing that the truth

24. Mihajlov, *Moscow Summer*, pp. 107–8. Former Soviet citizens report that some listeners interpret the black tomcat as a description of Stalin; others see it as referring to Sholokhov, the conservative novelist; still others regard it as a symbol of communist authority. Mihajlov also describes the circumstances surrounding publication of Okudzhava's third volume of verse, *The Merry Drummer*, in 1964. See also Mihjlov, "An Unperson Sings to the Russians," *New York Times Magazine*, May 13, 1966.
25. "Opustite, pozhaluista, sinie shtory," in Okudzhava, *Proza i stikhi*, p. 186.
26. K. Pomerantsev, "Bulat Okudzhava v Parizhe," *Russkaya mysl'*, December 14, 1967.
27. "Beregite nas, poetov, beregite nas," in Okudzhava, *Proza i stikhi*, p. 173.

cannot be refuted. He offered as evidence an incident that took place at a concert hall in Moscow. Okudzhava was invited by the organizers of the concert to ensure a full house for an evening of poetry reading by several poets of varying talent. The evening was recorded for television and radio, but someone ordered that Okudzhava's performance be cut. "So what have I got to deny?" he asked the committee.[28]

It would be an error, however, to assume that all Soviet leaders dislike Okudzhava's songs. Despite the censorship, many officials secretly enjoy listing to magnitizdat tapes. A striking illustration of this ambivalence comes from Warsaw. In 1967 the Soviet embassy protested when the first three prizes in a local contest of Soviet songs were won by young Poles who sang the songs of Okudzhava. When Okudzhava arrived in Warsaw for a visit a few weeks later, the embassy invited him to give a concert. One of the counselors told him: "You can't imagine how we love you here. Especially Averky Borisovich [Aristov, the ambassador], who collects tapes of all your songs." Okudzhava replied: "But in view of the fact that others express their official dissatisfaction over my songs, I must refuse you."[29]

Okudzhava was permitted to travel to Western Europe in the late 1960s.[30] But after 1970 the Foreign Committee of the Soviet Writers Union replied to all invitations from abroad that the poet's health would not permit a trip. In June 1972 Okudzhava was threatened with expulsion from the Communist Party, to which he had belonged since 1955, for "conduct unbecoming a Soviet writer and Communist." At a press conference in Moscow, Sergei Mikhalkov, chairman of the Russian section of the Writers Union, declared that Okudzhava had violated the party's rules by permitting émigré organizations to publish his works abroad with "emphatically anti-Soviet commentaries." Mikhalkov added that Okudzhava had turned down the proposal to correct his error by dissociating himself from the émigré activities.[31] Later that year, however, a statement by Okudzhava was published:

> For several years many organs of the press abroad have attempted to use my name for purposes that are far from unselfish.
>
> In this connection I feel that it is necessary to make the following statement:
>
> The criticisms that have been made of my individual works on the grounds of their content or literary qualities have never provided a basis for considering me politically compromised. For this reason I condemn as absolutely without foundation any attempts to present my work in a spirit hostile to us and to use my name for interests that have nothing in common with literary ones. Such attempts are on their author's conscience alone.[32]

28. Ignatiev, "Ternisty put' Bulata Okudzhavy," p. 10.
29. *Ibid.*
30. Pomerantsev, "Bulat Okudzhava v Parizhe," gives a report of Okudzhava's concert in Paris. I attended a concert he gave in Munich in January 1968 before an enthusiastic audience of Russian émigrés.
31. Radio Liberty newscast, Munich, June 30, 1972.
32. *Literaturnaia gazeta*, November 29, 1972. See also *Christian Science Monitor*, December 5, 1972.

Anatoly Kuznetsov commented after reading Okudzhava's protest that, as a person who himself had been forced to write such a document when he was still in the Soviet Union, he could appreciate Okudzhava's position.[33] Soviet writers whose work is published abroad are often under pressure to condemn the West's use of their material for alleged anti-Soviet ends. Actually, Okudzhava's statement is rather mildly worded; and as one analyst observed: "This time, too, Okudzhava, remaining true to himself, has pointed his finger not directly, but completely in accordance with the real situation, at those [in the Soviet Union] who are trying to use his name for 'interests having nothing in common with literature.'"[34]

By the early summer of 1974, however, Okudzhava's fortunes had taken a turn for the better. He was allowed to perform at closed concerts in clubs and institutes and was expected to visit East Germany. Moscow writers explained to foreign correspondents that the Soviet authorities, "perturbed by the number of formerly well-considered authors who encountered trouble and then tried to leave the country, had started a belated campaign to satisfy those who remain."[35] Okudzhava appeared to be one of the beneficiaries of this tactical shift in policy.

MIKHAIL NOZHKIN AND YULI KIM

Nozhkin and Kim deserve passing mention as two young bards who have become well-known for their statements on the contemporary Soviet scene.[36] Nozhkin, a motion picture actor, is not as prolific a song writer as Vysotsky, nor does his work possess the depth of content of Galich or Okudzhava. One of Nozhkin's basic themes is the daily humdrum existence of ordinary Soviet citizens. For example, he sings of Auntie Nyusha, a cleaning woman who "just keeps on sweeping, just keeps on dusting, / Just keeps on cleaning; after high-ranking ministers, after plain workers / From morning till night, from morning till night." He contrasts the lot of the charwoman with the Soviet Union's technological advances:

Reactors are roaring, as rockets are flying and radar surrounds us,
With the help of astronomy we reach for the stars,
While robots are walking along our sidewalks
Physics and mathematics are in full bloom

33. Kuznetsov, "Talks."
34. "Just Whom Are Gladilin and Okudzhava Criticizing?" (Research Department, Radio Liberty, Munich, January 15, 1973).
35. "Kremlin Rethinks Expulsion Policy," *Christian Science Monitor*, June 25, 1974.
36. Others whose works are popular include Yevgeny Kliachkin, Novella Matveyeva, Mikhail Ancharov, Yuri Vizbor, and Anatoly Ivanov. Magnitizdat is not limited, however, to these few bards. Thousands of ordinary Soviet citizens compose their own songs, tape them, and play them for friends. The craze has even reached the Soviet army. In "Vulgarity on a Magnetic Tape," *Krasnaia zvezda*, June 20, 1972, two colonels write indignantly about a private who distributed "ditties repulsive to a self-respecting person."

Not to mention electronics and cybernetics, but
Auntie Nyusha just keeps on sweeping.[37]

Yuli Kim is a young teacher—half Korean, half Jewish by birth—and the
son-in-law of Peter Yakir, for many years one of the leading Soviet
dissenters. Kim himself has played an active part in signing samizdat
protests against neo-Stalinist repression of civil and human rights.[38] His first
songs were heard in plays of the student theater of Moscow State University,
which he attended in the early 1960s. After graduation Kim taught Russian
language and literature at the physics and mathematics boarding school
attached to the university. In 1968 he was dismissed from his job and
forbidden to perform his songs, and he even lost a contract to play the
leading role in a film. Kim had joined in protesting the violation of legality in
the trial of Ginzburg and Galanskov, and together with Yakir and Ilya
Gabai had signed a appeal "to public figures who work in science, culture
and the arts."[39]

. One of the best examples of Kim's irreverent humor and social commentary is his "Song of the Social Science Teacher":

People all do as they should—
Go to sleep and eat their food,
Take turns working, then relaxing,
But for me it's really taxing
Teaching social science.[40]

The teacher complains that his students torment him with "sharp little
questions," which he attempts to handle by giving stereotyped answers
according to the approved Soviet pedagogical rules. "But they keep insisting:
'facts, man, facts, / Lay your arguments right on the line.'" In despair and
frustration, the teacher decides to commit suicide in an appropriate manner:

I'll lie down beneath the bookcase,
With *Das Kapital* above my head,
When the shelf begins to shake,
Marx will fall and strike me dead.[41]

---

37. Translated by Misha Allen in "Russia's Dissident Balladeers," *East Europe* 20, no. 11
(November 1971): 30. See also N. Cherkashin, "Zhivoe Slovo Pesni," *Krasnaia zvezda*,
January 12, 1974.

38. Peter Reddaway, ed., *Uncensored Russia* (New York, 1972), pp. 79–81, passim. Yakir
was arrested in June 1972 and tried in August 1973, along with Victor Krasin, on charges of
anti-Soviet activities. Both men were sentenced to three years in jail and three in exile.
Inasmuch as they confessed and recanted, however, their sentences were reduced and they were
released from prison in the fall of 1973.

39. "Obrashcheniie k deiateliam nauki, kul'tury i iskusstva SSSR," AS 14; English trans.
in *In Quest of Justice*, ed. Abraham Brumberg (New York, Washington, and London, 1970),
pp. 157–61.

40. "Pesnia uchitelia obshchestvovedeniia," Radio Liberty Tape Library, New York.

41. *Ibid.*

ALEXANDER GALICH

A brief paragraph in the official *Short Literary Encyclopedia*, published in Moscow in 1964, describes Alexander Arkadyevich Galich as a "Russian Soviet dramatist" and lists the names of several of his plays and film scenarios. The entry concludes: "G. is the author of popular songs about youth."[42]

Galich is a Jew, born Ginzburg in 1919. He was trained as an actor in the Stanislavsky school and served during World War II in a theatrical troupe that played for front-line soldiers. After the war Galich devoted himself to literature. Ten of his plays have been produced, but three of his best were not allowed to be staged. Since the beginning of the 1960s his major artistic contribution has been the creation of scores of poems, not so much about Soviet youth as about aspects of Soviet reality that are forbidden in officially approved works. In contrast to Okudzhava's plaintive lyricism, Galich's work bristles with political barbs. Where Okudzhava evokes a melancholy mood of alienation, Galich tells a pointed little story about a specific feature of Soviet life. From the standpoint of his popularity among people on many levels of Russian society as well as his remarkable talent as a writer and deep concern about the survivals of Stalinism in the Soviet Union today, Galich can be compared to Alexander Solzhenitsyn.

In a poem-song written at the beginning of the 1960s, entitled "We Are Not Worse than Horace," Galich described the contemporary situation in the Soviet arts with typical uncompromising candor: "Falsehood wanders from zone to zone, / Sharing Falsehood with its neighbor Falsehood." But at the same time: "What is sung in a low voice resounds, / What is read in a whisper thunders." Galich's theme is that the genuine artist needs no noisy openings of art exhibits and theatrical premières; it is sufficient for him to paint a picture that stands on an easel in his small room or to pound out four copies of his work on a typewriter or to dub his songs with a tape recorder:

There is no orchestra, no loge or tier,
No claque with its hullabaloo,
A "Yauza" tape recorder's here,
That is all, but it will do.[43]

---

42. *Kratkaia literaturnaia entsiklopediia* (Moscow, 1964), 2:45. Galich's real name is given in the *Teatral'naia entsiklopediia* [Theatrical encyclopedia] and in the appendix to the *Kinoslovar'* [Cinema dictionary]. None of the official sources mentions, however, his forbidden plays or poetry.

43. "My ne khuzhe Goratsiia," in A. Galich, *Pokoleniie obrechennykh* (Frankfurt, 1972), p. 162. More than 100 poems by Galich have been collected in this book, based on magnitizdat tapes of his songs. For additional information see L. Donatov, "Poiot Galich, poet Galich," *Posev*, 1969, no. 11 (November), pp. 52–54. Also see Gerry Smith, "Whispered Cry: The Songs of Alexander Galich," *Index* 3, no. 3 (Autumn 1974): 11–28.

What Galich has "sung in a low voice" includes such themes as the informer and the secret police in Soviet history. "Immortal Kuz'min" begins with the civil war period following the October Revolution. "Citizens, the Fatherland's in danger! / Citizens, the civil war's begun!" Brother fights against brother, and "the guilt is mine." But Kuz'ma Kuz'mich Kuz'min —Galich's prototype of the informer through various stages of Soviet history—drinks the best vodka, eats the best sturgeon, then "like a real patriot, a true son of the Fatherland," takes pen in hand to report to the authorities. Next comes the Nazi invasion of the USSR in 1941. Again the cry: "Citizens, the Fatherland's in danger! / Tanks advance on Tsarskoye Selo!" Everyone prepares for battle and death, feeling that it is "my war, my guilt"; but Kuz'min continues to eat, drink, and inform the secret police. In the next vignette Galich alludes to the Soviet invasion of Eastern European countries: "Citizens, the Fatherland's in danger! / For our tanks are now on foreign soil!" Again the average Soviet citizen shares the guilt for the war and deaths, but the "true patriot" Kuz'min keeps on informing.[44]

In "Leapfrog with Letters" Galich employs the device of a children's nonsense verse to describe the fate of the letters "A" and "B"—and since the word for "and" in Russian is the letter "I" three letters are actually involved in the tale. Three members of the Cheka (the first Soviet secret police) appear one evening and arrest "A" and "B" but leave "I" alone for the time being. They return after one year, but soon three men appear from the NKVD (a later name for the secret police, which still later became known as the KGB) and this time take away all three. They return in ten years:

But again came three in civvies,
In a car from the KGB,
A, I, B they took away, called them all "s.o.b."
A—forever disappeared
B—forever disappeared
I —forever disappeared
Forever and without a trace.
Now you understand what nonsense entered the lives of these letters![45]

In "Night Watch" Galich symbolically raises the question of a return of Stalin by fantasizing an eerie scene. While Moscow sleeps late at night, a monument of Stalin comes to life and stalks the streets with thousands of other statues and bits of statues as the drums roll in accompaniment:

I see the bronze generalissimo
Leading the fool's procession,
He goes out to the Execution Grounds,
"The genius of all times and peoples!"

44. "Bessmertny Kuz'min," in Galich, *Pokoleniie obrechennykh*, pp. 82–85.
45. "Chekharda s bukvami," *ibid.*, pp. 76–77.

And just as in the good old days
He reviews the parade of the freaks!
   And the drums roll!

Although the traces of Stalinism are fragmentary, they are quite capable
of being restored:

Here a boot crashes in a march tempo,
Here a piece of a mustache bristles!
The remains are rather faded,
But even a button is certain
That it will be of use if the time comes,
   And the drums will roll!

Dawn comes and the statues return to their places:

But the plaster ones lie there in hiding,
And though for a while they are maimed,
In the dust they preserve their aspect,
How they hunger to eat human flesh!
Then again they'll achieve their grandeur
   And the drums will roll![46]

"Dance Tune" describes the nostalgia of former executioners for Stalin.
They invite one another to drink cognac and eat caviar while they "quietly
but soulfully sing about Stalin the wise, our own, our beloved." They
reminisce about the good old days when there was order and things got
done. Galich sarcastically asks pity for these people: "Executioners also are
sad, / Take pity on hangmen, you folks!" They are impatient for Stalin to
return: "We are on guard, but when will it be? Let it be soon!" They appeal
to Stalin: "Arise, Father, and bring reason and sense."[47]

In "Poem About Stalin" Galich says: "I see that something is not right in
the world, / It would be good to be concerned with it." He appeals to his
listeners to resist the blandishments of leaders with ready-made formulas
who promise paradise on earth:

And although I am taking a risk
To be labeled a jester and fool,
Day and night there is one thing I say—
People, there's no need to fear!
Don't fear prison or a beggar's cup,
Don't fear pestilence or hunger,
Only fear the person who tells you
"I know how it must be!"

46. "Nochnoi dozor," *ibid.*, pp. 31–32.
47. "Pliasovaia," *ibid.*, pp. 95–96.

Who says: "People, follow me,
And I'll teach you how it must be!"[48]

And again at the end of this passage—which Galich calls a "chapter written while completely drunk and representing the author's digression"—the poet admonishes: "Drive him out! Don't believe him! / He lies! He *does not know* how it must be!"[49]

Galich's civic courage expresses itself throughout his work. "I Choose Freedom" is the title and leitmotif of a militant song in which he declares that he chooses not to retreat from the battle but to enter into the thick of it, remaining true to himself regardless of the consequences. He concludes: "I choose Freedom, / And know that I'm not alone! / And 'freedom' says to me: / 'Well then, get dressed / And let's take a walk, citizen.'"[50] Galich means that in contrast to his ideal of "Freedom," the real life of so-called "freedom" results in one's arrest and investigation.

"The Prospectors' Little Waltz" presents a clear statement of Galich's attitude toward those who get ahead by keeping quiet.

For a long time we've called ourselves grownups,
And abandoned our juvenile style,
And we're no longer searching for treasure
Far away on a fabulous isle,
In the desert or pole's frigid air,
Or by slow boat to heaven knows where.
But seeing that silence is golden,
We are prospectors, that's what we are.

Just keep mum—and it's rich you'll become!
Just keep mum, keep mum, keep mum.

And not trusting our hearts or our reason,
For safety's sake closing our eyes,
Many times, many ways we were silent,
Never nays, to be sure, always ayes.
Where today are the shouters and gripers?
They have vanished before they grew old—
But the silent ones now are the bosses,
And the reason is—silence is gold.

Just keep mum—number one you'll become!
Just keep mum, keep mum, keep mum.

---

48. "Poema o Staline," *ibid.*, p. 284.
49. *Ibid.*, p. 285.
50. "Ya vybiraiu Svobodu," *ibid.*, p. 34.

And now we're on top of the heap,
The speeches all give us a pain,
But under the pearls that we speak
Our muteness seeps through like a stain.
Let others cry out from despair,
From insult, from hunger and cold!
In silence we know there's more profit,
And the reason is—silence is gold.

That's how you get to be wealthy,
That's how you get to be first,
That's how you get to be hangmen!
Just keep mum, keep mum, keep mum.[51]

"Ask Questions, Boys" summons youth to insist "two hundred times and three hundred" that their fathers answer all their questions instead of keeping silent. Galich has in mind such unanswered questions as those concerning Stalin's era.[52] In "Song About Islands" the poet describes his ideal—a place where there is no sorrow, illness, or hangovers, where falsehood is not the law, where conscience is a necessity, where truth is achieved, not assigned.[53]

In "Without a Title" Galich asserts his responsibility as a critic of his times by replying to those who urge him not to judge:

So does that mean I should sleep peacefully?
Keep putting my five-kopecks in the subway?!
But when it comes to judging, who needs it?
"Why not just live and let live," they say.

No, that kind of formula for living
Is despicable to the core!
Are those who have been elected the judges?
I was not elected, but I am a judge![54]

Although the subject of Soviet forced labor camps surfaced in such officially approved works as Alexander Solzhenitsyn's *One Day in the Life of Ivan Denisovich*, the post-Stalin regime has prevented a forthright examination of this theme as evidenced by its violent reaction to Solzhenitsyn's latest book, *The Gulag Archipelago, 1918–1956*. Galich never served time in a camp, but many of his magnitizdat songs capture the atmosphere

51. "Staratel'ski val'sok," *ibid.*, pp. 13–14. See Gene Sosin, "Then Came Galich's Turn," *New York Times*, February 12, 1972.
52. "Sprashivaite, mal'chiki!" in Galich, *Pokoleniie obrechennykh*, p. 45.
53. "Pesnia pro ostrova," *ibid.*, p. 55.
54. "Bez nazvaniia," *ibid.*, p. 42.

of the camps and the mood of those citizens who returned from Siberia after Stalin's death. "Everything at the Wrong Time," which is dedicated to V. T. Shalamov, a writer of stories about labor camps, tells of two prisoners who are led off to be shot.[55] "Clouds" evokes the memories of twenty years spent in a camp as an unnamed former inmate sits in a bar and recalls how "I was frozen through and through for ages."

The clouds float on, the clouds,
To Kolyma, that dear land,
And they don't need a lawyer there,
For them amnesty is hopeless. . . .

And these days, just like me,
Half the country sits in taverns!
And our memories float to those lands,
The clouds float on, the clouds.[56]

"Song of the Bluebird" is a lament for lost years and for "our crippled lives" in various *Gulag* camps:

Not as soldiers, but as numbers
We died, yes, we died,
From Karaganda to Narym,
All the earth like one abcess,
Vorkuta, Inta, Magadan.[57]

Another forbidden theme that Galich treats is anti-Semitism in the USSR. One of his best-known songs, entitled "Warning," admonishes Jews not to sew fancy clothing in the hope of sitting like gentlemen in synod or senate; rather they should expect to "sit" (i.e., in prison or camp) and to be dragged off by guards for questioning instead of being allowed to make the traditional toast of "l'chaim" (to life). He concludes: "That is the truth, it's the truth I say, / Tomorrow, I fear, will be like yesterday. / Perhaps it could even more quickly come true, / So don't bother to sew any livery, Jews!"[58]

"Falling Asleep and Waking Up" begins with an epigraph containing a Yiddish phrase: "'nit gedaiget'—don't be upset, cheer up." Galich says that as he sleeps "a cold little voice from the bottomless past floats up." It is an old woman, like Pushkin's nursemaid, Arina Rodionovna, who reassures him: "Nit gedaiget, little son." She tells him that he can sleep peacefully because everything is in good order, there is laughter and music at Babi Yar

---

55. "Vse ne vovremia," *ibid.*, pp. 78–79.
56. "Oblaka," *ibid.*, pp. 69–70. Cf. Olga Carlisle, *Poets on Street Corners* (New York, 1968), pp. 350–52.
57. "Pesnia o sinei ptitse," in Galich, *Pokoleniie obrechennykh*, p. 71. Cf. Langland, Aczel, and Tikos, *Poetry From the Russian Underground*, pp. 96–99, 237–38.
58. "Predosterezheniie," in Galich, *Pokoleniie obrechennykh*, p. 54.

(the ravine outside Kiev where tens of thousands of Jews were massacred by the Nazis in September, 1941—an event played down by the Soviet regime). But the old woman adds: "Sleep, but clutch in your fist a weapon, / David's meager sling!" Galich concludes: "People forgive me out of their indifference, / But I do not forgive those indifferent ones!"[59]

This irreconcilable attitude toward those who are indifferent to past and present anti-Semitism is found in "The Train," dedicated to the memory of S. M. Mikhoels:

We no longer rattle like sabres
With indignation or rage,
We say hello to scoundrels,
Exchange greetings with informers,

We don't dash out to battle,
Everything's peaceful and just;
But remember: a train is leaving!
Today and every day. . . .

And only at times our hearts
Are pricked with sadness and wrath—
Our train is leaving for Auschwitz,
Our train is leaving for Auschwitz
Today and every day![60]

Galich reminds us, as did John Donne before him, that we cannot escape responsibility for the fate of others.

"Kaddish" is a lengthy and powerful threnody written in 1970 and dedicated to another victim of anti-Semitism, Janusz Korczak. Born Henryk Goldszmidt, he was a Polish Jew—a writer, physician, and teacher who, although given a chance to survive, chose to perish in the Nazi death camp of Treblinka in 1942 along with the children of the Warsaw orphan home where he taught. Galich describes how the Polish police-collaborators arrive at the home and interrogate the watchman, Piotr Zalewski, a crippled war veteran:

They asked him: "You're a Pole?"
And he said: "Yes, a Pole."
And they asked: "How is that?"
And he said: "Just so."
"But you, stumpy, want to live,

---

59. "Zasypaia i prosypaias'," *ibid.*, pp. 52–53.
60. "Poezd," *ibid.*, p. 48. Mikhoels, for many years the most famous Yiddish actor in the Soviet Union and director of the State Jewish Theater in Moscow, was murdered in January 1948 on Stalin's orders.

So damn it all, how come
You're playing nursemaid in a ghetto,
Like a kike with the children of kikes?"[61]

The cripple replies that Poland is inside the Jewish orphan home just as
much as it is outside:

"Well, then," they said, "The ball is over!"
And then they ordered: "Fire!"
And before he himself fell down,
His crutches fell,
And before peace,
And sleep and silence came,
He managed to wave his hand
To those watching at the window.
O, God grant me such an end,
Having drunk all pain to the dregs,
At the moment of my death to wave my hand
To those watching at the window![62]

The children are taken away to the railroad station for the trip to Treblinka:

The train departs on time at midnight,
The stupid locomotive puffs "Shalom!"
Along the station platform stands the riff-raff,
The riff-raff comes to see the train depart,
The train departs on time at midnight,
The train leaves straight for paradise,
The riff-raff cannot wait to pass the word
That Poland now at last is "Judenfrei."[63]

Galich comments on the recrudescence of anti-Semitism in postwar Poland,
first in a folk-tale digression:

A hundred years ago
In his palace a slovenly prince
Everywhere piled up such dirt
That he himself was unhappy;
And finally, getting very angry,
He summoned a painter.
"Isn't it time," said the prince,
"To paint this dirt some color?"

---

61. "Kaddish," *ibid.*, p. 293. The title is the Hebrew word for the mourner's prayer.
62. *Ibid.*, p. 294.
63. *Ibid.*

The painter said: "It's time,
It's time, O noble prince,
It's long past time."
And the dirt turned dirty-white,
And the dirt turned dirty-blue,
And the dirt turned dirty-yellow
Under the painter's brush.
Because dirt remains dirt
No matter what color you paint it.[64]

The indignant voice of the poet shouts to the souls of the dead who would return to their native Warsaw:

From the year 70 I cry to you!
"Pan Korczak! Do not return!
You will be ashamed in *this* Warsaw!" . . .

I beg you, Pan Korczak,
Do not return to Warsaw,
There's nothing for you to do in *this* Warsaw!
Gomulkomunculi play the buffoon,
Heroic mugs grimace,
The noisy riff-raff rushes to unclean power—
Don't return to Warsaw, I beg you, Pan Korczak!
You'll be an alien in your native Warsaw![65]

"Ballad of the Eternal Light" is prefaced by Galich's noting that "they tell me the favorite melody of the camp commandants in Auschwitz, the melody that was played whenever they led groups of prisoners to their death, was the song 'Tum-balalaika' [a favorite Yiddish folk song], which was played by the orchestra of prisoners." Galich then employs the phrase "tum-balalaika" as a bitter leitmotif of his song:

Tum-balalaika, play balalaika,
Song that they played when we went to our death!
Tum-bala, tum-bala, tum-balalaika,
Tum-bala, tum-bala, tum-balalaika,
Tum-balalaika, play balalaika,
Weeping and bursting apart is my heart![66]

"Requiem for the Unkilled" is also introduced by an epigraph: "My transistor was broken, so for forty-eight hours I received reports only from

64. *Ibid.*, p. 297.
65. *Ibid.*, pp. 298–99. See Lev Ventsov, "Poeziia Aleksandra Galicha," *Vestnik russkogo studencheskogo khristianskogo dvizheniia*, no. 104–5 (1972), pp. 222–26.
66. "Ballada o vechnom ogne," in Galich, *Pokoleniie obrechennykh*, p. 242.

the [official Soviet] radio centers. These reports naturally gave me a completely distorted idea about what was happening, and on the second evening I wrote verses that didn't correspond at all to reality."[67] Galich refers to the Six-Day War between the Arab states and Israel in June 1967. Convinced that the loss of over six million Jews during the Nazi holocaust would now be followed by the destruction of the Israeli Jews, whose number he symbolically estimates to be three and one-half million, the poet laments:

> Six and one-half million,
> Six and one-half million,
> Six and one-half million!
> But it should be exactly ten!
> Lovers of round numbers
> Should be glad to hear the news:
> That it's really very easy
> To burn and shoot and hang
> This pitiable remnant,
> Besides, one has experience![68]

The author complains that "the voice of good and honor / In our rational age is futile." He notes with bitterness that "blood is no dearer than oil, / And oil is desperately needed!" Finally:

> The tanks go into Sinai,
> And the sands are black with blood!
> Three and one-half million
> Will make an even number!
> That isn't very many—
> It's just the merest trifle![69]

Galich's versatility in handling the theme of anti-Semitism is seen in his witty "Story Heard in a Bar at the Station." Written in the form of a *chastushka*—a trochaic tetrameter as popular in Russian folklore as limericks are in English, with similar humorous and often salacious associations—the story is told by a Russian major, a member of the party, who loses his identification papers after a night of carousing. Still in a "disheveled state," he shows up at the documents bureau to apply for new papers and jokingly tells the clerk, "Just put down that I'm a Jew." He forgets all about it; but when his leave ends he is summoned before a personnel officer who calls him a "smartass" and accuses him of shirking his patriotic duty by trying to emigrate to Israel:

---

67. "Rekviem po neubitym," *ibid.*, p. 225.
68. *Ibid.*
69. *Ibid.*, p. 227.

We'll all slog, our faces ruddy,
To our happy future here,
While in Israel you bloody
Bastard munch on matzos there!
We're for peace and act like heroes,
Getting ready for the fray;
But, my friend, you're like Shapiro,
Want to goldbrick night and day.

The major tries to explain himself:

I, my stomach slowly sinking,
Say—though I can hardly breathe,
"Just a gag, I wasn't thinking,
Who the hell wants Tel Aviv!"[70]

But the personnel officer refuses to be convinced that the major did not plot to leave the country. Broken to private, expelled from the party, and fired from his job, the hapless fellow turns to his listeners:

Now at last I've made my mind up,
There's no other way to choose:
Could you fellows help me find a
Synagogue where there's some Jews?[71]

The technique of distilling into a few stanzas of poetry a satirical comment on Soviet reality is characteristic of many of Galich's songs. "Stories from the Life of Klim Petrovich Kolomiitsev, Shop Foreman, Bearer of Many Medals, Deputy to the Supreme Soviet" is a cycle of three such songs. In the first, entitled "Concerning How Klim Petrovich Spoke at a Meeting in Defense of Peace," the hero relates how one Sunday, while he is relaxing at home (with the help of vodka), an official car suddenly drives up and takes him to address a peace rally at the House of Culture. En route a prepared speech is thrust in his hands which he proceeds to read to the crowd with sincere conviction. However, by mistake he was given a text to be delivered by a widowed mother who demands, with the usual clichés, that the "Israeli warmongers" be brought to account and who asserts that she stands ready to fight for the cause of peace. Klim reads on, silently cursing the official who handed him the wrong text. But to his surprise he discovers that nobody in the audience has noticed the difference because they never

70. "Rasskaz, kotory ia uslyshal v privokzal'nom shalmane," *ibid.*, p. 223.
71. *Ibid.*, p. 224. Along with other Russian poets of Jewish origin such as Boris Pasternak, Osip Mandelshtam, and Yosif Brodsky, Galich has been attracted to Christian themes. Cf. "Rozhdestvo" and "Ave Maria" in his "Poem about Stalin," *ibid.*, pp. 275–87. See also the analysis of this poem by Archbishop John of San Francisco in "Stikhi i pesni sovetskogo podpol'ia," *Russkaia mysl'*, March 25, 1971, p. 7.

pay any attention to such speeches. All the same, he is enthusiastically applauded when he finishes. The local first secretary (who evidently was asleep during the speech) compliments him, saying, "You sure did give it to them like a worker, and you told it like it really is!" Klim concludes: "So that is the sad story."[72]

The second song is entitled "Concerning How Klim Petrovich Tried to Get His Shop the Award of 'Shop of Communist Labor' and, Failing That, Got Drunk." Klim protests that his unit has not received a deserved award for excellence in production (the plan was overfulfilled up to 1980) and indignantly takes his case to the authorities in Moscow. There he is told that it would not be proper to publicize this matter in view of what the shop produces: "You can imagine yourself the fuss / The BBC would make of such a fact!" Why is Moscow reluctant to bestow the honor on Klim and his coworkers? Klim tells us what they explained:

Well, sure, they say, you're right, they say,
Your production couldn't be higher,
But still, they say, what you make, they say,
Isn't cloth, after all—it's *barbed wire.*

Oh well, says I, I give up, says I!
I'm going, says I, on a drunk, says I![73]

In the third song, entitled "Concerning How Klim Petrovich Rebelled against Economic Aid to Underdeveloped Countries," Galich describes it as "a very tragic story, and Klim Petrovich tells it in a state of extreme irritation, so he permits himself several expressions not entirely parliamentary." Speaking in the coarse slang of a worker, Klim tells of a trip he took to Algiers with a Soviet trade union delegation. His wife packed cans of food in his suitcase in order to avoid spending money on food abroad. On arriving in Algiers, however, he discovers only cans of salty sprats, which make him groan with thirst. Next morning he shops in an Algerian store, angry at spending his valuable foreign currency:

So I step up to some señorita,
"Excuse please, combien, bitte-dritte,
You got a can here with some meat?"
And she nods her head yes, the damn shitter.

Klim rushes back to the hotel room:

---

72. "O tom, kak Klim Petrovich vystupal na mitinge v zashchitu mira," in Galich, *Pokoleniie obrechennykh,* pp. 263–65.
73. "O tom, kak Klim Petrovich dobivalsia, chtoby ego tsekhu prisvoili zvaniie 'Tsekha Kommunisticheskogo truda' i ne dobivshis' etogo, zapil," *ibid.,* pp. 266–68.

And there till the dawn's early light
I cussed like a dog through the night!
There wasn't no meat in the can!
There were just salty sprats in the can!

I looked, but I wasn't able
To find "made in Brazil" on the label,
Only "USSR, Leningrad,
One ruble, four kopecks, in marinade."

Klim returns home convinced that the Soviet Union is becoming impoverished through aid abroad, where the situation is "even worse, pardon me, than ours."[74]

In December 1971 Galich was expelled from the Soviet Writers Union. He was said to have been confronted by members of the organization's board with three accusations: that his uncensored works had been published abroad, that they had aroused wide interest in the West, and that he had insisted on making his views known to large groups of people in the Soviet Union. During the meeting the poet was addressed not as "Comrade Galich" but as "Comrade Ginzburg." His friends interpreted this as "an attempt by the writers union to emphasize the fact that he is Jewish and therefore potentially disloyal to the Soviet Union." Galich is said to have refused to speak in his own defense, although he confirmed that he was a "corresponding member" of the unofficial Committee on Human Rights founded in 1970 by Andrei Sakharov, Valery Chalidze, and other dissidents.[75]

Galich later gave Western correspondents in Moscow his own explanation for the expulsion. In 1971 the daughter of Dmitri S. Polyansky, a Politburo member, married a young actor. At the wedding reception, which was attended by many elite members of Moscow society, someone played a magnitizdat tape of Galich's songs. Polyansky is reported to have laughed at some of the songs, but later he ordered that Galich be punished. The Writers Union acted quickly to expel him, and the higher authorities advised those officers of the union who had voted against expulsion that the decision be made unanimous.[76]

---

74. "O tom, kak Klim Petrovich vosstal protiv ekonomicheskoi pomoshchi slaborazvitym stranam," *ibid.*, p. 269–71.

75. David Bonavia, *Times* (London), January 4, 1972.

76. Robert G. Kaiser, "Soviet Union's Dissident Troubadour," *Washington Post*, May 26, 1974. Kaiser also reported that Galich gave only one public concert. It took place in the spring of 1968 in Novosibirsk at a festival of balladeers. "Several thousand people heard it and responded with extraordinary enthusiasm. But the songs were too controversial and there was no chance that Galich could become a public performer." By the late 1960s even his closed concerts at the Moscow House of Writers were stopped. See also James R. Peipert, "Soviet Union's 'Bob Dylan,'" *Washington Post*, April 12, 1974.

The action of the Writers Union was followed by Galich's expulsion from the Union of Cinematographers and the Literary Fund, which pays pensions and sick-leave allowances to writers and artists. Thus Galich was deprived of access to regular income. Emigrés in the U.S. who received information from him reported that, in his mid-fifties, unemployed and having suffered four heart attacks, Galich was undergoing a difficult time. He remained true to his principles, however, and signed his name to several samizdat documents. For example, one called for the end to the death penalty in the USSR in the name of humanity; another alerted world public opinion to the dangers that would face Soviet samizdat writers after the USSR joined the Universal Copyright Convention in May, 1973; still another appealed to "people of integrity all over the world" to defend Solzhenitsyn from the regime's persecution of the Nobel laureate after the publication abroad of his *The Gulag Archipelago, 1918-1956* and before the writer was forcibly exiled.[77]

In Galich's "Song of Exodus," dedicated to friends departing for the West at the end of 1971, he expressed his love of Russia and his decision to remain there in spite of hardships:

You're leaving. Leave—
Through Customs and through clouds.
My hand's grown thin
From shaking hands goodbye. . . .

You flee these whiskered gangs,
The questionnaires, midnight alarms?
You're leaving? Leave, fly off—
And God be with you all.

Fly off to those uncertain truths
From truths long frozen in this ice.

77. "Obrashcheniie v Verkhovny Sovet SSSR ob otmene smertnoi kazni" [To the USSR Supreme Soviet on the abolition of the death penalty], AS 1197 (September, 1972); "Otkrytoe pis'mo v YUNESKO o reshenii SSSR prisoedinit'sia k Vseobshchei konventsii ob avtorskom prave v red. 1952" [Open letter to UNESCO concerning the USSR's accession to the 1952 Universal Copyright Convention], AS 1402 (March 23, 1973); "Obrashcheniie k chestnym liudiam vo vsem mire s prizyvom vystupit' v zashchitu A. Solzhenitsyna" [Appeal to people of integrity all over the world to defend A. Solzhenitsyn], AS 1541 (January 5, 1974). There were fifty-two signatories on the first document. Signers of the second document—an open letter to UNESCO—also included Andrei Sakharov, Igor Shafarevich, and Grigory Podyapolsky, all members of the unofficial Committee for the Defense of Human Rights. In part, the letter declared: "If [Soviet] censorship had previously been able to possess international legal force, Russian and world culture would have been deprived of the many wonderful works of [Anna] Akhmatova, [Boris] Pasternak, [Alexander] Solzhenitsyn, [Alexander] Tvardovsky, [Alexander] Bek, and other writers, composers, artists, historians, and publicists. It must not be permitted that this censorship now become capable of acting on a world scale, using the Geneva Convention." Other signers of the third document were Sakharov, Shafarevich, Vladimir Maksimov, and Vladimir Voinovich.

But leave behind your dead,
Do not disturb their sleep of death.

In Ponary and Babi Yar,
In mass graves still unmarked,
Just that pervasive burning smell
Will still persist for centuries.

In Kazakhstan and Magadan,
Beneath the snow and grass. . . .
Yet could there be some land more blessed
Than this—our present godless land? . . .

I'll stay . . . What's strange in that?
As usual I'll wave my hand.
So leave! But I'll remain.
I'll stay here in this land.
For someone must scorn weariness
To guard the peace of all our dead.[78]

However, by the beginning of 1974 his deteriorating health and material situation led Galich to request permission for a trip abroad. At first he was refused, leading him to write an open letter to the International Committee on Human Rights "on the deprivation of professional and civil rights." In it he cited passages from the UN's Univeral Declaration of Human Rights affirming the right of every person to leave his country and return to it. Galich charged that this right had been twice denied to him "on ideological grounds," that is, "as punishment for my attempt to express my own viewpoint, which differed on a number of issues from the official view." He continued:

More than two years since my expulsion from the Union of Writers and the Union of Cinematographers I am deprived of other professional rights: the right to see my work published, the right to sign a contract with a theater, film studio, or publishing house, the right to perform in public. When films are shown that were produced in past years based on my scenarios, someone's hidden hand cuts my name out of the credits. Not only am I untouchable, I am also unpronounceable. Only at various kinds of closed meetings I am forbidden to attend is my name sometimes mentioned, with insulting and abusive epithets added to it. I have only one right left: the right to resign myself to my complete lack of rights, to admit that at fifty-four my life is practically over, and to get my invalid's pension of sixty rubles a month and shut up. And keep waiting.

78. Elisavietta Ritchie, "Alexander Galich: Russian, Writer, Jew," *Washington Post,* January 28, 1973. The translation is by Mrs. Ritchie and Vadim Medish. Galich dedicated the poem to Victor and Galina Kabachnik in December 1971 on the eve of their emigration from the USSR; he called it "my sorrowful goodby present." Cf. "Pesnia iskhoda," in Galich, *Pokoleniie obrechennykh,* pp. 35–37.

In my position anything can happen. In view of the extreme danger of this position I am forced to turn for help to you, the International Committee on Human Rights, and through you to writers, musicians, theater and film people, to all who perhaps out of naïveté continue to believe that a person has the right to express his own opinion, has the right of freedom of conscience and speech, the right to leave his own country and return to it if he so desires.[79]

In May Galich applied for a visa to emigrate to Israel as a Jew. He had been long reluctant to take such a step, for it would mean that he could not return to the Soviet Union. On June 17 he reported that he had been given permission to emigrate to Israel and that the authorities had told him he must leave by June 25, two days before President Nixon was scheduled to arrive.[80] Galich and his wife arrived in Vienna in late June and declared their intention to live in Norway rather than Israel because they had visited Norway in 1961 and "immediately fell in love with the country."

Shortly before he received his exit visa, Galich was approached at a party by an elderly admirer who raised a glass of vodka to his health, saying: "We don't know if you will stay or go, but either way, the songs of Galich will remain here with us."[81]

VLADIMIR VYSOTSKY

Soviet citizens who have emigrated to the West in recent years say that Vladimir Vysotsky is probably the best known of all the poet-bards in the Soviet Union. They assert that if a statistical study of magnitizdat dissemination were possible it would reveal that Vysotsky has the greatest number of listeners.[82] Vysotsky, forty years old in 1974, is a well-known actor in the avant-garde Taganka Theater of Moscow.[83] He has also appeared in several films in which he sang his own compositions. In the mid-1960s a Soviet record was produced based on his songs from the film *Vertical*. Soviet critics of Vysotsky regard these works as differing markedly from the songs he plays in student clubs and at private gatherings of friends:

79. "Otkrytoe pis'mo 'V Mezhdunarodny komitet prav cheloveka' o lishenii professional'-nykh i grazhdanskikh prav ego i V. Maksimova," AS 1580 (February 3, 1974). See also Gene Sosin, "Alexander Galich: Russian Poet of Dissent," *Midstream*, 1974, no. 4 (April), pp. 29–37.

80. Christopher S. Wren, "Song Writer Says Soviet Will Let Him Go to Israel," *New York Times*, June 18, 1974.

81. Kaiser, "Dissident Troubadour." In September he began a concert tour of Western Europe and inaugurated regular weekly broadcasts to the Soviet Union over Radio Liberty, thus realizing his desire to maintain contact with his public at home.

82. Kabachnik, "Magnitizdat," no. 13, October 5, 1972.

83. One of his best-known roles is Hamlet in an unconventional production typical of the Taganka. Vysotsky opens the play with guitar in hand, singing the poem "Hamlet" by the play's translator, Boris Pasternak. See Charlotte Saikowski, *Christian Science Monitor*, February 16, 1972; Hedrick Smith, *International Herald Tribune*, March 2, 1972. See also Alexander Anikst, *Literaturnaia gazeta*, January 12, 1972.

Let us say it right out: those songs he sings on the stage raise no doubts, and we do not wish to speak about them. This actor has other songs which he performs only for "selected" people. Under the guise of art he offers Philistinism, vulgarity, and immorality. Vysotsky sings in the name of and on behalf of alcoholics, prisoners, criminals, depraved and inferior people.[84]

The authors of this newspaper attack cited examples of Vysotsky's magnitizdat songs that they considered reprehensible. One of them, "My Friend Has Left for Magadan," tells of a man who chooses to work in distant Magadan in eastern Siberia:

I know that some will ask, "What for?
Why give up everything you have?
What's out there but labor camps galore
Full of murderers, full of murderers?"
He answers them, "The rumors are untrue.
Moscow has as many murderers, too."
Then he packed a suitcase—only one—
And left for Magadan, for Magadan.[85]

Vysotsky's critics comment:

To go to Magadan and other regions in order to build and to cope with difficulties is a praiseworthy cause. But Vysotsky does not celebrate that. . . . In the name of what does Vysotsky sing? He answers the question himself: "for the sake of justice and only that." But in fact it turns out that this "justice" is slander of our reality. For example, one finds in his work no good words for millions of Soviet people who gave their lives for the Motherland. This is strange but true: judging from one of Vysotsky's songs the heroes of the Fatherland War are former criminals who . . . were practically the main force, and had it not been for them we would not have defeated the enemy.[86]

The critics were referring to "Penal Battalions," in which the poet pays tribute to wartime detachments of Soviet soldier-prisoners who were sent to fight in the front lines with little chance of survival:

The prisoner-soldiers have one law, one end,
Cut down and kill the Fascist knave,
If you don't catch a bullet in the chest
They'll pin a medal there for being "brave."[87]

84. G. Mushta and A. Bondariuk, "O chëm poiot Vysotski," *Sovetskaia Rossiia*, June 9, 1968.
85. Translated by Misha Allen in "Ballads from the Underground," *Problems of Communism* 19, no. 6 (November–December 1970): 29.
86. "O chëm poiot Vysotski."
87. "Shtrafnye batal'ony," Radio Liberty Tape Library, New York. This song is also included in a Western disc of Vysotsky ballads: VOICE Records, RTV 101R (1972).

Vysotsky frequently portrays sympathetically such alienated elements as thieves, prisoners, and labor camp inmates. In the ballad "The Leningrad Blockade," a thief inquires:

Brave citizens, what were you doing then,
When our city couldn't even count its dead?
You were eating caviar and bread, while I
Scrounged for cigarette butts instead.[88]

The thief complains that today, after the victory, "we could really live in clover, / If the volunteer militia'd let us be." He pleads with the *druzhinniki*, who patrol the streets of Soviet cities to preserve law and order: "I beg you kindly, citizens in armbands, / Don't lay upon my soul your grubby hands!"[89]

"Sunday" is an amusing account by a pickpocket who is arrested and questioned by the police—all on his day off when he wasn't "working":

"How many times have you been tried?"
"I'm not so good at counting."
"Well, are you a recidivist?"
"No, comrade, I'm Sergeyev."

Finally the thief signs the confession and comforts himself with the thought that "in the seven-year plan for catching hooligans and bandits / I've also made my modest contribution!"[90]

"The Criminal Code" describes with grim irony the mood of a thief as he pores over that piece of literature with which he is all too familiar:

Tales and plots of intrigues mean nothing to us . . .
We know it all no matter what you suggest we read.
I, for example, consider the best book in the world
To be our Criminal Code.
And whenever I have a sleepless night,
Or suffer from a heavy hangover,
I open the Criminal Code at random
And just can't tear myself away . . .
I never gave my friends advice
But I know that robbery could be charged against them . . .
I have just finished reading about it,
Not less than three not more than ten.
As you become immersed in these simple lines,
Novels of all times and lands lose their meaning.

88. Allen, "Ballads from the Underground," p. 28.
89. *Ibid.*
90. "Voskresny den'," in *Novoe russkoe slovo*, December 17, 1968.

It is full of barracks, long as sentences . . .
Scandals and fights, cards and cheating . . .
If I were not to see these lines for a hundred years,
I should still spot someone's fate in each one of them.
And I feel happy when a paragraph
May bring some luck, although not much, to someone.
And my heart throbs like a wounded bird
When I start reading up on my own case.
And my blood and temples feel as if they are being crushed,
Just as if the cops came to take me away.[91]

As Misha Allen has expressed it: "The prisoner has always had a special
place in the hearts of the Russian people, regardless of crime."[92] One of
Vysotsky's most popular songs, "Ze-Ka Vasiliev and Ze-Ka Petrov," gives
the flavor of life in a Siberian camp through the eyes of two inmates
(*zakliuchonny*, the Russian word for "prisoner," is abbreviated as "Ze-Ka"):

We're both done for and through fluke:
He for embezzlement and I for love of Xenia.
Xenia—I loved her, but we parted,
She was yelling and resisting.
The Cheka pounced on both of us,
And now Petrov and I are Ze-Ka inmates . . .
And in the camps there is no life at all,
Surrounded by railroad thieves and housebreakers
We are mistreated horribly by everyone
With passes made at us, the most peculiar.
And those in charge don't give a damn,
To them we're all the same Ze-Kas—
So we decided to escape one day
Or things would end for us quite badly,
Every day tormented by the criminals,
While the chief doctor wants us as his lovers.
And so the die was cast, escape we must,
But in the meantime we remain the same
Ze-Ka Vasiliev and Ze-Ka Petrov.
Four years we were preparing our escape,
Saved lots of food, it seemed like three tons in weight.
Even a sympathetic criminal type
Shared with us his meagre rations.
And so we left together hand in hand,

91. Translated by Misha Allen in "Songs a Hero Sings," *Toronto Globe Magazine*,
February 28, 1970.
92. Allen, "Russia's Dissident Balladeers," p. 27.

Our daring was applauded by the other Ze-Kas—
Along the tundra like lost orphan kids we wander,
Not along the roads but hidden paths.
Are we heading for Moscow or Mongolia?
My bastard mate had no idea, nor did I.
I showed him where the sun sets, that's the West,
But it was too late, the Cheka grabbed us,
Ze-Ka Vasiliev and Ze-Ka Petrov.
Our colonel was mentioned in reports,
That he recaptured two hardened criminals;
For us he got two medals and some cash,
And out of joy he kept on hitting us.
Years have been added to our term,
And now again we are the same Ze-Kas,
Ze-Ka Vasiliev and Ze-Ka Petrov.[93]

Like Galich, Vysotsky treats the theme of contemporary Soviet anti-Semitism in at least one well-known satirical song called simply "Anti-Semites." A young man wonders why he should bother to become a thief or a bandit when it is more socially acceptable to join the anti-Semites: "Although you can't say there are laws to protect 'em, / There's millions of people who gladly accept 'em." But before making his decision, the fellow tries to find out who these Semites are, and learns that they are "plain Jews." He is in a quandary, because he always admired Einstein and Chaplin. Besides: "Folks, please excuse me, but I got to thinkin' / What'll I do about Abraham Lincoln?" Moreover, he says, Jews include "My friend Rabinovich, the victims of fascism, / And, I might add, the founder of Marxism!" He is finally reassured when he is told that Jews drink the blood of Christian children, crucified God some time back, and stole last year's grain harvest from the people. So he decides: "Now I'm all ready to rob and rampage, / I'm beating the Yids and it's Russia I save!"[94]

In recent years the regime has imprisoned dissenters in insane asylums when it was not possible to prosecute them for violating Soviet law.[95] This subject is treated by Vysotsky in "Song of the Madhouse," which reflects the thoughts of a sane man imprisoned with genuinely mentally ill people:

93. Translated by Misha Allen in the brochure accompanying a recently produced disc, "Songs of the Russian Underground," Collector Records, Silver Spring, Md., 1972. This is a selection of ten songs unpublished in the Soviet Union, sung by Nougzar Sharia, a former Georgian actor and film director. Five of the songs are anonymous works about Soviet forced labor camps, the rest are magnitizdat songs of Vysotsky, Kim, and Kliachkin.

94. "Antisemity," Radio Liberty Tape Library, New York. The last couplet is taken from the slogan of the notorious "Union of the Russian People," a society whose "Black Hundreds" fomented pogroms in Russia before the Revolution.

95. Reddaway, *Uncensored Russia*, pp. 227–48.

I keep saying to myself, stop writing;
But I keep on.
Oh mother dear, dear friends of mine,
As I lie in this ward, they are ogling, stalking me:
I'm afraid to doze off, they might pounce on me.
These silent, incurable lunatics around me.

There are psychos of all sorts—quiet ones, filthy ones,
Starved and beaten as part of their cure.
But the one thing I find strange:
I am sure they walk around quite undeterred.
And the food that is brought to me,
These nuts devour without a word.

If only Dostoevsky, long deceased,
For his Death House Notes renowned by all,
Were to see them as they stand,
Banging their heads against the wall;
And if Gogol could be told
About our life of grief,
I am sure that even Gogol
Would stare at this in utter disbelief.

This is real misery, my friends;
But I spit on them, I do,
Those violent bitches around me,
Ready to trick me, ready to kick me,
Standing with their tongues hanging out;
By God, I haven't the strength to shout.
Yesterday in Ward Seven, down the hall,
Eight orderlies fought to subdue just one.
"Let me at America," he screamed and beat them black and blue.

I am not asking for fame or glory,
While I still have my health,
And my judgment is not yet impaired,
I don't know for how long—do you?
The woman who is chief physician here
Is a quiet sort, but her mind is not quite clear.
I tell her: "I am going mad."
She says: "Just wait a while my dear."

I am waiting but I feel that time is running out;
I've forgotten the alphabet, you see;
As for grammar cases, I remember two or three,
And therefore I say to I, to you, to thee,

Get him, take you, take I away,
Get me out of here today.[96]

Vysotsky's choice of themes is so diversified that his songs justifiably have been called "an encyclopedia of Soviet life today."[97] Although he has managed to avoid the treatment meted out to Okudzhava and Galich, perhaps because of his popularity as a stage and screen personality, Vysotsky is not immune to sharp criticism in the press. In March 1973 he was reproved by *Sovetskaia kultura*, an organ of the Communist Party Central Committee, for allegedly violating all esthetic and legal norms by cooperating with a theater director in a "commercial" deal. Under it he gave as many as sixteen concerts during four days in the industrial city of Novokuznetsk, and about a thousand people filled the hall at each performance. The Moscow correspondent of the *New York Times* commented:

> There was only an indirect hint that the real issue might be the content of some of his songs, rather than his concert arrangements. Either way, the intent of the attack seemed to be to curtail both his activities and his growing popularity.[98]

CONCLUSION

In their samizdat appeal "to public figures who work in science, culture and the arts," Yuli Kim and his fellow dissidents, Yakir and Gabai, declared:

> If there had been no "samizdat" in Russian literature, we would have lost Radishchev's novel [a famous uncensored work written during the reign of Catherine the Great], *Woe from Wit* of Griboyedov, and many poems by Pushkin. In our times as well, the solicitude of a group of readers toward the unpublished word will carry forward to better times the genuine creativity of our contemporaries.[99]

Such a judgment can also be applied to magnitizdat. The solicitude of countless collectors and reproducers of tape recordings is preserving the genuine creativity of the contemporary Soviet balladeers. In addition, shortwave broadcasts into the USSR serve as an effective medium for acquainting Soviet citizens throughout the country with these uncensored songs of dissent. Radio Liberty, for example, which devotes a considerable portion of its Russian language program schedule to readings and discussions of samizdat texts, also regularly broadcasts magnitizdat songs several times per week. Tapes of songs copied by recording machines inside the

---

96. Translated by Misha Allen in *Toronto Telegram*, February 17, 1971.

97. V. Maslov, "Tri znakomstva s Vysotskim," *Posev*, January, 1971, p. 57. Maslov then proceeds to list more than 30 separate topics chosen by Vysotsky from Soviet life.

98. Hedrick Smith, "Soviet Reproves Singer of Underground Songs," *New York Times*, April 2, 1973. Cf. *Sovetskaia kul'tura*, March 30, 1973.

99. AS 14. See also Pavel Litvinov, comp., *The Trial of the Four*, English text ed. Peter Reddaway (New York, 1972), pp. 241–46. Gabai committed suicide in October, 1973.

Soviet Union are brought to the West by tourists and émigrés and then played back to millions of shortwave listeners.[100]

It is not difficult to understand why the singing poets of magnitizdat are so popular with Soviet citizens on many levels of the society. Their songs articulate genuine attitudes, moods, and aspirations, in contrast to the synthetic output of official cultural media. "Authenticity, spontaneity, and human spirit"[101] fill the works of Okudzhava, Galich, Vysotsky, and others who, aided by the sophisticated artifacts of the technological-electronic era, are perpetuating the age-old quest for truth and justice so characteristic of Russian folklore, poetry, and song.

100. Radio Liberty estimates that in 1974 there were about 36 million privately owned shortwave receivers in the USSR, or one for every two families.

101. The quotation is from Telegin's samizdat work excerpted on p. 277 above.

CHAPTER NINE / LEGAL CONTROLS ON AMERICAN

PUBLICATION OF HETERODOX SOVIET WRITINGS /

PETER B. MAGGS

Recent changes in Soviet legislation and the recent accession of the Soviet Union to the Universal Copyright Convention have brought forth expressions of alarm from American publishers, authors, and newspaper commentators.[1] They have warned that the combined effect of these changes will be to give the Soviet state the power to use the American legal system to censor the publication of heterodox Soviet writings in the United States. The American fears have not been alleviated by the following statement by an authoritative Soviet commentator:

The possibility is provided (by the use of the legal means for copyright protection stipulated in the internal legislation of countries participating in the convention) for the prevention of the use of Soviet works for anti-Soviet purpose, for under the conditions of sharp ideological struggle in the modern world a number of publishers in the West have been so using Soviet works.[2]

The American commentators have argued that prompt counteraction, including legislation, is necessary to avoid such potential censorship. In the following pages I shall seek to examine the questions of the extent to which the legal situation has been changed; the dangers of such censorship at present; and the need for the proposed countermeasures.

---

1. Anthony Astrachan, "Concern Voiced in the U.S. at Soviet Copyright Law," *Washington Post*, March 23, 1973, p. A14; Anthony Astrachan, "Soviets Join Copyright System," *Washington Post*, March 1, 1973, p. H1; "Authors, Publishers Deplore Soviet Moves to Curb Dissident Writers by Copyright Laws," *Publishers Weekly*, March 26, 1973, pp. 47–48; Nicholas Bethell, "Authors' Rights, or Authors' Wronged," *Times* (London), March 2, 1973; Rhoda F. Gamson, "Moscow's Copyright Maneuver," *New Leader*, May 14, 1973, pp. 11–13; Leo Gruliow, "Soviet Copyright Loopholes Eyed," *Christian Science Monitor*, March 23, 1973; Leo Gruliow, "Soviets Ready Participation in World Copyright," *Christian Science Monitor*, March 12, 1973; "Moscow Amends Law on Copyright: Outflow of Dissident Writing is Apparent Target," *New York Times*, March 18, 1973, p. 5; "A Moscow Move to Restrict Publication," *Wall Street Journal*, March 16, 1973; "Reverse Copyright," *New York Times*, March 21, 1973; "Russians and Copyright—A Welcome Move, but a Host of Questions Remain," *Publishers Weekly*, March 12, 1973, pp. 32–33; Wolfgang Saxon, 'U.S. Authors Ask a Bar to Soviet: Seek to Block Copyright Actions in U.S. Courts," *New York Times*, March 25, 1973, p. 17; Alan U. Schwartz, "Russian Roulette," *ibid.*, March 10, 1973, p. 29; Hedrick Smith, "6 Soviet Intellectuals Warn of Danger in Moscow's Acceptance of World Copyright Law," *ibid.*, March 28, 1973, p. 15.

2. M. M. Boguslavsky, "Novoe v sovetskom avtorskom prave" [New developments in Soviet copyright law], *Sovetskoe gosudarstvo i pravo* [Soviet state and law], 1973, no. 7, p. 56.

Various types of heterodox Soviet writings are now being published in the United States. Some of these works merely fail to meet accepted Soviet standards of socialist realism; some are openly anti-Soviet. Some were once published by Soviet publishing houses but have since fallen into disrepute, some were informally distributed in typewritten and carbon copies within the Soviet Union, some have never been distributed there.

Given the past absence of copyright treaty arrangements, many such works have been published without the benefit of formal legal arrangements, though some have been published under private agreements with Soviet authors or their representatives. The continued viability of these publishing practices has been thrown into doubt by the adherence of the Soviet Union to the Universal Copyright Convention and by certain changes in Soviet law made at the time of adherence. Therefore it seems worthwhile to evaluate the legal framework under which foreign publication of works by Soviet authors will take place in the future in light of the changed situation. Such an evaluation must be highly tentative, however, since international and United States copyright law leaves many important questions to the discretion of individual authors and publishing houses and since at this writing it is too early to determine in detail what practices authors and publishers will adopt in reaction to the new legal situation.

CONTROLS IN SOVIET LAW

The Rights of the State and the Rights of the Author. Soviet copyright law and practice does not differ sharply from that in noncommunist countries with respect to the rights of the author.[3] The law gives the author the basic rights to publish, to secure the integrity of his work, and to receive fair payment. The rights of the state are protected by regulations providing for limitations upon payment in case the work was produced by the author under official government assignment, by a powerful but little-used or never-used section of the law giving the state the right to compulsory purchase of copyright, and by the general provisions of article 5 of the Fundamental Principles of Civil Legislation, which provides that rights under civil law are to be protected by law except to the extent that they are exercised to the contradiction of their purpose in socialist society.[4]

3. The primary sources of Soviet copyright law are Osnovy grazhdanskogo zakonoda-tel'stva Soiuza SSR i Soiuznykh respublik [Fundamental principles of civil legislation of the USSR and the Union republics], arts. 96–106, and corresponding articles of the civil codes of the Union republics. The most comprehensive treatise on Soviet copyright law is Dietrich A. Loeber, *Urheberrecht der Sowjetunion* (Frankfurt and Berlin, 1966). A recent work in English is J. A. Baumgarten, *U.S.-U.S.S.R. Copyright Relations Under the Universal Copyright Convention* (New York: Practicing Law Institute, 1973). An extensive older work in English is Serge I. Levitsky, *Introduction to Soviet Copyright Law*, Law in Eastern Europe, no. 8 (Leiden, 1964). The position of samizdat under Soviet law is covered in an excellent article by Dietrich A. Loeber, "Samizdat under Soviet Law," *Index* 2 (Autumn 1973): 3–24.

4. Fundamental Principles of Civil Legislation, arts. 5, 98, 100, 106.

Regulation of Transmission of Works Abroad. It is in the area of the regulation of transmission of works abroad that Soviet law differs most significantly from that in foreign countries. The differences are two: the state controls the transmission or sale of works abroad, and authors who transmit certain categories of works abroad are punishable. These controls can be examined separately for unpublished and published works.

In the case of unpublished works, Soviet controls on transmission abroad are of various types. One is control on the physical means by which the works are sent out of the country. Customs legislation forbids private parties from carrying works across the Soviet border to bring them to foreign publishers, and postal and customs regulations forbid the transmission of works of an "anti-Soviet character." These regulations create no problems for the author who wishes to transmit an approved work abroad. The author of an unapproved work, however, is faced with the danger that if he mails the work it will be seized by the Soviet postal authorities, and if he gives it to someone to take abroad it may be seized by customs authorities and he may be prosecuted for violating customs regulations.[5] Even after the work is physically transmitted to a foreign publisher, problems remain in giving him the legal publishing rights. These will be discussed later. Authors who transmit "anti-Soviet" works abroad for publication may be prosecuted criminally if the works are published, as was done in the cases of Sinyavsky, Daniel, and others.

NEW DEVELOPMENTS IN SOVIET COPYRIGHT POLICY

The New Legislation. On February 27, 1973, the Soviet government announced its adherence to the Universal Copyright Convention effective May 27, 1973.[6] Six days before the announcement, February 21, Soviet copyright legislation was amended.[7] The amendments provided for the issuance of supplementary administrative regulations;[8] since then regulations with respect to what works published by state agencies should bear copyright notices have been issued.[9] An office is being opened to deal with

---

5. Tamozhennyi kodeks Soiuza SSR [Customs code of the USSR], *Vedomosti Verkhovnogo Soveta SSR* [Gazette of the Supreme Soviet of the USSR], 1973, no. 20, item 242; V. Koldaev, "Otvetstvennost' za kontrabandu" [Liability for contraband], *Sovietskaia institsiia* [Soviet justice] 37, no. 9 (1973): 5–6.

6. "Soviet Union Joins Copyright Nations," *New York Times*, May 28, 1973, p. 6.

7. *Vedomosti Verkhovnogo Soveta SSSR*, February 28, 1973, no. 9, item 138 (hereafter cited as Soviet Copyright Amendments).

8. Soviet Copyright Amendments, par. 1.

9. Instruktsiia o poriadke primeneniia znaka okhrana avtorskogo prava na proizvedeniiakh literatury, nauki i iskusstva, izdavaemykh v SSSR [Instructions on the procedure for the use of the copyright protection symbol on productions of literature, science, and art published in the USSR], approved by Order 153 of the chairman of the State Committee on Matters of Publishing Houses, Printing and the Book Trade, March 28, 1973, *Biulleten' normativnykh aktov ministerstv i vedomstv SSSR* [Bulletin of Normative Acts of Ministries and Departments of the USSR], 1973, no. 7, p. 44.

foreign copyright matters.[10] New tax legislation and regulations have also been adopted to deal with international copyright royalties.[11]

The basic principle of the Universal Copyright Convention is to end all discrimination against foreign authors and works published abroad. The convention provides for the protection of unpublished as well as published works.[12]

The changes in Soviet copyright law include various technical amendments to assure foreign authors the minimum privileges guaranteed them under the convention—for instance, the limited privilege to prevent unauthorized translations of their works.[13] More closely relevant to the present essay, the legislation also contains provisions that many foreigners assume are designed to limit the foreign publications of works that Soviet authorities believe reflect unfavorably upon the Soviet Union. Two specific provisions of the legislation are cited in this regard. One says that the procedure for the transmission by a Soviet author of the right to use his work in a foreign country shall be established by Soviet legislation. The other adds references to "legal successor of the author" to certain sections that used to refer only to "the author."[14]

The first provision might seem to pose two threats: first, that new criminal sanctions would be available to the Soviet state to deter unapproved transfers of the right to publish;[15] second, that an approval of publication given within the Soviet Union in violation of such regulations might be held to be without legal effect in the United States.[16] In fact, however, the new legislation seems to have made no change in the situation of the Soviet author with respect to the criminal law. The new copyright

10. "Vo Vsesoiuznom agenstve po avtorskim pravam" [At the All-Union Copyright Agency], *Izvestiia*, December 27, 1973, p. 2, col. 7; English trans., *Current Digest of the Soviet Press* 25 (January 23, 1974), p. 3. See Hedrick Smith, "Soviets Form World Copyright Agency," *New York Times*, September 21, 1973, p. 3.

11. "O podokhodnom naloge s summ, vyplachivaemykh za izdanie, ispolnenie ili inoe ispol'zovanie proizvedenii nauki, literatury i iskustva" [On the income tax on amounts paid for the publication, performance, or other use of works of science, literature, and art], *Vedomosti Verkhovnogo Soveta SSSR*, 1973, no. 37, item 497; Theodore Shabad, "Soviet Increases Tax for Authors," *New York Times*, September 28, 1973, p. 6; "O stavkakh i poriadke vyplaty avtorskogo gonorara" [On the rates and procedures for payment of authors' royalties], *Izvestia*, February 20, 1974, p. 3.

12. The standard treatise on the Universal Copyright Convention is Arpad Bogsch, *The Law of Copyright Under the Universal Convention*, 3d rev. ed. (Leiden, 1968; New York, 1968). A copy of the Geneva version of the convention, to which the United States has acceded as well as the Soviet Union, may be found in the Bogsch work; in [1955] 3 UST 2731, TIAS no. 3324; or in 216 UNTS 132.

13. Universal Copyright Convention, art. 5, par. 1; Bogsch, *Law of Copyright*, pp. 56–81; Soviet Copyright Amendments, par. 4.

14. Soviet Copyright Amendments, pars. 1, 2, 3, 4.

15. Astrachan, "Soviets Join Copyright System," citing an article by Victor Louis in the *London Evening News*; Astrachan, "Concern Voiced in U.S."

16. See the argument made by the defendant in Bodley Head, Ltd. v. Flegon, [1972] 1 WLR 680 (Ch.), to be discussed in detail below.

legislation provides no criminal sanctions, and nothing in the present criminal codes makes violation of the state monopoly of foreign trade a crime. The new copyright situation has not affected the array of legal mechanisms available to the Soviet state for threatening and punishing authors who publish "anti-Soviet" works abroad. Nor is there any evidence to date that the recent Soviet adherence to the International Covenant on Human Rights has changed Soviet practice with regard to dissident authors.[17]

Legal sanctions against dissident Soviet writers whose works were published abroad have included in recent years criminal punishment for "anti-Soviet agitation and propaganda" and for lesser offenses, forced labor and internal exile under the antiparasite laws, and foreign exile and loss of citizenship under ad hoc legislation. In addition to these open and official actions, the government, according to well-documented charges, has used commitment to mental institutions as a means of pressure upon dissidents. A quasi-legal sanction that has been used in a number of instances has been dismissal from the Writers Union.

A policy of open criminal prosecution of dissident writers was initiated in 1966, one and one-half years after Khrushchev's ouster. Andrei Sinyavsky and Yuli Daniel were brought to trial for writing a number of works that had been published in the West under the pseudonyms "Abram Tertz" and "Nikolai Arzhak."[18] These writers were tried under article 70 of the Russian Criminal Code, which proscribes:

Agitation or propaganda carried out for the purpose of subverting or weakening the Soviet power or of committing particular especially dangerous crimes against the state, or the distribution, for the same purpose, of slanderous fabrications defaming the Soviet state and social system, or the distribution or preparation or keeping, for the same purpose, of literature of such content.

The writers at their trial disclaimed the anti-Soviet purpose necessary for conviction under this article. The judge, however, gave great weight to the use made by Western publishers of the defendants' writings. At one point in the trial, for instance, the judge asked Sinyavsky if the reactionary publishing houses would have published his works in such elegant format if they

17. *Vedomosti Verkhovnogo Soveta SSSR*, October 3, 1973, item 564. The Soviet Union did not adhere to the optional protocol to the covenant, which provides an enforcement mechanism. The texts of the covenant and the protocol are in 21 UN GAOR Supp. 16, at 52-58 (1966) (A16316). The covenant has not yet received the number of ratifications necessary for it to enter into force.

18. Harold J. Berman, *Soviet Criminal Law and Procedure: The RSFSR Codes*, 2d ed. (1972), pp. 81–83; Alexander Ginzburg, *Belaia kniga po delu A. Siniavskogo i Iu. Danielia* [White book on the case of A. Sinyavsky and Y. Daniel] (Frankfurt, 1967); Max Hayward, ed., *On Trial: The Soviet State versus "Abram Tertz" and "Nikolai Arzhak"* (New York, 1966); *Izvestiia*, February 11, 1966, p. 4; *Izvestiia*, February 16, 1966, p. 4.

had not been anti-Soviet.[19] A great deal of the trial discussion concerns the opinions of Western European and American critics of the defendants' works.

Harold J. Berman points out that this case employs an extremely broad interpretation of article 70. He suggests that the Soviet regime's discomfort with assigning the article such scope was the reason for the introduction later in 1966 of a new provision, article 190-1. This law prohibits defamation of the Soviet state without requiring an anti-Soviet purpose as an element of the crime.[20]

Another important trial was that of Yuri Galanskov, Alexander Ginzburg, and others.[21] Ginzburg's major offense, again under article 70, was apparently his compilation of the White Book containing a transcript of the Sinyavsky-Daniel trial and its subsequent publication in the West.[22] Thus once again publication of a dissident work outside the USSR led the authorities to severe retaliation. Since then criminal prosecutions have occurred regularly against persons who have allowed works regarded as anti-Soviet to be published in the West.[23]

Deprivation of citizenship has been used as a sanction a number of times in recent years against Soviet citizens who have published unapproved works in the West. In each case citizenship has been taken away by a special decree of the Presidium of the Supreme Soviet. Cases include those of Valery Tarsis in February 1966, Svetlana Alliluyeva in January, 1970, Valery Chalidze in December, 1972, Zhores Medvedev in August, 1973, and Alexander Solzhenitsyn in February 1974. In all the cases except that of Solzhenitsyn the deprivation came while the person involved was abroad. In Solzhenitsyn's case it occurred concurrently with his "expulsion" from the country.[24]

Some commentators appear not to understand the effect of such deprivation of citizenship on the possibility of return by the former citizen to the USSR. Soviet law places the question of entry by noncitizens in the discretion of the Ministry of Foreign Affairs. Normally it would probably refuse to grant entry visas to such former citizens, who furthermore would have well-founded apprehensions about what sanctions might await them if

19. Ginzburg, *Belaia kniga*, p. 236.
20. Berman, *Soviet Criminal Law*, p. 82.
21. "Biographic Notes," *Problems of Communism* 17, no. 4 (July–August 1968): 115–16.
22. See n. 18 above.
23. E.g., the cases of Vadim Delone, Vladimir Dremliuga, Victor Fainberg, Lidia Gorbanevskaya, and Pavel Litvinov, *New York Times*, October 18, 1968, p. 15; of Amalrik, *ibid.*, November 13, 1970, p. 1; of Anatoly Marchenko, *ibid.*, August 10, 1971, p. 8; of Levitin Krasnov, *ibid.*, September 19, 1971, p. 12; of Vladimir Bukovsky, *ibid.*, January 6, 1972, p. 3.
24. For Tarsis, *Vedomosti Verkhovnogo Soveta SSSR*, February 23, 1966, no. 8, item 135; for Alliluyeva, *ibid.*, January 7, 1970, no. 1, p. 10; for Chalidze and Medvedev, Theodore Shabad, "Expulsion by Soviet Highly Unusual Step," *New York Times*, February 14, 1974, p. 16; for Solzhenitsyn, *Izvestia*, February 15, 1974, p. 4.

they did succeed in returning. From the point of view of international law, however, every state has the duty to receive back its own nationals expelled from another state.[25] Since this is an international obligation, the Soviet Union cannot unilaterally deny it by depriving a national of his citizenship rights. Thus if a writer living abroad could persuade the country he was in to expel him to the Soviet Union, the Soviet Union would be compelled under international law to take him back.

The case of Solzhenitsyn goes beyond that of the other writers in that he was deprived of Soviet citizenship concurrent with expulsion rather than after he had left voluntarily. If he had been willing to risk the possible dire consequences of remaining (according to the *New York Times*, he was threatened with an indictment for treason, a capital offense, and was put under severe psychological pressure), he could have requested that West Germany refuse to receive him. Unless it had made a prior agreement to take him even against his will, West Germany could then have demanded under international law that the Soviet Union take Solzhenitsyn back.

Another possibility for state action against persons who publish abroad has been compulsory assignment to work under the antiparasite laws, which provide that each Soviet citizen is expected to work in the public interest and may be compelled to take a job if he does not do so voluntarily. Until recently such an assignment could have been coupled with banishment to some remote part of the country, though this provision has been changed, perhaps because of protests from the residents of the areas to which the "parasites" were sent. Since some dissident writers seemed to have no other occupation than writing, and since their kind of writing was not regarded under Soviet law as socially useful labor, such writers opened themselves to charges of parasitism. The two most notable cases of the use of the antiparasite laws against writers who published in the West were those of Yosif Brodsky and Andrei Amalrik. Each writer was sent for a substantial period of exile to a remote area, though each was released before the term of his sentence had expired, perhaps because of international protest.[26]

Soviet writers, prominent among them Zhores Medvedev, have complained of use by Soviet authorities of involuntary commitment to mental institutions as a means of bringing pressure upon writers not to publish certain types of works abroad.[27] While the Soviet government has taken many other types of measures against dissident writers quite openly, it has never admitted using this procedure against anyone who was not in fact mentally ill.

25. L. Oppenheim, *International Law*, ed. H. Lauterpacht, 8th ed. (1955), 1:646, 695.
26. Berman, *Soviet Criminal Law*, pp. 77–81; Samuel Kucherov, *The Organs of Soviet Administration of Justice* (Leiden, 1970), pp. 212–34; A. Amalrik, *Involuntary Journey to Siberia* (New York, 1970).
27. Berman, *Soviet Criminal Law*, p. 11, 88; Zhores and Roy Medvedev, *A Question of Madness* (London, 1971).

Since the Soviet citizen is dependent on the good will of Soviet administrative authorities for many aspects of his daily existence, the citizen who incurs the authorities' disfavor may find himself encountering a wide variety of difficulties. A notable example is the fact that Solzhenitsyn was refused a permit for residence in Moscow even after he married a resident of the city. Normally a permit is issued automatically in such a situation.

A number of Soviet writers who published disapproved material abroad have found themselves expelled from the Writers Union. Such action is not a legal sanction, since the union is not a governmental organization, but it does cause the writer considerable harm by denying him the substantial monetary and other benefits the union provides other established writers.

A recent Soviet decree issued to supplement the new copyright amendments provides that no Soviet author may give valid permission to publish abroad without the approval of Soviet authorities.[28] Does this mean that American courts would refuse to recognize the legal effect of any documents executed by Soviet authors that did not bear the official Soviet stamp of approval? The answer appears to be no. American courts would in all probability hold that the validity of the document was governed by American rather than by Soviet law, or that the Soviet restriction was against American public policy and would not be enforced.

They would have as an example a recent English case that concerned Solzhenitsyn's historical novel *August 1914*. A certain Alec (or Oleg) Flegon wrote to a number of publishers offering them a translation of the novel at very favorable terms. The Bodley Head Press sued as Solzhenitsyn's assignee to have Flegon enjoined from proceeding with publication. The press's rights rested ultimately on a power of attorney apparently executed by Solzhenitsyn in the USSR but providing that it should be governed by Swiss law. This power of attorney granted Solzhenitsyn's Swiss lawyer the right to dispose of publication rights for *August 1914*. One of the defenses argued for Flegon was that Soviet law forbade giving such powers of attorney and that therefore the power should not be recognized by the English court. The court held that the Soviet provisions were irrelevant and that since there was nothing in giving such a power repugnant to British or Swiss law the power would be given full legal force. After rejecting Flegon's other defenses, the court ruled for Bodley Head.[29]

The other change in Soviet copyright law, that involving reference to "the successor to the rights of the author," likewise does not make any significant change in the legal position of the Soviet author. The main reason for the change was probably to bring the Soviet Union into compliance with those provisions of the Universal Copyright Convention that envision the assignment of copyright. But Soviet citizens have always had the right to dispose

28. See n. 10 above.
29. Bodley Head, Ltd. v. Flegon.

of their copyright powers through the use of a power of attorney; little if anything is added by the additional right of assignment. It may well be true, as some American commentators suggest, that pressure will be brought on certain Soviet writers to assign their rights to state agencies so as to allow those agencies to oppose foreign publication of the works involved. Yet Soviet authorities could always have used a power of attorney for the same purpose.

New Soviet tax legislation was passed on September 12, 1973, to deal with the hard-currency incomes Soviet authors will now be earning.[30] The tax is 30 percent on royalties up to 500 rubles and 75 percent over that amount. This rather heavy tax rate would reduce the profitability of publishing material abroad but would not be a threat to the freedom of a Soviet writer if he paid the taxes. Failure to pay taxes in peacetime is not an offense under the Russian Republic Criminal Code. If an author sought to bring in royalties through unofficial channels to avoid paying taxes, however, he could probably be convicted under article 88, which governs foreign currency operations. This article provides severe penalties, including death, for aggravated violations.

Until and unless the United States and the USSR ratify the Convention on Matters of Taxation signed in June 1973, Soviet authors will have to pay both American and Soviet taxes on works published in the United States. That treaty would relieve Soviet authors from such American taxes.[31]

THE EFFECT OF SOVIET ACCESSION TO THE UNIVERSAL COPYRIGHT CONVENTION

How will the rights of the Soviet author and the Soviet state under United States law be affected by Soviet accession to the Universal Copyright Convention? The obvious effect will be on those American publishers who have been translating and publishing works originally published by Soviet state-owned publishing houses. To the extent that Soviet authors and publishers choose to protect their works by copyright, American publishers will have to negotiate royalty arrangements in order to continue translating and publishing the works involved. For heterodox Soviet writings that would not be published by regular Soviet publishers, the effects of the change in Soviet law are not so obvious. But many American commentators have seen ominous possibilities for use by the Soviet government of the copyright convention to suppress works it considers to be anti-Soviet in character.

The legal status of a work under the Universal Copyright Convention and American law depends on whether or not it has been published and, if it has

30. See n. 11 above.
31. *Department of State Bulletin* 69 (1973): 169.

been, on whether or not the published copies bear a copyright notice.[32] In the American copyright system an author can choose to have an unpublished work protected by state law or, for limited classes of works, by federal law. No formalities are necessary for protection under state common law, but registration is necessary to protect an unpublished work under federal law.

Many of the commentators on the recent Soviet copyright developments have apparently overlooked the whole area of common law protection. The law of every state in the United States has always forbidden the unauthorized copying or publication of unpublished works, and this law has made no distinction as to whether the owner was American or foreign.[33] While the universal copyright requires that such protection be provided, it adds nothing to the rights of foreigners in this respect under American law, since they are already fully protected.

The publication of a work with a proper copyright notice will result in protection of the work under United States federal law. Publication without such a notice, however, may result in loss of the opportunity for any United States copyright protection. It may therefore become crucial to determine whether or not the work has been published. Many *samizdat* (self-published) works are on the borderline between unpublished and published works. Such a determination therefore raises several serious legal and factual questions. What law governs the question of whether or not samizdat distribution constitutes publication—Soviet law, United States federal law, state law, or the Universal Copyright Convention? Exactly what constitutes publication under the applicable law? How can the extent of distribution within the Soviet Union be proved in an American court?

Consider first the question of the governing law. Article 6 of the Universal Copyright Convention provides:

"Publication," as used in this Convention, means the reproduction in tangible form and the general distribution to the public of copies of a work from which it can be read or otherwise visually perceived.

Article 2, paragraph 2 of the convention provides:

Unpublished works of nationals of each Contracting State shall enjoy in each other Contracting State the same protection as that other State accords to unpublished works of its own nationals.

Article 6 was designed to restrict the definition of published works. A restricted definition provides greater protection for authors. If publication is

---

32. A copyright notice is a short formal statement such as "© John Jones 1975." It serves to warn potential copiers that the book is protected by copyright.

33. Such protection was clearly established by the leading English case of Donaldson v. Beckett, 4 Burr. 2408 (HL 1774), which was followed in a leading early American copyright case, Wheaton v. Peters, 33 U.S. (8 Pet.) 591 (1834).

defined broadly as including any circulation of a work, authors might easily forfeit their copyrights through some very limited distribution. The definition in article 6 is designed to protect authors against such forfeiture. It might be noted, however, that the definitions of publication in the French and Spanish versions of the convention carry a slightly different emphasis: "la mise à la disposition du public d'exemplaires de l'oeuvre" and "el poner a disposición del publico ejemplares de la obra."

There would appear to be no conflict between this treaty provision and the American cases that have indicated that a work will still be regarded as unpublished and so protected by common law without formalities even though it has had a limited distribution.[34] Because of the very general nature of the treaty provision, it seems likely that the courts would rely on the precedents in American law to determine what constituted publication of a work by a Soviet author.

The question might well arise whether or not a samizdat distribution constituted publication. If it did and the copies distributed did not bear a copyright notice, the work would not be and could never be protected by copyright and so could be copied with impunity by American publishers. Everything would depend upon the particular facts surrounding its distribution. Proof of these facts, however, could be extraordinarily difficult because of the clandestine nature of samizdat distribution. Indeed, when the defense of prior publication was attempted in the English case involving *August 1914*, the defendant was unable to produce evidence that would satisfy the judge that there had been sufficient samizdat distribution to constitute prior publication.[35]

If a work has been published, the next question that must be asked is whether or not it bears a copyright notice. If it does in the form prescribed by the Universal Copyright Convention, it will be protected without further formalities in the United States and all other countries that are parties to the convention. If it does not bear a notice, all copyright protection is lost except under unusual circumstances and the work is thrown into the public domain.

The notice requirements of the Universal Copyright Convention are simple. Article 3, paragraph 1 provides:

Any Contracting State which, under its domestic law, requires as a condition of copyright, compliance with formalities such as deposit, registration, notice, notarial certificates, payment of fees or manufacture or publication in that Contracting State, shall regard these requirements as satisfied with respect to all works protected in accordance with this Convention and first published outside its territory and the author of which is not one of its nationals, if from the time of the first publication all the copies of the work published with the authority of the author or other copyright

34. M. B. Nimmer, *Nimmer on Copyright*, loose leaf (New York, 1963–74), § 58.1–58.3.
35. Bodley Head, Ltd. v. Flegon.

proprietor bear the symbol © accompanied by the name of the copyright proprietor and the year of first publication placed in such manner and location as to give reasonable notice of claim of copyright.

Article 2, paragraph 1 provides:

Published works of nationals of any Contracting State and works first published in that State shall enjoy in each other Contracting State the same protection as that other State accords to work of its nationals first published in its own territory.

Taken together, these provisions mean that copyright protection will be obtained under United States law if the work is first published outside the United States and the simple formalities mentioned in article 3 are complied with. Similar but slightly more onerous formalities are required under American law for works first published in the United States.

If the work has been published without a copyright notice, copyright protection for the work is usually lost irrevocably. But the effect of such publication depends on whether or not it was authorized, on where it occurred, and on a particularly doubtful question of United States copyright law that will be discussed below.

It is clear that, under United States law, publication with the consent of the author or other copyright proprietor, in the United States, and without a copyright notice, forever divests the author or proprietor of his copyright protection. It is likewise clear that publication without notice, but without the consent of the author or copyright proprietor, has no effect on his rights. In a number of instances it has been alleged that Soviet authorities sought to create difficulties for dissenting writers by having their works published abroad without copyright notices. Such a publication would have no effect on the legal validity of the author's copyright under United States law, though if it were widely distributed it could obviously affect the commercial prospects of an authorized version. An example is the publication in Europe of Svetlana Alliluyeva's *Twenty Letters to a Friend.* Unauthorized versions suddenly appeared in England, Germany, and Switzerland, and only rapid legal action by the authorized publisher prevented their publication and distribution.[36] Alexander Solzhenitsyn's attorney was likewise successful in suppressing an unauthorized German edition of his novel *August 1914.*[37]

A more difficult question arises if publication without notice occurs with the consent of the author but outside the United States. Dictum in a leading case states that even such publication would not prevent the author from obtaining American copyright protection by publication in the United States with an appropriate copyright notice and compliance with United States

---

36. *New York Times*, August 4, 1967, p. 26; *ibid.*, August 7, 1967, p. 21; *ibid.*, August 9, 1967, p. 36; *ibid.*, August 11, 1967, p. 29.
37. Loeber, "Samizdat under Soviet Law," p. 13.

registration formalities.[38] American copyright law, however, has since been amended as a result of American adherence to the Universal Copyright Convention, and the register of copyright has interpreted the amendments as providing that authorized foreign publication without a copyright notice now forfeits the author's right to a United States copyright.[39] This interpretation has not been tested in court and is disputed by the leading American writer on copyright law.[40] But given the position of the register of copyright, registration in this situation could be obtained only after litigation if at all.

The Effect of Soviet Ratification of the Universal Copyright Convention on Soviet Use of American Copyright to Control the Publication of Heterodox Works by Soviet Authors. Many commentators have suggested that the Soviet ratification of the Universal Copyright Convention has given the Soviet government new powers to censor American publication of unorthodox works by Soviet writers. I believe that such suggestions rest on two basic misconceptions: first, that such writings were previously unprotected by copyright law; and second, that American courts would automatically recognize Soviet government seizure of American copyrights of Soviet authors.

As was mentioned above, American law, by so-called common law copyright, has always protected the unpublished works of Soviet authors. Thus the possibility, that the Soviet government would either seize a Soviet author's rights or coerce him into filing a court action to prevent publication of his works is not a new threat; rather it has always existed.

On the urging of American authors and publishers, Senator John L. McClellan has introduced a bill in Congress to deal with the problems of Soviet state confiscation or coerced assignment of the rights of Soviet authors to American copyright.[41] I submit that the proposed legislation will not change existing law in any major way and will not solve the problems it addresses.

---

38. Heim v. Universal Pictures Co., 154 F.2d 480 (2d Cir. 1946).
39. 37 CFR Sec. 202.2(a) (3) (1972).
40. *Nimmer on Copyright*, § 89.41.
41. S. 1359, 93d Cong., 1st Sess. (1973). The bill would add a subsection (d) to 17 U.S.C. § 9:

(d) A United States copyright secured by this title to citizens or subjects of foreign states or nations pursuant to subsection (b) or (c), and the right to secure such copyright, shall vest in the author of the work, his executors or administrators, or his voluntary assigns. For the purposes of this title, any such copyright or right to secure copyright shall be deemed to remain the property of the author, his executors or administrators, or his voluntary assigns, regardless of any law, decree or other act of a foreign state of nation which purports to divest the author or said other persons of the United States copyright in his work, or the right to secure it; and no action or proceeding for infringement of any such copyright, or the right to secure it, or common law right in such work, may be maintained by any state, nation, or person claiming rights in such copyright, right to secure copyright, or common law rights by virtue of any such law, decree, or other act.

Consider first the case of Soviet expropriation of the rights of a Soviet author. Legal authorization for such expropriation has long existed in Soviet law, both criminal and civil. Under criminal law, confiscation of property without compensation is a possible penalty for a number of crimes.[42] Under civil law property illegally obtained or used may be confiscated under certain circumstances without compensation, while property needed for public use (including copyrights) may be expropriated with the payment of compensation.[43] One may consider two possible circumstances: where the expropriation is with adequate compensation, and where there is in fact confiscation without adequate compensation. In the latter circumstance a series of decisions makes it apparent that American courts would not recognize the confiscation either on the grounds that the situs of the right involved is in the United States, so that the Soviet government lacked the power to expropriate, or on the theory that it violated United States or state public policy.[44] A taking by the Soviet government with compensation seems quite unlikely. If such a taking were to occur, however, the doctrines just mentioned might well still be applied, though the argument for them would be weaker. In both the above situations, however, a third argument is applicable based on the concurring opinion in a recent leading case. This opinion argued that a copyright acquired solely for the purpose of suppressing publication of a work should not be enforced.[45] Thus the Soviet state might find itself without an enforceable copyright.

Much more likely and more dangerous is the possibility that the Soviet state might bring pressure on a Soviet author to proceed in his own name against publication of his work in the United States. The use of just such pressure was reported in a French case a few years ago.[46] In 1965 a Soviet writer, Anatoly Kuznetsov, sued a French publisher who had brought out an unauthorized version of his novel *The Continuation of a Legend*. He won the lawsuit. But in 1969, after defecting to England, he petitioned to have the judgment set aside on the ground that he in fact had had no objection to the publication but had been forced to sue by Soviet authorities.

If it were shown that an author was acting under duress or had acted under duress in granting a power of attorney, a court would be certain to give no legal effect to the actions performed under duress. The problem is

42. Such confiscation might occur, for instance, if an author was found to have violated such articles of the Russian Republic Criminal Code as 78 (contraband) or 88 (illegal foreign currency dealings).

43. Fundamental Principles of Civil Legislation, arts. 14, 31, 106.

44. United States v. Pink, 315 U.S. 203 (1942); Republic of Iraq v. First National City Bank, 353 F.2d 47 (2d Cir. 1965), *cert. denied*, 382 U.S. 1027 (1966), notwithstanding; First National City Bank v. Banco National de Cuba, 315 U.S. 203, 92 Sup. Ct. 1808 (1972).

45. Rosemont Industries v. Random House, 306 F.2d 303; 311 (1966), *cert. denied*, 385 U.S. 1009, 87 S. Ct. 714 (1967).

46. Samuel Pisar, *Coexistence and Commerce* (New York, 1970), p. 364 and p. 526, n. 10, citing *Daily Telegraph* (London), August 6, 1969, and *Le monde*, August 8, 1969.

that in the Soviet Union duress can take many forms that may escape detection and proof abroad. A foreign court may thus have no easy way to distinguish an author who is legitimately holding out to bargain for higher royalties from one who is acting under severe pressures from the Soviet state. One procedure in such circumstances would be to require the Soviet author to testify in person. This remedy would not be practical in all cases, however, because the expense of personal testimony might exceed the value of the copyright involved. Besides, the testimony still might not be free of suspicion of duress because the author might wish to return to the Soviet Union or might have family there.

PROPOSALS

The fact that recent developments have not increased the possibilities of Soviet censorship of what is published in the United States does not mean that there is no problem. The Soviet government has in the past engaged in serious and often successful efforts to prevent certain types of Soviet writings from being published in the United States. The problem is by no means new, and the threat has always been serious. The new copyright developments have simply served to draw attention to that threat.

The main remedies seem to require the same basic qualities as those approaches that in the past have resulted in some moderation of Soviet government efforts to suppress certain writings. These qualities are courage on the part of the Soviet writers involved and continuous effort and some financial sacrifice by American writers and publishers. The specific steps that need be taken, however, may differ somewhat from those taken in the past.

The Soviet writer who is determined to have his work published in America must avoid becoming an unwilling accomplice in efforts by the Soviet state to suppress such a work. He can do so both indirectly and directly. He can secure permanent indirect protection if he can organize broad samizdat distribution in the USSR of copies of the work bearing no copyright notices. The work, through the provisions described above, will then be considered to have been published under the universal convention and American law and to be in the public domain. Neither the author, the Soviet government, nor anyone else will then be able to prevent further publication of an American edition.

The Soviet writer can also secure protection directly by making a written assignment of his copyright to an American publisher. Such an assignment would prevail over any later attempt by the Soviet government to seize his copyright or to force him to sue in his own name, since once he had assigned his rights there would be nothing left for the Soviet government to take or for him to use as a basis of suit.

As was mentioned above, perhaps the greatest threat would be a situation where a writer was pressured by the Soviet government to sue in his own name to suppress an American publication of his works. If a Soviet writer had not taken one of the steps suggested above to divest himself of his copyright, he would have the final alternative of refusing to bow to such government pressure and of accepting the unpleasant consequences.

American authors and publishers could cooperate to prevent Soviet censorship of what is published in the United States. They could bring political pressure by publicly stating their solidarity with Soviet writers and protesting any specific Soviet repressive measures. They could take vigorous legal action to fight any Soviet steps to use the American courts as instruments of censorship. Finally, if Soviet writers voluntarily divest themselves of their copyright by one of the means suggested above, so as to put their works in the public domain and thus forever out of reach of Soviet authorities, American publishers should not react by denying to such writers the royalties available to writers approved by the Soviet government.[47]

---

47. After this chapter was written, an excellent work was published on Soviet-American copyright relations, John Baumgarten, *U.S.-U.S.S.R. Copyright Relations under the Universal Copyright Convention* (New York, 1973). I have commented on that work in an article, "New Directions in US-USSR Copyright Relations," *American Journal of International Law* 68 (July 1974): 391. Some of the other material from that article is found, in different form, in the present chapter.

4

PEOPLE OF THE
DEMOCRATIC MOVEMENT

CHAPTER TEN / **HISTORY AND THE DEMOCRATIC**

OPPOSITION / ROBERT M. SLUSSER

Subtle, complex, and many-sided, the relationship between samizdat and history is a factor of central importance for an understanding of the dissident movement in the Soviet Union. The emergence of these materials is itself, of course, a historical event of undeniable importance, just as each uncensored text constitutes a primary historical source that casts light not only on its immediate context but on Soviet society as a whole.

Two of the major tenets of the democratic opposition—the citizen's right to know the truth about his nation's past, and society's need for open publicity (*glasnost'*) concerning the victims of arbitrary oppression—are at the same time basic to historical research. It was a historian, Peter Yakir, who formulated most clearly the rationale underlying the latter principle:

Under Stalin there was always an iron curtain and no one knew what was going on here. Millions of people were destroyed and nobody knew anything about it. Now we try to publicize every arrest, every dismissal. We see in this the most important role—that is, informing people what is going on in our country and about these illegal acts. We consider this the main task today.[1]

Some of the most eloquent and effective leaders of the democratic movement have been historians. In addition to Yakir, who until his arrest in June 1972 held a position in the Institute of History of the Academy of Sciences, there is Andrei Amalrik, whose decision to cast his lot with the dissidents is a direct result of the uncompromising views he holds on the need for integrity in historical research.[2] Finally, in Roy Medvedev's monumental study of Stalinism *K sudu istorii* (Let history judge), samizdat has contributed to the appearance of a major work of historical scholarship, one that in all probability would never otherwise have reached the world.[3]

A study of the relationship between samizdat and history can thus be expected to cast light both on the dissident movement and on history as a field and as a professional discipline in the Soviet Union. The present article pursues a twofold approach to the problem. First, it surveys the many and

1. Interview with William Cole, *Survey*, no. 77 (Autumn 1970), p. 138.
2. *Survey*, no. 74–75 (Winter–Spring 1970), p. 96.
3. On the genesis and background of the book see Robert M. Slusser, "A Soviet Historian Evaluates Stalin's Role in History," *American Historical Review* 77, no. 5 (December 1972): 1389–98.

various forms in which history has been reflected in samizdat texts. Second, it inquires into the samizdat and other unpublished sources on which Medvedev drew in writing *Let History Judge*. Some possible avenues of future development will also be explored briefly.

SAMIZDAT AND HISTORY

Russian History before 1917. In a 1971 essay on what he calls "historiosophical" tendencies in samizdat literature, Dmitri Pospielovsky noted: "Until the recent past the basic materials in samizdat were protests against concrete cases of official arbitrary acts" together with "condemnation of Stalinism and calls to return to Leninist legality."[4] The reasons for this situation are not difficult to understand. The study of history for its own sake is a luxury the producers and consumers of samizdat literature can ill afford. When every text constitutes a real and present danger to its writer, its copyist and distributor, and its readers, there is little incentive for that disinterested investigation of the past which, to some, constitutes the principal motive force behind historical research. Under the conditions of present-day Soviet society, it is a wonder that there is so much history in samizdat, relatively speaking, and that it is so varied and, on the whole, so high in quality.

Pre-1917 Russian history has served in samizdat principally for the insights it affords into the evolution of modern Soviet society and as a source of perspective on long-term treads in Russian history. As elsewhere in samizdat, one is never far here from the dominant theme of so many samizdat texts, the problem of Stalinism.

One of the most widely reprinted and most influential samizdat texts falls into this category: Grigory Pomerants's essay, "O roli nravstvennogo oblika lichnosti v zhizni istoricheskogo kollektiva" (On the role of individual moral outlook in the life of a historical group). Originally presented as a paper at a meeting in the Institute of Philosophy of the USSR Academy of Sciences, Pomerants's essay is a noteworthy attempt to evaluate Stalin's career in the long perspective of Russia's past. Appropriately, since Pomerants is a philosopher rather than a historian, the essay is valuable for the probing of serious moral problems rather than for its historical content, which is marred by a number of factual errors.[5]

---

4. D. Pospielovsky, "Etika i istoriia: Istoriosofskie tendentsii v Samizdate" [Ethics and history: Historiosophical tendencies in samizdat], *Grani*, no. 81 (1971), p. 155.

5. Pomerants's essay first appeared in the samizdat journal *Phoenix 1966* and was reprinted in *Grani*, no. 67 (1968), pp. 134–43; *AS*, no. 547. An English translation appears in Abraham Brumberg, ed., *In Quest of Justice* (New York, 1969), pp. 323–30, and *Problems of Communism* 17, no. 5 (September–October 1968): 29–32. Examples of mistakes are an erroneous quotation from Lenin's *Testament* and the dating of a trip to France by Bukharin in 1937 instead of 1936.

Another quasi-philosophical discussion of Stalin and stalinism in their historical context is "O natsional'nom styde veliko-rossov" (On the national shame of the Great Russians) by an author using the pseudonym Alexander Ivanov. It explores the historical antecedents of the invasion of Czechoslovakia in 1968 and portrays Stalin as an unabashed Russian nationalist.[6]

Perhaps the most penetrating analysis of the historical roots of Stalinism that has appeared in samizdat is the essay "Rossiiskii put' perekhoda k sotsializmu i ego rezultaty" (The Russian path of the transition to socialism and its results), which has been widely but erroneously attributed to the prominent Soviet economist Eugene Varga (whence its popular designation the "Varga 'Testament' ").[7] The essay uses sociological data within a Marxist framework to explain why stalinism developed in Soviet Russia.

For some Soviet dissidents the traditions of the nineteenth century Russian revolutionary movement have provided a model and an inspiration. Thus Yevgeny Kushev's poem cycle *Dekabristy* (The Decembrists) is a direct reference to the Decembrist movement, the starting point of organized dissidence in modern Russian history. The title of the samizdat journal in which Kushev's poems first appeared, *Russkoe slovo*, itself constitutes a borrowing from the nineteenth century tradition.[8] The same journal circulated an article by N. Eidelman dealing with the Russian populist N. A. Serno-Solov'evich.[9] An even more direct use of the Narodnik tradition was the circulation of a polemical pamphlet from the 1870s by Varfolomei Zaitsev.[10] The role of students in the Russian revolutionary movement has been explored in a book-length work by the pseudonymous Ivan Ruslanov.[11]

By contrast, the early twentieth century, down to 1917, has attracted relatively little attention from samizdat authors despite the crucial significance of this period in the background of the Russian Revolution and the shaping of the Bolshevik Party. One of the rare samizdat texts to deal with

6. "Stat'ia Alexandra Ivanova k 90-letiiu I. V. Stalin—'O natsional'nom styde velikorossov'," *Politicheskii dnevnik 1964–1970* (Amsterdam, 1972), no. 63 (December 1969), pp. 589–94 (this publication is hereafter cited as *Political Diary*).

7. *Phoenix 1966, AS* 166; reprinted in *Grani*, no. 68 (1968), pp. 134–53. English trans. *New Left Review*, no. 62 (July–August 1970). The true author is not known.

8. *Russkoe slovo*, July 1966. Translation in *Problems of Communism* 17, no. 5 (September–October 1968): 97–98. The editors of *Russkoe slovo*, considered it to be the continuation after a century's lapse of the original journal founded in 1859. The first samizdat issue was reprinted in *Grani*, no. 66 (1967), pp. 3–34.

9. *Russkoe slovo*, July, 1966. English trans. in *Problems of Communism* 17, no. 5 (September–October 1968): 68–70.

10. "Neistovyi kholui, ili manifest lakeizma" [The violent lackey, or a manifesto of servility], an underground pamphlet first published in Geneva in 1877 in the journal *Obshchoe delo* [Common cause]. Listed under "Novosti samizdata" [New materials in samizdat], *Khronika tekushchikh sobytii* [Chronicle of current events], no. 9. Reprinted in *Posev*, December 1969, p. 58. *Khronika* hereafter cited as *Chronicle*.

11. "Molodezh' v russkoi istorii" [Youth in Russian history], *AS* 539. Reprinted in *Grani*, no. 68, (1968), pp. 157–89; no. 80 (1971), pp. 191–215; and no. 81 (1971), pp. 180–221.

this period is an article by O. O. Gruzenberg on the Beiliss case, a *cause célèbre* in the Russia of Nicholas II involving the charge of ritual murder against a Jewish defendant.[12] Gruzenberg, who is identified in samizdat sources as one of the defenders of Beiliss, writes that the ruling circles of tsarist Russia knew that Beiliss was innocent but permitted the trial to continue because of anti-Semitic tendencies in the administration.

The most massive uncensored work drawing on materials from this prerevolutionary period is Alexander Solzhenitsyn's epic work-in-progress on Russia in war and revolution. The first part, a novel entitled *Avgust 1914 g.* [August 1914], has been published in the West.[13]

Lenin and the Early Period of Soviet Rule. Samizdat interest in Lenin's historical role, usually seen in relation to his responsibility for stalinism, has been manifested principally in the *Politicheskii dnevnik* (Political diary). This journal has made available articles on such subjects as "O pokushenii na Lenina 1 ianvaria 1918 goda" (On the attempt on Lenin's life of January 1, 1918); "V. I. Lenin o svobode pechati i intelligentsii (V. I. Lenin on the freedom of press and the intelligentsia); "Lenin o Sovetskoi vlasti i diktature proletariata" (Lenin on the Soviet power and the dictatorship of the proletariat; "Lenin o iubileiaka (Iz zapisok Prof. I. Dashkovskogo)" (Lenin on jubilees (from the notes of Prof. Dashkovsky); and "Stat'ia D. Iu. Zorinoi 'Bor'ba V. I. Lenina za monopoliiu vneshnei torgovli'" (An article by D. Iu. Zorina, "V. I. Lenin's struggle for the monopoly of foreign trade").[14] Also relevant to the historical role of Lenin is another *Political Diary* article, "Vospominaniia M. P. Iakubovicha o G. E. Zinov'ev" (M. P. Iakubovich's recollections concerning G. E. Zinoviev), one of the few samizdat articles in this area in which the Lenin-Stalin relationship is not stressed.[15]

What appears almost certainly to be a previously unpublished letter by Lenin to the Politburo demanding increased repression of the Orthodox Church appeared in the samizdat journal *Khronika tekushchikh sobytii* [Chronicle of current events] accompanied by a comment that clearly indicated the editors' sensitivity to the question of Lenin's responsibility for the system of repression in Soviet society:

The letter is top secret [*sverkhsekretno*] and it would be difficult to find a source from which it could have reached samizdat. Therefore this letter must not be taken completely on faith [*na veru*]; it would be good to carry through an intensive

12. O. O. Gruzenberg, "Sram. (Vospominaniia o dele Beilisa)" [Shame! (Recollections about the Beiliss case)]. First issued in the samizdat journal *Obshchestvennye problemy* [Social problems], no. 9 (January–February 1971); appearance noted in *Chronicle*, no. 19; reprinted in *Posev*, October 1971, p. 21.

13. Russian text, Paris, 1971; English trans., London and New York, 1972.

14. *Political Diary*, no. 9 (June 1965), pp. 110–11; no. 55 (April 1969), pp. 555–58; no. 63 (December 1969), pp. 644–50; no. 67 (April 1970), pp. 660–61; no. 72 (September 1972), pp. 764–78.

15. *Ibid.*, no. 63 (December 1969), pp. 618–29.

textological analysis of the letter. Obviously, official propaganda will not fail to declare the document a forgery. But in samizdat, where there is complete freedom of research, it is necessary not to fall into the opposite extreme; if the genuineness of the document is established, the image of the first chairman of the Sovnarkom [Council of People's Commissars] will become more sharply defined in the consciousness of the broad public.[16]

Together with its extensive current political commentary, the *Political Diary* has provided a series of stimulating historical studies and articles. Taking them in roughly chronological order, the subjects of these articles include intraparty opposition to the Brest-Litovsk treaty in 1918; the mutiny of the Czechoslovak Legion in Siberia in the same year; the "Leninist levy," which brought hundreds of thousands of new members into the CPSU after Lenin's death; Dzerzhinsky's alleged part in the intraparty struggle in 1925, based on what is presented as a previously unpublished letter from Dzerzhinsky to Stalin and Ordzhonikidze; and Konstantin Ordzhonikidze's recollections of the circumstances surrounding his brother Sergo's death in February 1937. Along with all this the *Political Diary* provided a brief and regrettably superficial analysis of the "Letter of an Old Bolshevik," which at least served to bring to the attention of a new generation this important document on the background of the Kirov assassination and the Great Purge.[17]

Among unpublished manuscripts the *Political Diary* has circulated is a memoir-article by E. Drabkina, who served as Iakov Sverdlov's secretary in the first period of Soviet rule and who wrote about her impressions of that far-gone time. Another memoir consists of excerpts from a manuscript by "D. B." that deals with the period of the industrialization drive and is notable for its sympathetic portrayal of Bukharin.[18]

Other uncensored historical studies include an article on an episode in the history of early Soviet counterespionage, and "Kto ubil Trotskogo?" (Who killed Trotsky?), which is noteworthy for its attempt to break one of

16. V. I. Lenin, "Pis'mo chlenam Politbiuro" [Letter to members of the Politburo], February 13, 1922; summary, *Chronicle*, no. 9; reprinted, *Posev*, December 1969, pp. 57–58.

17. "Iz istorii Brestkogo mira. O pozitsii F. E. Dzerzhinskogo" [From the history of the Brest peace (treaty of 1918). Concerning the position of F. E. Dzerzhinsky], *Political Diary*, no. 30 (March 1967), pp. 235–37; "Iz istorii Chekhoslovatskogo korpusa v Rossii" [From the history of the Czechoslovak corps in Russia], *ibid.*, no. 55 (April 1969), pp. 561–69; "O tak nazyvaemom 'leninskom prizyve' v partii v 1924 godu" [On the so-called 'Leninist levy' in the party in 1924], *ibid.*, no. 46 (July 1968), pp. 482–83; "Iz istorii bor'by s oppozitsiei v 1925 godu" [From the history of the struggle against the opposition in 1925], *ibid.*, no. 30 (March 1967), pp. 237–41; "Iz vospominanii K. K. Ordzhonikidze o svoem brate, S. Ordzhonikidze" [From the memoirs of K. K. Ordzhonikidze about his brother, S. Ordzhonikidze], *ibid.*, no. 55 (April 1969), pp. 539–43; "O tak nazyvaemom 'Pis'mo starogo bol'shevika'" [Concerning the so-called "Letter of an Old Bolshevik"], *ibid.*, no. 25 (October 1966), pp. 154–64.

18. "Iz stat'i E. Drabkinoi, 'Na drugoi den' posle revoliutsii'" [From E. Drabkina's article "The day after the revolution"], *ibid.*, no. 50 (November 1968); *AS* 1008 (listed in table of contents; text not available); "Iz vospominanii D. B-go" [From the memoirs of D. B.], *ibid.*, no. 55 (April 1969), pp. 543–47.

the strongest taboos in Soviet historiography as well as for its ringing conclusion: "Long live historical truth, and down with the falsifications of history."[19]

A document of great historical and psychological interest, Bukharin's last letter, was circulated in *Phoenix 1966* and was included in *Let History Judge*. The letter was communicated orally to Bukharin's wife, A. M. Larina, while he was in prison being prepared for trial, was memorized by her, and eventually was written down and sent to the party Central Committee.[20]

The Central Position of Stalin. No one can study the uncensored, informally published samizdat literature long without becoming aware that the historical problem most passionately debated in dissident intellectual circles in the Soviet Union is the historical role of Stalin. This is understandable, since most members of the democratic opposition identify the repressive system under which they live with Stalin's career and personality. Medvedev's *K sudu istorii* [Let history judge], the most substantial samizdat work dealing with this question, will be discussed below.

A work of unique value is Svetlana Allilueva's *Dvadtsat' pisem k drugu* [Twenty letters to a friend], which for all its naïveté and occasional factual errors provided for the first time a sympathetic but on occasion sharply revealing picture of Stalin as an individual.[21]

The original Russian text of the most famous as well as the most influential analysis of Stalinism, Khrushchev's "Secret Speech" to the Twentieth Congress of the Soviet Communist Party, has circulated in samizdat. The *Chronicle of Current Events* helped clarify the genesis of the speech with a news item concerning the expulsion from the party of A. V. Snegov, a former security police official who helped provide the archival materials on which Khrushchev drew in preparing the speech.[22]

Remarkably effective as a philosophical exploration of the roots of Stalinism is an anonymous essay, "Ob Oktiabr'skoi revoliutsii i sozdannoi eiu politicheskoi sisteme (Dialog)" (On the October Revolution and the political system which it established [a dialogue]). Excerpts from an unpublished study of the early stages of Stalin's career by an Old Bolshevik, V. E.

---

19. R. I. Pimenov, "Kak ia iskal shpiona Reili" [How I discovered the spy Reilly], *AS* 1089; Ye. M., "Kto ubil Trotskogo?" [Who killed Trotsky?], *Tetradi sotsialisticheskoi demokratii*, 1965; English trans. in *Problems of Communism* 17, no. 5 (September–October 1968): 78–79.
20. Roy Medvedev, *Let History Judge* (New York, 1972), pp. 183–84, under the title "To a Future Generation of Party Leaders."
21. English trans., New York and Evanston, 1968.
22. N. S. Khrushchev, "O kul'te lichnosti i ego posledstviiakh" [Concerning the cult of personality and its consequences], *AS* 460. For the expulsion of Snegov see *Chronicle*, No. 21, reprinted in *Posev* 27, no. 11 (November 1971): 6.

Gromov's "Stalin: Mysli i fakty" (Stalin: ideas and facts), have appeared in the *Political Diary*.[23]
One of the most famous contemporary attacks on Stalin, F. F. Raskol'nikov's devastating "Open Letter to Stalin" of August 17, 1939, has been circulated both as an individual text and as one of the historical documents incorporated into Medvedev's *Let History Judge*.[24]
A fairly extensive group of samizdat texts consists of "open letters" warning against the rehabilitation of Stalin and the reestablishment of his system of internal controls. Authors of letters of this kind include the historians Roy Medvedev, Peter Yakir, and Leonid Petrovsky, the writer Lidia Chukovskaya, retired Maj. Gen. Peter Grigorenko, former party members Alexei Kosterin and Lev Kopelev, and a group of forty-three children of purged but subsequently rehabilitated communist party leaders. Among these documents the most striking, and from the historian's point of view the most valuable, is Yakir's "Open Letter" to *Kommunist*, in which he details Stalin's crimes and calls for the institution of charges against him under the RSFSR Criminal Code. Of closely related interest is Yakir's letter to the Secretariat of the International Historians' Congress in Moscow, dated August 16, 1970, which proposes the addition of several topics for historical research to the congress's agenda, including a comparative study of Stalin's and Hitler's roles in history.[25]

---

23. *Political Diary*, no. 55 (April 1969), pp. 558–61; "Iz rukopisi V. E. Gromova 'Stalin' (mysli i fakty)" [From V. E. Gromov's manuscript "Stalin (ideas and facts)"], *Political Diary*, no. 43 (April 1968), pp. 375–82.

24. Cited in Peter Reddaway, ed., *Uncensored Russia* (New York, 1972), p. 484; French trans. in *Samizdat 1*, pp. 93–101; text in *Let History Judge*, pp. 256–57.

25. (*a*) R. Medvedev, "Otkrytoe pis'mo v zhurnal 'Kommunist'" [Open letter to *Kommunist*], *AS* 131; reprinted, *Posev* 25, no. 6 (June 1969): 25–31, and *ibid.*, no. 7 (July 1969): 25–34.

(*b*) Peter Yakir, "Otkrytoe pis'mo v redaktsiiu zhurnala 'Kommunist' o reabilitatsii Stalina" [Open letter to the editors of *Kommunist* concerning the rehabilitation of Stalin], *AS* 99; *Posev* 25, no. 7, (July 1969): 57–60; English trans., *Problems of Communism* 18, no. 4–5 (July–October 1969): 102–4; *Survey*, no. 70–71 (Winter–Spring 1969), pp. 261–69.

(*c*) L. Petrovsky, "Pis'mo v TsK KPSS o reabilitatsii Stalina" [Letter to the CC of the CPSU concerning the rehabilitation of Stalin], *AS* 130; original text and English trans. in *Za prava cheloveka* (Frankfurt, 1969), pp. 45–98.

(*d*) Lidia Chukovskaya, "Pis'mo v redaktsiiu 'Izvestii'" [Letter to the editors of *Izvestiia*], *AS* 116.

(*e*) P. Grigorenko, "Pis'mo v redaktsiiu zhurnala 'Voprosy istorii KPSS'" [Letter to the editors of *Questions of the History of the CPSU*], *AS* 157; reprinted, London and Toronto, 1971.

(*f*) A. Kosterin, "Pis'mo v Politbiuro KPSS" [Letter to the Politburo of the CPSU], AS 62; English trans. in Cornelia Gerstenmaier, ed., *Voices of the Silent* (New York, 1972), pp. 411–14.

(*g*) L. Z. Kopelev, "Pis'mo sotrudniku venskogo zhurnala 'Tagebukh' o vozmozhnostiakh reabilitatsii Stalina" [Letter to a reporter on the Vienna journal *Tagebuch* concerning the possibilities of the rehabilitation of Stalin], *AS* 124.

(*h*) "Pis'mo 43 detei kommunistov, neobsnovanno repressirovannykh Stalinym, v TsK KPSS ob opasnosti neostalinizma" [Letter from 43 children of Communists unjustifiably purged by Stalin to the CC of the CPSU on the danger of neostalinism], *AS* 134.

Stalin's Role in World War II. Problems concerning Soviet participation in the Second World War, with special reference to Stalin's role as a wartime leader, have attracted the attention of a number of writers. One of the most noteworthy items in this area is a documentary compilation, "K voprosu o zakliuchenii sovetsko-germanskogo pakt o nenapadenii v avguste 1939 goda" (On the question of the conclusion of the Soviet-German nonaggression pact in August 1939). It provides Russian translations of six documents taken from the German diplomatic archives. Among them is the full text, never before published in the Soviet Union, of the secret supplementary protocol to the August 23 pact in which the signatories divided Eastern Europe into spheres of influence. The seventh and final document in the compilation is an excerpt from Vyacheslav Molotov's speech to the Supreme Soviet on October 31, 1939, in which he offered a justification for the pact.[26]

The circumstances surrounding the German attack of June 22, 1941, including Stalin's personal responsibility for the unpreparedness of the Soviet forces, are the subject of Ernst Henri's "Open Letter to Ilya Ehrenburg" of May 30, 1965.[27] The same problem is illuminated in a fascinating document, the transcript of a discussion in the Institute of Marxism-Leninism on February 16, 1966, of A. M. Nekrich's book *1941. 22 iunia* [June 22, 1941].[28] Nekrich's book brought to bear on the problem much information from Western sources not previously available to Soviet readers, and the discussion centered around the damage this new information might do to the Soviet public image not only of Stalin but the Soviet leadership in general.

Two samizdat articles focus on problems of Soviet policy formulation in terms of the role of Marshal S. M. Shtemenko, Stalin's chief of the General Staff. One, by a war veteran named Peter Dudochkin, was first given as a paper at a conference in the Kalinin Military-Scientific Society on December 11, 1968. The other argues that Shtemenko's book *General'nyi shtab vo vremia voiny* (The General Staff during the war), though designed to rehabilitate Stalin as a wartime leader, actually provides extensive materials for destroying the Stalin myth.[29]

(*i*) Peter Yakir, "Pis'mo v Sekretariat Mezhdunarodnogo kongressa istorikov v Moskve" [Letter to the Secretariat of the International Historians' Congress in Moscow], *AS* 640.

26. Contents listed in the *Chronicle of Current Events*, no. 10 (Reddaway, *Uncensored Russia*, p. 362); summarized, *Posev* 26, no. 1 (January 1970): 5.

27. Ernst Henri, "Otkrytoe pis'mo pisateliu I. Erenburgu" [Open letter to the writer I. Ehrenburg], *Phoenix 1966*, pp. 249–57; reprinted, *Grani* 22, no. 63 (1967): 192–203.

28. Nekrich's book was published in Moscow in 1965. For a translation of it and of the principal items in the controversy that arose over it, see Vladimir Petrov, *"June 22, 1941": Soviet Historians and the German Invasion* (Columbia, S.C., 1968).

29. Peter Dudochkin, "O glubine mysli, ubeditel'nosti i neoproverzhimosti slova" [Concerning depth of thought, convincingness, and irrefutability of the word]; R. Lert, "Shtemenko protiv Shtemenko" ["Shtemenko against Shtemenko"]; both listed under "Novosti samizdata" in *Chronicle*, no. 13, and in *Posev*, June 1970, pp. 36–37.

One of the most eloquent samizdat documents in this area is General Grigorenko's letter to the editor of a history journal. The letter takes up the controversy over Nekrich's book; its thrust is summarized in its samizdat title, "Sokrytie istoricheskoi pravdy—prestuplenie pered narodom" (Concealment of the historical truth is a crime against the people).[30]

The Khrushchev Era and After. The period of late stalinism, 1945–53, has thus far attracted little attention from samizdat authors, a situation strikingly parallel to that in the West. Also neglected is the period of the struggle for power following Stalin's death, 1953–57. By contrast, the Khrushchev era, 1957–64, and Khrushchev as an individual have been subjected to scrutiny by a number of samizdat writers. Short articles in the *Political Diary* have examined "N. S. Khrushchev kak gosudarstvennyi deiatel' i kak chelovek" (N. S. Khrushchev as a government figure and as a man), which records two attempts on Khrushchev's life not reported in the Soviet press; "Ob okruzhenii N. S. Khrushcheva" (On Khrushchev's associates), which emphasizes nepotism as a factor in Khrushchev's choice of advisers; "O iunskom plenume Tsk. KPSS v 1957 godu" (On the June 1957 plenum of the CPSU CC, (Central Committee of the Communist Party of the Soviet Union), a factual summary of the meeting at which Khrushchev overturned the coalition that had been formed against him in the party Presidium; and "O vneshnei politike N. S. Khrushcheva" (On N. S. Khrushchev's foreign policy), which stresses the risk-taking characteristic of his style.[31]

An interesting sidelight on the June 1957 meeting is contained in a samizdat article on Dmitri Shepilov, a former foreign minister. He switched to the anti-Khrushchev coalition before the final showdown and thereby earned special obloquy in party histories published during the Khrushchev period.[32]

Another contribution to the history of the Khrushchev period is a summary, apparently genuine, of Anastas Mikoyan's report to the Central Committee plenum in October 1964 explaining the reasons for Khrushchev's overthrow. A short notice on the Twenty-second Congress in 1961 provides the useful information, evidently based on testimony by delegates to the congress, that it was Khrushchev personally who raised the question of the "Antiparty Group" (i.e., the anti-Khrushchev coalition of 1957) and with it the subject of Stalin's crimes, thereby violating previous agreements in the party leadership and confronting the congress with a totally unexpected situation.[33]

30. Grigorenko, "Pis'mo v redaktsiiu."
31. *Political Diary*, no. 3 (December 1964), pp. 15–16; *Ibid.*, no. 9, pp. 106–9.
32. V. Gusarov, "I primknuvshii k nim Shepilov" [And Shepilov who joined them], *AS* 482.
33. "A. I. Mikoian ob Oktiabr'skom plenume TsK KPSS i o Khrushcheve" [A. I. Mikoyan on the October plenum of the CC CPSU and about Khrushchev], *Political Diary*, no. 3

Although samizdat provides much raw material for the historian of the Brezhnev-Kosygin period, historical materials as such are still infrequent. A noteworthy exception is an item in *Political Diary* that analyzes the conflict in the party leadership over the question of whether or not to rehabilitate Stalin as reflected in the speech Brezhnev delivered for the centennial of Lenin's birth. Also relevant is a well-informed report in the same journal of the abortive official plans for celebrating Stalin's ninetieth birthday in 1969 with extensive laudatory propaganda and the publication of a four-volume set of Stalin's selected writings.[34] Political developments for the period 1965–68 have been analyzed by B. Talantov in an article entitled "Sovetskoe obshchestvo" (Soviet society),[35] while the same period has been scrutinized in the light of the historical traditions of Bolshevism by an anonymous author in an article entitled "Transformatsiia bol'shevizma" (The transformation of Bolshevism).[36]

The Literature of Repression. In the long run the rich and extensive writings of samizdat authors on the system of repression may well come to be regarded as their greatest single contribution to history. Here one finds some of the truly unforgettable masterpieces of samizdat: Peter Yakir's laconic, harrowing account of his coming of age in Stalin's prisons and camps; Yevgenia Ginzburg's unsurpassed narrative of the impact of the Great Purge on a loyal rank-and-file party member; Andrei Amalrik's vivid and observant prisoner's-eye view of Soviet society in the mid-1960s; and Anatoly Marchenko's sobering panorama of the post-Stalin camps.[37] Overshadowing all other works in this field and warranting comparison with Dostoevsky's *From the House of the Dead* is Solzhenitsyn's fundamental study of the concentration camp system, *Arkhipelag Gulag 1918–1956* [The Gulag Archipelago, 1918–1956]. Like his short novel *One Day in the Life of Ivan Denisovich*, the only one of his novels which has been passed for publication by the Soviet censhorship, *Arkhipelag Gulag* is based in part on

(December 1964), pp. 5–8; "XXII-ii s"ezd KPSS" [The Twenty-second Congress of the CPSU], *ibid.*, no. 33 (June 1967), p. 280.

34. "Prazdnovanie stoletnego iubileia V. I. Lenina" [Celebration of the centennial jubilee of V. I. Lenin], *ibid.*, no. 67 (April 1970), pp. 661–64; "K predstoiashchemu iubileiu I. V. Stalina" [On the approaching Stalin anniversary], *ibid.*, no. 10; English trans. in Reddaway, *Uncensored Russia*, pp. 423–24.

35. *Posev*, September 1969, pp. 35–41.

36. Summarized, *Chronicle*, no. 8; reprinted, *Posev*, 2d special issue, December 1969, p. 39; Reddaway, *Uncensored Russia*, pp. 362–63.

37. Yakir, "Detstvo v tiur'me" [A childhood in prison], *AS* 1050; translation, London and New York, 1973. Ginzburg, *Krutoi marshrut, Phoenix 1966*; reprinted, *Grani*, vol. 22, no. 64 (1967), pp. 81–111, no. 65, pp. 51–99, no. 66, pp. 45–151; vol. 23, no. 67 (1968), pp. 71–88, no. 68, pp. 9–100; English trans., *Journey into the Whirlwind* (London and New York, 1967). Amalrik, "Nezhelannoe puteshestvie v Sibir'" [Involuntary journey to Siberia], *AS* 450; Russian text, New York, 1970; German trans. Hamburg, 1970; English trans., New York, 1970. Marchenko, *Moi pokazaniia* [My testimony] (Frankfurt, 1969); English trans., London and New York, 1969.

the author's personal experiences as a labor camp inmate, but it also incorporates first-hand data from several hundred other former prisoners.[38]

A special place in the literature about prisons and concentration camps is held by Varlam Shalamov's biting stories of prison life. His skillful narrative technique places him in the direct line of Russian prose masters from Gogol to Gorky. A prison report not unworthy of comparison with that of Yevgenia Ginzburg is Yekaterina Olitskaya's memoirs. This document provides an insight into the fate of one of the principal non-Bolshevik socialist parties, the Left Social Revolutionaries, during the pre-Stalinist stage in the evolution of the camp system. As Dmitri Pospielovsky has pointed out, Mme Olitskaya's book thus makes an indirect but nonetheless significant contribution to the great debate within the democratic opposition concerning Lenin's responsibility for the establishment of the system of repression.[39]

One samizdat journal, fittingly entitled *Prestuplenie i nakazanie* (Crime and punishment), has undertaken the herculean task of recording the names and actions of jailers and concentration camp officials, as well as those of Soviet citizens in various walks of life whose collaboration with the secret police played a sinister role in the purges.[40]

Some of the worst of the post-Stalin concentration camps, those in the Mordvinian Autonomous Republic, are described in Valentin Moroz's "Reportazh iz zapovednika imeni Beriia" (Report from the Beria reservation). Framed as a letter to deputies of the Ukrainian Supreme Soviet, it includes a striking passage on the suppression of Ukrainian historical scholarship by the KGB.[41] Another samizdat account of the Mordvinian camps is in Yuri Ivanov's personality sketches and biographies of fellow prisoners. A cycle of poems was issued in samizdat by Alexander Petrov-Agatov, a former member of the Union of Soviet Writers who spent from 1947 to 1967 in labor camps and was then rearrested after a single year's freedom.[42]

A useful contribution to an understanding of the techniques used by the secret police in preparing the show trials of the 1930s is Mikhail Yakubovich's "Pis'mo General'nomu Prokuratora SSSR" (Letter to the general

38. Pts. 1 and 2: Paris, 1973; English trans., New York, 1974. Pts. 3 and 4: Paris, 1974. See also the extract from Roy Medvedev's critique of the work—the first responsible evaluation of it by a Soviet historian—in the *New York Times*, September 7, 1973, p. 3.

39. Shalamov, "Rasskazy iz zhizni ze-ka" [Tales from the life of a prisoner], *Grani*, no. 76 (1970), pp. 16–83; no. 77, pp. 15–48. Olitskaya, *Vospominaniia* [Memoirs], *AS* 461; reprinted, Frankfurt, 1971 (2 vols.). Pospielovsky, "Razvenchannyi Lenin. O vospominaniiakh Ekateriny Olitskoi" [Lenin debunked. On the memoirs of Yekaterina Olitskaya"], *Posev*, February 1972, pp. 40–46.

40. Issues no. 2, 3, 5, and 7 have been listed in the *Chronicle*.

41. *AS* 249; English trans. in Michael Browne, ed., *Ferment in the Ukraine*, pp. 119–53.

42. Ivanov, "Lagpunkt 17-a," *AS* 488. Petrov-Agatov, "S nachala kolyma; potom Mordoviia" [From Kolyma to Mordovia], excerpts, *Grani*, no. 80 (1971), pp. 104–6; *Posev*, May 1961, pp. 54–56; *ibid.*, June 1971, pp. 54–56.

procurator of the USSR). It explains in absorbing detail the processes by which the defendants in the 1931 Menshevik trial, including Yakubovich, were prepared for their roles in court. A. S. Volpin's article "Glasnost' sudoproizvodstva" (Publicity of court proceedings) is a study of the secret police's and procuracy's procedure of obtaining false evidence by means of various forms of duress.[43]

The use of mental hospitals under control of the secret police, a tsarist practice revived and expanded by the post-Stalin regimes, has been studied in a number of samizdat works by authors themselves its victims. The rationale behind this system has been concisely and accurately defined by Vladimir Bukovsky:

The fact is that the inmates, the patients . . . , the prisoners, are people who have done things which from the point of view of the authorities are crimes but which are not criminal from the point of view of the law. And, in order in some way to isolate them, to punish them in some way, such people are declared to be insane and are detained as patients in these mental prison-hospitals.[44]

The biologist Zhores Medvedev's experience of forced incarceration in a mental hospital forms the basis of his book *Kto sumasshedshii?*, translated under the title *A Question of Madness*, which illuminates in graphic detail the working of the system.[45] The historian Roy Medvedev, Zhores's twin brother, has also written on the subject.[46]

Useful for an understanding of how the system developed is an open letter by S. P. Pisarev. A party member, Pisarev had the foolhardy courage to write directly to Stalin in January 1953 calling for a review of the "doctors' plot." He paid for his boldness with a three-year jail term, including one year in the notorious Serbsky Institute in Leningrad. The same subject forms the basis for M. A. Naritsa's *Prestuplenie i nakazanie* (Crime and punishment), one of a series of samizdat texts on the prison system by this much-imprisoned writer.[47]

An anonymous author, in an article entitled "Nevezhestvo na sluzhbe proizvola" (Ignorance at the service of arbitrary rule), has sketched the historical background of the use of mental hospitals for political repression from its nineteenth century origins to the recent past.[48]

43. Yakubovich, *AS* 150; shortened translation in R. Medvedev, *Let History Judge*, pp. 125–31. Volpin, *AS* 657.

44. Interview with William Cole, *Survey*, no. 77 (Autumn 1970), p. 140. Conditions inside a prison-hospital are described in *ibid.*, pp. 140–42. A samizdat manuscript by Bukovsky on the prison-psychiatric system has been published in French translation under the title *Une nouvelle maladie mentale en URSS: l'opposition* (Paris, 1971).

45. Translation, London and New York, 1971.

46. "Compulsory psychiatric treatment for political purposes," *AS* 1265, listed in Albert Boiter, "Report on new samizdat: first half of 1973," Radio Liberty Report, July 16, 1973, p. 6.

47. Pisarev, "V Prezidium AMN SSSR" [To the Academy of Medical Sciences of the USSR]; reprinted, *Posev*, November 1970, pp. 35–44. Naritsa, *Posev*, August 1971, pp. 35–42.

48. *AS* 1104; translated in *Survey* 19, no. 4 (Autumn 1973): 45–65.

To judge by the samizdat materials available in the West, their authors have done relatively little to study the actions, careers, and personalities of secret police officials. Several articles or documentary publications, some noted here, have dealt with incidents in Dzerzhinsky's career, but there seems to have been no sustained effort to understand his role as founder of the secret police. His colleagues and successors—Vyacheslav Menzhinsky, Henrikh Yagoda, Nikolai Ezhov, and Lavrenti Beria—have been almost ignored in official and unofficial Soviet literature alike. Perhaps the victims of the secret police have been too concerned with the immediate impact of their personal experiences to have much time to ponder the motives of the men (other than Stalin) who were responsible for their fate. It does remain surprising, nevertheless, to find virtually nothing in samizdat relevant to such recent secret police chiefs as Ivan A. Serov, Alexander N. Shelepin, Vladimir E. Semichastny, or Yuri V. Andropov.

The samizdat journal *Prestuplenie i nakazanie* (Crime and punishment) provides much that is of value for studying the operations of the secret police at lower levels. The *Chronicle of Current Events* has also frequently served the cause of history by publishing details on secret police operations.

One Chekist who has been singled out for special attention in samizdat writings is Andrei Sverdlov, the son of Lenin's colleague and staunch supporter Yakov Sverdlov, first organizer of the party secretariat. The younger Sverdlov, a secret police official for many years, acquired a reputation as one of the most treacherous, cruel, and vindictive members of that organization, with a special talent for the entrapment of young party members and his own friends and acquaintances as well as Bolsheviks from his father's generation.[49]

Other Areas. Turning to other themes, samizdat includes several penetrating analyses of long-term trends in Soviet society and politics, notably an essay by the nuclear physicist Valery Chalidze, "Klassovaia diskriminatsiia v sovetskom prave" (Class discrimination in Soviet law).[50] An author using the pseudonym Sergei Razumnyi has contributed a stimulating essay, "Rasstanovka politicheskikh sil v KPSS" [The disposition of political forces in the CPSU].[51]

Authors of samizdat have shown scant interest in the history of the international communist movement or in relations between the Soviet Union and its communist ally-satellites. The Brezhnev-Kosygin regime's decision to invade Czechoslovakia in 1968 touched off a series of demonstra-

49. "O neobychnoi sud'be chlenov sem'i i rodstvennikov Ya. M. Sverdlova" [On the unusual fate of members of the family and relatives of Ya. M. Sverdlov], *Political Diary*, no. 55 (April 1969), pp. 526–32; shortened trans., *Survey* 18, no. 3 (Summer 1972): 214–15.

50. Summarized in *Chronicle*, no. 11; reprinted, *Posev*, April 1970, p. 47.

51. *AS* 570; reprinted in *Posev*, May 1971, pp. 41–46; English trans., *Survey* 17, no. 2 (Spring 1971): 66–73.

tions and protests in the Soviet Union, which found their reflection in these materials.[52] But no general study of intracommunist relations, either party or government, has appeared. Hardly an exception is a brief note in *Political Diary* entitled "Oktiabr'skaia revoliutsiia i mirovaia sotsialisticheskaia revoliutsiia" (The October Revolution and the world socialist revolution), which argues that the Bolshevik Revolution actually delayed the development of the world revolutionary movement.[53]

Minority Nationalities and Parties. Some of the most valuable informally published materials, from the historian's point of view, deal with Soviet nationality policy. Three minority groups—the Ukrainians, the Crimean Tatars, and the Jews—have contributed the lion's share of this material. Other minority nationalities whose special problems have been treated include the Moslem peoples of Central Asia and the Hutsuls, an isolated ethnic group inhabiting the western Ukraine.[54]

While all these materials on minority groups offer something of value for the historian, what is directly relevant to the study of Soviet Russian history as a whole is the samizdat that raises broad questions of Soviet nationality policy as it has developed from the October Revolution to the present.

Perhaps the outstanding work of this kind is Ivan Dzyuba's *Internationalizma chi rusifikatsiia?* [Internationalism or Russification?]. This work makes a sustained effort to show that Soviet nationality policy under Stalin and his successors has departed from Leninist principles. It can thus be regarded as a contribution to the controversy over the relationship between Lenin and the Stalinist system, with the distinctive merit that in focusing on the nationality question Dzyuba has hit on one of the few policy spheres in which palpable differences between Lenin's and Stalin's policies can effectively be demonstrated.[55]

An essay on party ideologist Mikhail Suslov by a writer identified simply by his last name, Shel'ga, is relevant in this context. It concentrates on Suslov's complicity in carrying out repressive policies against national minorities during the Stalin period.[56]

An encouraging sign of a willingness on the part of some members of the democratic opposition to broaden the scope of historical investigation has been the appearance of several studies of non-Bolshevik socialist parties and

52. For example, A. Kosterin, "Pis'mo v Politbiuro KPSS" [Letter to the Politburo of the CPSU], October 24, 1968, *AS* 62, in which he resigns his CPSU membership in protest over the return of Stalinist methods.

53. Pp. 82–84, *AS* 1010.

54. Iu. B. Osmanov, "Prodolzhenie rasskaza" [The continuation of a story], *AS* 91, concerns attempts by the censorship to suppress his works about the Muslim areas of the USSR. On the Hutsuls, see V. Moroz, "Khronika soprotivleniia" [A chronicle of resistance], *AS* 411.

55. Translation, London, 1968.

56. "Suslov, M. A.," first issued in the samizdat journal *Kolokol*, no. 40; reprinted in *Posev* 24, no. 1 (January 1968): 12–13.

tendencies. *Political Diary*, for example, has made available an extract from the memoirs of I. K. Kakhovskaya, one of the last surviving Left SRs, who, in the period after the Twenty-second CPSU Congress, sent an account of the fate of the party's leaders to the CPSU Central Committee, the Council of Ministers, and the Procuracy.[57] Further light on the fate of the Left SR leaders has been cast by Yekaterina Olitskaya's memoirs (above, p. 339).

Various Historical Genres. Memoirs of general historical interest have not been numerous in samizdat, but one of the few to appear, Nadezhda Mandelshtam's *Vospominaniia ob O. E. Mandel'shtame* (Recollections of O. E. Mandelshtam), has already achieved recognition as a classic. In addition to its obvious value for a study of the life and work of the great Russian poet, Mme Mandelshtam's book provides what may well prove to be the sharpest analysis ever written concerning changes in the psychology, world-view, and values in Russian society during the first two decades of Soviet rule.[58]

In the field of the history of science, samizdat literature has been surprisingly weak—with one shining exception. The weakness is surprising in view of the prominence of scientists in the democratic opposition. But men like the nuclear physicist Andrei Sakharov and his colleague Valery Chalidze have preferred to assist the democratic movement through broad appeals for the defense of human rights in Soviet society and have drawn a sharp line between their work as scientists and their civil rights activities.[59] No doubt a prime consideration in this stance was the realization that anything they wrote for samizdat that touched on their work as scientists could be used against them by the authorities, thus endangering their usefulness to the democratic movement.

The great exception is, of course, Zhores Medvedev's book *Biologicheskaia nauka i kul't lichnosti* [Biological science and the cult of personality], which is a major contribution to the intellectual history of Stalinist Russia.[60]

The democratic opposition itself as a subject of historical study has given rise to some of the most effective uncensored writings. Outstanding in this category is the first part of Andrei Amalrik's *Prosushchestvuet li Sovetskii Soiuz do 1984 goda?* (Will the Soviet Union survive until 1984?), which has

57. "Iz istorii partii i rukovoditelei levykh eserov (zapiski i zaiavleniia I. K. Kakhovskoi)" [From the history of the party and leaders of the Left SRs (notes and declaration by I. K. Kakhovskaya)], *Political Diary*, no. 67 (April 1970), pp. 705–26.
58. English trans. under the titles *Hope against Hope* (New York, 1971) and *Hope Abandoned* (New York, 1973).
59. When the official attack on him sharpened in August and September 1973, Sakharov for the first time revealed some of his activities as a scientist, including his warning to Khrushchev in 1961 concerning the dangers of fallout from nuclear testing. See his article "This, Not That," *New York Times*, September 12, 1973, p. 43.
60. *AS* 452; republished, *Grani*, no. 70 (1969), pp. 127–66; no. 71 (1969), pp. 78–161; English trans., New York and London, 1969, under the title *The Rise and Fall of T. D. Lysenko*.

been acclaimed by Peter Yakir as being "in fact, the only [analysis] of such breadth and logic."[61]

A more recent article, "Iz istorii samizdata" (From the history of samizdat), provides a summary of the field from the first underground organizations in the post-1945 period through the early 1960s.[62] A brochure, "Intelligentsiia i demokraticheskoe dvizhenie" (The intelligentsia and the democratic movement), by K. Vol'nyi, has been described as characterized by the "naive messianism [which was] typical of the prerevolutionary intelligentsia in its earlier period." A document whose historical importance cannot yet be accurately assessed is the *Programma demokraticheskogo dvizheniia Sovetskogo Soiuza* (Program of the Democratic Movement of the Soviet Union), which purports to be based on negotiations among representatives of the Democratic Movement from Russia, the Ukraine, and the Baltic republics.[63]

History as a Professional Discipline. A small but significant group of samizdat texts deals directly with problems faced by Soviet historians in their research. One of these is Peter Yakir's letter to the Secretariat of the International Historians' Congress in Moscow (above, p. 335).

A clear recognition of the vital role historians must play in any broad civil rights movement in the Soviet Union is shown in an essay by A. Antipov, "Ot brozheniia umov—k umstvennomu dvizheniiu" (From a ferment of intellects to an intellectual movement). Analyzing the needs of the demo-cratic opposition, Antipov writes, "We need . . . basic studies dealing with . . . social, legal, moral, cultural . . . problems of our society, objective works on its entire history. . . . We must fearlessly study our own social organism—that is the urgent task which can only be carried out in common, under the conditions of live and free discussion."[64]

One of the most direct statements in samizdat of the historian's duty to search for and analyze the truth about the past objectively is a letter from a group of prominent historians to *Izvestiia*. That newspaper refused to publish it, but it appeared in *Political Diary*.[65]

The transcript of the discussion at a historians' conference of Nekrich's book on the outbreak of the Soviet-German war was mentioned above (p. 336). An equally revealing document that has been circulated informally is the transcript of a discussion concerning the mockup (*maket*) or draft

61. Amalrik, Amsterdam, 1969; English trans., *Survey*, no. 73 (Autumn 1969), pp. 48–79, and New York and Evanston, Ill., 1970, rev. ed. 1971. Yakir, "Otkrytoe pis'mo Andreiu Amalriku" [Open letter to Andrei Amalrik], *Chronicle*, no. 13; reprinted, *Posev*, June 1970, pp. 40–41; English trans., *Survey*, no. 74–75 (Winter–Spring 1970), pp. 110–11.

62. *Survey*, no. 77 (Autumn 1970), pp. 136–39.

63. Vol'nyi, *ibid.*, no. 3 (Summer 1971), pp. 180–91; see also Pospielovsky, "Etika," p. 178. *Programma*, Amsterdam, 1970.

64. Quoted in Pospielovsky, "Etika," p. 156.

65. "Pis'mo gruppy vidnykh istorikov v gazeta 'Izvestiia'" [Letter from a group of prominent historians to *Izvestiia*], *Political Diary*, no. 9 (June 1965), pp. 83–88.

version of the third volume of the *History of the CPSU*. The discussion, held in the Institute of Marxism-Leninism in 1966, developed into a struggle between neo-Stalinist and more objective historians over the presentation of evidence on such matters as the position adopted by Zinoviev, Kamenev, and Stalin on the eve of the October Revolution. The neo-Stalinist group blocked any attempt to bring the volume's treatment of the subject more closely into line with the facts.[66]

An important function of samizdat has been to acquaint its readers with contemporary Western historical writings to which they have otherwise been denied access. For example, translations of two chapters of Robert Conquest's book on the purges, *The Great Terror*, have been circulated.[67] So has a review of the book first published in *Encounter*.[68] For a time *Political Diary* provided a regular series of reviews of historical works by Western or émigré writers, including A. Avtorkhanov, Werner Hoffman, Leonard Schapiro, and Alexander Werth.[69]

The thirst for unbiased and objective historical analysis of Soviet history has been partially satisfied by the circulation of a Russian translation of a book by the West German historian Georg von Rauch, *A History of Soviet Russia*.[70] Along somewhat the same line, an article from the 1930s by the Cadet leader Pavel Milyukov, "The truth about Bolshevism," has been circulated by *Political Diary* with an editorial note describing it as "not without interest in many respects."[71]

66. "Obsuzhdenie maketa 3. toma istorii KPSS v Institute Marksizma-Leninizma pri TsK KPSS s uchastiem starykh bol'shevikov" [Discussion of the mockup of the third volume of the *History of the CPSU* in the Institute of Marxism-Leninism under the CC, CPSU, with the participation of Old Bolsheviks], *Phoenix 1966, AS* 466; reprinted, *Grani*, no. 65 (1967), pp. 129–56.

67. Noted in *Chronicle*, no. 19; *Posev*, October 1971, p. 21.

68. "O knige Roberta Konkuesta 'Velikii terror' (zhurnal 'Enkaunter,' 1968, noiabr')" [Concerning Robert Conquest's *Great Terror* (*Encounter*, November 1968)], listed under "Novosti samizdata," *Chronicle*, no. 14; *Posev*, November 1970. *Political Diary*, no. 50 (November 1968), carried a review of the book; table of contents in *AS* 1008.

69. (*a*) "O knige A. Avtorkhanova 'Tekhnologiia vlasti'" [Concerning A. Avtorkhanov's book *The Technology of Power*], *Political Diary*, no. 55 (April 1969), pp. 509–15. The judgment is severe: "As a whole the work of A. Avtorkhanov proves to be not merely anti-Soviet and anticommunist in spirit but extremely unreliable in its content. The author commits not only crude distortions but also deliberate fabrications."

(*b*) "Referat knigi V. Khofmanna 'Stalinizm i antikommunizm'" [Review of Werner Hoffmann's book *Stalinism and Anticommunism*], *Political Diary*, no. 46 (July 1968), pp. 434–41.

(*c*) "O knige L. Shapiro 'Ot Lenina k Stalinu'" [On L. Schapiro's book *From Lenin to Stalin*], *Political Diary*, no. 43 (April 1968), pp. 355–56. The review is of the French translation of Schapiro's book (Paris, 1968).

(*d*) "O knige A. Verta, 'Rossiia v voine 1941–1945 gg.'" [On A. Werth's book *Russia in World War II*], *Political Diary*, no. 43 (April 1968), pp. 352–55. Extracts from a review by V. Kulish first published in *Novy mir*, no. 3 (1968), pp. 273–78.

70. Reddaway, *Uncensored Russia*, pp. 377 (from *Chronicle*, no. 1), 383 (from *Chronicle*, no. 5).

71. "Stat'ia P. Miliukova o bol'shevizme" [An article by P. Milyukov on Bolshevism], *Political Diary*, no. 33 (June 1967), pp. 281–97; originally published in the émigré journal *Poslednie novosti* (Paris).

Belles-Lettres. By no means all samizdat contributions to history have been deliberately designed to serve that goal. Some of the most valuable texts from the historian's point of view have been those in the field of belles-lettres in which a historical background is used to explain or set off the immediate subject matter. Solzhenitsyn's novel *V kruge pervom* [The first circle], with its use of sharply dramatic scenes involving Stalin, the secret police chief Viktor S. Abakumov, and other high Soviet officials, is a striking case in point.[72] Effective as a work of fiction, *The First Circle* must be used by the historian with great circumspection and then rather as evidence of what a well-informed and highly intelligent Russian novelist believes about the inner workings of Soviet policy in the late Stalin period than as historically valid evidence on the subject.

The uncensored text of Anatoly Kuznetsov's World War II novel *Babi Yar* is subject to the same qualifications, though it has definite value as an eyewitness account of German occupation policies in the Ukraine.[73]

Another samizdat novel, Alexander Bek's *Novoe naznachenie* (The new assignment), portrays vividly the workings of the Soviet party-government bureaucracy. Its value for the historian is indicated by the fact that Roy Medvedev makes use of it in *Let History Judge* (below, p. 350). Broader in scope and more reflective in approach is Vasily Grossman's novel *Vsë techet* . . . [Everything flows—published in the West under the title *Forever Flowing*], a work Pospielovsky has justifiably characterized as "a historico-sociological analysis rather than a novel."[74]

THE SOURCES OF *LET HISTORY JUDGE*

Despite the wide acclaim with which it has been greeted in the West as an authentic expression of uncensored Russian scholarship, Roy Medvedev's massive study of stalinism, *K sudu istorii* (Let history judge), cannot be regarded as a typical samizdat work. It was not originally intended for clandestine circulation. During the six or more years it was in preparation its author, a Communist Party member since 1956, made no secret of the fact that he was at work on a historical study of Stalinism. When the manuscript was completed it was submitted to a regular publishing house. Meanwhile drafts of the work had been circulating, and when it was rejected for publication the author decided to make it available for internal circulation as well as for translation and publication in the West.

Manuscript Sources. In the preface to *Let History Judge* Medvedev describes as follows the sources used in its preparation:

72. Zurich, 1968; English trans., London and New York, 1968.
73. A censored version was published in *Yunost'*, 1966; English trans., New York, 1966. The uncensored text was circulated in samizdat (*AS* 771); English trans., New York, 1970.
74. Bek, Frankfurt, 1971. Grossman, Frankfurt, 1970. For the characterization, see Pospielovsky, "Etika," pp. 165–66.

This work is based on the numerous Soviet publications that have followed the policy of the XXth and XXIInd Party Congresses in examining Stalin's cult honestly and truthfully. I have also used many unpublished manuscripts—documents, memoirs, and eyewitness accounts—belonging for the most part to older Party members who survived the lawlessness of the 1930's and 1940's. These sources are especially important because many of Stalin's illegal orders and actions were not recorded in any documents during his lifetime. Some of the manuscripts I have used report deathbed testimony passed on to Party comrades in Stalinist camps and prisons. In the tortuous journey of such testimony, sometimes measured in decades, distortions and inaccuracies were inevitable. But it would be irreverence to the dead to cast aside their testimony as unreliable or unobjective, instead of carefully compiling and comparing their various accounts.[75]

Medvedev then lists by name fourteen "old Bolsheviks who placed valuable historical documents and memoirs at my disposal" and thanks an additional seven who, "along with many others, helped me with their documents and comments." Supplementing these twenty-one sources of unpublished material, moreover, are nearly one hundred individuals cited throughout the text either by full name or initials.

It is striking that the overwhelming majority of Medvedev's unpublished sources have not been identified in the West as samizdat materials. Thus in all probability they would never have come to general knowledge if Medvedev had not dug them out. A few examples will help make this point clear. One of the sources Medvedev cites most frequently on matters relating to the role of the security police is an unpublished manuscript by a secret police veteran, Suren O. Gazarian, entitled "Eto ne dolzhno povtoritsia" (This must not be repeated). There appears to be no trace of this work, however, in samizdat.[76] Similarly, the unpublished memoirs of E. P. Frolov, whom Medvedev identifies as a party member since 1919 and on which he draws repeatedly, is otherwise unknown in samizdat texts available in the West. The same conclusions apply to eighteen of Medvedev's twenty-one named sources of unpublished manuscripts. The three others—A. V. Snegov, M. P. Yakubovich, and L. P. Petrovsky—are known to have contributed to samizdat literature. A similar picture emerges from the nearly one hundred individuals identified in the text of *Let History Judge* as sources of unpublished material: thirteen of the group at most appear as authors of samizdat texts known in the West.

These facts point to several conclusions. First, they serve to emphasize the tremendous labor performed by Medvedev in seeking out and evaluating unpublished materials for his book. Without this toil there would have been only a slim possibility that any of these valuable historical sources would have been brought to general knowledge. By the same token, the inclusion of

---

75. R. Medvedev, *Let History Judge*, p. xxxiii.
76. In Slusser, "A Soviet Historian Evaluates Stalin's Role," p. 1395, I erroneously stated that Gazarian's memoirs had circulated in samizdat.

this wealth of authentic but unofficial historical data helped greatly to give *Let History Judge* its impressive depth.

Second, the very small proportion of known samizdat authors and manuscripts among Medvedev's unpublished sources focuses attention on an important fact that is not always adequately recognized. Most of those on whose unpublished manuscripts and recollections Medvedev draws are or once were party members or government officials. The fact that their memoirs, diaries, and other unpublished materials have evidently not circulated in samizdat seems to indicate how little such people have contributed to the dissident movement. With prominent exceptions such as General Grigorenko, people from the elite of Soviet society appear to have remained aloof despite their suffering under Stalin.

Other Unpublished Sources. In addition to manuscripts, Medvedev drew on several other types of unpublished sources. One was the publisher's mockup (*maket*), an advance copy of a book prepared for limited circulation and discussion prior to publication. Medvedev cites the mockup of the ninth volume of the *Istoriia SSSR s drevneishikh vremën* (History of the USSR from the most ancient times), which was prepared by the Institute of History of the Academy of Sciences in 1964 but later withdrawn for extensive alterations.[77] In its portrayal of the purge trials of the 1930s, as Medvedev points out, this draft text went further than any previous Soviet history in calling into question the verdicts reached at the trials. Medvedev made no use, on the other hand, of another *maket*, that of volume 3 of the *History of the CPSU* (above, pp. 344–45).

Another unpublished historical study that Medvedev cites is a symposium on the collectivization of agriculture. It was prepared by a team of scholars under the direction of V. P. Danilov in the Institute of History and accepted for publication in 1964, prior to Khrushchev's fall. After that event, however, the work was withdrawn, according to Medvedev, "for political reasons having nothing to do with scholarship."[78]

Medvedev also makes effective use of several stenographic reports of public meetings at which historical events or problems were discussed. Two such reports concern memorial ceremonies for victims of Stalin's purges: the Komsomol leader A. Kosarev, held on November 21, 1963, and the government official I. A. Akulov, the date of which Medvedev does not specify.[79]

Unpublished papers presented at conferences of historians or ideologists are among the sources used by Medvedev. An example is a paper by the historian N. N. Maslov, "Sostoianiia i razvitiia istoriko-partiinoi nauki v 1935–1955 g." (The condition and development of party-historical scholar-

77. R. Medvedev, *Let History Judge*, p. 182.
78. *Ibid.*, p. 101.
79. *Ibid.*, pp. 217, 308, 333.

ship in the period 1935–1955). This essay formed the basis of discussion at a joint meeting of the historiographical group and the methodological sector of the Institute of History of the Academy of Sciences on April 29, 1966. Also cited by Medvedev is a paper by A. V. Snegov that was presented at a conference held in the Institute of Marxism-Leninism June 26–28, 1966.[80]

Snegov is a figure of the greatest interest in regard to the interlocking spheres of the democratic opposition, the historical profession, and the secret police. *Chronicle* reported that he was expelled from the Communist Party in July 1971.[81] A veteran of the security police who served his own term behind bars during the Stalin years, Snegov developed after Stalin's death into a member of that rare species, a liberal intellectual with inside knowledge of the working of the secret police. He was named to an important position in the post-Stalin MVD under Khrushchev's patronage and repaid the favor by compiling materials from police archives that Khrushchev incorporated into his secret speech to the Twentieth Party Congress (above, p. 334).

Snegov took part in each of the two discussions by historians that gained clandestine circulation, that of Nekrich's book (above, p. 336) and that of the third volume of the *History of the CPSU*. Not surprisingly, the security police in their search for possible conduits for the transcripts turned their attention to Snegov. The *Chronicle* report of his expulsion from the party does not specify that he was identified as having played this role, but the circumstantial evidence pointing in that direction may well have contributed to his ouster.

In a few instances Medvedev used unpublished historical documents, evidently from the archives, even though he explicitly states, "I have not used the materials of any state or Party archives, of any 'special collection' or other limited-access depositories."[82] One of his unpublished documents is a letter by Lenin to G. L. Shklovsky in which Lenin complains of the difficulties he is experiencing in overcoming bureaucratic red tape. Another is an unpublished letter by Stalin to the Society of Old Bolsheviks rejecting their request to open an exhibition concerning his life and career on the ground that "such enterprises lead to the establishment of a 'cult of personality' which is harmful and incompatible with the spirit of the Party."[83]

Medvedev and Samizdat. In view of the fragmentary state of our knowledge of samizdat—to take a particularly striking example, we have fewer than a dozen of the first seventy-two issues of *Political Diary*—it

80. *Ibid.*, pp. 16, 499–500, 518.
81. See n. 22 above.
82. *Let History Judge*, p. xxxiii.
83. *Ibid.*, pp. 19, 547. On Stalin's letter Medvedev cites the Central Party Archive of the Institute of Marxism-Leninism.

would be hazardous to draw any far-reaching conclusions about the relationship of *Let History Judge* to samizdat. Nevertheless the available evidence suggests that in writing the book Medvedev deliberately avoided drawing on unofficially circulated materials. Toward the end of the book, it is true, he shows greater awareness of samizdat writings and a greater willingness to use them, citing, for example, texts by Pomerants, Bek, and Henri.[84] This may indicate either a change in Medvedev's attitude toward samizdat or the appearance of a greater number of materials relevant to his purpose as the work progressed. Of course, some of the most significant samizdat contributions to history—Olitskaya's memoirs and Dzyuba's study of Soviet nationality policies, for example—appeared too late for use in *Let History Judge.*

It is doubtful, however, that Medvedev's basic conclusions would have been significantly different had he had access to these and similar materials. In his following book, *De la democratie socialiste,*[85] written at a time when samizdat was already flourishing, Medvedev continued to follow the line of analysis presented in *Let History Judge.* Historical analysis is not prominent in the new book, but what is there continues to be framed in terms of the Lenin-Stalin relationship with a basic aim the exoneration of Lenin from charges of responsibility for the development of Stalinism. Medvedev attacks this problem at its most sensitive point, the political changes in the party regulations introduced at its Tenth Congress in 1921 for the purpose of preventing the development of factions. Admitting that these changes were made at Lenin's direct insistence, Medvedev argues that he intended them to be only temporary measures—as though historical causes are to be analyzed in terms of motives alone, without regard to the effects they produce.[86]

But exoneration of Lenin, important as it is, remains a subsidiary goal for Medvedev. His basic purpose in writing *Let History Judge*, it is clear, was to force the Communist Party and the Soviet historical profession to face the truth about Stalin's actions. "In the future," he writes,

Stalin will never be forgiven his monstrous crimes. Neither will those historians, political leaders, and writers, who lacked the courage to study the history of Stalin's crimes, be forgiven. Transient political considerations cannot justify this silence.[87]

Yet Soviet historians and party ideologists have adopted exactly such a silence as the only feasible line of defense against the demand by Medvedev and others for a thorough and searching historical analysis of Stalinism and

84. References to manuscripts by G. Pomerants, *ibid.*, pp. 323–24, 376, 429, 556, 565. Reference to A. Bek's novel *Novoe naznachenie, ibid.*, p. 419. References to manuscripts by Ernst Henri, *ibid.*, pp. 471, 439–40.

85. Roy Medvedev, *Kniga o sotsialisticheskoi demokratii* (Amsterdam, 1972); French trans., Paris, 1972; English translation, New York, 1975.

86. *Ibid.*, pp. 83–90, 165–66.

87. R. Medvedev, *Let History Judge*, p. 274.

its roots. An entire epoch in the history of Russia, the Stalinist period, has in effect been declared off limits to Soviet historians.

SOME FUTURE PERSPECTIVES

Far from the least of Stalin's crimes was his nearly successful effort to destroy the integrity of the Soviet historical profession. During the period of his dominance Soviet historians were never allowed to forget the brutal power of the .Communist regime to force them to support whatever version of the historical record it chose to present. In the long run, because the regime found it impossible to dispense with their expertise, the historians managed to preserve a comparatively large degree of autonomy. Following Stalin's death, with sporadic but powerful assistance from a few maverick party leaders such as Khrushchev, they have even regained some of the professional élan lost under Stalin. Since Khrushchev's overthrow in 1964, however, new restrictions and something like the old system of curbs have been established. The most serious barrier is the limitation on serious historical research into the Stalinist period. An authoritative recent survey of the tasks of Soviet historiography by a leading party ideologist, Sergei Trapeznikov, glorifies Lenin's role in history and stresses the need for *partiinost'* in the work of Soviet historians but says not a word about Stalin or the urgent historical problems of his era.[88]

An even sharper warning to Soviet historians not to submit the Stalinist period to critical analysis was contained in a report by Vladimir N. Yagodkin, ideological secretary of the Moscow city party committee. The report was presented at a conference on "The Ideological Struggle in Historical Science" in the Institute of History of the Academy of Sciences on June 14, 1973. According to Yagodkin, any "revisionist" idea in history is by definition inspired by foreign agencies for the purpose of disrupting the Soviet system, even though the historian who proposes the idea may sincerely believe that he developed it independently on the basis of a study of the historical evidence. Combating the view that the stalinist period represented in any way a setback for the development of socialism in the USSR, Yagodkin demanded that "*all*—and I repeat, *all*—stages in the development of our Soviet society must be regarded as 'positive.'" He thereby warned Soviet historians not to look into such touchy matters as the cost in human lives of Stalin's policies in the collectivization drive, the Great Purge, or the period immediately preceding the German attack of June 1941.[89]

---

88. S. Trapeznikov, "Sovetskaia istoricheskaia nauka i perspektivy ee razvitiia" [Soviet historical scholarship and the prospects for its development], *Kommunist*, no. 11 (July 1973), pp. 68–86.

89. A summary of Yagodkin's report was circulated in samizdat (*AS* 1461); English trans. in Christian Duevel, "A high-ranking CPSU official corroborated Sakharov's warning on détente," *Radio Liberty Dispatch*, September 6, 1973, pp. 5–6. For a summary report on the

A similar message is conveyed in an authoritative article recently published by three historian-academicians, I. I. Mints, M. V. Nechkina, and L. V. Cherepnin. It skirts the issue of Stalin's role in history by obliquely referring to the responsibility of Soviet historians to help overcome "the negative consequences of the cult of personality."[90]

The party's determination to discourage or suppress serious historical scholarship on the Stalinist period presents the democratic opposition with its greatest challenge and its greatest opportunity in the field of history. Roy Medvedev's *Let History Judge* and Solzhenitsyn's *The Gulag Archipelago* constitute a magnificent response to that challenge. Will they be followed by other works of similar caliber? Will the professional historians of the Soviet Union turn to the now well-established samizdat channels to present the results of their "revisionist" studies of the Stalinist period? One may hope that these things will come to pass. At the same time, however, one must soberly recognize the extraordinary efforts the Soviet regime is making to keep the historians on a tight leash and to stamp out the samizdat movement as a form of historical research and record. The arrest and trial of Peter Yakir, the suppression of *Political Diary* and *Chronicle*, and the closing down of several other samizdat journals have seriously impaired the ability of the democratic opposition to study historical problems or to record facts of historical significance.

Also relevant is the dying off of an older generation of scholars whose willingness to resist the cruder forms of political control served as a partial check on the party ideologists and their KGB watchdogs. A salient example is the medievalist academician S. D. Skazkin, who died in April 1973. Skazkin, who completed his graduate work at Moscow University two years before the Bolsheviks seized power, was one of the historians who in 1966 signed a letter warning the party leaders against the rehabilitation of Stalin.[91]

Skazkin's death, the apostasy of Yakir, the resentencing of Amalrik, articles and reports like those of Trapeznikov and Yagodkin—all these events constitute a series of ominous warnings to Soviet historians and democratic dissidents. Yet to succeed in stamping out the historical sense among the Soviet intelligentsia would require the reestablishment of the full

conference, see *Voprosy istorii*, no. 8 (1973), p. 173, where the full title of Yagodkin's report is given: "Ideologicheskaia bor'ba v istoricheskoi nauke i zadachi uchenykh-obshchestvovedov Moskvy" [The ideological struggle in historical science and the tasks of the scholar-students-of-society of Moscow].

90. "Zadachi Sovetskoi istorichesko nauki na sovremennom etape eë razvitiia" [The tasks of Soviet historical scholarship in the contemporary stage of its development], *Istoriia SSSR*, no. 5 (1973), pp. 3–16 (quote at p. 4).

91. See Slusser, "A Soviet Historian Evaluates Stalin's Role," p. 1390. For Skazkin's obituary, see *Voprosy istorii*, no. 6 (1973), pp. 219–20.

stalinist purge machinery, and it seems doubtful that the present Soviet leadership really wants to go that far. Short of that dire eventuality, the regime is likely to find it impossible to cut off completely the flow of historical materials into samizdat channels. If that prognosis is correct, the historian concerned with Russia's past will continue to find samizdat a rich source of information.

CHAPTER ELEVEN / ANDREI SAKHAROV: THE

CONSCIENCE OF A LIBERAL SCIENTIST / PETER DORNAN

Hope springs eternal in the human breast; | Man never is, but always to be blessed.—Alexander Pope, *An Essay on Man*

This study will examine the development and shifts in emphasis in several of the political views of the Soviet physicist and academician Andrei Sakharov. After a brief look at the man as scientist and citizen it considers his position on the issues of intellectual freedom, the nationality question, religious freedom, ideology, and Soviet foreign policy. It also treats his year-long duel with the KGB (Committee of State Security) and views him after the involuntary exile of Alexander Solzhenitsyn. Throughout the discussion it will be essential to remember that Sakharov's views are not dogmatic opinions; always subject to revision, they are based on reason and compassion.[1]

1. This study grew out of the paper "Academician Sakharov—Despairing Optimist of the Human Rights Movement, June 1968–June 1972," Radio Liberty Research Paper no. 196/72 (Munich, 1972). Its main sources are the following samizdat documents written by Sakharov:
(1) *Razmyshleniia o progresse, mirnom sosushchestvovanii i intellektual'noi svobode* [Reflections on progress, peaceful coexistence, and intellectual freedom, hereafter *Reflections*], June 1968, *in Arkhiv samizdata* [Samizdat archive, hereafter *AS*] 200, as registered by the Research Department of Radio Liberty (Munich). First published in English by *New York Times*, July 22, 1968; the translation used here, with modification as required, is Andrei Sakharov, *Progress, Coexistence, and Intellectual Freedom*, ed. Harrison E. Salisbury (New York, 1968), which also appears in *Sakharov Speaks*, ed. Harrison E. Salisbury (New York, 1974), pp. 55–114. This translation should be used with caution, for it contains a number of inaccuracies. A Russian edition has been published by Possev-Verlag (Frankfurt, 1968).
(2) "Pis'mo A. D. Sakharova, V. F. Turchina i R. A. Medvedeva Brezhnevu, Kosyginu i Podgornomu" [Letter of A. D. Sakharov, V. F. Turchin, and R. A. Medvedev to L. I. Brezhnev, A. N. Kosygin, and N. V. Podgorny, hereafter "Letter of Three"], March 19, 1970, *AS* 360. English trans., *Survey* 16, no. 3 (Summer 1970): 160–70 and *Sakharov Speaks*, pp. 116–34. The text, written in collaboration with the physicist Valentin Turchin and the teacher-historian Roy Medvedev, has a Marxist flavoring that in all likelihood reflects more Medvedev's viewpoint. In *Reflections* (p. 64) Sakharov had hinted at differences of approach, if not of ultimate goals, between the two men; in *Sakharov Speaks* (p. 116) he notes that the text no longer "fully" reflects his position. Presumably the text is a compromise of the three minds, but for purposes of discussion here it is assumed that its contents are Sakharov's views too in March 1970.
(3, 4) "Pamiatnaia zapiska A. D. Sakharova L. I. Brezhnevu" [A. D. Sakharov's memorandum (literally aide-memoire) to L. I. Brezhnev, hereafter "Memorandum"], March 5, 1971, and "Posleslovie k 'Pamiatnoi zapiske' A. D. Sakharova" [Afterword to A. D. Sakharov's "Memorandum," hereafter "Afterword"], June 1972, both in *AS* 1136. English trans., *Survey* 18, no. 3 (Summer 1972): 223–40 and *Sakharov Speaks*, pp. 135–58. Both texts were made available to Western correspondents in Moscow in the week of June 19; *New York Times*, June 23, 1972.

SCIENTIST AND CITIZEN

To honor the seventieth birthday of his mentor and colleague, the Soviet physicist and Nobel Prize winner Igor Tamm, Sakharov wrote a brief article entitled "Scientist and Citizen" for *Izvestiia* in 1965. He attributed Tamm's tremendous popularity with the scientific intelligentsia to his "passionate love for science" and "passionate irreconcilability with everything false in science and in life." He also emphasized three qualities that Tamm instilled in his students: "profundity of thought, perseverance, and principle-mindedness

---

The addressee of the "Afterword" became known through Sakharov's interview on Swedish television (see below). Sakharov summarized the contents of the "Memorandum" in his open letter of March 30, 1971 to the USSR minister of internal affairs, N. A. Shchelokov (*AS* 609), in which he protested new violations of human rights.

(5) "Zametki o besede ot 16.8.73 s pervym zam. general'nogo prokurora SSSR Generalom M. P. Maliarovym" [Notes on talk of August 16, 1973, with General M. P. Malyarov, first deputy procurator general of the USSR, hereafter "Talk with Malyarov"], n.d. [between August 16 and 18, 1973], *AS* 1463. English trans., *New York Times*, August 29, 1973; *Index* 2, no. 4 (Winter 1973): 19–23; and *Sakharov Speaks*, pp. 179–92.

(6) "Zaiavlenie zarubezhnym korrespondentam, oprovergaiushchee obvinenie sovetskoi pressy o iakoby vozrazhenii ego protiv razriadki mezhdunarodnoi napriazhënnosti" [Statement to foreign corespondents rejecting Soviet press accusation of his alleged opposition to détente, hereafter "Statement on Press Accusation"], September 8, 1973, *AS* 1482. English trans., *Times* (London), September 10, 1973; *New York Times*, September 12, 1973; *Index* 2, no. 4 (Winter 1973): 29–30; and *Sakharov Speaks*, pp. 208–10 (where text is misdated September 12).

(7) "Zaiavlenie po povodu R. i Zh. Medvedevykh" [Statement on R. and Zh. Medvedev, hereafter "Statement on Medvedevs"], November 20, 1973, *AS* 1505.

(8) "Otkrytoe pis'mo Predsedateliu KGB Iu. V. Andropovu" [Open letter to KGB Chairman Yu. V. Andropov], November 28, 1973, *AS* 1511, which assumes full responsibility for his wife's nonappearance for further interrogation.

(9) "Zaiavlenie o reshenii priniat' priglashenie dlia sebia i chlenov svoei sem'i posetit' SShA" [Statement on decision to accept invitation for himself and members of family to visit the USA, hereafter "Statement on Invitation"], November 30, 1973, *AS* 1512.

(10) Introduction, dated December 31, 1973, to the collection *Sakharov Speaks*, pp. 29–54; the Russian text used is that published under the title *Sakharov o sebe—Sakharov about Himself* (New York, 1974), hereafter *Sakharov o sebe*. The text was circulating in Moscow by early March 1974; *New York Times*, March 5, 1974.

(11) "Zaiavlenie 'O pis'me Aleksandra Solzhenitsyna "Vozhdiam Sovetskogo Soiuza"'" [Statement on Alexander Solzhenitsyn's *Letter to the Leaders of the Soviet Union*, hereafter "Statement on Solzhenitsyn Letter"], April 3, 1974, *AS* 1655. English trans., *Times* (London), April 16, 1974.

Other major texts used include two interviews Sakharov has given to Western correspondents, a press conference, and an article by Hedrick Smith, former chief of the Moscow bureau of the *New York Times*:

(1) Interview to Jay Axelbank of *Newsweek* on October 26, 1972. An English translation exists in two versions: a condensed text in *Newsweek* (international ed. was used), November 8, 1972, p. 13, and a fuller text in the Sunday *Observer* (London), December 3, 1972. The shorter text contains material not in the longer one while the latter contains at least one mistake (Nixon visited the USSR in May, not February).

(2) Interview to Olle Stenholm of Sweden, probably in late June 1973, first broadcast on Swedish radio and television July 2, 1973 (hereafter cited as interview on Swedish television). The transcribed Russian text of this taped interview is the version used and cited in this study; it is registered as *AS* 1455. First published in a reportedly uncut version in Swedish in *Dagens nyheter*, July 3, 1973, the text has since appeared in at least eight other versions: English, in

[*printsipial'nost'*]."[2] This tells much about Sakharov, even as it does about Tamm. In a second commemorative article, written by Sakharov and two physicist colleagues for the journal *Uspekhi fizicheskikh nauk* (Successes of the physical sciences), Sakharov recalled:

> The years of I. Ye. Tamm's work in the field of thermonuclear synthesis are especially unforgettable for one of the writers of these lines (A. D. S.), who then had the fortunate opportunity to live and work side by side with [Tamm]. In particular, it was precisely in this period that they together began Soviet work (on a theoretical plane) on a controlled thermonuclear reaction in a strong magnetic field and also participated in other work bordering on the problem of thermonuclear synthesis.[3]

The second article stresses Tamm's opposition to Lysenkoism, notes his public work "in the reconciliation [*sblizhenie*] of peoples" and in efforts "to restore justice when he sees it violated," and mentions his participation in "the Pugwash movement," the series of informal conferences, chiefly of scientists from East and West, held annually since 1957 to air problems of science and world affairs.[4] When Tamm died in 1971, Sakharov recalled him as "a man who was the measure of decency in science and in public life."[5] The moral

---

brief excerpts in *Times* (London), July 4, and *New York Times*, July 5, and in fullest versions in *Index* 2, no. 4 (Winter 1973): 13–17 and *Sakharov Speaks*, pp. 166–78; German, in extensive excerpts in *Der Spiegel*, July 9 (probably based on the *Dagens nyheter* text), in fullest version in A. D. Sacharow, *Stellungnahme* (Vienna, Munich, Zurich, 1974), pp. 43–55 (this collection of texts is not identical with that in *Sakharov Speaks*); French, in extensive excerpts in *L'express*, July 17–22, 1973 (apparently also based on the *Dagens nyheter* text); Russian, in *Novoe russkoe slovo*, July 14–17, 1973 (a translation of the *Spiegel* text), and *Posev*, 1973, no. 8 (August), pp. 6–10 (based on the original Russian tape, this text contains stylistic changes for the printed page). While all published versions give the sense of the interview, there are discrepancies among them and in most of them mistakes, and all the material must be used with utmost caution. This writer has listened to a copy of the Russian tape.

(3) Sakharov's press conference of August 21, 1973, held at his Moscow flat for about a dozen foreign correspondents. The Russian text was not available, but there are at least three versions in translation: English, by the Associated Press in *Times* (London), September 5, 1973 (the version cited hereafter as press conference of August 21, 1973); *Index* 2, no. 4 (Winter 1973): 25–29; and *Sakharov Speaks*, pp. 194–207 (where the expected date of return of Bochkov, head of the prison hospital at Chernyakhovsk, is misprinted September 1 instead of 10); German, in *Stellungnahme*, pp. 165–75.

(4) Hedrick Smith, "The Intolerable Andrei Sakharov," *New York Times Magazine*, November 4, 1973, pp. 42 ff.

Not treated in this study are Sakharov's views on the class nature of Soviet society or those elements of his political thinking that have remained relatively constant: peaceful coexistence; adoption of a press and information law, including abolishment of censorship; abolition of anticonstitutional laws and directives violating human rights; amnesty for political prisoners; complete destalinization; and extension of economic reform. These appear in his summary proposals at the end of *Reflections*.

2. A. Sakharov, "Uchionyi i grazhdanin" [Scholar and citizen], *Izvestiia*, July 8, 1965.

3. V. L. Ginzburg, A. D. Sakharov, and Ye. L. Feinberg, "Igor' Yevgen'evich Tamm: K semidesiatiletiiu so dnia rozhdeniia" [Igor Yevgenevich Tamm: For the seventieth anniversary of his birth], *Uspekhi fizicheskikh nauk* 86, no. 2 (June 1965): 354.

4. *Ibid.*, pp. 353, 356.

5. V. L. Ginzburg et al., "Pamiati Igoria Yevgen'evicha Tamma" [In memory of Igor Yevgenevich Tamm], *ibid.* 105, no. 1 (September 1971): 163.

qualities Sakharov attributes to Tamm as scientist and citizen seem to have rubbed off on himself. Very likely the example of the older man has been the most powerful human influence of Sakharov's adult years.

Andrei Dmitrievich Sakharov, one of the fathers of the Soviet hydrogen bomb, was born May 21, 1921.[6] Until publication in 1974 of his autobiographical foreword to the collection *Sakharov Speaks* it was not even known that Sakharov is a native of Moscow. The son of a physics instructor at the Lenin Pedagogical Institute, Sakharov had the good fortune to grow up in a warm and healthy family atmosphere of mutual respect.[7] In 1942 he graduated from Moscow State University, where he presented, according to one unidentified American source, "the most brilliant thesis ever offered in physics" at the university. For the remainder of the war he worked as an engineer in a war factory.[8] In 1945 Sakharov entered the P. N. Lebedev Physics Institute in Moscow to study under Tamm, who was head of the institute's Theoretical Division and the country's leading scientist in quantum mechanics. Before the end of 1947, when he obtained his doctoral degree, he published his "first major scientific contribution," the paper "Generation of the Hard Component of Cosmic Rays," which was probably a part of his doctoral dissertation.[9]

The following spring, in 1948, Sakharov became a member of the Soviet research team working on a thermonuclear weapon.[10] During this year he produced at least three papers: "Electron-Positron Interaction in Pair Production," "The Excitation Temperature in Plasma of a Gaseous Discharge,"[11] and one that reported his study of a nuclear reaction catalyzed by mu mesons in liquid deuterium.[12] Two years later, in 1950, Sakharov and Tamm achieved

6. *Biograficheskii slovar' deiatelei yestestvoznaniia i tekhniki* [Biographical dictionary of figures of the natural sciences and technology] (Moscow, 1959), 2: 201 (hereafter *BSD*). Biographical treatment of Sakharov in Soviet encyclopedias can be traced in the following: *Entsiklopedicheskii slovar'* [Encyclopedic dictionary] (Moscow, 1955), 3: 172, 4 lines; *Bol'shaia sovetskaia entsiklopediia* [Large Soviet encyclopedia], 2d ed. (Moscow, 1955), 38: 165 (hereafter *BSE*), 5 lines plus 6-line bibliography of three articles of 1947–48; *BSD*, 8 lines, with first mention of day and month of birth, plus same 6-line bibliography; *Malaia sovetskaia entsiklopediia* (Small Soviet encyclopedia), 3d ed. (Moscow, 1960), 8: 229, 7 lines (same as in *BSD*); *Entsiklopedicheskii slovar'*, 2d ed. (Moscow, 1964), 2: 353, 3 lines.

7. *Sakharov o sebe*, p. 4, and Smith, "Intolerable Sakharov," p. 51.

8. Louise Campbell, "Sakharov: Soviet Physicist Appeals for Bold Initiatives," *Science* 161 (August 8, 1968): 557–58. For the work in the war factory see *Sakharov o sebe*, p. 5.

9. The year of the doctoral degree and the view on his first major scientific contribution are in the introduction by Salisbury to *Progress, Coexistence, and Intellectual Freedom*, p. 11. "Generatsiia zhestkoi komponenty kosmicheskikh luchei" is in *Zhurnal eksperimental'noi i teoreticheskoi fiziki* [Journal of experimental and theoretical physics, hereafter *ZhETF*] 17, no. 8 (1947), as cited in *BSD*.

10. *Sakharov o sebe*, p. 6.

11. "Vzaimodeistvie elektrona i pozitrona pri rozhdenii par," *ZhETF* 18, no. 7 (1948); "Temperatura vozbuzhdeniia v plazme gazovogo razryva," *Izvestiia Akademii Nauk SSSR: seriia fizicheskaia* 12, no. 4 (1948), both as cited in *BSD*.

12. In *Otchiot FIAN* [Report of the Physics Institute of the Academy of Sciences], 1948, as cited in a letter to the editor by Ya. B. Zel'dovich and A. D. Sakharov, "O reaktsiiakh, vyzyvaemykh mu-mezonami v vodorode" [On mu meson reactions in hydrogen], *ZhETF* 32, no. 4 (1957): 947–49.

a breakthrough when they proposed "the application of an electrical discharge in a plasma, placed in a magnetic field, to obtain a controlled thermonuclear reaction"—the theoretical foundation of the use of thermonuclear energy for peaceful purposes.[13] Within another three years, on August 12, 1953, the Soviet Union tested its first nuclear device using the thermonuclear fusion reaction of the hydrogen bomb.[14]

Two months later, on October 23, Sakharov was elected a full member of the USSR Academy of Sciences.[15] He thus became at age thirty-two the youngest scientist ever to reach this prestigious station, and without having been a corresponding member (as Tamm, elected academician the same day, had been for twenty years). Sakharov's election, coming so soon after the Soviet test, was as much a reflection of his value to the country as a recognition of his brilliance as a scientist. In his first reported interview with a foreign correspondent in October 1972, Sakharov recalled his role in developing the Soviet H-bomb as follows:

Yes, I suppose my contribution . . . was one of the most important. My role was great but not exclusive. No one man developed our bomb. There are many I worked with whose names are not known. And I wouldn't have been known, either, if my beliefs had not put me outside the Establishment.[16]

Since the mid-1960s Sakharov's published scientific work has been concerned chiefly with the origin and structure of the universe. He developed a hypothesis "on the creation of astronomical bodies as a result of gravitational instability of an expanding universe," published in early 1965 under the title "The Initial Stage of Expansion of the Universe and the Appearance of Nonuniformity of the Distribution of Matter."[17] In 1966 Sakharov and a colleague contributed a hypothesis on the quark phenomenon; it appeared under the title "Quark Structure and Masses of Strongly Interacting Particles."[18] Sakharov's latest known contribution to theoretical physics is his paper "Antiquarks in the Universe," submitted January 15, 1969, to the Joint Institute for Nuclear Research at Dubna. Here he attempts to "explain why the universe seems to be almost entirely made up of matter, with no

---

13. *BSE* 41: 578. For Sakharov's nonmilitary research see *Sakharov o sebe*, p. 6.

14. Confirmed by an announcement August 19 by the U.S. Atomic Energy Commission; *New York Times*, August 20, 1953.

15. *Vestnik Akademii Nauk SSSR* [Herald of the USSR Academy of Sciences, hereafter *Vestnik*], 1953, no. 11 (November), p. 12. Sakharov was one of four new academicians whose biographies were *not* featured in this journal during the next five months.

16. Axelbank, in *Observer*.

17. A. D. Sakharov, "Nachal'naia stadiia rasshireniia vselennoi i vozniknovenie neodnorodnosti raspredeleniia veshchestva," *ZhETF* 49, no. 1 (7) (1965): 345–58.

18. Ya. B. Zel'dovich and A. D. Sakharov, "Kvarkovaia struktura i massy sil'novzaimodeistvuiushchikh chastits," *Yadernaia fizika* [Nuclear physics] 4, no. 2 (August 1966): 395–406.

substantial amounts of antimatter" by hypothesizing "a universal sea of neutral antiquarks."[19]

The appearance of his treatise *Reflections* in mid-1968 has assured Sakharov a prominent place in the history of Soviet dissent. His voice, joined in the public mind (at home and abroad) to that of Solzhenitsyn, gave a new dimension to dissent. These two now became the most powerful spokesmen in the country for justice and humanity. Solzhenitsyn out of Stalin's camps had

19. As reported and explained in *New York Times*, August 7, 1969. The study reached the U.S. in one of the institute's "communications." Eight other published articles (three of them popularized) by Sakharov have been located:

(1) "Teoriia magnitogo termoiadernogo reaktora (chast' II)" [Theory of a magnetic thermonuclear reactor (part II)], in *Fizika plazmy i problema upravliaemykh termoiadernykh reaktsii* [Plasma physics and the problem of controlled thermonuclear reactions], ed. M. A. Leontovich (Moscow, 1958). The work, executed in 1951, is reproduced from the 1958 collection in *Uspekhi fizicheskikh nauk* 93, no. 3 (1967): 564–71.

(2) With R. M. Zaidel', V. N. Mineev, and A. G. Oleinik, "Eksperimental'noe issledovanie ustoichivosti udarnykh voln i mekhanicheskikh svoistv veshchestva pri vysokikh davleniiakh i temperaturakh" [Experimental research of shock wave resistance and of the mechanical properties of matter under high pressures and temperatures], *Doklady AN SSSR* [Proceedings of the USSR Academy of Sciences] 159, no. 5 (1964): 1019–22. The results of the research were reported at a conference on high pressures in the Institute of Chemical Physics in May 1963.

(3) With R. Z. Liudaev *et al.*, "Magnitnaia kumuliatsiia" [Magnetic "cumulation"], *ibid.* 165, no. 1 (1965): 65–68. The journal received the paper August 23, 1965.

(4) "Vzryvomagnitnye generatory" [Explosion-magnetic generators], *Uspekhi fizicheskikh nauk* 88, no. 4 (1966): 725–34.

(5) "Rekordy magnitnykh polei" [Magnetic field records], *Izvestiia*, April 30, 1966.

(6) "Magnitnoe pole vzryva" [The magnetic field of an explosion], *Tekhnika-molodiozhi*, 1968, no. 8 (August), p. 5.

(7) "Vakuumnye kvantovye fluktuatsii v iskrivlionnom prostranstve i teoriia gravitatsii" [Vacuum quantum fluctuations in curved space and the theory of gravitation], *Doklady AN SSSR* 177, no. 1 (1967): 70–71. The journal received the paper August 28, 1967.

(8) "Sushchestvuet li elementarnaia dlina?" [Is there a length element?], *Fizika v shkole* [Physics in school], 1968, no. 2, pp. 6–15.

In 1971 Sakharov responded to a questionnaire distributed to Soviet scientists and scholars by the organization committee of the symposium CETI-71 (Communication with extraterrestrial intelligence), which was held at the Biurakan Astrophysics Observatory in Armenia September 6–11, 1971. It is not clear whether Sakharov actually attended the symposium. His responses to two of the questions, however, are interesting for what they reveal about his approach to a new scientific problem.

In reply to the question "What directions should be developed in research on the problem of extraterrestrial civilizations?" Sakharov pointed to "flagrant gaps in our basic ideas" about space and types of emissions. However, he wrote, "doubts must not discourage us from attempting to receive signals by gradually increasing the sensitivity (and the cost) of receiving equipment and by expanding the methodology of searching. Only thus can we sooner or later count on success."

Commenting on the question "What are the possible consequences of contact?" Sakharov saw no "danger in obtaining information from extraterrestrial civilization" if man assimilates it properly. "The creation of an artificial 'superbrain,' due to feedback, is far more dangerous. Somewhat crudely, one can say that for the intelligent and the good all additional knowledge is of benefit, while for the stupid and the evil . . . nothing can either help or harm. Being an optimist, I am for the persistent search for extraterrestrial civilizations." L. M. Gindilis, "CETI-71," *Zemlia i vselennaia* [Earth and the universe], 1972, no. 2 (March–April), p. 49, and "Anketa CETI" [CETI questionnaire], *ibid.*, no. 4 (July–August), pp. 57, 61.

reached this point through literature, Sakharov out of the technical elite through science. The one seemed to embody the suppressed anger of the masses, the other the suppressed reasoning of the intelligentsia.

Sakharov took a decade to reach this position. His start on the road of dissent can be marked provisionally in 1958. To Axelbank he explained: "I developed a moral consciousness gradually in the 1950s. I suppose the turning-point came when I sent a letter of protest to the Government against our atomic tests in 1958—and again in 1961."[20]

In 1958 the Soviet Union had conducted two series of tests, January 23–March 22 and September 30–October 25.[21] In 1961 a series of large-scale tests was conducted September 1–October 23, when a thermonuclear bomb in the range of thirty megatons was exploded on Novaya Zemlya. At the Twenty-second Congress of the Communist Party of the Soviet Union, Nikita Khrushchev announced that a fifty-megaton bomb would be exploded despite worldwide protests. It was detonated October 30.[22]

On July 7, between the two 1958 test series, the Soviet journal *Atomnaia energiia* (Atomic energy) received Sakharov's paper "Radioactive Carbon from Nuclear Explosions and Nonthreshhold Biological Effects." In the paper, published in the December issue, Sakharov estimated the amount of genetic damage that had resulted from tests already conducted and that would appear in the future even if no more tests were held. He took the position that "the continuation of tests and all attempts to legalize nuclear weapons and their tests are contrary to humanity and international law." His reasoning to answer his own question "What moral and political conclusions should be drawn from the figures cited?" provides insight into the nature of his moral stand made public in 1968:

One of the arguments advanced by proponents of the theory of the "inoffensiveness" of tests is that cosmic rays cause doses of radiation larger than doses from tests. But this argument does not alter the fact that the suffering and deaths of hundreds of thousands of victims, including those in neutral countries and in future generations, are additional supplements to the suffering and death already occurring. Two world wars also added less than 10% to the death rate in the twentieth century, but this does not make war a normal phenomenon.

Another argument disseminated in the literature of many countries reduces itself to this: that the progress of civilization . . . causes the sacrifice of human life. Casualties of the automobile are frequently cited as an example. But the analogy here is not precise, and not legitimate. Automobile transportation improves the condition of people's lives; it is the cause of accidents only in individual cases due to the carelessness

20. Axelbank, in *Observer*.
21. For the 1958 tests see *New York Times*, January 24–March 23 and October 1–26. For Andrei Gromyko's announcement of the Soviet decision to halt tests but with a threat of renewal if the United States and Britain ignored the Soviet overture, see *ibid.*, April 1. Two low-yield tests were conducted on November 1 and 3; *ibid.*, November 8 and 17.
22. For the 1961 tests see *ibid.*, September 2–October 24, October 29, 31.

of individuals, who are thereby criminally liable. But accidents caused by tests are the inescapable consequence of each explosion. In the author's view, the unique specific in the moral aspect of the given problem consists of the complete impunity from crime, because it cannot be proved that radiation is the cause of death of the individual in each specific case, and likewise because our offspring are totally defenseless against our actions.

The cessation of tests will directly preserve the life of hundreds of thousands of people and will have a far greater indirect importance by helping to reduce international tension and decrease the threat of nuclear war—the basic threat of our era.[23]

Sakharov's 1958 protest took the form of a confidential letter, presumably in late September,[24] to the physicist Igor Kurchatov (until his death in February, 1960, the chief scientific administrator of the Soviet nuclear weapons program) in which he argued for cancellation of the October tests. Agreeing to intervene, Kurchatov flew to see Khrushchev, then on vacation at Yalta, but to no avail. Sakharov tried again in the summer of 1961, sometime before September 1, when Khrushchev assembled top atomic scientists to announce the need for a new series of tests in support of foreign policy. This time, in a note passed to Khrushchev, Sakharov insisted that technically the tests were unnecessary and that to break the three-year moratorium on atmospheric tests would mean renewal of the armaments race—"a far more serious matter than building a wall in Berlin." But Khrushchev rejected the argument.[25]

Sakharov tried a third time in September 1962, when a routine but powerful test, technically unnecessary, was planned. After several weeks of ineffective pleading, he telephoned Yefim Slavsky, USSR minister of medium machine building (whose ministry oversees the Soviet nuclear weapons program), on the eve of the test and threatened resignation. Deceived by the minister's apparent assurance that the test had been canceled, Sakharov in desperation telephoned Khrushchev, then in Ashkhabad. But the latter equivocated, saying he would check with Frol Kozlov. By the time Kozlov spoke with Sakharov the next day the test had already taken place.

The experience was a psychological turning point in Sakharov's life. In 1973 he could still recall his feeling of frustration: "I had an awful sense of powerlessness. I could not stop something I knew was wrong and unnecessary. After that, I felt myself another man. I broke with my surroundings. It

23. A. D. Sakharov, "Radioaktivnyi uglerod yadernykh vzryvov i neporogovye biologicheskie effekty," *Atomnaia energiia* 4, no. 6 (December 1958): 576, 580.
24. The logical date is late September, for the test series began September 30. *Sakharov o sebe*, p. 8, does not specify the month. Smith, "Intolerable Sakharov," p. 51, dates the letter in October. Sakharov referred to it during his September 8, 1973, press conference with 14 foreign correspondents; see Theodore Shabad, *New York Times*, September 9, 10; Robert Kaiser, *Washington Post*, September 9, 14; Michael Parks, *Baltimore Sun*, September 10; Victor Buist's Reuter dispatch of September 9.
25. Smith, "Intolerable Sakharov," p. 54; *Sakharov o sebe*, p. 8.

was a basic break. After that, I understood there was no point in arguing."[26] Commenting on his own mental outlook at the time, Sakharov has said:

The atomic question was always half science, half politics. . . . [It] was a natural path into political issues. What matters is that I left conformism. It is not important on what question. After that first break, everything later was natural.[27]

In the years 1950–68, Sakharov told Axelbank, "I had money . . . , title, and everything which my work enabled me to have. But I had a very tragic feeling." It would be incorrect, however, to conclude that Sakharov was developing a guilty conscience. When Axelbank asked whether he regretted his contribution to development of the hydrogen bomb, he replied: "It is difficult to explain it in a couple of words. What was obvious twenty years ago, now isn't so obvious. Then the US had the bomb, we didn't. . . . It's hard to answer."[28] His reply is consistent with an earlier report on his views: "Sakharov has told Western scientists that he worked on the Soviet H-bomb program quite mindful of the negative aspects of Stalinism, but convinced that bipolarity would be more conducive to world peace than a monopoly of power by any one country."[29]

1958 was also the year in which Sakharov first spoke out in the mass media on a social issue. Together with Zel'dovich, he joined the public debate on Khrushchev's proposed education reforms. These would have required all pupils in their final year of secondary education to spend one-third of their time in factory or farm work. Instead, Sakharov and Zel'dovich propounded, in *Pravda* of November 19, "the need to create a network of special schools with a bias in the natural sciences and mathematics," arguing against such an interruption in the education of children with a talent for mathematics and physics at the critical ages of 14 and 15: "Many major discoveries and valuable research are effected by talented scientists at the ages 22–26. . . . To delay the training of such people means . . . to harm the development of science and technology." They also demanded a "radical revision" of the entire school

26. Smith, "Intolerable Sakharov," pp. 54, 56; *Sakharov o sebe*, p. 9. Nine- and 13-megaton tests were conducted on Novaya Zemlya September 21 and 25, 1962, respectively; *New York Times*, September 16–22, 26. In Khrushchev's version of the telephone talk with Sakharov he recalled that Sakharov had addressed an appeal to him as chairman of the Council of Ministers "to cancel the scheduled explosion and not to engage in any further testing, at least not of the hydrogen bomb." Sakharov is then quoted directly: "As a scientist and as [a] designer of the hydrogen bomb, I know what harm these explosions can bring down on the head of mankind." *Khrushchev Remembers. The Last Testament*, trans. and ed. Strobe Talbott (Boston and Toronto, 1974), p. 69.

27. Smith, "Intolerable Sakharov," p. 56.

28. Axelbank, in *Observer*; also Sakharov's September 8, 1973, press conference (references at n. 24 above).

29. Walter C. Clemens, Jr., "Sakharov: A Man for Our Times," *Bulletin of the Atomic Scientists* 27, no. 10 (December 1971): 51. See also *Sakharov o sebe*, p. 6, and Sakharov's September 8, 1973, press conference. Sakharov evidently finds some consolation in having contributed to the 1963 partial test ban treaty. *Sakharov o sebe*, pp. 9–10; Smith, "Intolerable Sakharov," p. 56.

program, especially in these fields, to introduce subjects relevant to the modern world such as the theory of probability, analytical geometry, vector analysis, and computer principles.[30]

In 1964 Sakharov raised his voice during a vote crucial to the future of the biological sciences in the Soviet Union. In June he participated in the decisive stand against Lysenkoism taken at the general meeting of the Academy of Sciences. The biological section of the academy had voted for the election of Nikolai I. Nuzhdin, a corresponding member and, acording to Zhores Medvedev, "an unprincipled, active supporter of Lysenko," as a full member in genetics. The academy's statutes, however, required a confirmation vote by a general meeting of its full members. During the debate prior to this vote Sakharov called on "all those present to vote so that the only yeas will be by those who, together with Nuzhdin, together with Lysenko, bear the responsibility for the infamous, painful pages in the development of Soviet science, which fortunately are now coming to an end."[31] The vote was 22 or 24 for and 126 against Nuzhdin. By his action Sakharov placed himself squarely on the liberal side of a political conflict that had stunted the growth of a major science in the USSR for nearly a quarter of a century. Because of his forthright stand Sakharov was criticized for the first time in the Soviet press. With a sneering reference to him as "an engineer by speciality" Mikhail Ol'shansky, president of the All-Union Academy of Agricultural Sciences, described him as "incompetent and naive [*malosvedushchee i ne v meru prostodushnoe*]."[32] Ironically, Sakharov's stand against Lysenkoism was soon afterwards lauded by the new collective leadership at the Communist Party's Central Committee plenum of October 1964, which confirmed the removal of Khrushchev.[33]

It was in this period that Sakharov met the biologist Zhores Medvedev and his twin brother, Roy, a historian. Ol'shansky's main target had been Zhores, who sought out Sakharov as an ally in his war against Lysenkoism. Sakharov read a samizdat text for the first time—Zhores's work on Lysenkoism. In 1966 he met Roy and was among the first to read his study of Stalinism. Despite their subsequent differences on questions of principle, Sakharov has acknowledged his debt to the brothers.[34]

30. Ya. Zel'dovich and A. Sakharov, "Nuzhny estestvenno-matematicheskie shkoly" [Schools for the natural sciences and mathematics are needed], *Pravda*, November 19, 1958.

31. Zhores A. Medvedev, *The Rise and Fall of T. D. Lysenko*, trans. Michael Lerner (New York, 1969), pp. 215, 217, citing the stenographic record.

32. M. Ol'shansky, "Protiv dezinformatsii i klevety" [Against misinformation and slander], *Sel'skaia zhizn'* [Rural life], August 29, 1964. Sakharov recalls the attack in *Sakharov o sebe*, p. 10.

33. Zhores Medvedev, "A. D. Sakharov i problema mirnogo sotrudnichestva" [A. D. Sakharov and the problem of peaceful cooperation], *Novyi zhurnal* [The new review], no. 113 (December 1973), p. 215; a slightly revised text in English translation under the title "The Sakharov I Knew" appears in Sunday *Observer* (London), July 7, 1974.

34. Zh. Medvedev, "Sakharov," pp. 215–16; *Sakharov o sebe*, p. 10. R. Medvedev's samizdat work "Pod sudom istorii" [Let history judge], 1962–68, *AS* 1060, is published in English under the title *Let History Judge: The Origins and Consequences of Stalinism* (New York, 1971).

With the fall of Khrushchev and the formation of collective rule under Brezhnev, Kosygin, and Podgorny, Soviet society witnessed a flurry of efforts by the party to rehabilitate Stalin. On the eve of the Twenty-third Congress of the Communist Party of the Soviet Union, Sakharov for the first time put his signature to an open group appeal, copies of which circulated in samizdat. Right after the Sinyavsky-Daniel trial, probably in February, he joined twenty-four other leading intellectuals in a letter to Brezhnev to voice opposition to the rumored rehabilitation of Stalin. They foresaw "the danger of serious divisions within Soviet society" and "the threat of a new split in the ranks of the world communist movement, this time between us and communists of the West."[35] Stalin was not rehabilitated at the congress, but manifestations of neo-Stalinism became more evident as the year 1966 progressed. Articles 190-1 and 190-3 were added to the Criminal Code of the Russian Soviet Federated Socialist Republic by a decree of September 16 (as were corresponding articles to the codes of the other Union republics). Article 190-1 treated deliberate fabrications defaming the Soviet state and social system and article 190-3 group activities disturbing public order. Twenty-one intellectuals addressed an open appeal to the deputies of the RSFSR Supreme Soviet not to approve the decree, and Sakharov was one of the twenty-one. The articles, they argued, were "contrary to Leninist principles of socialist democracy" and, "if approved, . . . might be an obstacle to realization of the liberties guaranteed by the USSR Constitution."[36] The articles were approved.

Within weeks of the arrests of Yuri Galanskov and Alexander Ginzburg, Sakharov "sent an appeal to the Party's Central Committee on February 11, 1967, asking that the Ginzburg-Galanskov case be closed." This was the first time Sakharov interceded in an attempt to right the violated civil rights of individual citizens.[37]

From 1950 to 1968 Sakharov "resided and worked in a remote, secret city," although he maintained his Moscow apartment. He told Axelbank he had "worked on secret projects for the Government for twenty years. . . . I have not done theoretical work for twenty years because I was involved in practical defense work" (but cf. pp. 357–58 above). The publication abroad of *Reflections* led to the loss of his security clearances in August 1968, and he returned

---

35. "Pis'mo 25-ti deiatelei kul'tury Brezhnevu o tendentsii k reabilitatsii Stalina" [Letter of 25 cultural leaders to Brezhnev on possible rehabilitation of Stalin], n.d. [mid-February 1966], *AS* 273. In reporting the letter in *New York Times*, March 21, 1966, Peter Grose wrote that it had been sent "more than a month ago."

36. "Obrashchenie gruppy intelligentov (21 chelovek) k deputatam Verkhovnogo Soveta RSFSR v sviazi s vvedeniem v UK RSFSR statei 190-1 i 190-3" [Appeal of 21 intellectuals to deputies of the RSFSR Supreme Soviet concerning amendment to the RSFSR Criminal Code by articles 190-1 and 190-3], n.d. [soon after September 16, 1966], *AS* 159. Both appeals were signed by the academicians I. Ye. Tamm and M. A. Leontovich; another, Ya. B. Zel'dovich, signed the appeal of 21.

37. *Reflections*, p. 64. See also *Sakharov o sebe*, p. 11.

to Moscow.[38] Although not a party member, he was invited before the academy's party committee, it was reported in late 1968, for what may have been an attempt to expel him from the academy.[39] In its issue of April 30, 1969, the samizdat *Chronicle of Current Events* carried the following item: "The Ministry of Medium Machine Building, at which Sakharov was a consultant, has dispensed with his services. Now Sakharov holds a post only at his own institute [Lebedev], where no security pass is required." Sakharov also dates his return to his old institute from 1969. Zhores Medvedev recalls this telling exchange between institute director Dmitri Skobel'tsyn and Sakharov:

Skobel'tsyn: We are taking you in the hope that you will stop making political statements.
Sakharov: I will not speak out if there will be no serious reasons for doing so.[40]

The seminars he attends at the Lebedev Physics Institute are "more passive than active," Sakharov told Axelbank. "They had to provide me with some work, because they didn't want any scandals involving me." The fall 1972 seminar on quantum theory and elementary particles was open and unclassified.[41]

Thanks to Axelbank and to those correspondents who followed him, particularly Hedrick Smith and Olle Stenholm, the world has a picture of Sakharov in his private surroundings. He comes through as an extremely modest man, with simple tastes and no hobbies except for an interest in skiing. He has three grown children by his first wife, now dead. They are two daughters, who are married, and a son who was probably born in 1957. He married Yelena Georgievna Bonner-Alikhanova, a pediatrician of a mixed Armenian and Jewish background, in the fall of 1970 "after they met outside the courthouse where a dissident scientist [the Leningrad mathematician Revol't Pimenov] was on trial." She is an aunt of Eduard Kuznetsov, a Jewish dissident whose death sentence at the December 1970 Leningrad trial of "hijackers" was commuted to fifteen years in special-regime labor camps; her mother spent the years 1937–53 in Stalin's camps and in exile.[42] Sakharov has two stepchildren. Tatiana Ivanovna Semionova, born in February 1950, was a

---

38. Axelbank, in *Observer*; *Sakharov o sebe*, p. 13. According to Zh. Medvedev, Sakharov lost his security clearances because *Reflections* was published "in the Russian émigré press in Paris and Frankfurt"; "Sakharov," p. 218. *Russkaia mysl'* published the text August 1 through 29, 1968, and Possev-Verlag in August.

39. Reported by Eugene Rabinowitch, who attended the September 1968 Pugwash Conference in Nice, France, as cited by Victor Cohn, *Washington Post*, November 10, 1968.

40. *Khronika tekushchikh sobytii* (hereafter *Chronicle*), no. 7 (April 30, 1969), *AS* 196; *Sakharov o sebe*, p. 13. Medvedev dates the exchange, perhaps mistakenly, in the first half of 1970; "Sakharov," p. 219.

41. Axelbank, in *Observer*.

42. *Ibid.* Pimenov and the puppet-theater actor Boris Vail were sentenced in October 1970 by the Kaluga oblast court. Sakharov attended the trial; *Chronicle*, no. 16 (October 31, 1970), *AS* 500; *Sakharov o sebe*, pp. 14–15. On Bonner's relationship to Kuznetsov and on her mother

student in good standing at Moscow University until expelled from the evening department of the faculty of journalism in early October 1972. She is married to Yefrem Vladimirovich Yankelevich, born in June 1950, a graduate of the Institute of Communications, whose field is communications theory. In June 1973 he was forced to leave his job or face dismissal. Sakharov's stepson Alexei Ivanovich Semionov, born in August 1956, had been a student in good standing in a special physics and mathematics school in Moscow until expelled in the winter of 1973. In July 1973 he was refused admission to Moscow University after his entrance exam in Russian literature had been purposely downgraded, but in the fall he was finally allowed to enter the Lenin Pedagogical Institute, the same institute at which Sakharov's father had taught physics.[43]

Sakharov has expressed concern for his new family. "I am just worried about the consequences of my actions for those near to me, my family," he told Axelbank. At another point he added, "They are afraid to touch my children or me because of my position, but they go after Tania and Yelena." Throughout 1973 this became a major concern for Sakharov. In the spring of 1973 Princeton University invited him to be a visiting scholar and Yefrem and Alexei were offered scholarships by the Massachusetts Institute of Technology for the fall term. In early 1974, however, Sakharov announced that he was abandoning the projected visit, at least for the time being.[44]

Sakharov has been awarded a Stalin Prize and a Lenin Prize and has been honored three times as a Hero of Socialist Labor. He was elected a member of the American Academy of Arts and Sciences in May 1969 and a foreign associate of the American National Academy of Sciences in April 1973. No evidence has been found that he has ever traveled outside the USSR.[45]

---

see Smith, "Intolerable Sakharov," p. 61. Yelena Bonner is the author of a note on the son of the poet Eduard Bagritsky in *Yunost'* [Youth], 1962, no. 7 (July), pp. 58–59, and of an article in *Neva*, 1961, nos. 3–4 (March–April).

43. For data on the stepchildren, see Axelbank, in *Observer*; Hedrick Smith, *New York Times*, May 3, 1973 (where Yankelevich is described as an electrochemical engineer); *idem*, "Intolerable Sakharov," p. 64; press conference of August 21, 1973; and *Sakharov o sebe*, pp. 23–24.

44. For the invitation see Sakharov, "Statement on Invitation," and Smith, *New York Times*, May 3, 1973. For the abandonment of the U.S. visit, see Sandro Scabello's report of a February 21 telephone interview with Sakharov in Leningrad, *Corriere della sera*, February 22, 1974.

45. Sakharov's awards are indicated in *AS* 273. For his honors by the American academies see UPI dispatch of May 15, 1969, and John Walsh, "National Academy of Sciences," *Science*, May 11, 1973, p. 576. The information in *Prominent Personalities in the USSR: A Biographical Directory* (Metuchen, N.J., 1968), p. 536, that Sakharov attended the "2nd International Atomic Conference" in Geneva in 1958 is evidently incorrect. He is not listed as a member of the Soviet delegation in vol. 1 nor as the author of a paper presented at the conference in vol. 33 of *Proceedings of the Second United Nations International Conference on the Peaceful Uses of Atomic Energy Held in Geneva 1 September–13 September 1958* (Geneva, 1958). Tamm, it can be noted, did participate; for his lecture see *ibid.* 1: 408–13.

THE QUESTION OF INTELLECTUAL FREEDOM

In *Reflections* (1968) Sakharov advances two interdependent theses—"the division of mankind threatens it with destruction" and "intellectual freedom is essential to human society"—which he applies to the state of the world. While the danger to all mankind of "universal thermonuclear war" is the general theme of *Reflections*, the danger implied in the second thesis applies more particularly to Soviet citizens. "Freedom of thought," he writes, "is the only guarantee of the feasibility of a scientific democratic approach to politics, economics, and culture." And further on: "Today the key to a progressive restructuring of the system of government in the interests of mankind lies in intellectual freedom. This has been understood, in particular, by the Czechoslovaks. . . ."[46]

It is to the second thesis that Sakharov devotes more and more of his thinking since 1968. In *Reflections* the ethical issue of the value of the individual is tied to the second thesis: "The threat to intellectual freedom . . . is a threat to the independence and worth of the human personality, a threat to the meaning of human life"; and:

The prospects of socialism now depend on . . . whether the moral *attractiveness* of the ideas of socialism . . . will be the decisive factors that people will bear in mind when comparing socialism and capitalism, or whether people will remember mainly the limitations of intellectual freedom under socialism or, even worse, the fascist-like regimes of the cult.[47]

In the "Letter of Three" (1970) intellectual freedom becomes utilitarian, a means to resolving the economic problems at home: "Without reforms in management, information, and openness [*glasnost'*], the economic measures [i.e., the 1965 reform] cannot be carried out in full." And: "The scientific approach [to solve the economic problems] requires complete information, unbiased thinking, and creative freedom."[48] The "Letter of Three" conveys a mood of greater urgency and growing alarm at the leadership's failure to take positive action: "Now we have a chance to take the correct road and carry out the necessary reforms [proposed in the text's fifteen-point model program]. Within a few years it will perhaps already be too late." Too late for what? To prevent "a victory of the tendencies of rigid rule by fiat, of 'tightening of the screws,'" for such a victory "not only will not solve any of the problems, but on the contrary . . . will lead the country to a tragic deadend. The tactic of passive waiting will in the final analysis lead to the same result."[49]

46. Pp. 27, 29, 67.
47. Pp. 59, 71; emphasis in Russian text only (see Russian ed., p. 35).
48. Pp. 5, 6.
49. Pp. 12–13.

In the "Memorandum" (March 1971), by contrast, the moral issue is dominant. Sakharov reformulates this issue far more forcefully: "The fundamental goal of the state is the protection and security of the fundamental rights of its citizens. The defense of human rights is higher than other goals."[50] The example of Vladimir Bukovsky may have been decisive in Sakharov's thinking here. On January 18, 1972, in his appeal to Brezhnev and R. A. Rudenko, procurator general of the USSR, to annul Bukovsky's sentence, Sakharov writes: "Only the moral health of a people is the true pledge of the country's viability for creative labor and for facing up to future tests."[51]

In the "Afterword" (June 1972) the higher priority of the value of the individual is now completely self-evident to Sakharov: "It seems to me now, to a still greater degree than before, that the one true guarantee of the preservation of human values . . . is the freedom of convictions of man, his moral striving for good." Whereas in the "Memorandum" Sakharov could avoid direct reference to the events of 1968 in Czechoslovakia, in the "Afterword" he can no longer. Looking back to date the beginning of the "reexamination" of his views, he notes the year 1968: "For me personally the beginning of that year was marked by work on *Reflections on Progress*, while the end, as for all of us, was marked by the roar of tanks on the streets of unsubdued Prague." He still favors the convergence of the socialist and capitalist systems as the alternative to the destruction of mankind; he still "assigns decisive importance to the democratization of society, to the development of *glasnost'*, legality, and the safeguarding of basic human rights"; he still "hopes for the evolution of society . . . although my prognoses have become more reserved." But now, recording his waning optimism, he cries out his disappointment:

With pain and alarm I am compelled to note, following a largely illusory liberalism, a renewed intensification of restrictions on ideological freedom, of the urge to suppress information not under state control, of persecutions for political and ideological reasons, of deliberate exacerbation of nationality problems.[52]

What had happened? The most immediate cause was the arrest of Peter Yakir on June 21, 1972.[53] Within two days Sakharov's "Memorandum" and "Afterword" were carried in the Western press. A few months earlier had occurred the trial of Vladimir Bukovsky (January 5, 1972) following his year-long detention. Sakharov had not been admitted to his trial, and all efforts to rescue him from injustice had failed.[54] More and more in the

50. P. 5.
51. The text is in *Chronicle*, no. 24 (March 5, 1972), p. 4, *AS* 1100.
52. "Afterword," pp. 12–14.
53. Robert G. Kaiser, *Washington Post* and *International Herald Tribune*, June 22, 1972.
54. Sakharov protested Bukovsky's arrest in an open letter of March 30, 1971, to Shchelokov; *AS* 609. He signed a joint appeal of the Moscow Human Rights Committee of July 4 to the Fifth World Congress of Psychiatry; *AS* 1015. On November 29 in a supervisory complaint to Rudenko he demanded an end to infringement of Bukovsky's right to a defense;

period since mid-1968 Sakharov had been drawn into the world of the particular by the immediacy of the problems of the persecuted and the oppressed. In October 1972 he told Axelbank that "one cannot be inactive when people are perishing from increased repressions." When asked why he continued to struggle if he thought it so futile, Sakharov replied: "Because for us it is not a political struggle. . . . It is a moral struggle for all of us. We have to be true to ourselves."[55] For Sakharov, then, a man's ethical position in the final analysis is measured by his actions.

THE NATIONALITY QUESTION

Setting the nationality question in the frame of "the threat to intellectual freedom," Sakharov in *Reflections* (1968) writes: "Nationality problems will long continue to be a reason for unrest and dissatisfaction unless *all* departures from Leninist principles which have occurred are acknowledged and analyzed and firm steps are taken to correct all mistakes." This assertion appears, in the Russian text, as a footnote to a passage condemning the incomplete rehabilitation of the Crimean Tatars (by the law of September 5, 1967, "On citizens of Tatar nationality who lived in the Crimea"): "Is it not disgraceful to continue to restrict the civil rights of the Crimean Tatar people who lost about 46% of their population (mainly children and old people) in the Stalinist repressions?"[56]

Whatever "Leninist principles" may mean to Sakharov at this stage, one inference is clear—the nationality policy as developed under Stalin must be abandoned. One observer has found Sakharov's views in 1968 to be "in striking agreement" with those of the Ukrainian Ivan Dzyuba: "While Dzyuba writes [in 1965] that 'nobody in the Ukraine advances the slogan of "independence" today,' he nevertheless points out that 'the Constitution of the USSR guarantees the Republics the right to secede from the Union.'"[57]

Chronicle, no. 23 (January 5, 1972), p. 3, *AS* 1075. On December 12, with fellow members of the Moscow Human Rights Committee, he appealed to the chairman of the Moscow city court to be admitted to Bukovsky's trial "to observe in person the workings of justice in this case, which has aroused great public interest"; *ibid.*, p. 4. In a joint letter of late December to Rudenko and V. I. Terebilov he argued that neither Bukovsky's television interview nor the medical documents he had sent to Western psychiatrists could be regarded as "libelous," since the former was "based on what he saw and heard and experienced himself" while the latter were "copies of genuine documents"; A. Sakharov *et al.* to USSR procurator general and USSR minister of justice, n.d. [late December 1971], *AS* 1283. Finally, on January 18, 1972, he appealed to Brezhnev and Rudenko to annul the sentence; *Chronicle*, no. 24, p. 4.

55. Axelbank, in *Observer*.

56. P. 66; emphasis in Russian text only (see Russian ed., pp. 33–34). On the law, see the anonymous document reviewing the struggle by the Crimean Tatars for rehabilitation and the right to return to the Crimea, "Vsenarodnyi protest" [An all-people's protest], addressed to CPSU Central Committee, USSR Supreme Soviet, USSR Council of Ministers, and the Soviet public, n.d. [soon after January 31, 1969], p. 3, *AS* 379.

57. Michael Browne, in his introduction to the collection of documents *Ferment in the Ukraine* (London, 1971), p. 26, citing Ivan Dzyuba, *Internationalism or Russification?* (London, 1968), p. 56.

In *Reflections* Sakharov does not actually discuss the problem of self-determination, which for the USSR poses the problem of the right of secession. He comes close to it, however, in developing his four principles which the USA and the USSR must "apply universally" if mankind is to escape from the threat of thermonuclear war. Principle 1 asserts: "All peoples have the right to decide their own fate with a free expression of will. This right is guaranteed by international control over observance by all governments of the Declaration of Human Rights."[58] But the principle is concerned chiefly with relations among *states*.

The "Letter of Three" (March 1970) devotes two of the fifteen points in its model program for political and economic democratization to the nationality question. One proposes "abolition of the mention of nationality in passports and official questionnaires."[59] This would serve the needs of Jews in the USSR, but it hardly satisfied the editors of the samizdat journal *Ukrain'sky visnyk* (Ukrainian herald), who wrote in issue no. 5: "Proposals of this sort were put forward in Khrushchev's time and were seen in the Union republics as a desire to make further encroachments on their sovereignty."[60]

The second point sets down a minimal program for all the less numerous peoples of the USSR who have been repressed in the past: "Restoration of all rights of nations [*natsii*] forcibly resettled under Stalin. Restoration of national autonomy of resettled peoples and granting them the opportunity of return settlement [*obratnoe pereselenie*] (wherever this has not been done up to now)."[61]

The "Letter of Three" also raises the specter of China. Clearly its authors are writing with the Sino-Soviet border clash along the Ussuri River in March 1969 still fresh in their minds:

What awaits our country, if a course for democratization is not set? . . . Exacerbation of nationality problems, for in the national republics the movement for democratization in process from below is inevitably becoming nationalistic [*natsionalisticheskii*]. This prospect is especially threatening when one considers the danger of Chinese totalitarian nationalism (which danger we consider historically to be temporary, yet very serious in the coming years).[62]

In March 1969 the young dissident historian and publicist Andrei Amalrik had told Anatol Shub, Moscow correspondent of the *Washington Post*, that "unless there is a radical change of policy and we go back to Lenin's principles (permitting independence for the Finns, the Balts, etc.) all

---

58. P. 41 (Russian ed., p. 12).
59. P. 9.
60. As quoted by *Chronicle*, no. 22, p. 33 (a readable copy of *Ukraïn'sky visnyk*, no. 5, has not reached the West).
61. "Letter of Three," p. 9.
62. *Ibid.*, p. 12.

these people will see the war with China as a signal to rise against what they consider Russian colonialism."[63] One wonders just how much of Amalrik Sakharov has read. To take just one example, in his letter of December 18, 1967, to the editor in chief of *Izvestiia*, Amalrik argued that "war with Communist China, [Soviet] territorial pretensions in the West and the Orient, and moral weariness from war may lead to a regeneration of separatist tendencies still hidden at present, first of all in the Baltic area, the Transcaucasus, and Central Asia."[64]

By March 1971 the pressure of the Jewish demand for the right to emigrate forced itself on Sakharov's thinking. Perhaps his first public expression on this problem is to be found in his appeal to President Nixon and Chairman Podgorny just after Mark Dymshits and Eduard Kuznetsov had been sentenced to death at the December 1970 Leningrad trial of alleged hijackers. On December 28 Sakharov argues and pleads with Podgorny:

One must bear in mind that the reason the condemned attempted to hijack a plane was the restriction by the authorities on the legal right of tens of thousands of Jews wishing to leave the country. I categorically reject the accusation of treason to the Motherland as without relation to the act of the condemned. . . . [To execute Dymshits and Kuznetsov] would be unjust cruelty. Soften the punishment of the other accused.[65]

It is thus a logical development for Sakharov to list the nationality question among the "urgent questions" in his "Memorandum" (March 1971). He proposes "the adoption of laws that ensure the simple and unhindered right of citizens to leave and return to the country" and "abolition of directives restricting this right and contravening the law."[66]

He reiterates his defense of the less numerous peoples by urging "adoption of decisions and laws on the complete restoration of the rights of peoples exiled under Stalin."[67] He has also signed at least six other documents on this subject. The first was his note of March 16, 1972, to the

---

63. *International Herald Tribune*, March 31, 1969, as cited by Browne, *Ferment*, pp. 26–27.

64. Amalrik asked, "What could the Soviet Union do not to be isolated in the face of possible aggression?" and sketched a tentative policy: "First, cease to spread its influence by means of organizing and participating in conflicts. . . . Second, strive for relations with other countries which would be based on mutual interests and a community of goals. . . . Third, establish genuinely friendly relations with the USA. . . . This . . . would lead [the USA] to a better understanding of USSR interests and would make the two great powers the guarantors of a durable peace. Fourth, try to obtain a situation in Europe which would be stable and without constant pressure from the USSR." AS 1044. Here in miniature is the convergence thesis of Sakharov's *Reflections*; but it cannot be demonstrated that Amalrik is actually the fountainhead of Sakharov's thinking in this area.

65. A. D. Sakharov, "Prezidentu SShA R. Niksonu; Predsedateliu Prezidiuma Verkhovnogo Soveta SSSR N. V. Podgornomu" [To R. Nixon, president of the USA, and N. V. Podgorny, chairman of the Presidium of the USSR Supreme Soviet], December 28, 1970, *AS* 512.

66. P. 3.

67. *Ibid.*

Moscow Human Rights Committee "On the Problem of Restoring the Rights of Individuals and Peoples Violated under Forced Resettlement." It is a brief but detailed seven-point proposal to take action after thorough study and discussion of the problem. Besides historical studies, Sakharov wants analyses of the current situation, for example the facts of discrimination against the Crimean Tatars, Volga Germans, and Meskhi with respect to residence permits, employment, education, and the right to acquire property. He also wants to know why those demanding the restoration of such peoples' rights are being persecuted. He is interested in such factors as "the role of the general ideological course of great-power chauvinism" and "overt violence as a method of political play on prejudices and base instincts."[68] Following discussion of the note and an opinion from Chalidze on it, the committee voted April 13 to send an appeal to the Presidium of the USSR Supreme Soviet. The appeal, dated April 21, calls on the Presidium "to help restore the rights of the Crimean Tatar people and the Meskhi (and other peoples [narodnosti] and groups) to reside in the territory from which they were forcibly and illegally exiled."[69] A third document is Sakharov's letter "On Discrimination against the Crimean Tatars" (as he refers to it in the "Afterword" addressed to the USSR minister of internal affairs.[70]

Sakharov has catalogued "unresolved" problems in the field of human rights in his statement of December 5, 1973, accepting the 1973 Human Rights Prize awarded by the International League for the Rights of Man. Noting "many problems of national equality," he lists the Crimean Tatars, Volga Germans, and Meskhi among peoples who "cannot return to their native lands."[71] In a January 1974 joint appeal (which he signed as "member of the Council of Directors of the International League for the Rights of Man") Sakharov calls on the UN Secretary General, Kurt Waldheim, "by all means possible to encourage the return to the homeland of the Crimean Tatars, who are being detained administratively in banishment against the unambiguously expressed will of this people."[72] And in his statement (April 1974) on Solzhenitsyn's *Letter to the Leaders of the Soviet Union*, he counters the latter's view that the Russian people have been the main victims of the regime's tyranny: "Such actions as forcible genocide deportation

68. A. D. Sakharov, note to the Moscow Human Rights Committee "O probleme vosstanovleniia prav lits i narodov, narushennykh pri nasil'stvennom pereselenii," *AS* 1251; English trans., *Sakharov Speaks*, pp. 237–38.

69. Human Rights Committee, appeal "Prezidiumu Verkhovnogo Soveta SSSR" [To the Presidium of the USSR Supreme Soviet], *AS* 1254. Esenin-Volpin also signed the appeal, according to *Chronicle*, no. 25 (May 21, 1972), p. 38, *AS* 1130.

70. "Afterword" p. 15.

71. Text is in *Khronika zashchity prav v SSSR*, nos. 5–6 (November–December 1973), p. 62; English trans., emended to include Meskhi, in *Sakharov Speaks*, p. 229.

72. A. Sakharov et al., "Obrashchenie k K. Val'dkhaimu s pros'boi sposobstvovat' vozvrascheniiu na rodinu krymskikh tatar" [Appeal to K. Waldheim to encourage the return of the Crimean Tatars to their homeland], n.d. [January 1974], *AS* 1725. For date of text see UPI dispatch of May 24, 1974.

[*deportatsiia-genotsid*], the struggle against national-liberation movements, and suppression of national culture—this has been even basically the privilege of precisely the non-Russians!"[73]

In the eighth thesis of the "Memorandum"—"the field of law"—he advises "elimination of obvious and concealed forms of discrimination—on the basis of belief, nationality, and the like."[74]

It is in the ninth thesis of the "Memorandum"—"mutual relations of the national republics"—that Sakharov comes to the heart of the nationality problem. He now proceeds to discourse openly on self-determination:

Our country has proclaimed the right of a nation [*natsiia*] to self-determination up to separation [*otdelenie*]. The Soviet government sanctioned realization of the right to separation in the case of Finland. The right of Union republics to separation is proclaimed by the Constitution of the USSR. However, there is a vagueness about the guarantees of the right and of the procedure which provides for its preparation, necessary discussion, and actual realization. In fact, even discussion of such questions is frequently persecuted.[75]

These are precisely the points made by Ivan Dzyuba: "After all, the Constitution of the USSR guarantees the Republics the right to secede from the Union, which means that it recognizes every citizen's right to advance the idea . . . and to argue the case for it." And: "The very notion of independence, as applied to the republics, has long since been made a weapon of intimidation."[76] The Ukrainian dissident historian Valentin Moroz in his "Report from the Beria Reservation" (April 15, 1967) uses the same argument: "My comrades and I were convicted for 'propaganda directed at separating the Ukraine from the USSR.' But article 17 of the USSR Constitution clearly states the right of each Republic to secede."[77]

Sakharov argues that discussion of the subject would be not only lawful but useful to the state: "A juridical analysis of the problem and adoption of a law guaranteeing the right to separation would be of major internal and international importance as corroboration of the anti-imperialistic and anti-chauvinistic nature of our policy." He finds "no massive tendencies in any republic to secede"; moreover, any such tendencies would "undoubtedly weaken yet more with time as a consequence of further democratization in the USSR." He has "no doubt that a republic that seceded . . . for one reason or another by peaceful, constitutional means would fully preserve its ties with the socialist community of nations."[78]

73. Sakharov, "Statement on Solzhenitsyn Letter," pp. 2–3.
74. P. 10.
75. *Ibid.* Article 17 of the Constitution reads: "The right of free secession [*vykhod*] from the USSR is reserved for every Union republic." *Konstitutsiia SSSR* (Moscow, 1970), p. 7.
76. Dzyuba, *Internationalism or Russification?*, p. 56, cited by Browne, *Ferment*, p. 26.
77. "Reportazh iz zapovednika imeni Berii," April 15, 1967, *AS* 249; English trans., Browne, *Ferment*, p. 124; Ukrainian trans., *AS* 957.
78. "Memorandum," pp. 10–11.

This approach to the problem of self-determination is very much like that of Svyatoslav Karavansky, who wrote on September 25, 1965: "Perhaps under the present conditions of the development of the communist movement it would be expedient for the Ukrainian socialist nation to be a separate socialist unit in the common socialist camp?"[79] The similarity of approach is even more striking when it is realized that Sakharov will have something to say about Karavansky's wife, Nina Strokata.

At this point it will be interesting to compare Sakharov's *Reflections* (1968) and "Memorandum" (1971) with the *Program of the Democratic Movement of the Soviet Union* (1969) on the nationality question. A textual comparison suggests an interplay of thought, although there is no concrete evidence that Sakharov and the authors of the *Program* were in fact in dialogue. In *Reflections*, as has been indicated, Sakharov asserts that "all peoples have the right to decide their own fate with a free expression of will [*svobodnym voleiziavleniem*]. This right is guaranteed by international control over observance by all governments of the Declaration of Human Rights."

The *Program* holds that "self-determination of nations [*natsii*] of the Soviet Union must be secured by their right of appeal to the UN with the demand for a referendum to be conducted freely as an outpouring of the will of all the people [*vsenarodnoe voleizliianie*] under obligatory supervision of UN observation commissions." It proclaims as one of the goals of the Democratic Movement "complete self-determination and free expression of will [*svobodnoe voleiziavlenie*] by means of a referendum."[80]

In the "Memorandum" Sakharov notes that "our country has proclaimed the right of a nation to self-determination up to separation." But, as has just been seen, he does not particularize as to method (for example, referendum), although he suggests a series of steps—open discussion, juridical analysis, adoption of a law—and insists that the method be "constitutional."

Sakharov goes on to argue that because "the economic interests and defense potential of the socialist countries are . . . all-embracing and will undoubtedly deepen all the more with mutual noninterference of the socialist countries in the internal affairs of one another," he sees nothing dangerous in discussing the question. He seems to be saying to Brezhnev that he can never forget August 1968 in Prague but nevertheless again urges him to take up the program.

Sakharov finds support for his proposals in international law. In the thesis "the field of law" in the "Memorandum" he recommends "considera-

---

79. From Karavansky's petition to Gomulka, cited by Browne, *Ferment*, p. 26. See also Vyacheslav Chornovil, ed., *The Chornovil Papers* (New York, 1968), p. 184; Ukrainian trans., AS 462, p. 123.
80. "Programma demokraticheskogo dvizheniia Sovetskogo Soiuza," signed anonymously by "Democrats of Russia, the Ukraine, and the Baltic Region," 1969, AS 340, pp. 14, 45; published in Amsterdam, 1970.

tion of the question of USSR Supreme Soviet ratification of the Covenants on Human Rights, adopted by the Twenty-first Session of the UN General Assembly" on December 16, 1966.[81] These are the International Covenant on Economic, Social, and Cultural Rights and the International Covenant on Civil and Political Rights. It is noteworthy that both covenants give pride of place to the nationality question. Paragraph 1 of article 1 of both reads: "All peoples have the right of self-determination. By virtue of that right they freely determine their political status and freely pursue their economic, social, and cultural development."[82]

On December 26, 1970, Sakharov and his colleagues of the Moscow Human Rights Committee had agreed that "to develop a social system for the defense of [human] rights [in the USSR] the committee recognizes as of paramount importance: legal education, including the propagation and explanation of the Universal Declaration of Human Rights and of the Covenants on Human Rights."[83] It is noteworthy that as early as April 1967 Moroz had caught the significance of the UN covenants for the Soviet nationality question: "The right of every people to secede is laid down in the Covenant on Civil and Political Rights."[84] In his introduction (December 1973) to *Sakharov Speaks* and in a February 1974 interview given to the *Sunday Times* (London), Sakharov refers to Moroz's "Report from the Beria Reservation" as the latter's camp memoirs.[85] (In both instances the context is cruelty of punishment and severity of labor camp conditions, not the nationality question per se.) While it thus appears that he has read Moroz, just when is not known, nor can the extent of its influenced be determined.

81. P. 10.
82. For the official English text of the two covenants see *Yearbook of the United Nations 1966* (New York, 1968), pp. 419–31; for Russian texts see V. L. Israelyan, ed., *Sovetskii Soiuz i OON 1961–1965 gg.* [The Soviet Union and the UN 1961–65] (Moscow, 1968), pp. 611–35. The Soviet government signed both covenants on March 19, 1968 (*Times* [London], March 20) and ratified them on September 18, 1973 (*Vedomosti Verkhovnogo Soveta SSSR* [Bulletin of USSR Supreme Soviet], no. 40 [October 3, 1973], article 564, reported in *Pravda*, September 26). In "Memorandum," Sakharov also recommends "accession to the Optional Protocol to the covenants." Actually the protocol, also adopted December 16, 1966, is only to the second covenant. The importance of the protocol is that it provides an avenue of appeal to the international community through the UN Human Rights Committee (created by the Covenant on Civil and Political Rights) for an individual claiming violation of his rights as set forth in the covenant (for the official English text of the protocol see *Yearbook 1966*, pp. 431–32). The Soviet government has up to now ignored the protocol, arguing that for the UN Human Rights Committee to receive or make recommendations on a complaint from an individual who is subject to the jurisdiction of a state party would constitute interference in the internal affairs of the state. For Soviet treatment of the issues of noninterference and implementation of the covenants see, e.g., Israelyan, *Sovetskii Soiuz i OON*, pp. 265–66.
83. The text is in Chalidze's journal *Obshchestvennye problemy* [Social problems], no. 8 (November–December 1970), p. 11, *AS* 660.
84. From his "Report from the Beria Reservation," cited by Browne, *Ferment*, p. 124.
85. *Sakharov o sebe*, p. 16, and A. D. Sakharov, "Interv'iu, dannoe gazete 'Sandi taims', o vysylke A. Solzhenitsyna i o 'Moskovskom obrashchenii'" [Interview given to *Sunday Times* about A. Solzhenitsyn's exile and about the "Moscow Appeal"], February 20, 1974, p. 1, *AS* 1593.

Between March and September 1971 Sakharov expressed growing concern over violations of a citizen's human right to leave the country. He supported Chalidze's appeal of May 20, 1971, to the Presidium of the USSR Supreme Soviet "concerning persecution of Jewish repatriates in the USSR." Chalidze lectured the Presidium on the essence of Zionism: "It is no more than the idea of Jewish statehood. . . . Zionism is represented in the [Soviet] press as an anticommunist and anti-Soviet trend, whereas the concerns of Zionism are deeply national." Sakharov, together with Tverdokhlebov, writes in a postscript to Chalidze's appeal: "We are in agreement with the conclusions of Chalidze's letter and join the appeals to cease persecution of repatriates and not to violate the right to leave the country."[86]

On September 20, 1971, Sakharov himself addresses an open appeal to the Presidium. Perhaps for the first time he signs a document of his own as "member of the Human Rights Committee, A. Sakharov, Academician." In the appeal he calls on the Presidium "to take the initiative . . . to obtain adoption of laws that resolve the problems of exit in a democratic spirit—whoever desires must have the opportunity to leave and, if his desire changes, to return without hindrance—in accordance with universally recognized human rights." Sakharov does not limit the problem to Jewish "repatriates":

Soviet citizens of Jewish as well as of many other nationalities—Russians, Ukrainians, Germans, Armenians, Lithuanians, Latvians, Estonians, Meskhi-Turks, and others—striving to leave for personal, national, or other reasons, have for years been receiving refusals without any grounds, refusals that for many have turned their lives into a constant torment of expectation.[87]

He focuses on some of the well-known trials of May–August: that of Simas Kudirka, the Lithuanian "whose entire guilt was an attempt to remain abroad," sentenced "for treason to the motherland" to ten years; that of Dmitri Mikheev, a postgraduate student in physics at Moscow University, sentenced to eight years "for attempting to leave the country by exchanging documents with a foreigner"—Sakharov was present at his trial in Moscow and finds the case "analogous in its legal aspect" to those of Kudirka and the ten Leningrad "hijackers"; and those of the Jewish "repatriates" Reiza Palatnik in Odessa (sentenced to two years) and Valery Kukui in Sverdlovsk (sentenced to three years).[88]

86. The full text is in *AS* 625.

87. *AS* 694.

88. A samizdat transcript of Kudirka's trial is *AS* 679. Kudirka, according to Sakharov, was released August 23, 1974, by decree of the Presidium of the USSR Supreme Soviet; Christopher Wren, *New York Times*, August 31, 1974. On Mikheev, see *Chronicle*, no. 21 (September 11, 1971), p. 2, *AS* 1000. On the trials of Palatnik and Kukui, see *Chronicle*, no. 20 (July 2, 1971), pp. 14–17, *AS* 675. After their release both were granted exit visas; Palatnik arrived in Israel December 21, 1972 and Kukui, April 9, 1974. UPI dispatch, December 21, 1972, and Reuter dispatch, April 9, 1974.

It is revealing that Sakharov chooses to speak first of Kudirka, widely known as a symbol of the nationality problem in Lithuania. He notes various reasons motivating individuals in their desire to leave and broadens his comments to cover the basic human right of every Soviet citizen to leave and return. Because the courts usually treat such cases as "treason" and deliver harsh sentences, Sakharov recommends that the article on treason in the criminal code be reworked so as to "prevent that unlawful extension of the concept [of treason] now prevalent in legal practice." He links the issue of the right of some citizens wishing to leave with the freedom of all Soviet citizens: "Freedom to leave . . . is a necessary condition for the spiritual freedom of all." In his "Afterword" (June 1972) he refers the reader to this appeal, which he cites as his letter "On freedom to leave the country," rather than repeat his views on the subject.[89]

But Sakharov returns to the topic again and again. To Stenholm in mid-1973 he points to the "absence of the right to leave and return" as an example of "our isolation from the outside world," which is "having a very pernicious effect on domestic life." For Sakharov it is axiomatic: "The right to leave . . . is one of the conditions necessary for the country somehow to develop along healthier lines."[90] In late fall 1973 he reacts strongly to Roy Medvedev's view that acceptance by the United States Congress of the Jackson Amendment would worsen prospects for emigration.[91] And in April 1974 he elaborates further on his axiom:

A democratic solution of the problem of the freedom to leave the USSR and to return—for [all peoples]—is very important inasmuch as with such a solution it will become impossible to retain the other antidemocratic institutions in the country, the need will arise to bring living standards closer to Western [standards], and conditions will arise for the free exchange of people and ideas.[92]

As Sakharov himself observes, fifteen months separate his "Memorandum" from his "Afterword" and his decision to make both texts available to the world public. In the "Afterword" he points to "deliberate exacerbation of nationality problems" as one of the factors contributing to his decision. Among the "alarming" signs of this he mentions "the wave of political arrests in the first months of 1972," many in the Ukraine. He also takes note of major political trials in the first half of 1972, particularly those of

89. P. 15.
90. Interview on Swedish television. See also press conference of August 21, 1973; "Statement on Press Accusation"; Sakharov to U.S. Congress, September 14, 1973, in support of the Jackson Amendment (first reported by Agence France-Presse, Reuter, and UPI dispatches, September 15, 1973; Russian text not available; English trans., *Sakharov Speaks*, pp. 211–15); and his statement of December 5, 1973, accepting the 1973 Human Rights Prize (Russian text in *Khronika zashchity*, nos. 5–6, p. 62).
91. Sakharov, "Statement on Medvedevs"; R. A. Medvedev, "Ocherk 'Problema demokratizatsii i problema razriadki'" [An essay "The problem of democratization and the problem of détente"], October 1973, p. 14, *AS* 1500.
92. Sakharov, "Statement on Solzhenitsyn Letter," p. 10.

Bukovsky in Moscow and Strokata in Odessa (May 4–19).[93] Sakharov is undoubtedly aware that Nina Antonovna Strokata is the wife of Svyatoslav Karavansky, the long-persecuted Ukrainian writer. The special emphasis Sakharov gives her is thus additional evidence that he may be familiar with Karavansky's writings.

Information on the wave of arrests, searches, and interrogations in the Ukraine in January–April 1972 was also reported to Sakharov in a letter of May 1972 from a "group of Soviet citizens" in the Ukraine. The letter was addressed to the Moscow Human Rights Committee, as well as to the USSR and Ukrainian Supreme Soviets and the editors of *Izvestiia* and *Literaturna Ukraïna*. According to *Chronicle*, no. 25, the sole source of information about the letter, it was received by the committee; hence Sakharov was cognizant of its contents, although he makes no reference to it in his "Afterword." After discussing the "complexity" of the "decades of Stalinist tyranny," a "social plague" that led to the rise of the NKVD as "a state within a state," the letter warns in particular on the nationality question: "Suppression of national self-consciousness, numerous arrests of notable representatives of the Ukrainian intelligentsia, threats, blackmail, persecutions, and incessant searches on a massive scale—all this recalls with dread that the year 1937 began in 1933, began with repressions against leading figures of the national cultures."[94]

In his interview on Swedish television (mid-1973) Sakharov touched guardedly on the nationality problem. Because of the size of the USSR he believes that the country "can never be completely uniform," but he admits that "it is almost impossible to know what is happening due to the lack of information and of contact among particular groups of peoples." Yet he is able to say that "nationalist tendencies in the border areas . . . are very strong, although it is extremely difficult to discern whether or not they are positive in each particular case." Without explaining what would be a negative "nationalist tendency," Sakharov limits himself to an inferred definition of a "positive" tendency: "Here and there, for example in the Ukraine, these tendencies are very closely linked to aspirations for democratization; also in the Baltic area, where religious and national trends consistent with demands for democratization are interwoven." Finally, he concedes incomplete knowledge: "In other regions it is perhaps not like this; we do not know the details."[95]

At a glance, Sakharov may seem to take a big step on the nationality question in his statement (April 1974) on Solzhenitsyn's *Letter to the Leaders of the Soviet Union*. He agrees with the latter's marginal note on the subject, which he summarizes as repudiating the "forcible retention of the

93. "Afterword," p. 14. For samizdat transcript of Bukovsky's trial see *AS* 1077; on Strokata's trial see *Chronicle*, no. 25, pp. 2–3, *AS* 1130.
94. Pp. 10–11. For discussion of the letter as a possible KGB provocation see p. 000 below.
95. P. 6.

national republics within the structure of the USSR." He admits that he has "involuntarily strengthened Solzhenitsyn's accent on [this] point, which seems to me to be exceptionally important from moral and political points of view."[96] But actually he does not go beyond the stand taken in the "Memorandum" (March 1971), when he raised the Soviet constitutional "right of self-determination up to separation."

THE QUESTION OF RELIGIOUS FREEDOM

Sakharov devotes no special attention to religious freedom in *Reflections* (1968), although the subject comes naturally under one of his summary proposals: "All anticonstitutional laws and decrees violating human rights must be abrogated."*Reflections* does refer to the Universal Declaration of Human Rights, but the context is one of peoples as nation-states, not religious groups.[97]

In the spring of 1969 two samizdat documents appeared that may have influenced Sakharov's subsequent thinking, although there is no real proof of it. The first is Solzhenitsyn's essay "Easter Procession," which describes the disruption of an Orthodox Easter service by a group of young atheist rowdies.[98] The second is the comment on *Reflections*, dated March 12, 1969, by the Orthodox priest Sergei Zheludkov. Zheludkov welcomes *Reflections* but believes it overemphasizes economics, technology, and politics. To Zheludkov the problem of intellectual freedom is essentially a religious problem.[99]

Probably far more important in shaping Sakharov's subsequent thinking on the subject of religious freedom was another event of 1969, the arrest of Anatoly Levitin-Krasnov on September 12. Levitin is a lay Orthodox religious writer whose collected essays "Stromaty" (Miscellany) appeared in samizdat in 1968. One essay is a lengthy analysis of different political trends. As one student of Levitin's writings has said:

He calls the latest and newest trend *neohumanism*, a personalistic *Weltanschauung* centered on the living, concrete, and free human personality, in the name of which

---

96. Sakharov, "Statement on Solzhenitsyn Letter," p. 6. Sakharov adds: "Solzhenitsyn gives this thesis in a footnote only." Solzhenitsyn had written: "Nor can there by any talk of the forcible retention within our country of any borderland nation"; A. Solzhenitsyn, *Pis'mo vozhdiam Sovetskogo Soiuza* [Letter to the Leaders of the Soviet Union] (Paris, 1974), p. 28, *AS* 1600.

97. Pp. 87, 41.

98. "Paskhal'nyi krestnyi khod," *AS* 544; text also in A. Solzhenitsyn, *Sobranie sochinenii* [Collected works] (Frankfurt, 1969). Sakharov and Solzhenitsyn have known each other at least since late August 1968; Zhores A. Medvedev, *Desiat' let posle "Odnogo dnia Ivana Denisovicha"* [Ten years after *One Day in the Life of Ivan Denisovich*] (London, 1973), pp. 111–12.

99. "K 'Razmyshleniiam ob intellektual'noi svobode': Otvet akademiku A. D. Sakharovu" [Concerning *Reflections on Intellectual Freedom*: A reply to Academician A. D. Sakharov], *AS* 331.

people of goodwill are uniting in the struggle for a democratic world structure in the broad sense of the word, in the struggle against all forms of tyranny and exploitation.[100]

That Sakharov is familiar with Levitin's writings and was to take a personal interest in his fate will become evident below.

Like *Reflections*, the "Letter of Three" (March 1970) does not treat religion per se. Point ten of the fifteen-point model program, however, would "guarantee public organizations and groups of citizens the opportunity to establish new printing organs."[101] This freedom presumably would extend to groups wishing to publish religious periodicals.

On February 26, 1971, Sakharov's colleague Chalidze supported a group of over 1,400 Orthodox believers from Naro-Fominsk (Moscow oblast) who for the previous forty years had been denied permission to register as a religious association. After the group's appeal to Father Pimen (now patriarch of the Russian Orthodox Church) had been rejected by the latter's secretary they turned to Chalidze. In a letter to Pimen, Chalidze expressed surprise that he had not supported the group vis-à-vis the local authorities who were "disregarding the law."[102]

Almost immediately after Chalidze's letter the problem of religious freedom assumes a prominent place in Sakharov's writings. His "Memorandum" (March 1971) places religious persecution high on the list of "urgent questions." His call for a general amnesty for political prisoners includes "those condemned . . . for religious reasons," and he views as "intolerable" all "psychiatric repressions for . . . religious reasons." He now defines "freedom of convictions and conscience" as one of the essentials for "the happiness of people." In his thesis on the "exchange of information, culture, science, and freedom of convictions," he urges the adoption of decrees to "guarantee the real separation of church and state and real (that is, guaranteed juridically, materially, and administratively) freedom of conscience and religion."[103]

Here it is necessary again to note the recommendation in the "Memorandum" that the USSR Supreme Soviet ratify the two UN covenants on human rights. Article 18 of the Covenant on Civil and Political Rights concerns religious freedom.[104]

---

100. Dimitry Pospielovsky, "The Ideational and Programmatic Work of the Democratic Opposition," Radio Liberty Research Paper no. 218/70 (Munich, 1970), p. 3.

101. P. 9.

102. V. Chalidze, "Glave Russkoi Pravoslavnoi Tserkvi mestobliustiteliu Ottsu Pimenu" [Letter to acting head of the Russian Orthodox Church, Father Pimen], February 26, 1971, *AS* 599. The request of the 1,450 believers to register as a religious congregation is *AS* 764, formerly registered as *AS* 439. An attack on the group by a Naro-Fominsk newspaper shortly before Chalidze wrote his letter is reported by *Chronicle*, no. 20, p. 31.

103. Pp. 2, 5, 9.

104. *Yearbook 1966*, p. 426.

On May 19, 1971, Sakharov attended the one-day trial of Levitin-Krasnov. Levitin had first been arrested in September 1969 and sent to Armavir; the Krasnodar krai court refused to take up the case in view of violations of legal norms; this refusal was upheld by the RSFSR Supreme Court; and in August 1970 Levitin was released. But the investigation continued, and Levitin was again arrested in Moscow May 8, 1971.[105] Four days after the trial, on May 23, Sakharov appealed to Podgorny to alleviate Levitin's fate. From this appeal it is evident that Sakharov is familiar with Levitin's writings:

The articles by Levitin for which he has been charged in fact express the viewpoint, natural for a believer, on the moral and philosophical meaning of religion; they state opinions on present-day internal church problems and also discuss from loyal and democratic positions problems of the freedom of conscience. In expressing his religious convictions and setting forth actual facts, Krasnov-Levitin can in no way for this be accused of spreading false, let alone deliberately (i.e., from his viewpoint) false fabrications. Criticizing individual aspects of existing legislation on problems of religion . . . he can in no way be accused of calling for noncompliance with the laws, inasmuch as he calls for their improvement by legislation.[106]

But Sakharov heard no response. On August 12 he again appealed, this time together with his colleagues of the Human Rights Committee, to the deputies of the USSR Supreme Soviet: Levitin "has propagated his beliefs and defended the right of people to believe in God and to perform religious ceremonies. Let there be one less sufferer for his beliefs.[107] Again the appeal was fruitless. Levitin was dispatched to an ordinary-regime labor camp in Sychiovka (Smolensk oblast).[108]

Exactly two weeks after Sakharov's second appeal for Levitin, on August 26, the Roman Catholic priest Juozas Zdebskis was arrested in Lithuania. From this date the rising tide of protest by the Catholic population and their priests in the Lithuanian SSR was regular reported in *Chronicle*. One example concerned a memorandum addressed to Brezhnev in January 1972 by 17,054 persons complaining of infringements of the rights of believers, the exile of bishops, dismissals of believing teachers, and the destruction of churches. Sometime between October 24 and November 10, 1971, Chalidze appealed to the Presidium of the Lithuanian SSR Supreme Soviet on behalf of Zdebskis. Before March 5, 1972, Sakharov himself received two letters from groups of believers in Chernigov oblast (Ukraine), one Catholic and the other Orthodox, both requesting help in the opening of churches.[109]

105. Levitin's story can be followed in *Chronicle*, nos. 15, 17, 20–22.

106. The text is *AS* 685.

107. As quoted by *Chronicle*, no. 21, p. 9.

108. Levitin was released May 8, 1973, on completion of his sentence. *Khronika zashchity*, no. 3 (June–September 1973), p. 30; *Chronicle*, no. 29 (July 31, 1973) (New York: Khronika Press, 1974), p. 62, *AS* 1701. He was allowed to emigrate in September; Reuter dispatch, September 21, 1974.

109. *Chronicle*, nos. 21–25, *AS* 1000, 1038, 1075, 1100, 1130.

There was also a series of clashes between crowds and the militia in the weeks following the self-immolation of the youth Romas Kalanta on May 14.[110] Kalanta's banner was "freedom for Lithuania," but the undertones of the protesting crowds were religious—freedom for Catholic Lithuania.

It is therefore not surprising to find Sakharov taking a strong stand against religious persecution in his "Afterword" (June 1972):

In its consequences one of the most serious violations of human rights in our country is without doubt the persecution and destruction of religion, which have been carried out persistently and brutally for decades. Freedom of religious convictions and religious activity is an integral part of intellectual freedom in general. Unfortunately, recent months have been marked by new instances of religious persecution, in particular in the Baltic area and in other places.[111]

Sakharov apparently was not yet prepared at this time to link the nationality and the religious questions. By mid-1973, however, he did link them, as is apparent in the discussion of nationalism above.

Sakharov's view of religious freedom now stands fully revealed. While the factors that moved him to this view are not so clear, they probably included the fate of Levitin-Krasnov and his humanistic writings, situations like those in Naro-Fominsk, and the Lithuanian events.

A QUESTION OF IDEOLOGY

Sakharov uses the term Leninist four times in *Reflections* (1968). Three of these are in footnotes in the Russian edition but are incorporated into the text in the English translation (which may lead an English reader to overvalue the term's significance to Sakharov). In all but one instance the use is trivial; the exception is in a footnote on nationality problems, which he says "will continue to be a reason for unrest and dissatisfaction unless *all* departures from Leninist principles which have occurred are acknowledged and analyzed and firm steps are taken to correct all mistakes."[112]

The context is a discussion of the incomplete rehabilitation of the Crimean Tatars. From this it can be deduced that in applying the term "Leninist principles" to nationality policy Sakharov is calling for a minimal program of autonomy for the less numerous peoples. But it cannot be deduced that he is also applying the term to nationality policy for the larger peoples (that is, the Union republics). His stand of self-determination for them, as has already been seen, is based on the Constitution, not "Leninist principles." And now the discussion is moving away from the term Leninist—this is precisely the point. It has no real meaning for Sakharov.

110. *Chronicle*, nos. 25–27 (May 20, July 5, October 15, 1972), *AS* 1130, 1155, 1200.
111. P. 15.
112. *Reflections*, Russian ed., p. 34; English trans., p. 66. The other instances are: Russian ed., pp. 25, 32, 45; English trans., pp. 56, 64, 81.

In the "Letter of Three" (March 1970) the term is not used directly, but the ideology is certainly implicit in the statement that "democratization, in being carried out under the leadership of the CPSU in cooperation with all strata of society, must retain and strengthen the party's leading role in the economic, political, and cultural life of society."[113] The Marxist flavoring in this work, as has been suggested, more likely reflects Roy Medvedev's thinking than Sakharov's (see n. 1 to this chapter). In any event the term Leninist does not appear in the "Memorandum," the "Afterword," or other available writings of Sakharov. His explanation to Axelbank (October 1972) of the change in his political views indicates why:

When I wrote [*Reflections*] I was a little idealistic. . . . I wrote from what you call a position of abstraction. . . . I called myself a socialist then, but now I have modified my beliefs. What I stand for now is contained in the ["Afterword"] to the "Memorandum." . . . I would no longer label myself a socialist. I am not a Marxist-Leninist, a Communist. I would call myself a liberal.[114]

SEVERAL QUESTIONS OF FOREIGN POLICY

In *Reflections* (1968) Sakharov considers the possible consequences of the Chinese Cultural Revolution. One of five main dangers to civilization he sees pertains to the China of 1968—"a spreading of mass myths that put entire peoples and continents under the power of cruel and treacherous demagogues." Given these dangers, any action further dividing mankind is "madness and a crime." Therefore "only universal cooperation" under certain conditions will preserve civilization. These conditions are "intellectual freedom and the lofty moral ideas of socialism and labor, accompanied by the elimination of dogmatism and pressures of the concealed interests of ruling classes." But a footnote adds that "ideological peace cannot apply to those fanatical . . . ideologies that reject all possibility of rapprochement, . . . for example, ideologies of . . . Maoist demagogy." Thus he agrees with his country's stand on China: "In the presence of the 'disease' [of Maoism] formal unity [of the world communist movement] would be a dangerous, unprincipled compromise." However, "the split . . . to some extent represents the way to treat the 'disease'. . . . The Chinese people are now in much greater need of the unity of the world's democratic forces to defend their rights than in the unity of the world's communist forces in the Maoist sense."[115] Actually, then, the road to preservation is not by "universal cooperation" but by cooperation, convergence, of all *democratic* forces.

Sakharov finds a direct connection between the China question and neo-Stalinism in the USSR. The following passage (in the Russian text it

113. P. 1.
114. Axelbank, in *Observer*.
115. *Reflections*, pp. 27–28, 58. Cf. Russian ed., p. 4.

comes immediately after a discussion of the need to remove neo-Stalinists from the Soviet political scene) reveals the direction of his thinking:

The full picture of the tragedy in China is unclear. But in any case, it is impossible to look at it in isolation from the internal economic difficulties of China . . . , in isolation from the struggle by various groups for power, or in isolation from the foreign political situation—the war in Vietnam, the alienation [*razobshchionnost'*] in the world, and the inadequate and lagging struggle against Stalinism in the Soviet Union.[116]

Sakharov has thus prepared the ground for further reflection on the relationship between the China question and the battle for human rights at home.

In the "Letter of Three" (March 1970) the China question is both a moral and a material one: "It is of utmost importance to strengthen the moral and material stand of the USSR in respect of China and to increase our means [*vozmozhnosti*] to influence the situation in this country indirectly (by example and by technical and economic aid) in the interests of the peoples of both countries." If the Soviet leadership does not democratize Soviet society, the "Letter of Three" foresees "the danger [to the USSR] of Chinese totalitarian nationalism," which may be only temporary but will nonetheless be "very serious" for the coming years. Aside from democratization at home,

we can counter this [Chinese] danger only by increasing or at least by maintaining the existing technological and economic gap between our country and China, by increasing the ranks of our friends in the world, by offering the Chinese people the alternative of cooperation and aid. This becomes evident when one considers the great numerical superiority of the potential adversary and his militant nationalism, as well as the great length of our eastern frontiers and the sparse population of the eastern regions.[117]

In his "Memorandum" (March 1971) Sakharov clarifies his view of the China question. The Near East and Vietnam are "urgent questions," but they may be settled by compromise; and West Berlin, given "the changed relations with the FRG," may no longer be a trouble spot. Not so China, which is his country's "fundamental foreign policy problem." Reiterating suggestions made in the "Letter of Three," Sakharov recommends

proposing to the Chinese people [he does *not* say government] the alternative of economic, technical, and cultural aid, fraternal cooperation, and joint advancement on the democratic road, always leaving open the possibility of this road for the development of relations. At the same time [we should] take especial care to ensure the security of our country, avoid all other possible foreign and internal complications, and carry out our plans to develop Siberia, bearing in mind the indicated factor [China].

116. *Ibid.*, p. 58.
117. "Letter of Three," pp. 10, 12.

Solution of the China question, as in "Letter of Three," is made dependent on democratization at home. But the formulation is now much starker. There is only one way to avoid conflict with China: "Only by concentrating [our] resources on domestic problems . . . will the country be safeguarded from possible exacerbations with China."[118]

By mid-1973 Sakharov has radically modified his appraisal of the China question. To Stenholm of Swedish television he says that in the "Memorandum"

I treated the China question . . . in a tone I would not employ today. Perhaps I would not write on it at all today, for as before our relations with China are completely incomprehensible to me. . . . Today I would no longer in any way want to accuse China of aggressiveness. But I also did not make it clear there. But perhaps there was an element of exaggeration of a China threat.[119]

Exaggerated because of his fears for democratization at home; in the "Memorandum" a Soviet solution of the China question was made dependent on this factor. In mid-1973, however, Sakharov sees China to be "simply an earlier stage of development of our society." China today is concerned "more with revolutionary self-assertion within the country and in the whole world than with ensuring, for example, the well-being of its people."[120]

Indirectly and very briefly, in his "Statement on Solzhenitsyn Letter" (April 1974), Sakharov accounts for his reappraisal of the China problem. Disagreeing with Solzhenitsyn, who "believes that our country (because of the struggle for ideological supremacy and because of demographic pressure) is threatened, and very soon, by total war with China for the territory of the Asian part of the USSR," Sakharov recalls that he too "at one time had paid tribute to similar fears in my 'Memorandum.'" But, he continues, "most experts on China, as it seems to me, share the judgment that for a relatively long time to come China will not have the military capacity for a major war of aggression against the USSR, and it is difficult to imagine that adventurers will turn up who would now drive China to such a suicidal step."[121]

It is rather clear from these two statements—to date there is no other evidence—that Sakharov had been studying the momentous developments affecting the future of China during the fall and winter of 1971–72: the end of the Cultural Revolution, or at least of its first phase; the removal of Marshal Lin Piao from the Peking stage; the entry of the Chinese People's Republic into the UN; and President Nixon's visit to China in late February 1972. In *Sakharov o sebe* (December 1973) he reveals his regret at not having altered the text of the "Memorandum" when he released it fifteen months after having written it:

118. "Memorandum," pp. 3, 6.
119. Interview on Swedish television, p. 9.
120. *Ibid.*
121. "Statement on Solzhenitsyn Letter," pp. 5–6.

In particular, I did not change the treatment of the problem of Soviet-Chinese relations—something I regret. Today I still do not idealize the Chinese variant of socialism. But I do not regard as correct the evaluation in the "Memorandum" of the threat of Chinese aggression against the USSR; in any case, the China threat cannot serve as justification for the militarization of our country and the absence of democratic reforms in it.[122]

Repeating almost verbatim this last thought a few months later, he adds that "one can even speculate that exaggeration [*razduvanie*] of the China threat is one of the elements of the Soviet leadership's political game."[123]

While Sakharov had thus discarded the "China threat" as a real danger sometime between March 1971 and June 1972, in this period he was reexamining his entire approach to Soviet foreign policy, for despite removal of that "China threat" the pace of repression at home continued to accelerate. The first indication that his views were changing is to be found in the "Afterword" (June 1972) in remarks concerning the May 1972 Soviet-American agreements made during Nixon's Moscow visit: "One wants to believe that these agreements have not merely a symbolic meaning."[124] In October 1972, to Axelbank, Sakharov already links the threat to democratization at home with the possible course of East-West détente. Since Nixon's visit in May 1972, he finds that "things have got worse. The authorities seem more impudent, because they feel that with a détente they can ignore Western public opinion, which isn't going to be concerned with the plight of internal freedoms in Russia."[125]

In mid-1973 on Swedish television, after Brezhnev's visits to West Germany and the United States, Sakharov phrases this idea differently: "If one speaks of the West, then each time we do not understand whether it is a desire to help us or, on the contrary, a kind of capitulation, a play at our expense because of the internal interests of people of the West."[126]

Any lingering doubt as to his meaning is dispelled at his press conference of August 21, 1973:

> Détente without democratization, a rapprochement when the West in fact accepts our rules of the game . . . , would be very dangerous . . . and wouldn't solve any of the world's problems, and would mean simply a capitulation to our real or exaggerated strength. It would mean an attempt to trade, to get from us gas and oil, neglecting all other aspects of the problem. . . . By liberating ourselves from problems we can't solve ourselves, we could concentrate on accumulating strength, and as a result, the whole world would be disarmed and facing our uncontrollable bureaucratic apparatus. . . . That would be . . . encouragement of closed countries,

122. *Sakharov o sebe*, pp. 20–21.
123. "Statement on Solzhenitsyn Letter," p. 6.
124. P. 16.
125. Axelbank, in *Observer*.
126. Interview on Swedish television, p. 6.

where everything that happens goes unseen by foreign eyes behind a mask that hides its real face. No one should dream of having such a neighbor, and especially if this neighbor is armed to the teeth.[127]

His insistent linking of international détente to internal democratization was thus made clear to the entire world. At the end of the year in *Sakharov o sebe* he writes of his "duty to point out all hidden dangers of a false détente, a collusive détente, or a capitulation détente, and to call for the use of . . . all efforts to achieve real convergence, accompanied by democratization, demilitarization, and social progress."[128]

It is now possible to suggest an explanation for Sakharov's approach to Soviet foreign policy. The key is democratization at home. Whatever external force endangers the course of democratization becomes for Sakharov the main external danger of the moment. Until Nixon's visit to China that danger was the China of "Maoist damagogues" because it was a potential ally of Soviet internal neo-Stalinists. Since Nixon's visit to the USSR, and especially since Brezhnev's visits to West Germany and the United States, Sakharov evidently believes that danger may become a West more concerned with trade and superficial cultural relations than with the "plight of internal freedoms in Russia." As long as Sakharov "supported" official Soviet foreign policy, which represented China as the main external danger to the country, he was allowed to live in relative peace. Now he has changed course and has dared to conduct a dialogue with the West in which the sincerity of Soviet foreign policy is impugned, and over the heads of the authorities. The regime has therefore tried to end this dialogue of candor.

The converse of the explanation suggested—that whatever external force encourages democratization at home should be supported—can be applied to Sakharov's stand on the Jackson Amendment and his proposal of an International Council of Experts. The U.S. Senate's adoption of the Jackson Amendment, which would make the relaxation of Soviet-American trade dependent on free emigration from the USSR, Sakharov explained at his press conference of August 21, 1973, "looks like the minimum step, which is important not only by itself, but as a symbol of the fact that détente with the Soviet Union does not preclude some kind of control on this country so that it could not become a danger for its neighbors." The great importance Sakharov attaches to the amendment is evident from the fact that in mid-September 1973 he addressed the U.S. Congress directly. In an open letter he argues that the amendment

is made even more significant by the fact that the world is just entering on a new course of détente and it is therefore essential that the proper direction be followed from the outset. This is a fundamental issue, extending far beyond the question of

127. Press conference of August 21, 1973.
128. P. 27.

emigration. . . . The amendment does not represent interference in the internal affairs of socialist countries, but simply a defense of international law, without which there can be no mutual trust.[129]

The proposal for a council appears in the "Memorandum." Sakharov suggests that the Soviet leadership take the initiative, and thereby the credit, in proposing "the creation (under UN auspices?) of a new consultative International Council of Experts on the problems of peace, disarmament, and economic aid to needy countries, on the defense of human rights, and on the protection of the natural environment." Such a council would have "maximum independence from the interests of individual states and groups of states" and be granted international status by means of an "international pact" that would "obligate the legislative and governmental bodies to consider the council's recommendations." These recommendations would have to be "open and public, and sound"; decisions on them by national bodies would also have to be "open and public."[130] The vast scope of the council's work would clearly embrace all aspects of his two theses developed in *Reflections*.

Why under United Nations auspices? Suggestive of Sakharov's attitude toward the UN is the closing paragraph of the letter of greeting from the members of the Moscow Human Rights Committee and its experts Alexander Esenin-Volpin and Boris Tsukerman, which was addressed to U Thant on the occasion of the dinner given in his honor by the International League for the Rights of Man in New York in January 1972:

We think that the years of U Thant's period in office as Secretary-General have seen a marked increase in the authority of the UN in the efforts made by all mankind to defend human rights. There are many who hope that in the future the United Nations will be able to defend human rights not only when the party guilty of their violation is weak, or the complaints of the victim are well known, but above all where the evil done is especially great.[131]

What are the sources of Sakharov's proposal? Several can be cited as possibilities. First, in the post-Hiroshima world there have been innumerable proposals for international controls by international panels—the Baruch Plan of 1946, to name just one.[132] Second are the Pugwash confer-

---

129. *Sakharov Speaks*, pp. 213–14.
130. "Memorandum," p. 7.
131. For the full text of this letter, dated December 2, 1971, see *Dokumenty Komiteta prav Cheloveka: Proceedings of the Moscow Human Rights Committee, November 1970–November 1971*, intr. by John Carey (New York, 1972), pp. 243–44. The passage is also quoted by *Chronicle*, no. 23, p. 30. Sakharov and seven other advocates of civil rights appealed to the new secretary general, Kurt Waldheim, during his visit to the USSR July 17–22, 1972, on behalf of the Jewish mathematician Vladimir Gershovich, who had been refused an exit visa four times since 1971. Extensive excerpts from this appeal are in *International Herald Tribune*, July 22/23, 1972. Gershovich emigrated from the USSR in October 1972.
132. The plan would have instituted an International Atomic Development Authority with "managerial control or ownership of all atomic energy activities potentially dangerous to world

ences, informal international sessions of experts who assembled originally to exchange ideas on how to prevent nuclear war. Sakharov's mentor, Igor Tamm, attended the 1962 session in London.[133] It can be noted that the host of the initial conferences was the American industrialist Cyrus Eaton, whom Sakharov describes positively in *Reflections*.[134] In 1969 American scholars requested that Sakharov be allowed to attend the Pugwash session in Sochi, but his name was not on the delegation list and he did not attend.[135]

Third is the experience of the Moscow Human Rights Committee, formed only four months before Sakharov set forth his proposal in the "Memorandum." He and his original colleagues Chalidze and Tverdokhlebov—and later the mathematician Igor Shafarevich and the geophysicist Grigory Podyapolsky—were themselves lay jurists, a consultative council aspiring to become legal experts in the field of human rights with the self-assigned task of studying and propagating the ideas of such rights.[136] Finally, the "Letter of Three" had proposed "the creation under the directing bodies at all levels of *consultative* scientific *committees*, including *highly trained specialists* from various fields."[137]

In the "Afterword" (June 1972) Sakharov affirms the importance he attributes to his proposed Council of Experts. He considers it a practical proposal, "provided there is broad international support, for which I ask and appeal not only to Soviet but also to foreign readers."[138] If the Soviet leadership could pursue "peaceful coexistence" with the West and at the same time clamp down on dissidents at home, why could not the academician also use "peaceful coexistence" with the West to combat the regime's stepped-up repression? Sakharov may well have felt that such a council would provide him and other dissidents moral support and greater security in their battle for human rights in the Soviet Union.

SAKHAROV UNDER KGB PRESSURE

Sakharov was openly criticized in a major Soviet newspaper, *Literaturnaia Gazeta*, on February 14, 1973. This was only the second time he had ever

---

security" and exclusive powers of inspection and of sanctions. The text of the plan is in Chalmers M. Roberts, *The Nuclear Years: The Arms Race and Arms Control, 1945–70* (New York, 1970), pp. 123–33.

133. Clemens, "Sakharov," p. 6.

134. P. 79.

135. Bryce Nelson, "A. D. Sakharov: Soviet Physicist Believed to Have Been Punished," *Science* 164 (May 30, 1969): 1043; *New York Times*, October 23–30, 1969.

136. The text of the committee's statement of principles is in A. D. Sakharov, A. N. Tverdokhlebov, and V. N. Chalidze, "Printsipy Komiteta prav Cheloveka" [Principles of the Human Rights Committee], November 4, 1970, *AS* 448, and in *Chronicle*, no. 17, *AS* 555. This issue of *Chronicle* also contains 'Reglament Komiteta prav Cheloveka" [Statutes of the Human Rights Committee], as does Carey, *Dokumenty*, pp. 16–18.

137. P. 9; emphasis added.

138. P. 16.

been attacked in public and the first since the fall of Khrushchev. Events both before and since then suggest that throughout 1973 the KGB was developing a case against Sakharov for "anti-Soviet activity." It appeared to be touch-and-go whether Sakharov would be indicted for a "political crime," would be judged mentally incompetent (his wife was reported to have said on July 3 in a telephone conversation from Moscow that Sakharov "risks internment in a psychiatric hospital"),[139] or would be banished (in the spring he was invited to be a visiting scholar for the 1973-74 academic year at Princeton).[140] Of course it is also possible that no case at all was planned, merely simulation of one with the intent to intimidate.

Sakharov told Axelbank (October 1972) that Khrushchev had once "ordered the authorities to find compromising material on me. . . . He told them 'Sakharov is against testing the bomb, he pokes his nose into politics. He must be given a lesson.'" The story dates from the late summer of 1964, when Khrushchev was losing the battle for Lysenko.[141] But after the removal of Khrushchev the order presumably was quietly filed away.

In 1967 the KGB did attempt in some way to incriminate Sakharov. The attempt involved the preliminary investigation of Ginzburg and Galanskov, and Alexei Dobrovolsky was its instrument. Sakharov writes in *Reflections* that his appeal of February 11, 1967, to the party Central Committee that the case against Ginzburg and Galanskov be closed went unanswered. "Only much later" he learned that

there had been an attempt (apparently inspired by Semichastny, the former chairman of the KGB) to slander the present writer and a number of other persons on the basis of instigated false testimony. . . . Subsequently the testimony of that person—Dobrovolsky—was used at the trial as evidence to show that Ginzburg and Galanskov had *ties with a foreign anti-Soviet organization*, which one cannot help but doubt.[142]

Reiterating his concern over the regime's abuse of psychiatry in the "Afterword" (June 1972), Sakharov singled out "the case of the poet Lupynis in the Ukraine" among "new facts of psychiatric repression."[143] Anatoly Ivanovich Lupynis had been arrested May 28, 1971, after having recited poetry at a meeting May 22 at the Shevchenko Memorial in Kiev to mark the centennial of the return of Shevchenko's remains to Kiev from St. Petersburg. During the investigation two witnesses testified that Lupynis had allegedly given them works by Sakharov to read. According to *Chronicle*, No. 22, "photocopies of articles by Sakharov, taken from the KGB

139. *L'express* (Paris), July 16–22, 1973, p. 58.

140. This range of possible punishments for dissidents was mentioned at the press conference of August 21, 1973.

141. Axelbank, in *Newsweek*. This passage is not included in the fuller version in *Observer*. Khrushchev addressed the first sentence to the ideologist Mikhail Suslov and the second to the KGB chairman, Semichastny; Smith, "Intolerable Sakharov," p. 59.

142. Pp. 64–65; emphasis added.

143. P. 15.

archives, were attached to the case." In October 1971 Lupynis was sent to the Serbsky Institute of Forensic Psychiatry in Moscow and diagnosed as schizophrenic. Returned to Kiev, where his trial was held December 28, he was then sent for compulsory treatment to the prison psychiatric hospital in Dnepropetrovsk.[144]

Had the KGB again tried to incriminate Sakharov, this time through Lupynis, either directly or indirectly? Is this the real reason Lupynis was silenced and dispatched to a prison psychiatric hospital? Is this why Sakharov had singled out Lupynis alone among the "new facts of psychiatric repression"? The evidence is incomplete.

The anonymous "group of Soviet citizens" from the Ukraine who had addressed their May 1972 letter to the Moscow Human Rights Committee began their concluding paragraph as follows:

We make a point of noting the considerations that have forced us to divulge our names only to the Human Rights Committee in the USSR. . . . We answer for the authenticity of the information. . . . We are sick of anonymity. But the situation is such that at any manifestation of public activity the organs of the KGB reply with immediate repressions. . . . We would be prepared to give our names . . . were there even the slightest hope of the text being published in full.

The sole source for the letter, *Chronicle*, no. 25, reported that it had been *received* by the committee and had also been *addressed* to the supreme soviets of the USSR and the Ukraine and the editors of *Izvestiia* and *Literaturna Ukraïna*. Because of the intensified activities of the KGB the anonymity of the authors is understandable. Yet the question arises: Why would anyone want to put Sakharov and his colleagues in jeopardy by deliberately announcing that the names of the anonymous authors were known only to the committee? It cannot be excluded that the letter was a provocation by the KGB against the committee as a functioning body or against one or more of its members. On the other hand, would the compilers of *Chronicle*, presumably all responsible dissidents, have published the letter if there was reason to suspect its authenticity?

On November 15, 1972, Sakharov disclosed what looked like another attempted provocation against him. In an "Open Appeal" to psychiatrists of the world he announced that the young psychiatrist Semion Gluzman of the Ukraine had been accused of "distributing my work on the Czechoslovak question." He added, "But I have no such work." According to *Chronicle*, no. 28, "a photocopy of a certain article on the Czechoslovak question" had been attached to the Gluzman case, "one witness mentioned such a work," and its "authorship was unwarrantly attributed to Academician A. D. Sakharov." After a week-long trial Gluzman was sentenced October 29,

144. *Chronicle*, no. 22, p. 19; no. 23, p. 29; no. 25, p. 34. Born in 1937, Lupynis was first sentenced to six years in 1956. He received an additional four years while in Dubrovlag in Mordovia and was released in 1967.

1972, by the Kiev oblast court to seven years in a strict-regime camp plus three in exile.[145] While the severity of the sentence was probably the chief reason for Sakharov's rapid response to news of it, a contributing motive may have been the way his name had been brought into the trial.

During the week of Gluzman's trial Sakharov gave his first interview to a foreign correspondent, Jay Axelbank of *Newsweek*, on October 26. Excerpts were published in the American weekly's issue of November 13; the Sunday *Observer* (London) carried a fuller version December 3, and the Russian émigré journal *Posev* carried a retranslated summary based on the two English texts in its January issue.

Sakharov described himself as "a little idealistic" when he had written *Reflections*" (1968): "Remember that Czechoslovakia had not yet been invaded. I wrote from what you call a position of abstraction. Now I know many more things and am a much more disappointed man." Aware that his remarks would appear in the foreign press, Sakharov nonetheless for the first time openly criticized the very nature of the regime. Since 1968 "he had come to realize," to use the paraphrasing of Axelbank, "that the practice of socialism in Russia . . . had proved 'a grave disappointment,' and that even the theory of socialism . . . did not offer the solutions for mankind's ills." Furthermore (Sakharov is now quoted directly), "the redeeming aspects of Soviet society do not come from anything peculiar to our system but from the nature of society itself." Yet "in ten years nothing will change. This country could perish, but it still would be the same." Sakharov went on, as has been seen, to question the method the regime seemed to be applying in executing its foreign-policy course of East-West détente (see pp. 386–87 above). A reaction from the "authorities" was inevitable. Through Axelbank Sakharov also disclosed to the world that "nobody bothers me except when the KGB follows me every now and then." But the pressures were already mounting. He had been detained for the first time by the militia for participation in a demonstration September 6 outside the Lebanese embassy held to object to the Soviet government's failure to protest the murder of the Israeli atheletes at the Munich Olympics. His stepdaughter had just been expelled from Moscow University, and his stepson's expulsion from a special secondary school would follow in the winter. "I know what could happen," Sakharov said cryptically, "but I prefer not to discuss it here."[146]

On January 23, 1973, Sakharov and his wife appealed to Yuri Andropov, chairman of the KGB, for the release on their personal surety of their friend Yuri Shikhanovich, a former Moscow University mathematics teacher who

145. A. D. Sakharov, "Otkrytoe obrashchenie k psikhiatram vsego mira s prizyvom vystupit' v zashchitu Semiona Gluzmana" [Open appeal to psychiatrists of the whole world to speak out in defense of Semion Gluzman], November 15, 1972, *AS* 1221; *Chronicle*, no. 28, December 31, 1972 (New York: Khronika Press, 1974), p. 19 (*AS* 1700).

146. Axelbank, in *Observer*; on September 6 demonstration, *New York Times*, September 7, 1972.

had been held incommunicado in Lefortovo prison since his arrest four months earlier. The warrant for his arrest had stated, according to *Chronicle*, no. 27, that "for a number of years he has systematically saved, reproduced, and disseminated anti-Soviet literature"; he was charged with anti-Soviet activity under article 70 of the RSFSR Criminal Code. During the search of Shikhanovich's flat Sakharov and other friends arrived, *Chronicle* reported, but "were not allowed into the flat or permitted to say goodbye to him." Samizdat copies of the Sakharovs' plea for Shikhanovich reached Western correspondents in Moscow February 11.[147]

Three days later open criticism of Sakharov appeared in the Soviet press. It is in the middle of the full-page article "And What Next? Reflections on Reading Harrison Salisbury's New Book" by Alexander Chakovsky in *Literaturnaia Gazeta*. Writing at the midway point between the first and second series of Brezhnev-Nixon talks, Chakovsky deals primarily with the possibilities of East-West détente, faintly praising Salisbury's book *Many Americas Shall Be One* (published in 1971!). In treating Salisbury's discussion of ways to check the American "military-industrial complex," Chakovsky pauses to belittle Sakharov and his treatise *Reflections*:

> [Salisbury] examines several suggested "prescriptions," including the so-called "declaration" by the Soviet scientist Sakharov.
>
> At one time I read this concoction published in the Western press. It seemed to me to be a naive conglomeration of selected passages from the Gospel, Rousseau's *The Social Contract*, the Soviet and American constitutions, and one's own wishful thinking. . . . I found nothing new in the ways Sakharov proposes to achieve peace on earth, or, in particular, in the main "way"—the establishment of a "world government" to which "everyone" so to speak would be subject: Soviet workers and kolkhozniks and Texan oil kings. . . .
>
> *This Sakharovian utopia*, already long since being *used in the West for anti-Soviet purposes*, disgusts me not because of its "goodness," but because of the demonstrative coquettishness and pose of a man who stands majestically "above the battle," waves an olive branch fanlike, and benignly accepts compliments from that very military-industrial complex which regards the harmless political idiocy of saints [*iurodstvo*] with condescension, but . . . on the other hand simply destroys everyone who really threatens its power.
>
> For the sake of justice it must be said that Sakharov's "prescription" evokes an ironic sneer from Salisbury, although he cannot refrain from complimenting its author.[148]

But Chakovsky failed to inform his Soviet readers that Harrison Salisbury was the author of the foreword to the English-language edition of

147. Yelena Georgievna Bonner and Andrei Dmitrievich Sakharov to chairman of the Committee of State Security, *AS* 1244; also *Khronika zashchity*, no. 1, p. 49; reported in Reuter and UPI dispatches of February 11 and Hedrick Smith, *New York Times*, February 12, 1973.
148. A. Chakovsky, "Chto dal'she? Razmyshleniia po prochtenii novoi knigi Garrisona Solsberi," *Literaturnaia Gazeta*, February 14, 1973; emphasis added.

Sakharov's *Reflections*. And so the insinuation of "anti-Soviet" activity distilled in ridicule became the opening move of a press campaign to arouse Soviet public opinion against a father of the Soviet H-bomb turned champion of human rights. At the same time Chakovsky's piece served a purpose that Sakharov explained at a press conference: "Articles regarding myself, which have been published in the Soviet press, are . . . very likely meant as warnings from the KGB's point of view." Similar attacks against Sakharov had already been delivered at closed lectures and seminars for upper strata of the intelligentsia.[149]

The day the public read Chakovsky's attack on Sakharov, Foreign Minister Andrei Gromyko addressed a letter to René Maheu, director general of UNESCO, announcing Soviet accession effective May 27 to the Universal Copyright Convention of 1952. Decree no. 138 (dated February 21, 1973), which modified Soviet copyright law, was made public March 14.[150] Soviet advocates of human rights immediately realized that the decree might be used to restrict publication in the West of Soviet works deemed to be "anti-Soviet." Within a week, on March 22, Sakharov and five other prominent intellectuals responded with an open letter to UNESCO. They welcomed the Soviet decision to accede to the convention for its possible "advancement of the cause of free exchange of information and contribution to the reduction of mutual distrust and . . . cultural rapprochement among peoples." But at the same time they expressed concern lest Soviet law on the monopoly of foreign trade be "used to restrict or even suppress entirely the international copyrights of Soviet citizens." Soviet censorship, they said, "must not be allowed to function on an international scale."[151]

The following day, March 23, Sakharov appeared for his first interview with the KGB. Ostensibly the invitation was to discuss the January letter on Shikhanovich, but Sakharov's suggestion that his wife be present was rejected, although she had also signed the letter and Soviet law requires two citizens as guarantors. Most of the hour-long session with two KGB officers (identified as Lieutenant Colonel Galkin and a higher-ranking officer named Frolov) concerned Sakharov's public work, described as "personal activities" in all three reports of the interview. He was informed that he was "not morally sound" and that his membership in the Moscow Human Rights Committee was "slander" against the Soviet Union, since it implied the need to defend human rights in the USSR. In addition, he was criticized for

149. Press conference of August 21, 1973; for reports on the lectures, see Hedrick Smith, *New York Times*, February 15, 1973.

150. Reuter and UPI dispatches of February 27 and Andreas Freund, *New York Times*, February 28, 1973; Decree no. 138, "O vnesenii izmenenii i popolnenii v Osnovy Grazhdanskogo Zakonodatel'stva Soiuza SSR i Soiuznykh Respublik" [On changes and additions to the Fundamentals of Civil Legislation of the USSR and the Union Republics], *Vedomosti Verkhovnogo Soveta SSSR*, February 28, 1973, art. 138; also reported briefly by *Izvestiia*, February 23, 1973.

151. Andrei Sakharov *et al.*, "Otkrytoe pis'mo v YuNESKO," *AS* 1402.

attempts to attend political trials (he had been barred from the courtroom since January 5, 1972, when he was denied admittance to the trial of Vladimir Bukovsky) and for his comments to foreign correspondents, in particular for the fact that his interview with Axelbank had been published in the "anticommunist" émigré journal *Posev* in West Germany. He was also advised that Westerners were really interested in him "only for anti-Soviet purposes."[152]

According to all available accounts of the interview, Sakharov was not explicitly told to stop his human rights activities. Given the subjects discussed, however, the inference that he do so was rather clear. Friends of Sakharov also believed the KGB might have intended to intimidate him. At his August 21 press conference Sakharov explained that "the institution of so-called warnings [has] become common in the practice of the KGB and associated organizations in respect to dissidents." He recalled that in March "I was told that Shikhanovich had also been warned without drawing the appropriate conclusions. What was meant, apparently, were the searches of his home."

The phrases used by the KGB officers warrant an interpretation.

"*Not morally sound*" neatly disposed of Sakharov's efforts to obtain the release of his friend Shikhanovich; the phrase also had the ring of Chakovsky's "political idiocy of saints." The word "sound" is used in three English language reports on Sakharov's session with the KGB; the Russian word used is not known, but was probably *zdorovii* (healthy, sound). "Not morally healthy" is close to "morally unhealthy," which with sleight of hand may easily become "*mentally* unhealthy." Lieutenant Colonel Galkin had also been an investigator on the Shikhanovich case. Witnesses interrogated in that case were asked whether they had observed any deviations from the norm in Shikhanovich's psyche. The nature of the questions suggested that efforts were under way to commit Shikhanovich to a psychiatric hospital. He was, in fact, later declared mentally ill by a medical commission of the Serbsky Institute of Forensic Psychiatry and committed by a Moscow city court to a general psychiatric hospital.[153] Sakharov is an avowed close friend of Shikhanovich. Moreover, had not the "mad poet" Lupynis been "caught" with the works of that "political idiot" Sakharov? If given a free hand, the KGB could easily "prove" that Sakharov too was "mentally ill." After all, the KGB thrives on association; to invent relationships is its *raison d'être*.

152. For the KGB summons see *Sakharov o sebe*, p. 23. Reuter and UPI dispatches of March 24 and Hedrick Smith, *New York Times*, March 25, 1973, reported the interview. Article 94 of the RSFSR Code of Criminal Procedure calls for a minimum of two guarantors; *Ugolovno-protsessual'nyi Kodeks RSFSR* (Moscow, 1967), p. 33.

153. On Galkin and the witnesses, interrogation, *Khronika zashchity*, no. 2 (April–May, 1973), pp. 10, 11; on findings of the medical commission, Ye. Bonner, G. Podyapolsky, and A. Sakharov, "Otkrytoe obrashchenie" [Open appeal], July 5, 1973, *AS* 1445; on the court decision, *Khronika zashchity*, nos. 5–6 (November–December 1973), pp. 18–19.

As for "slander," the KGB could easily extend the charge to cover much of Sakharov's public work. Even Sakharov's participation in the "minute of silence" on Moscow's Pushkin Square on Soviet Constitution Day December 5 could be declared a slanderous act, inasmuch as its function was to test the constitutionally guaranteed right of assembly.[154]

The warning by the KGB officers that Westerners were interested in Sakharov "only for anti-Soviet purposes" is similar to Chakovsky's "Sakharovian utopia . . . used in the West for anti-Soviet purposes." To link Sakharov to the "anticommunist" journal *Posev* because it published the interview given to Axelbank when in fact Sakharov gave the interview to an American correspondent for an American journal is but one step removed from the charge frequently leveled at political dissidents of "transmitting anti-Soviet material of slanderous content for publication in the journal of an anti-Soviet organization." Bukovsky, for example, was sentenced January 5, 1972 under article 70 of the RSFSR Criminal Code for, among other things, having "communicated slanderous information to foreign correspondents."[155]

On April 13 Sakharov received a strange letter from Peter Yakir, who had been in Lefortovo prison since his arrest June 21, 1972. In Yakir's handwriting and over his signature but misdated April 3, 1972, the letter was delivered by a "man in the uniform of a counselor of justice from the procuracy." An anonymous postscript to a copy of the letter circulating in samizdat describes the delivery and calls attention to the many spelling errors in the original. The 500-word letter purports to be a friendly warning to Sakharov to avoid the mistakes Yakir had made.

having begun with opposition to . . . restalinization . . . , I gradually took the direct road of anti-Sovietism. . . . I was the author and coauthor of many letters that contained unjustified generalizations openly slandering our social and state system. I saved, reproduced, and distributed anti-Soviet literature and transmitted to the West diverse information, which was openly tendentious and frequently slanderous, and in many instances called for a struggle against our existing system. . . . Before my arrest I also spoke out . . . in defense of condemned friends and persons unknown to me. Now . . . I am persuaded that I frequently defended people who had committed serious crimes, imagining them to have been victims of individual arbitrariness and lawlessness. Letters and other documents written by me and my circle, after reaching the West, were immediately . . . used by open and concealed adversaries for propagandistic purposes against our Motherland. . . . Especially zealous in this respect were such mouthpieces of anticommunism as Radio Liberty and NTS, an organization not unknown to you. . . . The NTS ideologists have used any negative

154. On the 1972 "minute of silence," AP dispatch in *New York Times*, December 6, 1972. Sakharov first participated in a "minute of silence" demonstration in 1971; *Chronicle*, no. 24, p. 23.
155. A samizdat transcript of the Bukovsky trial is *AS* 1077.

manifestation in our country to slander the Soviet system. Illustrative of this is the statement by one NTS leader that in combatting the Soviet state everyone is useful—from the mad terrorist "Ilin to Sakharov." . . .

Since 1968 your name likewise has not been absent from the pages of their propagandistic press. They immediately set to work to print a pamphlet . . . in which your *Reflections on Peaceful Coexistence* [*sic*] appeared together with their program calling for the overthrow of the existing regime in the USSR. Thus our enemies have used our names in every way for their own purposes. . . . I will be infinitely happy if what I have written will afford you the opportunity to avoid the mistakes and pitfalls I was unfortunately unable to avoid and realized too late. I would very much like to hear your views on the substance of the questions touched upon. This letter has been written by me personally.[156]

According to Soviet law, letters written by persons arrested and under investigation can be delivered only with permission of the investigator.[157] The document in question is the only letter from Yakir known to have been delivered before his trial. For purposes of this discussion it is immaterial whether Yakir wrote the letter himself or from dictation, how the KGB broke him, and why he submitted.[158] Had he not been in the hands of the KGB in Lefortovo for nearly ten months it is inconceivable that he could have written such a text. The essential point here is that the KGB wanted to convey its message to Sakharov. Did the KGB follow up its March 23 interview with the Yakir letter because Sakharov had remained unpersuaded? Had the KGB originally planned a Sakharov-Yakir con-

156. Yakir to Sakharov, April 3, 1973, *AS* 1425. The letter was reported to be circulating in samizdat by AP and UPI dispatches of May 2 and by Hedrick Smith, *New York Times*, May 3, 1973. NTS (Natsional'nyi Trudovoi Soiuz, or National Labor Union) is an organization of primarily Russian émigrés whose social and political platform is generally supported by the independent monthly *Posev*, published in West Germany by the publishing house Possev-Verlag. Ilin was the man who shot at a car carrying Soviet cosmonauts on January 22, 1969, possibly in the belief that Brezhnev and Podgorny were inside.

157. *Khronika zashchity*, no. 2, p. 11.

158. Shortly before his arrest Yakir had told David Bonavia, former Moscow correspondent of the London *Times*, that if arrested and "if they beat me, I will say anything—I know that from my former experience in the camps. But you will know it will not be the real me speaking"; *Times*, June 23, 1972. Bonavia's account was corroborated by Yakir at the September 5 press conference following the Yakir-Krasin trial; Edmund Stevens, *Times* (London), September 6, 1973. But even without resorting to physical torture the KGB could threaten him with the arrest of his beloved daughter Irina and play on his addiction to alcohol. "Known widely as a heavy drinker," as Hedrick Smith reported (*New York Times*, December 11, 1972), Yakir was in a real sense a broken man even before arrest. Yet it appears that during the first five months of imprisonment he did not break completely. But in early December it was learned that he had twice been hospitalized in prison following deprivation of alcohol, after which he had begun cooperating with the KGB; Smith, *ibid.*; Robert G. Kaiser, *Washington Post*, December 3, 1972. An open letter from Adel Naidenovich, the former wife of Vladimir Osipov, describes him as of December 19. She says she "was put on [her] guard by the glassy look in his eyes"; "Poslednie vesti o Petre Yakire" [The latest news on Peter Yakir], Moscow, December 23, 1972, *AS* 1423. Andrei Dubrov also describes him on December 7 in "Ochnaia stavka s Petrom Yakirom" [Confrontation with Peter Yakir], Moscow, January 24, 1973, *AS* 1424.

frontation for March 23 which for unknown reasons had to be canceled? Be that as it may, the Yakir letter contains, in somewhat different guise, all the known ingredients of the March 23 interview.

"From the mad terrorist 'Ilin to Sakharov'" is the equivalent of "not morally sound." To link Sakharov to a "mad terrorist" is on the face of it more far-fetched than to link him to his friend Shikhanovich, already "becoming" mentally ill. Yet if it suited the authorities to declare Ilin mad for what may have been an act of political terrorism, it might also suit them to declare Sakharov mad.

More obviously ominous is the emphasis in the Yakir letter on the NTS. An old and reliable weapon of the KGB, the NTS has been used as the "foreign connection" in many political trials. Would it work once again for the KGB against the academician, who dared to brush off as "primitive ideas" about international relations the warning by one of the KGB officers that the West was interested in Sakharov "only for anti-Soviet purposes"?

Like Chakovsky, the Yakir letter refers to *Reflections*, though with a small difference in tone. Yet the objective is the same: the NTS, that "mouthpiece of anticommunism," used *Reflections* "for their own purposes." The letter insinuates that because the NTS published Sakharov's *Reflections* in a pamphlet with its own program, calling for overthrow of the Soviet regime, *Reflections* must in some way be connected with the NTS program, and hence the NTS with Sakharov.

There are two seemingly personal elements in the Yakir letter. The acknowledgement of thanks with which the letter opens ("having learned of your coming out in my defense") suggests that the KGB found it "useful for its own purposes," to borrow a favorite phrase of the KGB, to inform Yakir of Sakharov's action. The Russian word used, *vystuplenie*, is too general a term to be able to identify the type of action referred to, let alone the particular action. Although there may have been others, the only action known that could fit the *vystuplenie* is Sakharov's signature to an open group letter of fifty-two in Yakir's defense sent to the party Politburo and the Presidium of the USSR Supreme Soviet in July 1972. The group letter, interestingly enough, asserted that "only those who equate Stalinism with Soviet authority can accuse Yakir of anti-Sovietism."[159] "Anti-Sovietism" is precisely the essence of the *mea culpa* of the Yakir letter. The Yakir letter's invitation ("I would very much like to hear your views . . .") is patently naive. Did the KGB really imagine that Sakharov would be interested in starting a correspondence? This line looks more like an oblique hint that the KGB would like to continue its March 23 interview.

The KGB had thus so set the stage that within two months of Chakovsky's article Sakharov had every reason to regard as serious the possibilities

159. Excerpts from the letter are in *Chronicle*, no. 27, p. 33. A list of signatories is in a note to *ibid.*, which says there were 51, while a Reuter dispatch of July 27, 1972 says there were 52.

of indictment for a political crime or of commitment to a psychiatric hospital. The door to a third possibility, banishment abroad, was opened in March when Sakharov was invited to be a visiting scholar for the 1973–74 academic year at Princeton. The fate of his former committee colleague Valery Chalidze, deprived of Soviet citizenship in mid-December while in the United States, immediately comes to mind. In mid-January Sakharov had explained his position on the case. To Sakharov it was "evident from the outset that for a private person to obtain permission to give unofficial lectures [abroad] . . . , and at that together with his wife, was absolutely unprecedented. Even for a Soviet citizen in high position a private family trip is an exceptional event." After he and another committee member, Shafarevich, met "resistance" from Chalidze in efforts to dissuade him from making the trip, arguing probable loss of citizenship, Sakharov concluded that "evidently the lifting of Chalidze's citizenship had in some sense been arranged between the authorities and Chalidze himself."[160] The alternative was probably imprisonment.

As far as Sakharov was concerned, however, the events of the winter of 1972–73 did not intimidate him. The summer saw a repetition in aggravated form of the winter sequence. In the spring he spoke out in spirited defense of Amalrik; of a fellow academician, the Jewish physicist Veniamin Levich; and of the ethnic German Friedrich Ruppel, who had been trying to win repatriation to West Germany.[161] He next granted, probably in late June, a second interview to a foreign correspondent (Stenholm), this time daring to appear before a foreign television audience, albeit in neutral Sweden. He was well aware that Amalrik, Bukovsky, and Yakir, all of whom had preceded

160. Sakharov learned of the invitation during a March telephone conversation with friends in the United States; Hedrick Smith, *New York Times*, March 25, 1973. Chalidze resigned from the committee September 4, 1972; arrived with his wife in the United States November 23 to deliver a series of lectures on human rights in the USSR; and was informed December 13 by an official of the Soviet consulate that he (but not his wife) had been deprived of Soviet citizenship by the Presidium of the USSR Supreme Soviet; *Chronicle*, no. 27, p. 37; *Khronika zashchity*, no. 1, pp. 23–26. For Sakharov's position see the document "Ot Komiteta prav Cheloveka" [From the Human Rights Committee], n.d. [January 1973], *AS* 1246, reported circulating in samizdat by Hedrick Smith, *New York Times*, January 18, 1973.

161. For the defense of Amalrik see Moscow Human Rights Committee [Sakharov, Podyapolsky, and Shafarevich], "Obrashchenie Komiteta prav Cheloveka k mirovoi obshchestvennosti s prizyvom vystupit' v zashchitu Andreia Amalrika" [Appeal . . . to world public opinion to speak out in defense of Andrei Amalrik], May 22, 1973, *AS* 1436; A. Sakharov, "Otkrytoe pis'mo Genrikhu Belliu ob A. Amal'rike i L. Ubozhko" [Open letter to Heinrich Böll about A. Amalrik and L. Ubozhsko], Moscow, May 27, 1973, *AS* 1521. For the defense of Levich see A. Sakharov, "Otkrytoe pis'mo rektoru Tel'-Avivskogo universiteta Prof. Iuvalu Neemanu . . ." [Open letter to Professor Yuval Neeman, president of Tel-Aviv University . . .], Moscow, May 30, 1973, *AS* 1522, appealing for "a wide international campaign" to demand the release of Levich's 25-year-old son Yevgeni, a brilliant physicist who was inducted into the army though seriously ill. Sakharov mentioned the case in his interview on Swedish television, p. 12. For the defense of Ruppel see A. Sakharov, "Telegramma L. I. Brezhnevu v podderzhku Fridrikha Ruppelia" [Telegram to L. I. Brezhnev in support of Friedrich Ruppel], May 18, 1973, *AS* 1634; English trans., *Sakharov Speaks*, p. 241.

him on Western television, were now in camps or prison. The Yakir "invitation" to correspond was thereby indirectly rejected.

Going far beyond what he had told Axelbank, Sakharov set forth to Stenholm his views concerning the undemocratic nature of the Soviet system. Socialism in the Soviet Union was "simply state capitalism," while the society's main defects were "the lack of freedom" and "the bureaucratization of government." At the same time he described himself to Stenholm as a liberal—"a 'gradualist,' if you like"—arguing against any total reorganization of the Soviet state.[162]

The interview was broadcast July 2, 1973. The regime's initial response came only ten days later, on the twelfth, when the press agency TASS carried the article "Purveyor of Slander" by its political commentator Yuri Kornilov. The article appeared six days later in *Literaturnaia Gazeta* (between *Newsweek*'s publication of the interview given to Axelbank and the appearance of Chakovsky's article there had been a time lag of three months). Kornilov asserted that "the entire activity of Sakharov as a purveyor to the reactionary press of calumny against the Soviet Union is dictated by a . . . desire to slander his own country." The interview "merely confirms that [Sakharov's] 'ideological baggage' . . . contains nothing but groveling before the capitalist system and a collection of malicious fabrications about the Soviet system." Sakharov was also accused of treating "questions on which he is utterly ignorant."[163]

The August issue of *Posev* with a text of the interview on Swedish television appeared in late July. By early August the writer Vladimir Maksimov considered the position of dissidents in general, and that of Sakharov in particular, so precarious that he issued an appeal to world public opinion through an open letter to Heinrich Böll. The outside world was urged to act to save Sakharov, "the honor and conscience of contemporary Russia," before it was too late.[164]

A week after Maksimov's appeal Sakharov was summoned for a second interview with the authorities, this time with the first deputy procurator general, Mikhail Malyarov, and an unnamed assistant. Sakharov reproduced the seventy-minute session from memory and gave it to foreign correspondents August 18 so that unlike the March interview it is available in a detailed report. Describing his talk as a warning to be taken "in all seriousness," Malyarov presented Sakharov with a bill of particulars that was an unmistakable response to the interview on Swedish television. Indeed, the interview was, as Sakharov put it at his press conference five days later, "the straw that broke the camel's back." He was accused of

162. Interview on Swedish television, p. 9.
163. Yu. Kornilov, "Postavshchik klevety," *Literaturnaia gazeta*, July 18, 1973.
164. Maksimov, "Otkrytoe pis'mo Genrikhu Belliu" [Open letter to Heinrich Böll], Moscow, August 4, 1973, *AS* 1457.

"giving [foreigners] material for anti-Soviet publications," of having "renounced the socialist system in our country," of adopting in effect the same anti-Soviet subversive position as *Posev*, and of responsibility for "beginning to be used . . . also by foreign intelligence." Only the last charge was new. Malyarov's allegation that Sakharov knew Yakir well was possibly another attempt to involve him in the Yakir trial, which was to open at the end of the month. Finally, by his assertion that "any state has the right to defend itself," Malyarov threatened that if need be the regime would apply the relevant articles of the criminal code—190-1 and 70—against Sakharov.[165]

The talk with Malyarov, it is interesting to note, contains nothing that could be interpreted as a threat to commit Sakharov to a psychiatric hospital. On the other hand, an August 19 dispatch, quoting Sakharov's friends, reported that he "fears that the increased official pressure on him is a prelude to his incarceration in a prison or a mental hospital." Six weeks earlier, on July 3, Sakharov's wife had warned by telephone from Moscow that he "risks internment in a psychiatric hospital. . . . The chief assistant [possibly Frolov] of KGB chairman Yuri Andropov told a prisoner whom he had interrogated: 'I spoke with Sakharov recently. He did not seem normal to me.'"[166]

The breakdown of his mental capacities was implied in the following explanation of Sakharov's "death as a creative personality," the result of his withdrawal from scientific work:

Generally the process of such a "degeneration" of the personality proceeds very painfully and leads to an open or concealed deformation of the capacity for soundly judging one's actions. Here the hypertrophical syndrome of self-assertion comes into effect automatically.

This gobbledygook is buried in a commentary for foreign consumption distributed by a Soviet press agency on August 30, just after a major press and radio campaign against Sakharov had been launched (see p. 403 below).[167]

Around September 23 to 25, two weeks after the campaign had stopped, unnamed Soviet officials passed the story that Sakharov "isn't quite normal" to several Westerners in Moscow. "His ideas suggest some sort of mental instability," they added. There was a report that he would soon be required to submit to a medical examination. These reports sound like the work of

---

165. Sakharov, "Talk with Malyarov."

166. On report by Sakharov's friends, UPI dispatch of August 19, *International Herald Tribune*, August 20, 1973. On Bonner's warning, *L'express* (Paris), July 16–22, 1973, p. 58. According to David Floyd, the prisoner was Bukovsky, the reported words of Andropov's assistant were that Sakharov was "not quite normal," and the telephone call was "a message to friends in the West" sent on July 4 (cf. July 3); *Daily Telegraph* (London), July 5, 1973.

167. Alexander Miklashevsky, "Who is he, Andrei Sakharov," Novosti, August 30, 1973.

the KGB. That an attempt had been made to start or test a rumor in this period is evident from Sakharov's remarks to an English television audience on September 24. Speaking by telephone, he said that while he would like to go abroad for several months it would be "terrible" to have to leave the country permanently. "But if it came to a choice between myself and members of my family going into a mental hospital or going abroad, then I would choose abroad." But thereafter the issue of Sakharov's mental health receded into the background.[168]

The trial of Peter Yakir and Victor Krasin finally opened behind closed doors August 27. After their arrest in June and September 1972 respectively they had become the authorities' chief instruments in the crackdown on *Chronicle*. Once they began to cooperate under interrogation, they incriminated others as well as themselves. Over 200 persons were interrogated during the preliminary investigation. The line developed at the trial was the one foreshadowed in Yakir's letter to Sakharov in April 1973 (see pp. 396–97 above). For their cooperation the two men received light sentences—three years in confinement plus three years in exile each. The appeals court lifted the prison terms, and in mid-October Krasin was sent to Kalinin and Yakir to Ryazan to serve their terms of exile.[169]

Sakharov's name was linked to the trial in two TASS reports. The first report appeared August 29, the day the press and radio campaign against him moved into high gear. At the trial, according to TASS, "it was discovered that Yakir had met [Sakharov] many times at farewell banquets given by foreign correspondents after they [had been ordered to leave] the Soviet Union for violating the status of journalists." The second item reported that Sakharov's name was mentioned frequently at the trial and that his "materials . . . were used by the accused in anti-Soviet propaganda."[170]

Yakir and Krasin were presented to the Soviet and foreign public at an extraordinary press conference September 5. Press, radio, and television were on hand. Here they reiterated the line of the trial in prepared statements and in answers to questions. The most interesting personage presented at the conference, however, was Malyarov. Asked what might happen to the outspoken critics of Soviet policy, Malyarov replied that "Sakharov does not enjoy any immunity by which he would not be

168. On the first rumor about Sakharov's mental health, Robert G. Kaiser, *Washington Post*, September 26, 1973. On the second rumor, AP dispatch of September 24, 1973, *New York Post*, September 24. On Sakharov's telephone interview to BBC television, Reuter dispatch of September 24, 1973.

169. *Chronicle*, no. 27, p. 13; *ibid.*, no. 30, pp. 69–71. Reuter and UPI dispatches of November 1, 1973, reported that Sakharov had refused to speak to Yakir, who phoned him from Ryazan.

170. On the first report, TASS, August 29, 1973, and *New York Times*, August 30, 1973. On the second report, Ye. Maiorov, TASS correspondent, "Na sudebnom protsesse v Moskve" [At the court trial in Moscow], *Izvestiia*, August 31, 1973.

accountable for criminal activities against the state." As to the possible consequences, he declared:

We shall not decide that question now. I only want to emphasize again that nobody can be exempt from responsibility for a crime committed against the Soviet state. In particular academician Sakharov and Solzhenitsyn, as well as some others, must remember what they have received from the Soviet state. They must remember that they are Soviet citizens and they must not tear up the roots of the tree whose fruit they have been enjoying so well.

But he ignored a written question on which part of the Criminal Code forbade meetings with foreigners (Yakir had listed such meetings among his "illegal" activities).[171]

Questioned about the trial and press conference in a telephone interview broadcast by a Dutch radio station September 7, Sakharov replied that his information was incomplete. "I am very sad. These people have been broken. I have never been in their situation, and I do not assume the right to judge them." At the same time he pointed out that much of what they had said was untrue, especially Yakir's assertion that things were normal in Soviet psychiatric hospitals. It was difficult to explain their behavior, but "I know that Yakir had a difficult life. . . . After the arrest of his father he spent 18 years behind bars. He grew up in absolutely inhuman surroundings. After that I cannot accuse him of anything. I pity him and I pity his family." Yet in mid-September a *Pravda* article could group Sakharov and Solzhenitsyn together with Yakir and Krasin as part of "a handful of individuals remote from the people and alien to their interests."[172]

The press and radio campaign against Sakharov began seventy-two hours after his August 21 press conference. In volume and duration it exceeded the anti-Pasternak campaign of 1958 and recalled the Stalinist press of the mid-1930s and 1940s. It opened as the August 24 Moscow evening edition of *Izvestiia* published a TASS report of a *L'humanité* article critical of Sakharov for his statements made August 21, and the 7 p.m. Radio Moscow press review featured the *Izvestiia* item. On the twenty-seventh TASS used an article and a letter to the editor in the Austrian communist party organ *Volksstimme* in the same way. The next evening *Izvestiia* and Radio Moscow featured a letter of indignation signed by forty members of the USSR Academy of Sciences.[173]

171. Alain Jacob, *Le monde*, September 7, 1973; Edmund Stevens, *Times* (London), September 6, 1973; Gordon F. Joseloff, dispatch for UPI, September 5, 1973.

172. Sakharov interview to Jan Bezemer, professor of Russian history at Amsterdam University, as reported by Karel van het Reve, Sunday *Observer* (London), September 9, 1973; V. Bol'shakov, "Kto stoit na pozitsiiakh 'kholodnoi voiny'" [Who favors "cold war"], *Pravda*, September 15, 1973.

173. "'Nekii "gumanist" vystupaet protiv razriadki': stat'ia Iva Moro v 'Iumanite'" ["A certain 'humanist' comes out against détente": Yves Moreau's article in *L'humanité*], *Izvestiia*, international ed., August 25, 1973; "Protiv kogo on boretsia?" [Against whom is he fighting?],

The two TASS reports and the letter of forty contained most of the charges cited during the campaign: Sakharov opposes the government's policy of détente; he defames the Soviet state structure and distorts Soviet reality; he appeals to reactionary imperialist circles of the West for help, in effect has become an instrument of hostile propaganda; he has lost contact with his people and his country; he wants to wreck the European Conference on Security and Cooperation (Phase II of the conference was to open in Geneva September 18). On September 8, with an unsigned TASS article "To be a Soviet scientist means to be a patriot," a survey of letters of protest received by Soviet press and broadcast media, the campaign ceased.[174]

If the authorities had hoped to frighten Sakharov and his supporters into silence, they failed. Among the statements in his defense was a proposal by Shafarevich, Galich, and Maksimov that Sakharov be awarded the 1973 Nobel Peace Prize. Describing him as "an outstanding fighter for real democracy, for the rights and dignity of man, and for a genuine not an illusory peace," they added that "the downtrodden and the humiliated look to him for hope and strength. Though not a dogmatic believer, he represents an example of truly Christian behavior on earth." The same proposal was made by Solzhenitsyn in his article "Peace and Violence."[175]

Sakharov, who had been on the beach at Gagra, Georgia, when the storm broke, returned to Moscow no later than September 4. He now granted telephone interviews almost daily to newspaper, radio, and television correspondents of the West. On the fifth he told the second program of West German television that protests by Böll, Grass, and others would be helpful, but that these should not concern him alone. On the sixth he told the editor of the Rotterdam newspaper *Algemeen Dagblad* that he was no more afraid than at other times and believed that world public opinion would protect him. On the seventh to the *Bild-Zeitung* of Hamburg he said that "an appeal [from Brandt] to the Soviet government would certainly help us." On the eighth, at a press conference with fourteen foreign correspondents, Sakharov called the major theme of the campaign—that he was against détente—"an unscrupulous play on the antiwar feelings of the nation which suffered the most from the Second World War."[176]

Pravda, August 28, 1973; "Pis'mo chlenov Akademii nauk SSSR" [Letter from members of the USSR Academy of Sciences], Radio Moscow, August 28, 1973, 2130, *Pravda* and *Izvestiia*, international ed., August 29, 1973.

174. "Byt' sovetskim uchionym—znachit byt' patriotom," *Pravda* and *Izvestiia*, international ed., September 8, 1973.

175. For excerpts from proposal by Shafarevich *et al.*, Theodore Shabad, *New York Times*, September 8, 1973, UPI dispatch of September 7, 1973. A. Solzhenitsyn, "Mir i nasilie" [Peace and violence], Moscow, September 5, 1973, *AS* 1479, p. 9, first published by *Aftenposten* (Oslo), September 10, 1973, English trans., *Index* 2, no. 4 (Winter 1973), pp. 47–51. The proposal was seconded by many statesmen and scholars in the West. On September 10 the chairman of the Nobel Institute, August Schou, announced that nominations for the 1973 prize had been closed February 1; UPI dispatch of September 10, 1973.

176. On Gagra, Vincent Buist dispatch for Reuter, September 9, 1973. Chalidze spoke by telephone with Sakharov September 4; *New York Times*, September 6, 1973. For September 5

Why the press campaign against Sakharov was stopped is not clear, but several factors can be suggested. One of these was the Soviet government's concern for the success of the Conference on European Security and Cooperation. European statesman had already started to speak out in defense of Sakharov and Solzhenitsyn. Suggestive of Soviet sensitivity was the way a TASS report of September 9 singled out two European neutrals for criticism. In distorting the situation concerning dissidents in the Soviet Union, it said, "some statesmen in Sweden or Austria . . . try to link their statements with the Conference." A few days earlier the Austrian chancellor, Dr. Bruno Kreisky, had described Sakharov as a symbolic figure in a battle for scientific freedom and the Swedish foreign minister, Krister Wickman, had stated that the campaign against Sakharov and Solzhenitsyn did not serve the cause of détente.[177]

Another factor was the regime's concern lest American technical aid be withdrawn. On the eighth, Dr. Philip Handler, president of the American National Academy of Sciences, sent two cablegrams to his Soviet counterpart, Mstislav Keldysh, following a meeting of the academy's executive council. The shorter message warned that "harrassment or detention of Sakharov will have severe effects upon the relationships between the scientific communities of the USA and the USSR and could vitiate our recent efforts toward increasing scientific interchange and cooperation." The longer message stated that it was "with great dismay that we have learned of the heightening campaign of condemnation of Sakharov for having expressed, in a spirit of free scholarly inquiry, social and political views which derive from his scientific understanding." The import of the final paragraph of the longer message could not possibly be misunderstood:

Were Sakharov to be deprived of his opportunity to serve the Soviet people and humanity, it would be extremely difficult to imagine successful fulfillment of American pledges of binational scientific cooperation, the implementation of which is entirely dependent upon the voluntary effort and goodwill of our individual scientists and scientific institutions. It would be calamitous indeed if the spirit of détente were to be damaged by any further action taken against this gifted physicist.[178]

---

telephone interview conducted in German over West German television, unpublished transcript. For September 6 interview with editor Bert van Oosterhout conducted in German, *Die Welt* (Hamburg), September 7, 1973, and *Times* (London), September 8, 1973. For September 7 interview, Deutsche Presse Agentur (DPA) dispatch of September 7, 1973, reporting *Bild-Zeitung* (Hamburg) was to carry text September 8. Willy Brandt issued a cautious statement to the effect that he felt allied with those "who are endangered because of their convictions," but later added that he would favor détente "even if Stalin were still the first man in the Soviet Union"; *New York Times*, September 9, 1973, DPA dispatch of September 12, 1973. For September 8 press conference, Sakharov, "Statement on Press Accusation."

177. Buist dispatch for Reuter, September 9, 1973. For Kreisky's statement, Reuter dispatch of September 3 in *Times* (London), September 4, 1973. For Wickman statement, *Süddeutsche Zeitung*, September 7, 1973, and Reuter dispatch of September 10, 1973.

178. For Handler's short cable, *New York Times*, September 10, 1973; for the longer cable, press release of September 9, 1973. On September 9 Wilbur D. Mills, the former chairman of

A third factor may have been that the authorities themselves realized the campaign had not been convincing. As Litvinov and Shragin said in a statement of support for Sakharov: "In the absence of the Iron Curtain our internal affairs appear to the whole world such as they are and not as one would want to picture them." In late September there were reports that speakers at closed party *aktiv* meetings were admitting that the campaign had been a mistake: Sakharov was not a danger to Soviet society and should be ignored.[179]

Although the letter-writing campaign was not resumed, the press continued sniping at Sakharov from time to time. In September he unwittingly gave the press an occasion to accuse him of supporting the military junta in Chile, which overthrew the leftist Allende government September 11. On the eighteenth, when it appeared that the Marxist poet Pablo Neruda might be in danger, Sakharov, Galich, and Maksimov penned a moving appeal to the new government to safeguard the poet's freedom: "The violent death of this great man would darken for a long time what your government has proclaimed to be the era of the rebirth and consolidation of Chile."[180]

L'humanité and the Italian communist party organ *L'unità* interpreted this sentence to mean that the authors of the appeal themselves believed the junta would usher in this era. TASS carried this distortion and omitted all reference to Galich and Maksimov. *Pravda* published the TASS dispatch September 25 after a curious delay of three days. Telephoned by a foreign correspondent, Sakharov explained that he could not take a position on the junta because "Chile is too far away"; the appeal had been motivated "strictly by humanitarian considerations."[181]

In mid-October the press pounced on Sakharov again, this time for his comments on the Arab-Israeli War. On October 11, in an interview to an unidentified Lebanese correspondent, Sakharov asserted that Egyptian and Syrian military action had started the war. This conflicted with the official Soviet policy, which termed Israel the aggressor. Moreover, when asked what steps the United States and other Western countries could take to end

the Ways and Means Committee of the U.S. House of Representatives, warned that he would oppose liberalization of trade with the USSR "if the price is to be paid in the martyrdom of men of genius like Solzhenitsyn and Sakharov"; *New York Times*, September 10, 1973.

179. Excerpts from Litvinov-Shragin statement as quoted by AP dispatch of September 14, *International Herald Tribune*, September 15, 1973, and Reuter dispatch of September 14, *Times* (London), September 15, 1973. On *aktiv* meetings, Hedrick Smith, *New York Times*, September 28, 1973.

180. A. Galich, V. Maksimov, and A. Sakharov, "Zaiavlenie novomu pravitel'stvu Chili v zashchitu P. Nerudy" [Statement to the new government of Chile in defense of P. Neruda], September 18, 1973, *AS* 1488, where Sakharov's name is listed third, English trans. *New York Times*, October 3, 1973, and *Sakharov Speaks*, pp. 243–44, where Sakharov's name is listed first.

181. "Nedostoinaia pozitsiia" [Unworthy position], *Pravda*, September 25, 1973; on delay of *Pravda* use of TASS dispatch, Robert G. Kaiser, *Washington Post*, September 26, 1973; on Sakharov's comment, *ibid.*, and Theodore Shabad, *New York Times*, September 26, 1973.

the war, Sakharov replied: "Call upon the USSR and socialist countries to abandon the policy of one-sided interference in the Arab-Israeli conflict, and take retaliatory steps if this policy of interference continues."[182]

On the sixteenth *Pravda* distorted this passage to accuse Sakharov of "calling on imperialist states to 'take retaliatory steps against the Soviet Union' because it is giving aid to Arab states in repulsing the Israeli aggression." It then quoted a *L'unità* comment that "Sakharov always sides with imperialism. Yesterday he sided with the Chilean insurgents, today with Israel. . . . But this time the case is far worse: it is an open call to foreign states 'to take steps' against his own country in order to make it change its policy."[183]

Now something entirely new happened to Sakharov as a direct consequence of his statement on the Near East war. On October 21 Sakharov was described as "badly shaken" in three accounts by foreign correspondents who saw him some hours after two men claiming to be members of the Palestinian nationalist Black September movement had held him, his wife, and his stepson hostage for over an hour. The men cut the telephone wire and forbade the family to answer the doorbell. The intruders gained entrance by speaking German, then spoke in Russian, one quite well. One of the men never removed his coat. "Underneath there was a bulge," said Sakharov. "It seemed there was a pistol there. He never took his hands off it." Accusing Sakharov of being "under the influence" of his wife, they demanded that he change his views on the Arab-Israeli conflict. At one point Sakharov's wife asked, "Do you want to kill us?" One of the Arabs replied, "We can do worse things than kill you." Although warned not to mention their visit to anyone, Sakharov said he notified the police several hours later. Four men came to the apartment, but it was Sakharov's impression that they were not very serious.[184]

As soon as he learned of the incident Solzhenitsyn penned an angry letter of support to Sakharov. It was his view that "with the blanket physical and telephone surveillance put on you such an assault is impossible without the knowledge and encouragement of the authorities." Sakharov agreed a month later that "Solzhenitsyn's assumption seems right to me in all probability."[185]

182. Andrei Sakharov, "Beseda s livanskom korrespondentom v Moskve ob arabsko-izrail'skoi voine" [Interview with a Lebanese correspondent in Moscow on the Arab-Israeli war], October 11, 1973, *AS* 1490, English trans. *New York Times*, October 17, 1973, and *Sakharov Speaks*, pp. 224–26.

183. "Antisovetskaia vykhodka" [Anti-Soviet prank], *Pravda*, October 16, 1973; TASS in English, October 15, 1973.

184. AFP dispatch of October 21, 1973; Vincent Buist dispatch for Reuter, October 21, 1973; *New York Times*, October 22, 1973. In *Sakharov o sebe*, p. 24, and *Sakharov Speaks*, p. 51, the incident is mistakenly placed in "late September."

185. Alexander Solzhenitsyn, "Pis'mo Andreiu Sakharovu" [Letter to Andrei Sakharov], October 28, 1973, *AS* 1491; Van Vinar, telephone interview with Sakharov, *Die weltwoche* (Zurich), November 28, 1973. On November 28 Sakharov showed reporters a letter he had

In mid-November Sakharov was subjected to a new form of pressure but one he had mentioned as a possibility to Axelbank a year earlier. On the thirteenth his wife, Yelena Bonner, was summoned by the KGB for interrogation. The pretext for the summons was to discuss the Sakharovs' offer of October 28 to Andropov to stand surety for Victor Khaustov. The offer was "not serious," KGB officer Sokolov said at this session, because "it had become known abroad" and because she was "essentially a codefendant of Khaustov and Superfin."[186]

At a second session, on the nineteenth, Bonner acknowledged that she had transmitted the prison diaries of her nephew, Eduard Kuznetsov, to the West. This, it appeared, was the KGB's real interest in her.[187] In support of Yevgeny Barabanov, a young art historian who had openly admitted sending samizdat texts to the West, Bonner stated that she too had done so. "I believed and still believe it to be my duty," she said. "What would the world know of our life if no one did this?" Simultaneously Sakharov and Podyapolsky issued a similar statement.[188]

In this session and others on November 20, 23, and 27, Colonel Syshchikov, KGB investigator from Orel oblast, tried to ensnare Bonner in "the criminal actions of V. Khaustov, G. Superfin, and Ye. G. Bonner"—first as an accomplice, then as a witness, finally as a sympathizer. The fates of Superfin, Khaustov, and Kuznetsov, whose original death sentence could be reimposed, depended on her, Syshchikov warned. As a mother she should consider the fate of her children. When she refused to give testimony (it was not clear whether it might be used against her) she was told that "the guards can be called" and that possibly she was mentally sick. He continued that she

received from Beirut threatening him with another visit by Palestinians if he continued his "policy of confrontation with Arab countries"; AFP dispatch, November 28, 1973.

186. Yelena Bonner, "Zaiavlenie po povodu doprosov 13, 19 i 20 noiabria 1973 v KGB" [Statement on KGB interrogations of November 13, 19, and 20, 1973], November 20, 1973, *AS* 1506. On pretext for summons, *Chronicle*, no. 30, p. 79; also implied in *AS* 1506. On Sakharovs' offer, Ye. Bonner and A. Sakharov, "Pis'mo Yu. V. Andropovu s pros'boi otpustit' na poruki Viktora Khaustova" [Letter to Yu. V. Andropov requesting Victor Khaustov's release on surety], October 28, 1973, *AS* 1496.

187. Reuter and UPI dispatches of November 20, 1973. The diaries record Kuznetsov's confinement in the Leningrad investigative prison October 1970–May 1971 and in the special regime camp in Mordovia June–November 1971; they reveal the process of interrogation and attempts by the KGB to set the accused of the Leningrad trial of "hijackers" against one another. According to one account, the manuscript of the diaries was smuggled out of the Mordovian camp in November 1971, was transcribed on six different typewriters in Moscow, and reached Paris in July 1972, where a "righteous" man refused to divulge it for two months. It appeared in excerpts in Italian, *L'espresso* (Rome), October 12, 1972; in English, *News Bulletin on Soviet Jewry* (Tel-Aviv) 3, no. 2 (October 2–31, 1972), pp. 14–16, which relates the above account as told by *L'espresso*; and in French, *L'express* (Paris), December 18–24, 1972, pp. 80–86. The complete Russian text, Eduard Kuznetsov, *Dnevniki* [Diaries], was published by Les éditeurs réunis (Paris, 1973).

188. Yevgeny Barabanov, "Zaiavlenie dlia pressy" [Statement for the press], September 15, 1973, *AS* 1475; Yelena Bonner, "O zaiavlenii Barabanova" [Concerning Barabanov's statement], September 19, 1973, *AS* 1477; A. Sakharov and Grigory Podyapolsky, "O zaiavlenii Yevgeniia Barabanova" [Concerning Yevgeny Barabanov's statement], September 19, 1973, *AS* 1476.

would have to speak anyway and not as a witness; moreover, she was only harming her husband. On the twenty-seventh, when she declared that she would not appear for the next day's session because there was no point in the interrogations, Syshchikov threatened to send a truck for her and "all your anti-Soviet friends and foreign correspondents."[189]

It was at this point that Sakharov intervened. In his open letter to Andropov November 28 he described Syshchikov's actions against his wife as "a form of pressure" on himself and declared: "I object to her being summoned . . . and I assume full responsibility for her nonappearance." He advised Andropov "to explain to your subordinate" that it was illegal to interrogate his wife as a witness if he considered her to be an accomplice, pointless if the person had good reason not to testify, and "immoral to subject a sick person who is a war invalid to many hours of exhaustive interrogation accompanied by threats." As to the accusation that she had kept and transmitted the diaries, "this can in no way be considered a crime by generally accepted legal standards and in accordance with the Declaration of Human Rights."

Following the third interrogation session Bonner held a press conference November 21. Here Sakharov was asked whether he thought that the interrogation was "a way to get at him." He replied: "That's the way I would evaluate it, but of course I can't say for sure." According to another account, Sakharov "viewed the sudden interest shown by the KGB in his wife as part of the general campaign against him for his outspoken criticism of Soviet society." On the twenty-fourth in a telephone interview he was asked by an Italian correspondent: "Are they trying to blackmail you through your wife?" Sakharov responded: "Undoubtedly. It can last for years, no one knows."[190]

In this period Sakharov had to shoulder yet another burden. On November 7 the world learned about Roy Medvedev's latest samizdat article "The Problem of Democratization and the Problem of Détente," dated October 1973. The article attacked Sakharov's thesis linking détente with democratization while the regime was also attacking his position, albeit for different reasons. Thus what has become known as the great debate among Soviet dissidents (including former Soviet citizens now residing in the West) burst into the open.[191]

---

189. Sakharov, "Open Letter to Andropov" (see n. 1); Bonner, "Statement on KGB Interrogations"; UPI dispatch of November 20, 1973; Reuter dispatch of November 21; DPA and UPI dispatches of November 24; AFP, Reuter, and UPI dispatches of November 27.

190. On Sakharov's direct reply, Christopher S. Wren, *New York Times*, November 22, 1973. The second part of the reply was evidently dropped from Reuter report in *Times* (London), November 22. On Sakharov's second remark, Reuter dispatch of November 21, *Times* (London), November 22, 1973; cf. Tony Conyers, *Daily Telegraph* (London), November 22. Sakharov's telephone interview to F. S. Alonzo in Stockholm, *Corriere della sera*, November 26, 1973.

191. R. A. Medvedev, "Problema demokratizatsii i problema razriadki," October 1973, *AS* 1500.

Medvedev rejected Sakharov's view that before agreeing to détente the West should set minimal conditions. Détente was important in itself. Although at present détente had brought no extension of the democratic freedoms, in the long run it would "undoubtedly encourage" them because it would increase the influence of world public opinion on the internal policies of the great powers. "The basic impulses" for democratization, however, would have to come from within Soviet society, including its leaders. Adoption of the Jackson Amendment and American denial of the most favorable conditions of trade were examples of outside pressure that would worsen Soviet-American relations and the prospects for emigration. Appeals to the West ought to be addressed to circles of the left, not the right, for the latter were mainly interested in using arbitrary acts by the Soviet regime as a means to discredit their own left oppositions and communism and socialism in general.[192] Roy's twin brother, Zhores, speaking before the Royal Institute of International Affairs in London on the thirteenth, made essentially the same points. He added, however, that his differences with Sakharov were over strategy, not principles.[193] On the same day Bonner was summoned by the KGB for her first interrogation.

It must have appeared uncanny to Sakharov's supporters that the appearance of the Medvedevs' criticisms coincided with the renewed pressure on Sakharov by the KGB. His supporters were enraged, especially Maksimov. On the eighteenth he telephoned to the West a biting open letter to the brothers. He chastized them for lack of shame at "raising a hand against . . . the moral pride of Russia—Academian Sakharov and Alexander Solzhenitsyn, and just when the danger of their death [had become] a daily reality. Good Lord, come to your senses! Isn't it too much? And one more thing—for whom are you working!" At the very least they could have shown "a sense of gratitude"—presumably by keeping quiet, thought Maksimov, recalling that both Sakharov and Solzhenitsyn had spoken out to obtain the release of Zhores from a psychiatric hospital in mid-1970.[194]

Agursky also lashed out at weaknesses in the brothers' arguments in his article "Where the Brothers Medvedev Are Right and Where They Are Wrong."[195]

192. *Ibid.*, pp. 4–5, 14, 15–16, 20. Medvedev also criticized statements by Solzhenitsyn, Maksimov, and (possibly) Agursky.

193. Reuter dispatch of November 13, 1973, *Times* (London) and *Guardian* (London), November 14. Zhores had published a pessimistic article on the prospects for dissent following the Yakir-Krasin trial, "Konets 'inakomysliia' ili urok na budushchee?" [The end of "dissent" or a lesson for the future?], *Novy zhurnal*, no. 112 (September 1973), pp. 298–307, also *Novoe russkoe slovo*, November 4, 1973; a condensed English trans. appeared under the title "Dissent/Medvedev Speaks," Sunday *Observer* (London), September 9, 1973.

194. Vladimir Maksimov, "Otkrytoe pis'mo brat'iam Medvedevym" [Open letter to the brothers Medvedev], n.d. [no later than November 18, 1973], *AS* 1507. Maksimov dictated the text by telephone November 18 to a correspondent of *Daily Telegraph* (London), q.v. November 19, 1973.

195. M. S. Agursky, "V chiom pravy i nepravy brat'ia Medvedevy," Moscow, November 17, 1973, *AS* 1508.

On the twentieth, the day his wife was interrogated for the third time, Sakharov announced in a brief statement his basic disagreement with "many of the assertions and the general direction" of the Medvedevs' statements. He agreed with the evaluations of Agursky and Maksimov. "By their pragmatism," Sakharov wrote, "the Medvedevs have set themselves against those who are waging a moral struggle for the right of man to live and think freely." The moral nature of his demands, such as the release of political prisoners, freedom to emigrate, and freedom of convictions, were prerequisites of a healthy Soviet society. He disagreed emphatically with the way the Medvedevs downgraded the role of free emigration, and he questioned Roy's call to limit appeals to the West to circles of the left. Appeals should be addressed "to all honest people whatever their political persuasions." The following day Sakharov told reporters that Roy had brought him a copy of his article, but his wife commented that this version was "much softer than the one he put out later."[196]

Sakharov's emotional reaction to the Medvedevs' statements is hard to determine. *Sakharov o sebe*, the account of his political development, does indicate, however gently, that his friendship with the brothers had cooled. It says: "Whatever form my relations and disagreements on matters of principle with the Medvedevs may have taken subsequently, I cannot minimize their role in my own development" (see p. 363 above). If the friendship had not cooled, the word "relations" would be superfluous. Perhaps the essentials of the emotional, as distinguished from the political, aspect of the former friendship were disclosed by his wife in a remark caught by at least one correspondent at her November 21 press conference: "The KGB says that our activities stand in the way of democratization and of détente. This is only an emotional observation, but I cannot help but notice that this is the same position the Medvedevs hold." It reflects her bitterness of the moment, but the idea may have passed through Sakharov's mind too.[197]

One indication that KGB pressure through Bonner had eased was the way Sakharov disclosed to foreign correspondents on November 29 that on the twenty-first he had finally taken the first step required of a Soviet citizen seeking an exit visa to travel abroad—a request for a character reference from his place of work, the Lebedev Physics Institute. He had not mentioned this important fact, the newsmen were quick to observe, during Bonner's press conference on the twenty-first. Had he done so, his action would certainly have been interpreted to be the result of the current KGB pressure. Sakharov emphasized that he had made his decision some time before—"a month ago" according to one account, "five weeks ago" according to

---

196. Sakharov, "Statement on Medvedevs"; on Bonner's comment, Robert Evans dispatch for Reuter, November 24, 1973.

197. *Sakharov o sebe*, p. 10. On Bonner's remarks, Michael Parks, *Baltimore Sun*, November 26, 1973.

another. Five weeks before was about the time of the Black September harassment.[198]

Sakharov stated that he had "decided it was time to do something. The situation here has become very critical" ("very tense," according to a second account). He wanted to deliver a series of unpublished lectures on the theories of gravitation and elementary particles at Princeton University "for a few months" ("three to six months," according to several accounts), but for some of the time he wanted to listen to lectures because he had been "under such nervous pressure." It was his impression that the authorities might regard the visit as "a good step," but he also realized the risk that he would be deprived of his Soviet citizenship. But he emphasized his wish to retain Soviet citizenship and to return. "My place—for moral, social, and personal reasons—is in my native land," he said. He added that he would leave only if his wife and stepchildren accompanied him; he had also applied for a visa for his two-month-old grandson.[199]

On the twenty-first, Sakharov continued, he had received a personal invitation for himself and his family from Professor Herman Feshbach of the Massachusetts Institute of Technology. The invitation was visaed by Henry Kissinger. "Inasmuch as the invitation meets Soviet official requirements and has such authoritative support, I decided to make use of it." He showed the correspondents the legal form Feshbach had mailed him. Four invitations had been extended by Princeton University. Sakharov received the first one, an offer to be a visiting professor for the 1973–74 academic year, in the spring. He also received an invitation no later than September 4, probably the fourth one mailed in late August. This one had been made by Professor Marvin L. Goldberger, chairman of Princeton's department of physics.[200]

Reaction among dissidents in Moscow to the news of Sakharov's decision to request documentation for an exit visa was mixed. Veniamin Levich, corresponding member of the academy, supported Sakharov's efforts as a test case. He believed that the authorities' response "will be interpreted by many as a sign of what is the actual way of further [scientific] development

198. On the November 29 press conference, Julian Nundy dispatch for Reuter, November 29, 1973; UPI dispatch of November 29; Christopher S. Wren, *New York Times*, Robert G. Kaiser, *Washington Post*, and Tony Conyers, *Daily Telegraph* (London), November 30. Sakharov's silence on the character reference was reported by Nundy and Wren; "a month ago" by Kaiser; "five weeks ago" by Conyers. On the character reference see also Sakharov's "Statement on Invitation," the contents of which he made known to the correspondents November 29.

199. "Very critical" and "for a few months" by Kaiser (see n. 198); "very tense," subject of lectures, "three to six months," and "nervous pressure" by Conyers; Sakharov, "Statement on Invitation"; on conditions of departure, Kaiser; on grandson, Nundy.

200. On Feshbach and first Princeton invitation, Sakharov, "Statement on Invitation"; on legal form, UPI dispatch (see n. 198); on number of Princeton invitations and receipt of the fourth, which was confirmed by Chalidze, Kathleen Teltsch, *New York Times*, September 6, 1973.

of international cooperation." On the other hand, one unofficial artist stated: "If he really goes, it means they [the authorities] have won. As long as he stayed here and continued to speak out, it meant he was winning."[201]

On Soviet Constitution Day, December 5, Sakharov participated in the "minute of silence" protest on Pushkin Square, as he had in 1971 and 1972. The same day he was awarded the 1973 International Human Rights Prize by the International League for the Rights of Man. At a session of the league in New York his statement of acceptance was read on his behalf by Feshbach. On a single page Sakharov recapitulated the major problems of human rights still unresolved in the Soviet Union and expressed the hope that "awarding the . . . Prize to a Soviet citizen is evidence that international attention to assuring human rights in our country will increase and have a deep influence."[202]

Two days later Sakharov and his wife voluntarily entered Academy Hospital on Lenin Prospect for three-week medical checkups—he for aggravated high blood pressure and she for acute toxicosis caused by a thyroid condition—and a much-needed rest. The nervous strain from the constant pressure throughout the year had begun to tell. While in the hospital Sakharov curtailed drastically but did not cease completely his public work.[203]

To end the year Sakharov dated his introduction to the collection *Sakharov Speaks* December 31. The date marked his survival in 1973: his moral courage supported by world public opinion had forced the KGB to a draw. His request for a character reference posed a new dilemma for the regime. This dilemma would be resolved indirectly by action the regime would soon take not against Sakharov but against Solzhenitsyn.

As the new year opened, two TASS articles portrayed the writer as a traitor whose work *The Gulag Archipelago*, published in Paris in late December, libeled the country.[204] The Soviet press and radio continued a high-pitched campaign against Solzhenitsyn until his arrest February 12 and banishment the following day.

Sakharov immediately spoke out in defense of Solzhenitsyn's right to publish abroad and his right to live and publish in his own country as well. In a January 5 statement he and four other Moscow intellectuals asserted

201. Levich's open letter to the world scientific community, as quoted by UPI dispatch of December 10, 1973; on the views of the artist, Hedrick Smith, *New York Times*, December 2, 1973, and *International Herald Tribune*, December 3.

202. For Sakharov on Pushkin Square, UPI dispatch of December 5, *Times* (London), December 6, 1973; on award, *Khronika zashchity*, nos. 5–6, pp. 61–62, and *Sakharov Speaks*, pp. 228–29.

203. *Sunday Times* (London), December 9, 1974, and Alexander Galich's telephone call of December 5, as reported in *Russkaia mysl'* [Russian thought] (Paris), December 13, 1973. The Sakharovs were released December 28.

204. Sergei Kulik, "Otraviteli atmosfery razriadki" [Poisoners of the atmosphere of détente], TASS, January 2, 1974; Kiril Andreev, "Otshchepenets: gnev bessiliia" [Renegade: The anger of impotence], TASS, January 3, 1974.

that "the right of an author to write and publish what his conscience and duty as an artist dictate is one of the most basic in civilized society. This right cannot be limited by national frontiers."[205]

Typical of Sakharov's many comments supporting Solzhenitsyn throughout the winter is one made January 20 during a telephone interview given to *La tribune de Genève*:

I would like to believe that the book *The Gulag Archipelago* will be widely read not only in the West but also in the USSR and will become the stone that will finally crack the ice of mistrust and lack of understanding created by lies, wickedness, cowardice, and stupidity. This stone has been cast by a powerful and sure hand.[206]

On the day of Solzhenitsyn's banishment, according to Bonner, Sakharov decided against the trip to the United States.[207] The same day he, his wife, and eight other Soviet intellectuals compiled a "Moscow Appeal" in which they demanded:

1. Publication of *The Gulag Archipelago* in the USSR and making it available to all our countrymen;
2. Publication of the archival and other materials which would give a full picture of the activity of the Cheka-GPU-NKVD-MGB;
3. Formation of an international public tribunal to investigate the crimes which have been committed;
4. Protection of Solzhenitsyn against prosecution and the opportunity for him to work in his native land.

Arguing that "all people on earth need to know the truth of what happened in the USSR," they asked "all mass information media to disseminate [their] appeal" and "all public and religious organizations to form national committees for the collection of signatures."[208]

A week later Sakharov explained in a telephone interview granted to the *Sunday Times* of London that their aim had been to make not a "pragmatic document" but rather "a moral appeal." The appeal, he believed, "showed the approach of a live democratic movement in the USSR for the defense of moral values of all mankind." Sakharov's defense of Solzhenitsyn was thus an essential part of the moral battle they were both waging. As he said the next day in another telephone interview, this time to the *Corriere della sera*: "Solzhenitsyn had and will continue to have a very important role [to play] for our cause. His moral conceptions deserve great respect."[209]

205. A. Sakharov *et al.*, "Obrashchenie k chestnym liudiam vo vsem mire s prizyvom vystupit' v zashchitu A. Solzhenitsyna" [Appeal to honest people throughout the world to speak out in defense of A. Solzhenitsyn], January 5, 1974, *AS* 1541.

206. Interview granted to Henri-Paul Deshusses of *La tribune de Genève*, January 20, 1974, p. 2, *AS* 1579; French trans., *La tribune de Genève*, January 24, 1974.

207. Hedrick Smith, *New York Times*, February 14, 1974.

208. A. Sakharov *et al.*, "Moskovskoe obrashchenie" [Moscow appeal], February 13, 1974, *AS* 1584.

209. A. D. Sakharov, "Interv'iu, dannoe gazete 'Sandi taims', o vysylke A. Solzhenitsyna i o 'Moskovskom obrashchenii' " [Interview granted to *Sunday Times* concerning A. Solzhenit-

On March 20 Sakharov and Shafarevich made available to foreign correspondents the samizdat volume "Live Not by Lies," a 194-page anonymous compilation of Soviet press and radio attacks on the novelist and of letters and documents in his support. The two academicians endorsed the volume with a brief foreword in which they said: "The great number of voices, among them people who have no protection from prosecution, shows how illusory were the hopes of those who thought Solzhenitsyn's influence on the country's spiritual life would diminish."[210]

One reason for putting aside the invitation to the United States became clear when, on February 27, Sakharov's wife underwent an operation in Leningrad, where she had been undergoing treatment for what he called a hyperthyroid condition.[211] A second reason—the fate of his stepchildren's applications for exit visas to the United States—was discussed by Sakharov in his open letter of March 29 to the academician Engelhardt.[212] A third reason, as Bonner had reported, was Solzhenitsyn's involuntary expulsion, which left Sakharov alone as the major figure of dissent. Seated at his wife's bedside in their Moscow flat three weeks after her operation, Sakharov told foreign correspondents that since Solzhenitsyn's banishment he had "given up thoughts of taking his family to the United States."[213]

Still other factors may have been concern for the fate of their friend Shikhanovich, who was still in a psychiatric hospital, and concern over the possible involvement of his wife in the forthcoming trials of Khaustov and Superfin. And in fact at both trials Bonner's name did come up. Khaustov's sentence of March 6 alleged that she had been an accessory in transmitting the Kuznetsov diaries, while Superfin at his trial on May 13 doubted the authorship of statements the prosecutor attributed to her and insisted that he alone had been responsible for the transmission of the diaries.[214]

While the health of his wife and the defense of Solzhenitsyn were his major preoccupations in the early months of the year, Sakharov continued to speak out for others who were oppressed or threatened with reprisal. A few examples: the essayist Lydia Chukovskaya, when ousted from the

syn's exile and the "Moscow Appeal"], February 20, 1974, pp. 2–3, *AS 1593*; English excerpts in *Sunday Times* (London), February 24, 1974; Scabello, *Corriere della sera*, February 22, 1974.

210. As quoted by Christopher Wren, *New York Times*, March 21, 1974, and Roger Leddington in AP dispatch of March 20, *Stars and Stripes*, March 22.

211. Reuter dispatch of February 28, 1974.

212. P. 2, *AS* 1651.

213. As quoted by Leddington, March 20.

214. Although a medical commission agreed March 25 to Shikhanovich's release from the hospital, he was not released until June; Andrei Sakharov and Yelena Bonner, "Otkrytoe obrashchenie k druz'iam Iuriia Shikhanovicha" [Open appeal to the friends of Yury Shikhanovich], June 1, 1974, *AS* 1741; Peter Osnos, *Washington Post*, June 27, 1974. For Khaustov's trial in Orel March 4–6, see *Khronika zashchity*, no. 8, pp. 8–9, and Pavel Litvinov's statement published in Rome March 19 in which he asserts that Khaustov was sentenced "mainly" for transmitting the diaries (*ibid.*, p. 7). For Superfin's trial in Orel, May 12–14, see *ibid.*, no. 9, pp. 7–10, and "Protsess nad Superfinom: kratkaia zapis'" [The trial of Superfin: a brief transcript], n.d. [not before May 13, 1974], *AS* 1823, p. 7.

Writers Union for having supported Sakharov in 1973; the poet and scenarist Alexander Galich, when denied permission to visit a relative in the United States; the writer Victor Nekrasov, after his Kiev apartment had been searched for forty-two hours and his personal archives and manuscripts seized; the mathematician Leonid Plyushch, on the verge of death due to mistreatment in the Dnepropetrovsk prison psychiatric hospital; Victor Khaustov, on the day of his sentence. The very day of his wife's operation he put his name to a group appeal for Vladimir Bukovsky, threatened with a new transfer to Vladimir prison.[215]

In April Sakharov broadened the great debate on détente and internal democratization. To the astonishment of the dissident community and the outside world, and perhaps to the Soviet authorities too, he came out in open disagreement with Solzhenitsyn over the future of their country and of the world in a critique of the novelist's *Letter to the Leaders of the Soviet Union.* He again paid homage to Solzhenitsyn for his "uncompromising, accurate, and deep illumination of the sufferings of the people and the crimes of the regime" depicted in *The Gulag Archipelago* and called him "a giant in the struggle for human dignity." But he was deeply distressed by the pervading note of Great Russian nationalism, an "enthusiasm for developing the virgin lands," and the appeals to patriotism and Orthodoxy in the letter. In particular, he disagreed with Solzhenitsyn's idealization of pre-Soviet Russia:

The spirit of slavery together with contempt for foreigners and peoples of other origins and faiths which has existed in Russia for centuries I consider to be the greatest of misfortunes, not a sign of national well-being. Only in democratic conditions can a national character develop capable of a rational existence in a world of ever-growing complexity.[216]

215. Andrei Sakharov, "Zaiavlenie v zashchitu Lidii Chukovskoi po povodu yeio iskliucheniia iz Soiuza pisatelei SSSR" [Statement in defense of Lydia Chukovskaya concerning her exclusion from the USSR Writers Union], Moscow, January 9, 1974, *AS* 1544; A. Sakharov, Ye. Bonner, and V. Maksimov, "Obrashchenie v Mezhdunarodnyi PEN-klub i Yevropeiskoe soobshchestvo pisatelei v sviazi s otkazom v razreshenii na vyezd v SShA Aleksandru Galichu" [Appeal to International Pen Club and European Writers Association in connection with refusal to Alexander Galich of permission to visit USA], Moscow, January 16, 1974, *AS* 1546; A. Sakharov, "Zaiavlenie 'V Mezhdunarodnyi komitet prav cheloveka, v Pen-klub, Genrikhu Belliu, mezhdunarodnyi obshchestvennosti' v zashchitu V. Nekrasova i drugikh" [Statement "To the International Human Rights Committee, PEN-club, Heinrich Böll, and international public opinion" in defense of V. Nekrasov *et al.*], Moscow, January 19, 1974, *AS* 1549; *Khronika zashchity*, no. 7, p. 29; T. Velikanova *et al.*, "Obrashchenie k raznym mezhdunarodnym organizatsiiam s pros'boi vystupit' v zashchitu V. Khaustova" [Appeal to various international organizations with request to speak out in defense of V. Khaustov], March 6, 1974, *AS* 1667; A. Sakharov *et al.*, "Obrashchenie k Lige zashchity prav cheloveka v zashchitu V. Bukovskogo" [Appeal to the International League for the Rights of Man in defense of V. Bukovsky], Moscow, February 27, 1974, *AS* 1622.

216. Sakharov, "Statement on Solzhenitsyn Letter," pp. 2–11. Cf. Andrei Sakharov, "Mir cherez polveka" [The world in fifty years], May 17, 1974, published in English under the title "Tomorrow: The view from Red Square" in *Saturday Review/World*, August 24, 1974, pp. 12 ff. The article was written especially for the journal's fiftieth anniversary issue.

Practical considerations force this narrative to end here. Sakharov's activities of course continue as of this writing, and therefore a complete assessment of his extraordinary career must await the future. No delay is necessary, however, to say that he will stand for all time as the champion of his countrymen's aspirations for their rights as men and of the need for a humane approach in dealing with the individual and groups of people. Well aware that a balance of power rules the world, Sakharov is equally aware that power without compassion is insufficient to secure the survival of mankind.

Galich summed up the new situation well when he welcomed the debate as "a positive step forward in the development of our spirit"; quoted by Andrew Nagorsky in *Newsweek* [international ed.], April 29, 1974, p. 16. The regime's sensitivity about the debate can be gauged from a lampoon which dismissed it as "this delirium, this discussion from the beyond, from the realm of darkness" and rejected "the reproach of the BBC that we are not informing our readers about one of 'the main discussions of the century' "; I. Petrov, "Potomki 'Chiornomortsev' " [Offspring of "the residents of Chiornomorsk"], *Literaturnaia gazeta*, May 1, 1974.

CHAPTER TWELVE / **NO PROTEST: THE CASE OF THE PASSIVE MINORITY** / GEORGE FEIFER

On a musky evening in the autumn of 1968, a young writer from Voronezh then living with his mistress near Gorky Park took me to a gathering of friends—"party" is far too formal for Moscow evenings of this sort—in the apartment of an older writer better known by the intellectual community for his samizdat poetry and satirical sketches than his published novels. The flat was in a sprawling new cooperative development that was already decaying although the last units had been completed only the previous winter. We walked up four dank flights of stairs—one lift was out of order, the other had been shut down in the practice of conserving electricity after midnight —and into the warm welcome of the host and his wife, who opened their arms although we had come unannounced. Because I had met them several times previously on Sunday countryside outings and because we had close friends in common, my presence as a foreigner disturbed neither them nor the atmosphere of almost vibrant openness and candor typical of Russians of this type when gathered among their trusted friends (*svoi liudi*) and shut off from all the double talk, crudeness, and resentful suspicion of the outside "them."

We pushed through the jumble of clothes hanging in the hall and into the smoky bed-sitting room, a replica of hundreds inhabited by the small circle of Moscow's "smart" young intelligentsia. Furnished with an eclectic assortment of cheap pieces, the room was further cramped by icons, old prints, and broken tsarist artifacts propped between tables, chairs, the sagging studio couch, and drearily papered walls. A substantial collection of books, largely yellowed prerevolutionary volumes and Western literature unpublishable in Russia, spilled from the bookcases into untidy piles on the floor, where they were surrounded by empty bottles and an accumulation of dirty dishes. Two other friends sat happily among this hospitable disorder: a Chekhovian, blond-bearded artist and a balding doctor with an English tweed jacket and a supply of Gitanes. In the kitchen two young graduate students without a room of their own were, we imagined, making love.

For those who have enjoyed such evenings with Moscow friends, my limitations in evoking their unaffected intimacy—an ambiance in which one feels miraculously at home with oneself and fellow men—will be no obstacle to visualizing the mood of this particular occasion. It is no less true for being a commonplace that what distinguishes Russian social relationships is naturalness, artlessness, and "sincerity": an atmosphere in which *falsh* (phoneyness or insincerity) is rare because friends, and even recent acquaintances, feel supremely at ease with one another. On this evening, too, no one felt a need to appear successful, clever, or profound; the principal compulsion was to be and enjoy oneself according to one's mood. We smoked to Bach preludes, danced to tapes of Western pop songs, drank the remains of the vodka, wine, and cognac. While some couples told funny stories or flirted, others seriously debated English youth's fascination for the mysticism of the East.

Inevitably the conversation turned to the invasion of Czechoslovakia several months earlier. Although the seven Russians present had felt little but dissatisfaction toward the Soviet government and, increasingly, the Soviet system in general in previous years, the events in Czechoslovakia (together with the swing toward greater domestic orthodoxy and repression, discernible some eighteen months earlier) promoted their resentment to bitterness and contempt. Ignoring the instinct for caution that normally makes light of such matters in larger than *à deux* gatherings even of close friends, they expressed sullen condemnation of the country's political condition and leaders. Russia was termed "barbaric," "desperately backward and dark," and "a [politically] medieval country ruled by medieval tyrants." Because of its implications for my friends and all their liberal cosmopolitan kind as well as its more direct suffocation of the "Prague spring" they so admired, the invasion itself was held in abhorrence. The spectacle of the Soviet tanks, in fact, was so symbolically and crushingly evil, yet it so vividly personified the mentality of the Politburo–First Oblast Secretary muzhiks who ruled the USSR, that little was said about it. The silence in which we drained our glasses rang louder than many anguished words.

During the next three years (the last time was in July 1971) I met the participants of that evening several times individually. As the hard line in Soviet domestic affairs was made harder and intellectuals' despair over their own condition and the future of Russia grew correspondingly deeper and more morbid, their bitterness turned toward anger. In degrees varying according to personality (the young Voronezh writer dreamed of machinegunning the Politburo in a sensitive anatomical area), each of the seven now despised the Soviet system with a conviction that took them close to contempt for Lenin and the revolution, to new dimensions of alienation and disaffection. Their aversion to the Communist Party had spread to Marxism-Leninism, and now several were no longer certain they still believed in socialism itself, long the ultimate social good despite its perversions by bullying rulers.

Yet none of them took any part whatever in what is known as the "Democratic Movement" or even seriously considered participation. As carefully as they followed the real course (as opposed to the *Pravda* picture) of domestic and international events, and as strongly as theirs differed from the official Soviet interpretation—as clearly, in short, as they saw the vast establishment of Soviet rule as a front for a thick-witted and, when provoked, cruel dictatorship by village louts—they were neither "dissidents," "protestors," "signers" (*podpisanki*), nor even "nonconformists" in any institutional sense. Instead their response was to seek the individualist and ineffectual comfort expressed in the increasingly popular saying "we silently hate" (*my tikho nenavidyem*).

Why such people take no part whatever in a movement extolled in the West as a shining fight for good against evil in the most heroic circumstances is the phenomenon I propose to explore here. My interest, if this is not obvious, is not in these seven friends alone nor in the score or so of Muscovites I know best, all highly intelligent, cynical, witty, and (by Soviet standards) well informed. I am concerned about the social stratum they represent, the counterpart to my own in London and New York. Their state of mind, I believe, warrants contemplation not only for what it might reveal about this highly select segment of the Soviet population itself but also about the condition of the country as a whole. Irrespective of the accuracy of my observations—which, by the nature of things, must be an intensely subjective interpretation of sadly limited evidence—I believe that Soviet dissent cannot be seen in anything approaching true perspective without somehow accounting for the 99.9 percent who have so far abstained.

It must be said at the start, however, that I shall not attempt any explanation of why the Soviet *majority* has stood aloof. It seems to be that, together with a conviction that they have never had it so good, deep criticism-of-the-government-is-the-work-of-effete-intellectuals patriotism keeps the Soviet, especially the Russian, working class far from any consideration of dissent. The peasantry might well feel itself less well rewarded by the system, but it appears so atomized and so in the grip of its collective farm boards and radios—so sunk in provincial oblivion and political backwardness—that the very concept of resistance, not to speak of somehow organizing it, is farfetched. When it can be afforded, vodka is more likely than earthly plans to provide comfort. Despite what the peasant might stand to gain from democratization, his Mother Russia patriotism—which inclines him to regard the Democratic Movement much as Radio Moscow would describe it; treachery by ungrateful eggheads under the influence of outside agitators—might be even more intolerant than that of the factory worker. But these broadest of generalizations should not be taken as anything more than that. My personal knowledge of Russian workers and peasants, not to speak of the "broad masses" of the nationalities, is scant; one hand is enough to count the heart-to-heart talks I have had with Soviet citizens wholly outside the intelligentsia.

On the other hand, my friendships with Muscovites of the kind already described, people who (apart from adjusting themselves to the relative social stiffness) would find themselves instantly at home at the dinner parties of

Western editors, artists, and television producers, are as long-standing and trusting as those of any Westerner I know. And it is among these Russians, who sometimes refer to themselves as the "one percent" in terms of sophistication and cosmopolitan outlook if not measurable intellectual achievement, that the relative *lack* of protest seems telling. If they, free as they are of the hold of ignorance, obscurantism, and Soviet interpretations (which, without again laboring the point, the majority seems to me not to be), feel unable or unwilling to take any positive steps toward their own salvation, what will be the effect upon the Democratic Movement?

But before taking up this sketch, at last, of the attitudes of Moscow's "silent haters," another personal explanation must be offered. That I have seen little inclination to express dissent among the people who might be expected to have the greatest enthusiasm for it means neither that I am pleased by this situation nor that I am "on the side of" the authorities who are determined both to repress and to belittle the dissent that does exist. That a statement so obvious need be made is connected, although indirectly, with some of the factors that appear to discourage some Muscovites, at least, from taking a stand—or that perhaps serve as a pretext for their not doing so. Several years ago I reported that the great majority of Russians regarded the Sinyavskys, Daniels, Ginzburgs, and Galanskovs less as freedom-fighting heroes than as sniveling intellectual traitors. By at least implying that these brave men were sacrificing themselves for popular causes, I wrote, Western correspondents were seriously misleading their readers. I was thereupon accused by more than one Soviet specialist of serving the interests of the KGB by understating the resistance to Soviet rule. Such nonsense might easily be ignored except that, as I have suggested, it appears to bear on the plight of the one percent. The same intrigue, accusation, rivalry, denunciation, and suspicion that drift into some parts of the world of Western Soviet specialists pollute much more heavily the atmosphere of intellectual Moscow. This point will be raised in its natural sequence below. For the moment it is enough to say that my subject here, the abstention from overt dissent, gives me neither personal nor professional pleasure. Even from the narrowest point of view of capturing readers' interest, how much happier I would be to write about the dramatic protest of heroes instead of the nebulous dullness of nonprotest practiced by ordinary people like myself. Nor is it much comfort in this respect to remember that at any given moment history consists far less of what is changing than of what remains the same. Nevertheless, someone should speak for the tiny intellectual minority's silent majority in whose crow-eating ranks, *mutatis mutandis*, most of the writers as well as the readers of these essays would find themselves.

Surely there is no need to elaborate here on by far the most important cause of inertness. My Moscow friends who knew everything and did nothing except withdraw, wisecrack, and wordlessly despise were afraid of reprisals. And, of course, they had every reason to be. I can add nothing to the general knowledge of the KGB's power to hunt down and punish active dissenters except that this was wholly taken for granted by the people I knew. Unwilling to be martyrs, they saw no third alternative. To put it crudely, their beliefs were not nearly strong enough to allow them to bear the suffering of labor camps. They themselves had something to say about the "Russian disease" of fatalism; but their judgment of the chances of avoiding retribution for public dissent seemed rationality itself.

Yet their attitude toward dissent offers more material for rumination about the Soviet Union than this realistic fear of palpable danger. At the time of the invasion open protest had existed for almost two years in Moscow. Western observers were discussing it enthusiastically and at great length; some wrote about little else. It was called a movement, a wave, even a crusade. From their crowded Moscow flats my friends saw it in a distinctly different perspective. They felt that even I, whose primary interest in Russia lay elsewhere, made too much of the fanciful activities of the idealistic few. Why all my questions about the protestors and their ideas? What had they, those young Don Quixotes, to do with the country's real life and reasonable perspectives?

In one respect, at least, this skepticism was prescient. While foreign attention to the manifestations of protest swelled, together with speculation about the movement's potential influence on society and government, my pessimistic friends predicted, even in 1968 and 1969, that the dissidents would be quickly silenced by imprisonment or exile. Although the roundup was less swift than they had foreseen, it indeed advanced very far in the next few years with the notable exception of Sakharov and one or two other special cases with illustrious names.

Are my friends' long-term predictions as accurate? For the principal source of their pessimism lay not in the government's ability to crush dissent but in the nation's ability to sustain it. They felt that democratic movements are futile at this stage in Russia's history because the people are not ready for them. If merely the dictatorship had Russia in the grip of bigotry and reaction, this would offer some grounds for hope and an incentive to political action. But far worse than this, the country as a whole was backward and "dark."

This viewpoint rests on a depressing appraisal of the Russian people's political maturity. The comments of that autumn evening in 1968 are enough to illustrate this—although many I heard (but did not record) in later years were even more gloomy.

The host: "This country is so desperately backward politically, so reactionary and dark, there isn't a real chance of change. We go from brutality to brutality—because brutality *breeds* brutality. We haven't yet reached a take-off point for democratic government."

My friend from Voronezh: "Politically this is a medieval country. We are living in the Middle Ages, ruled by tyrants with modern methods but medieval minds. The Politburo hunts witches and burns heretics at the stake—because the Russian people are still ready to believe in witches and heretics."

The doctor: "Look, it's one thing that dissidents are treated as mad by the government. Maybe some Politburo types genuinely believe they're mad —which, of course, is worse. But the worst of it, the truly terrible thing, is that *the people*, too, are convinced that the dissidents are crazy or out to cheat them. The poor, oppressed people for whom the dissidents think they're sacrificing themselves. . . . *You* tell me what has changed. Chaadeyev declared insane by Nicholas I, and the *narod* believed that the *narodniks* were whacky. Russia's burden has always been in the horrifying pitiful people, who are so repressed that they tremble at any progress not measured in potatoes they can touch. Compared to the West, this backwardness is probably growing relatively worse."

Running through these comments—which, to repeat, were milder versions of what I heard during the following three years—was a deep despair about the possibility of significant change and a corresponding doubt of the wisdom (in the circumstances, better to say conviction of the romantic folly) of committing oneself to senseless protest. Making a symbol—or spectacle—of oneself, my friends believed, would alter nothing except in their own lives. No benefit to the country would accompany their destruction; no constructive impression or piquing of conscience would be produced on the People any more than on their Leaders. It was their reading of the general level of political consciousness that had brought these members of the Moscow intelligentsia to this state. They felt that the popular Russian political mind was no less medieval than the Politburo's—was, in fact, as much the cause of the dictatorship as its effect. Again, their attitude is most forcefully expressed in almost random quotes:

"Russians can be the kindest and most generous people in the world, and in personal relationships the most democratic and egalitarian. But they can't live without a tsar."

"Most people, meaning *the* people, simply can't conceive of political democracy. They understand quantitative changes perfectly well: more or less suffering, a tighter or looser squeeze, a harsher or more benevolent leader. But only within the system, with someone up above giving or taking back. The idea that they might decide for themselves is simply beyond their comprehension."

"What's missing in the political consciousness of the Russian people is everything democratizing and liberalizing in the last seven hundred years of Western history, from the Magna Charta, the French Revolution, and down to the hippie movement. In certain ways this makes Russia a better place to live. Life is more easygoing and in some ways more honest here. But politically it's been disastrous. While Europe became adult with its renaissances and reformations, we stayed slaves—like retarded children—under the Tatar yoke. The result is hopeless political backwardness; we simply never grew up."

"Communism will no doubt fall some day—although that day is not now in sight. Communism is an anachronism, socially, economically, politically—in almost every way. It's terribly out of date, ultraconservative, rigid, backward, *afraid*. One day people's hopes will soar, communism will fall, and we'll all rejoice. Wrongly. Because what will replace it? Something more or less the same, more or less in keeping with the environment and attitudes here. In other words, more darkness."

"The most meaningful single sentence about Russia is still the opening to Trotsky's *Russian Revolution*: 'The fundamental and most stable feature of Russian history is the slow tempo of her development, with the economic backwardness, primitiveness of social forms and low level of culture resulting from it.' Of course Russia has changed since then—but in keeping with what Trotsky wrote: in keeping with Russia's essential inertia. The revolution shifted the locus of power and ownership of property, but it didn't change the underlying characteristics of Russia and Russians."

In later years the comments became even more melancholy in proportion to the retreat to orthodoxy from Khrushchev's tentative liberalization and the yet deeper plunge of the intellectuals' mood. "Russians yearn to be slaves," an internationally known cultural celebrity told me in 1969. "They understand nothing else; the subjugation satisfies not only a preference for the familiar but also a deep emotional or spiritual longing. A longing to be submissive—even submissive to harsh authority. Because that way they gain redemption for their sins, and the notion of sin is at the core of the Russian character. Russians are a deeply religious, mystical, superstitious people, even though the church has been destroyed as such."

"Are you mad?" charged a less celebrated friend in 1970. "Are you suggesting that I should be? That I should sacrifice myself for 'the people' who don't give one damn about my 'funny' ideas about freedom and dignity? Please read some history before speculating about this country's future. Tolstoy's serfs stubbornly refused to be 'tricked' when he offered them their freedom. Others turned *narodniks* over to the police. Yes, I love my people, for all their trusting, pitiable gullibility and endurance to mistreatment. But I'm not yet demented enough to risk my head trying to 'help' them. Do you understand that they feel *I'm* the enemy—not the brutes who enslave them?"

By 1971 the dismay over popular political lethargy was tinged with bitterness, and my friends' tendency to withdraw into inner, private worlds was justified not only as a necessity but as a positive virtue. "By sacrificing ourselves for a people who do not even understand our goals, let alone want them for themselves," a friend explained, "we would only be helping the leadership in *its* goal of quashing people who think creatively and independently. Now is not the time. I don't know when it will come, but when it does, Russia will need a genuine, *living* intelligentsia. To participate now in quixotic protests and visionary movements would be not only hopeless but stupid. To speak of a duty to our serfs without proposing realistic ways to end their serfdom of the mind is too shallow to interest me in discussion."

All this, I emphasize again, was told me by people *not* involved in the Democratic Movement and therefore perhaps less well informed about political currents than the highly politicized protestors. But in late 1972 no less a personage in the movement—and one fearlessly clear-thinking about the country—than Andrei Sakharov validated my friends' pessimism if not their despair over the people's backwardness as its cause. "Our struggle is really useless and senseless," said Dr. Sakharov. "In ten years, nothing will change. This country could perish, but it still would be the same. We know we cannot change anything really, despite all the things I write. . . . No, I am not a pessimist, I am a born optimist. I am just making an objective analysis of the situation."

So much for my Moscow friends' attitude toward the Russian masses. It can be summarized by the old aphorism that no people unwilling to fight for its own freedom can attain it—or is worthy of it. The Russian people, by contrast, is not only happy with the heavy hand of dictatorship but actually requires it.

My confidants' despair in this regard was so cosmic that it seemed to color their attitude towards the purpose of life itself. What use is a struggle to free a people that receives freedom fighters as traitors? Why sacrifice oneself for it and its pitifully propagandized perception of the world—for a people fond of its own chains?

Whether this despair is justified is a separate question. My rare confidential talks with Russian "plain folks" sometimes persuaded me that disaffection, if not dissent, was much more widespread than my Moscow friends imagined. But some conversations with workers convinced me that, if anything, my friends underestimated the stubborn political obtuseness of the *narod*, so grateful for its own servile condition as long as the party prevented hunger and war.

In any case, my judgment about this is largely irrelevant—as, in a way, was that of my Moscow friends. It might be said that their pessimism reveals more about their own state of mind than the state of Russia. Perhaps, like the fiercely self-critical American student-cultural-intellectual circles of the mid-1960s, they violently overreacted, as such people often do, to the turn of events. Both countries, it may be, took a small backward step while the mood of the haute intelligentsia wildly plunged. Intellectuals everywhere, Russians among them, may be inclined to exaggerate the shortcomings of their own country and social system and to ignore its virtues and accomplishments. Perhaps because it is a more serious matter there, it is not as clever or smart to bemoan the Establishment in Russia as it is in most Western countries; but the same tendency to disparage one's own exists as in left-wing circles everywhere in the world.

But, as I've suggested, all this is in one sense beside the mark. For no less than other people, the Muscovites I knew lived not according to the facts but according to their perception of them. And they perceived their own people as enormously backward and encased in a tough hide of semireligious mysticism that only long exposure to the fresh air of world knowledge and sophistication might corrode. Whether or not the situation bordered on the hopeless, they saw it as such.

Partly because of this, no doubt, they did not behold the open dissenters in quite the same heroic light as radiates from many Western reports of their activities and persecution. Their splendid courage was of course conceded, together with the rightness of their cause. Certain individuals were esteemed for their humility and unposturing good will. But as a group, the freedom fighters extolled in Western news media inspired little enthusiasm *as potential leaders*. It is one thing to admire self-sacrifice, quite another to commend it, not to speak of wishing to join.

What was it in the prominent dissenters that prompted my friends' qualms? To some degree they were vexed by the protestors' seemingly talmudic argumentation and, occasionally, personal-cum-ideological squabbles over the movement's direction and Russia's deserved political future. Although conceded as inevitable in Soviet conditions—although, moreover, some of the liberal-social-democratic analyses and platforms closely approached their own vague hopes for Russia—the very phenomenon of internal wrangling, sometimes embellished by remote-sounding theories about the nature of man and of the political process, depressed them. Some saw in this a confirmation of the dissidents' romantic-illusory temperaments. It was as likely to provoke associations with the factionalism of tsarist émigrés and the disaster to which this helped lead as to the healthy conflict of ideas and the parliamentary democracy they thought they wanted.

There were also personal factors. While some dissenters, it bears repeating, were profoundly admired for their astonishing bravery and "purity" of motive, others were considered self-righteous, self-interested, and even arrogant. The kind of puerile idealism and holier-than-thou stance that a part of the American liberal intelligentsia ascribed to some early protestors against the Vietnamese war was also attributed to certain Soviet dissenters. Their protests (said members of the nonparticipating Moscow intelligentsia) revealed as much about their own emotional angst—their need to expiate a sense of personal guilt—as anything about the "objective" political situation. Their personalities sometimes made even their noble ideals insufferable.

Moreover, the dissenters acted from a mixture of motives—nothing in any way surprising or reprehensible, of course, but a phenomenon that helped explain the reservation that some provoked. The loudest call that several seemed to be answering was to prove themselves to their small circle of like-minded friends. "I can't escape the feeling," said a Moscow artist, "that several of the most tragic cases are driven by a special need for self-sacrifice. Whatever else they are doing—and for all my skepticism, I won't deny that it *may* eventually turn out to be vastly helpful—they are also seeking their own redemption. No harm in that, of course. But my own need for self-expression takes different forms."

"These good people have a need to *do* something about our condition," said the artist's friend. "To express their own moral outrage, to purify their own souls. Fine. But this is hardly a plan of action. Why don't they join the party and burrow from the inside? Perhaps because, although possibly more effective, that would be less personally satisfying than unfurling a banner for two seconds on Pushkin Square."

Some felt that several prominent dissenters had an unmistakable suicidal streak. This was the most serious charge.

These thoughts were most forcefully put to me in 1971 by an erudite young man with as clear a picture of the dictatorship's power in all its brutal and subtle forms as anyone I'd met in Russia or abroad. Yet like my closer friends, he stood on the sidelines.

"Distance lends a certain perspective to the dissident phenomenon—but largely the perspective of oversimplification. From the foreign colony and from Western capitals, certain correspondents write about our 'protestors,' with the implication that these are shining men and selfless heroes. (I don't know any Western Soviet specialists personally, but with some, their search, their crusading mentality, suggests something about their own personalities. Might they be compared to those Russian intellectuals who bury themselves in some preoccupation five thousand safe kilometers from our own borders?)

"If only because such Western writers do not treat, presumably because they don't know about, such things as ego, self-righteousness, rivalries, personal motives, arrogance—the aspects that historians will examine when it is time for a more analytical view—the impression of dissenters is inevitably misleading. I myself know few, but among these is one man who is supercilious and vainglorious—who even lies. Yet in Western press reports about him, he is pictured only as a martyr (which he profoundly wants to be).

"It's a curious situation. For all the reasons you know well, we ordinary Russians lacking martyr complexes don't write about dissent and dissenters. Certain Western specialists *do* write, and perhaps for personal reasons about which you perhaps know too little. I'm not saying the situation is parallel, but so much of what went terribly wrong in the Western judgment of Soviet reality in the 1920s, 1930s, and 1940s was simply because they couldn't see social phenomena with their own eyes. Didn't know people *as people*. They talked in terms of categories, social movements, and, above all, theories —and left out the human stuff, the factors which guide most people's daily lives. Then it was "social reconstruction"; now it is "dissent." I repeat: the mistakes are equal neither in force nor in substance, but if your Soviet specialists were to spend time with some of our protestors, drink with them, listen to their plans and problems, observe their characters and the 'revolutionary-romantic-self-purifying' elements in them, they might understand why some inspire principally themselves. . . .

"I think great political naïveté is your most serious mistake. In the old days, many experts analyzed socialism and Bolshevism, not knowing who the socialists and Bolsheviks were: what kind of *people*, as opposed to what slogans they shouted. Now you do the same, but the other way round. Why do you forget that the dissenters too are mortals, some moved by envy, rivalry and vainglory? *Why do you assume that their oppression and persecution by a primitive state makes them ipso facto splendid people?* Lenin too was oppressed, you know. American blacks are oppressed, and not all professors are eager to join *them* in their struggle."

Ought this to be taken as more than a clever man's apologia for his own moral "copout"? I have no evidence to support or refute his judgment of Russian dissenters, but my experience of Western writing about dissent—the prism through which many of us perceive the phenomenon—suggests that at least some of the young historian's reflections deserve consideration. It seems to me—and now I am digressing for a moment into pure opinion —that those Soviet experts who write almost exclusively about dissidents sometimes put their subjects in an unreal perspective.

What is it that makes certain experts passionate about injustice in a distant land, yet seemingly indifferent to other forms in their own countries? Have they any (concealed) associations to émigré organizations? Have they a vested professional or psychological interest in Soviet dissent? Does it represent something in their emotional constitutions? These are not, if the pun can be tolerated, academic questions. The atmosphere of struggle and mission has been transmitted from dissent itself to some Western circles involved with its description and interpretation. This is understandable, even laudable—except when it distorts our vision. But I know Westerners who, although dubious of several protestors' personalities, refrain from expressing their judgment in writing. They have been intimidated: they fear accusation of hampering the cause. Thus is uncomfortable information suppressed. Where have we heard before that the full truth is a luxury we can't afford during this time of struggle? Do they visit Russia and spend time with average people partaking in ordinary pleasures and struggling with prosaic daily problems? If not, because of either their own wishes or exclusion by the Soviet authorities, do they take account of the distinct difference in tone between commentators writing from on the spot and those writing from their Western offices? (About Eastern Europe, too, a large majority of reporters who write from "outside" their beat produce articles with a considerably more political and critical slant not necessarily out of personal motivation but because most sources available in the West are more hostile than those in the country itself.) Even some Moscow correspondents feel constrained from reporting the unthinkable: that several celebrated protestors have considerable personal quirks and seem less than totally admirable. And whispers in Western academic halls accuse certain authors of being "proregime" or "antidissident"—or, ugliest (and most Soviet!) of all: "serving the interests" of communism or the KGB.

One sad example may make this point clear. For many years Moscow correspondents were well aware that Peter Yakir (like other prominent dissidents) often exhibited unfortunate qualities in addition to his many splendid ones. His drinking, loud talk, and apparent urge to flirt with danger—not to mention his occasional gross rudeness—made some evenings with him in Moscow flats exasperating and grotesque, while others could be exalted and exhilarating. But presumably for fear of attack by the establishment of specialists in Soviet affairs, or perhaps out of the higher goal of reluctance to damage "the cause," reporters refrained from mentioning these complexities, and Yakir continued to be presented in the single dimension of a persecuted, courageous freedom fighter.

In the spring of 1973, however, a free-spirited Canadian correspondent recounted several incidents of intolerable behavior by Yakir. In this case, drinking and rudeness were minor peccadilloes compared to Yakir's unsolicited accusation—which, in Soviet conditions, can lead to an extremely unpleasant road—that one of the correspondent's friends was a KGB agent. To the Canadian's article a respected Anglo-American Soviet expert and leading supporter of dissenters replied, in effect, that it was a lie. This authority had not set foot in Moscow since well before protest emerged as a phenomenon. He had never laid eyes on Yakir, let alone spent an evening with him. Yet his response was to deny the evidence of the correspondent's eyes, and to do it by personal abuse and character assassination, those most Soviet methods. Nor did any other Soviet expert protest at this outrageous but representative treatment. It grew naturally in the atmosphere of scholarship with political ends, just as accusation of treachery is so much a part of émigré politics.

Later, however, ways had to be found to explain Yakir's fall as a hero. (Many simply avoided analysis of this.) This embarrassing turn of events could have been escaped by not slipping into partisanship in the first place, that is, by not assuming, as many have tended to do, that a dissenter is ipso facto a person of unimpeachable virtue. One way to avoid damaging disillusionment is not to feed on illusions in the first place. At the same time, it is too much to expect dissenters, after all they endure, to be saints. Moreover, such an attitude encourages the false notion that Western support for these brave, wronged people (which now more than ever seems to me pathetically timid) is dependent on their goodness rather than on what should be their inherent rights. Illusions are harmful in so many ways!

Needless to say, the principal issue is not Yakir but the question of involvement versus full and honest reporting. But paradoxically, the danger of overinvolvement is not only the obvious one to Western standards of journalism and scholarship but also to the democratic cause itself. What is needed least of all is romanticization or idealization of the movement. This encourages, as it often has in the past, mistakes in interpretation (outsiders will expect such splendid people to attract more followers) and, when it is finally revealed that idiosyncrasy of personality played some part in their drive, an overreacting disillusionment. I believe we are old enough to understand that warts make brave men no less so.

No one knows better than I the conflict inherent in writing about such matters. The Soviet government does savagely punish courageous men and women seeking elementary civil rights. The victims do deserve our support as well as our sympathy. We all root for the dissenters; it's impossible not to, any more than it is possible to refuse to smuggle out a letter from a Muscovite in trouble to his friends who have emigrated to Paris or London. But some root much more than others and are involved very much more. It is difficult to see how the roles of advocate and scholar can be kept from conflict unless one assumes that nothing at all negative need be said about a man if he is a dissenter.

Of course this is nonsense. Perhaps the answer to those who want to be both scholars and fighters is that they should not attempt to be both simultaneously. To help the cause, take a trip to Russia, if that is feasible, and see what service one can offer there, or find a place for some supporting role in the West. Certainly this is admirable. But when writing, do not compromise with the complex truth, even the truth of dissenters as they are, not as one might want them to be. For albeit in service to the highest of causes, any portrayal of them that omits all mention of (entirely natural) personal foibles and petty jealousies is inevitably misleading. As helpful as it is as encouragement to the lonely campaigners themselves and as an alarm to a slumbering world, it has serious shortcomings as a record for contemporary analysts and future historians. It distorts as war propaganda does, and in both cases the greatest consequences are apparent only later.

A dictatorship does impose special obligations on reporters and commentators. Dissenters *are* in deep distress; there *is* a moral duty to help them. In a real way their fight is for all of us. But the tendency of some to judge writing in this field in terms of its immediate effect on the political situation—what will or will not "serve the interests of" the regime or KGB—is unfortunate on all counts. It not only insults our own intelligence (upon reflection, does anyone really believe the one-dimensional portraits?) and harms the West by distorting its perception but provides no long-term benefits to the dissidents themselves. Reducing complex and subtle matters to the level of shallow journalism encourages them to entertain false notions about themselves and their place in the world and to make wrong assessments in their own plans for action.

With the destruction of so much of the movement, clear thinking for right assessments is more important than ever. Was it right, for example, to unfurl a banner on Red Square protesting the invasion of Czechoslovakia? Or was this an act of personal gratification, which for the sake of several seconds of freedom provoked fear, hatred, and repressive measures that have actually pushed Russia away from the movement's own democratic goals? Would it not have been better, if far less personally satisfying, to acknowledge Russia's despotic conditions—and the popular mood, which is anything but encouraging to "radicals"—and settle for millimeters of progress instead of risking everything on stirring but, to the large majority, quixotic gestures? Would it not be worthwhile to work in a library, for example, even to joining its party committee, and to advance cautious arguments for allowing this or that book to be placed on the shelves? Much can be said for this plodding approach, especially in hindsight. The young protestors, of course, could not have been certain that the people would show so little interest in, let alone support of, their ideals. And the publicity their brave actions attracted did throw a clear diagnostic light on Soviet society for the outside world. These questions are for the dissidents themselves to decide, of course. My point is that they can best be helped not by mere publicity for their courageous acts but, in addition, by thoughtful, intelligent analysis that might better help them attain the most realistic perception possible of themselves in relation to their country and the outside world.

If all this strikes the reader as an irrelevant digression, I suggest he ignore it and consider but one comprehensive factor. Can he remember an account of the dissenters' activities (aside from David Bonavia's *Fat Sasha and the Urban Guerilla*) that treats them as anything but oppressed victims and heroes? Compare this with Tolstoy's description (in *Resurrection*) of the Russian revolutionaries of his age, with their strong sociological and psychological parallels to contemporary dissidents. "Learning more about them, Nekhludov became convinced that they were not villains one and all, as some imagined them, and not heroes to a man, as others considered them, but ordinary people among whom were, as always, good, bad and average individuals. Among them were people who had become revolutionaries because they sincerely considered themselves obligated to fight existing evil; but there were others who had chosen this activity because of egotistical, vainglorious motives." And remember that for all the abuse and scorn poured on George Orwell at the time, his account of the Spanish Civil War is most valuable today precisely because it did not fall into the expected pattern of black and white, heroes and villains. Orwell kept complex matters complex despite the passion of the moment and although he was a fighter.

The foregoing was intended to suggest why some dissenters appear less magnificent to my Russian friends than to Western analysts who are farther removed from the drama's protagonists and who have vastly less to lose. A simpler way to say it is that fighters for freedom often appear more shining to readers of accounts of their struggles than to the sharers of their kitchens and bathrooms (and not only in Russia, as participants in the American civil rights movement of the mid-1960s will testify). But neither this reality nor despair for the Russian masses contributes as much to the Moscow intelligentsia's political impotence as their unwillingness to abandon what they have for the sake of a cause that is unattainable (as they see it) in their lifetime. In one sense this is simply a restatement of the first and most important reason for their abstention: fear of reprisals. But there is fear and fear, there are reprisals and reprisals. A closer look at precisely what my Moscow friends and their counterparts do not want to risk might reveal more about the setting and the prospects of organized dissent as well as about their own life styles.

When I first wrote extensively about Russia during the appearance of the new phenomenon of protest I was reproached for exaggerated pessimism, specifically for downplaying the movement. Some critics felt I had underestimated the significance of the protestors and signers, who, it was said or implied, were the opening wedge of an extraordinary new development. These brave souls, the argument went, had demonstrated that the political consciousness and the courage of Russian sufferers had been awakened. Soon they would be joined by large numbers of intellectuals and the creative intelligentsia, perhaps even the keener sectors of other social strata. To this I could only reply weakly that no one *I* knew was pulling on his boots in preparation for the good march. On the contrary, they were closing their doors to shut out the nastiness they wanted to forget and were turning up their radios to drown out the occasional gnashing of their own teeth.

Since then reliable evidence has appeared that in this respect my friends were representative of a large part of the intelligentsia. In 1972, Dr. Sakharov observed sadly that the best-placed Russians in creative work and elsewhere were obstinately clinging to their privileges rather than involving themselves in a struggle against violations of human rights. In a later interview his wife put it more bluntly: 'Everybody here worries about his job." In mid-1973 Sakharov directly confirmed my friends' opinion. "You can hardly call it a movement," he said of protest.

It was not corporal punishment my friends feared but the loss of precious privileges, rewards, and comforts. That these may seem small by Western standards does not diminish their appeal to the holders; in all countries the narrowest distinctions of status, recompense, and living standards are often the most treasured. Besides, in the Soviet context, money to shop in peasant markets and access to the Cinema Club with its private showings of foreign films are not small things at all. They are the difference between a limitlessly dreary material and intellectual poverty, which "bleak," "drab," and "depressed" are too weak to describe, and at least a measure of pleasant living.

It is into the sanctuary of their cooperative flats—a secluded world of their own work and careers, their personal friends and families, their private interests and intellectual pursuits—to which my friends have retreated. The phenomenon of withdrawal is too well known to require description here. Elsewhere I have tried to convey the flavor of behind-the-closed-door Moscow life at this level, drawing attention to the compensations—easy sex, easy conversation, relaxed attitudes towards oneself and one's friends—as well as the disgust, feelings of impotence, and buried rage. But several points that seem to bear on these people's inclination to try to forget rather than to fight deserve mention.

For one thing, they are among the most alienated social groups in the world. Whether applied to a pair of socks or a new ballet, the adjective "Soviet" has become a sneering pejorative. Everything "Sov" (to use the hip short form) repels them. But in a perverse way, the loathing for politics and for the Soviet compulsion to politicize everything in society that accompanies this alienation extends to "good" politics as well. Despite its ideals, the Democratic Movement is political, therefore dirty and to be avoided.

There is a corresponding tendency toward hedonism. Since no significant democratization will come in their lifetime, attention is focused on what *can* be attained: a tolerable wine and palatable roast for tonight's dinner, or a new Zhiguli automobile (determinedly called "Fiat") for countryside picnics. The greater the despair, the more significance is attached to the pleasures of eating, drinking, and acquiring hard goods; and the greater the significance given these matters, the sillier it seems to risk them for illusory political causes. This cycle may have healthy roots in the legendary Russian attention to the simple delights of food and drink, but its current manifestation seems to contain an element of losing-oneself-in-pleasure self-deception. Having a good time has been elevated to almost a philosophical good. "What the hell are you talking about with your 'movements' and 'platforms'? Real people live for tonight."

But at tonight's fling, or tomorrow's, another factor will operate further to discourage any thought of joining the dissenters. Year by year in the late 1960s and early 1970s the fear of informers grew, even among jolly mates. En route to a typical evening of food, drink, ragged dancing, intellectual banter, and riotous political jokes with one trusted Russian friend, I would be warned about someone expected later. "He's a fine chap, good for stories and laughs, very knowledgeable about poster art and Etruscan pottery. But for your own good, watch yourself with him. Tell him nothing serious about yourself. I have no real evidence; it's just that he gets around too much, behaves himself too 'loosely' not to have permission for it—for which he probably informs in return." Later the subject of these melancholy thoughts would take me aside to repeat them almost word for word about the man with whom I came. It is this atmosphere of suspicion and guarded denunciation which, alas, has drifted into some Western circles of Soviet specialists.

At these Moscow evenings, an occasional (and guarded) outburst from a heavily drinking participant put the blame for the refusal to become involved on himself—on the curse of passivity and fatalism that plagues the Russian intelligentsia. "Everyone's having a grand time, yes—but don't let that fool you. Inside we're all sick, full of hate and disgust. We hate those bastards at the top . . . and hate ourselves too. A handful of martyrs are brave enough to protest openly—and we don't even lift a finger for them, we have parties like this to try to *forget* them. . . . We stand by while they're sent to their camps. That's what's inside us, behind the merry façade; pain and disgust, guilt and hate. . . . I drink to the real heroes of this country, the people in the camps—but that's all I do about it: drink."

"It would seem we have nothing to lose but our chains," said my friend the writer from Voronezh sadly. "But despite Marx, this was never true of the workers—or of us. Workers are afraid to lose their jobs and food, no matter how grueling and miserable. And we, the intelligentsia, are afraid to lose the little half-comfortable niches we've carved out for ourselves. It's pitiful, you know: instead of fighting the good fight (which only *we* can win from inside Russia; no foreign influences can ever win our war), we content ourselves with the few bones thrown our way and grumbling about our masters."

"There is a deep longing to *do* something at last," said my instructor friend at the institute. "Of course, doing something means going to a [labor] camp. But still, everyone's haunted by the feeling he should be doing more. We know that's wrong, and we'll sit around complaining about it in our comfortable little flats. The only way Russia will change is if people like us work and sacrifice for change. *But the Russian intelligentsia is not made for action.* We're lazy, perhaps cowardly. And selfish! It all adds up to self-disgust. We probably deserve our own condition."

But these rare "Russian" confessions put the everyday political attitude of my friends in a too-dramatic light. Their ordinary mood is better understood in terms not of the Russian national character but of a universal tendency to seek refuge in private affairs when no course of action seems feasble to help right public wrongs. On a recent visit to New York I noticed a similar condition among member of the publishing, professorial, and public relations intelligentsia. This was a profound depression about the future of the city accompanied by a furious pursuit of the private interests of career, family, and recreation and a shutting out of futile thoughts about the causes of the grave social malaise. Years of steadily worsening conditions had reduced the city to a stage of siege. People were afraid to allow their children out of doors even in daylight. Yet the inclination was not to sally forth into the public arena with reforming zeal but the contrary, to barricade one's family in patrolled cooperative apartments and to find personal escapes from crime, drugs, racial tensions, jungle schools, and other symptoms of the affliction. The danger of violence and the security precautions against it in homes, shops, and offices seemed so unavoidable that they were taken for granted. Although the city was felt to be in the process of destruction by oppressive forces, there was less and less talk about the situation—not only about cures, of which there seemed to be none, but about the problems themselves. The primary solution was to earn the $30,000 salaries needed for guarded flats, good restaurants, intellectual hobbies, private schools, and country houses.

It goes without saying that the differences between New York and Moscow are greater than the similarities. What struck me was the common tendency at the moment to seek escape from community problems that individuals felt powerless to resolve by retreating to a protected inner world of private comfort and interests. In Moscow the inner world extends well beyond the new car and the recently acquired flat with the separate room for the children and granny. Other possessions—collections of Western records and books; pants suits for the new, relatively smart generation of wives —provided hours of enjoyment. And the privilege of lunching at the journalists or the cinema workers union with their new bars (the counterpart to the expense account meal?) was topped by access to tickets to a closed showing of *The Godfather*. Intellectual interests played as great a role: with patience, contacts, and money, one could acquire a respectable library of prohibited books. Even political interests were important to some: a good Japanese receiver (placed next to the sleek Japanese tape recorder) could pick up a good number of foreign stations. Work too was important—not the hack efforts submitted to the painters or the writers union but canvases for oneself and one's friends and manuscripts for the desk drawer. Above all, my friends wanted to be left alone. If they continued to be so and could maintain minimal contact with all things official while devoting maximum time to their friends, hobbies, and pleasures, life would be tolerable, as good as possible in the circumstances. What was wholly intolerable was the thought of being stripped of everything that allowed them not only their prized physical comforts but a measure of civilized standards and intellectu- ally satisfying pursuits. Who knew better than they what it was like to be exiled from Moscow and live with the Russian masses on a worker's wages?

Nothing in the foregoing is intended to suggest that my friends' attitude is either prescient or virtuous. As suggested earlier, Russian intellectuals and "practitioners of the free professions" seem to me as self-centered and biased as those of any Western country. Perhaps they are more so—and more given to cynicism, "left-wing" antagonism towards authority, and a my-country-is- always-wrong presumption—than in countries where resentment of this kind is diffused through its free expression. Certainly the discernment, even the moral outlook, of this kind of Russian is affected by the dictatorship's suffocation of cultural and intellectual life. Inwardly enraged by its subjugation, the haute intelligentsia simultaneously nurses its grievance of being misunderstood and mistrusted by the masses. None of this contributes to sound judgment.

As for virtue, the comments of an underground activist (presumably writing in 1971) are enough to underline the grave weaknesses of my friends' plan of "action." A samizdat "Social-Democratic Agitational Leaflet" says: "An individualist will tell you that political opposition is hopeless. The answer would seem to be clear: given this attitude and sensing (which he often does) the disastrousness of the situation, he should join the party and serve the system with faith and truth, strengthening and improving it wherever possible. Oh no, nothing of the kind! The whole world can go to hell, but for people who join the party, he feels only contempt. He can't go one way, can't go the other: can't strengthen the system, can't reform it. What he can do is 'just live,' foaming at the mouth in anguish over the unjustness of things."

To this devastating critique I can only answer—without in any way refuting it—that during my last heart-thumping visits to Moscow (I was gathering material for a book bound to displease the Soviet authorities) the more I wondered whether *I* would make the sacrifices required of dissent, the more I felt I would withdraw precisely to my friends' theoretically indefensible middle ground. And few Western Soviet specialists I've met or read since have impressed me as the kind of people who, in Soviet conditions, would do anything more than "just live."

On the other hand, neither is anything in the foregoing intended to suggest that the Democratic Movement has had *no* salutary effect on the Muscovites I have in mind. Over the past five or six years they, like most of the Western intelligentsia, have become far more aware of the dictatorship's essential nature. "Suddenly it's become blazingly clear," a (different) young historian told me. "The country is rotten inside and out. Evil and filthy. A medieval prison run by sadists and crooks." For this considerable growth in understanding the self-sacrificing protestors who challenged and were struck down surely deserve the greatest credit.

More than this: all my friends and presumably the social stratum they represent, perhaps even some urban clerks and workers, believe at some deep level that the dissenters are right. The great gap now lies between this knowledge and a willingness to act upon it. To end the abstention, some change in the system must occur that will encourage my friends to feel that political opposition is no longer wholly hopeless and that the masses can at least begin their education. This change could be the appearance of a liberal faction in the Politburo, perhaps, or of another Khrushchev—even a man who understands the *economic* folly of sustaining the present rigidity. The last time I saw them none of my friends saw the remotest evidence of such a development (except for the possibility of a ruinous but perhaps liberating war with China). But they confessed that they knew almost nothing about the intrigues at the highest level of party and government, where good as well as bad things might be happening. And while most felt there was no "objective" reason why Soviet rule could not continue in roughly the same form for another fifty years, some thought that under the continued pressure of nationalism and relative economic failure the whole system might collapse overnight. Their pessimism caused several sober Muscovites to doubt in such a case whether anything better would rise up from the *narod* to replace the present knout-cum-obscurantism. But if liberal-democratic voices have at least a chance of a hearing amidst the roar of the chaotic masses in social breakdowns, they will be those that have been debating and practicing in the underground.

That these thoughts about dissidents derive almost wholly from eye-and-ear evidence is in one sense a severe limitation. On the other hand, a lack of just such personal observation may lead to an even greater distortion of perspective. I cannot forget one elderly Muscovite's tale of her first encounter with Bolshevism in 1918. While a French lesson was in progress in a small provincial gymnasium, a man in muddy boots entered, introduced himself as the school's new commissar, and proceeded to instruct the French tutor in new teaching methods. Most of the students understood instantly what kind of person this was who, in bullying and ungrammatical Russian, was giving instructions about teaching a language not one word of which he knew. The elderly lady felt strongly that had the Western intelligentsia known the social development and attitudes of this commissar and his colleagues, much of its abstract and rather grandiose speculation about Bolshevism—and socialism, the future of mankind, and other subjects—would have been seen to be superfluous and illusory.

What I am suggesting is that who becomes a dissenter and who shuns involvement despite his convictions seems a more complicated question than I would have imagined—but also a simpler one. The decision is made by recognizable *people* reacting to the pressures of their personalities and social forces. Amidst the quite different pressures of academic examinations of the phenomenon, perhaps such a truism bears mentioning.

CONTRIBUTORS

Frederick C. Barghoorn is professor of political science at Yale University. His publications include *The Soviet Image of the United States* (1950), *Soviet Russian Nationalism* (1956), *Modern Political Parties* (with Sigmund Neumann, 1956), *Soviet Cultural Diplomacy* (1960), *Soviet Foreign Propaganda* (1964), *Politics in the USSR*, 2nd ed., 1972, and several monographs, chapters, and articles in scholarly symposia and journals. Aided by a Guggenheim Fellowship, he is presently completing a major study on political dissent in the USSR.

Howard L. Biddulph teaches communist politics and government in the Political Science Department at the University of Victoria, Victoria, British Columbia. He has been review editor of *Canadian-American Slavic Studies* and is the author of several published articles and of a forthcoming book, *Public Opposition in the Communist Polity*. Professor Biddulph holds a Ph.D. degree in government and the Certificate of the Russian and East European Institute at Indiana University. He has also taught at Rutgers University and Indiana University.

Walter D. Connor is an assistant professor of sociology and an associate of the Center for Russian and East European Studies, University of Michigan. He is the author of *Deviance in Soviet Society: Crime, Delinquency, and Alcoholism* (1972) and also a contributor to the *American Sociological Review, Problems of Communism*, and other journals. His current interests include the management of political and nonpolitical forms of deviance in communist countries, and aspects of social stratification and mobility in Eastern Europe and the USSR.

Peter Dornan is a member of the policy staff at Radio Liberty in Munich. He holds an M.A. degree from the University of Chicago and attended the Russian Institute, Columbia University. Mr. Dornan has also worked with the Chicago Housing Authority, the Survey Research Center of the University of Michigan, and the Research Program on the USSR of the Ford Foundation.

George Feifer, a free-lance journalist and novelist living in London, is a graduate of Harvard College and of Columbia University's Russian Institute. He spent a year as an exchange student at Moscow University and frequently traveled to the USSR thereafter both for scholarly research and on journalistic assignments. Mr. Feifer's major publications are *Justice in Moscow* (1964), *Message from Moscow* (1969), *The Girl from Petrovka* (1971), *Solzhenitsyn: A Biography* (with David Burg, 1972), *Our Motherland* (1973), and the forthcoming *Moscow Days*. He contributes to many American, British, and European newspapers and magazines, especially, during the most recent years, to the *Sunday Times* of London.

Theodore Friedgut is director of the Soviet and East European Research Center at the Hebrew University of Jerusalem. Dr. Friedgut received his B.A. and M.A. degrees at the Hebrew University and his doctorate in political science from Columbia University. He was an exchange fellow at Moscow State University and has traveled widely in the USSR, particularly in Georgia. His publications include a contribution to *Columbia Essays on International Affairs* (1970), a chapter, "Community Structure, Political Participation and Soviet Local Government: The Case of Kutaisi," in H. W. Morton and R. L. Tőkés, eds., *Soviet Politics and Society in the 1970's* (1974), and articles in scholarly journals. Dr. Friedgut is presently at work on a book on Soviet local and community politics.

Gayle Durham Hollander is currently a fellow of the Radcliffe Institute and research fellow of the Russian Research Center, Harvard University. She holds a Ford Faculty Fellowship for Research on the Role of Women in Society to work on a book, *Political Equality for Russian Women: The Russian Social Democratic Labor Party and the Communist Party of the Soviet Union*. She is an associate professor of political science at Hampshire College and lecturer in government at Smith College. She received an M.A. degree in regional studies (Soviet Union) from Harvard University in 1964 and a doctorate in political science from the Massachusetts Institute of Technology in 1969. Her publications include *Soviet Political Indoctrination: Developments in Mass Media and Propaganda since Stalin* (1972), five monographs on Soviet communications (published by the Center for International Studies at the Massachusetts Institute of Technology), a chapter on Soviet communications in the *Handbook of Soviet Social Science Statistics* (edited by Ellen Mickiewicz, 1973), and several articles in scholarly journals.

Barbara Wolfe Jancar is an associate professor of political science at Union College and the executive director of International Science Exchange, a private consulting firm. She was formerly on the faculty of Skidmore College and has also taught at the George Washington Center at Newport, R.I. Dr. Jancar graduated from Smith College and did her graduate work at Columbia University (M.A., Ph.D., and certificate, Institute on East Central Europe). Her publications include *The Philosophy of Aristotle* (1963, 1966), *Czechoslovakia 1971* (1970), *Czechoslovakia and the Absolute Monopoly of Power* (1971), two major monographs on problems of mental health and regional development in upstate New York, and several articles in *Orbis,*

East Europe, and other scholarly journals. Presently she is completing a book tentatively entitled *Women under Communism: A Comparative Analysis*.

George L. Kline is professor of philosophy at Bryn Mawr College. His most recent book is *Religious and Anti-Religious Thought in Russia* (1968). Mr. Kline made six research visits to the Soviet Union between 1956 and 1968.

Peter B. Maggs is professor of law at the College of Law, University of Illinois, and an associate of the Russian and East European Center of that university. He is a graduate of Harvard College and Harvard Law School and a member of the District of Columbia bar. Professor Maggs was an exchange student at Leningrad State University (1961–62), Fulbright Scholar in Yugoslavia (1967), and an exchange scholar at the USSR Academy of Science (1972). His publications include two books, *The Soviet Legal System* (with John N. Hazard and Isaac Schapiro, 1969) and *Disarmament Verification under Soviet Law* (with Harold Berman, 1967), and articles in law reviews and other scholarly journals.

Robert M. Slusser is professor of history at Michigan State University. He is the author of *The Soviet Secret Police* (with Simon Wolin, 1957), *A Calendar of Soviet Treaties, 1917–1957* (1959) and *The Theory, Law, and Policy of Soviet Treaties* (1962) (both with Jan F. Triska), *Soviet Foreign Policy, 1928–1934: Documents and Materials* (with Xenia J. Eudin, 1966), and *The Berlin Crisis of 1961* (1973).

Gene Sosin is director of broadcast planning at Radio Liberty in New York City, where he heads a special projects division that prepares radio programs based on Soviet samizdat documents. He received B.A., M.A., and Ph.D. degrees from Columbia University, along with the certificate of the Russian Institute. His publications include "Children's Theater and Drama in Soviet Education," in E. J. Simmons, ed., *Through the Glass of Soviet Literature* (1953), and "Then Came Galich's Turn," *New York Times*, February 12, 1972. Dr. Sosin collaborated with John Gunther in revising *Inside Russia Today* (2d ed., 1962).

Rudolf L. Tőkés is professor of political science at the University of Connecticut and associate editor of *Studies in Comparative Communism*. He received his higher education at the Law School, University of Budapest, Western Reserve University (B.A.), and Columbia University (M.A., Ph.D., and certificate, Institute on East Central Europe). Formerly on the faculty of Wesleyan University (1964–70), he has held a visiting appointment at Yale University (1968, 1972, 1974) and was a senior fellow at the Research Institute on Communist Affairs, Columbia University (1969–71). His publications include *Béla Kun and the Hungarian Soviet Republic* (1967), *Soviet Politics and Society in the 1970's* (contributor and editor with H. W. Morton, 1974), chapters in collective volumes, and articles and reviews in *Problems of Communism, Slavic Review, Studies in Comparative Communism, East Europe, Etudes,* and other scholarly journals. Professor Tőkés is presently completing the second volume of his history of the Communist Party of Hungary.

INDEX

THE JOHNS HOPKINS UNIVERSITY PRESS

This book was composed in PTS Times Roman text and Univers display type by Jones Composition Company, from a design by Susan Bishop. It was printed, on 60-lb. Warren 1854 regular paper, and bound by The Maple Press Company.

Library of Congress Cataloging in Publication Data

Main entry under title:

Dissent in the USSR.

   Includes bibliographical references and index.
    1. Dissenters—Russia—Addresses, essays, lectures. 2. Russia—Politics and
government—1953–   Addresses, essays, lectures. I. Tőkés, Rudolf L., 1935–
DK274.D57   322.4'4'0947   74-24391
ISBN 0-8018-1661-0